CATHOLIC WOMEN AND MEXICAN POLITICS,
1750–1940

Catholic Women and Mexican Politics, 1750–1940

Margaret Chowning

PRINCETON UNIVERSITY PRESS
PRINCETON & OXFORD

Copyright © 2023 by Princeton University Press

Princeton University Press is committed to the protection of copyright and the intellectual property our authors entrust to us. Copyright promotes the progress and integrity of knowledge. Thank you for supporting free speech and the global exchange of ideas by purchasing an authorized edition of this book. If you wish to reproduce or distribute any part of it in any form, please obtain permission.

Requests for permission to reproduce material from this work should be sent to permissions@press.princeton.edu

Published by Princeton University Press
41 William Street, Princeton, New Jersey 08540
99 Banbury Road, Oxford OX2 6JX

press.princeton.edu

All Rights Reserved
First paperback printing, 2024
Paperback ISBN 9780691264578

The Library of Congress has cataloged the cloth edition as follows:

Names: Chowning, Margaret, author.
Title: Catholic women and Mexican politics, 1750–1940 / Margaret Chowning.
Description: Princeton : Princeton University Press, [2023] | Includes bibliographical references and index.
Identifiers: LCCN 2022021222 (print) | LCCN 2022021223 (ebook) |
    ISBN 9780691177243 (hardback) | ISBN 9780691235424 (ebook)
Subjects: LCSH: Catholic Church—Mexico—History. | Catholic women—
    Political activity—Mexico—History. | Cofradías (Latin America)—Mexico. |
    Church and state—Mexico—History. | Women—Mexico—Social conditions. |
    Mexico—Religious life and customs. | Mexico—Politics and government—1810– |
    BISAC: HISTORY / Latin America / Mexico | POLITICAL SCIENCE / General
Classification: LCC BX1428.3 .C46 2023 (print) | LCC BX1428.3 (ebook) |
    DDC 282/.72082—dc23/eng/20220615
LC record available at https://lccn.loc.gov/2022021222
LC ebook record available at https://lccn.loc.gov/2022021223

British Library Cataloging-in-Publication Data is available

Editorial: Priya Nelson and Barbara Shi
Production Editorial: Nathan Carr
Jacket/Cover Design: Chris Ferrante
Production: Lauren Reese
Publicity: Alyssa Sanford and Charlotte Coyne
Copyeditor: Natalie Jones

Jacket/Cover Credit: Portraits by Hermenegildo Bustos. (Top row, left to right): Eustasia Parra de Murillo (1886), Vicenta de la Rosa (1889), Ramona Pérez (1888). (Bottom row, left to right): Rómula Torres (1899), Albina Villanueva (1889). Courtesy of Instituto Nacional de Bellas Artes y Literatura. (Bottom right): Portrait of Mauricia Hernández (1887). Courtesy of Museo Regional de Guanajuato Alhóndiga de Granaditas.

This book has been composed in Miller

To my sister Jane

CONTENTS

Acknowledgments · ix
Archives Consulted · xiii

INTRODUCTION   1

PART I   THE LATE COLONY AND THE
              AFTERMATH OF THE WARS FOR
              INDEPENDENCE   17

CHAPTER 1   "Under No Circumstances Shall a Woman
              Be Elected": Gender Roles in Colonial Urban
              Cofradías   19

CHAPTER 2   "Our Fears That the Cofradías Will Disappear
              Are Not Unfounded": Gender, Lay Associations,
              and Priests in the Aftermath of the Wars for
              Independence, 1810–1860   45

PART II   THE ERA OF THE REFORM   71

CHAPTER 3   "We Ladies Who Sign Below Wish to Establish
              a Congregation": Priests, Women, and New Lay
              Associations, 1840–1856   73

CHAPTER 4   "Throwing Themselves upon the Political
              Barricades": Catholic Women Enter National
              Politics in the Midcentury Petition Campaigns   97

CHAPTER 5   "The Intervention of the Faithful Was an
              Unavoidable Necessity": Lay Organizing and
              Women, 1856–1875   123

CHAPTER 6   "We'll See Who Wins: Them with Their Laws,
              or Us with Our Protests": The *Ley Orgánica* and
              the 1874–1875 Petition Campaign   147

PART III	THE PORFIRIATO	173
CHAPTER 7	"Excellent Assistants of the Priest": Women and Lay Associations, 1876–1911	175
CHAPTER 8	"The Men Are Somewhat Preoccupied. Fortunately, the Mexican Woman Carries the Standard of Our Beliefs": Women and Catholic Politics in the Porfiriato	206
EPILOGUE	Catholic Women and Politics, 1910–1940	232

Appendix · 253
Notes · 257
Bibliography · 325
Index · 353

ACKNOWLEDGMENTS

I FIRST FLOATED the core idea behind this book when I interviewed for my job at Berkeley in 1992. Six years later, after I managed to transform my dissertation into my first book, I turned to researching this one, and quickly came upon the extraordinary materials on the convent of La Purísima Concepción that caused me to change plans and put *Catholic Women* on the back burner. After *Rebellious Nuns* was published in 2006, I finally returned to this book, though I continued to cling to the idea that a book about "Catholic women" in the nineteenth century should include nuns; I didn't fully give up on that conceptualization of this book for another decade, after it finally became clear to me that this would result in a six-hundred-page book with an unnecessarily cluttered narrative. In other words, this book has been a long time in the making, and has taken many twists and turns.

In this lengthy period of research and writing, I have incurred many debts. To be honest, I've forgotten the names of some of the people who helped me decades ago, like the young Franciscan who supervised the Archivo Histórico de la Provincia Franciscana de Michoacán in Celaya, which I visited when I still thought more nuns were in my future. He was helpful in the archive, but I am also grateful to him for inviting me to lunch in the monastery. The meal (fish, pickled carrots, beans, and tortillas) was served in the kitchen by a tandem of gentle, pious laywomen who clearly saw cooking for and serving the Franciscans as a sweet privilege. This gave me an early glimpse at one (not all, I was already discovering) of the "types" of women I was writing about, women whose dedication to the church was, to me, mysterious, even unfathomable. This was the reason I wanted to study them. I hadn't really understood the wealthy people in my first book or the nuns in my second, either, until I wrote about them, and even then I'm sure I didn't really "get" them, but at least the challenge of trying to get inside their heads kept me interested for years. I apologize to this priest, these laywomen, and everyone else whose name I neglected to write down when I was first helped by them.

The National Endowment for the Humanities and (several times) the University of California made research and writing possible. So did the staffs at the Archivo General de la Nación and the archiepiscopal archives of Michoacán, Guadalajara, Oaxaca, and México. Going above and beyond just being helpful, archivist and scholar Lic. Glafira Magaña Perales, in Guadalajara, let me use her office in the afternoons after the archive was closed so I could squeeze in more hours. Also literally giving me space to work, Martín Sánchez at the Colegio de Michoacán in Zamora let me use a corner of his office while I made my way through the Archivo General de la Congregación Hijas de María

Inmaculada de Guadalupe. And similarly, the staff at the Branson Library at New Mexico State University, which holds microfilm of the entire archdiocesan archive of Durango, made room for me to work and gave me a dedicated microfilm reader one hot summer in Las Cruces. No one needed to clear space for me at the Archivo Histórico del Arzobispado de México, which was already set up as a lovely place to work, but archivist Marco Antonio Pérez Iturbe was immensely helpful, alerting me to the existence of the 1896–97 parish surveys for the archbishopric, which form a big part of chapter 7, and then pulling and photocopying them for me. Marco also gave me a copy of his own excellent master's thesis.

I usually prefer to do my own research. I love archives, for one thing, and besides, I don't always know what I'm looking for until I find it, making it hard to be sure a research assistant has not skipped over some small thing that I would treasure. But over the years I have relied on a number of my (at the time) graduate students. Nicole von Germeten, Pablo Palomino, Germán Vergara, Stephanie Ballenger, and Sarah Selvidge, in addition to being valued fellow scholars and friends, all contributed hours of their time in Mexico City or Morelia. Thanks also to Lorena Ojeda Dávila for setting me up with two of her students from the Universidad de Michoacán who did some newspaper photographing for me, and thanks to both of them, Dulce Ávila and Claudia Martínez.

Far too many people to acknowledge have read chapters or listened to me try out parts of the argument in presentations at numerous panels and workshops and presentations over the years and have provided encouragement and feedback, but there are a few whose comments or questions stand out as really changing the way I was thinking or arguing. Some of them probably do not even remember making a comment at all; others will definitely remember the slog through early versions, and to you I am especially grateful. I thank Peggy Anderson, David Blackbourn, Lina Britto, Matthew Butler, Vera Candiani, Brian Connaughton, Jessica Delgado, Heather Fowler-Salamini, Rebecca Herman, Emilio Kourí, Brianna Leavitt-Alcántara, Kate Marshall, Pablo Mijangos, Ana Minián, Luis Murillo, Matt O'Hara, José Juan Pérez Meléndez, Paul Ramírez, Elena Schneider, Yuri Slezkine, Mauricio Tenorio, Mary Kay Vaughan, and Eddie Wright-Ríos. Eddie also very generously shared his research notes on the 1908 Oaxaca parish survey, which I used extensively, and located the image of Catholic women signing petitions that appears in chapter 4. He has been a consistent friendly interlocutor through two of his books and now two of mine.

I am profoundly grateful to Silvia Arrom, William B. Taylor, Brian Stauffer, John Tutino, and one anonymous reader for Princeton, all of whom read the entire manuscript with great care. Their detailed comments were so important in the final stages of the manuscript preparation. Silvia also heroically helped me work through what an epilogue should be at the very last minute.

Toward the end of the process, Felipe Galindo, an exciting artist in his own right, helped me locate the family of Eduardo del Río (Rius), who gave me permission to use one of his images in the epilogue. I thank him and them (Citlali del Río and Micaela Flores). I'm also grateful to Dr. José Eduardo Aréchiga and David Ramos for permission to use their photography.

Thanks also to the editors at *Past & Present* for allowing me to use substantial parts of my 2013 article, "The Catholic Church and the Ladies of the Vela Perpetua," which appear in chapters 1, 2, and 3. Priya Nelson, Barbara Shi, and Nathan Carr were great to work with at Princeton.

Irv Scheiner understood Catholic women even less than I did when I started this project, which happened to be the first summer he went with me to Mexico after we had started our relationship the previous February. So the beginning of this book coincided with the beginning of my oh-so-happy life partnership. And sadly, the (near) end of this book coincided with his unexpected death in May 2021. He would have liked to see the book all the way through. I miss him every day, and it's hard to know how I'll get my next book in shape without his great curiosity, his smart questions, and our near-daily conversations about how to think about and write history. Luckily our wonderful blended family (four children and eight grandchildren) fills my life with joy even in his absence.

I dedicate this book to my sister Jane. Jane's frustrating role as a woman with natural leadership abilities who was committed to a church that did not even allow female servers at Sunday worship was the inspiration for this book. Her faith allowed her to accept this institutionalized undervaluing of her abilities, even as her intellect and personality resisted it. I am happy to report that her church has finally recognized her talents and those of other women, and now allows them to help lead the church (only 175 years after the Mexican women in this book!). She has been my partner in navigating the pleasures and pain of what life has to offer for over 60 years.

ARCHIVES CONSULTED

Archivo del Catedral de Morelia (ACM)
Archivo de la Congregacion Hijas de Maria Inmaculada de Guadalupe (Zamora, Michoacán) (ACHJMI)
Archivo General Histórico del Poder Ejecutivo de Michoacán (AGHPEM)
Archivo General de la Nación (AGN)
Archivo Histórico del Arzobispado de Durango (AHAD)
Archivo Histórico del Arzobispado de Guadalajara (AHAG)
Archivo Histórico del Arzobispado de Michoacán (AHAMich)
Archivo Histórico del Arzobispado de México (AHAMex)
Archivo Histórico del Arzobispado de Oaxaca (AHAO)
Archivo Histórico del Congreso del Estado de Michoacán (AHCEMich)
Archivo de Notarías de Morelia (ANM)
The Church of Latter Day Saints online family search records
Hemeroteca de Morelia
Hemeroteca Nacional Digital de México (online)

INTRODUCTION

RELIGION FIGURED IN four of the major wars Mexico endured after its independence from Spain in 1821.[1] In none of them were the proper roles of Catholicism and the Catholic church in Mexican society the only issues that drove people to take sides. But they were significant, and they were the ones that generated "culture wars" before the military battles began and after they were over. As we know from our twenty-first-century experience in culture warring, questions of profound cultural significance—the nature of marriage, the role of the state in the lives of families and individuals, the extent to which the public practice of religion is permitted by law, gender equality, school choice and prayer in schools, religious liberty vs. civil rights (all present in nineteenth- and early twentieth-century Mexico as well)—can become intensely political even in the absence of armed conflict. Mexico was in a state of cultural warfare from the middle of the nineteenth century to at least the middle of the twentieth. At times the debates were more intense than at others, and always, behind the polarizing discourse, there were Catholic liberals and liberal Catholics and a whole, complicated spectrum of belief and behavior, but the taking of sides and rhetoric ginning up partisan divides over religion and church were never absent.

Catholic women were fully engaged in the culture wars that bookended and permeated the hot wars. They were part of the public attack on tolerance of other religions in the middle of the nineteenth century, and in the defense of religious liberty as a way to safeguard Catholic institutions and values after 1867. They worked mainly behind the scenes to advance the church's political agenda during the long Díaz dictatorship (1876–1911), and returned to the center of the political stage in very public ways after the Revolution in the 1910s, 1920s, and 1930s. Most historians agree that Mexico's delay in granting women full suffrage (until 1953) was directly linked to their perceived dedication to the church and Catholicism. A high-ranking Mason expressed liberal fears when he warned about the dangers of female suffrage in 1931: "Twenty-five thousand women coming before the Chamber to demand the vote for women! How horrible! If they attain their objective, we shall soon have a Bishop for President!"[2]

This book explores the connections between Catholic politics (the defense of church and religion) and gender in Mexico from the mid-eighteenth to the mid-twentieth century, though its center of gravity is the century from 1810 to 1910. At the broadest level, it is concerned with two questions that have preoccupied historians since it became clear—no later than the 1980s—that secularization was not a necessary part of modernization. How have religion and the churches that organize religion survived and even thrived since the nineteenth century? And does gendering the question provide fresh answers?[3]

The first question has been asked surprisingly infrequently by political historians of Mexico (or any other part of Latin America), despite the pervasive political power of the Catholic church everywhere in the region. For many Catholics and conservatives, both in the past and in the present, the answer is clear: the multiple challenges of the modern world *require* religion as a moral compass.[4] But for the most part, it is a liberal, secular narrative that has dominated the construction of national histories in Latin America. For Mexico, the outlines of this narrative were first framed in the nineteenth century, and later largely accepted by revolutionaries and progressives, who on the topics of the church and religion quite resembled nineteenth-century liberals. In their answers to the question of why religion and the Catholic church have endured, they have been largely dismissive: religion was and is more of a residue of colonialism than an ongoing source of personal meaning and empowerment. The church, in this story, comes across as pesky, stubborn, and venal rather than a continuing repository of political or moral power. This understanding of church and religion as irrational, lacking legitimacy, and destined to fade away has led liberals and progressives to tell the story of the history of Mexico in a way that has marginalized Catholic politics and Catholic actors. One does not have to agree with the church's positions or favor the strengthening of religious rights in order to see that to downplay the historical importance of these actors is misleading.

The same liberal history-writing project has also marginalized women, as national histories commonly do. To the extent that women figure in the liberal story, they are, with a few notable heroic exceptions, mothers. These are either admirable mothers who raised good liberal citizens, or retrograde mothers who raised resisters of the liberal project. In neither case are they themselves direct agents of change. They are timeless in these roles. Men, by contrast, change and progress. With their "natural" inclination to "modern" thinking and greater involvement in the secular worlds of business and politics, they slowly abandoned the church, or at least the most inimical of the church's teachings, beginning in the late colonial period. (This view privileging liberal men also tends to dismiss male indigenous peasants, who are seen as the only men who as a group failed to emancipate themselves from the hold of the Catholic church.)

For Mexico, the discursive marginalization of women has yielded a particularly skewed picture of historical change, especially where religion and the Catholic church are concerned. What if, following US historian Ann Braude, we center women, and pay more attention to the ways that women supported the church than to the ways that men abandoned it?[5] This perspective shift shapes the narrative arc of this book. The capsule version goes like this. After independence from Spain (1821), denied full rights as citizens in the new nation, women forged their own form of "citizenship" in the church: they aimed to become, and did become, both more included and more equal to men in church institutions, as well as more obligated and responsible for maintaining family and community piety, than they had been in the colonial past. These "reactionary feminists," as Edward Wright-Ríos calls them, then entered the political arena on behalf of the church, defending it and their religion as fiercely as many men defended the nation.[6] The conventional wisdom is that it took the Mexican Revolution of 1910 to open up spaces for large numbers of women to act politically in meaningful ways in Mexico. But while that does seem to be true for liberal or radical women, this book shows that Catholic women had aggressively entered national politics by the 1850s. The church's struggle to survive disestablishment and to remain relevant in the nineteenth century became women's struggle. Thus the politically active Catholic women of the 1920s who so concerned our Mason were the product of historical processes set in motion in the colonial period and dramatically shaped between 1810 and 1910. Catholic women's actions put the story of the church's survival as a political actor in the nineteenth and twentieth centuries in a new perspective.

An important vehicle—indeed, I argue, a crucially important vehicle—through which Catholic women helped the church survive was the lay association or confraternity (*cofradía* in Spanish). After the outbreak of the wars for independence in 1810, male-led lay associations declined significantly in number and activity, for reasons that are explored in chapter 2. In response to the post-independence debility of these associations, women created new and different lay associations whose distinguishing feature was female leadership. These associations proved to be extremely popular and proliferated rapidly, especially in parts of the country where the wars had most damaged the older ones, at first to the chagrin of the ecclesiastical hierarchy (archbishops and bishops) and with the lukewarm support of at least some parish priests—who needed these new associations but were not sure they wanted to deal with women in positions of local power—but later with the enthusiastic encouragement of both priests and bishops, as women's domination of lay associations spread throughout the country.

The appeals for women of founding, joining, and leading lay associations were manifold, from the social to the spiritual. But social and spiritual satisfactions could also be earned elsewhere, for example by practicing great personal piety, or by making donations to the church. What the associations did uniquely—and what the women who reinvented and led them envisioned—was to build and sustain a literal community of the faithful at the parish level. This was not the metaphorical community of all believers that was imagined by Catholic intellectuals and church doctrine, but rather an actual, bounded group of Catholics, formed to provide crucial support to the parish church and its priest. The priest, in turn, supported families and the lay associations in the all-important project of moralizing the children of the parish, inculcating "Catholic values" (rarely spelled out, but including not just understandings of right and wrong but also an emphasis on the social good, the community, and faith over individual interest, the nuclear family, and science) that made certain children would grow up to be pillars of the community and, after independence, the nation.

This understanding that without religion children would grow up as selfish individuals without a moral center combined with the relatively new expectation that moralization was the responsibility of the mother and the priest (and not, as in the past, the father; this is another point explored in more detail in chapter 2). The urgency of the task of moralization grew as liberal and secular challenges to previously unquestioned Catholic values mounted in the post-independence era. Thus two changes—the transfer of responsibility of Christianization from father to mother, and the building political strength of secular liberalism—give us the core explanation not only for why women formed new associations beginning in the 1840s, but also for why women continued to found, join, and dominate them throughout the nineteenth and twentieth centuries. Lay associations gave women an essential tool with which to support their churches, defend Catholic values, promote their community's spiritual well-being, and moralize their children, vital projects for which they were understood and understood themselves to be responsible.

These associations served the implicit political role of keeping Catholicism alive and vibrant at the grassroots. But the new women-led lay associations also served a more explicit political role: around the middle of the nineteenth century, I argue that they formed the organizational base for women's movement into the national political arena in defense of the church, in the form of major, highly visible petition campaigns. Thus Catholic women, as members and leaders of lay associations and as mobilizers of nonmembers, formed a crucial bridge between the late colony, with its strong male support for and participation in the church, and the last decade or so of the nineteenth century. At that time Mexico experienced its version of Catholic revival and men once again became interested in defending the church, as a way to oppose liberal dictatorship and liberal models of modernization (though without returning in large numbers to Catholic associational life). The Mexican church's recovery thus had an important homegrown, gendered dimension. By this time women, especially as members of lay associations, were firmly ensconced at the right hands of priests whose diminished ability to act publicly—in a climate of anticlericalism and in a material context of diminished resources—they had compensated for with faith-nurturing and parish-supporting activities at the grassroots, and vocal advocacy at times of political crisis.

The Colonial Urban Cofradía

What exactly was a lay association (*cofradía*) in the late colonial period, when this story begins? In both indigenous villages and Hispanic towns and cities, the church had, from the early sixteenth century, encouraged the formation of lay associations. The central role of both indigenous and urban cofradías was to organize devotional practices that honored a saint or a divine figure (usually Christ or Mary in one of her many devotional titles), but while there was overlap, indigenous cofradías were quite different from the urban ones that are the focus of this book.[7]

In the towns and cities, cofradías generally sponsored a special mass one day a month, and most participated in citywide processions, notably Corpus Christi, during which the images to which the association was devoted were taken out of the church and paraded solemnly through the streets on the shoulders of select members.[8] Almost all put on an annual "function" that might include a procession, sermons, music, extra candles for the church, luminarias, fireworks, bullfights, and refreshments.

These out-of-the-ordinary events on the calendar provided a special and invigorating spiritual and community experience. People looked forward to them, praised them when they were carried out with appropriate pomp, and criticized them when they weren't. Cofradías spent a significant portion of their income to make sure they were not seen as skimping on the drama and lavishness of the annual functions. The Cofradía del Rosario in Valladolid, for example, in the late eighteenth century purchased a new set of armor for the Roman centurions that accompanied the Virgin in procession (seated on her new throne), hundreds of fireworks, and a bull for the bullfight in her honor, all in order to "enhance the splendor of the titular functions of the cofradía."[9]

Besides organizing devotions and sponsoring the annual function and the special monthly masses, urban cofradías provided members a "good death." Members earned indulgences that reduced their time in purgatory. They prayed for each other when death was at hand, and lit the path of the Host with candles and luminarias as it was transported to the homes of the dying. Sometimes the cofradía provided valued embellishments to the administration of viaticum to its members: the Cofradía del Santísimo Sacramento of Durango, for example, had on retainer a marching band that accompanied the Host as it visited the houses of the moribund. (The band featured two French horns, a double bass, a drum, a bass drum, and two clarinets, and commanded a substantial yearly stipend of over 550 pesos.)[10] Members also joined their *cofrades'* funeral corteges and attended anniversary masses. Besides these aspects of a good death, many of the larger cofradías went farther, operating as burial societies. This meant that they guaranteed members a coffin, shroud, burial fees, and a burial as well as a one-time cash payment to survivors, often fairly significant (as much as three to four months' wages for the poorest members).[11]

These popular cofradía-sponsored practices (masses, processions, sermons, fiestas, transport of the Host, funeral and anniversary masses, death benefits) had to be paid for.[12] Some cofradías were purely devotional and existed on alms, but many, and a majority of the largest ones, were supported by initiation fees, membership fees, and rental or interest income produced by houses, lots, and funds that members had bequeathed or donated to the organization over time.[13] Some, like the Archicofradía del Santísimo Sacramento in Mexico City with its late colonial endowment of over 500,000 pesos, were extremely wealthy.[14] The income from these investments was used for upkeep on the properties that the cofradía owned, as well as to fulfill their spiritual obligations. Most of the larger cofradías and even some of the smaller ones thus spent and took in a good bit of money, and their finances were complicated enough to require a business manager (mayordomo). Chapter 1 provides more details, but the point I wish to emphasize here is that the colonial cofradías had spiritual and public functions that were expensive and that required a good bit of administration, and for this reason were seen as necessarily led by men.

Settings and Actors

The book is set in urban Mexico. By "urban" I mean not only the large cities that are usually the settings for urban histories, but also the larger mestizo or Hispanic towns, in the neighborhood of 2,000–3,000 inhabitants and up.[15] In these cities and towns, there were multiple cofradías in different parish churches and in the convents of the male and female orders. In late eighteenth-century Mexico City, for example, with a population of about 137,000, there were probably at least one hundred cofradías.[16] In the city of Guanajuato, with a population of about 27,000, there were twenty cofradías; in San Miguel el Grande, a villa of about 14,000, there were fifteen; and in smallish Puruándiro, with around 4,400 inhabitants, there were four.[17]

In both the mestizo towns and the neighborhoods of the larger cities, people knew each other. Their lives came together at numerous points almost on a daily basis: in the streets, in the markets, in the churches, and in lay associations. A majority of urban dwellers probably belonged to one of the cofradías in their town or neighborhood, and some of them belonged to more than one, making cofradías microcosms of colonial society: most were racially and socially diverse, with both men and women represented.[18] They included workers (servants, municipal workers, laundresses, seamstresses, food sellers, and lower-prestige artisans like cobblers, masons, tanners or smiths, market sellers, and other plebeians); elites (merchants, ranchers, estate owners, high-ranking people in both the ecclesiastical and municipal bureaucracies); and "respectable" people, or *gente decente*, neither workers nor, quite, elites. Some in the middle groups were educated and practiced professions based on that education (teachers, scribes, notaries); others might be shopkeepers, artisans in higher prestige crafts, or managers and privileged employees of the businesses owned by elites.

The women who are the primary actors in this study were either elites or gente decente: solid, pious, cross-wearing, bourgeois women, like those on the cover of this book, women painted by Hermenegildo Bustos in and around Guanajuato in the second half of the nineteenth century. These were the founders and officers of the female-led cofradías, and the organizers and possibly authors of the pro-Catholic petition campaigns of the mid to late century. Simple arithmetic makes it clear that lower-status urban women were also members of these cofradías and signers of these petitions, since there were far too many members/signers for all of them to have come from elite or middling families. These lower-class women were perhaps known to or acquainted with the women who were the leaders of the associations. They might have been their servants, or they were shopkeepers and laundresses and seamstresses with whom the higher-status women came in contact during their daily routines, and many of them were probably women who did not personally know any of the officers of the cofradía or the organizers of the devotions, but knew someone who did. They were a racial mix, but certainly included many more African-descended and Hispanized indigenous peoples than the overwhelmingly white and mestizo women who were the leaders of the new cofradías. But they are elusive. Their words and individual actions rarely show up in the archives. The reader should try to keep their presence in the associations in mind even when I cannot account for them in very satisfying detail. As a result of the murkiness of class and race within the documents concerning associations, I use these frameworks of analysis sparingly.

Influences

First and most obvious, this book has connections to both gender studies and religious studies. My main goal, as it is the goal of most historians, is to complicate and reveal the complexity of driving themes in these theoretical traditions—in my case, especially the theme of the feminization of piety—showing how they operate and change over time, in different places, among different groups. Chapter 2 includes a longer discussion of the feminization of religion in the Mexican case, but since the debates over how to view this phenomenon are multiple and unresolved, it may be helpful to say a few words here, by way of framing the reading experience.

Religion seems, throughout the Western world, to have become more and more the social domain of women in the nineteenth century. By "social domain of women," scholars mean two things: that religious vocations soared among women in many Catholic countries, while declining among men; and that women became increasingly numerically dominant in religious practices and institutions (sometimes referred to as the feminization of the pews). A third understanding of the feminization of religion comes from scholars' observations of changing religious language and symbols, which they have argued became more "feminized" in the nineteenth century.

Some scholars have tried to go beyond gathering and analyzing empirical evidence and have endeavored to make the feminization of religion into a theoretical construct or master narrative, often operating in tandem with secularization. They have attributed causation to multiple factors: enlightened ideas about the irrationality of religion that led men (but not women) away from the church; the rise of the market economy that required men to be increasingly away from their communities, leaving women behind to preserve church and family; liberal ideas about the separation of church and state and the assignment of the church to the private sphere; republicanism, which gendered citizenship and concretized the notion of separate gender spheres; the expansion of the masculine public sphere (clubs, societies, and so on), drawing men away from church organizations; and, in the case of Catholicism, the actions of the church itself, which has been seen as reacting to threats to its dominance by recruiting women, rendering Jesus, for example, into a more gentle and feminine image, and introducing new devotions aimed at women, thus making the feminization of religion an intentional action on the part of the church.

This brief recap of the variety of definitions of the feminization of religion—should we define it as stylistic or discursive change, or as something more demographic and social?—and of the multiple causes offered to explain it already suggests that as a theory, the feminization of religion is impossibly messy. And this just scratches the surface. Others problems include dating the various kinds of feminization (one could make an argument for the beginnings of both discursive and the demographic feminization as early as the sixteenth century and as late as the twentieth century); accounting for male religiosity and female irreligiosity; accounting for class differences among women and/or the devout; ascertaining whether a presence in the pews necessarily implies great piety; and accounting for women who were not displaced from the public sphere. Further, as a theory, feminization can be seen as reifying gender at a time when many scholars are looking to complicate it. The concept of the feminization of religion as a discursive change cannot be very useful unless we have relatively firm definitions of what is feminine and what is masculine, and these have been shown to change over time and from place to place.[19]

However, there is no question that at the very least the demographic phenomenon of greater female dominance in church institutions—Protestant, Catholic, and Jewish—existed. It existed in Mexico, too, as I have already made clear, and here it had important implications for Mexican politics and, at a scholarly level, for how we periodize Mexican history.[20] This book advances the ideas that the feminization of religion was integral to the mobilization of Catholics in culture wars against liberalism in the era of the Reform; and that the Reform, because of its assault on church and to a considerable extent religion, deepened and hardened cultural divides even more thoroughly than did the Revolution of 1910. As a theory, then, the feminization of religion is not tenable. But as a way to think differently about Mexican history, it is helpful.

Besides work on gender/women and religion/church, a number of different literatures on politics have helped me make sense of the Mexican evidence. Because of my core interest in lay associations and their possible role in shaping women's political actions and thinking, I have mined the historical and sociological literature on associationalism and politics for insights and comparisons.[21] An argument in this literature particular to women's associations is that they are important in raising consciousness of women's issues and women's culture, and empowering women to speak out on political matters of concern to their sex, even if the reasons for any given group to have been founded in the first place were not particularly political. My own interpretation of the connection between women's lay associations and the petition campaigns in which women participated, as the reader will see in chapters 4 and 6, is based partly on the theoretical contributions of this literature, since direct evidence—for a variety of reasons spelled out in the chapters—was hard to find.

Another important argument in the writing on the relationship between associations and politics is that clubs, societies, and other groups help develop habits of cooperation across kinship or occupation as they elect officers and/or create bylaws or constitutions. Associations, then, were inherently political, a point of obvious importance for this book. Women members and officers, especially after the rise of all-female associations or female-led associations, developed leadership and other skills, amassed social capital, and formed a group identity outside of the family through their participation in associations (just as men did). They also had to learn to defend their associations against the ubiquitous presence of a priest as the director of the association.[22] Both priest and church had an interest in controlling the associations, and tensions between members/officers and ecclesiastical authorities provided proving grounds for women as political actors. Yet women's lay associations never, in my research, fundamentally challenged the "right" of the priest to supervise their operations. Lay associations were not, then, leading a trend toward democracy, and arguably their success reinforced the anti-democratic (a point made skillfully by Stefan-Ludwig Hoffmann about Germany in the nineteenth century), even as they did bring women previously excluded from politics into this arena.[23]

Studies of political conservatism in the West that highlight important roles for religion and gender have also been helpful.[24] Many of these studies usefully emphasize the extent to which people have viewed churches and religion as defenders of "family values" (as they are sometimes labeled in the US). They also explore how religious conservatives have successfully characterized liberal individualism as a threat to the family, a point that was made implicitly by the female founders of associations by the very act of forming a group to restore community piety, and was made explicitly and repeatedly by Mexican women in the petition drives they participated in as signers and organizers. When the liberal (or, later, revolutionary) state could be painted as undermining the family, the church became the main institutional resource for protecting it, and religious practice the means by which God was enlisted in the project. As prime defenders of religious practice, Catholic women and the associations to which they belonged became pillars of anti-liberal and anti-revolutionary movements in Mexico.

One assumption that has long informed most literature on politics, and that I very firmly share, is that politics is much more than the actions of statesmen and politicians and military leaders, extending well beyond the electoral arena. As Susan Moller Okin put it in 1979: "The exclusion from 'politics' of all that is domestic, familial, private, personal, and sexual clearly depends on the exclusion of women and cannot be sustained once women are included as full and equal partners in either political theory or political practice."[25] For Latin America, the literature that points to women as direct political actors, at least before their enfranchisement, is small and is overwhelmingly concentrated on the twentieth century.[26] But thinking of women's indirect or informal impact on politics as powerful and meaningful gives us a bigger canvas. In the case of Mexico in the nineteenth and early twentieth century, when politics to a considerable extent revolved around whether religious values and institutions were deemed worthy of protection or destruction by competing armies or parties, the women who cleaned the church or planned the parish raffle or taught in the parochial schools or led lay associations became important political actors. They preserved and extended religious community at the local level—a political act, even if it was unconsciously so. Sometimes they entered the political arena quite self-consciously, but even when they didn't, they were acting politically.

Finally, I should address a key concept in much work on women in politics. Most scholars nowadays recoil at the long-dominant assumption that Catholic priests manipulated gullible female parishioners, assuming instead that women had "agency."[27] "Agency" is, of course, a core concept of social/political historians, and it is surely important to evaluate historical evidence with the idea that subaltern people might have possessed or devised tools they could use to "negotiate" with those in power. But at the same time, it seems to me that the hyperaware search for agency can be (and frankly often has been) as distorting as assuming that subalterns have none. In my story, there are times when women unmistakably act as "agents," but at other times it is not clear whether it is they or priests or some other male authority who are dominating a certain situation—if indeed any one group is dominant—and I never discount the possibility that priests, as well as other male Catholic leaders, tried and succeeded in getting women to do what they wanted. Time and context matter, and sometimes in this book the stereotype of the manipulative priest is shown to be more or less accurate. That stereotype's counterpart, the clueless and fickle woman, is less likely to show up in the archival record and there are not many examples of such women in this book, although there are certainly women for whom their priests were great and much-admired allies in the Catholic versus secular culture wars.

Historiography

When I first began this project some twenty years ago, there was very little written about women's relationship either to the church or to politics in Mexico in the nineteenth century (and not much about nineteenth-century women in any historical context).[28] There was a fairly robust literature on church-state relations and the thinking of Catholic intellectuals and the clergy, but it was based on the assumption that the actions of the church in the national arena were influenced by ideas and institutional self-interest, and were largely independent of the laity, certainly of the female laity.[29] Although the number of studies that strive to understand the connections between women, the church, and Mexican politics remains minuscule, there are now more relevant works, especially for the twentieth century.[30] For the nineteenth, we have the first major book-length analysis of a lay association in Mexico, Silvia Arrom's *Volunteering for a Cause*, on the Ladies of Charity, and Edward Wright-Ríos's *Searching for Madre Matiana*, both of which successfully integrate religion, gender, and political change.[31]

The literature on the Catholic church and religion in Mexico in the nineteenth and twentieth centuries is mature enough to have developed a mutually respectful debate around whether conflict (what I have called "culture war") or coexistence is the best framework through which to engage the changing roles of Catholicism in modern Mexico.[32] In large part the answer depends on what is meant by "Catholicism." The ecclesiastical hierarchy? Catholic intellectuals? Ordinary Catholics? There is a body of excellent work that rejects the "old" culture war arguments, which depicted the hierarchy as bitterly opposed on philosophical grounds to the modern state, and instead emphasizes cooperation and negotiation between these actors.[33] A modernizing church, these authors show, could and did work with a modernizing state. Another tendency in the recent literature on Catholicism, however, is to burrow into local religious cultures—featuring the laity, not taking their acquiescence for granted—and here authors have found what we might broadly classify as "secularizing" actions by the state (e.g., the establishment of public schools that were forbidden to teach religion) or even "modernizing" actions by the church itself to be deeply troubling to ordinary people.[34] As historian José Alberto Moreno Chávez emphasizes, these were not just rural folk resentful of anyone who took their religious practices away from them, but also urban Catholics who had a different understanding of "modernity" from positivist and progress-oriented liberals, and who sought a "utopia in which everyone would be converted to a single faith and would comport themselves in accordance with its morality."[35] This book is about such ordinary Catholics and the ways they could wield power and influence politics. In fact, I see the power of the church hierarchy to confront or coexist with the state as dependent on demonstrations of loyalty to the church on the part of the laity, without which the hierarchy's negotiations in the political sphere would have no teeth.

Methods and Sources

The book interweaves two approaches. First, it is a social history of women in lay associations, using pedestrian materials like membership lists, parish surveys, financial records, and correspondence among leaders of lay associations, priests, and bishops or other diocesan officials. Who joined these institutions and why? How did women function within them? Were power relationships with priests and other male authorities confrontational? Deferential? Collegial? Did class differences between women and priests matter, and how? In pursuit of this kind of source I primarily used the archiepiscopal archives of Mexico, Michoacán, Guadalajara, Oaxaca, and Durango, as well as documents in the National Archive that ended up there following the transfer of documents during and after the Reform.[36]

Second, it is a study of political action and discourses, of how petitioners and the liberal and conservative press had gendered agendas and used gendered language in the political arena. Here the sources are quite different: the petitions themselves, the partisan press, debates in the national congress, speeches. I relied especially on the partisan press to evaluate the response to the petitions; it allowed me to follow polemical calls and responses between opposing newspapers, over a period of days or weeks. I found the back-and-forth to be especially useful in understanding the issues as people defined them in real time.

Both of these approaches—social history and analysis of political discourse and behavior—can fruitfully be employed separately, but together they are far more powerful. Social history can establish that women assumed new roles in local church institutions, for example, but it cannot help us understand whether or why they became politically active, or what was at stake when they did. Similarly, bringing gender to the surface of politics is an important scholarly task, but gendered political discourses are made more intelligible when paired with gendered social and institutional histories. When liberals wrote about the church "hiding behind the petticoats" of its female supporters (see chapters 4 and 6), for example, it is easy (and no doubt correct) to interpret this as an attempt to diminish the church by feminizing it. But if we know something about institutional and social changes in the relationship of women to church, the phrase takes on additional meaning: it becomes not only the use of gendered language to dislodge the church's patriarchal power and shift it to the state, but also liberals' recognition of social—and political—realities. New alliances between women and the church, in other words, gave the church some of the power that the liberals hoped to undermine by caricaturing its relationship to women.

Organization

It is standard practice at the end of an introduction to lay out the organization of the book. In this case it is particularly important that the structure of presentation be made clear to the reader at the outset. The dual social history/political history approach that is the core of this book's methods requires an organizational scheme that is not quite as straightforward as one that is either simply chronological or thematic. Parts I, II, and III do proceed chronologically: Part I deals with the late colony and the aftermath of independence; Part II with the era of the Reform (1856–75); and Part III with the Díaz period (1876–1910). But within Parts II and III, the chapters advance along two different fronts, alternating a social history story and a political story. So, beginning with chapter 3, chapters on changes in women's relationship to the church and to lay associations (the odd-numbered chapters) are followed by chapters devoted to the role that Catholic women and lay associations played in politics (the even-numbered chapters). An alternative organization might have grouped together the social history chapters and the political discourse chapters. But I firmly believe that the social and the political constantly informed each other. In other words, cross-fertilization between women's joining practices and women's political practices is an essential part of my story, and the organization of the book needed to reflect that.

Part I (the first two chapters) establishes key contexts. Chapter 1 deals with women in colonial lay associations, and demonstrates the importance of women for those male-led associations. This is something like a background chapter, although, unlike many such chapters, this one is squarely based on archival material. Chapter 2 accounts for the collapse or near-collapse of the cofradía system analyzed in chapter 1 in the five decades after the crisis of the independence wars beginning in 1810. It establishes the regional and gendered breakdown of that system, and it probes the origins and nature of the "feminization of piety" in Mexico from 1810 to 1860.

Part II consists of four chapters on women's lay associations and their role in politicizing their members and their communities in the context of the lead-up to and aftermath of the 1856 liberal reforms. The liberal *Reforma* in Mexico, beginning in 1856, moved to aggressively secularize society and economy, so much so that it led to a civil war, a church-sponsored foreign intervention, and another war to expel the invaders. It was more punishing toward the church than any of the liberal measures taken by governments elsewhere in Latin America, calling for (among other things) the nationalization of church wealth (not just the forced sale of church property) and the expulsion of nuns from the convents. Chapter 3 has least to do with these political changes since it begins in 1840, so sixteen years before the Reform government took power. But it is focused on the rise of new, female-led lay associations in the center-west, and as such puts in place the structures from which Catholic women were positioned to move into politics if they saw the need to do so. Its (rough) chronological pair, chapter 4, moves from these local religious institutional changes to the national political level. It analyzes two petition campaigns: one in 1849 and one in 1856, both against religious tolerance, in both of which political petitions were presented from Mexican women. I explore whether the presence of new female-led lay associations had something to do with the decision to petition, and I analyze both liberal and conservative receptions of Catholic women's move into politics, mainly in the press. As the reader will see, the liberal response is quite predictable and sounds much like responses to activist women elsewhere in the West (that is to say, disparaging and dismissive). But the conservative response was necessarily more subtle, and as a result is more interesting.

The second pairing of chapters in Part II begins with chapter 5. This chapter deals with the impact of the liberal Reform on lay associations, explaining the apparent paradox that in an era of intense anticlericalism and episcopal timidity, lay associations for both men and women, but especially women, flourished and diversified. The chapter covers the period from 1856 to 1875, and I characterize this as a kind of "golden age" of local organizing and local autonomy of women-led lay associations. Chapter 6 returns to the national political arena with an analysis of another petition campaign in 1875 in which women participated, this time much more broadly than in the earlier campaign. Like chapter 4, it makes the case that lay associations were once again important promoters of these campaigns, and it discusses changes in the ways the liberal and Catholic press dealt with the reappearance of women in the political arena.

Part III deals with the thirty-five-year regime of Porfirio Díaz, the "Porfiriato." From the Catholic point of view the regime was a mixed bag. Díaz sought "conciliation" with the church as part of a broader project to stabilize the country, which gave a church weakened by two wartime losses the political space to regroup. But as a Mason and a liberal hero, Díaz was not inclined to go beyond conciliation with the church, refusing to overturn the laws of the Reform. As a result, the cultural/political conflicts that had been so front and center in the previous twenty years continued a low-grade churn. Chapter 7 genders the development of lay associations during the Porfiriato, documenting the continued dominance of women in lay associations and the difficulties of getting men to participate. This period featured an increasingly dense set of ecclesiastical networks; regular meetings of priests to discuss theological and other questions; the publication of *Boletines Eclesiásticas* intended to inform priests and interested laymen of national and international events; Catholic conferences to which women were not invited; and Vatican training for Mexican priests. The Catholic press also expanded its reach. In other words, these were years of reassertion of priestly and masculine power in the church and in pro-church secular society. These moves constituted the church's (and their allies in the press) best efforts to reestablish colonial-style gender hierarchy and gender segregation, and to treat the performance of piety in lay associations as gender neutral (against all evidence, as any parish priest could attest). The chapter's pair, chapter 8, deals with the (still strongly female-dominated) lay associations' key roles in promoting the church's political projects during the Porfiriato, especially religious education, the Catholic press, and keeping Catholic practice as visible and publicly present as possible. The perceived "morality" of Catholicism versus the moral neutrality of liberalism—many of whose advocates persistently contrasted their "scientific" and "rational" worldview with that of Catholic "fanatics"—was at the center of these projects.

In pairing the rise of women-led and women-dominated lay associations in the 1840s with the rise of politically active Catholic women around the same time, this book tells a new story. It also provides a genealogy for the militant and highly visible Catholic activism in the 1910s, 1920s, and 1930s, which is taken up in the epilogue. Women's political activism in the decades after the 1910 Revolution is generally written about as if it were something new, something that grew out of openings for women provided by the Revolution itself (as liberal women's activism seems fairly clearly to have done). A genealogy—unlike mere "background"—should show us a new way of thinking about something not only in the past, like the activism of Catholic women in the early part of the century, but also in the present. Historicizing and gendering the question of the survival of religion in Mexico does that, as I hope the following chapters show.

PART I

The Late Colony and the Aftermath of the Wars for Independence

CHAPTER ONE

"Under No Circumstances Shall a Woman Be Elected"

GENDER ROLES IN COLONIAL URBAN COFRADÍAS

ON MAY 21, 1724, the dues-collector for the Cofradía de Nuestra Señora del Tránsito set out on his Sunday rounds. One of his first stops was the residence of Rafael Romero, where he collected the small weekly membership fee from five people in Romero's household: Rafael himself, his sister Francisca, his daughter María Francisca, and Joseph Nicolás and Pedro Nolasco, almost certainly servants. The collector continued, in the course of a long day, to call on nineteen other households. Most of them were comprised of couples like Francisco del Castillo, a tailor, and his wife, Juana Francisca, but there were also mothers and children, like Ysabel de la Barquilla and her daughter María Peres; siblings who lived together, like Doña Ysabel and Doña María de Aguilas; and other complex households whose relationships are impossible to penetrate, like that of María de la Concepción, whom the collector tracked down "in the corral, along with Felipa de Santiago and Luisa Antonia and Manuel Antonio and Felipa de la Cruz and María Francisca and Micaela Petrona."[1]

In addition, dues were collected from twenty-seven members who did not pay as part of a household, and who did not share surnames with any other members, including Manuela de los Santos *la biscochera* (pastry-maker), Pasquala de San Joseph the vegetable seller, and María Martínez, with whom he caught up in the barber shop. Strikingly, these twenty-seven apparently independent, single members included twenty-five women and only two men.[2] All told, this Sunday's collection brought in dues from sixty women and twenty men. This was a slightly higher proportion of women to men than collections from other days of the week—perhaps on Sundays the collector checked in at homes more than at places of work, and perhaps during the week he found more men than women in workplaces (we know he located Diego Lopes the sombrero maker, Manuel Calderón the tailor, and Blas Pavón the muleskinner on Saturday, for example). Nonetheless, the overall gender balance in this cofradía was a lopsided 70 percent women and 30 percent men.

The church that housed the image of the Virgen del Tránsito, to whom the above cofradía was dedicated, was a parish church in the poor residential district of San Pablo, to the east of the main plaza of Mexico City, and only about 10 percent of the membership carried the honorific *don* or *doña*. About eight blocks to the south was the church of the parish of Santísima Trinidad, where another cofradía with a somewhat different social profile was housed: the Cofradía de Nuestra Señora de la Guía. The membership of this cofradía was more socially mixed than that of the Cofradía del Tránsito, with about 30 percent of its members dons or doñas.[3] Among the cheese sellers, fireworks manufacturers, barbers, shoemakers, banner-makers, and other petty commercial and artisanal occupations, there were also five priests, a lawyer for the high court, several master artisans, and a number of storeowners. However, while the female-dominant gender profile of this cofradía was not quite as pronounced as that of the Cofradía del Tránsito, women nonetheless formed a solid majority in this cofradía as well: in 1727–28, dues were collected from thirty-six independent women and fifteen independent men, and the overall percentage of women members in the 1720s was 61 percent.

A third example, this one from the 1760s and 1770s, gives us yet another social and gender profile. Some three-quarters of the members of the Cofradía de la Purificación, founded in the chapel of San José de los Españoles in the convent church of San Francisco, in a wealthy neighborhood to the west of the *zócalo* (the central plaza of Mexico City), were dons and doñas. They included the Mariscal de Castilla and his wife, as well as many prominent merchants and royal and ecclesiastical officials. Several of the non-elite minority were their servants, who paid with the household, though there were also some independents, mainly petty merchants with stalls on or near the zócalo—Pedro Vasques with his seed stall (*puesto de semillas*) in the plaza grande, for example, or Juliana Antonia Sánchez, who sold street food in the nearby Plazuela del Volador, across from the viceregal palace. However, despite the presence of several priests and many unmarried merchants—who boosted the number of independent men in this cofradía to forty-two, compared to thirty-five independent women—women still formed a slight majority (52 percent) overall because of the outsized presence of women and girls in household groupings (aunts, mothers, daughters, and their servants).[4]

Are these three cofradías representative of the hundreds of urban cofradías in late colonial New Spain? Were female majorities "normal" in the last century of the colony? Did social status affect gender balances, as the evidence from this small sample—the slight female majority in the elite Cofradía de la Purificación, a larger one in the less elite Cofradía de la Guía, and a much larger one in the much-less-elite Cofradía del Tránsito—suggests? Is the fact that the data from the Cofradía de la Purificación comes from the 1760s and 1770s rather than the 1720s a crucial difference? Finally, is Mexico City a unique case, or were there similar patterns in provincial New Spain?

In order to answer these questions, I used four types of documents: *libros de cornadillo* or *libros de cobranza*,[5] the account books kept by dues collectors (two of the three examples above were drawn from these books); treasurers' account books, as distinct from those of the individual collectors;[6] *libros de asiento*, or membership lists;[7] and *patentes*, or certificates of membership, the document issued upon joining and then turned over by survivors after the death of the holder, in order to collect survivor benefits (see Figure 1.1).[8] To my knowledge no historian has employed these four sources systematically to develop a social profile of urban cofradías.[9]

These sources allowed me to compile gender and status information on sixty-two cofradías in six bishoprics over the last century of the colonial period. The results are summarized in Table 1.1, and they provide some answers to the empirical questions posed above. First, the female majorities in the three cofradías profiled at the beginning of this chapter were not aberrations. In Mexico City I was able to locate good information on twenty-seven mixed-sex cofradías, between one-fifth and one-third of all the cofradías in the city, depending on whether we base our count on the period before or after the 1794 purge and consolidation of Mexican cofradías. Of these twenty-seven, only two did *not* have a female majority.[10] Overall, the mixed-sex Mexico City cofradías in the eighteenth century and the first decade of the nineteenth century averaged female majorities of over 63 percent (median 65 percent).

Outside of Mexico City, the story was similar.[11] The pattern of female majorities was somewhat more dispersed in the provinces than in Mexico City—that is, there were more extremes at both ends of the spectrum.[12] Still, over three-quarters of the mixed-sex provincial cofradías had female majorities—not as high as the 93 percent of Mexico City cofradías with female majorities, but a clear pattern nonetheless. Many of the women in these cofradías appear to have been single, independent women, though the nature of the records I used—the patentes and the lists of members especially—makes it difficult to establish marital status and age.

If region did not seem to matter much, what about status, a factor that did seem to play a role in the three examples that opened the chapter? I defined elite cofradías as ones in which at least half the membership were dons and doñas. For Mexico City I found data on ten elite cofradías, and for the provinces I found data on eleven. There was little difference between the two regions; in the Mexico City elite cofradías, women comprised 59 percent of the membership, and in the provinces, 58 percent. The fourteen identifiably non-elite cofradías in Mexico City and the seventeen in the provinces were also quite similar in their profiles; for Mexico City the average female majority in the non-elite associations was, as the three examples at the beginning of the

PATENTE

DE LA COFRADIA, Y HERMANDAD, QUE CON el Título de la Santísima Trinidad está fundada en el Hospital de Indios Othomies de esta Ciudad de Santa Fé, del Real, y Minas de Guanaxuato en el año de 1729. y trasladada à la Iglesia de San Juan Bautista el de 1766.

Yo Juan Xavier Pacheco Mayordomo de la Cofradía, que con Título de la Santísima Trinidad está fundada en el Hospital de Indios Othomies de esta Ciudad de Santa Fé de Guanaxuato, y trasladada à la Iglesia de S. Juan Bautista (como arriba se expresa) digo, que recibí por Hermana à D.ª Ana M.ª Teresa Betanzos à quien me obligo à asistir à su entierro con el Estandarte, cera, y el Señor Capellan, y toda la Comunidad de la Archi-Cofradía de la Santísima Trinidad, como tambien una Misa cantada; y asimismo participa de los Sufragios de la Cofradía; con obligacion, de que ha de dár quatro pesos, y quatro reales por su asiento, y dos reales cada un mes de cornadillo; y ha de rezar todos los dias tres Padre nuestros, y tres Ave Marias à la Santísima Trinidad, por los Hermanos vivos, y difuntos, y en falleciendo un Hermano ha de rezar lo dicho por su alma; y para que conste dí la presente en dicha Ciudad en 16. dias del mes de Diciembre del año de 1792.

Juan Xavier Pacheco
Mayordomo

Juan José Quixos
Sec.

FIGURE 1.1. Patente from the Cofradía de la Santísima Trinidad de Guanajuato, 1792. Photograph by Dr. José Eduardo Vidaurri Aréchiga.

Table 1.1. Percentage of female members in urban cofradías, approx. 1700–1810*
(numbers rounded)

	Elite**	Non-elite	Unable to determine
Mexico City			
	62 (1753–93)	54 (1688–1748)	83 (1780–1810)
	86 (1780–1819)	65 (1670–1719)	68 (1730)
	66 (1760–1809)	61 (1720s)	66 (1730–50)
	65 (1700–30)	66 (1700–29)	
	62 (1797)	61 (1690–1710)	
	53 (1762–74)	52 (1777)	
	28 (1750–85)	70 (1724)	
	46 (1717–19)	59 (1750–69)	
	65 (1786)	78 (1700–20)	
	59 (1750s)	72 (1771)	
		67 (1710–29)	
		65 (1730)	
		60 (1712)	
		67 (1719)	
	59 percent (n = 10)	64 percent (n = 14)	72 percent (n = 3)
Provincial New Spain* **			
	55 (1760–99)	60 (1770–99)	27 (1750s)
	51 (1790–1810)	65 (1805)	75 (1791)
	63 (1770–1809)	64 (1805)	72 (1786–94)
	57 (1805)	61 (1805)	51 (1770)
	80 (1805)	75 (1805)	65 (1787)
	36 (1805)	63 (1805)	72 (1767)
	65 (1770–1800)	49 (1805)	70 (1799)
	59 (1805)	72 (1750–1800)	
	82 (1743)	60 (1805)	
	39 (1743)	75 (1767–98)	
	50 (1799)	40 (1728–29)	
		34 (1738–91)	
		66 (1780s)	
		51 (1802)	
		50 (1763)	

Continued on next page

Table 1.1. (*continued*)

	Elite**	Non-elite	Unable to determine	
Provincial New Spain*				
		54 (1810)		
		73 (1800–1809)		
	58 percent (n = 11)	59.5 percent (n = 17)	62 percent (n = 7)	
All factors combined				61 percent (n = 62)
Combined by social status				
Elite				58.5 percent (n = 21)
Non-elite				62 percent (n = 31)
Unable to determine				65 percent (n = 10)
Combined by region				
Mexico City				63 percent (n = 27)
Provincial New Spain				59 percent (n = 35)
Combined by date**				
1680–1749				62 percent (n = 18)
1750–1810				61 percent (n = 43)

Sources: For Mexico, AGN, AHAMex, and Belanger, "Between the Cloister"; for Michoacán and Guadalajara, AHAMich and AHAG; for Oaxaca, AHAO, and Guardino, *Time of Liberty*; for Puebla and Veracruz, Records of the Church of Latter-Day Saints.

* Among the cofradías I included three Third Orders of the Franciscans or Dominicans. Third Orders were named in reference to the First Order (male religious, that is, members of monastic orders) and Second Order (female religious, that is, nuns). They were lay associations that shared many practices of cofradías (collective devotions, obligations to other members at the time of their deaths, yearly dues), but some members took vows of chastity or other secondary vows, were allowed to wear habits upon death, and had other practices that were not shared by cofradías such as a year-long novitiate. For some purposes, therefore, it would not make sense to include them in a study of cofradías, but since I aim here only to capture rough gender balances in lay associations, I think it makes sense to include them.

** I defined "elite" as cofradías in which at least half of the members carried the designation *don* or *doña*.

*** Archdiocese of Mexico outside of Mexico City and dioceses of Michoacán, Guadalajara, Durango, Puebla, Veracruz, Oaxaca

**** One cofradía discarded for this measure since the statistics spanned the whole century

chapter suggested, slightly higher (at 64 percent) than in the elite cofradías (at 59 percent). But in the provinces it was close to identical (58 percent elite vs. 59.5 percent non-elite). Overall, excluding region as a factor, there was only a modest difference between female majorities in elite versus non-elite cofradías. The former averaged 58.5 percent and the latter 62 percent.

Finally, we wanted to know whether change over time produced any difference in the presence or size of female majorities. It did not. The female majorities in the first half of the century, at 62 percent, were almost exactly the same as the majorities in the second half of the century, at 61 percent. It is possible that the various royal and ecclesiastical assaults on the cofradías late in the colonial period discouraged people of *both* sexes from becoming cofradía members, since my data are not good indicators of absolute numbers of members. This is an argument made by historian Juan Javier Pescador, using data on several cofradías in the parish of Santa Catarina in Mexico City.[13] He specifically blames perceptions that because of financial problems related to government interference in their operations, the cofradías could no longer be assumed capable of covering burial expenses and survivor benefits. This argument is also made by historian Brian Larkin, who documents fewer mentions of cofradía membership and declining donations to cofradías in Mexico City wills over the eighteenth century, attributing these patterns to increased penetration of "enlightened" ideas that led some testators to reject baroque religiosity in favor of a more individual and personal religion.[14] Both Larkin's and Pescador's methods have limits—Pescador's because of the small number of cofradías involved, and Larkin's because of the indirect nature of ascertaining cofradía membership from wills (styles of testating—what it was common to mention in a will—could and did change) and also because of the relatively small numbers of wills made by women. There is frankly no method that would yield truly clean results; it is not feasible to accumulate reliable data on a sufficient number of intact cofradías (that is, ones that were not joined together with others or moved from one church to another), over time, to allow superior comparison. But even if it seems that there was some pulling away from the cofradías in the late eighteenth century—compared to, say, the middle of the seventeenth century, when enthusiasm for cofradías and for communal displays of religiosity in general seems to have been at its height—it is clear that there was not a wholesale and dramatic abandonment of the cofradías, and that if there was any abandonment it was not primarily male. Cofradías remained popular, and gender balances within the membership did not change much right up to the outbreak of the wars for independence.

The female majorities in cofradías will surprise most readers, since until recently the assumption was that Mexican (as well as European) cofradías were all or mostly all male in their membership.[15] This assumption was understandable. Most of what we know about cofradías comes from the legal records of their business dealings or from the court cases in which they were involved, and the officers who acted on behalf of the cofradías in these contexts were always men. Reinforcing this assumption that cofradías were masculine institutional spaces is the fact that for Mexico, there has been particular attention paid to the cofradías whose membership *was* exclusively male or heavily male-dominated—for example, those comprised of flagellants, priests, or ethnic Spaniards.[16] It is not surprising, then, that the functions women served in the cofradías we now know they dominated, their relationships to men and to priests, and their reasons for joining have not been probed.

Gender Roles in the Cofradías: Men

All cofradía members, both men and women, were expected to attend the special masses sponsored by the organization and to participate in funeral masses for other members. Beyond that, however, cofradía activities seem to have been highly gendered. What women members of a cofradía expected from the institution and what they contributed is hard to excavate from the sources, so it may be helpful to begin with the roles that men filled. In that light, women's functions in the cofradía will come into sharper relief.

Cofradías, as we saw in the introduction, were highly visible in towns and city neighborhoods, and men were highly visible within them. Most obvious, men participated actively when the image to which the cofradía was dedicated left the church in procession. Men who formed part of the processional cortege had formal roles, including but not limited to carrying the image on its platform through the streets. Banners and standards organized the members of the cortege, and active participants might wear a costume or uniform. Participating in processions was one of the most spiritually meaningful parts of being a member of a cofradía. This was a solemn event and a direct conversation with God. It was also socially meaningful; it was witnessed by the entire city, and prestige accrued to those who carried the image and to those who were placed in particularly favored positions close to the image. These appear always to have been men.

Second, men elected other men as members of the governing boards (*mesas*) in an annual *junta*. All male members of the cofradía could vote (as we will see below, it is unclear whether women had the right to vote, much less whether they took advantage of it). Most cofradías elected a fairly large number of deputies; twelve was a common number. The governing board, which usually met monthly, made important decisions about the cofradía's activities. Some of these were business decisions—for example, whether to sell or rent property owned by the cofradía. In other cases the mesa decided how the charitable funds administered by the cofradía would be distributed. Historian Jessica Delgado, for example, shows the surprising extent to which members of a cofradía's board might try to micromanage which young girl in one of the

FIGURE 1.2. "El traslado de las monjas dominicas a su nuevo convento de Valladolid," anon., 1738. Note the image of the Cofradía del Santísimo being carried in the procession in the center right. The painting strives to show all ethnic groups, from "barbarous" Indians in the foreground to African-descended people and "civilized" Indians on the right, but the only women are the nuns themselves, and the women looking on from the balconies. Image reproduced by permission from the Instituto Nacional de Antropología e Historia and the Museo Regional Michoacano.

Mexico City *colegios* would receive a dowry from the cofradía to enable her to marry, and might even interfere in her choice of husband.[17] The mesa was also involved in settling legal disputes that involved the cofradía. A business manager, or mayordomo, was elected by the male members of the cofradía (or sometimes by the governing board). This person kept the books, collected rents and interest, and in general took care of the day-to-day business of the cofradía.

Cofradías took pride in recruiting elite men. When prominent men chose to join a particular cofradía, it was thought to validate the cofradía's spiritual worth, as well as to ensure "good government" of the organization. The Cofradía del Santísimo Sacramento in the small town of Salvatierra (present-day Guanajuato), for example, endeavored to attract socially prominent men as members because "religious piety shines especially brightly when it is practiced by persons of the highest distinction, and the public is greatly edified by witnessing their piety, and for these important reasons the cofradía must always ensure that responsibility for its growth and good government is in the hands of subjects of this class."[18] The well-to-do were seen as more disinterested, more trustworthy, than the less well-off. The Cofradía del Santísimo Sacramento of Fresnillo (Zacatecas), for example, having ballooned to seven hundred members by 1777, decided to contradict its own constitution—which called for the mayordomo to be elected by a vote of the whole membership, in what would inevitably be an unwieldy process—and instead to trust the selection of a mayordomo to the twelve officers of the cofradía. Under the circumstances faced by the cofradía, including its rapid recent growth, it was especially important for officers to be "elected from among the most distinguished subjects," as the cofradía secretary wrote to the archbishop.[19] All four Mexico City cofradías that were exclusive to peninsular Spaniards— the Cofradía de Aranzazu for Basques (men from Viscaya and Navarre); the Cofradía del Santo Cristo de Burgos for men from Cantabria; the Cofradía de Balbanera for those from La Rioja; and the Cofradía of Santiago for the Galicians—were said to be "in good shape because the *cofrades* are the most important and wealthiest men from each of these nations."[20] Similarly, although the various Third Orders of Mexico City in 1794 resisted allowing the archbishop to review their books, he not only let this mild rebellion slide but also gave them the benefit of the doubt, presuming their financial situation to be advantageous "because of the many . . . rich men that belong to them."[21]

Having wealthy mayordomos and officers was necessary because they might need to cover the cofradía's expenses out of their own pockets for a year or two if necessary, in case of a natural disaster, epidemic, or economic crisis that greatly reduced income or increased expenses. This was especially important in resource-poor cofradías like the Cofradía de los Esclavos y Acompañamiento del Santísimo Sacramento in Mexico City, which consistently spent more than it took in.[22] The cofradía had multiple obligations including sponsoring numerous masses, Holy Week celebrations, the last day of the Forty Hours celebration, oil for the lamp, lanterns and luminarias to accompany the Host when it was transported to the sick, as well as twenty-five pesos and a High Mass for each of the cofrades who died. The weekly contribution of the members was not enough to sustain these costs, and so to "maintain the necessary decency in the Sanctuary, we have relied on . . . the officers of the Cofradía, who have supplemented the cofradía's funds, risking that they will never be repaid."[23]

The risk was probably seen as worth taking by the men on whom it fell, since it reflected well on their piety, their wealth, and their social standing. Indeed, several scholars of cofradías have emphasized that cofradías provided spaces of sociability that could advance social standing and allow members to consolidate business or family connections.[24] This was true for the well-to-do, but it was also true to a certain extent for poorer men, who may not have hobnobbed with the rich during the cofradía's functions and meetings, but who might have been able to solidify patronage or business relationships in the context of shared cofradía membership.

Gender Roles in the Cofradías: Women

What roles did women play in the cofradías that they dominated numerically? Why did so many of them join cofradías? Without widespread recognition in the literature that female majorities existed, it is to be expected that these questions have not been asked. Historian David Carbajal López's work on women in cofradías in Mexico and Spain is the only other scholarly attempt of which I am aware to take up the question of gender roles in urban cofradías, and I draw on his work here gratefully but cautiously ("cautiously" since he includes all cofradías and not just urban ones, and since his conclusions are based upon the provisions in a cofradía's constitution and not on direct or even indirect evidence of what actually occurred).[25]

First, no matter their wealth and social prestige, Hispanic and mestizo women were never members of the governing boards in the mixed-sex cofradías to which they belonged (despite the fact that there was rarely a specific constitutional prohibition against their election).[26] While there were a few cases of female leadership of indigenous or *pardo* cofradías in the seventeenth century, they had become rare to nonexistent by the middle of the eighteenth. Men in these cofradías, according to historian Nicole von Germeten, increasingly "rejected female leadership, perhaps because it made their organizations look very different from confraternities led by their social betters of European descent."[27]

There were a few cases in which a woman served as the mayordomo of a cofradía, almost always because her husband had occupied the position and she was left in charge of his business affairs after his death. In these cases the cofradía usually replaced her quickly with a male mayordomo. But sometimes it was convenient to allow her to stay on the job because the cofradía owed her husband's estate a sum that would not be easy to raise quickly. This was the case with Doña Rita Michaela García, who was owed 392 pesos by the Cofradía del Santísimo Sacramento in Tulancingo (present-day Hidalgo) in the 1760s. When he visited Tulancingo, Archbishop Francisco Lorenzana permitted her reelection, but "only on the condition that she never attend the meetings of the officers" (which mayordomos ordinarily did) and that she "not mix in any of the other actions that are appropriately carried out by Men, and that when the said debt is paid, new elections should be held, and under no circumstances shall a Woman be elected."[28] In short, we have to stretch to find much evidence of female cofradía leadership, even as mayordomos.

As Lorenzana's comment suggests, the underlying principles governing lay interaction in cofradías (and elsewhere) were not only that women should not govern men but also that men and women should not mix in public. These rules prevented female leadership (and help explain why female mayordomos were occasionally tolerated, since their work was not done in a group, and while they managed financial affairs, they did not need to mix with men) and also colored women's experience in other cofradía activities, including processions. But before turning to this aspect of women's participation in cofradía activities, we should consider the phenomenon of separate women's and men's cofradías. These provided a solution to the problem of "mixing," but of course their structure inevitably required female officers to govern the women's group.

One of the very small number of all-female cofradías was the Cofradía del Rosario formed by the nuns of the Convent of San Bernardo in Mexico City in the first half of the eighteenth century, to which the secular women living in the convent as their companions or servants could also belong.[29] It was governed by nuns who held offices like those in the other rosary cofradías. Although nuns frequently belonged to cofradías established in their convent churches, one that was established *within* a convent, with a full complement of female officers, was unusual. A female branch of the Escuela de Cristo, a penitential cofradía, appears to have been theoretically possible, though the response to the question of whether or not there were any all-female Escuelas in Mexico City in a 1797 royal interrogatory was negative.[30] The other cases of separate female groups all involve indigenous or African-descended women, perhaps an artifact of pre-Hispanic and African relative gender parallelism. The Cofradía del Virgen del Camino in Orizaba (Veracruz) was made up of young, unmarried indigenous women (although their fathers seem to have been the main directors of the group).[31] Finally, a *cofradía de pardos* (African-descended people) in Parral (Chihuahua) had parallel male and female branches. A throwback to an earlier time when this kind of arrangement was common in the Afro-Mexican urban cofradías, this particular group of *madres* (as the female members were called) showed up in the records because it had been marginalized by a city ordinance—supported by the priest—that moved the cofradía's nighttime procession on Holy Friday to the afternoon. This change kept intact the participation of the male section of the cofradía, but the madres, whose responsibility had been to pay for the wax with which the procession was illuminated (for which they spent much of the year collecting alms), were out of a job when candles were no longer needed. The elected Madres Mayores and Menores were livid—a rare example of women in the cofradía context not only protesting but using quite intemperate language to do so.[32]

None of these cases, with the exception of the Cofradía del Rosario in the convent (which was all-female by design of the nuns, but adhered in every other way to the practices of the mixed-sex rosary cofradías outside the convent), involved an independent group of women who decided to form their own cofradía. That was not a model in play in Mexico before the turn of the century (as we will see below).[33] Instead, they were adjuncts or auxiliaries to men's groups.

Was separate in any way equal? We can gain some insight into this question from the detailed rules governing men's and women's Third Order associations. Third Orders were associations of laypeople who lived according to certain rules established by the First Orders (e.g., Franciscans or Dominicans or Carmelites, to name the most common in Mexico) for their affiliated lay groups. These associations were not, then, confraternities, but as lay associations connected to a church they bore similarities to them, and I utilize their published rules here to get at gender roles within lay groups more generally.

As in the communities of the First (male) and Second (female) Orders, there was a separate structure of governance for both men and women. In the Third Order of Dominicans in Mexico City in the 1770s, for example, both the men's section and the women's section had a prior(a) and a sub-prior(a), as well as twelve advisers, two *celadores* (alms collectors), and a novice master/mistress (who trained and acculturated new members). But the rest of the offices were not parallel. The men's group elected a master of ceremonies, a treasurer, an advocate (*abogado*), a secretary, and a pro-secretary, all positions absent on the women's side, while the women's group included an assistant in charge of the residential quarters (*Vicaria de Casa*) that did not have a male equivalent. Both groups, meanwhile, named caregivers to the sick (*enfermeros*), but the women provided five compared to two for the men; and the women also supplied five assistants to the Divine Cult (*Vicarios/as del Culto Divino*), who were responsible for caring for the altar of the church and the paraphernalia used in ceremonies, to the men's two. In addition there were six female and no male sacristans—another position that called for domestic labor (cleaning, mending, dusting, etc.).[34]

This breakdown of duties, in which the women's group was not involved in anything to do with money or legal disputes or public representation of the organization, and instead disproportionately assumed duties that revolved around healing and housekeeping, was roughly similar to the duties of female and male officers in the Third Order of Carmelites of Toluca in 1736: there, too, no female equivalent of the treasurer or secretary existed.[35] In no Third Order organizations were women officers allowed to attend the meetings of the executive boards during which the business of the organization was conducted.[36] This was true, of course, of all cofradías that were male-led, since only officers attended the private business meetings, but the exclusion is especially notable in the Third Orders since they did have female officers.

In some of the Third Order organizations, there were also meaningful restrictions on women that did not apply to men. For example, neither married women nor young single women could wear the habit of the Order, a meaningful privilege: married women "in order to avoid an indecency, unless they are of an age in which they cannot conceive," and single women because "they are on a path to marriage, unless they have taken a vow of perpetual virginity, to which the spiritual director must attest."[37] In what may have been a common practice that was not spelled out in most cofradía constitutions, it was stipulated in the constitution of the Third Order of Carmelites of Toluca that after the monthly meetings of all members, the women should take Communion only after all the men had finished.[38]

In all cofradías, women were treated differently from men when it came to participating in processions. They were never, probably needless to say, invited to carry the cofradía's image in procession when it left the church, nor the banners or emblems of the organization. They were not "active" participants in the processions in the sense that they had no assigned place in relation to the image, and they did not wear costumes or uniforms (though they may have worn an insignia identifying them as members). Their role in the larger processions in which many cofradías participated, like Corpus Christi, was purely that of spectators, since only a select number of members marched and there was not space for all members (see Figure 1.2). In smaller processions in which only one image was paraded, women participated by following behind the formally constituted part of the procession.[39]

Some of the most important activities of the cofradía—accompanying the Host when it was carried to the homes of the dying, and joining the funeral corteges of members—were generally off limits to women if they were either pregnant or single, both conditions that made it unseemly for them to "wander through the city (*vagar por la Ciudad*)," as the Archicofradía del Santísimo Sacramento in Oaxaca put it.[40] Pregnant women should instead stay home and say an Our Father and an Ave Maria for the moribund when they heard the signal of the bells telling the other cofrades to join in viaticum.[41] In a new Eucharistic cofradía founded in Durango late in the century, the constitution stated that all members were expected to participate in half-hour vigils before the Blessed Sacrament, "but for women who cannot leave their homes [because of pregnancy], it will be sufficient to carry out the vigil at home."[42] Similarly, the Cofradía del Rosario in Veracruz admitted women but did not allow them to participate in the nocturnal Rosary that was the principle activity of the cofradía.[43] Women may have occasionally attended the annual meetings at which officers were elected, since at least in some cases they received indulgences for doing so, though it is probable that this was discouraged, by custom if not regulation, since mixing of the sexes in public was discouraged. It is even less likely that women took advantage of the "right" to vote, since it was not indulgenced (although none of the dozens of constitutions that I have read with particular attention to this point specifically exclude women from voting, and Carbajal López for Spain only found one such explicit exclusion).[44]

None of this means that women were not valued as cofradía members. As the example of the Third Order and its differential functions for men and women suggests, women in cofradías performed important tasks that men could not or would not perform. In the adornment of churches and care of the image associated with the cofradía, women members had specific and indispensable roles to play: mending the clothing worn by the image, stitching and embroidering new garments as well as altar cloths and drapes; dusting and cleaning the altar; polishing the silver; sweeping the church; filling the altar with flowers (both live and artificial).[45] In the proposed Congregación de Esclavos y Esclavas de Guadalupe in Irapuato (Guanajuato), the female members of the cofradía were explicitly given the responsibility of cleaning the church every Saturday.[46] In the staging of processions, women likely worked behind the scenes to be sure that the image cared for by the cofradía was bejeweled, well-clad, framed by flowers, and ready for public adoration before it was solemnly carried out of the church and into the street. We know that women got together to sew and ornament the awnings that covered images in the procession of Corpus Christi in Mexico City.[47]

Their gendered labor on behalf of the cofradía was surely understood and valued by women as advancing and strengthening the Catholic faith. The importance of beautifying the churches and carrying off celebrations with the greatest pomp and dignity possible, for the greater glory of God and to enhance the zeal of the faithful, were constant elements of the broader discourse. Splendor, as Brian Larkin makes clear, was not just an embellishment but was rather at the core of worship and of pleasing God.[48] And besides beauty, there was also "decency," a word used repeatedly by ecclesiastical visitors to churches and cofradías in judgment of the manner in which the cofradía's spiritual inventory was maintained. Decency, as much or more than splendor, was probably the responsibility of the women of the cofradía.

What, besides this surely gratifying sense of contributing to the care and maintenance of the image and church associated with the cofradía, and the spiritual power that came from proximity to the altar and sacred images, did women get out of membership? The most important reason to join a cofradía, of course, was to aid salvation. The encouragement and support of cofrades who visited and prayed for the dying, escorted the body to its grave, and said masses for the souls of dead members every year were thought to comfort the dying, steel them to resist temptation, shorten their time in purgatory, and enhance the possibility of salvation.[49] Though men, naturally, also sought salvation, Larkin argues that there was a gendered dimension to the search for it. He demonstrates that by the late eighteenth century, at least among the better-off people of Mexico City—those who had sufficient property to justify writing a will—salvation was beginning to be understood as more an individual than collective responsibility, and one result was fewer mentions of cofradía membership and fewer donations to cofradías among testators. But women, he argues, remained more committed than men to the tenets of baroque Catholicism, presumably including the efficacy of the collective prayers of the cofradía (although he does not provide gender breakdowns specifically for cofradía membership among testators across the eighteenth century).[50] Thus, Larkin seems to be saying, to the extent that men continued to join cofradías and to pay their weekly or monthly fees in order to maintain their good standing, they did so for increasingly worldly reasons (sociability, prestige), while women—who could not derive prestige from leadership of the cofradía and could only to a very limited extent make or solidify social and business connections through association with other members—continued to join because they valued the cofradía's assistance in achieving a "good death" and salvation.

A "good death" aided salvation but there was also, of course—as there was for men—a material component to it. As we saw in the introduction, many cofradías paid for a coffin, shroud, and burial for deceased members, and they also offered fairly substantial survivor benefits. These protections were significant to all but the wealthiest cofrades, men or women; but poor women, and especially poor single women—who outnumbered poor single men in most urban areas—may have found them particularly attractive, since many of them had recently arrived in the cities or towns and might not have families who could be depended on to be sure that their deaths were dignified and proper. The arrival of young, single women from the countryside, swelling the numbers of women versus men in the cities, partly explains why there was a relatively high number of single or independent women who joined cofradías, but the appeal of the cofradías' commitment to provide a good death when these women had few family resources to rely on should not be discounted.

The cofradía also provided a particular kind of social community for women. Of course cofrades shared an identity and a social community with all the other members, male and female; this was inherent in the nature of the cofradía. As Larkin puts it, not just salvation but also "social cohesion" was the "ideal" outcome of the collective devotion expressed during processions, as well as at other times when cofradía members came together.[51] But in their preparations for a celebration and in the weekly maintenance of the church and image, working together in common purpose, women also developed a gendered community within the larger community. The female majorities in the cofradías meant that these communities were large and probably quite diverse. We cannot know how they functioned or the extent to which they *did* function as a group, but likely the higher-status women took on unofficial leadership roles, providing them a kind of social validation or prestige that was vaguely akin to that enjoyed by the male leaders of the cofradía. In fact, the responsibility of caring for the dress and ornamentation of images was a formalized honor for an elite woman in some cofradías like that of Covadonga in Mexico City, where the constitution called for a "señora from the most illustrious families of this court" to be named as "camarera" (here meant as a lady-in-waiting in attendance upon the image of Our Lady of Covadonga) by the governing board.[52] Even in those cofradías that did not appoint an elite attendant, it is not difficult to imagine a collective female effort to prepare the cofradía's image for its annual fiesta, one in which some women bossed others around, even as all women were subject to the dictates of the cofradía leadership and the priest in the final preparations for bringing the image into the street.

In sum, cofradías reproduced corporate society in that they were both inclusive and hierarchical. They were inclusive in that they welcomed women, in part for the important and valuable domestic work that needed doing, and in part because the presence of large numbers of women gave meaning to the inclusive language of the constitutions and undergirded the ideological premise on which the cofradías were based: that they represented the entire community. It is not surprising that we see more than a few cofradías, notably those to which males were especially drawn (disciplinary cofradías, for example), going out of their way to make sure that women joined. The Hermandad de la Sangre de Christo in Guanajuato, for example, allowed wives to join for free; the penitential Cofradía del Santo Entierro de Christo in Sayula (Michoacán) allowed women to join for half the men's fee; and the Cofradía del Santísimo Sacramento in Tizapan el Alto (Jalisco) charged women two-thirds of the men's fee.[53] With a substantial female membership, the ideology of confraternal community was preserved even for cofradías that were socially or racially exclusive (e.g., the four cofradías in late eighteenth-century Mexico City that were open only to Spanish immigrants).[54]

But they were also hierarchical, especially along lines of gender; if cofradías reproduced corporate principles, they were also microcosms of patriarchy. While women seem to have accompanied the Host to the dying alongside men, and they obviously attended Mass with men, within the cofradía there were times and places where men and women did not even come into contact with one another. Women performed different tasks within the cofradía; women were excluded from the meetings of the governing boards and perhaps from the annual meetings; men and women may not have taken Communion at the same time; they did not process side by side even in the smaller processions.

The many cases we know of in the colonial period in which women in various contexts challenged male precedence or acted independently of men (founding schools or convents, running businesses or haciendas, exploiting the court system for ways to undermine husbands or fathers, expressing political opinions, leading village rebellions) make me suspect that women in cofradías may have sought more ways to influence cofradía management than the records show.[55] But the archives that I have consulted are silent on any such challenges, not to mention on the question of whether many or any female cofrades resented the fact that they could not assume leadership roles or work or march alongside men. Female insubordination is the sort of thing that might be remarked upon by priests in their correspondence with the bishops (as happened fairly frequently in the nineteenth century, as the chapters below show), but I found very little. Even in the one case in which we do see women speak up—the Afro-Mexican women in Parral (see the case above), who were extremely angry about their group's exclusion from the annual celebration while the men's group was able to continue their participation—they did not challenge the men's prerogatives, only the priest's and governor's judgment in cutting them out.

All we can say is that hierarchy was a rule most women members of urban cofradías seemed to accept. Did it matter, then, that they formed the majority of the membership in most cases? I think it did, though perhaps more for the long term than during the colonial period. Looking ahead to the post-independence period, female majorities in the colonial cofradías meant that many, perhaps even most, urban women had the experience of belonging to an organization that held regular elections and public meetings, even if they were not included equally in those activities. They also had the experience of working with a group of women within the cofradía to advance its interests. As we will see in chapter 3, women were early organizers of alternatives to the traditional cofradía. At least one explanation for this was that they had experience in the colonial cofradías, with their associative culture, their constitutions that spelled out rights and duties, and their election of officers.

The Cofradía in the Late Eighteenth Century

Cofradías came under attack by both the state and the church in the last third of the eighteenth century.[56] As also happened in many other Catholic countries, the royal government of Spain in the 1760s began a campaign to reduce, control, and reform cofradías, which it saw as political loose cannons (because they heightened local loyalties in an era of a centralizing state), economic drains that impoverished members while contributing nothing to the state by way of taxes, and overexuberant "motors of irrational superstition."[57] Meanwhile, the church had its own cofradía agenda, which converged with that of the state in some respects. Broadly, both church and state were keen to reduce the number of cofradías associated with the monastic orders and to elevate those that served the parishes. Church reformers saw the parish, not the convents, as the appropriate locus of community piety, and the parish priests, not the friars, as the appropriate supervisors of this piety. In his own parish, the well-trained and dedicated priest could assure that alms or cofradía resources went to support sacramental functions and not alcohol or fireworks; he could set up schools, visit the sick, care for the spiritual and material well-being of his parishioners as a shepherd with a flock of sheep.[58] By 1795 Archbishop Núñez de Haro had reduced the number of cofradías in the archbishopric of Mexico from over nine hundred to around five hundred, either by combining two or more of them in order to create a more viable single institution (one that was often housed in the parish church rather than the convent church), or demoting them to the status of *hermandades*, simpler brotherhoods without the privileges enjoyed by a constituted cofradía.[59]

Both church and state were also determined to tone down the lavishness of the annual functions that the cofradías sponsored. The crackdown on cofradía celebrations appears chiefly to have been motivated by the changing tastes and ideals of the European eighteenth century and the attempt to respond to Protestant criticisms of Catholic "excess." It was part of a broader movement of Catholic reform that aimed "to redefine the balance in Catholic practice between ritual action and pious contemplation in favor of the latter," as Larkin puts it.⁶⁰ Reform projects were designed to minimize exterior displays of piety such as processions and pilgrimages, and to downplay the rituals and artistic traditions that appealed strongly to the senses and emotions (the use of fireworks, music, incense, gold and silver ornamentation, candles, evocative paintings and images of Christ's and Mary's suffering), in favor of dignified interior prayer, quiet meditation, restrained art, and decorous ceremonies. A variety of processional practices were banned (for example, processions that left too late in the day to return before dark; processions that included giant balloons and floats; processions that left the city streets and ventured into the countryside). It was thus clear that the direction of reforms on the part of both crown and church was toward sanitizing the popular religiosity associated with the cofradías, forcing the sale of the properties that supported their objectionable activities, and clearing out dysfunctional cofradías, however that term was defined by church and crown officials.

However, the ability and even, ultimately, the willingness of the crown and church to enforce these and other anti-cofradía measures—whose logical conclusion was a contraction in the number of cofradías in any given region and the diminution or elimination of some of the most popular festivals and religious practices—was less than the bluster of the language used to articulate them. Successful foot-dragging protected more cofradía wealth than the crown got its hands on. Although it is certainly the case that the 1804 Consolidación law, which forced church institutions to sell property and call in loans and then lend the proceeds to the crown, alerted everyone to the vulnerable situation of cofradías that depended on rents from property and capital out on loan to survive, cofradías still made up a significant presence in the cities and towns.⁶¹ The processions and fiestas they sponsored continued. Priests continued to defend and to rely on them, and people continued to join them.

Women in the Late Eighteenth-Century Cofradías

Carbajal López's study of cofradía constitutions submitted for royal review suggests that over time, women's roles in cofradías became even less rich and varied than earlier in the eighteenth century because royal officials became hypervigilant about preserving separation of the sexes.⁶² But two new cofradías proposed very late in the colonial period called for expanding roles for women in ways that are worth exploring in some detail, because of the precedents they provided for post-independence changes, but also because of what they tell us about the penetration into Mexico of European ideas about public roles for women and women's capacity for leadership. The first was the Real Congregación del Alumbrado y Vela Continua del Santísimo Sacramento (the Royal Congregation of the Illumination and Continuous Vigil of the Blessed Sacrament).⁶³ This lay association was proposed in January 1789, by two members of the court of

Charles IV. Aware of the special devotion that the king and Queen Luisa had for the Blessed Sacrament, and of their practice of "sitting with the Santísimo every day and hour that their many occupations allowed," these (male) courtiers decided to formalize the vigil in the royal chapel in Madrid—in other words, to set up an organization that would be responsible for making sure that the vigil was "continuous" (by which they meant that two people would sit for half-hour shifts during all the hours that the chapel was open).[64] The goal was "to excite in the hearts of the Faithful the most fevered affection for the Blessed Sacrament, and to pray for the health of the King and Queen and the royal family, for the wisdom of the government, and for the spiritual and temporal well-being of the Monarchy." The king was so pleased with the congregation that he proclaimed that it should be extended to all the parishes of his kingdoms. This was, then, a lay initiative (on the part of the members of the court), typical of the foundation of a cofradía, but it was unusual in that it was the king who directly authorized it and commanded its expansion.

The Madrid Real Congregación was led by an all-male officer corps.[65] But when the project was presented to the archbishop of Mexico, Alonso Núñez de Haro, he—following the recommendation of Juan de Cienfuegos, the archbishop's vicar general and also the priest of the parish of San Sebastián, whose church would house the new cofradía—made a crucial change: in Mexico City, he decided, the mesa should include a separate section for women.[66] "Zeal and Devotion," Cienfuegos had counseled, would best be "excited among the Women" if there were "officers of their sex who attend to [inspiring this zeal] and to stimulating the growth of the Congregation."[67]

The crown was evidently nonplussed by this addition of female officers, and the archbishop's innovation gave rise to a lengthy exchange among himself, the king and other royal officials, and the officers of both the Real Congregación in Madrid and the one in Mexico City. In these documents the issue was referred to in a de-sexed way as the "increase in the number of officers" in the Mexico City Real Congregación, but there is no question that it was about the presence of women, as the archbishop himself made clear in a September 19, 1794, letter to the new viceroy, the Marqués de Branciforte.[68]

Núñez de Haro began the letter by pointing out that he had complied with the royal charge, in 1791, to canonically establish the new cofradía, and he reported that it had attracted enough members to begin the continuous vigil in March 1793. (Separate letters describe the enthusiasm with which the new devotion had been received in the parish of San Sebastián.)[69] In a part of the correspondence that was not included in the file, it appears that the king had complained that the Mexico City congregation had begun to carry out the vigil without submitting its constitution to him. The archbishop countered that he did not need to send such a constitution because the congregation had been founded "on the same rules and constitutions as the Real Congregación founded in the royal chapel in Madrid," which had obviously already been approved by the king. The only "incidental difference" (*diferencia accidental*) between the Mexico City and Madrid constitutions, he wrote, "is the number of officers on the [two] Mesa[s]." But this was "not a substantial alteration" of the original constitution, he continued, as was clearly demonstrated by the fact that the number of officers in the Madrid congregation itself had been "increased to 51, when it used to be five."[70]

His insistence that the Mexico City congregation operated by the same constitution as the Madrid one was a clever maneuver on Núñez de Haro's part. As we have seen, there was no explicit exclusion of female officers in any cofradía constitutions—it was just understood that women were not suitable candidates—and the Madrid constitution was no exception. There was, however, in clause six a provision for an increase in the number of officers if the Junta decided it was necessary "for the good management of the congregation."[71] This is the clause that had been used to justify the expansion of the Madrid executive board: the massive increase in the number of officers by 1794 was necessary because of the "various matters that have arisen in the extension of the Real Congregación to all the dominions of His Majesty."[72] The archbishop agreed with this reasoning: "in every location officers ought to be chosen who are best capable of assuring the good governance and growth of the Real Congregación." "I myself," he continued innocently, "named a Vice Hermana Mayor,[73] two [female] counselors and one [female] alms collector," expecting that, "bound by these titles, they would dedicate themselves even more to the cult of the Blessed Sacrament, and excite others of their sex to enlist in the Congregation." Again, he reiterated, "these purely incidental changes" were made in the spirit of clause six, which allowed the size of the mesa to be adjusted "according to the circumstances of each place and the state of the Congregations." Moreover, not only clause six but also "natural reason" and precedent justified the addition of extra (female) officers. Besides the precedent of the Madrid mesa's expansion, another locally driven change in practices had been authorized by the archbishop of Seville, when he told his flock that the length of the vigil, set at half an hour in the original constitution, could vary "depending on the circumstances of the congregants." In short, the archbishop interpreted the Madrid constitution as anticipating that the interests of each cofradía might be served differently in different situations, and in his judgment the particular circumstances in Mexico City required women on the executive board.

What were these particular circumstances? Why did the archbishop feel it necessary to include women? One possibility is that he was annoyed at the king's intervention in the foundation and mandated expansion of this new cofradía. A recent royal requirement that crown officials preside over cofradía meetings had been poorly received by both laymen and the church, and later documents in this packet of materials on the Real Congregación show that the archbishop was indeed protective of the autonomy of the San Sebastián congregation vis-à-vis both the crown and the Madrid congregation.[74] Adding women as officers subtly diminished the Real Congregación's aggressive maleness (the huge number of noble, male officers; the rapid expansion to all the realms of the kingdom) and arguably diminished the importance of the enterprise. Women officers in the Mexico City Real Congregación, in this scenario, would best be interpreted as pawns in the jurisdictional skirmishes between church and crown that cropped up periodically during this period. But this interpretation is not fully compelling; the action was too subtle by half if this was its intent, and in any event, for the gender-hierarchy-bound church to make a stand against royal overreach by inventing female officers seems implausible.

It also seems unlikely that the archbishop was primarily motivated by a firm belief that women could and should be leaders of cofradías. It is possible that he was merely assuaging royal nervousness about female officers, masking a conviction that it was time for women to assume more responsibility for the organizations that they dominated numerically, when he made it clear that the female officers' honorifics were "titles in name only; they cannot call meetings or mix in the government of the congregation, because this is reserved for officials of the governing board [*junta*], just as in the original rules and constitutions."[75] But it seems more probable that "titles in name only" were exactly what the archbishop thought right and natural. It was one thing to flatter prominent and active women in colonial society by recruiting them to the governing board, where their energy and prestige would attract others to join, but quite another that they should actually hold power.

The best interpretation of the archbishop's actions is that socially prominent women officers were perceived as crucial to the task of signing up the requisite numbers of participants to make the vigil a success. We should remember that the initial suggestion that women should be made officers did not come from the archbishop, but rather his vicar general, Cienfuegos, who was also, importantly, the parish priest of San Sebastián. It was his church that stood to gain prestige if the new organization became a big success. But it was also his church that would lose face if the vigil fell apart. Unlike most cofradía practices, in which the number of people who actually accompanied the Host in viaticum or joined a procession mattered relatively little, the whole concept of a "continuous vigil" required that sixty people show up on time for their shifts, all day long, every day.[76] If it failed, it failed quite visibly. Cienfuegos made a recommendation that he saw as essential to the success of the new cofradía: to not only include women officers but also make them responsible for "exciting the women" and "ensuring the growth of the organization."[77] Mexico's history of female majorities in cofradías was surely on his mind.

Was offering prominent women empty honorifics in this new cofradía a significant innovation from the perspective of the relationship between women and the church? On the one hand, it can be seen as merely having created a women's auxiliary with quite limited responsibilities (mainly, it appears, encouraging other women to join). Beyond this, there is no evidence that even this small movement toward more equality between men and women in the cofradías resulted from women lobbying for inclusion, and the participatory experience of both the women members and the women officers was impoverished compared to that of the officers in most cofradías, who were elected by their peers. Here they were named by the archbishop, who was acting in service of the church's interests and convenience.

Nonetheless, it seems an important step that the concept of a separate women's group within a proper cofradía (not a Third Order organization), even if it was auxiliary to the men's group, was established. And it is also significant that before the profound disruptions of the independence era—which, as we will see, changed the whole calculus of power within the cofradías—a precedent had been set for a new kind of alliance between elite women and the church, one that went beyond individual women donating money to various church institutions. Finally, it is quite likely that the presence of female officers in the Real Congregación paved the way for a second late colonial organization that much more clearly envisioned a larger and non-auxiliary role for women in pious associations, closely resembling the activist women's charitable organizations in Europe.[78]

That organization was the Asociación de Señoras en la Ciudad de México, which probably never got off the ground because of the outbreak of the wars for independence just a bit more than five years after the initial proposals for its foundation were made. But that it was proposed in the first place gives us—much more than the presence of female officers in the Real Congregación—a sense that women in colonial Mexico were not only aware of European precedents for all-female lay associations that operated independently of any male organization, but that they aspired to form such an organization themselves.[79] The circumstances of its founding, as was true also in the case of the Real Congregación, suggest that the church, while by no means transformed in the late colony into an advocate of new roles for women in the religious/civic public sphere (after all, the archbishop had gone out of his way to reassure the crown that the female officers in the Real Congregación had no power), was both more open to those new roles and *perceived* as being more open to them than the state was.

The documentation on the proposed association begins with an annoyed letter from Viceroy Iturrigaray to Archbishop Francisco Xavier Lizana, dated December 28, 1804.[80] The viceroy wrote that "by accident, I discovered that in a house outside of this capital, on two occasions, various distinguished Ladies met with Your Excellency to discuss the establishment of a charitable association dedicated to the pious exercise of assisting women patients in the Hospitals, under the denomination of Oblatas; and now those Ladies have presented themselves to me, with a list of their Associates and with the constitution that will govern them, soliciting royal approbation. I write to you, Your Excellency, requesting that you inform me of exactly what happened and what is your opinion of the proposal." Lizana responded that in fact he had only met with the women once, but that it was indeed in a private house (though inside the walls of the city). He had traveled to meet them because he did not think it was appropriate for the women to come to the archiepiscopal palace. "I advised them," he continued, "that in order to carry out their idea they needed royal approval . . . And since you ask me what I think of this project, I can only tell you that the establishment of this pious Association offers advantageous results for both Religion and the State, which have been achieved in all the Populations in which it has been introduced."[81]

The list of associates included thirty-nine ladies, among them five Marquesas. The constitution that they had adapted from the Asociación de la Caridad in Madrid—more on this below—identified the primary goal of the association as to provide charity to poor women in the hospitals, though they also hoped in time to engage in other pious projects such as teaching the catechism in girls' schools, inspecting the progress that the girls made in learning domestic skills, and encouraging the girls by bringing them small rewards for their achievements. The ladies understood, however, that these secondary charitable activities would have to wait until the organization was well established: "Although there are other Women who need our charity, such as those in the Poor House, the Insane Asylum, and others," decisions about whether to expand to include them would be made at a later date. The first priority was the hospital, where they would serve the patients dinner and supper, as well as make their beds, comb their hair, and bathe them. They would also seek to identify other poor, sick women in the community, in order either to take them to the hospital or to aid and help them in their own homes.[82]

There was a formal religious component to the association. On the last Sunday of every month, all the ladies would attend the same church, where they would take Communion. Later that afternoon they would gather for a special spiritual exercise "only for Women," to be assisted by "at least six priests, with surplices," consisting of a quarter hour of interior prayer, a brief sermon "not to exceed half an hour," and a recitation of the Stations of the Cross before the Host, "praying for the needs of the Church, the happiness of our Monarchy, and the fervor of the Ladies."[83]

The constitution called for the president (*hermana mayor*) and twelve board members (*vocales*) to be elected in a secret vote of the whole membership. The hermana mayor, in particular, should combine "charity, zeal, inclination, and love for the goals of this establishment," as well as good health and the ability to devote all her time to it. Four of the board members would be the immediate deputies of the hermana mayor, and the other eight would be voting members of the board, among whose duties was to vote (secretly) on each prospective new member. The twelve board members plus the hermana mayor would choose a secretary and a treasurer, and unless the archbishop agreed to become the principle "spiritual director" of the association, they would also select the priest who would serve in that capacity.[84]

Any woman was eligible to join the association, as long as she was "respectable" and lived in Mexico City or its environs. By no means was the organization envisioned as ideally comprised only of the titled and the super-rich (though those were the organizers). In fact, in order to attract "poor and devout" women, the ladies insisted that there be no set fee for membership, and that members be able to deposit their contributions, in whatever amount corresponded to their ability to pay, in an alms box, so that no one would know how much they had given. The poorer women, the ladies wrote, would "compensate [for their lack of monetary contribution] with their good example and their personal services, edifying the rest [of the ladies] and maintaining the vigor and spirit of the Association." This, the ladies wrote, is how they understood the Madrid organization to function.[85]

The importance of encouraging "poor and devout" women to join so that they would provide "personal services"; the prioritizing of hospital work, with a secondary emphasis on promoting girls' education; the inclusion of monthly religious services "for women only" at a church later to be determined; and the use of a Madrid model all suggest a connection (either direct or imitative) to the charitable organizations founded by Vincent de Paul and his many female associates and cofounders in seventeenth-century France: the Sisters (sometimes called "Daughters") of Charity, and the Ladies of Charity. These two groups cooperated with each other, with the Sisters providing the nursing services for which the charity was known, and the Ladies more involved in administration and fundraising.[86] The Sisters and Ladies in France, like the Mexico City group, prioritized hospital work but also branched out into girls' education (as the Mexico City women said they wanted eventually to do). The Sisters physically lived in community, and for this reason were considered an active monastic order, while the Ladies worshipped together (as the Mexico City group insisted on) but did not live together.[87] To judge by the available documents on the Mexico City proposal, the founding ladies did not intend to create an order-like group of Sisters (nor, as chapter 3 makes clear, could they have done so because of the absence of a branch of the Vincentian male order to supervise them), but it is clear that, functionally, they saw a difference between their own roles and those of the "poor but devout" members they hoped to attract. These poorer members would act as the Sisters did, while they themselves would fill the administrative and fundraising functions of the Ladies. Lending further credence to the idea that the vague "Asociación de la Caridad" in Madrid that the Mexico City ladies said was their model was in turn affiliated with the Vincentian Daughters of Charity is the fact that the French Sisters, by now fully formed as an uncloistered religious community, arrived in Spain in 1789, after the Revolution drove them out of France, and arrived in Madrid a decade later.[88] This is about the right timing to have influenced the late-1804 proposal submitted by the Asociación de Señoras of Mexico City.

The Asociación de Señoras, in short, by aligning themselves with the goals and adopting the practices of the European Ladies of Charity—including electing their own officers, raising their own funds, and directing their own charitable operations—was the first Mexican pious association that proposed to exist as a freestanding entity, not just as an auxiliary to men's groups. It is very clear that the women themselves sought the new foundation. It may have been a late development, compared to European women's long-standing role as leaders of charitable organizations, but the changes in the relationship between women and the church that it portended were greatly accelerated by the outbreak of the wars of independence, so that by the mid-nineteenth century, as we will see in chapter 3, Mexican women had more than "caught up" with their European peers.

Conclusion

Despite the signs of change that these two organizations hinted at, it should be reiterated that one seems never to have got off the ground (the Asociación de Señoras), and that male leadership in the other was always more important than female leadership, and became more lopsidedly-male over time (the Real Congregación). These failures or weaknesses of women's organizing, combined with what we know about gender roles in the traditional cofradías, make it clear that the proper nature of things in lay associations—both as experienced by members and as understood by the church—was gender hierarchy. Women were included in many cofradías, but catholicity (in the sense of universality, the principle that led to both sexes and all races being accepted as members in many, probably most cofradías) was not democracy. Despite repeated use of inclusive language in the constitutions ("all the cofrades" were required to respond to the bell that called them to the homes of a dying brother or sister; "all the cofrades" must attend the monthly and yearly functions; "all the cofrades" would receive the same death benefits; "all the cofrades" should vote for the officers at the annual public meeting), a relatively rigid principle of gender hierarchy seems to have governed the day-to-day relationships and activities of the cofradías.

The archives give no indication that women chafed under this gender regime, at the same time that they contain ample evidence that women valued the cofradías' presence in their lives and communities. Loyalty to the cofradías is reflected in women's membership levels and in their pattern of gifting to the cofradías (beyond the scope of this chapter but significant).[89] A threat to the cofradías' existence—such as that posed by the wars for independence—would be a threat to women's spiritual satisfaction and in some cases material well-being.

CHAPTER TWO

"Our Fears That the Cofradías Will Disappear Are Not Unfounded"

GENDER, LAY ASSOCIATIONS, AND PRIESTS IN THE AFTERMATH OF THE WARS FOR INDEPENDENCE, 1810–1860

IN 1845 THE PARISH PRIEST of San Miguel de Allende, José Alejandro Quesada, wrote to the bishop's office, in despair: "There were happier times when this town abounded in pious and well-to-do people who formed cofradías in order to make their piety manifest. But the revolution of 1810 caused the loss of part of their interests and now, after many years, everything is very changed."[1] San Miguel was not alone. The wars for independence and the long depression that followed caused a massive contraction of cofradía income everywhere, and led in some parts of the country to the disappearance of cofradías altogether.

The first part of this chapter offers an overview of the financial impact of the wars for independence on urban cofradías. The second part analyzes changes in gender balances among the membership, placing the shift to even greater female majorities in a global context of the "feminization of religion" elsewhere in the Western world. In section three I turn to the question of whether the financial and gendered impacts of the wars were regional. Eric Van Young observes that the insurgent decade offered a "kaleidoscopic impression of widespread disruption and/or outright destruction," and his distinction between "disruption" and "destruction" is an important one.[2] There was significant damage to the economy virtually everywhere, but it was worse in some areas than in others. The focus in this section is on regional differences in the ways that the male leadership of cofradías responded to the crisis.[3] The last part of the chapter analyzes the impact of failing cofradías on the well-being of parish priests and their assistants, who were the beneficiaries of solid, functioning cofradías and whose situation suffered significantly when the cofradías faltered.

Cofradías and the Financial Crisis Beginning in 1810

Why did the wars for independence cause such damage to cofradías? As the quote from the San Miguel parish priest that opened the chapter indicates, the problem was partly that wealthy people who consistently donated to cofradías—donations most cofradías relied upon to absorb some of the costs of the important annual fiesta—were themselves greatly damaged by property destruction, the shutdown of credit markets, the interruptions of commerce, and, perhaps most fundamentally, the flooding of abandoned silver mines, the motor of the economy. But there were other factors, too: members fell behind on their dues, and fee collectors quit because their commissions were not worth the effort they had to expend to collect them. Debtors were unable to pay interest on cofradía loans, and renters of cofradía-owned houses and lots fell behind in their rents.

During the insurgent decade some cofradías tried to raise money by selling nonessential silver or tapestries or paintings that had been donated to the cofradía. In Zacatecas, a church fire produced an opportunity: the priest wrote that the cofradías of his parish were "completely exhausted of funds, and we have no other alternative but for the Cofradía de Dolores, which possesses a melted silver lamp valued at 800 pesos, to sell it and lend the funds to the others."[4] The leaders and business managers were called upon to finance the core operations of the cofradía—that is, death benefits and the costs of annual religious functions—out of their own pockets. This of course had also happened in the colonial period, but now the scale of reliance on the piety, generosity, and liquidity of the officers was on another order of magnitude.

In 1822 the new national government requested that the church provide a report on the state of cofradías in the nation. The responses were not encouraging. The six cofradías in the district of Santa María del Azúcar, in the bishopric of Puebla, for example, listed assets totaling 13,428 pesos, but "the majority of these debts are in bankruptcy, and the rest are secured on properties that are almost ruined, so that it is not possible to collect even half the interest."[5] In the same bishopric, in the district of Córdoba, four of the six cofradías had no funds and owed their mayordomos for the expenses he had absorbed on their behalf.[6] None of the Guanajuato town of Valle de Santiago's four cofradías had any capital left after all the properties that served as collateral for cofradía loans were destroyed in the insurrection.[7] By the 1820s there was also a clear crisis in the urban rental markets, in which cofradías were major actors. If roofs made of crude wood shingles were not regularly patched and replaced, and if adobe walls were not whitewashed, damage could be swift and disastrous, and a property became impossible to rent.

A decade later, cofradías in many parts of the country were still suffering from the effects of war and depression. A report on the assets and income of the Cofradía del Divinísimo Señor Sacramentado in Piedragorda (Guanajuato) in 1832 illustrates both the way the economic problems that arose during the insurgency could linger, and the increasingly untenable position of the mayordomo. According to the parish priest, the cofradía's assets consisted of:

- 100 pesos, recognized by the residents of the city of Pátzcuaro, whose interest has not been paid for over 25 years
- 620 pesos, in urban property, on which only 18 pesos a year in rent is paid by the city council for the two rooms it occupies, since the rest is in ruins
- 200 pesos, owed by D. Buenaventura Castañeda, of Morelia, on a property in bankruptcy for over 25 years
- 1,000 pesos, owed by D. Manuel Vaca Coronel, of Morelia, who for an equal amount of time or more has not paid interest
- 500 pesos, owed by the widow of D. José Ygnacio Benites, of León, slow but current
- 300 pesos, owed on the estate of D. Joaquín de Nava, of Piedragorda, current
- 2,000 pesos, owed, current but slow to pay
- 2 vacant lots, which produce 10 reales (1.25 pesos) a month

In sum, the report noted that "this cofradía only counts as income 160 pesos a year, with which it must cover vital expenses of 600 pesos for masses, singers and music, and the cofradía's principal functions of Holy Week, the Ascension, and Corpus Christi, and for this reason the Mayordomo spends from his own pocket 400 pesos a year."[8]

There were exceptions, of course. The Cofradía del Rosario in Colima managed to balance spending and income most years, as did Morelia's Cofradía del Rosario (the one belonging to Blacks; the one belonging to whites was another matter) in the mid-1820s, and all five cofradías in the city of San Luis Potosí in the early 1830s claimed small surpluses.[9] But for every exception there are dozens of examples of cofradías whose income was less, sometimes a great deal less, than its expenses, and whose assets had suffered sometimes-severe losses during the insurgency and into the post-independence period.

The cholera epidemic of 1833 was an additional blow. The epidemic began in Tampico, a central Gulf coast port, and from there spread to the populous center-western regions that had already been hard hit by the insurgency. The first city in the interior to be hit was San Luis Potosí, then the epidemic spread to Zacatecas, Aguascalientes, Guadalajara, Morelia, Guanajuato, and Querétaro by early August. From these cities it traveled to Mexico City and then to

Veracruz and Oaxaca. One report claimed that half the population of some towns in the center-west had died either from cholera or the ongoing wars.[10] This is unlikely, since the death toll from cholera was about 10 percent in Guadalajara and under 8 percent in Oaxaca. Still, some smaller towns surely experienced very high mortality rates. Dr. Francisco J. Estrada's memoir of his time as an army physician gives some sense of the disease's toll on one small town. In the town of Apaseo (Guanajuato), Dr. Estrada reported that he and a colleague went up and down the road looking for food, knocking on the doors of all the houses. "We found nobody in all that unfortunate town, where cholera had caused such ravages that the few inhabitants who remained alive had fled, leaving their homes abandoned. When we entered the main square, we saw some mules grazing, each one with a corpse on its back."[11] There is no question that the epidemic had a significant impact, perhaps especially in the center-west, given its early spread there. Church records for the archbishopric of Michoacán are full of references to places where there were not enough healthy priests to confess the dying.[12]

Because most of the largest cofradías were obligated constitutionally to pay for their members' "good deaths" (shroud, coffin, masses, burial) and also to pay a survivor benefit, epidemics had always been costly.[13] But this particular epidemic came at a time when the Mexican economy and cofradía finances were still extremely vulnerable. Survivors showed up at the office of the treasurer to claim their death benefits, and the only way some cofradías could raise the funds to fulfill these obligations was to sell off the cofradía's remaining possessions or, increasingly, income-producing properties. The Cofradía del Santísimo in Piedragorda (Guanajuato), for example, sold its mule train, used to transport the Host, for 200 pesos.[14] The Cofradía del Rosario in Morelia asked for a license to sell a silver altar plate, specifically in order to pay death benefits.[15] The Cofradía de la Merced, also in Morelia, wanted to sell a silver stand on which an image of the Virgen de la Merced was placed, or, alternatively, a damask wall hanging; this sale was approved, but it was not enough and in December 1833 the cofradía had to mortgage its urban property to pay for death benefits and masses for sixty deceased members. Ultimately even this measure was not sufficient to cover the death benefits, and the cofradía had to cancel its annual function that year, alienating the faithful (according to disenchanted members of the board) and threatening the viability of the cofradía.[16]

The accounts of the meetings of the governing board of the Cofradía del Santísimo in Tepotzotlán, north of Mexico City, show how the cholera epidemic could affect even wealthy, high-functioning cofradías.[17] Elections in 1826 had gone smoothly. The cofradía was able to assist primary schools for both boys and girls with 8 pesos a month; it organized a children's choir "to give luster to this Parish and its functions" and donated 300 pesos in order to increase the number of organists and singers; it spent funds to improve the church's appearance, acquiring new paintings, fixing the cemetery gates, and melting down some old silver that "does not provide enough splendor" and investing the proceeds in more magnificent ornaments. All this added up to a staggering 40,000 pesos. Early in 1833, right before the epidemic hit, the cofradía was feeling a little financial pressure and the governing board voted to call in at least one of two large debts and to replace two "apathetic and inefficient" debt collectors, but there was no sense of panic. As late as May 1833, the mayordomo proposed cutting down on the use of gunpowder during processions and other rituals, but only because the resulting savings, he hoped, could be used to hire extra musicians "for greater pomp." But in August, as the epidemic was hitting, the cofradía had to call in debts in order to pay for the unusually large number of death benefits it had to cover. By April 1834 there were said to be no funds in the treasury, and in September, despite income from debts and properties that totaled over 3,000 pesos a year, which would ordinarily be sufficient for the cofradía's expenses, the bulk of the income had to go to pay the death benefits of the many deceased members. The epidemic had left the cofradía over 9,000 pesos in debt. The language of despair over finances and the difficulties of debt collection continued to permeate the records of the meetings, and finally, in 1838, the cofradía was forced to turn over houses and rural properties to the Colegio de Tepotzotlán to pay back almost 25,000 pesos it had borrowed to cover the unusual expenses during the epidemic.

The epidemic and the post-1810 depression exposed flaws in the colonial cofradías' investment strategy, which had prioritized accumulating and renting out small, local properties for the steady income they provided. A lower-priority part of the strategy was to lend money locally (often to members). Before 1810 this strategy made sense: rental property was thought to be potentially more lucrative than lending, since interest was capped at the nonusurious rate of 5 percent and no such stricture applied to rents. But circumstances had obviously changed after 1810, as the mayordomo of the Cofradías de San José and Ánimas in Pátzcuaro clearly articulated in his early 1830s request to sell "four small, ruined houses" and three plots of land. "Given the limited income from these properties," he wrote, "and the amount of work that it takes to collect that income, it seems to me that it would be better to sell them." He went on to explain that

> at first glance this would appear to be contrary to the cofradía's interests, because it is easy to understand that income from rents ought to exceed income from interest . . . [but] there are no permanent renters for either class of property . . . and we cannot even find temporary renters for some; and when we do we have to keep the houses in good repair, and sometimes there are losses from tenants who simply disappear without paying what they owe.[18]

Other mayordomos, in the wake of the epidemic, were coming to agree that selling property was preferable to maintaining and renting it out.[19] The records of the 1830s hold hundreds of requests for licenses to sell off their property.[20] In fact, as historian Jan Bazant points out, concern that the church would sell too much property, thus reducing the government's ability to extract future loans, "explains the frequency of the laws which prohibited the Church from selling its possessions without the permission of the government."[21]

Still, reluctance to reduce the economic base of their cofradías by selling property persisted even after the cholera epidemic. Discussions in the books of the Cofradía de Jesús Nazareno in Amecameca (state of Mexico) in the 1820s and early 1830s came back repeatedly to whether or not the cofradía should sell an inn and its adjacent lands that had historically provided the cofradía with a good income, but by 1826 threatened to fall into "terrible ruin" for lack of maintenance. These proposals, however, were rejected by the board right up to the end of the account book in 1833, six months after the epidemic hit the region.[22] The church, for its part, had also been historically antagonistic to divestment, and its position, too, was slow to be abandoned. Repeatedly we see bishops refusing to authorize the sale of property or recall of debts; instead, they instructed the cofradías to sacrifice, to try harder to collect alms and dues, to economize in their celebrations—anything but erode their financial base.[23] As Archbishop Diego de Aranda of Guadalajara put it in 1853, one of his duties and the reason he regularly visited the parishes of his diocese was to "protect the assets of the church."[24]

Economizing, however, was also deeply unattractive, and many mayordomos refused to do so, since they were the ones who would be held responsible for impoverished and unsatisfying celebrations, and would have to suffer guilt and the whispers of the populace when these celebrations did not measure up in splendor to those in past memory. José María Arriaga, for example, the mayordomo of the Archicofradía del Santísimo Sacramento in Pátzcuaro (Michoacán) in 1855, professed great anguish because despite his best efforts, he had only been able to provide "a shadow of the previous religious solemnities . . . a poor and sad homage to our Lord and Master."[25] María Luisa de Buendía, the mayordoma of the Cofradía del Santísimo Sacramento in Amecameca in the mid-1830s (after the death of her husband) agreed: "Although it is true that no one ought to spend more than he has . . . [and] some expenses . . . could be reduced by cutting back on the decoration and luster of the Function, this would weaken devotion, and it is therefore better that the mayordomo make up the difference with his own funds rather than risk the erosion of the faith and piety and support of the members."[26] In short, from the point of view of many mayordomos and governing boards, selling property was not desirable, but it was preferable to putting on a less splendid celebration or, even worse, failing to fulfill obligations to its members and their survivors, which would surely exacerbate the losses in membership that many cofradías were already experiencing. They understood that in many ways selling off assets was shortsighted, but at the same time, loss of membership was also a road to disaster.

Adding to financial imperatives that made selling cofradía property more and more attractive was the direction of political change. All governments after independence were penurious, and both liberals and conservatives, once in office, sought ways to tap the church's propertied wealth. Liberal regimes grounded their demands in the principle of the superiority of private property. Conservative regimes defended the right of the church to own property, but needed the financial help of the church and for this reason were also a danger to the church's assets; even if they did not threaten to privatize church property, they frequently exercised their "right" to demand loans from church institutions that were calibrated on the basis of the wealth of the institution. Cofradía business managers with any degree of savvy could see that owning property was increasingly a political as well as à financial risk.

In sum, by the mid-1840s—in response to the conditions of the post-1810 depression or the cholera epidemic or political factors or all three in combination—many cofradías had lost economic power because they had been forced to sell off at least some of their property. In some cases the governing boards probably hoped that they could recover from this blow. Others, I argue below, were considering extinction as a real possibility; in these cases the sale of property should be seen as a kind of liquidation of assets before the shutdown of an enterprise that had outlived its usefulness, that was under a political attack that was unlikely to cease, and for which (as we will see in the next chapter) there were already substitute organizations in operation that were better suited to the current situation.

Gender and the Crisis of the Cofradías

Shrinking membership in cofradías was commented upon frequently after 1810.[27] The bishop of Michoacán in an 1836 *visita* to Pénjamo (Guanajuato) noted that no new members had entered the Cofradía del Divinísimo Señor since the 1810 revolution.[28] In the southwestern town of Teloloapan (today the state of Guerrero), in 1851 the former cofradía of the Santísimo and Rosario was said by the parish priest to have insufficient funds to cover its expenses, "because of the fact that so many members separated from the cofradía many years ago, with very few remaining."[29] Ygnacio Villegas, the fee collector for the Cofradía de San José in Morelia, lamented in 1838 that the cofradía had been reduced to only forty-one members. There used to be many more members, Villegas said, but they had been "erased" from the rolls of the cofradía for not paying their fees, although he had gone to their houses and warned them many times that this would happen.[30]

Why did the cofradías shrink? As Donald Stevens shows, priests certainly considered impiety to be a much more serious problem after independence than in the colonial period.³¹ But we do not have to go so far as to assert that impiety or secular thinking had increased in order to account for growth in the number of people who just couldn't see a powerful reason to renew membership in the cofradías or join in the first place. Likely much more important was the perception that the cofradías were no longer reliable when it came to providing death benefits and survivor benefits and arranging for good deaths.³² If cofradías could not guarantee a good death, there were serious material and spiritual implications, surely discouraging membership. It is also possible that some of the mayordomos who resisted cutting back on the exuberance of cofradía-sponsored celebrations were right, and that less lavish annual functions may have made joining less attractive. Combined with the difficulty many people faced in keeping up with even the modest fees charged by most cofradías in a context of war, instability, depression, and labor insecurity, it is easy to understand why people might drift away or chose not to join.

Reduced membership, however, was not the only notable change; another story was an increased gender imbalance in favor of women, sometimes quite strikingly so. By 1840, for example, a Morelia census revealed that the 836-person Archicofradía de Nuestra Señora de la Merced was 82 percent female; the Archicofradía del Rosario was 83 percent female (436 women and 89 men); and the Cofradía de Nuestra Señora del Tránsito, with a total of 187 members, was 71 percent female.³³ Of the 55 new members of the Cofradía del Santísimo Sacramento in Aguascalientes after 1815, 73 percent were women.³⁴ The elite 223-member Concordia del Sr. S. José in Mexico City in 1813 was 82 percent female; in the 1750s this cofradía had been about 60 percent female.³⁵ A sample of 160 patentes for the Cofradía del Tránsito in Durango indicates that 84 percent of the people who joined between 1810 and 1850 were women; in 1800 the membership had been 63 percent female.³⁶ As Table 2.1 shows, detailed information on 31 cofradías between roughly 1810 and 1860 shows that on average, 70 percent of the membership was female, a substantial increase from the average 61 percent female majorities in the late colonial period.

Given the solid evidence for declining membership totals overall, it is probably safe to assume that this pattern owed mainly to male abandonment and/or failure to join in the first place, and not to more women joining. The question then becomes: why should men leave the cofradías at a higher rate than women? Why did women stay?

Many contemporaries saw impiety as a particularly male phenomenon. As the priest of Turicato put it, the men "are extremely immoral," and "only confess when they marry and when they die . . . the women know their doctrine better, go to Mass more often, and in general are martyrs their whole lives with such husbands."³⁷ Wartime conditions also colored the gendered expectations of impiety. "How am I to behave toward these Libertines?" asked the priest of Zacapu, José Vicente Navarro, in 1823, singling out the scandalous behavior

Table 2.1. Percentage of female members in cofradías, approx. 1810–60

	Elite*	Non-elite	Unable to determine
Archbishopric of Mexico			
	67 (1810–32)	66 (1810–35)	83 (1820–48)
	62 (1842–50)	60 (1838)	79 (1830–60)
	80 (1820–39)		
	67 (1810–29)		
	82 (1812–13)		
Bishoprics of Michoacán and Guadalajara			
	68 (1815–34)	82 (1840)	
	83 (1840)	87 (1843)	
	71 (1840)	72 (1832)	
	76 (1855)	70 (1852)	
	83 (1838)	40 (1830s)	
Campeche			
			82 (1819)
Puebla			
	67 (1824)		
Oaxaca			
	53 (1832)	55 (1835)	60 (1824)
		67 (1837)	50 (1815)
Durango			
	84 (1810–49)		52 (1844)
	80 (1860)		
	75 (1810–60)		
	79 (1830s)		
Combined by region			
	74 (16)	67 (9)	68 (6)
Combined by region and social status			
			70 (31)

Sources: For Mexico, AGN, AHAMex, and Belanger, "Between the Cloister"; for Michoacán and Guadalajara, AHAMich and AHAG; for Oaxaca, AHAO, and Guardino, *Time of Liberty*; for Puebla and Veracruz, Records of the Church of Latter-Day Saints.

*I defined "elite" as cofradías in which at least half of the members carried the designation *don* or *doña*.

of soldiers and officers quartered nearby: "they no longer try to mask their impiety" and have been heard proclaiming that "there is no Hell, and that the Holy Sacrifice of the Mass is a chimera."[38]

But this interpretation risks assuming that women are fundamentally more religious than men. Most scholars now reject this assumption, and I propose a more plausible, better historicized, story. As men and some women drifted away from the cofradías for the financial and spiritual reasons just given, those left behind became even more protective of the cofradías than they had been before. In fact, they saw, in the changed material circumstances of the post-independence church and the emergence of a still-vague (at this point) challenge to Catholic values in the form of liberal and/or secular values, an increasing need for cofradías. The widespread perception of a growth in impiety—whether true or not—made Catholic moralization and socialization into the church all that much more important.[39] Cofradías not only supported church and priest; they also had a direct role in imparting a love of the church and Catholicism to children, introducing them to Catholic public practices from an early age, connecting them to the local Catholic community, and bringing them into a relationship with the priest. Cofradías were not the only means by which to socialize a child into the church, but they were particularly effective.[40] Children associated cofradías with ritual, spectacle, fun (the fireworks, the music, the food associated with the annual functions), and dramatic solemnity (the processions, the candles and torches that lit the church during these functions). (Some of these elements of cofradía practices would carry over into the new female-led associations that we will begin to analyze in chapter 3; others were replaced by new ways for children and youth to feel included.)

Socializing children to be good, moral Catholics was important, even profoundly important, to most men and women, in an era of great political disruption when the integrity of the family and the Catholic faith were seen as bedrocks of what little stability remained.[41] Thus it was not dismissiveness of religion (still rare at this time) that brought about a seemingly-mutually-agreed-upon new religious division of labor, but rather a desire to support religious unity. This new division of labor assigned the duty of instilling religious values in children to women.

Why did this happen? In the colonial period the patriarch of the family had been the one who ensured the Catholic education of his dependents. For some, women, far from capable of imparting Catholic values, were, as historian Erika Pani puts it, "weak in character and disposed to drag men down the path of sin."[42] But two phenomena that emerged since the late colony combined to shift this view of patriarchal responsibility. The first was the emergence of the ideology of separate spheres. The concept of a public sphere where issues of common interest could be debated rationally was, in this thinking, mainly occupied by men (as the main producers and consumers of newspapers, as the large majority of denizens of taverns or coffeehouses, as economic actors on the go, as members of a polity), required the idea of a separate, private sphere, occupied mainly by women.[43] "Enlightened" thinking assigned religion to this private or domestic sphere, where women with (ideally) sound religious educations would be in charge of modeling and instilling good moral values.[44] The second phenomenon was republicanism, which defined citizenship around military service and electoral politics, both of which excluded women. Men were increasingly understood as the ones who would properly take part in the rough-and-tumble world of politics (and also the rough-and-tumble world of the market economy). Female citizens in a republic, meanwhile, were treated differently in new constitutions from male citizens, most obviously because those constitutions denied them the vote or the right to hold political office. Republicanism, then, reinforced and concretized the emerging view that separate spheres were correct and natural.

These gendered ideologies were not Mexican in origin and indeed in some ways were not entirely appropriate for Mexico, whose market economy was in the doldrums until at least the late 1830s. But they strongly influenced Mexican political culture, which was unified in its embrace of republicanism and the exclusion of women from politics.[45] Add to this the way that liberal discourses that began to take shape in Mexico in the late eighteenth century aimed to remove the church from public power (economic, political), and the combined effect was to push religion and women more and more together in the imagined private sphere. The actual experience of women was of course quite different; economic separate spheres were fictions for poor women and even for many in the middle and upper groups. But the idea that religion should be the responsibility of women caught on because it was attractive to both men (who were thought to no longer have time for the still-important duty of Christianizing their families) and women, who welcomed being assigned such a crucial role. There was a sense in which in some countries (and most clearly France) the identification of religion with women was "derogatory," and as we will see in later chapters some Mexican liberals also intended to denigrate religion by associating it with women, and to dismiss women as good citizens because of their religiosity.[46] But more commonly, at least in the first half of the nineteenth century, Mexican men and women embraced the division of labor that put women in charge of the religious education of the family.

This story of women taking over the responsibility of Catholic moralization helps us historicize what some non-experts and even some scholars have assumed is a "natural" and timeless inclination on the part of women to be more religious and more church-oriented than men. In the Mexican case, defending the cofradías became the job of women after independence; they took it on willingly because they saw the potential loss of cofradías as a threat to their families' faith and connection to the church, and to the impartation of Catholic values to their children. As we will see in later chapters, attention to the dangers to children, youth, and family of the failure to support the church was an important theme in Catholic women's petitioning and letter-writing throughout the period covered in this book.

There was another interesting feature of the gender imbalance in favor of women after 1810: women became more prominent in the elite cofradías (those in which more than half the members carried the honorific *don* or *doña*) than in the non-elite ones. In the late colony, elite and non-elite cofradías had roughly similar female majorities, with the non-elite ones having a slightly higher proportion of women, at 62 percent, compared to 58.5 percent for the elite cofradías (see Table 1.1). But in the post-1810 period, this picture flipped. Women came to dominate in elite cofradías, with an average of 74 percent of the membership, over 25 percent more than in the colony (see Table 2.1). In the non-elite cofradías, female majorities increased, but not nearly so dramatically. After 1810 they made up 67 percent of the membership, up less than 9 percent from the colony. In other words, female majorities increased in all cofradías, but the loss of men was more striking in the elite cofradías than in the non-elite ones.

Why would more men in elite cofradías drop out than in non-elite ones? Again, we can only speculate, but I think there are three possible answers. First, for the well-off men in elite cofradías, the masculinizing public sphere was a real thing: they were increasingly presented with a new world of alternative associations. Even in the late colony we can begin to detect the appeal of new voluntary associations, with the foundation of scientific societies, economic societies, and Masonic lodges. After independence other new associations proliferated.[47] These may have seemed not just new but also more modern than cofradías, as they were often borrowed from countries that many Mexicans wished to emulate (England, the US, France). They were also male spaces, meaning that for middle-class and elite Mexican men, modernity equated to masculinity. Cofradías, as we saw in chapter 1, even before the financial difficulties of the post-1810 period, were spaces shared with if not dominated by women.

Second, men in elite cofradías in the colonial period had benefited not only from the social and business connections they could make, but also in more material ways from access to the wealth of the cofradía. Often cofradía loans went to members. Rental of income-producing properties might well be granted to members. When a decision to sell a property was made, the price might be made sweeter for a member.[48] But when the cofradía's finances collapsed, as happened with so many of them, those benefits were no longer available, and membership lost some of its appeal for elites who could afford to borrow, rent, and buy.

Third, as we will see in the next section, for the men who served as officers in these cofradías, difficult financial conditions might translate into personal loss, not just the absence of an opportunity for personal gain. The loss of male leadership, in turn, further weakened the cofradías, in a kind of cycle of decline.

Male Leadership and Cofradía Finances: Regional Patterns

The withdrawal of men posed a problem for the smooth operation of the traditional cofradías, which as we have seen were very dependent on men as fee collectors, officers, business managers, and for key roles in processions. These cofradías functioned like businesses, as money-lending, property-owning entities, with the legal and administrative apparatuses that those activities demanded. It was unthinkable for women to assume duties as deputies, treasurers, or legal representatives of the cofradía (other than the occasional mayordoma). Thus, as the number of men in the cofradías shrank, the pool of men who could be elected to office and carry out the essential duties of the cofradía also diminished.

This situation could be finessed to a considerable extent. As long as there were enough men to carry the image in the annual procession, and enough men to staff the officer corps, the cofradía could carry on even with highly unequal gender balances. But a smaller pool of men from which officers could be drawn was a potentially serious problem. A crucial element in determining the fate of the traditional cofradías, then, was whether or not the leadership of the cofradías remained intact. As we will see, the phenomenon of male leadership had strong regional dimensions: in some regions, officers tended to stick with the cofradía even as membership shrank and the rank and file became more female, while in others there was a crisis of leadership, as mayordomos and officers simply abandoned the organization.

In the archbishoprics of Durango and Oaxaca—the first in the north and the second in the south—as elsewhere, the decade of insurgency was difficult for cofradías. The governing board of the Archicofradía del Santísimo Sacramento del Altar in Durango, for example, reported in 1818 that "despite the devotion of the Contributors," the funds of the Archicofradía had "diminished notably because of the calamities of the times . . . and the losses that many Individuals of this City have experienced as a result."[49] According to its mayordomo, the Cofradía de Nuestra Señora de las Nieves in Oaxaca City was left in March 1817 "without even a half a real in its treasury," and "abandoned and forgotten by the Faithful," with only sixteen members left.[50]

But even in the difficult 1820s and 1830s, there was a clear pattern of mayordomo and mesa stability in these archdioceses. The mayordomo of the

Cofradía de la Santísima Trinidad in Chihuahua noted in 1832 that in the past twelve years he had accumulated a 1,498-peso credit against the cofradía. However, he had continued to serve.[51] In Oaxaca the mayordomo of the Cofradía de la Preciosa Sangre de Cristo not only chose to stay in his post but was able to pay for repairs to houses owned by the cofradía in the 1830s and buy new items for the church (notably a new velvet drape with gold trim for the altar).[52]

And in both archdioceses by the late 1830s and 1840s there was an increasing number of positive signs. Mayordomos observed that debtors had resumed service on their loans. José Guadalupe Beltrán of Valle de Allende in Chihuahua, who had taken out a loan from the Archicofradía del Santísimo in the 1820s and had accumulated over 2,300 pesos in interest by 1844, began making payments of back interest in that year; while he still owed 984 pesos, the mayordomo was optimistic that the rest would be paid soon.[53] In 1840 borrowers from the Cofradía del Rosario in Hidalgo (Durango) owed a total of 6,700 pesos and back interest totaling 3,758 pesos, but three out of the five borrowers were now making regular payments.[54] New cofradías were being formed (for example, a Cofradía del Santísimo in the Mineral de San Pedro de los Chalcuihuites, on the border between Zacatecas and Durango, in 1844, which had signed up forty-nine men and fifty-three women); established cofradías were spending freely on nonessentials like fireworks, flowers, singers, and musicians; they were running small surpluses; and some were even resuming lending practices.[55]

In Oaxaca the 1830s and 1840s saw continuing recovery and even a degree of prosperity. In 1831 the Archicofradía de Nuestra Señora de Juquila set minimum guidelines for the opulence of its three-day-long annual function, which should be "as magnificent as it has always been; the Temple will be illuminated with around 300 candles"; the procession should be lit by 150 *hachas* (large candles or torches) and 200 small candles; the Virgin should be carried by eight priests or, if this was not possible, by eight men of the highest social distinction.[56] Throughout the 1830s the Cofradía de la Preciosa Sangre de Cristo did very well financially, consistently running surpluses despite some fairly extravagant spending. The mayordomo was able to stage an annual function with a rich menu of music (organ, tambourine, chirimía, many singers), food, and drink, including sherry from Málaga and two pounds of iced cookies (*soletas encaladas*), a feast for the governing board, incense, floral arches, and many candles and torches.[57]

In short, in neither archdiocese did I find evidence of difficulty replacing mayordomos or reluctance to serve as either deputies or mayordomos. Instead, to judge by the extant records, the urban cofradías of Oaxaca and Durango, despite experiencing the general tendency toward larger female majorities after independence, continued to be managed successfully by a reduced but committed number of men who took their turns as officers and produced displays of community piety that seem to have been nearly the equivalent of the colonial celebrations.

Cofradías in the archdiocese of Mexico offer a more ambiguous picture than those in Durango and Oaxaca, with evidence of both stability and near-chaos in the leadership ranks. But on balance many more seem to have survived than disappeared, with their leadership more or less intact. In Tlalpan (now part of the Federal District) the Cofradía del Santísimo had virtually disappeared in the mid-1820s, leaving the practice of Catholicism in the town in a state of "complete abandonment and decadence." But in 1854 the parish priest suggested its reestablishment, and the townsfolk, including the twelve men he tapped to serve as the governing board of the cofradía, met this idea with much enthusiasm.[58] New cofradías were founded, as in the central mountain town of Temascaltepec (southwest of Toluca) in 1843, where a new Cofradía del Santísimo, with the particular purpose of transporting the Host to the houses of the dying, was founded; the costs of illumination and music, so that "Our Lord leaves the church with the greatest possible pomp," would be assumed by the twelve members of the governing board.[59]

In other places, however, male leadership seems to have wobbled in its commitment to the cofradía. Sometimes this was because of financial disaster. The Cofradía del Santísimo y del Rosario in Teloloapam (Guerrero), which fell into trouble when two sugar mills that served as collateral for the cofradía's main assets were destroyed in the insurgency, is one clear example. By the early 1850s the cofradía could not muster enough members of the board to carry out the administration of the cofradía.[60] But in several other cases on record, the crisis of leadership was less about men trying to protect themselves from financial obligations associated with the cofradía, and more about trying to benefit personally from their role as managers of the cofradía's assets. In 1840 one of the deputies of the Cofradía del Santísimo Sacramento in Jilotepec (northwest of Mexico City), Ygnacio Santos García, wrote to the parish priest, worried about the "notable abandonment" of the interests of the cofradía and about the "inactivity" of the members and deputies of the governing board. He demanded that the mayordomo of the cofradía, José María Aguirre, render his accounts for the three years during which he had served in this position. The priest tried four times to call the deputies to a meeting to discuss the state of the cofradía, but in vain; there were not enough men present at any of those meetings to follow up on García's complaint or Aguirre's response, thus leaving the interests of the cofradía in limbo. Almost four years later, in 1844, García again articulated his concern that "the majority of the Deputies refuse to even come to the meetings, notwithstanding repeated efforts on the part of the parish priest to get them to do so."

This sounds very much like the abandonment of leadership positions that was pervasive, as we will see, in the archdioceses of Michoacán and Guadalajara, except for one thing: this cofradía was not impoverished. Instead, it owned an unspecified amount of real estate and held mortgages totaling about 4,000 pesos. Rather, the crisis of male leadership here seems to have been a story of corruption. The mayordomo (at least according to the priest) collected interest in an inadequate and unproductive manner, probably (the priest thought) because he was favoring those who had borrowed the money in the first place. "In effect, many of the members that comprise the Board have borrowed from the cofradía, without the Mayordomo having kept the proper documentation." The reason the deputies were impossible to call to meeting was because they wanted to keep things as they were: "the members of the Board cooperate to maintain disorder and deformity in the administration of the institution."[61]

Corruption and indifference, more than financial crisis, also seem to have played a role in the problems experienced by the Cofradía de Jesús Nazareno in Amecameca. The governing board was difficult to convene in the 1820s and early 1830s. On record is an episode in 1827 when the priest rang the church bell, "as is customary," to call the deputies to meet, and waited in vain all afternoon for them to show up, before finally giving up at seven thirty when only the mayordomo and one deputy had responded. By the 1850s the male leaders were still blasé about taking care of the cofradía's business: it was hard, the perhaps-not-entirely-objective parish priest asserted, "in our unfortunate epoch, to find men who take care of [the cofradía's] interests with the piety and efficacy necessary for their conservation."[62] But here, as in the case of Jilotepec above, the deputies of this cofradía had stuck with the cofradía. It still existed. It still had interests, if poorly, indeed corruptly, handled.

The situation was very different in the center-western archdioceses of Michoacán and Guadalajara (states of Michoacán, Guanajuato, Jalisco, Tepic, Colima, and parts of San Luis Potosí, Zacatecas, and Aguascalientes). There the crisis of leadership did not stem so much venality as from self-protection. The poor financial situation of the cofradías removed any temptation for the corruption-minded to remain in the cofradía leadership since there was so little income to skim or loan capital or rental property to manipulate.

Why were cofradías in the center-west worse off than those elsewhere? The answer lies partly in the extent of damage to the economy during the insurrection, during which this region was especially devastated.[63] It was here that the insurrection began, with Father Miguel Hidalgo's call to arms in Dolores (Guanajuato) in September 1810. Here is where it directly involved the largest proportion of the population. Unlike the more heavily indigenous center and the south, where many communities did not join the insurrection and in consequence large areas were relatively unaffected by property destruction or major labor disruption, in the center-west, dominated by Hispanic/mestizo cities and towns, rebel bands operated almost everywhere. Here is where it lasted the longest. Pacification of the parts of the center, south, and north that had rebelled was complete by 1815 or 1816 at the latest, whereas in the center-west pacification was not achieved until 1820. And here is where the most prosperous silver mines were located. These were largely undermaintained, flooded, and eventually abandoned over the course of the wars; they were extremely difficult to revive later, effectively eliminating the driving force of the regional economy. The damage was bad enough in the center-west that church lenders in the bishopric of Michoacán, which included the future states of Michoacán and Guanajuato, took the extraordinary step of forgiving interest that accrued during the insurrection for those who had suffered significant losses.[64] To my knowledge this is the only bishopric in which that arrangement was made.

The lasting effects of the damage done to property, credit networks, commercial circuits, and productive capacity of the mines made recovery of the cofradías extremely difficult. There were many cofradías in this part of Mexico, a function of the large number of small Hispanic-mestizo towns that were founded after the European discovery of silver, but for the most part their business portfolios were quite modest, certainly compared to the cofradías in Mexico City or Puebla, and they would not easily withstand lengthy periods of depression. A mayordomo or officer might very well be willing, as we saw in the other regions, to stick with a cofradía for which a future rosier than the present could be imagined. But in many cofradías in the center-west, no such future beckoned. Hence we see conscious decisions to refuse to serve, and even to extinguish, the cofradías. Here I interpret these decisions as the results of financial weakness and the burdens of leadership. But as I will argue in chapter 3, paired with male withdrawal, especially in the center-west, was female strength that made preservation of the old and dysfunctional cofradías less imperative.

I have already indicated some of the unique characteristics of the center-west: the destructive and long-lasting insurgency with its big impact on the silver economy, and a large number of Hispanic-mestizo towns, as opposed to indigenous villages. But I want to emphasize the extent to which these towns were founded on the basis of European Catholic traditions, and to which the wealthy and the middling folks (this was also a region of small farmers or *rancheros*) living in the center-west supported these traditions. Thus although I show the particularly steep decline of many cofradías here, it also should not surprise us to see pious attempts to resuscitate older cofradías and devotions. For example, the Cofradía de San José in Morelia had lost an unknown but clearly large number of members after the insurrection, and in 1838 consisted of only forty-one members, thirty-four of them women.[65] However, a year later there was a movement to "re-establish" the cofradía, and a number of prominent men agreed to serve on the governing board.[66] This effort was moderately successful; in 1855 there were seventy-seven members.[67] Eighteen were men and fifty-nine were women. Seventy-seven members does not exactly represent a magnificent rebound from "many more" than forty-one that the cofradía had before 1810, but it is respectable.[68]

Still, despite a number of new foundations, overall the number of traditional cofradías seems clearly to have been shrinking. In 1856 there were reported to be only "insignificant" numbers of cofradías in the entire archbishopric of Guadalajara; "many consist in little more than furniture or a bit of invested capital, more than a few have disappeared altogether."[69] This is almost certainly an exaggeration; the adjective "insignificant" comes from a report commissioned by the liberal government that was produced by priests, so there was motivation to hide cofradías and their resources. All the same, priests had to supply a believable number of cofradías since there was also motivation for the government to take aggressive measures to locate hidden resources, and I think we can take it as likely that the number of cofradías in Guadalajara was in fact quite a bit smaller than during the late colony. In partial confirmation of this pattern of disappearance—this time from an ecclesiastical source who had no reason to hide the presence of cofradías, and in fact had every reason to try to present them as still functional, even if they weren't—in Sayula, on the border between Jalisco and Michoacán, seven out of the eight cofradías that had been visited by the bishop in 1802 had disappeared by 1832, and no new ones had replaced them as late as 1853.[70] In Michoacán the colonial cofradías that were present during an 1831 survey had almost completely disappeared by the next comprehensive survey in 1896, and given the multiple comments about their financial weakness by priests at the time of the 1831 survey, it is extremely likely that they failed soon after that survey was completed.[71]

In the center-west, as elsewhere, after 1810 mayordomos did what the colonial mayordomos had always done: assume the burdens of paying for cofradía functions. But as years of income imbalance took their toll and debts owed to mayordomos mounted up, cofradías began to have trouble finding someone who would agree to serve. In 1822 the parish priest of San Felipe (Guanajuato) wrote in response to a questionnaire from the bishop's office that "the deplorable ruination that this villa suffered in the past revolution has left [all three of the parish cofradías] so decayed that every single one lacks a mayordomo."[72] In response to the same 1822 questionnaire, the priest of Chilchota (Michoacán) noted that two of the town's five cofradías "could not find a single cofradía member who wanted to serve as mayordomo."[73] Vicente Casas Navarrete, the priest of Guadalcazar (San Luis Potosí), noted in 1824 the "state of inaction" and "near dissolution" to which the mesa of the Cofradía de Nuestro Amo had arrived, and provided an example of the dissension: at the meeting to elect a mayordomo there was a two-hour discussion that finally came back around to the idea that the present mayordomo should remain in the position, upon which he protested that he "did not want to get involved in anything more" and resigned.[74]

The cholera epidemic, as we have seen, set back a number of cofradías and psychologically seems to have been a turning point for some mayordomos, since the 1830s and 1840s are particularly rich in cases in which the mayordomos gave up.[75] In 1844 the priest of Lagos (Jalisco) explained that the funds of the Archicofradía del Santísimo could not cover expenses, "and for this reason no one wants to serve as mayordomo, because of the money it costs out of pocket."[76] In 1850 the parish priest of Silao decided to seek a single mayordomo to run all the cofradías of the parish, since only one had a mayordomo (the Cofradía del Divinísimo, which, the priest predicted, would probably lose him very soon), and the others were utterly lacking someone to collect their debts. The problem was "lack of willingness to serve" (at least on the part of people who would serve with "integrity and purity"). So the priest named a general mayordomo, the same person who was charged with collecting the tithe, and agreed to pay him an extraordinarily high commission (12.5 percent).[77] The priest of San Miguel de Allende (Guanajuato) used almost exactly the same language in 1851 in making what he called the "radical proposal" of asking the bishop to name a single person as "general mayordomo."[78]

The pressures of declining membership and financial shortfalls could lead to disagreements among the members of the governing board as to how to respond. In 1832 the deputies of the Archicofradía de la Santísima Trinidad in Tacámbaro (Michoacán), trying to save money, took upon themselves some of the work of sacristans and servants, which one member, Francisco Avila, found embarrassing and "not appropriate to my station." When the others tried to expel him for his failure to take on duties that all the other officers had been willing to shoulder, "he insulted us, disturbing all order and calm, and stood up, and pounded the table, and shouted, 'For the love of God, Blessed Mary and all the saints, am I to allow this absurdity to destroy my family [reputation]?'"[79] Finances also divided the governing board of the Cofradía de la Merced in Morelia. In 1840 three members of the mesa wrote to the *provisor* complaining that they had taken it upon themselves to aid the mayordomo (who they said was not really qualified to carry out his duties) in fixing some of the disorder of his account books, looking for ways to increase the cofradía's funds and find ways to economize, but,

> instead of improving the situation, the only thing that has come of their efforts is that some [of the other] individuals on the Mesa despise them, and this has awakened an intolerable anarchy within the board, so that some insult others and even the Padre, without preserving the harmony that ought to exist in these corporations, and without showing respect and consideration . . . They try to get their way with rudeness and sarcasm, to the extreme that more than once someone has said that if another individual didn't side with him he would beat him up. This, Sir, is the state of discord in which the cofradía exists.[80]

Also in Morelia, the priest who supervised the Cofradía de San Roque in 1848 begged the bishop to authorize a completely new governing board, since the present deputies "are in a constant battle among themselves, and they also contradict the mayordomo, and he them." The priest even offered to pay the costs of the cofradía in its first year with a new mesa, since otherwise he was afraid that no one would agree to serve, given the "public discredit into which the cofradía has fallen because of the ruination of its property and the scarcity of its funds. They fear, with good reason, that such discredit will contaminate them."[81]

The final and particularly telling example is the one that opened this chapter, the case of the cofradías in the town of San Miguel de Allende. This town, probably not coincidentally, had been the birthplace of the most important new female-led pious association five years earlier, the Vela Perpetua, and as we will see in chapter 3, the Vela immediately flourished. But the traditional cofradías were in trouble. Many had been "reduced to mayordomías," meaning that there were no meetings and no members—just a mayordomo who did the best he could to carry out at least a few of the functions that the cofradía used to sponsor. The priest, José Alejandro Quesada, said he felt it was his duty to try to resurrect some of these cofradías, but he was not very optimistic that this would be possible, and indeed it wasn't.[82] In 1852 Quesada's successor, Maximiano Moncada, called for all but two of the San Miguel cofradías to be disbanded and converted into *obras pías* (simple pious works), since the others were too "decadent" to revive.[83]

Priests

Loss of cofradía resources, leadership, and members not only affected the way that religion was practiced in Mexican towns, but also had a direct impact on priests. In this section of the chapter, I examine what had happened to priests since the late colony, since priests' cooperation, support, and initiative were crucial elements of the new solutions to the problem of how to organize and stimulate local piety that we will turn to in chapter 3.

The priesthood in the late colony was a career with complex prospects. On the one hand, it was as desirable a career as ever, to judge by the number of young men choosing to become ministers. The secular clergy in the archbishopric of Mexico and the bishopric of Guadalajara increased by about one-third between 1750 and 1810, and this rapid rate of increase is almost certain to have also characterized the bishopric of Michoacán.[84] Although there was not a corresponding growth in the number of parishes in which recently ordained priests could be placed, young men continued to enter the seminaries and compete in the examinations to become priests, sometimes failing multiple times, hoping, perhaps, to have their perseverance recognized by the bishop with an appointment as an interim priest, while others, unwilling to wait for a parish, accepted a position as a priest's assistant, with the expectation that this would provide them at least a modest income and allow them to help their families.[85] Those who were placed in poor parishes hoped in time for promotion to a wealthier and more desirable one.

Many historians have emphasized the increasing financial difficulties priests experienced in the late colony, due to this "excessive" growth.[86] The secular clergy was structured as a pyramid, and virtually all the growth in numbers happened in the middle and lower ranks of the pyramid, where opportunities to thrive economically were limited.[87] All told, as many as half of all ordained ministers may have lived precariously, piecing together bits of income here and then, and sometimes even falling into poverty.[88] In the parish of San Luis Potosí, for example, in 1791 there were reported to be twenty-eight priests in residence, only nine of whom held parishes or positions as vicars or chaplains.[89] This meant that nineteen were living solely on the income from benefices or trusts (*capellanías*).[90] Fifteen of these had incomes of 200 pesos a year or less—about half the salary that most vicars earned, much less than most parish priests, and probably only about three times what an unskilled worker might earn.[91]

One of the things that made life without a parish position tolerable for poorer priests was cofradías, and at least partly for this reason priests without parishes almost always chose to live in larger towns and cities. There multiple cofradías guaranteed a rich, varied religious culture, with some opportunity for padding one's income by means of fees paid by the cofradías for conducting special monthly masses, services during the annual function, and funeral masses at the death of members.[92] In San Miguel el Grande (Guanajuato), for example, fifteen cofradías helped support the twenty-nine priests who lived in the small city; and in Celaya (Guanajuato), with fifteen cofradías, there were twenty-two priests.[93] The curate of Santa Cruz Acatlán (Mexico City) reported in 1791 that without the support of the cofradías, priests without an independent income "would find it necessary to resign what would then be an intolerable burden of their ministry, as has happened in many parts."[94] In other words, if cofradías faltered, priests' fortunes could also be expected to suffer.

When the wars for independence broke out, parish life, along with economic life, was jolted apart. Many male parishioners left to join the insurgency, along with a fairly large number of the lower clergy, who followed their colleagues Father Miguel Hidalgo and Father José María Morelos into battle.[95] Other priests and parishioners left their parishes to shelter in larger towns and cities. Father Juan Bautista Figueroa, the revered priest of Zinapécuaro, probably exaggerated when he wrote in 1835 that "all of the Priests fled to take refuge in the Capitals," and that he alone "stayed to consume with my Flock the bitter bread of the Insurrection and to defend their lives and interests."[96] But his statement gives us a sense of the unmooring of parish life after 1810.

Even after soldiers and priests returned home, things did not return to any sort of pre-independence status quo, and indeed the problems priests had suffered in the later decades of the colony only grew worse. If some priests had risen up in 1810 because of their dissatisfaction with a Bourbon regime that actively aimed to diminish their public power, as argued by William B. Taylor, after independence they were surely disappointed because the new municipal, state, and national governments were much inclined to try to reproduce, or even expand, Bourbon intrusiveness on priests' domains.[97] Several historians have found that after independence, municipal and state authorities made more demands on priests, put more restrictions on their power, and even brought suits against them.[98] In an extreme case, the parish priest of San Luis Potosí claimed in the early 1830s that when he and his vicar tried to stand up to municipal authorities who refused to return cofradía wealth they had appropriated in the late 1820s, he suffered such "cruel personal persecution at the hands of these immoral men with their repeated insults, grotesque slanders, and even attempts on my life" that he was forced to ask the state governor to allow him to move his residence to the hacienda of Bocas, where he would be safe.[99]

Priests also suffered from increased resistance on the part of cofradía officers to attempts to oversee the use of cofradía funds. One case from 1846 reveals particularly well the priest's frustration with his lack of control over mayordomos and parishioners, as well as the financial repercussions of the decline of the cofradías.[100] The case took place in Morelia, where the bishop's office had recently made it a requirement for cofradías to get the priest's approval before paying out survivor benefits. Father Ramón Magaña applauded this requirement. It was necessary, he wrote, because some cofradía members, "although they are alive, pretend to be dead, sending someone else to present their certificate of membership to the mayordomo, with the goal of receiving money that is meant for [their survivors] after their deaths . . . Others conspire with the mayordomo to split the benefit." The mayordomo of the Cofradía del Rosario, he continued, was particularly egregious in his "effort to destroy order and harmony," and Magaña asked the bishop to "make an example of those like him, who dare to make fun of their Priest." Meanwhile, seven other mayordomos of Morelia cofradías wrote a letter agreeing with their colleague from the Cofradía del Rosario that the bishop's order was "onerous and contrary to the interests of the cofradías." Since time immemorial, they said, cofradías had had the right to deal directly with the families of the cofrades who died, and this practice must continue "so that these pious establishments do not disappear." The priest, Magaña, then revealed what may have been his true objection to the independent behavior of the mayordomos. When the Morelia mayordomos bypassed his authority, they undercut his ability to be sure he was paid his just due for conducting burials and services for deceased members. Here is Magaña again: "Without this disposition [that priests have to approve survivor benefit payments], the priest will not receive a single peso from those cofrades who have died, and then I will find myself in even greater misery than is already the case."

The inability of the cofradías to pay for funerals and burials of cofradía members, or their outright refusal to do so, was a common complaint by priests.[101] In the past, cofradías had operated as a kind of buffer between priests and parishioners. When the cofradía had the responsibility of paying priests' fees, the priests were insulated from complaints by parishioners that they were overcharging for these services, and members were protected from voracious priests. But now, with the decline of the cofradías, more parishioners were exposed directly to the fees charged by priests for administration of the sacraments. The most famous case occurred in 1851 when the senator from Michoacán, Melchor Ocampo, demanded the reform of parochial fees, citing the case of a worker on his own hacienda who could not afford the fees charged by the priest for the burial of his son. According to Ocampo, the priest told the grieving father that "if he did not want to pay for the service, he could very well 'salt and eat' the body of his dead son."[102] Because of the shocking language that Ocampo quoted the priest as using, this case created a major stir, ratcheting up anticlericalism at a time when the church was already under attack for supposedly having done less than it might have to help repel the American armies that invaded Mexico in the war with the US (1846–48). The exchanges between Ocampo and the "anonymous priest of Michoacán," who defended the priest's actions (if not his words), have usually been interpreted within this political context of growing liberal criticism of the church and clerical intransigence. But the shrinking incomes of priests and the decline of the cofradías that had previously protected priests from parishioner anger over burial fees puts the case in a slightly different light. Whether the parish priest actually did address the boy's father with such inflammatory words, the likelihood is great that he charged the boy's father exorbitant burial fees—perhaps expecting that Don Melchor would pay them on behalf of his employee—because he was frustrated with his own financial situation. If the child had been a member of a cofradía (and there were several in nearby Maravatío, though I doubt there was one on the Hacienda of Pateo itself), the fees that the priest charged might well have been paid by the cofradía.

A letter from Father Félix de la Fuente, the interim priest of Apaseo, provides more insight into the financial situation of priests by midcentury.[103] As an interim priest, he was obligated to turn over one-quarter of his emoluments to the curia, and De la Fuente had done so.[104] But he accompanied his payment with a statement declaring that it would not be possible for him or any other interim priest to continue to turn over this much of his income. As he wrote: "The miserable state of priestly income in this Diocese is well known to Your Excellency. . . . Virtually the only compensation we receive comes from Marriages. . . . In my first two months here I received not a single penny, and in the next three, after expenses, I was left with only 60 pesos. . . . I have even had to reduce the salaries of my vicars and the rest of my dependents."[105]

There was one final factor that worsened priests' overall well-being after 1810. Because of a disagreement (not resolved until 1831) between the Mexican government and the Vatican over who had the right to make new ecclesiastical appointments, in many dioceses there were no bishops and therefore no permanent appointments of parish priests.[106] This meant that the number of interim priests—with all the insecurity and relative lack of authority that interim status brought—increased considerably almost everywhere during this decade.[107] By the mid-1820s Michoacán only had nine permanent priests when it should have had 122.[108] In Guadalajara, the colonial bishop was long lived but died in 1824. Between 1824 and 1830 the number of interim priests increased from sixteen to fifty-three, representing over a 30 percent drop in the number of parishes with a permanent priest.[109] As late as 1850 over one-quarter of Mexico's 1,222 parishes were filled by interim priests.[110]

The multiple pressures on priests—as well as the new opportunities for young men in careers that opened up after the end of colonial rule (law, medicine, journalism, the military, public service, politics)—greatly diminished the "supply" of curates in the post-independence era, compared to the colonial era of oversupply. In 1800–1801 the bishop of Michoacán had ordained over one hundred ministers every year, but by the early 1820s ordinations had skidded to a virtual halt, and even in the early 1840s, with an active bishop in place, ordinations had only returned to an average of forty-five a year.[111] There were no longer large numbers of underemployed ministers who could be brought in either as vicars to assist the priest in his ministerial duties or as temporary assistants during feast days or annual functions. As a result parish priests often found themselves ministering by themselves or with little help to a population that was much larger than the colonial priests had served. The ratio of ordained ministers to population in the bishopric of Michoacán rose from about one priest for every 1,375 parishioners in the 1790s to about one for every 3,000 in the 1820s and 1830s.[112] This had an obvious negative impact on priests themselves, and an equally obvious negative impact on local devotion.

The future for priests, under the existing status quo, did not look hopeful, either for them personally, or for their churches, or for their communities. It was under these circumstances that, presented with the opportunity to welcome and help form new pious associations, with new and enthusiastic leaders and a stable income entirely devoted to the parish churches, priests began to shed their old ideas about women's roles in cofradías.

Conclusion

This chapter has shown that after 1810, when financial crises meant that cofradías could no longer provide the same spiritual satisfactions and material advantages as they could in the colonial period, they struggled to retain old and attract new members. There were two important characteristics of this broad pattern. First, this struggle was gendered. Everywhere in Mexico cofradías (and especially elite cofradías) had trouble holding onto men. Piety and traditions of membership tied many men to the cofradías for years, but before the Reform they proved, on balance, to be less loyal than women, either joining less often or leaving or both. Second, the struggle was regional. If preventing men from leaving the cofradías was a problem everywhere, it was especially acute in the bishoprics of Michoacán and Guadalajara (the center-western states of Michoacán, Guanajuato, and Jalisco) because of the duration and severity of the insurgency in this region. Here cofradías lost men not only as members but also as leaders and business managers, putting their survival (and not just their smooth functioning) in jeopardy. The next chapter explores how responses to the weaknesses and failures of the cofradías were likewise regional and gendered.

PART II

The Era of the Reform

CHAPTER THREE

"We Ladies Who Sign Below Wish to Establish a Congregation"

PRIESTS, WOMEN, AND NEW LAY ASSOCIATIONS, 1840–1856

AS THE ECONOMY BEGAN a weak but noticeable rebound in the late 1830s and 1840s, many cofradías in the north, center, and south more or less recovered by infusing colonial leadership structures and forms of organization with new funds and energy (though as we saw in chapter 2, the new energy sometimes came from leaders' desire to profit from managing the new funds).[1] In these regions women tended to form larger majorities in the cofradías than in the colonial period, but structurally not much changed, and men continued to provide leadership. In the center-west, however, as this chapter will show, the revival of lay associationalism had a different look, as women took a more active, leadership role in promoting local piety and assisting parish churches than women in the rest of the country either wished, or were allowed, to play.

The emergence of women as key actors in local religious culture happened in three ways, all of which represented new or newish approaches to organizing lay piety. First, women increasingly formed separate branches of traditional cofradías, which allowed them some freedom to operate without having to wait for weak or even nonexistent male leadership to act. This strategy built on the model of the Real Congregación (chapter 1) in the sense that it embraced a parallel male and female structure.[2] Second, women welcomed the foundation of new service organizations brought from Europe, specifically the associations sponsored by the Vincentian order, the Sisters of Charity and the Ladies of Charity. The Vincentian model involved close supervision by more than one male cleric, but it held the promise of a fair degree of local autonomy as the associations matured.

The third innovative way in which women responded to the weakness of the colonial cofradías was to form new pious associations with themselves as the officers. In the early part of the period this pattern was represented, most strikingly, by the Vela Perpetua, modeled after but fundamentally different from the Real Congregación. The Vela's constitution required that it be led by women officers, upending the traditional relationships between women, men, and priests in lay associations. It spread quickly throughout the center-western bishoprics of Michoacán and Guadalajara after its foundation in 1839 and by the time of the Reform was a cornerstone of urban religious culture in the region. All three new ways of organizing local piety—though particularly the Vela, because of its autonomy, its high visibility, its female officers, and its sheer numbers—contributed to the transformed public and self-image of Catholic women, especially in the center-west, by midcentury.

The role of priests in shaping and creating these new roles for women was crucial. If a new pious association was to be "canonically erected," the priest's endorsement was the key element in diocesan and then papal approval. If he did not get around to seeking formal authorization (and he might not—even in the colonial period the process was slow and was sometimes postponed or deemed unnecessary), the association might nonetheless function perfectly well. But no local group—especially a group of women—could operate effectively and openly without the consent and at least a minimal degree of participation of the priest. Although women often designed or proposed new parish organizations, priests, too, initiated new foundations with women in key roles, as we will see. In supporting or promoting new women's lay associations, then, priests managed to overcome strong cultural (both general and ecclesiastical) preferences for gender hierarchy and disdain for women's capacity to organize, administer, and lead. The relationship between priests and women in the new associations varied from place to place, but in the Hispanic/mestizo towns that are the main subject of this book, priests and the officers of the new organizations seem most often to have partnered with each other as relative equals. Sometimes this partnership was contentious. The agendas of laywomen and those of priests did not overlap perfectly. But both ultimately rested on the shared perception that by themselves, priests could not bring about the reinvigoration of local religious practices that they and their female parishioners desired.

New Women's Lay Associations from Independence to the Reform

WOMEN'S AUXILIARIES

As we saw in chapter 1, in most colonial cofradías men and women were governed under a single administrative structure with exclusively male officers. It was not until the splashy launching of the Real Congregación del Alumbrado y

Vela Continua del Santísimo Sacramento in 1793 that a major cofradía, one that the king wished to see established in every parish, was designed with a separate women's branch.[3] The Real Congregación's women's auxiliary, as we saw, was not equal to the men's in either the number or variety of officers, but it did create a distinct space for women's activities. It is unclear how many Congregaciones were formed before the wars for independence broke out or how long they lasted after independence, after which of course they no longer enjoyed the royal imprimatur that gave them such cachet in the late colony. The foundation documents of the first Vela Perpetua in San Miguel in 1839 suggest that at that time there were still active congregations in Querétaro and Mexico City (probably the original one in the church of San Sebastián), and we know that there was also one in Orizaba as late as 1840.[4] There were likely others.[5] Thus the parallel male and female structures in the Real Congregación continued after independence to provide an example of a different and somewhat more egalitarian and autonomous way for women to be included in cofradías.

In the immediate aftermath of independence, most cofradías—both the older ones and the small number of newly formed ones—seem to have maintained the old mixed-sex (*ambos sexos*) structure. But beginning in the 1830s one almost aggressively male cofradía began to experiment with female branches or auxiliaries. This was the Santa Escuela de Cristo. The core practice of the Santa Escuela was the *banquillo*, or docket, a kind of public confession in a dimly-lit room, followed by the ritual extinguishing of candles and group self-flagellation with whips.[6] The banquillo was not suitable for a mixed-sex cofradía—if women were to engage in extreme penitential practices, it would only be appropriate within a single-sex setting, most likely a convent—and indeed the constitution's wording was unambiguous: the Santa Escuela was open only to men, whose preeminence was "clear and unquestionable."[7]

By the middle of the nineteenth century, however, there were at least four women's Escuelas de Cristo in a relatively tight geographic cluster in the center-west (Morelia, Celaya, Salamanca, and Valle de Santiago, the first in Michoacán and the other three in Guanajuato).[8] The existence of this cluster makes it unlikely that these were the only four Escuelas de Señoras in Mexico. Instead, their presence in these relatively small populations (only Morelia could claim to be anything like a city) suggests that the notion of a women's Escuela had become normalized by the mid-1840s. Unfortunately, these are the only women's branches of the Escuela that I have been able to document. They may be hard to locate in the archives because they were not perceived as clearly requiring a separate license from the men's branches. As the case below suggests, a priest might well have allowed or encouraged the formation of such a group, intending to formalize it later once he had evidence that it was viable and functioned well, but never quite got around to doing so.[9]

Despite the dearth of broad data on women's Escuelas, we do have some good detail about the origins and functions of one of them, the Escuela de

Señoras in Salamanca. Five years after the 1839 foundation of an Escuela for men, "ninety-odd ladies" requested permission from their parish priest to write to the bishop asking him to authorize the establishment of a Santa Escuela de Señoras in their town.[10] The priest approved, and he accompanied their letter with one of his own, assuring the bishop that the women's and men's spiritual exercises would be held at different times so that complete segregation was maintained. Both Escuelas met every eight days in the church of El Señor de las Tres Caídas. This church had been extremely run-down when the associations settled there: it had only one altar, there was no fence around the cemetery, and it lacked ornamentation and sacred utensils. But once the Escuelas were established, members raised money for a decent fence for the cemetery, five new altars, and ample provisions for the church. This provides a very clear and specific glimpse into the difference an active lay association could make in the life of a parish and its priest.[11]

Why might women have decided to form their own Santa Escuela in the 1840s? The answer may lie in some key changes that were made to the constitution of at least one men's Escuela in the mid-1830s. The congregation that met in the convent of Espíritu Santo in Mexico City voted, in 1836, to make significant changes, or "adiciones," as they were called in the printed constitution, to do with the banquillo.[12] "There is no thing so solid that it is not subject to change," the amendment began. Although it was "indisputable," it continued, that the banquillo was the most efficacious method of correction of errors, it had become "almost impracticable." People "in this day and age" were "weak-willed and disinclined to suffer the humiliation, confession of one's own faults, penitences, and all the rest" in the banquillo, and as a result, far from achieving what it was meant to, it was counterproductive and threatened the very existence of the cofradía.[13]

The *Obediencia* (the name given to the leader of the congregation) of the Mexico City Santa Escuela had come up with a solution: the banquillo would be suppressed, and instead the members would be required to participate in a "spiritual conference."[14] In the new system, members would not be asked to talk about their defects or failings or anyone else's (as had been the case previously), but rather they would be "tenderly and gently" questioned about material from a text that they were supposed to have studied beforehand.[15] If the person being examined did not answer the question properly, the Obediencia would explain where he went wrong "in a very prudent manner so as not to cause embarrassment."[16] The member being examined would not be called to the docket, but rather would remain where he was sitting, simply taking a knee when he was called upon. There was no discipline afterward. The physicality of the banquillo was done away with.

I suggest that while the document made it clear that these additions were meant to make the cofradía more attractive to men, they also had the effect of making it more accessible to women. Although there was no mention of admitting women or encouraging an Escuela de Señoras at the convent of Espíritu Santo, it is easy to imagine that the concept of a "tender and gentle" spiritual conference or retreat was compatible with an Escuela for women. It is possible, of course, that the changes were limited to this one men's Escuela. Unfortunately, I have not been able to find any post-1836 Mexican Escuela constitutions, so whether any other men's Escuelas followed the lead of the Espíritu Santo branch of the Escuela I cannot say.[17] But the amendments were so revolutionary that word of them must have gotten around to other groups, some of whom had probably encountered the same problems that the changes made by the Espíritu Santo Escuela were meant to address. They would surely have found it easier to adopt these changes once the precedent had been set by the Espíritu Santo Escuela. Moreover, the timing of the amendments lines up well chronologically with what we know about the new foundations of both women's and men's Escuelas in the four towns above (none of which had colonial Escuelas, so we know that the men's groups as well as the women's were new). If more men's Escuelas were founded with kinder and gentler practices, it stands to reason that Escuelas de Señoras might have cropped up alongside them. Priests, like the one in Salamanca, were the beneficiaries.

In order to try to understand what a women's Escuela might look like, let's turn to a 1797 interrogatory concerning the Escuelas de Christo in Mexico City. One respondent noted that benefactors from two (male) Escuelas in Mexico City funded a day of retreat every month for women in the chapel dedicated to the Santa Escuela.[18] This was not considered by the respondent to be a separate women's Escuela, since he explicitly stated that there were no Escuelas de Señoras in the city, but the 1836 amendments calling for a spiritual conference instead of the banquillo brought the core practices of the Escuela closer to those of spiritual exercises or spiritual retreats. There is similar evidence from the late eighteenth century in Zacatecas of the Santa Escuela sponsoring ten-day spiritual retreats for both men and women (separately, of course).[19]

The 1840s, however, was when separate men's and women's spiritual retreats began to appear in large numbers in the documentation. There had been "casas de ejercicios" in the late colony, but they were mainly run by the Jesuits and most (though not all—there was one in Lima, Peru, dedicated to women) were intended for the use of priests.[20] But around 1840 a house was built in Silao (in Guanajuato, near the cluster of Escuelas de Señoras) that was either meant exclusively for women or was shared between men and women, just as the church of the Tres Caídas in Salamanca was shared by the men's and the women's Escuela.[21] In 1847 it created a scandal because the priest who had built the casa and supervised the spiritual exercises had apparently allowed girls to help with the Mass. Estimates of female attendance at these exercises were impressive, ranging from four hundred to six hundred. Although spiritual retreats for women were not lay organizations and are therefore somewhat outside the scope of this book, it is worth noting their rise during this period, as part of a picture of patterns of parallel male and female lay devotionalism, and as a way to fathom how a women's Escuela could exist.

In sum, although the number of cofradías with parallel female structures still seems to have been quite modest during this period, the 1840s and 1850s did see the expansion of the Real Congregación model into a pattern that would later gather even more steam. Given the relatively few known examples, it is impossible to make a strong case for a regional bias, but for what it is worth, most of them were found in the center-west, the region that also gave rise to the most experiments with separate male and female casas de ejercicios.[22]

THE VINCENTIAN ASSOCIATIONS

Already widespread in Catholic Europe, in the 1840s and 1850s female Vincentian organizations came to Mexico, including the Sisters of Charity (the Hermanas de la Caridad, an order of nursing and teaching nuns) and the Ladies of Charity (Señoras de la Caridad). Although the lay Vincentian associations, like the women's auxiliaries, did not dramatically increase in number until 1863, their impact in the 1840s and 1850s was greater than their numbers because of the publicity they commanded and especially because of the much-ballyhooed entrance into Mexico of the Sisters of Charity. It therefore makes sense to begin with a short account of the arrival and impact of the Sisters.[23]

The Sisters were an order of active nuns founded in France by St. Vincent de Paul and St. Louise de Marillac in the seventeenth century. The order was forcibly disbanded during the Revolution, then revived in 1830. They were brought to Mexico in 1844 by a collaborative effort between Dr. Manuel Andrade, who had studied medicine in Paris and thought that Mexico's struggling hospitals could benefit from the Sisters' nursing expertise; Father José Guadalupe Romero, an activist priest with a parish in Silao; the ex-Countess Ana Gómez de la Cortina; and the sisters Faustina and Julia Fagoaga. The three women funded the project and Julia Fagoaga later joined the order.[24]

Great anticipation surrounded the arrival of the eleven founding sisters from Madrid (nuns from Spain were chosen because they would have no language difficulties in Mexico). When they finally embarked on their journey after initial efforts to bring them to Mexico over two years earlier, every move was tracked in minute detail in the press. The over-the-top ceremonies that greeted them as they passed through towns and cities on their way to Mexico City (despite their professed preference for modest celebrations) were described in long paragraphs in most newspapers. Booksellers stocked copies of *The Life of St. Vincent de Paul* to honor them, and a poem about these saintly "godsends" was printed and then reprinted in the press.[25] The liberal newspaper *El Siglo Diez y Nueve*, at least in the beginning, was almost as approving as the conservative press, since the Sisters, with their dedication to nursing and teaching, represented a welcome change from "useless" cloistered nuns.

Despite the excitement around the arrival of the Sisters, the expansion of the order in Mexico was constrained by the limited number of nuns that were allowed by the Vincentians and the royal government to leave Spain. We know of several towns that built or arranged housing for the nuns they hoped to attract, only to be disappointed. The city of Morelia, for example, prepared for the arrival of a group of Sisters in 1850, but in the end not enough arrived from Spain to make the project viable at that time.[26] The villa of Tulancingo (Hidalgo) was in the process of building a school and a house for the group of Sisters they hoped to attract in 1854, but this project also failed.[27] As Mexican novices became nuns, however, the resupplying of the Sisters from Europe became slightly less crucial. By 1860 the Sisters had at least one house in ten different towns and cities, where they operated hospitals, schools, orphanages, and hospices.[28]

The Sisters are relevant to the story of women's lay associations in part because of the positive public attention they brought to new roles for women in Mexican society—including having authority over male doctors on the wards of the hospitals—but also, more directly, because the Ladies of Charity were related to them.[29] Ideally (as in France and Spain), the Ladies worked with the Sisters as lay volunteers, visiting homes that the Sisters had identified as needing charitable assistance. So, we might expect that where the Sisters went, the Ladies would follow. But just as there was a bottleneck to the expansion of the Sisters—the limited number of nuns that the Casa Central in Madrid was willing to send to Mexico—there was a serious external impediment to the development of Ladies of Charity conferences (as the lay associations were called). This was the fact that the women's conferences had to be founded and directed by the Congregación de la Misión, the male order of Vincentian priests, and that order was not established in Mexico until 1845, after the arrival of the Sisters, and was not canonically approved until 1851.[30] Men's conferences could be established autonomously—and in fact it was the first men's conference in Mexico City, led by Dr. Andrade (who had been so active in bringing the Sisters), that put in motion the petitions to the government to allow the male order of Misioneros to come to Mexico—but a group of pious and charitable women could not simply decide to found a Ladies' conference.

After the first men's conference was established, their number expanded relatively rapidly.[31] I have found no direct evidence to suggest that Andrade or the other promotors of Vincentian charitable organizations in Mexico had a master plan for a gendered division of labor in which Mexican women would become Sisters (nuns) and Mexican men would join the conferences, but it does appear to be the case that the Vincentians' priorities were to found a women's order and laymen's conferences, not laywomen's conferences. Even after the arrival of the Misioneros, without whom the Ladies' conferences could not exist, there were not enough Misioneros to direct multiple conferences. These roadblocks would disappear after 1863, but for the time being they greatly limited the expansion of the Ladies of Charity.

Moreover, even when a new group received the male support it needed, there was an ongoing commitment required of more than one male cleric or official, and that, too, may have discouraged new foundations. The first meeting of the León (Guanajuato) branch shows the extent to which the foundation of the Ladies' conferences was a complex organizational undertaking. Present in the "general assembly" of the group that met in the house of the president, Doña Ignacia Ceballos de Cánovas, were the parish priest, the district governor (*jefe político*), and the vice-rector of the seminary. The ladies voted not only on their own officers but also on which Vincentian priest would serve as their "director" and which would be his substitute. Further, they needed to name a male *procurador* (a lawyer or agent) and a substitute for him. The speech made by the priest who was their director included a tribute to two other priests, one now deceased, who he said had "established" the organization that he now directed.[32] The involvement of multiple priests, a lawyer, and the district governor made this women's organization both more formal and less autonomous than the female branches of the Santa Escuela and others, which as we have seen might not even be authorized by the bishop.

These two related factors—the priorities of the Vincentian order and their Mexican sponsors, and the requirement that the Ladies must be supervised by multiple male actors—ensured that there were not too many formally constituted women's conferences by 1860. The first Ladies' conference was not founded until Puebla in 1848, and chapters followed in Guanajuato, León, and Toluca.[33] These seem to have been the only urban women's conferences officially established before 1863.[34] There is some evidence to suggest that there might have been informal Ladies' charitable groups—proto Ladies' conferences—that were in existence but not yet official. There was a group in Silao in 1845, for example, that called themselves the Señoras de la Caridad. Although their affiliation is unknown, they were contributors to a fund to build the house in which the Sisters would live and teach, so they may very well have envisioned themselves as Ladies of Charity–like, even without formal recognition.[35] However, no matter precisely how many women's conferences existed, the number was surely much smaller than the number of women who wished to participate, to judge by the rapid growth of the women's conferences after 1863 when the impediments to local foundations were eliminated.

In the meantime, a much simpler-to-establish and simpler-to-manage lay association, the Vela Perpetua, tapped into the enthusiasm for association that many Catholic women apparently felt, but that was hard to accommodate through the structures we have looked at so far.

AUTONOMOUS WOMEN-LED ASSOCIATIONS: THE VELA PERPETUA

In April 1840 the parish priest of San Miguel de Allende, José Manuel Fernández, received a letter that began: "We Ladies who sign below wish to establish a congregation dedicated to carrying out a daily and continuous vigil before the Blessed Sacrament."[36] This was a deceptively simple opening line for a radical proposal. First, it was highly unusual for a group of women to approach a priest with a plan for a new lay association.[37] This alone was notable. But the short constitution for the association, which the ladies appended, contained more surprises.[38] It began: "Thirty-one señoras will be named as *cabezas de día*" (day leaders, i.e., those who were in charge of organizing the vigil for one specific day of the month), and from their number the cabezas would elect a president (hermana mayor), secretary, and treasurer. In other words, the constitution did not just tolerate women officers—it required them. And it continued with more innovations: the men who wanted to join would be obligated to pay a fee, sit vigil on Holy Thursday, and also sit vigil "on any other day that they are told by the *cabeza* to do so." The ladies were proposing a cofradía in which the officers would *always* be women, and that men could join but in which they would be governed and told what to do by female officers. Even if women telling men when they must participate in the vigil seems a small thing in substance, in principle it was gender-role-upending.

The ladies had mentioned in their petition that the vigil would be "in imitation of that which is practiced in various other cities of our Republic." This was a calculated effort on their part to disguise the innovations of their proposal by likening it to the Real Congregación of 1793, which as we have seen was still in existence in at least a few places. If their cofradía was "in imitation" of one that had already been approved, they surely reasoned, there would be less reason to turn them down. And in fact the central practice of the two cofradías (the two-by-two half-hour vigil in front of the Blessed Sacrament), some of the language (e.g., the title of "hermana mayor"), and the names of the two groups (officially the San Miguel version was Congregación del Alumbrado y Vela Continua del Santísimo Sacramento—borrowing all but the "royal" from the Real Congregación) were identical. But lopping off the entire male-officer structure of the Real Congregación made this a fundamentally different organization from the one brought to Mexico from the court of Madrid in 1793, and the San Miguel ladies, and their priest (who strongly supported the proposal), were surely quite well aware of this.

So were the bishop's advisers who reviewed the petition. In the diocesan capital of Morelia, there appears to have been considerable confusion about what to do. The first to see the petition was the bishop's chief legal adviser (*promotor fiscal*), who tepidly applauded the new foundation before passing the petition on to the bishop.[39] In most cases the bishop would then have gone along with the recommendation of his promotor, but he asked another adviser, his provisor, to have a look at it. This legally trained vicar was clearly conflicted. On the one hand, the Vela's constitution came squarely up against the norm of gender hierarchy in church institutions and in cofradías in particular. Mixed-sex cofradías simply did not elect female officers. Women could not govern men. On the other hand, the Vela promised to bring at least fifteen hundred people a month into the parish church outside of the Mass, to establish a presence in the church every hour of the day, and to do so without need for overworked priests to cajole or organize their flocks.[40] A new kind of lay organization that promised to revive community piety and would involve many people was attractive.

The provisor could not decide. Why not, he must have thought, buy some time by deferring the decision to the civil authorities? The district prefect found the project "laudable," but the provisor nonetheless required the ladies of San Miguel to resubmit their request to the governor of the Department of Guanajuato.[41] Perhaps he thought the ladies would give up, but they did not. When it came his turn to rule on the proposed new association, the governor, apparently also torn, decided to appoint a special departmental junta to discuss the case. Finally the matter was decided when the junta evaluated the Vela petition positively. Both the priest and the prefect were "individuals who inspire our confidence," the junta wrote in its decision (saying nothing about its confidence in the ladies); furthermore, the Vela did not mix the spiritual with the political or civil, nor—with its quiet, inside-the-church practices—did it threaten to "disturb the peace."[42]

This complicated set of delays and confusion was understandable, since the Vela was different from anything that had come before. But once it was approved, the San Miguel Vela took on a new life as a precedent of its own. When the Vela spread less than two years later to the bishopric of Guadalajara, its prior approval by the bishop of Michoacán smoothed the path for the bishop of Guadalajara, who became an advocate (in fact, he used his first pastoral letter in 1854 to urge the foundation of a Vela in every parish).[43] By 1860 around ninety Velas had been founded in the many small Hispanic cities and towns of the dioceses of Michoacán and Guadalajara (about one-third of the towns where Velas were founded had populations less than six thousand and almost all of them were under twenty thousand). I am aware of no precedent in the history of Mexican cofradías for the enthusiasm with which the Velas were received or the rapidity with which they proliferated (see Figure 3.1).

In its early phase the Vela spread when women and/or priests heard about it from colleagues, friends, or family in relatively nearby towns, to judge by the geographical patterns of foundation. The first ten Velas founded formed three distinct clusters: one was comprised of San Miguel (1840), Silao (1841), and Guanajuato (1842). The second was Acámbaro, Zinapécuaro, and Maravatío, all by 1841. The third was Pátzcuaro (1842), Santa Clara (1842), and Tacámbaro (1843) (see Figure 3.2). The Morelia Vela, founded in June 1843, was

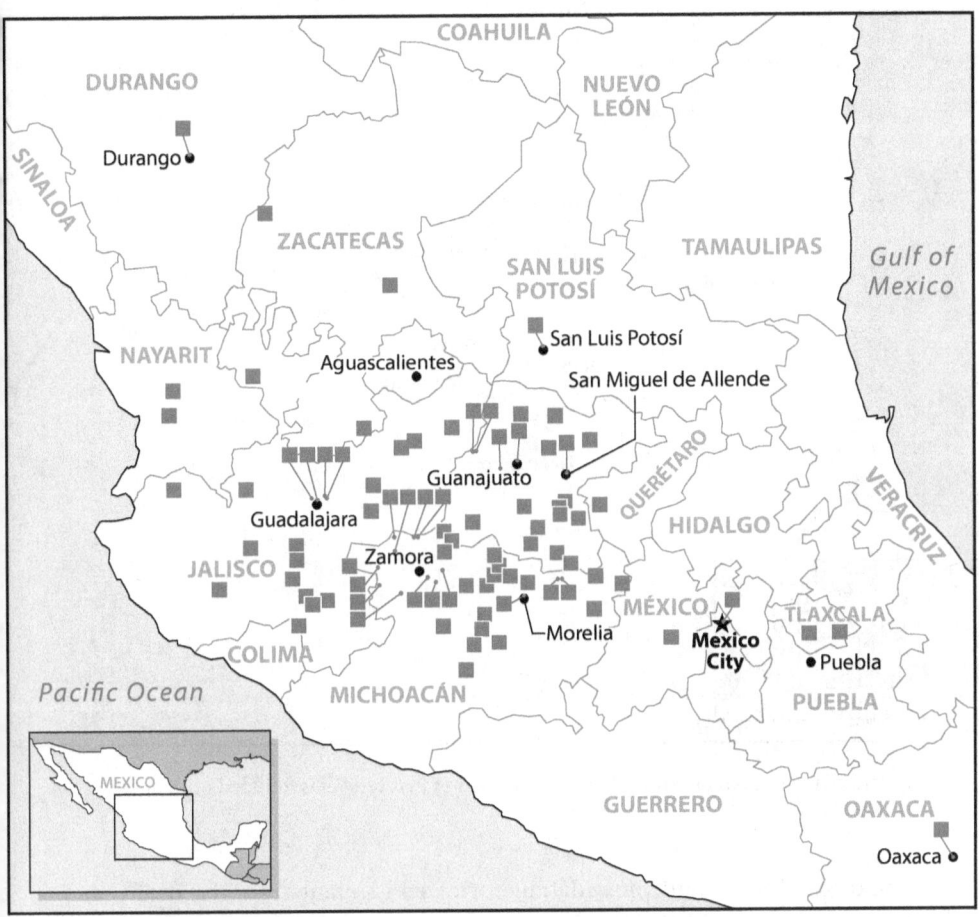

FIGURE 3.1. Map of central Mexico. Location of Velas founded between 1840 and 1860 (see Appendix for the places these Velas were established and the dates of their foundation).

positioned in between the second and third of these clusters, and it appears that once the Vela was established there it quickly jumped to a neighboring diocesan capital, Guadalajara, in July. After mid-1843 there was still some tendency for new foundations to move from one nearby town to another one (for example, by 1845 there were Velas in Celaya, León, San Luis Potosí, and Dolores Hidalgo in the bishopric of Michoacán, all towns within close radius of San Miguel), but there was a somewhat less distinct clustering pattern as the news of the Vela spread in other ways and more of a network pattern emerged, almost blanketing the temperate parts of the states of Michoacán, Guanajuato, and Jalisco, where most of the small towns were located.

The highly local origins of the new cofradía are also suggested by the slightly different names and different constitutions written for each of the early Velas.

FIGURE 3.2. Map of central Mexico. Location of first ten Velas founded in 1839–43.

The original San Miguel foundation borrowed its name from the Real Congregación: it called itself the Congregación del Alumbrado y Vela Continua del Santísimo Sacramento. In Guanajuato in 1842 it was called the Cofradía o hermandad de la Vela y Alumbrado Perpetuo al Santísimo Sacramento; in Pátzcuaro it was the Congregación llamada del Alumbrado y Vela Perpetua del Santísimo Sacramento; and in several towns, including Jungapeo as late as 1853, it was known as the Velación Perpetua al Señor Sacramentado.[44] There was also much variety in the details of the constitutions. In Michoacán and Guadalajara in the 1840s and 1850s, while the major features of Vela constitutions were consistent from town to town, some supported the feast of the Ascension instead of Corpus Christi; some required their members to accompany the Blessed Sacrament when it was exposed in procession, while others required them not to; some called for the priest to appoint new cabezas de día, while others gave this power to the hermana mayor. Most wrote their own preambles. Some permitted men to join, while others did not. Even in Guadalajara, where separate male and female Velas were the rule, the early Velas were not always sure how to handle the issue of men's participation. In Lagos, for example, in 1843 the women's Vela asked the bishop to clarify if they were or were not allowed to admit men.[45]

The question of who, within each town, was the driving force behind the impressive spread of the Vela—insistent ladies tired of belonging to decaying traditional cofradías where their power to encourage Catholic practice was limited, or frustrated priests trying to gin up religious practice (and especially to support the cult of the Santísimo Sacramento, the fundamental devotional practice in any given parish) by tapping into women's energies—is worth considering since we have rich information on the lead-up to Vela foundations. Fernández, the parish priest in San Miguel, made it clear that the Vela was the ladies' idea. When he forwarded their petition to the bishop's office, he appended this message: "Persuaded by the justice of this petition and happily inspired by it, I confess that it fills me with edification and I judge that it would be scandalous not to foment it or to refuse to cooperate."[46] The pleased-but-surprised tone of his comment suggests, or was meant to suggest, that the ladies were out ahead of him. But the *cura* in remote Tepic, by contrast, wrote that he had "convoked a sufficient number of Señoras" to form a Vela in December 1843, implying that founding the Vela was his idea, and this impression is strengthened by the fact that he had some trouble keeping the officers from resigning (one of the few cases in which there was not ongoing enthusiasm for the Vela Perpetua).[47] In Pátzcuaro, also, the priest assigned himself the role of organizer: "Desiring to promote the cult of the Santísimo Sacramento ... I have endeavored to excite the zeal of the leading ladies of that city to establish the Congregation called the Alumbrado y Vela Perpetua del Santísimo."[48] Other examples on both sides abound: the priests in La Barca and Tlazazalca (both in Michoacán) seem to have been the instigators, while the ladies of Lagos (Jalisco) were in the lead.[49] It was the cura of Zinapécuaro (Michoacán) who in 1847 petitioned ecclesiastical authorities to establish a Vela there, but in Yuririapúndaro (Guanajuato) the priest wrote that "varias Señoras principales" of the town planned to solicit the foundation of the Vela; and in Zinaparo, Tingüindín, and Jungapeo (all in Michoacán), too, the petition was presented as a result of the "desires of the populace" that a Vela be established in their towns.[50] In Mexico City one woman, Salvadora García de Vara, was personally responsible for obtaining the permission of the priest, ecclesiastical authorities, and civil authorities. The priest of the Sagrario, Manuel Ignacio de la Orta, depicted himself as simply going along ("in this era when impious men heedlessly vilify the Sacrament ... far from opposing such a laudable proposal, I am very agreeable").[51]

In all these cases we should be careful not to read the language of the documents as transparent. A priest who claimed to be the organizer of the Vela might think it unseemly to concede power or autonomy to his (female) parishioners, even if they were the moving force, while a priest who assigned agency to the ladies might have felt it was important to preserve the idea that lay organizations were the product of lay organizing, even if it was he who quietly promoted the Vela. Perhaps the most important point is that there was clearly collaboration between priests and the upper- and middle-class ladies who overwhelmingly composed the leadership of the early Velas. In other words, we stand to lose insight into the process of Vela foundation by trying to put too fine a point on the question of agency. It does not matter much whether the ladies were the first ones to come up with the idea, or whether the priest suggested it. The one thing that is clearly important is that the ecclesiastical hierarchy was not involved. These were local collaborations between women and parish priests.

Both priests and the ladies of the parish stood to gain from their new partnership. From the priests' point of view, the Vela inspired enthusiasm and energy in parish organizations and brought hundreds of people into the church every week. Beyond this, as we will see shortly, it provided a new source of much-needed funds. From the ladies' point of view, the Vela Perpetua offered opportunities to deepen their faith by contemplating the miracle of the Eucharist outside of the Mass. Vigil sitters, unlike participants in the Mass, could think of themselves as "visiting" Jesus, keeping him company when the church (especially in small provincial towns) might otherwise be empty, thinking of him as a friend. The chaplain of the cathedral of Durango, in support of the Real Congregación, had observed that vigils allowed Jesus to be "less alone" (*más acompañado*).[52]

There was also the clubbiness of the meetings, the snob appeal of the company of leading ladies of the town, the social interaction that was part of the rather daunting task of organizing an all-day, every-day vigil, the challenge of good management and professional record-keeping, the pride that came from funding parish projects (including projects designed by the ladies themselves), the pleasing sense of self-importance from having been given the responsibility to protect and accompany the Blessed Sacrament on a daily basis, in the past entrusted only to men and only on special occasions. (This complex mix of faith, sociability, and the opportunity for women to exercise their talents and ambitions also characterized the motivations for entering a convent, as many students of female monasticism have demonstrated.) Most of all, there was the sense of pride and relief that they had rejuvenated community religious practices in their parishes. The priest was not the only one who valued the Velas' recentering of the church in the community; the women did too. As we will see in chapter 4, women were exceedingly fearful of the weakness of an institution that they saw as crucial in the protection of their families and the moralization of their children.

How did the key innovation of the Vela—its female leadership—work out in practice? As we have seen, the Velas *required* the officers and the cabezas to be women.[53] The original San Miguel *reglamento* (statutes) had specifically permitted men to join, but limited their participation as *veladores* (vigil sitters) to Holy Thursday or any other day they were told to sit. Later Velas in

Michoacán, however, included both male and female daily veladores, under the governance of the cabezas de día and the hermana mayor. The two-by-two pairs were never mixed, but under a single Vela organization it became quite common for men to serve as veladores from 6:00 p.m. to 9:00 p.m. This was welcomed by the women as a way to extend the devotion into the evening hours. Not too many Velas provided the names of all the people who signed up to sit vigil (they were only required to give the names of the cabezas de día), but in 1843 the Vela in Morelia did, and the list of approximately 1,350 people included some 960 women and 390 men. Doña Josefa Juárez, for example, had signed up 35 women and 11 men to fill the hours for which she was responsible on Day One of every month.[54]

It is remarkable how easily the men who became members of the Vela Perpetua appear to have accepted female leadership. I have not turned up a single complaint by male veladores against the woman who governed them, and I have found several cases in which men seem to have gone out of their way to express not just acceptance but admiration for female leaders. In San Diego del Bizcocho (Guanajuato), for example, an 1853 complaint against the priest (for charging too much for his services) was signed by eight men who identified themselves as members of the Vela Perpetua. It began: "ever since this holy devotion was established in this place ... it was embraced by all of the parishioners with the greatest enthusiasm, and people of both sexes enlisted with great passion and good will," and went on to say that "the Señora who is in charge of the funds employs and distributes them with complete dedication to the devotion."[55]

The Michoacán model of a single, mixed-sex Vela with female officers continued to make some clerics nervous, as it had when the San Miguel foundation was proposed. Though ecclesiastical authorities had tolerated the upending of the principle of gender hierarchy that was implicit in the constitutional structure of the Michoacán Vela, four years later, in the town of Lagos in the bishopric of Guadalajara, the first separate Vela for men was founded, creating a constitutional model that became dominant in Guadalajara and was increasingly adopted in Michoacán as well.[56] The Vela de Señoras remained the more central institution, since its obligation was to keep the vigil during the hours that the church was always open, from 6:00 a.m. to 6:00 p.m. The Vela de Señores operated as a kind of men's auxiliary, extending the vigil from 6:00 p.m. to 9:00 p.m., as the male members of the Velas had done in Michoacán, though there they had done so under the leadership of women, without a separate organization.

The way the Velas functioned in the archdiocese of Guadalajara allows us to compare the popularity and the organizational effectiveness of the separate Velas for men and women. As they had in Michoacán, women clamored to join. Although only two women were required to fill each shift, in Lagos in the 1840s four or five women at a time were keeping vigil, giving rise to anxiety that all five would not earn the promised indulgences, which were automatically granted to the two mandatory *veladoras*. (Complaining that the women had refused to listen to him, the priest requested that the bishop reassure them that *everyone* who sat vigil would earn the indulgence.)[57] The Vela in the city of Guadalajara also attracted more veladoras than required by its constitution, and on top of their monthly fees, members of this Vela seem almost to have competed with each other to contribute items, from the expensive to the modest, to adorn the chapel where the Blessed Sacrament was displayed.[58] The inventory that was passed from one treasurer to the next in 1850 went on for several pages, with careful annotations of what each member had given and how much it had cost.[59]

Several of the women's Velas were singled out for praise by the bishop for their efficient organization. Of the Guadalajara Vela, for example, Bishop Diego de Aranda wrote: "The efficacy in the management of [the society's] interests and the orderly presentation of documents that support the account books . . . reflect the splendid education and piety that characterize not only the Hermana Mayor and Treasurer, but also all of the ladies that form that society."[60] Of the treasurer of the San Juan de los Lagos (Jalisco) Vela de Señoras, his secretary gushed: "The Bishop gives thanks to Señora Doña María Aleja Jimenes de Castro for the exactitude, fidelity, order, and good management with which this devotion . . . has been conserved."[61]

Many of the Velas de Señores, by contrast, were constantly in danger of collapse. They had persistent staffing troubles. The lists of cabezas that the priest was supposed to turn over to the bishopric sometimes left half or more of the days of the month blank. Their collections, while expected to be smaller than those of the Señoras since they had (and needed) fewer participants, were frequently disappointing. Much more often than the women's groups, their accounts were described in pastoral visits as poorly prepared, and they were more likely to be characterized by the priest as "decaída" (in decay). Sometimes the bishop contrasted the men's groups to the women's in an apparent effort to shame the men into action. The women's group in Arandas (Jalisco) was managed with great care, the bishop commented, but the men's group lacked cabezas for some days of the month, and sometimes collected as little as two reales, either because the veladores did not show up or because no one kept track of the funds.[62] The women of Aguascalientes presented accounts that showed a surplus of 452 pesos, reflecting the "well-formed and duly documented" accounts produced by Doña Ygnacia Olavarrieta, but Archbishop Pedro Loza sent the men's account book back to the treasurer to clean it up.[63] The men's groups were usually founded later than the Velas de Señoras in any given parish, sometimes just by a few months but sometimes by years, suggesting some feet-dragging. Often the priest did double duty as the president and treasurer of the Vela de Señores, perhaps a sign that the men of the parish were less committed to taking leadership responsibility than the women. In Zapotlán el Grande (Jalisco), for example, in 1873 the bishop scolded the priest for not presenting the accounts of the Vela de Señores, "nor did the cura give a reason for this, despite the fact that he ... has been [acting as treasurer] since who knows when, and he has been receiving the alms of the veladores, as apparently there is neither an Hermano Mayor nor a treasurer."[64] The Velas de Señores, then, tended to flounder. Over time most men's groups stayed on the books, and some were successful, but they were almost invariably eclipsed by the women's Velas.

So far we have been discussing the Vela in the center-west. There is a good reason for this: if priests and women in the dioceses of Michoacán and Guadalajara were immediately enthusiastic about the Vela Perpetua, that was not the case elsewhere. In Mexico City the first Vela Perpetua was not established until 1848, and Salvadora García's early, lonely foundation in the Sagrario did not spread in Mexico City until the early 1870s.[65] Foundations in the rest of the archbishopric of Mexico were also late and few.[66] When the Vela Perpetua did begin to proliferate in the archbishopric in the 1870s, the language of the foundation documents clearly indicates that this was an unfamiliar process; we see the same variety and confusion of constitutional provisions that were common in the early years of mass foundations in Michoacán and Guadalajara in the 1840s, before the method of establishing a Vela became streamlined and a clear model was in place.[67] Eventually the archbishop's office, weary of revising the flawed (as the office saw them) reglamentos of dozens of proposed Vela constitutions, insisted that all new foundations follow the model that Doña Salvadora had presented in 1848.[68] It is interesting to note that her petition made a point of stating that she had modeled her constitution on that of the Vela in Guanajuato, which had in turn been modeled on the San Miguel Vela. The path to the Vela Perpetua that had begun with the Real Congregación's foundation in 1793 in Mexico City had come full circle.

Elsewhere in the republic Velas were also scarce. The first Vela in Oaxaca was not founded until 1855 in the sagrario of Oaxaca City, and I have located no other new foundations in Oaxaca until the 1870s.[69] Terry Rugeley does not mention any Velas in Campeche or Yucatán in his discussions of cofradías there.[70] The bishop of Puebla first approved the establishment of a Vela in Tlaxcala and Huamantla in 1854, but these were not only late foundations; they were also quite different from the ones in Michoacán and Guadalajara, since the Huamantla constitutions called for thirty-one men as hermanos mayores and thirty-one women in the same capacity, and it called for the treasurer of both to be elected from among the men.[71] In other words, the Puebla/Tlaxcala version of the Vela was envisioned more like a cofradía with a women's auxiliary than like the original center-western Vela with its guaranteed female officers.[72]

Relationships between Women and Priests in the New Associations

Women may have been allies of priests in the project to resurrect and strengthen community piety, but this does not mean that there were no disputes between the curas and the lay organizations. There were, and when they occurred, women were not afraid to stand their ground and defend their organization. I have argued elsewhere that there was a mode of interaction between nuns and other religious women and priests that was characterized by rights-awareness, discursive equality with male ecclesiastical authorities, and willingness to engage them in argument, not just in moments of great crisis but also on an everyday level.[73] Given its ordinariness, and given the fact that female religious communities were porous places where many of the residents (servants, *niñas*, schoolgirls) came and went regularly, and where information flowed relatively freely (despite futile efforts to control it) through the "conventual grapevine" and "underground network[s] of communications," this self-defensive mode of interaction between women living in community and their male supervisors was surely something with which women and others outside the female religious communities were quite familiar.[74] If community seems to have given religious women the motivation and confidence to assert themselves in the face of men's unreasonableness or negligence, the same might hypothetically happen with the new communities of women in lay associations.

And it did. When parish priests tried to exercise more control over them than the ladies were willing to concede, women adopted something very like the "talking back" mode of interaction.[75] Further, when they stood up to priests, as the examples below show, priests, at least in this period, had no choice but to accept the consequences of the ladies' defiance.

Most of the disputes involved money. One of the consequences of declining financial resources of the cofradías was resistance on the part of the mayordomos to help support the parish churches, as they tried to reserve the dwindling resources of the cofradías for the members and not divert it for upkeep of the churches. Time and again priests lamented the depletion or exhaustion of the Fábrica Espíritual (building fund) to which the colonial cofradías had regularly contributed. As the priest of La Huacana (Michoacán) put it in 1854, as soon as he arrived in the parish as a new priest, he set about establishing a Vela Perpetua "because the advantages that result from such an association have always seemed to me of great importance; besides being a means to foment public piety, it counts with a secure common fund, more or less substantial, which is much needed in this parish because its Fábrica Espíritual is impoverished."[76]

As the Velas amassed funds, priests were grateful for their assistance, financial and otherwise. The projects that the ladies enjoyed supporting were often ones priests themselves might prioritize: beautification, replacement of deficient sacred objects and utensils with newer ones, and repair of decaying buildings. The parish priest of Arandas (Jalisco), for example, in 1850, gladly accepted money from the Vela for a new oil lamp and for the repair of the "unusable" organ.[77] The Vela of Ario (Michoacán) in the 1850s paid for the ringing of church bells to resume and the clock to be repaired, and bought some bronze candlesticks, a censer, lace for the altar table, flowers, and other ornaments.[78] The Pátzcuaro Vela in the late 1840s paid for nails, whitewash, a new door and doorframe, a new table, workers' salaries, and an organist for the afternoon mass.[79] The inventory of gifts by the Guadalajara Vela to the parish included numerous candelabra, a 250-peso rug brought from Mexico City, ornamented wooden chests and tables, a German clock that was in constant need of repair, crystal vases, numerous altar cloths and embroidered linens, and many arrangements of artificial flowers.[80]

But the age-old conflicts over lay association autonomy, especially where money was concerned, also surfaced. The parish priest of Lagos (Jalisco), Clemente de Sanromán, like other priests, at first welcomed the Velas, both men's and women's, to his parish. But he quickly became resentful of their wealth and financial independence. "Four, six, even eight people sit vigil during the same half hour," he complained, "all turning over [to the Vela treasurer] the monetary contribution that the devotion requires . . . while the parish itself received not even a *ramillete* [bouquet of flowers] in return." He himself often went unpaid for his services, he said, "because they [the officers] claim that the association has no funds."[81] So he began to hatch a plan to push back against the "disdain that the Vela and its President show him, and the outrageous diminishment of the authority of the parish." The treasurers of the Velas consistently refused to turn over the collection to him for safekeeping, he wrote to the bishop, and if he asked for an account of their expenses, they refused, and "the poor Priest is presented to the pueblo as an enemy of all that is good and all that is religious and all that is pious." He decided to leverage his priestly role, rather than always go along with their requests for celebration of the Mass. Local enthusiasm for the Vela had led to multiple requests for permission to observe "with all possible pomp and solemnity" events that Sanromán complained were not even in the liturgical calendar, like the anniversary of the founding of the Vela itself (for which, he added bitterly, additional collections were held).[82] So when the date for that particular celebration came around, he refused to celebrate the Mass unless the Vela agreed to pay him in advance. His plan didn't work. The Vela did not cave in; the function was not celebrated; and Sanromán was back where he started.[83]

In a similar case, Rafael Herrera, the priest of San Diego del Bizcocho, asked the Vela to increase its contribution to the Mass to four pesos, in light of the fact that it had accumulated so much money. The ladies responded that "their treasury is not his store," accusing him of abusing power and, for good measure, of interfering in their elections. Though after several angry exchanges he responded that he "desired to put an end to disputes with women," he could not resist a final salvo: if he had in fact interfered in the last elections, he wrote, "Doña Florentina Garate would never have been elected Hermana Mayor."[84] In 1850 the priest of Jaral (Guanajuato), José de Jesús Robledo, was also locked in a battle with the hermana mayor. "The administration of this institution," he fulminated, "has passed from the hands of the priest to the hands of a woman, who functions as an arbiter of and superior to the priest. She is the one who ordains and disposes whatever she judges to be convenient to the Vela.... She has bought some items for the cult, but these are only to be used when she allows it, or if I beg and plead, so that the Host ... is subject to the will of the Señora.... In verbal conferences and in two letters I have reproached her for her absolutism, telling her that she has been put in charge of the *veladoras*, but she has not been put in charge of the Church."[85]

In a case involving the ladies of the Pátzcuaro Vela, the hermana mayor, Doña María de la Luz Sierra, threatened to resign over the issue of who controlled the funds of the Vela. She argued her case in a lengthy and well-crafted letter to the priest, Victoriano Treviño. Before Treviño had arrived in the parish, she wrote, the Vela had undertaken the ambitious work of rebuilding the church, "rescuing it from its miserable and abandoned state and transforming it into the beautiful building we see today." But now Treviño, who had previously offended the women of the Vela by calling them "impertinent women," wanted to dictate which projects the Vela would pay for. He demanded that instead of paying for the repair of the roof of the sacristy, the Vela should finance repairs on the roof of the baptistery. As the ladies saw it, the sacristy roof repair prevented the ruination of a large part of the wall of the church, whereas the baptistery roof repair "only serves to protect a hallway that is of little use other than as a place for you to drink your *chocolate* and distract your imagination with the agreeable vistas that the location presents." "I do not consider myself capable of sustaining a harmonious relationship with you," Doña Luz wrote, "and so I have decided to relieve myself of the task of leading the Vela." Treviño seems to have backed down.[86]

These disputes between Vela members and priests show that the women who comprised the Vela leadership were not prepared to submit to any more priestly interference than their male counterparts had been willing to do in the colonial period; both women and men leaders valued institutional autonomy. They also show the extent to which the Velas had become forces in their parishes within a short period of time. An important contribution to the parishes was monetary. But the Velas also made a social contribution, in the sense that they provided an exciting new voluntary association that galvanized the female population (and many men as well); and a spiritual one, in the sense that community piety received a spark, a new focus and a new energy that it had often lacked in the years of declining cofradías after 1810.

Non-Catholic Associations

Before turning in the next chapter to the political importance of the new Catholic women's associations founded in the 1840s and 1850s, it may be helpful to establish whether there were other voluntary associations, not associated with the church, that were developing alongside the lay associations discussed here. Besides the new Catholic associations, were women also joining nonreligious clubs or secular societies, as men were? Were these organizations founded and run by women? Was there a broad-gauged joining fever of which the lay associations examined here were simply a part?

The answer to these questions is: "not really," "almost never," and "no." As for joining, Carlos Forment's massive study of voluntary associations in Mexico documents some male-led new clubs and societies that women were allowed to join, and that they did join. Of these, the Juntas Patrióticas that organized patriotic celebrations all over the country seem to have been the most widespread.[87] But the numbers were very small; perhaps equally important, these associations also had male members, and men were always the officers. Since I have argued that the fact of women's majorities in the mixed-sex cofradías of the colonial period had significance because they meant that women had experience within male-led organizations that helped them form their own cofradías later, organizations like the Juntas Patrióticas are worth noting, but they were nowhere near as numerous as the colonial cofradías, and thus their ability to serve as a training ground for women to form their own secular societies was quite limited.

The most visible non-church-affiliated, all-female association was the women's auxiliary of the Compañía Lancasteriana, the organizing and financing entity that operated the Lancaster school system. The association was established in Mexico in 1822, and twenty years later, in 1842, the Compañía Lancasteriana de Señoras was founded (consisting of the wives of the male members, according to historian Anne Staples).[88] The role of the Señoras in the association was to provide instruction for women in the prison school in Mexico City, to hand out end-of-the-year prizes in girls' schools, and to examine prospective teachers on their ability to teach sewing. These functions limited the number of Juntas de Señoras that could exist outside of Mexico City. Although by the early 1850s there were Lancaster schools in many parts of the country, there were no prison schools in the smaller cities and towns. There were also fewer Lancaster girls' schools than boys' schools at this time in provincial Mexico, diminishing the need for the Junta de Señoras in its role as supervisor of sewing classes. And since a men's Junta was needed in any given locale because it, and not the women's Junta, examined the female teachers for the girls' schools in all subjects but sewing, an autonomous Junta de Señoras was impossible. When a woman joined a Lancaster society, then, she and her fellow female members were supervised by the men's societies that necessarily existed in their towns.

Besides the Lancasterian auxiliary, Silvia Arrom has shown that the municipal government of Mexico City was occasionally favorable toward female charitable boards—not exactly a club or association, but clearly a recognition of new roles for women.[89] A fourteen-member Junta de Señoras assisted the Mexico City Junta de Caridad in 1828; a women's board supervised the Foundling Home from 1836 to 1846; another Junta de Señoras was created to help protect female artisans against imports in 1844; and a women's board oversaw the Hospital for Demented Women in 1844.[90] But none of these groups was founded by women, and women did not even join them voluntarily. Rather, they were appointed. Furthermore, in three of the four cases the duration of these organizations was short. The Junta de Señoras (Caridad) only lasted one year before it was disbanded; the Junta de Señoras (artisans) also appears to have been short lived; and the women's board that oversaw of the Hospital for Demented Women is only known to have existed for a year. As Arrom puts it: "Support for women's taking on this limited public responsibility was extremely tentative. Most philanthropic organizations founded during this period were male, and the three documented female groups probably had few members. . . . Indeed, as soon as it was able, the Mexican government took back some of the duties it had delegated to women."[91]

Outside of Mexico City there seem to have been even fewer examples of women forming associations. The ones I've found are few and not very meaningful. There is no evidence of municipal governments outside of Mexico City inviting women to form ongoing charitable organizations, much less widespread organization of non-church-affiliated women's groups, for any purpose.[92] There was some repetition of the pattern of naming women to short-term appointments. During the war with the US, for example, the governor of San Luis Potosí named María de Jesús Lacaves de Cabrera to head a commission to collect food and supplies from among "her sex"; but this was a one-time appointment, there was a parallel men's commission, and the governor also named a man to work alongside Doña María de Jesús.[93]

By highlighting the sparseness of women's non-Catholic organizations, I do not mean to suggest that the 1830s, 1840s, and 1850s saw no changes in women's lives in the secular sphere. Historian Anne Staples points out that this was an era in which women were out of the house and in the world much more than was the case in the colonial period.[94] By the 1830s newspapers were running ads, at least in Mexico City, for several shops that catered to women (*peluquerías, perfumerías,* etc.). Female literacy was sufficient to permit the publication of magazines for women beginning in the early 1840s (though edited by men).[95] But by comparison to devout Catholic women, women from, say, liberal families or with anticlerical inclinations just did not have much opportunity to join, much less found, non-church-related organizations.[96] Female associationalism remained strongly identified with the church, both within the traditional cofradías, and in the new women-led associations that were beginning to take hold.

Conclusion

In the world of business, innovation can come in the course of expansion, as workers and owners tinker with how to do things better. But innovation also happens under the opposite circumstances, when things are going poorly and improvements in processes or systems are essential to the survival of the enterprise.[97] Cofradías were not businesses, but the second of these rules, I argued in this chapter, seems to apply: when the cofradías faltered badly (chapter 2), we see innovations in Catholic associationalism beginning in the 1840s.

Other factors, of course, also help explain the new associational landscape. For one, all three types of women-headed lay associations discussed in this chapter had roots in colonial experiments; there was, in other words, already a move in the direction of larger roles for women before the financial and leadership crisis of the cofradías. The Vela Perpetua was a radical variation on the Real Congregación of the 1790s; the women's auxiliaries like the Santa Escuela also drew on the parallel structures of the Real Congregación, as well as the Third Orders; and the Ladies of Charity had a distant European model and a Mexican precursor, the Asociación de Señoras (chapter 1).

But a colonial pattern tending increasingly to acknowledge and utilize women's enthusiasm for lay associations does not explain the regional dimension of innovation in the 1840s. Theoretically a difference in the leadership of the center-western dioceses might figure here, and it is true that the bishops of Guadalajara and Michoacán in the 1840s—Diego de Aranda and Juan Cayetano Gómez de Portugal—appear to have been unusually supportive of the new female organizations.[98] Nonetheless, this chapter showed that the initiative for the foundation of the Velas (and the handful of women's auxiliaries for which we have evidence) came from women and priests at the parish level, not the bishops. To the extent that Aranda and Gómez de Portugal appear to be more encouraging of women-led associations than bishops elsewhere, it is because they were presented with more requests for licenses from the parishes. Those requests came, in turn, because of the dysfunction of the traditional ways of organizing lay piety. That is, they were gendered, regional responses to the gendered, regional crisis of the traditional cofradía.

Once established, the most nimble and easiest to found of the new associations, the Vela Perpetua, spread extraordinarily rapidly in the bishoprics of Michoacán and Guadalajara. But all three types of new associations were well-suited to the times, in two senses. First, they were simple in their financial structures, not requiring property ownership or great wealth to sustain their practices. In the 1840s when these associations were founded, property-owning cofradías had not yet been suppressed, but the pitfalls of pious associations that depended on wealth and property had already been amply demonstrated by the fate of the traditional cofradías after 1810. The model of the non-property-owning cofradía, however, was not new; in the colonial period these purely devotional cofradías had been fairly numerous. The fact that the new women's associations were not property-owning, then, makes them appropriate for the times but does not fully explain why a brand new type of association was needed.

The second and most powerful reason is that the female-led associations were better designed to take advantage of women's strengths than the traditional cofradías. This was not only because the leaders commanded more power than women had enjoyed as mere members, but also because the associations were built on practices that meshed well with women's daily lives and fit nicely within the accepted scope of their public behavior. The women of the Vela eagerly embraced the vigil (a practice that took place inside the church, at a time of the day chosen by the member, which required a quiet and prayerful demeanor) in place of the procession (which took place in public, sometimes at night, occupied several hours, and involved music and fireworks as well as other side activities inappropriate for women). The women of the Santa Escuela found meaning and excitement in the spiritual retreat and the examination of conscience, something associated with the daily schedule of nuns. The Ladies of Charity put the home visit, and its opportunity to save souls, at the center of their new devotionalism. In all three cases, instead of the raucous fiestas that accompanied the annual function, members celebrated the everyday presence of Jesus in their lives, their literal closeness to him during the vigil or the retreat, and their spiritual closeness as they emulated him in their charitable work. Women founded the new pious associations as organizations that they could not only lead, but whose religious practices were compatible with their preferences and culturally sanctioned spheres of activity, and stood to strengthen piety in the community just as well if not better than the traditional cofradías had done before the crisis.

CHAPTER FOUR

"Throwing Themselves upon the Political Barricades"

CATHOLIC WOMEN ENTER NATIONAL POLITICS
IN THE MIDCENTURY PETITION CAMPAIGNS

ON JULY 12, 1856, Antonia Eguren submitted a petition to the constitutional congress signed by ninety-six women, urging the congress not to include religious tolerance in the new constitution.[1] Doña Antonia identified herself as an "hermana de la Vela" and noted that most of the female signers of the petition also belonged to the organization.[2] Because the petition weighed in on a constitutional matter—in other words, it operated in the realm of politics—she was careful to deny that the women wished to "establish rights, much less try to stir up public opinion on such an important matter . . . which would be judged as absurd and against all reason because it is so inappropriate for our sex." But, she continued, as ladies of the Vela, they felt "obligated to manifest, simply and frankly, our Catholic faith" by sending this petition.

It appears that membership in a female-led lay association played a role in the decision of these women to express a political opinion. Was this an isolated case, or did the proliferation of women's Catholic associations in the 1840s and 1850s (chapter 3) have anything to do with the fact that by the late 1840s a surprisingly large number of Catholic women—mainly as "señoras" of a given town—also signed petitions like the one Antonia Eguren submitted, against liberal efforts to legislate religious tolerance in Mexico?

The scholarship on the topic of whether membership in voluntary associations promotes and enlarges access to political power is especially strong for men, perhaps because it is relatively easy to draw the connections between earning social capital in associations and spending it in politics when the subject of the inquiry can participate in politics in multiple and highly visible ways. It is harder to evaluate the connection between women's associations and women's political engagement when women could neither vote nor hold office. But while studies have shown that women's political activism in the US and Europe was not an automatic or universal outcome of joining, they have also made clear that being a member of, say, a literary society could feed moral outrage that could in turn translate into the establishment of societies with political aims, whether opposing slavery, protesting Indian removal, or condemning drink.[3] In other words, while it is neither true that before they had the vote all politically-minded women came out of a background in an association, nor that all associations produced political women, the literature nonetheless suggests a connection.

In this chapter I argue that Catholic women's associations in Mexico played important roles in the process by which women moved from encouraging local piety (an action with political implications but little consciousness of such on the part of the women involved) to entering national politics by means of active petitioning (a consciously political action, no matter denials like those in Antonia Eguren's petition to the effect that the signers did not mean it to be). It is logical that women's lay associations played important roles as instigators and implementers in these campaigns: after all, as we saw in chapter 3, women had recently come into their own as instigators and implementers of new voluntary associations. Additionally, in later twentieth-century protest movements lay associations are well known to have organized or "articulated" protest campaigns.[4] But I prefer not to rely solely on logic or read backward from the post-revolutionary era to the mid-nineteenth century, so I have sought other ways to understand the role of associations in political organizing. Unfortunately, direct evidence is not too plentiful, for reasons I will explain later. Doña Antonia's up-front acceptance of authorship of the anti-tolerance petition as a member of the Vela was, it turns out, unusual. Nonetheless, there are clues that, without proclaiming that they were doing so, women's religious associations did play a strong role in petition drives, which were the main way (short of armed movements) that people exerted political pressure and tried to achieve political goals outside of the electoral cycle.

The chapter begins with a discussion of the importance of petitioning in colonial and nineteenth-century Mexico and of women's petitioning before the major 1856 campaign. It then turns to that campaign, analyzing the public/press reception of the petitions. The goal of this section is to understand changes in the ways gender operated in the political arena when women self-consciously entered it. It will surprise no one to learn that many in the liberal press insisted that women were duped by priests into signing the petitions they submitted. And the liberal critique of women entering politics will sound familiar to most readers, since some of the same themes were struck in the US and Western Europe in the nineteenth and twentieth centuries. But how the liberal press pushed that point of view, the extent to which they might have been right that priests were much-involved in producing the women's petitions, and, most important, how the Catholic press wrote about Catholic women in politics are clearly relevant to the questions of whether and how organized groups of women became involved in the petition campaign, and what the impact of that involvement on the broader political conversation might have been. If the liberal reaction is predictable, the conservative reaction is less so. Next, the chapter moves toward the question of what role the lay associations played in the petition campaign by examining the themes and form of the petitions themselves, looking for clues as to authorship. Finally, the last section presents the case for a direct relationship between the petitions and the lay associations discussed in chapter 3.

Petitioning before 1856
PETITIONS IN THE COLONIAL WORLD AND THE EARLY REPUBLIC

Historians have recently turned their attention to petitioning as a way of expanding the meaning of politics beyond high politics and outcomes.[5] Especially helpful is the recent study by Daniel Carpenter of petitioning in the early US, *Democracy by Petition*. Carpenter argues that petitioning allowed many different voices, including those of women, to be heard and attended to in the political arena. It was transformational because it "reshaped the agenda of politics (procedural democracy), the terrain of politics (organizational democracy), and the assumptions of politics (cultural democracy)."[6]

I am not sure all the same claims could be made for Mexico if a similar comprehensive study of nineteenth-century petitioning were to be made, but there is no question that petitioning was important, and that the nature of its importance changed from the colonial period to the post-independence period. In colonial Mexico, petitioning played a key role in preserving stability. It softened rigid hierarchies of authority, allowing ordinary people to bypass intermediate levels of power and take their grievances, whether as an individual or as a group, to a higher authority who might be more sympathetic or in a better position to take action (for example the viceroy, the king, a bishop). Church and state archives are full of petitions from indigenous villages, artisans, merchants, city councils, and other bodies looking for help in defending their corporate interests, as well as abandoned women asking for protection or financial assistance from a bishop, widows pleading for a pension from the state, mothers and fathers seeking a scholarship to the seminary for their son, underaged young men soliciting the early right of majority, priests hoping to be transferred to a parish with a more congenial climate, and every other imaginable individual request.

As Susan Zaeske points out, "natural law assumed that all subjects ... possessed the right of petition and that rulers ... were obliged to receive and respond to petitions."[7] For sixteenth-century Mexico, Adrian Masters has recently shown that hundreds of petitions from all manner of colonial subjects were not only heard, but their language was transplanted into decrees; in fact, the vast majority of imperial decrees came from petitions.[8] As reports from officials became more regular later in the colonial period it seems likely that petitioning as a major source of legislative inspiration diminished, but the expectation remained that petitions could influence or become law. In sum, it is clear that petitioning worked well during the colony, when the distant crown or the bishop had reasons to value petitions as a way of finding out what was going on, when decrees based on petitions were easy to issue if they were deemed to have merit, and when the king or the bishop could accede to one petition and deny a similar one the next week if he chose to do so.

Collective petitions, as opposed to individual ones, were a subset of the larger body of petitions. Most of them articulated local and group-specific grievances, such as a merchant's group in a certain city requesting relief from certain kinds of taxation. A further subset of these collective petitions was comprised of those that weighed in on national or imperial policy. Very often these petitions were submitted by more than one group, and together they constituted a petition campaign. There were not too many of these political petitions in the colonial period, much less ones that could be characterized as part of a campaign. The most famous were the petitions from corporate groups all over Mexico in opposition to the Consolidación de Vales Reales in 1804—the requirement that the church call in loans, sell property, and lend the proceeds to the crown—a campaign that succeeded in bringing about important changes in the way the Consolidación operated.[9] But after independence, seemingly coordinated political petitioning began to proliferate, creating problems that had not existed or had not been too serious in the colony.[10]

The post-independence political petitions were landmines. The expectation that petitions would be heard and acted upon was one problem.[11] Individual and many collective petitions could be forwarded to an appropriate official or ministry for consideration, but political petitions were another matter. They could not, either logistically or politically, be easily brought to a vote in the national or even state congresses. How could the congress vote on multiple petitions that all endorsed a major policy change, but in slightly different language and with slightly different demands? Moreover, did the petitions represent the "will of the people" or just the organizational acumen of a small number of people, somewhat analogous to the calls to our representatives that we are regularly urged to make on behalf of one cause or another? The calls, and the petitions, had some meaning, but it was not always easy to discern. Seeking clarity (and hoping the results would vindicate their preferred course of action), deputies in the congress of Michoacán in the mid-1830s, faced with a large number of petitions calling for a change of the system of government from federalism to centralism—a change most of them did not favor—went so far as to do the arithmetic on the number of inhabitants of the towns that had sent petitions, to see whether they represented a majority of the state's population.[12]

An even more serious problem was the fear that when men assembled to discuss and sign a petition, the meeting could turn into a rebellion. Will Fowler and his team identified sixty-five "pronunciamientos" issued between 1824 and 1853 that used the word "petition" in the text of their public statements; clearly the line between the fundamentally pacific intent of a petition and a call to arms was blurry.[13] How to guard against this danger? While it was relatively easy for monarchs to simply forbid collective petitions or restrict the number of people who were allowed to sign, it was unpopular in a liberal republic to narrow the constitutionally protected (as they saw it), "sacrosanct" (a word used often) right of petition, and doing so risked defeating the peace-preserving purpose of the limitation.[14] The press and members of the congress repeatedly called for regulation of the right to petition, but they usually did so without providing concrete suggestions. One early proposal was to limit the right to individuals or to corporations whose grievance or request was peculiar only to that group and was not a broad-gauged issue shared across regions or even the whole country; in other words, it was a proposal to ban the political petition.[15] But this proposal went nowhere. As one legislator put it in 1833, regulation was "such an arduous and delicate enterprise that no Mexican legislative body has attempted it."[16] Moreover, a vague right to petition—rather than a precisely delineated one—served many people well because, as *El Universal* put it in 1850, "questions like which issues were citizens allowed to petition about, and what obligations did this right, so solemnly guaranteed by the constitution, impose upon the congress?" could be left up in the air, while decisions about whether to approve or reject a petition could remain subject to partisan interests.[17]

Petitioning was fairly intense during the first fifteen years after independence. The expulsion of Spaniards from Mexico in 1829, the conservative Plan de Jalapa in 1830, and especially the "change of system" from federalism to centralism in 1835 all provoked petitions from across the country, usually authored by the residents and/or *ayuntamientos* of a city or town. After centralism replaced federalism in 1835, political petitioning seems to have weakened (probably because there was no confidence that the centralist state, with its narrow definitions of "citizenship" and "rights" and its dissolution of state congresses, would pay any attention), but it did not disappear, and when the 1824 federalist constitution was restored in 1846, an updated version of it once again clearly stated that citizens had the right to petition.[18] Thus when the first big wave of religious/political petitioning began in 1848, the right to petition was well established, if still unregulated.

WOMEN'S PETITIONING BEFORE 1856

While women were frequent writers of individual petitions, collective petitioning by women in the colonial period and the first two and a half decades after independence was quite rare. There were some petitions from wives protesting the expulsion of their Spanish husbands in 1829.[19] In 1833 a group of some forty women in Guadalajara signed a petition urging the derogation of a law that threatened to expel their husbands, sons, and fathers from the state of Jalisco.[20] In the same year there was an unusual "pronunciamiento" of women in the town of Zacatlán (Puebla), in which some one hundred forty women signed a document declaring that they were willing to take up arms in defense of the state government.[21] Other than these I know of no other political petitions written by women, much less any petitions they wrote as part of broad-gauged political campaigns.

Since even women's petitions that arose out of immediate threats to their families (like the expulsion of husbands) were uncommon, it was a bit of a shock when I found groups of women from three different cities contributing to a political petition-writing campaign in early 1849 against a colonization project that would disestablish Catholicism as the official religion of Mexico (that is, establish *tolerancia de cultos*). One orator in 1856 claimed that "thousands" of petitions against religious tolerance were sent to the congress; this was an exaggeration, probably a gross exaggeration, since the orator's purpose was to suggest that if there were thousands of petitions in 1848–49, the fact that there were many fewer than this in 1856 indicated growing acceptance of the idea of tolerance.[22] I think it is likely that there were no more than two hundred.[23] Unfortunately, a fire in 1909 burned many of the documents archived by the congress, including petitions from both 1848–49 and 1856.[24] But no matter exactly how many petitions there were, the topic of religious tolerance commanded a lot of attention in the press.[25]

The issue arose at this time because of soul-searching about the disastrous loss of half the national territory of Mexico to the US in 1848 and what should be done in response. One answer, proposed by some delegates from Veracruz, was to promote colonization.[26] Mexico, their reasoning went, needed colonization in order to become prosperous enough to prevent future humiliating losses, and colonists would not come if they had to convert to Catholicism in order to participate in the Mexican economy and polity. Opponents of this call for religious tolerance mounted a furious defense that was couched primarily in nationalist terms: religious unity was the only thing keeping Mexico intact, and an invasion of non-Catholic foreigners would threaten this national unity. There was also concern expressed that since the foreigners would likely be young men, they would want to marry Mexican women and this would bring disruption to the Catholic family, the "anchor of social peace."[27]

With objections to this perceived threat to the family at their center, three petitions were submitted by women: the señoras of Orizaba, Oaxaca, and Querétaro.[28] (There were also petitions from the men of these cities.) The first to appear was the one from Orizaba, submitted on December 28, 1848, to the congress and published a month later in the Catholic organ *La Voz de la Religión*. In twelve pages, over two consecutive issues, it sounded many of the themes that would later appear in the 1856 women's petitions, especially the danger to the Mexican family and to Mexican women of tolerance. The Oaxaca petition was much shorter but struck similar themes, as did the long Querétaro petition. (I will have more to say about the content of the petitions below.)

Oddly, these petitions were scarcely noticed in the press. Women had always been understood to have the right to petition, but the fact that here they were doing so as a group, which was unusual, and on a subject of national political import, which was unprecedented, was remarkable, and yet it was rarely remarked. I have found only three relatively neutral mentions of the women's petitions. The first was a short comment in *El Universal*, a conservative paper, in which the editors noted that they had received word of a petition signed by one thousand women in Orizaba.[29] They closed the comment with an exclamation point, probably to emphasize the novelty of a petition from women, though possibly just to underline the large number of signatures. The second was also a short comment, this time from the liberal paper *El Monitor Republicano*, that the "fair sex of Oaxaca has submitted a petition against religious tolerance, but we should pay little attention to these documents since it is well known with what ease the men of the sacristy dominate women."[30] The third comment, from *El Observador Católico*, was a longer defense of the women of Oaxaca, whom *El Monitor* had accused of not being able to think for themselves and not being savvy enough to identify their own interests.[31] This was rude and disrespectful, *El Observador* wrote. The rest of the article mainly reiterated the points made in the Oaxaca petition itself. This was the last mention of the women's petitions.

Why did these three petitions not make much of a stir? Perhaps it is because they were such a small part of the campaign against religious tolerance at this time (just three out of at least forty published petitions and possibly as many as two hundred that were submitted). Additionally, their petitions came well after earlier condemnations of the colonization project had been published, including pastorals and petitions written by men in large cities. (The *vecinos* of Puebla were the first non-churchmen to petition; theirs was published in mid-November 1848.)[32] An even more likely factor was that the liberal stance in favor of religious tolerance was not as strong as it would become just six years later. *El Siglo Diez y Nueve* commented in connection with the petition from Guadalajara that even men who figured in the "first ranks of the ultra-liberal party" were enemies of religious tolerance.[33] In the end, the colonization project, which would have required changing Article 3 of the 1824 constitution protecting Catholicism as the state religion, never came to a vote and does not seem to have gained the support of any delegation except the one from Veracruz that introduced it in the first place. Hence the threatening strangeness of women entering the fray may not have seemed dangerous enough for liberals (other than the one-sentence notice in *El Monitor*) to speak out against them. But for whatever reason, the women's political petitions, novel as they were, did not register on the national psyche, and indeed in 1856, one author, somewhat panicked about the appearance of women's petitions during that campaign, commented, mistakenly, that they were an unprecedented phenomenon.[34]

The 1856 Campaign against Religious Tolerance

If in 1849 the proposal for religious tolerance was relatively easily defeated, the world had changed by 1856. Three years earlier, in 1853, the church had been discredited when it involved itself directly in bringing former president Antonio López de Santa Anna back from exile, and tolerating or even encouraging his most blatantly illiberal time in office (out of his eleven stints in the presidency). The next year the liberal revolution of Ayutla began and the famous Reform liberals took over the government. In 1856 they wrote several radical new laws mainly directed against the church (though also against the landholding indigenous village), and then called a constitutional convention to write a new document that would reflect the changes in Mexican liberalism since the writing of the first liberal constitution in 1824 and provide a framework within which the new laws of the Reform could be implemented.[35]

Religious tolerance was a natural proposal for inclusion in such a constitution. Most liberals, who dominated the constitutional congress (since conservatives had refused to serve in a process they saw as rigged), viewed the concept of a state religion as anti-modern (though this does not mean that they did not approve of religion, which most of them did).[36] Although some moderates were unsure that Mexico was prepared for religious tolerance, others argued that allowing other religions besides Catholicism to freely practice their faith was both a practical and philosophical necessity for a country that aspired to modernization and modernity (more or less the same reasoning as that behind the colonization effort seven years earlier). The laws of the Reform had already been bitterly denounced by the church and the Catholic press. But religious tolerance, with its end to the privileged and protected position of Catholicism in Mexico, would represent another severe blow.

Article 15 on religious tolerance was passionately debated in the press, in public meetings, and on the street, culminating in heated hearings at the congress.[37] Drawing on Francisco Zarco's account of the proceedings (Zarco was a major figure in the congress and the editor of the leading liberal newspaper *El Siglo Diez y Nueve*), historian David Gilbert describes the scene: every day between July 29 and August 5, "the visitor's galleries were packed with spectators, including many women, who applauded, cheered, or booed the delegates depending on the position they adopted in their speeches.... At times the delegates were showered with scraps of paper from above, on which were written threats like 'Death to the Heretics' or encouraging statements, like 'long live the Reformation.'"[38] Although Gilbert is right that both sides were represented in the galleries, reports from newspapers across the political spectrum strongly suggest an overwhelmingly anti-tolerance crowd, whipped up, according to the liberal press, by "agents of the sacristans" circulating among them.[39]

In early July the commission named to study Article 15 had begun to receive a number of petitions, virtually all of which argued—as they had in 1848 and 1849—against religious tolerance. Again, the 1909 fire destroyed our ability to estimate with much accuracy how many of these petitions were submitted, but Zarco himself referred to a "chubasco," or downpour, of anti-religious tolerance petitions.[40] The daily accounts of congressional business (*crónicas parlamentarias*) published in several newspapers listed the petitions officially received by the congress, and since both liberal and conservative newspapers reported the same lists, we can suppose they give us an accurate official number: between July 10 and August 15, the crónicas reported that forty-four petitions had been received by the congressional commission.[41] Others, however, did not make it into the crónicas, for reasons that varied. Some petitions were just never counted officially, and we only know about them because they were referenced elsewhere. We can't know how many fall into this category. Others went straight to a willing publisher, in some cases because by the time they were likely to be counted in the discussion the vote on the measure would already have taken place, and in other cases probably because they figured to make more of a splash as published petitions than as another document for the congress to shelve. (María Cruz Romeo Mateo, writing about a petition campaign in Spain against religious tolerance at almost exactly the same time, observes a similar divide between petitions sent to the Cortés—some from or signed by women—and those sent directly to the Catholic press, which she sees as having "clear propagandistic ends.")[42] I know of ten petitions that fall into this category, most from the state of Jalisco.[43] Using both liberal and conservative newspapers and a number of libraries that hold pamphlet literature, I can account for sixty-seven petitions through the end of September.

As had been the case in 1848–49, the majority of the 1856 petitions were written by male citizens of towns and cities. But seven years later, more women were involved: now seventeen of the sixty-seven known petitions came from women, and this time the fact of their existence was very much *not* ignored in the press or in the congress. Señoras from the following cities and towns submitted petitions: Mexico City, Morelia, Guadalajara, León, San Luis Potosí,

Toluca, Lagos, Guanajuato, Pátzcuaro, Silao, San Miguel de Allende, Zacatecas, Puebla, and Etzatlán (Jalisco).[44]

Even more important than the fact that some of the most important cities in Mexico were represented is that the women's petitions seemed to kick off and even to inspire the whole campaign. On July 7, under the headline "Mexican Women Turn into Bloomers"—"bloomers" was an epithet used in the US to ridicule early feminists who had adopted the liberating "Turkish" pants-dress—*El Republicano* wrote that they had received advance notice that the "leading ladies" of Mexico City were going to submit a petition against Article 15.[45] "Now all that is missing is for them to form a club in order to solicit certain rights, like the *bloomeristas* of our neighbor to the north." Sure enough, two days later the *Diario Oficial* recorded the Mexico City ladies' petition as the first received and recorded by the constitutional congress, despite one deputy (García Granados) who tried to block it because, he said, it was not known whether the ladies had the permission of their husbands to sign or "whether women enjoy the rights of citizens, including the right of petition."[46] The petition was received with "astonishment," according to *El Monitor Republicano*, even as the liberal paper feverishly called for verifying all the signatures in light of "well founded reports" that there were fishy methods used to obtain the signatures, that the majority of the names were "unknown," and that some respectable women had complained that their names were used without permission.[47] In time *El Monitor* acknowledged that the Mexico City petition and others were signed by "distinguished ladies," and it reprinted an article from a Guadalajara newspaper that called the petition a "notable and unprecedented occurrence, the first of its type among us," under the headline "Article 15 of the Constitution: The Political Importance of Women."[48] But the first reaction of the liberal press was panic.

As men's petitions began to follow the women's, almost as if in imitation of them, the public amazement increased. "What will our colleagues in the liberal opposition say when they learn that the strong sex has added its voice to that of the weaker one?" the conservative daily *El Omnibus* gloated, in reference to the fact that the petition by the women of Mexico City preceded the men's petition by several days.[49] In Morelia, too, the women's petition came before the men's: unfortunately, wrote a despondent correspondent of *El Monitor Republicano*, "the fair sex has succeeded in encouraging their male counterparts [*el sexo feo*] to follow their example."[50] The women's petitions from Toluca, Silao, and Guanajuato all seem to have preceded those submitted by the men from the same towns.

It is hard to tell how much effect the petitions, either in general or from women, had on the proceedings of the congress, which rejected a vote on religious tolerance—effectively killing it—in a 67-44 vote on August 6. Although some orators' references to expressions of "the will of the people" obliquely acknowledged the petitions, they were rarely mentioned directly by the more moderate speakers, the ones who ended up voting against religious tolerance.

José María Lafragua, one of these moderate delegates, did note later that he came to see religious *intolerance* as "in the public interest," because tolerance, he feared, "would be violently resisted by five million Indians and a million and a half women."[51] He did not make specific reference to the women's petition campaign, but we know that the petitions had an impact on the congress from the liberal delegates' and the liberal press's efforts to discredit and ridicule them.[52] The liberals simply protested too much for us to avoid the conclusion that they were quite rattled by the entrance of women into the national political arena.

Gender and Protest in Liberal Discourse

Unlike in 1849, when the liberal press scarcely noticed or acknowledged the women's petitions, now liberals from moderates to radicals took the "famous" women's petitions seriously.[53] It was a world turned upside down: "when the weaker sex leaves her sphere in order to take part in public matters, she is as out of place as a member of the stronger sex dedicating himself to domestic chores."[54] The liberal goal was to lessen the significance of the women's petitions. One way they did this was quite simple: although a large majority of petitions were written and signed by men (forty-nine out of the sixty-six we know of), many of the liberal press accounts mentioned only the "representaciones de las señoras." Although the novelty of women entering the political process and the fact that the women's petitions preceded the men's may account for the press downplaying the more familiar phenomenon of petition-writing by men, it is surely the case that highlighting the women's petitions was also a deliberate attempt to feminize, and thus, they thought, diminish, the whole process. One of the few comments on a men's petition (the one from Mexico City) used a similar belittling tactic, claiming that a third of the signatures were those of Spaniards "who have no business in our affairs," and another third were from boys.[55]

Another strategy was to portray the church as so desperate that it was forced to turn to women for support—also feminizing petitioning on this subject. The "feminine sex" was the church's "last resort," *El Interés General* (Puebla) wrote.[56] The church "hides behind the weaker sex, the sex that ought to be protected by the stronger one" wrote *El Heraldo*.[57] José María Mata, speaking before the constitutional congress, characterized the church as "seeking out simple and naive women ... now that they can't find support among men so easily as in the past."[58] Francisco Zarco echoed this theme, and his speech (with the deputies' reactions to it) was printed in *El Monitor*: "The clergy," he orated, "not finding enough support among the men, has gone in search of it from the women," and

> from some [women] they have extracted their signatures by using the element of surprise, from others by demanding compliance, from some perhaps by appealing to their vanity, and from all of them by deception,

making them believe that religion was in danger, telling them that we [Liberals] are going to erect temples to Venus in the plaza, to reestablish human sacrifice to Huitzilopochtli, to establish polygamy, to dissolve the institution of marriage. (Laughter.) Poor ladies! For good reason they became alarmed, they did not want to be abandoned by their husbands, nor live in the harem with his new wives, nor be immolated on the sacrificial stone, nor allow their daughters to become prisoners of the Mohammedans. (Laughter.)[59]

Another major theme in liberal discourse was that politics was an inappropriate place for women. (This was of course true in the West in general.) Some men writing in this vein took the tack of characterizing women as too good for politics, or above them. *El Monitor Republicano* in 1856 wrote: "We are very sorry that our beautiful countrywomen have been forced to take part in political-theological debates.... Woman is an angel sent by God to earth to console the unfortunate and alleviate pain. Why do you want to convert her into a dark inquisitor, without a heart . . . ?"[60] *El Interés General* weighed in with the opinion that "it is despicable that the sinister faction would force the more lovely half of humanity, whom we could never view as our enemy, whose weakness makes them vulnerable, to enter the bloody arena of politics."[61]

El Interés then added another twist that was commonly adduced: female ignorance and naivete. "As strangers in the terrain of politics, we suspect that when the fair sex speak of these matters, it is without understanding what they say."[62] *El Monitor Republicano* wrote that the "men with cowls" have undermined "the decorum and timidity that are natural to women, so that they will throw themselves upon the political barricades, without regard for how ridiculous this makes them look."[63] And a disdain for women's abilities to form opinions on political topics was implicit in the comments of Francisco Zarco, who thundered that "some are of the opinion that the legislator ought to capitulate to the concerns of the masses and I will never be of this opinion.... Are we to wait to see what women and their confessors opine on the big questions of the day?"[64]

Politics was also said to turn women ugly. For *El Interés General*, involvement in politics transformed women into "rigid antagonists" who "argue, tire you out, and pester you with their undigested ideas."[65] Ignacio Ramírez's speech before the constitutional congress on July 7, 1856, referred to a "phalanx of hussies [*mugerzuelas*] descending upon us to discuss religious tolerance."[66] How exactly women were changed by having participated in the campaign was strongly generational: young women tended to be portrayed as having been corrupted, while married women became disobedient to their husbands, and older women, "those well-aged ladies [*jamoncitas*] who have already counted their twenty-five Aprils or more," became fanatics about petitioning because "it gave them a way to pass the time."[67]

The liberal messages, then, were that politics were too difficult for women to understand; that women were above politics; that women were innocent and vulnerable to manipulation and deceit; that women were harridans who understood exactly what they were doing. These are some mixed messages. Even the most direct attempt to understand what was going on, José María Vigil's essay "The Political Importance of Women," was quite confused. On the one hand, Vigil thought that the most significant feature of women's entry into politics was their ability to use tears and batting eyelashes to influence men, who were able to resist logic and cogent analysis but not the wiles of a woman. "How can he remain impassive before a creature so beautiful, so kind, with her hair loose . . . her dress in disarray, who implores him that 'not now and not ever must he consider religious tolerance.' Impossible!"[68] But then he went on to say that the "initiation of women into politics has a real and positive importance, because it is a step in the direction of the political emancipation of women," which was overdue and on balance a good thing. Women's "political and social abjection, sooner or later, will fall, because it is unnatural, given that there is no difference in women's and men's intellectual abilities." Finally, returning to his theme of female seduction, Vigil weakly concluded that he wished women had entered politics for a better cause, and he ended by putting his hopes in the congress, who, he said, would be able to resist these "modern Eves."[69]

Gender and Protest in Conservative Discourse

The conservative press also had to come to terms with women's entry into politics, since although they were gleeful, they didn't really believe that women belonged in politics any more than the liberals did. Vigil rightly pointed out that it was ironic that the conservative *El Omnibus* should be so enthusiastic about women participating in politics, since this was "an idea that ought not fit with their principles" of upholding hierarchies and disdaining democracy.[70] Conservatives took four paths to making the petitions work for them. First, they emphasized that women entered politics reluctantly. "The ladies of Mexico have never interfered in even the most limited way before," wrote *El Omnibus*, and would not do so now but for the grave threat of Protestant churches "in which errors and lies are taught" being established "alongside churches that adore The Crucified One."[71]

Second, conservatives emphasized the respectability and therefore the education and astuteness of the women who signed. "The exposition that the ladies of this capital have submitted to congress was signed by something like 2,000 women, and among the signatures are the names of the principal families of the city, such as Alamán, Iturbe, Icaza, Paredes, Algara, San Román, Escandón, Tornel, Mier y Terán, etc., etc., etc. And *El Monitor* and *El Heraldo* still claim they didn't know what they were signing!"[72] (The conservative papers also emphasized the respectability of the men who signed: "This proves that the respectable class of society, that is, the class that is thoughtful, that lives on their work and does not aspire to live on the public treasury, that has morals and good habits, is against Article 15.")[73] The only reason some respectable women did not sign, wrote another author, is that they did not know about the petition in time, and if they had they gladly would have signed.[74]

Third, conservatives drew a distinction between intervening in *politics* and intervening in *religion*.[75] Commenting on the liberals' questioning whether the signers of the petitions had their husbands' or fathers' permission, one writer argued that "in matters of religion not only do women not need [permission] to sign, but they can sign even against the will of their husbands or fathers. Although sacred scripture is not the great strength of our wise and amiable colleagues [in the liberal press], we cannot believe that they are unfamiliar with what Jesus told Matthew in chapter 10, verse 37: He that loveth father or mother more than me is not worthy of me: and he that loveth son or daughter more than me is not worthy of me."[76] *El Omnibus* reported that when Sr. García Granados had made the point that women hadn't sought male permission to sign, his voice was drowned out by guffaws from the gallery.[77]

Finally, the conservative press in 1856 highlighted the liberal press's disrespect for women. "In yesterday's session," wrote *El Omnibus*, while the petition of the señoras of Mexico City was being read to the assembly, "some pseudo-liberal and impolitic—in every sense of the word—deputies coughed, sneezed, gesticulated, and exchanged knowing looks with each other, smiling sardonically."[78] The same paper accused the liberal *La Esperanza* of having "insulted the ladies of Lagos for having opposed tolerance, calling them ignorant, enemies of good manners, promoters of divorce and other things."[79] And Ignacio Ramírez's use of the word "mujerzuelas" to refer to the women who signed one petition came in for bitter criticism.[80]

All this was intended to counter the liberal disparagement of the entire petition campaign as something cooked up and managed from start to finish by priests. The conservative press insisted that the signers of the petitions were not ignorant or manipulated, but rather respectable and pure women who knew exactly what they were doing. They had agonized about whether or not to enter politics, and in the end had chosen to defend God and the church. Significantly, then, the conservative press made the decision in 1856—as it had not in 1849—to accept women, probably with some misgivings, as partners in their core political projects, just as we saw in chapter 3 that parish priests had, perhaps reluctantly, made the decision to accept women as leaders of lay associations in their towns and neighborhoods.[81]

The Petitions

Let us turn to the women's petitions themselves. I am interested in whether the themes struck in the women's petitions are different from those in the men's petitions, as well as in any clues about how they came into being:

whether, as Romeo Mateo suspects for the Spanish petition campaign against religious tolerance in 1855 and 1856, the hierarchy of the church was involved; or whether, as the same historian finds for another petition campaign in 1869, it was laypeople, "and especially laywomen," who were behind the campaign.[82] Because of the real possibility that it served as a model or inspiration for not only the other two 1849 petitions but also the 1856 ones, I will begin with the long petition from the women of Orizaba, which was the first of the 1849 petitions.

This petition sounded the general themes that the later petitions would also take up: the dangers to women, marriage, family, and the Mexican nation (more or less in that order, although they were all understood as intimately connected) if religious tolerance were mandated. It began by raising fears about bringing to Mexico "inhuman sects" that "only know how to oppress women, enslave women, and degrade women."[83] Many examples of the inhumanity of such sects were given, some from Greece and Rome but also from the contemporary US, where the petition pointed out that masters could put female slaves to death; and from Germany, where even the Protestant Madame de Staël was said to have admitted that the easy availability of divorce undermined marriage.[84] Henry VIII, whose rejection of Catholicism permitted murderous behavior toward his many wives, was of course cited.[85] The introduction of non-Catholic sects would bring not only callous discarding of wives and rampant divorce but also harems and infanticide.[86] Catholicism, and only Catholicism among the world's religions past and present, "liberated" woman from the "unlimited power that man held over her," exalting her as a worthy companion of man, enriching her with the splendid title of "Señora," and making her no longer a slave.[87]

Much of the petition was concerned with this historical and cultural comparison of the position of women under Catholicism to their position under all other religions, with the emphasis on women's roles in marriage. But the threat to marriage was naturally a threat to the family, and the threat to the family was a threat to the nation. The petition concluded this logical extension from the well-being of women to the well-being of the nation by invoking the biblical story of the wise woman of Tekoa. In that parable, the unnamed wise woman convinced King David not to allow his son Absalom to be killed for having killed his brother, since as she knew from her own tragic and almost-identical experience, this would bring only the terrible loss of both sons. Like the woman of Tekoa, the petition went, Mexican women had lost one of their sons in the war with the US: territorial integrity. But they had another son who could still be saved: Catholic integrity.[88] "Turn back this colonization project; do not sanction the introduction of heterodox sects into the Republic and by this means cause us to lose our Catholic integrity just as we have lost our territory.... This is the very patriotic objective of this petition."[89] In sum, when women and the institution of marriage were not protected from men's weaknesses and disrespect, the family and therefore the nation suffered mightily. To underline the point, the petition put Catholicism at the center of nationalism, as conservative writers and thinkers had been doing for decades, but it asserted that the link to Catholic marriage and the Catholic family was crucial.[90]

Were these petitions actually written by women? This question has preoccupied the handful of historians who have analyzed the 1856 women's petitions (most very briefly, one in a short article).[91] (No one has written about the 1849 petitions.) Did women write the petitions or didn't they? Though these historians are careful to make sure readers know that they believe that women were capable of writing them, they don't come down firmly on the issue. Susana Sosenski (the author of the one article-length study), in particular, seems conflicted; perhaps as a feminist historian she is unwilling to stand by her statement early in the article that it is unlikely that women wrote the petitions, and she retreats into the conclusion that it is "difficult" to know.[92] Edward Wright-Ríos, too, sees the petitions as "a shrewd, coordinated public relations campaign" and a "clever strategy to convey widespread feminine sentiment," suggesting that men were the authors and strategists, but he also calls the petition process "an effective means of women's political participation."[93]

For a book like this one that aims to analyze how women entered the political arena, the question of authorship is significant. Based on my own analysis of the petitions, I conclude that some, including the earliest ones, were likely written by men, probably priests, though I am open to the idea that some of the later ones had female authors. My reasoning is as follows.

As my brief encapsulation of the Orizaba petition shows, it was wholly oriented to women's central roles in preserving social order and even nationhood. Despite this feminist (of a sort) focus, however, I do not think it is at all likely that the Orizaba petition was written by a woman or women. First, it was signed and submitted just two days after the men's petition from Orizaba. This does not necessarily mean that the two petitions were written in tandem, but it is suggestive. More telling is that the men's petition—in a rare move—briefly signaled the themes that the women's petition would stress. Unlike almost all the other men's petitions in 1848–49, the Orizaba men's petition talked about the sanctity and indissolubility of marriage under Catholicism, in contrast to sects that believed marriage to be a dissolvable contract; about the likelihood of polygamy becoming established in Mexico if the opinions of "Melancton [sic] and the other founders of the Reformation" were followed; and about the national tragedy that would result when women were "abandoned once they are past their prime," leaving families broken apart and incapable of serving as the bedrock of society.[94] I suspect that the author or one of the authors of the men's petition expanded this short section into the multi-page women's petition, padding it with numerous historical and biblical allusions and with a number of Latin phrases. That some of both the history and the Latin was wrong (admittedly, mistakes in the latter could have been the fault of the typesetter) does not erase the clear impression that this petition was authored by someone with theological, literary, and historical learning (and a strong desire to showcase it).

There were plenty of women, of course, who were well-educated and were elegant writers—we met one in chapter 3, the president of the Pátzcuaro Vela Perpetua, María de la Luz Sierra—but the citations in this petition went beyond what women, especially in a provincial city like Orizaba, would likely be able to have at their command. Obviously I cannot be certain, and even women who did not have a lot of formal schooling could have been familiar with some of the personages and events cited in the petition (such as the woman of Tekoa) from sermons or pastoral letters they had heard read aloud, which would have provided a bank of references on which women writers could draw. The question of which references that to our ears seem arcane might have been part of the almost everyday religious currency of the time is a real one. But the timing of the women's petition right after the men's and the repetition of themes, and to a certain extent also the swashbuckling tone, makes me suspect a male author or authors. I have a nomination for the author: the prolific, verbose, and combative José Joaquín Pesado, an Orizaba native and prominently featured signatory to the men's petition. Pesado was later the editor of the Catholic newspaper *La Cruz*, a journal that had a similar predilection for historical arguments, Latin phrases, and exaggeration for effect.[95]

If the Orizaba petition was not written by a woman or women, what about the petitions that followed? Obviously with the Orizaba petition as a model it is possible that women in other towns might borrow ideas and themes and write up a petition more or less on their own. Female authorship or partial authorship, in other words, may have been more likely once there was a prototype petition. There is not as much repetition among the women's petitions as the liberal press liked to make out, but there is definitely some thematic sameness. We know that whoever the authors of the Oaxaca and Querétaro petitions were, they were aware of what Orizaba had produced: the Oaxaca petition began by stating that it was written "in imitation of the noble example of our *compañeras* in the Villa de Orizaba," and the Querétaro petition began theirs by saying that "Orizaba and Oaxaca have spoken and spoken well: no tolerance!"[96]

I think it's possible that some women felt uncomfortable signing a petition that was as strident and unapologetic as the Orizaba petition was, and that they insisted on framing the petition using a different tone, perhaps even themselves writing parts of the petition. Both the Oaxaca and the Querétaro petitions adopted a much more deferential tone than the one from Orizaba, more feminine and "appropriate" for women. The women of Oaxaca wrote: "We who sign form the weaker sex . . . we are uneducated and lack schooling; what could we possibly add to this subject that the finest writers in Mexico have not already said? Only that we can make public our emotions with the simplicity and candor that is peculiar to us women."97 The Querétaro petition also used extreme humility as a tool to make the point that even though women were not really equipped to join the public discourse, it was nonetheless important to do so: "We women are subject to man; we have value only as his other half; we are weak and feeble, nothing without him. . . . and we are content in this state in which our Creator put us. The only reason we lament our insignificance is because it prevents us from confirming our faith and our Catholicism in a more energetic, real, and positive way."98

However, I still think that authorship of the Oaxaca petition, because of the continued emphasis—alongside moments of extreme modesty—on proving a point using obscure literary and historical allusions that most women were unlikely to be able to deploy or feel comfortable deploying, was probably male.99 If these had been the same allusions as in the Orizaba petition, I would be more open to the idea that women were the authors, but since they are different references, I think we are looking once more at a petition that was primarily written by a man or men. The Querétaro petition is less pretentious in its references, but it is long, complex, and historically aware in ways that make its main parts, too, likely to have been written by a man. Furthermore, the deference expressed in both petitions is to my ear suspiciously over-the-top, almost as if it were a male-authored version of what he thought women should or would say, though it is true that deference had always been a key element in petition-writing, whether by men or women.

Some of the 1856 petitions had a peculiar, mixed tone, almost as if female authors began the petitions and concluded them, but turned over the middle section—the "proofs"—to men. These seem to have taken cues from the 1849 Orizaba petition, including expressing a fear of "Mahometismo," and an equally strange alarm at the prospect of idolatry and even a return of human sacrifice (as it happens, a theme articulated frequently by José Joaquín Pesado, whom I proposed as the author of the Orizaba petition).100 The petition from the ladies of Morelia was especially similar to the Orizaba petition. It was singled out by Francisco Zarco as possessing "so much erudition, so many disquisitions, so many theological labyrinths . . . that it is not reckless to think we see the influence, and perhaps the pen, of the distinguished archbishop Sr. D. Clemente Munguía."101 The Morelia petition does not in fact include "theological labyrinths," but it does display the kind of mastery (or manipulation) of history that made the Orizaba petition of 1849 seem more the product of an author with a worldly education and a propensity for showing off than something written by deferential women making their first foray into national politics. (It may be worth noting that Munguía was a patron of Pesado.)

There were several petitions, however, that had internal stylistic coherence and sounded very much like the kind of document that an educated woman or women might have written. The key example here is the petition from the ladies of Mexico City. It was short, dignified, and sincere. Like the 1849 petitions it staked the grounds of the debate firmly on territory that the authors felt belonged to women: the integrity of the family and the role of the women as guardians of religion. But it did so without resorting to artifice or example.

> If ever it is appropriate for the weak voice of women to be heard before the august national assembly, it is without doubt on a vital matter of particular concern to our sex.... How can her voice fail to be heard when it comes to resolving the question of which ought to be the religion of our adored *patria*? ... We do not mean to insinuate ourselves into the difficult questions of politics, which are foreign to our sex; we do not pretend to give advice to the representatives of the nation on the subjects of forms of government, or administrative systems, or on your many other preoccupations.... We come only to ask for that which we love more than life: ... the preservation of our religious beliefs, and the preservation of the integrity of our families ... [which we fear] will be fatally divided on points of religion.... How can we watch our children abandon the sainted and true religion in which we raised them? How can we view with indifference the defection of our dear husbands? How can we remain calm while our brothers waver? How can we bear to see temples of other religions established in our communities? No, please no, even imagining such a thing fills us with horror.[102]

Significantly, I think, this petition stuck to the issues to which women were intimately connected: marriage and family. There is no mention of the link between marriage, family, and nation, only a glancing reference to "our adored *patria*." Indeed, the petition pointedly refuses to engage in politics (as was true of most of them); it was written, the author(s) said, because of "a vital matter of particular concern to our sex," not because of a vital matter of particular concern to the nation. Put another way, women could be and were patriotic, but petitions that were written in their own words seem more likely to focus on the family and the local community, since these were the places women particularly felt the threat to Catholicism, than on the nation (as the Orizaba petition did). Other 1856 petitions that followed the Mexico City ladies' example in their brevity, relative lack of pretense, and focus on "women's issues" include the other two petitions from groups in Mexico City, and the ones from Toluca, Silao, San Miguel de Allende (despite one reference to Mahometismo), and San Luis Potosí.[103]

All this is a long way of demonstrating that as satisfying as it would be to know who wrote the petitions, it is impossible to know. But authorship is not everything. If we broaden the question of women's participation to include the whole range of actions needed to produce a petition—of which authoring it is only a part, and arguably not even the most important or interesting part—we can use other means to reach a richer understanding of the petition campaign(s).[104] A petition needed more than an author. A petition also entailed collaboration between the prospective signers and the author(s), and it needed to mobilize people to collect signatures. I propose that lay associations played an important role in these areas. The insights that we gleaned in chapter 3 about how women related to men and to priests and how their changing roles in lay associations affected those relationships as well as their roles in the community may be able to help us link their associations with the petition campaign.

Connecting Lay Associations to the 1856 Petition Campaign

Did local women play a role in urging their priests to take up a cause about which they felt strongly, and did they then support them in the process of writing and circulating the petitions? The women we met in chapter 3 would not have been shy about doing so. Indeed, *El Observador Católico* suggested in 1849 that a collaboration between women and priests was just common sense. Women, the editor opined, "have as much capacity to think for themselves, to reflect, to make judgments, and to decide their position as men," but when it came to authoring a petition on a topic of such importance, "why would they not consult the clergy, just as you would consult a doctor if you were looking for a remedy for cholera?"[105] This kind of instigating or collaborative role for women might account for the mixed tone of some of the petitions (if some women took part in authoring a petition), but it might very well be present whether or not women wrote a single word. Even those petitions whose texts seem most clearly to have been written entirely by men almost certainly reflected consultations with women for the simple reason that writing a petition as if it were coming from women was risky unless you had lined up women in advance who would buy into the content of the petition. Without this assurance of female support, without female collaborators and consultants, a petition could fail in embarrassing fashion.

This leads us to the second, related question: mobilization. The reason petitions made both monarchs and republicans nervous is that they physically brought men together for the purpose of drawing up, discussing, and then signing a petition; the fear of an assembly turning into a rebellion was real.[106] Women's petitions were obviously not signed at a group assembly. And yet they contained large numbers of signatures. While a few of the petitions were signed by a relatively small number of women (under one hundred), most had many more signatures: the first Mexico City petition numbered around two thousand signatures; the Guadalajara petition had over six hundred; Lagos had over six hundred fifty in two separate petitions; Toluca had over three hundred; and Silao, Guanajuato, and Etzatlán each had around two hundred.[107] Collecting them represented a major organizational undertaking.

CATHOLIC WOMEN ENTER POLITICS [117]

FIGURE 4.1. Satirical cartoon of Catholic women signing petition. From a framed clipping on display at the Museo del Estanquillo, newspaper unknown. The legend reads: Evangelista—Pero Señor Periodista, como quiere V. que ponga quinientas mil firmas cuando apenas hay aqui cuarenta Señoritas? (Scribe: But Mr. Journalist [from the Catholic newspaper *La Sociedad*], how can I put down 500,000 signatures when there are scarcely 40 Ladies?) Periodista—Eso no importa Señor Secretario, las Señoritas pueden multiplicar las firmas a su antojo, pues firman por sus generaciones pasadas, presentes, y futuras. (Journalist: That doesn't matter, Mr. Secretary, the Ladies can multiply the signatures as much as they want, since they sign for past, present, and future generations.)

Although liberals liked to suggest that priests were coercing signatures outside the church, this picture does not ring true, because the public spectacle of priests (or, as in Figure 4.1, scribes hired by a Catholic newspaper) publicly collecting signatures or even supervising their collection would prove the liberals' point. For the sake of avoiding negative and dismissive reportage, the process of collection of women's signatures absolutely had to be managed by women.

If women managed the process, where and how did they collect the signatures? Door-to-door visits by "commissions" of women who collected signatures from the inhabitants is the likely method. "Respectable" women felt comfortable walking the streets in pairs or groups, visiting homes of acquaintances, and at each home they could plausibly collect signatures from all females in the household, making this system reasonably efficient. This is probably the reason that many of the signatures contain clusters of family names: reading the lists, I imagine mothers, grandmothers, daughters, wives living in a household all signing together. Most of the explicit mentions of the home-visit collection method come from the second petition campaign, as we will see in chapter 6, but there are three clear references to collections of signatures by home-visit commissions (or as the liberal press called them, "agents") in 1856. One comes from Mexico City, where in early July, just before the petition campaign against tolerance began, *El Monitor Republicano* wrote that "certain agents" had received "a sum of money for having collected signatures from women by entering private and even tenement houses and obliging the women to sign a petition without telling them what they were signing." The petition was against the Lerdo Law, the law calling for the forced sale of church property. The next day, the paper "confirmed" that this had happened, and that the "commissioned agents" had been telling women that they were sent by very respectable ladies. *El Monitor* claimed to have in their possession letters from "various" of these women who had been lied to by the agents, and that they would soon publish them, but they did not (causing *El Omnibus* to mock them for not telling everyone who the "monitorianas" were).[108]

The second mention of home visits comes from Morelia, where a provincial correspondent of the liberal newspaper *El Monitor Republicano* made fun of the fact that men were now copying the women by designating agents to "go around collecting signatures."[109] The wording of the statement seems unambiguously to suggest, as did the previous example, that the collectors of signatures went to the signatories, presumably to their homes, rather than setting up in a central location.

A third reference to women's role in collecting signatures comes from a comment by liberal deputy and intellectual Ponciano Arriaga about a woman who had complained to him about being pressured by other women to help collect signatures for an anti-tolerance petition.[110] This is the only mention that clearly indicates that the signature collectors were women, though in the first two cases it seems unlikely that a commission of men would have bragged about being sent by distinguished women, or that such a commission would have been invited into private homes for the purpose of soliciting signatures from women. Furthermore, as we will see in chapter 6, there is a fair amount of evidence from the 1870s to suggest that the signature collectors were women.

In the mention of signature collection by Arriaga, the women doing the pressuring were identified by him as members of the Vela Perpetua. Direct evidence that the Vela or any other women's lay association was involved in the petition campaign is scanty; the Arriaga reference and the Vela-originated petition discussed at the beginning of the chapter are the only two cases in which we have direct assertions that women's lay associations played a role in the campaign. In one other case, Puebla, we know that a petition was sent by a women's group (but not a lay group), the Sisters of Charity.[111] Another tidbit of evidence, much more indirect, comes from one of the three 1849 petitions, the one from Querétaro, which was signed by thirty-one women.[112] This is suggestive because the constitution of the Vela Perpetua called for thirty-one "cabezas de día." Of course the fact that there were exactly thirty-one signers could be a coincidence, but we know that there was a Vela in Querétaro by 1849 so it is possible that this petition was signed at one of the monthly meetings.

That the Velas and other women's organizations might be involved in the petition campaign makes sense because of their demonstrated organizational skills, their close and collaborative contact with priests, and their large membership, which could make collecting signatures a relatively easy extension of their devotional duties. But since their goal was to enlist more women than just the members of the society itself—not only because this produced more signatures but also because it made the petition seem more widely popular and less closely linked to the church—any petition spearheaded by a women's lay association would be submitted as one coming broadly from the señoras of X city, rather than just X association in that city. The result is that direct evidence that women's lay associations were active in the petition process is elusive.

The indirect evidence, however, is compelling: of the seventeen cities from which the 1849 and 1856 petitions came, sixteen are known to have had at least one women's association (see Table 4.1). Thirteen of the seventeen had a Vela Perpetua and another (Orizaba) had an active women's auxiliary of the old Real Congregación, the precursor of the Vela.[113] Four had a formal association of the Vincentian Ladies of Charity to complement the work of the Sisters of Charity in their towns or cities, and in addition to these four cities where there were both Ladies and Sisters, the Sisters had houses in six more (probably implying active, if informal, laywomen's groups, as we saw in chapter 3). Oaxaca was the only petition-sending city that is not known to have had any women's lay associations or houses of the Sisters of Charity in 1849 when the petition was sent (although a Vela would be established there in 1855). Obviously this extremely high correlation between petitioning and early-established Catholic women's associations does not prove that these associations were instrumental in instigating, collaborating, coauthoring, or circulating petitions. It is certainly arguable that both Catholic women's increased organizing and increased political profile stem from the same root cause—the changing, deepening relationship between women and the church—but that they are not causally linked. But the presence of women's lay groups almost everywhere petition drives were organized, in light of the logistical and political difficulties that a single priest or even a group of priests would have encountered in mounting a complex project like a petition campaign, is strongly suggestive, especially when combined with the bits of evidence that home visits were a key instrument of signature collection.

Table 4.1. Cities/towns that sent petitions in 1849 and 1856 and the location of women-led associations

Petitions	Vela Perpetua (year founded)	Ladies of Charity	Sisters of Charity
Mexico City	X	X	X
Guadalajara	X		X
Toluca		X	X
León	X	X	X
Morelia	X		
Silao	X		X
San Luis Potosí	X		
Lagos	X		X
Querétaro	X		
Puebla			X
Guanajuato	X	X	X
Zacatecas	X		X
Pátzcuaro	X		
San Miguel de Allende	X		
Etzatlán (Jalisco)	X		
Oaxaca			
Orizaba	X (Congregación del Alumbrado)		

Sources: I date the presence of the Vela Perpetuas using documents in the archiepiscopal archives of Mexico, Michoacán, and Guadalajara, usually the documents that were generated when these associations were founded. But in two cases (Zacatecas and Etzatlán) I did not find foundation documents, but I did find clear references to the existence of a Vela by 1865. For Zacatecas, *El Siglo Diez y Nueve*, September 24, 1848, 2, "Caridad y Religión del Bello Secso Zacatecano"; for the Ladies of Charity, Arrom, *Volunteering*, 78; for the Sisters of Charity, *Historia de las Hijas de la Caridad*.

Conclusion

Any Mexican woman in the first half of the nineteenth century who lived in a sizeable town or city had access to political news and opinions through sermons, reading, gossip, and in conversations with each other, their priests, and men in their social circles. This was true during the colonial period—as we know from the number of women who were prepared in 1810 to participate in the wars of independence—and, with the expansion of the press, it became even more true after independence.[114] All the same, women rarely participated in political petition campaigns in the 1820s or 1830s.

Two things changed in the 1840s. First, political debates sharpened substantially after the war with the US. As these debates centered more and more on the role of the church and Catholicism in Mexico, a large number of women for whom the church's presence in their lives was important on a daily basis found that politics mattered deeply to them. This was a subject upon which many women—not just an unusually aware and politicized minority—could easily generate their own passionate opinions, and upon which they felt duty-bound, as Catholic women, to hold an opinion and indeed to express that opinion in private. But expressing opinions in private and expressing them in public were two different things. Another thing that had changed in the 1840s was the nature of women's associational life, especially in the center-west. Lay associations arguably provided both a vehicle and a support group (to use an anachronistic phrase) that allowed women to make the big move from the development of strongly held private opinions to public political action.

Women in seventeen cities and towns made this move in 1849 and 1856. Examining the way the women's petitions were received in the press in 1856 shows us that their action was understood as significant. The stakes were high. Gender hierarchy in lay associations, as we have seen, had already been challenged by 1849, but gender hierarchy in families had gone unquestioned across the political spectrum until, in the 1856 petition campaign, the church and the Catholic press gave women permission to act politically without their husbands' permission. They encouraged women to think for themselves and if necessary to express their political opinions "against the will of their husbands or fathers."[115] This stance posed a challenge to both the idea that husbands ruled their wives and to the idea that politics, more than any other realm of the public sphere, was inappropriate for women.

In the US at about the same time, as women's rights advocates began to demand suffrage and equality, some of the language that was used to attack them was quite similar to the language used in Mexico against Catholic women: politics would turn women into ugly creatures; the political sphere was no place for women. But there was one big difference. In the US, according to R. Marie Griffith, some women's rights defenders argued that the family needed to be rethought; this allowed critics to accuse them of destroying the traditional family.[116] In Mexico, however, the first women to enter politics did so in order to defend the traditional family. Put another way, women's right (and duty) to speak out in Mexico was aligned with the interests of the family. This forced Mexican liberals into an uncomfortable position, since they, like conservatives, as Pablo Mijangos y González puts it, "assumed the existence of a profound relationship between marriage, family, and social order."[117] In other words, in a very real sense liberals and conservatives were competing over who could best be seen as protecting the family and thus protecting the nation.

From the liberal point of view, the best way to compete with the church's, and women's, message that the church was the primary defender of the family and the liberals the destroyers of family was to claim a defense of the family on different grounds, that is, to insist that women must stay out of politics. Family was only safe when women stayed at home as wives and mothers. Now, it is no doubt true that most Catholics also preferred that women stay at home, and it is also true that liberals were quite comfortable with unequal gender relations, despite their rhetoric of inclusion and equality more generally. But in this moment, in the heat of the responses to the women's petitions, liberals committed themselves to a politics of unequal gender relations from which they could not extract themselves easily. In fact, the revolutionary government after 1910 continued to cling to it, denying women full voting privileges until 1953.

This liberal discursive strategy helps us understand why liberal women did not counter the views expressed in the Catholic women's petitions. We saw in chapter 3 that non-Catholic associations were relatively few, so there was only a very thin associational base from which to launch a female defense of religious liberty or a defense of liberal policy as good for the family. But liberal attacks on Catholic women's petitions, on the grounds that women were stepping into terrain they did not understand and should under no circumstances enter, also contributed to the inability of liberal women to develop an alternate political discourse to that of Catholic women. In 1849 *El Observador Católico* wrote that the liberal press would never tire of calculating the number of signatures if women had been petitioning in favor of progressive causes.[118] But I don't think this is true. Liberals were forced to insist vehemently that women must stay out of politics, a position they stuck with for many decades.

The conservative position, by contrast, was more flexible, not because it wanted to be, but because it had to be. The church had already been forced to commit to more gender equality than it had ever allowed in the colonial period. The acceptance of lay associations headed by women not only paved the way for churchmen to accept women in different social roles, but also, perhaps, allowed them to see them in political roles. In a perfect world, from the conservative point of view, neither women presidents of lay associations nor women in politics would be necessary. But that was not the world in which the church existed in the middle of the nineteenth century.

For their part, it is clear that the ladies who founded the early female associations like the Vela were not self-consciously political, at least not before the late 1840s. Their primary goal was to revive local piety after the long-lasting financial disasters of the wars of independence and in light of the weakness of the traditional cofradías. But in the process of founding and administering new lay associations, they had put themselves in a position to make the petition campaign a reality.

CHAPTER FIVE

"The Intervention of the Faithful Was an Unavoidable Necessity"

LAY ORGANIZING AND WOMEN, 1856–1875

THE TWO DECADES from the Reform to the eve of the dictatorship of Porfirio Díaz saw recurrent political crises. After the War of the Reform broke out in late 1857, the liberal government passed even more radical anticlerical legislation than the laws of the Reform that had given rise to the war in the first place: religious tolerance (after having been rejected just two years earlier by the constitutional congress), the nationalization—not just the forced sale—of church property and mortgages, the suppression of cofradías, the requirement for civil matrimony and civil registry of births and deaths, the secularization of cemeteries, an end to religious work holidays, the prohibition against religious activities outside the church, the ex-claustration of nuns and friars, and secular education.

When the civil war finally ended in late 1860, the liberal government, in part because of a depression brought on by wartime disruptions and the swamping of land and housing markets with the sudden influx of church property after 1856, could not pay its debts to its European creditors. Among these creditors was France, which seized the opportunity to invade Mexico in 1862. In 1864, recruited by conservatives, including prominent members of the Mexican church, and supported by the French army, Archduke Maximilian of Austria became emperor of Mexico. It was not until 1867 that the French withdrew and conservative Mexican forces supporting Maximilian were defeated. Even then, regional rebellions and unrest continued to mark the period through the 1870s.

Despite, or (as I will argue) in part because of, this massive political and economic turmoil, this period saw a significant increase in the number of Catholic lay associations. Although laymen were more present in this process than they had been in the 1840s and early 1850s, women founded the majority of all new associations and women's lay associations remained the most vibrant and enduring feature of the local religious landscape. This chapter accounts for and analyzes this explosion of lay associations, with particular attention to women's groups, in the post-Reform period. It stops at 1875 partly because this was the last year before the dictatorship of Porfirio Díaz created yet another new political environment to which the church and lay associations would need to adjust; and partly because 1875 was the year of a second major national petition campaign—against the elevation of the radical laws of the Reform to constitutional status—in which women played an even more important role than they had in the 1856 petition movement, making this a good place to pause before chapter 6's analysis of that campaign. As in chapter 3, the final section provides a brief discussion of nonreligious women's associations by way of comparison to the Catholic associations, and speculates as to why the former remained so sparse.

The Expansion of Lay Associations in a New Context

There were three main reasons why so many and such a variety of new Catholic associations were founded during this period. The first was simply that as part of an increasingly powerful global move toward associationalism—founding clubs or societies based on shared interests (whether economic, political, cultural, recreational, or religious)—Mexican men began to form similar groups. Association had of course always been a marked tendency in Mexico, with its cofradía tradition, and freedom of association was protected by custom and by inference in the 1824 constitution as well as explicitly in the 1857 one. But now that pattern of behavior blossomed. Carlos Forment counts over one thousand new, overwhelmingly male, mainly nonreligious associations formed in Mexico between 1857 and 1876, most of them local and short lived, but still an impressive number.[1] The thousands, "perhaps millions," of Mexicans who joined these voluntary associations, according to Elías Palti, formed an "authentic civil society."[2] The author of the 1874 statistical guide to Mexico City agreed: "The spirit of association," he wrote, "that antidote to the poison of egoism, is a thermometer that marks the degree of a people's culture, and is a powerful bond of brotherhood. By making gross individualism disappear, it promotes the interests of the group, crowns the legitimate ambitions of the members, and advances the progress of the nation."[3]

The other two factors specifically address the question of why *Catholic* associationalism was so strong. The first was the need to replace the traditional cofradías that were suppressed by the liberal government in 1859. As we saw in chapter 3, the financial weakness of traditional cofradías in the center-west had opened the door to experimentation with new kinds of pious associations in that region in the 1840s and 1850s, and now, because of the actions of the liberal government, much the same phenomenon occurred at a national level. The old property-owning, mutual-aid-oriented cofradías having been banned, laypeople began to promote new, non-property-holding associations that would carry on the devotional practices of the old cofradías. (The mutual aid function of the old cofradías would eventually be filled by new, secular mutual assistance associations, thus dividing the functions of the old cofradías between two associations. Secular mutual aid organizations did not begin to flourish, however, until the growth of the urban working classes a little later in the century.)[4]

The second factor was an emotional response on the part of both priests and the laity to the threat to the church and the Catholic religion posed by the installation in 1867 of a liberal regime that faced no organized opposition. This perception grew, of course, out of the heated debates over religious tolerance discussed in the previous chapter, but also out of the implementation of the laws of the Reform, which, where they were strictly enforced, brought a wholesale diminution of the church's everyday presence in Mexican society. The prohibition on public displays of religiosity was especially jarring and unnerving to the pious. After 1867 and until his death in 1872, Benito Juárez backed off strict enforcement of some, but by no means all, of the Reform legislation, and Catholic anxieties were confirmed when his successor, Sebastián Lerdo de Tejada, resumed a vigorous anticlerical policy, culminating in the elevation of the laws of the Reform to constitutional status in late 1874.

Some historians have de-emphasized the tensions between liberals and Catholics. They point out that most liberals were Catholics; that a large number of pro-church Catholics accepted the principles of economic and political liberalism; and that much of the hierarchy was pragmatic and forward-looking, preoccupied with trying to figure out how to survive and maneuver under the new conditions.[5] Further, as Claudio Lomnitz observes, liberalism itself became blurry, more "compromised and diffuse" after 1867 as a result of having soundly defeated its organized opposition, so that enlisting "liberalism" as part of a dichotomy is to assign it a singularity that did not exist.[6] I do not dispute these points, but if we are seeking the motivations of the laypeople who founded new religious associations during this period—that is, a group self-selected to value highly the daily presence of the church and religion in their lives—the perceived need to defend Catholicism against a government that was trying to reduce that presence was very much a factor. That "liberal" ideology was slippery and capacious, and that for some liberals it included an appreciation of a certain kind of Catholicism, was not relevant to those Catholics who were not prepared to listen to any kind of argument that one could be both anticlerical and Catholic. The language used in founding documents fully bought into the binaries rejected by historians. A new Vela Perpetua in Acuitzio established in 1863, for example, explicitly stated that it was being founded in order to give thanks for the recent triumph of Catholicism (with the arrival of the French) over the "Devil of liberalism."[7] The reasons given for the founding of one of the new associations that spread rapidly after 1868, the Sociedad Católica, were to counteract the "hypocritical propaganda" and "persecution" of the government and to bring "new triumphs for Catholicism."[8]

This kind of apocalyptic language was also the rule in Catholic Europe, where the revolutions of 1848, the Risorgimento, and the Paris Commune had already made clear the dangers of liberalism and the other godless isms.[9] A different, less defensive response to the same fears was the promotion, by both clergy and laity in Europe, of a "devotional revolution": exciting new practices (the Miraculous Medal, the Immaculate Conception, the Rosary, group pilgrimages to old and new shrines), and the foundation of confraternities and pious associations that organized and systematized these practices.[10] New lay societies and congresses in Europe promoting Catholic education and Catholic charity also appeared. These practices and associations served as models and inspiration for Mexican laymen and laywomen facing their own crisis. The Mexican Sociedad Católica, for example, openly acknowledged that the "good example" of European societies and assemblies (such as the Congresses of Mechlin in Belgium in 1863 and 1867) spurred them to form their own association.[11] In sum, the failure of the old, the threat of godlessness, and the appeal of the new—all in the context of a general enthusiasm for associationalism—combined to produce a flurry of foundations of new Catholic lay societies.

I should say a bit more about two factors I have not included: the roles of the papacy and the Mexican hierarchy in stimulating Catholic associationalism. Neither is irrelevant. Pius IX contributed both by perfecting a rhetoric and framing a policy of unbridgeable division between Catholicism and all the other evils of the modern world (liberalism, Freemasonry, Protestantism, communism, socialism), and by encouraging the new devotions as a way to ignite Catholic fervor and participation. Despite this, the pope was far away, there was no concordat with the Mexican state, the Mexican bishops did not wish to relinquish their autonomy from the papacy (resisting the presence of a papal nuncio, for example), and thus the influence of the pope was necessarily indirect.[12] A larger and much more direct role for the Vatican in influencing what associations formed in Mexico would not come until later, with the push for "Romanization" in the later nineteenth century, including the training of a generation of priests and future bishops at the Vatican and papal encouragement of the controlled globalization of new Catholic practices (chapter 7).

As for the bishops, Jorge Adame Goddard expresses the view of many historians of Catholicism when he writes that without bishops and archbishops, "the Mexican church could do very little between 1867 and 1876."[13] Although I do not agree that the church, broadly construed, did "little" during this period,

I do agree that the bishops were not at the center of things. Some of them had been defeated twice, in the War of the Reform and in the war against the French Intervention, and all of them suffered the blow to Catholicism represented by the restoration of liberal rule in 1867. Some spent years in exile. When they returned in the early 1870s they focused on managing their relationships to the papacy on the one hand and the new liberal government on the other, wishing not to unnecessarily antagonize either.[14] For the most part, even the zealous bishops of the new dioceses created in the 1860s (for example, Zamora and León), even if they wanted to get closely involved in the foundation of hard-to-control and potentially illegal lay associations, were at least temporarily constrained by the Reform laws' limits on their ability to do so.[15] As an adviser to Archbishop Pelagio Antonio de Labastida put it in 1874, just three years after Labastida's return from exile, "in light of the explicit and far-reaching language of the law [of 1859 that suppressed cofradías], who among us would believe that it is safe in the present circumstances to undertake the foundation of any pious congregation?"[16]

The bishops were in an awkward position. In principle they approved of lay associations that defended and modernized Catholicism, and of efforts being made by the laity to manipulate and utilize the principle of religious liberty against which they had fought so long (but now needed to defend in order to stay relevant). But at the same time they were concerned because supervision of these new associations in the prevailing political climate "was impossible, or at least very difficult."[17] Moreover, the leaders of the new associations themselves actively sought distance from the hierarchy, in order, they said, to protect their projects and to maintain the freedom of action that was necessary to carry out their goals. "They came to believe," Provisor Lic. Joaquín María Díaz y Vargas wrote in 1873 of the founders of the Sociedad Católica, "that in the tragic circumstances that surround the Church, the intervention of the faithful was an unavoidable necessity . . . and they believed that this intervention either ought to be entirely independent of the hierarchy, or at most ought to be dependent on them weakly and indirectly."[18] Like the papacy, the bishops would later be an important influence on which associations were formed and how they were controlled. But for now I see this as another period—like the decades from the 1810s to the 1850s—during which the burden of protecting Catholic practice at the community level fell primarily on the priest and the community itself, and another period during which Catholic women and their priests were disproportionately willing to assume this burden.

The Old Cofradías

Before turning to the new lay associations that proliferated in this period, we should recognize that not all traditional cofradías disappeared.[19] Although they had supposedly been suppressed and most of them did go underground for a while, it appears that as long as they did not openly try to hold onto their wealth and property, there was tolerance, at least in some cities, for their resurfacing after some years had passed. This was the case with the Archicofradía del Santísimo Sacramento in Durango, which began to reorganize in 1872 after not having convened since 1858; now the deputies were looking for ways to survive under "completely changed circumstances from those under which this corporation was erected in the middle of the last century."[20] Many other cofradías' adjustments were also made necessary by the nationalization of their wealth and property, but even those that had always been purely devotional and had existed on donations now had to adapt to a situation in which *all* lay associations were competing for alms.

Indeed, stepped-up, better-systematized alms collecting was crucial if the old cofradías (as well as the new associations) were to survive. This necessity led at least one prominent traditional cofradía, the Archicofradía del Santísimo Sacramento in Oaxaca, to formalize a women's branch, with the explicit aim of bringing women's energies more effectively to bear on solving the financial and other problems that they faced. According to the transcripts of the board meetings, beginning in 1869 there was a lively debate over whether they should distribute candles and allow women to join the inside-the-cathedral procession of Minerva, because not enough men were participating.[21] They also had a financial problem: the male deputies were complaining about being sent out too often to collect donations.[22] In 1875 the board decided to address both the alms-collection problem and the attendance problem by creating a separate formal structure for women "in order to promote the cult and so that they can collect alms" (which, it carefully stipulated, "they will put in a locked money-box and turn over to the Mayordomo every month"). Besides sending out women to solicit donations, they also enjoined the new organization to form an Honor Guard to stand by the Host and thus improve the visibility of the cofradía in the church.[23] Unlike the enthusiastic women who founded the Vela Perpetua and clamored to take part in the vigil, the female members of the Oaxaca cofradía seem not to have been all that eager to form a separate society. The acts of the cofradía for several years include plaintive comments from the male officers wondering what was going on with the women's group, why were they taking so long to form, and where was the Honor Guard? By 1882 the latter still had not materialized. According to the president of the women's society, Encarnación Maqueo, this was because the ladies refused to join until the mayordomo purchased an appropriate rug and candelabras.[24]

The Spread of New and "Old" Pious Associations

Despite the fact that some traditional cofradías managed to survive, however, by far the more common response to the weakness of the old cofradías and the perception of an urgent need for lay action was to found new associations.

There were two types of new lay associations in this period. The first was devotional associations that one joined in order to promote one's own spiritual advancement (no doubt among other more worldly reasons, as we saw in the case of the Vela Perpetua in chapter 3). The second was service associations, like the Ladies of Charity, that were dedicated to the relief of the spiritual and temporal needs of others. (After 1891, when Pope Leo XIII called for the creation of lay associations dedicated to charity and evangelization, what I am calling "service" organizations would be called "social action" organizations, but it is anachronistic to use that term here.) Both types of association spread rapidly during this period, and although, as we will see, the liberal press tried to paint each of them as representing very different kinds of Catholic womanhood, in fact there seems to have been quite a bit of overlap among the membership and it is clear that both had immense appeal to women.

DEVOTIONAL ASSOCIATIONS

The Vela Perpetua continued to experience rapid growth during this period, and remained among the most exciting and most popular new devotional associations, as it had been in the period from 1840 to the mid-1850s. In the archbishoprics of Michoacán and Guadalajara from 1856 to 1875, there was an average of three new foundations a year, which on the surface seems a reduced pace compared to the period from 1840 to 1856. But in 1863 the new bishoprics of Zamora, León, and Zacatecas were carved out of the old archbishoprics, and new record-keeping began in the new diocesan capitals. If I had been able to systematically use the archives of these new bishoprics in order to make a more apples-to-apples comparison with the earlier period, it is clear the numbers would be quite a bit higher, almost certainly the equal of the nearly five new foundations a year that was the pace of Vela foundation in the original archbishoprics from 1840 to 1856, and probably more than that, given the historically very high levels of devotionalism in Zamora and León in particular.

There was growth not only in the center-west but also elsewhere. Right before the Reform and increasingly during this period, the Vela began to go national. Foundations in Oaxaca City (1855), Jilotepec (archbishopric of Mexico, 1855), and Tlaxcala and Huamantla (bishopric of Puebla, both 1854) were indications that enthusiasm for the Vela was beginning to spread outside of the center-west by the mid-1850s. Another small clue that the Vela was poised for national expansion is found in a sarcastic report in the liberal newspaper *El Siglo Diez y Nueve* about a supposedly unpopular priest in the northern town of Saltillo (Coahuila) who in 1856 needed signatures on a petition in order to contest his defeat in an election. Unable to line up much support, he turned to an "original" strategy: he told his parishioners that they were signing a document requesting that a Vela Perpetua be established in their town. This "fraud," the newspaper commented, produced a surfeit of signatures.[25] It is highly unlikely that this actually happened as reported, but the fact that *El Siglo Diez y Nueve* thought it made for an amusing way to disparage priestly political ambitions assumes that their readers would find the story of a northern city's population leaping at the chance to establish a Vela to be credible. By 1868 national interest was sufficient to justify the publication and widespread distribution of a booklet written for members of the Vela Perpetua, giving them advice about how to use their half-hour vigil wisely (among other things by meditating on a poem entitled "La amistad de Jesús Sacramentado" or "The Friendship of Jesus in the Eucharist").[26]

The Vela Perpetua founded in the Sagrario of the Mexico City Cathedral in 1848 was joined in the early 1870s by two other Velas in the capital city.[27] Elsewhere in the archbishopric there were at least fourteen more foundations during this period.[28] In the north, Velas were established in Guaymas, Hermosillo, Ures, and Alamos in Sonora; Cosalá and San Sebastián [Concordia] in Sinaloa; Durango, San Dimas, and San Pedro Chalchihuites in Durango.[29] There are certain to have been others in the north that my sources don't reveal, and perhaps also in Puebla and Oaxaca, where I know of only five new Velas founded during this period (in addition to the three foundations in 1854 and 1855).[30] Nonetheless, despite the apparent weakness of the appeal of the Vela in Puebla and Oaxaca, this adds up to thirty-three known new foundations outside the center-west from 1854 to 1875—not the outburst of foundations that would come later (or that had already happened in the center-west), but a clear sign of increasing national scope.

The Vela's model of putting close and extended physical proximity to the Eucharist at the center of the organization's practices seems to have inspired a number of groups that were altogether new, with no pre-Reform presence at all. In 1873, for example, a new association was founded whose core practice was sitting with the Blessed Sacrament during siesta time, when Jesus would otherwise be alone.[31] The Guardia de Honor, the devotional society that the Oaxaca Archicofradía del Santísimo tried to get its female members to found, also operated on the principle of accompanying and adoring the Host. In both of these cases the organizations were comprised exclusively of women (in fact, most of the Guardias de Honor were composed of women, though they could theoretically be made up of men, and during the Porfiriato we see a few such examples). The Vela also inspired imitation in its core practice of holding all-day vigils, even when the object of the devotion was not the Blessed Sacrament. A new association in Durango in 1873 dedicated to San José divided the months into groups headed by women called "regentas" (as opposed to the Vela's nomenclature of "cabezas"), and these women organized groups of thirty-one people, mainly women but also some men and priests, to honor the saint each day of the month.[32]

Another inspiration for new devotional cofradías during this period was the proclamation of the doctrine of the immaculate conception of Mary in

1854. Although there were several Marian lay associations founded during this period, by far the most important of them was the Vincentian association of the Daughters of Mary, or Hijas de María.[33] The original Hijas association was composed of girls in the schools run by the Sisters of Charity. Although the Sisters were most famous (and most controversial) as nurses, they ran many schools, some stand-alone, some attached to their hospitals or orphanages.[34] After 1863, with the suppression of Mexican convents, the Sisters—who were the only religious order permitted by the liberals to remain in the country, in light of the fact that they were not cloistered and served useful social purposes—began to expand their educational operations significantly, taking up the slack from the now-defunct convent schools. In addition to the free schools they ran, they founded a number of colegios, adopting the familiar colonial convent-school model of combining paying students who boarded at the school with day pupils who attended for free. Before 1863 there had been eight schools run by the Sisters, mainly free schools for poor girls, who claimed to have been teaching over twenty-five hundred niñas.[35] Between 1863 and 1874 they opened eighteen more schools and more than doubled the number of girls they educated.[36]

Along with the regular curriculum, the Sisters were teaching these six thousand or so girls the "enchanting" rituals of the Mes de María (Month of Mary—May), including the "moving" ceremony in which teenage girls, "weeping with emotion," received the medals that "identified them as the daughters of the mother of God."[37] (The reference is to the Miraculous Medal, which was revealed by Mary to a French nun in 1830.)[38] The Hijas were meant to renounce dance, theater, novels, and "exaggerated or immodest styles of dress."[39] There was considerable emphasis on their innocence and virginity, and some explicitly-stated hopes that a large number of them would choose to become Sisters when they grew up.

We don't know for sure when the Sisters in Mexico began organizing these girls into associations. The French Sisters had been forming such associations in each house "by way of trial" in the 1840s and were given papal permission in 1847 to formalize the organization.[40] Since there were some French Sisters in Mexico and a majority of the Spanish Sisters had been trained in France, it is possible that there was some "trial" organization of Hijas in Mexico too. But at the latest, we know that the Asociación de Hijas de María was formalized in 1861.[41] Six associations had been established by 1862, and there were thirty-six by 1875.[42] In 1871 it was agreed that all the separate associations in different schools should be united into a single national organization.[43] In time, the Asociación de Hijas de María would transform from an organization of schoolgirls into an association that included both unmarried and married laywomen and that was practically ubiquitous in Mexico as well as in the American Southwest.[44] This transformation almost certainly happened when girls, as they aged out of the schools, remained in the organization, eventually making it logical for adult, married women to join even if they had not become members when they were schoolgirls.[45]

SERVICE ASSOCIATIONS

Besides the Vela, another pre-Reform women's association that vastly increased in numbers during this period was the Ladies of Charity, who had had such a difficult time getting off the ground in the 1840s and 1850s. In fact, it appears that the foundations discussed in chapter 3 did not survive the Reform; it was only with the arrival of the French in Mexico City in 1863 and the subsidies and encouragement provided by the imperial government of Maximilian that the women's conferences of St. Vincent de Paul made a second and much more successful appearance in Mexico.[46] Silvia Arrom has painstakingly pieced together the story of the Ladies (as well as the men's conferences), and she documents a "dramatic expansion" from their reestablishment in 1863—when a Vincentian father, Francisco Muñoz de la Cruz, convened twenty-three "principal ladies of the capital's Christian and cultured society"—to 1875, when they reached over four thousand active members in some three hundred chapters throughout the country.[47] There were also over ten thousand honorary male and female members (including priests, doctors, phlebotomists, pharmacists, etc.) who either contributed their time or made donations.

The men's conferences also expanded during these years, but less impressively: their membership grew from around five hundred at the time of the Reform to around twenty-eight hundred in 1875 (this would be the high point for the men's conferences), organized into 126 conferences, with fewer than seven hundred honorary members.[48] Already in 1870, as Arrom points out, in some places where they had been established early on, the men's conferences were beginning to dwindle.[49] Thus the men's groups by 1875 were established in fewer than half the number of parishes or towns as the women's, and had less than a quarter of the affiliates (including both active and honorary). According to Arrom, the men's groups were supportive of the women's, and where both were established—for example, in Mexico City, where in the mid-1870s there were 17 men's conferences and 19 women's—we can suppose that the relationship between them was cooperative, perhaps even close. But since nationally there were over 170 more women's groups than men's by this time, outside of the bigger cities it is clear that quite a few women's groups did not have a male counterpart. The towns with only a women's group were certain, then, to have had considerable autonomy in founding and managing their organizations.

Most of what we know about how the Ladies operated comes from official sources, which Arrom reminds us can "erase the agency of the women themselves."[50] To get beneath the surface of the Vincentian chronicles she emphasizes comments in the annual reports about the importance of the energy and leadership of the female officers, and highlights evidence that "some conferences were not founded by priests at all but by some of the strong woman presidents," for example, the conference in Malacatepec, whose *presidenta* revived the old pre-Reform Toluca conference "to the point of duplicating its members and its income."[51] Given what we know about women's sometimes-dominant roles in founding Velas (chapter 3) and the statistics that make it clear that many of the Ladies' conferences were founded without the participation of a male counterpart, Arrom's emphasis on women's initiative seems well-placed. Indeed, despite the facade of a "modern" integrative bureaucratic structure—its system of local, regional, and national councils—on the ground it is likely that many, and probably most, of the women's conferences operated largely on their own, whether or not they had a male counterpart. Further, because the conferences (both women's and men's) were supposedly "entirely secular in their organization and administration," it is possible that priests did not play an overweening role, especially since, like the Velas, the leadership of the Ladies' conferences tended to be women from the most prominent local families, women who were willing to stand up to a priest who was too intrusive.[52] Priests were certainly among the honorary members in any given chapter, and they were the spiritual directors of the organization, but theoretically they were not supposed to be involved in the management of funds or the activities of the group.

As they had flocked to the Vela Perpetua in the center-west for a variety of reasons, women were attracted to the opportunities provided by the Vincentian conferences to join, congregate, act, and lead—on behalf of the church, but also for their personal satisfaction. As Arrom comments, many conferences added offices, apparently to accommodate women's desire to occupy them (second vice presidents, pro-secretaries, sub-treasurers).[53] These women received public accolades and commendations from the church, and as providers of needed social services and Catholic charity, they were valued even by liberal society (at least to a point) in a way that the devotional associations like the Vela Perpetua were not, as we will see in more detail below. As had the women of the Vela, they gained experience as organizers, administrators, budget managers, public speakers, and defenders of their own organizations.[54]

A new service organization that in many ways resembled the conferences of St. Vincent de Paul was the Sociedad Católica. Like the Vincentian conferences, the Sociedad Católica was nationally organized (with local chapters, regional centers, and a national center in Mexico City); it was devoted to the idea that Catholicism could best be defended through charitable and social work; and it had a parallel women's group that followed the previous establishment of the men's group. Also like the Vincentian conferences, the Sociedad Católica de Señoras soon far eclipsed the men's Sociedad in number of members and number of chapters.

The origin story of the Sociedad Católica begins in June 1867, with the execution of Maximilian, an event so painful, the founders said, that even the faithful were filled with "discouraged despair."[55] Seeing, however, that in Europe, Catholics were taking action, a group of friends got together in the Hotel Iturbide on November 29, 1868—a group Brian Stauffer calls a "who's who" of the Conservative party—to discuss a proposal for a new association that would promote Catholicism in every possible legal way.[56] By Christmas they had elected the president of their new society, and it began to operate in January 1869.[57] The women's group, authorized by the men's constitution, was established a month later.[58]

Cecilia Bautista García has argued that the foundation of the Sociedad Católica marked a "watershed" moment because it represented a new kind of religious organization whose existence was based on liberal principles and civil rights.[59] The Sociedad itself made a similar claim: "we have come together under the protection of the nation's [liberal] laws to work in common for the propagation of moral and religious ideas."[60] I think this interpretation, while strictly correct, unavoidably downplays the illiberalism of the group. It is clear that the group's strategy was to operate close to the edge of government tolerance for their activities, sheltering behind its guarantees of freedom of speech, freedom of religion, and freedom of assembly, daring liberals to clamp down and thus reveal their "hypocrisy." The men's 1877 *Memoria* recounted such an act of daring in Oaxaca, when the presidents of the men's and women's groups co-organized a "Public Assembly" held at the Colegio Católico, at which poets and orators, "filled with love of the Holy Virgin, electrified the audience."[61] The presidents of both groups were then ordered to be arrested for having celebrated a religious act outside of a Catholic church. The president of the men's group was "by happenstance" out of town, but the señora who was the president of the women's Sociedad was arrested, and the spectacle of a "weak woman accepting prison with the ardor of a martyr" made for excellent political theater.

As this incident illustrates, the Sociedad Católica had a complex relationship to the liberal state. On the one hand, the Sociedad clearly meant to use liberal laws protecting assembly and speech to its own advantage. And it was a "secular" organization in the sense that it did not have priests as directors (only members). On the other hand, the members called themselves a religious community and made a point of saying that they had been particularly offended by the government's dissolution of earlier religious communities, that is, convents and monasteries, and that they intended their organization to recover as much of the "monastic legacy" as the law allowed.[62] They also were appalled by the laws that had stripped the church of its property and wished to find a way for the church to regain its wealth.[63] In short, while the Sociedad seems to have operated relatively independently (in a structural sense) of the church, at the same time it was dedicated to preserving as much of the church's power as possible. It did not represent an especially liberal brand of Catholicism; according to *La Luz de Monterey*, the "primary goal of the Sociedad is to mold the hearts and minds of Mexico's youth," turning "tender plants into leafy trees that will bear rich fruit for the Church and the State"; only "secondarily" was the goal to practice charity.[64] The liberal newspaper *El Monitor Republicano* was, I think, correct when it said in 1873 that "it is well known that the Sociedades Católicas belong more to politics than to religion."[65]

Several historians have surveyed the organization and activities of the Sociedad, so I offer here just a brief summary.[66] The range of activities was quite broad and ambitious, and included reinforcing religious faith and practice among Catholics of all ages; making sure youths were indoctrinated in the faith; promoting Catholic education (to save as many children as possible from the "poisoned springs" of a religionless public school education); supporting Catholic newspapers and founding press organs; and stimulating the "cult," by which was meant adorning and maintaining the churches themselves, founding devotional societies, and helping to fund religious functions.[67] These, as we will see in chapter 8, became the key features of the church's political project in the Porfiriato.

A comparison of the men's 1877 *Memoria* and the women's 1874 report suggests greater local diversity of activity in the women's groups than in the men's.[68] Of course it is possible that this was because the men's report was written by a single author, Licenciado Sebastián Alamán. It was based on data submitted to him by the various chapters, but he wrote it up with his own style and spin. In other words, it is possible that Alamán homogenized the men's activities somewhat in the interest of making the organization seem more uniform, more consistent in their adherence to the structure of the different commissions (originally these commissions were dedicated to promoting religious observance (*culto*) doctrine, schools, and the Catholic press, with others such as prisons added later), and more "national." The women's 1874 report, by contrast, did not have a strong authorial voice and mainly consisted of lists of their accomplishments submitted by the individual chapters. This method might enhance distinct local flavor, whereas Alamán's strong voice might conceal it. All the same, it is striking how much difference there was from women's chapter to chapter in terms of what and how they contributed to the adornment and cleaning/upkeep of the churches, which church functions they supported, which religious congregations or cofradías they helped establish, who was served by spiritual retreats and exercises (themselves? the poor? others?), how much energy was put into visiting the poor and sick, what kinds of money-raising activities they engaged in (raffles? lotteries? manufacture of small crafts to sell?). The fact that these activities varied so much suggests a strong degree of local autonomy.

The most obvious difference between the men's organization and the women's, however, was the rapid spread and perseverance of the latter and the decline of the former. By 1874 the women's groups had over ten thousand members and 151 chapters.[69] The men's Sociedad Católica had only about two thousand members nationwide in 1877 (admittedly after the 1876 "revolution" that brought Porfirio Díaz to power and that the men claimed had disrupted their organization), and only 38 chapters submitted reports on their activities.[70] Although more men's chapters than this had been established in the enthusiastic aftermath of the founding, it appears that their failure to report in 1877 meant they were basically inactive. Stauffer writes that the male chapter of the Sociedad in Zamora "quickly floundered and was overtaken by the female auxiliary."[71] Something like this must have happened all over the country. (Readers may recall from chapter 3 that many of the Velas de Señores also failed.) Adame Goddard, following contemporary comment and some discouraged language in the 1877 report of the men's Sociedad, wrote that the organization was on its last legs at that time.[72] But if this was true of the men's groups, we know that many of the women's Sociedades were active well into the 1890s—the Oaxaca City and Puebla chapters were still going strong in 1899—even though the national organizational structure seems to have collapsed with the decadence of the men's group.[73]

What was the relationship between the two national Catholic women's service organizations, the Ladies of Charity and the Sociedad Católica de Señoras? Did they coexist, cooperate, or were they rivals and competitors for members, donations, or prestige? The sources tell us little about perceived differences in prestige, though I think we might infer that the Ladies of Charity, with the more established international presence, had an edge.[74] This is suggested by an 1871 case from Tlalpan, in which the "principal" ladies of the town met with the archbishop and they agreed to establish "a conference of St. Vincent de Paul, or at least the Sociedad Católica."[75] I think we can also assume that where the two similar organizations were established in the same city, they were competing for many of the same funding sources and members (Mexico City, with its multiple separate neighborhoods, would be an exception). Both organizations needed women with a religious frame of mind and a fair amount of disposable time, since the Ladies of Charity spent hours visiting the poor and helping the sick, and the ladies of the Sociedad Católica taught doctrine, distributed newspapers, established schools and sometimes taught in them. These were more time-consuming activities than those required of rank-and-file members in devotional associations. So it makes sense that out of the 149 different towns or cities where the Sociedad Católica de Señoras was established in 1874 and the 92 where the Ladies of Charity are known to have operated in 1878, there were only 19 in which both of the women's charitable organizations existed.[76] In one case—Arandas, one of the smaller cities among these 19—the women must have been working extra hard to keep both societies going, because in 1874 it was noted in an episcopal visitation that "the [female] members of the Sociedad Católica are the same as the members of the Conference of St. Vincent de Paul, only with different Presidents and Dignitaries."[77]

The relationship between the service organizations and the devotional lay associations such as the Vela Perpetua, on the other hand, was more complementary. In the minds of prospective female members, the desire to promote their own spirituality and the desire to help others do so were absolutely connected. In fact, one of the activities in which the Sociedades Católicas were most likely to engage was to found devotional associations. Quite a few chapters noted that they had established the "exercise of the Good Death," a set of prayers and practices that contemplated a Christian death, and five had founded an association dedicated to organizing those practices on a systematic basis (the Congregación de la Buena Muerte).[78] We have several explicit statements about the compatibility and shared membership between the Sociedad Católica and the Vela Perpetua, and it would not surprise me to learn that dual membership in these organizations was close to ubiquitous where both organizations existed.[79]

This makes for an interesting contrast to the way that the liberal press portrayed the members of service organizations versus the way they depicted the members of the devotional associations. No doubt following the same impulse that had led the liberals to permit the Hermanas de la Caridad to stay in Mexico after all other convents were uncloistered—that is, that they provided important social services—moderate liberals seem, at least at first, to have accepted and sometimes even lavished praise on the Catholic service organizations. A piece in the liberal *El Monitor Republicano* in 1872 clearly illustrates the latter point of view. Refuting an "outrageous" comment by a Cuban commentator to the effect that Mexico had plenty of soldiers but not enough "matronas," the author fumed that Mexico abounded in *matronas*, which he defined as mothers of virtuous and noble families. Anyone who had seen the ladies of the Sociedad Católica, "these archangels of beauty," "descend upon the jails, swarm the hospitals and schools, and fly wherever misfortune demands their help"; or anyone who had seen "the thousands of afflictions that the ladies of the conferences of St. Vincent have cured, or seen them in the huts of the miserable, on their knees on the floor bringing sustenance to the mouths of the sick or removing their gloves to treat their ulcers" would know that Mexico has matronas! In fact, the author concluded with high praise, "it is almost impossible to find a señora or señorita who does not belong to a philanthropic association," and by this it is clear that he meant "Catholic" philanthropic associations.[80]

By contrast, women who spent hours in the church instead of in the homes of the needy (presumably including members of the devotional societies, though they were rarely named as such) were objects of ridicule or at best, as we saw in chapter 4, characterized as passive, ignorant, and often as old and "dried up." "Religion and religiosity," the raison d'être of the devotional associations, were, according to liberals, "old women's business," the province of "fanatical *beatas* and vulgar old women."[81] Catholic charity was one thing; for liberals it brought the church closer to the primitive Christianity that many of them admired. But wasted time spent on "fanaticism" was quite another.

THE RELATIONSHIP BETWEEN PRIESTS AND THE NEW ASSOCIATIONS

Did the women who led the associations continue to have the same kind of fundamentally collaborative but occasionally tense and conflictual relationship with priests that we saw between the ladies of the Vela Perpetua and their priests in the 1840s and 1850s? The simple answer is that there seems to have been at least as much, if not more, partnering, but perhaps somewhat less conflict. The Velas and the Sociedad Católica provided crucial material support to parish priests (as the Velas always had done): adornment and cleaning of the church, purchases of needed accessories, funds for repairs of the church or construction of new architectural features. We saw in chapter 3 some of the financial help provided by the Velas to the parishes, and now the Sociedad Católica got involved in the same kind of assistance. The Sociedad Católica of Toluca, for example, embroidered altar cloths for the church and bought a new canopy to shelter the Host; the San Sebastián del Potosí members created four dozen "magnificent" arrangements of artificial flowers and bought a cast iron handrail for the presbytery; in Zacatecas the ladies of the Sociedad paid for plastering and gilding an altar in the cathedral; Jiquilpan's chapter bought a carriage so that the Host could be carried to the homes of the dying; and in Tampico the Sociedad paid for music at all the church functions.[82]

But the service organizations also went beyond contributions to the parish church to promote Catholicism in multiple ways. At least fifty chapters of the women's Sociedad Católica founded or provided monetary support for parochial schools. Many of them also sponsored retreats and spiritual exercises, and all of them helped catechize. The Ladies of Charity spent the bulk of their funds on visiting the poor and the sick and offering them direct aid, but evangelization was not separate from charity: their 1878 report noted that from among the poor families and sick people they had visited and the orphans, schoolchildren, and abandoned children they cared for, they had persuaded almost fifteen thousand to take First Communion and over fifteen thousand to confess.[83] In fact, according to one harsh critic, the families "protected" by the association were subject to a kind of "slavery": "they are given a little bad rice and a few other grains of food, not even sufficient for two days, and in exchange for this 'charity' the most minor and private events of their households are monitored and observed, making them a blind instrument of the conference's desires."[84] Charity masked religious fervor, the author continued, and gained adherents for *mochismo* (extreme religious conservatism).

The archived exchanges among women's groups, priests, and bishops continue to include some disputes, but the number of them seems to have dropped off from the earlier period when women-led lay associations were still quite new and the relationship between female officers and priests was still being worked out. Further, the disputes that were registered tended to be less about money (as they had been in the earlier period) than about religious politics, and involved women's groups organizing on the side of the priest against some other official, or on the side of one priest against another, not so much as before against priestly interference in their affairs. The Vela Perpetua of Chavinda, for example, defended the "impeccable" Father José Ignacio de la Cueva against accusations that he had spent an exorbitant sum on Corpus Christi celebrations, when in fact he had only used what the Vela treasurer turned over to him.[85] Stauffer details two additional cases from Michoacán. One was a joint campaign in Jiquilpan by the Sisters of Charity, the women's Sociedad Católica, and members of the Vela Perpetua, joined by some male vecinos, to oust one priest (preferred by the local indigenous population, among others) in favor of another.[86] Another involved the fate of a priest in Coeneo, whom the women of the Vela supported in an 1873 letter to the archdiocesan secretary in Morelia, against complaints by indigenous villagers.[87]

In another telling case, in Cuautitlán in 1872, Eustaquia Guerrero, president of the women's Sociedad Católica, spoke out firmly against the men's Sociedad.[88] According to Doña Eustaquia, because of the "notorious malfeasance of D. Pomposo Patiño, president of the Sociedad, and D. José Orozco, president of the Hospital, and various other members [of the men's Sociedad]," she would be forced to submit her resignation because she "could not look with indifference at the abuses they committed against the Church, our Holy Religion, and our priest." Besides insulting the priest and the Señoras "and all those who do not go along with their ridiculous ideas," she continued, these men were speculating with the alms collected by the Sociedad. She and the other women who signed with her asked the archbishop to replace these scoundrels with "other persons who are honorable and truly religious." The archbishop immediately wrote the priest to ask if what the ladies had written was true, and he replied that he was "mortified" to say that it was, and that the men had demanded not only alms collected by the Sociedad de Señoras but also the funds of the Vela Perpetua (one of the associations that the women's Sociedad had founded). Sra. Guerrero, he said admiringly, had "resisted" in light of the fact that this money was dedicated exclusively to the promotion of the vigil and the adornment of the church. This case shows not only a women's group defending the priest, but the priest acknowledging that the funds the women had collected were their own and neither at the disposal of the men's Sociedad nor, presumably, at his own.

Naturally there were still some cases in which priests and women's groups were at loggerheads. The women of the Vela Perpetua and the Sociedad

Católica in Coalcomán, for example, coauthored several petitions asking the bishop for personnel changes in their city; among others, they wished to replace a priest whom they consider "cold," in favor of someone "who understands and wants to direct our religious societies." The priest they were trying to get rid of, Stauffer believes, "simply objected to the influence wielded by the women."[89] Similarly, although we have to read between the lines of the complaints by Bernardo Villagelin, parish priest of Tacuba, because we don't have the words of the Ladies of Charity themselves, it is not hard to see that they lacked the deference that the priest thought he deserved. "When I received this parish," he wrote in 1874, "I found already established an Association of St. Vincent de Paul . . . but it was completely disorganized because of continual in-fighting among the Señoras. I tried to reorganize them, but they have continued as before, and now things have become impossible because they refuse to give alms and they don't want to attend meetings and they are constantly resigning their positions without finding anyone to take their place. . . . This association has made the poor priest into a toy that is at the caprice of these Señoras."[90]

But these cases that hold echoes of the disdain for women that priests regularly displayed in the 1840s and 1850s were not only relatively rare but also concerned with more idiosyncratic problems than the rather ubiquitous fights over money in the earlier period. Why did disputes diminish and change in character? First, the idea of women in leadership positions in lay associations had had a chance to become normalized; priests had become accustomed to the modest power exercised by women's groups. Second, the idea that women-led lay associations had a right to manage their own funds had been defended often enough by diocesan authorities that priests largely stopped trying to interfere, realizing that their parishes would benefit more from treating the women with at least superficial respect than if they fought them and their organization. Third, they had grown dependent on the women's groups, in large part because they began to see them as more reliable than men's groups: they had more longevity, they were better at raising money, and they more consistently devoted it and their time to the parish. (See the case above in which the men's Sociedad Católica of Cuautitlán was accused by the women and the priest of speculating with the funds they collected.) In the 1840s and 1850s priests may have thought that these women's groups would not last, and that they ought to tap their funds while they could, before either the group disbanded or the women frittered away the money. By the 1870s the priests could see that the women's groups were here to stay, that they were dependable sources of support, and that losing them would be disastrous on many levels, from the financial to the religious. Father Silvestre Verdusco put it clearly when in 1876 he was asked either to document the origins and episcopal authorization of the women's Escuela de Cristo in Salamanca, or disband it.[91] Verdusco strongly advised, even pleaded with, the bishop's office that the ladies' Santa Escuela, which had been established in the 1840s, be legitimated, even though he had not been able to locate the original authorization from the bishop in the archive. Without the women's Escuela, he wrote, Catholic practice and faith would greatly diminish in Salamanca, since the Señoras numbered well over one hundred, and all of them were very active in the association. Moreover, he wrote, if he tried to suppress the organization there would be "great scandal, and much grumbling and resentment against the Priest."

Did the disputes quiet by 1875 because priests had learned how to manipulate women? Or because women officers and leaders of the associations had figured out how to manipulate their priests? Or should we put the emphasis on the idea that they had learned how to cooperate? The latter seems the most satisfying and consistent interpretation of the archival record. Time plus experience showed both parties that they had much to gain and little to lose from partnering toward common goals: beautification of the churches, increased community participation in religious practices, moralization of the youth in Catholic schools, and delivery of charity to the parish needy—all of which were ways to defend and protect the church at the local level. The rapid expansion of service organizations in Mexico during this period—organizations that were not structured as subservient to priests—strengthened the notion that women and priests were expected to operate as relative equals within local religious cultures. "Manipulation" of one party by the other implies that one forced the other to do something that either they did not want to do or they did not understand, and I see little evidence of this in any of the documents I have examined. In fact, this was a kind of golden age of parish autonomy and cooperation, in the sense that the needs of the parish were identified by local women and priests, and acted upon. As we will see in chapter 7, later changes in the power dynamics among parishes, dioceses, and the Vatican altered this balance so that the needs of the parish were identified more from above than by the priests and women of the parish itself—or at least that was the intent of the Vatican and many of the bishops.

NON-CATHOLIC WOMEN'S ASSOCIATIONS

Chapter 3 closed with a short effort to place the expansion of Catholic women's groups in the 1840s and 1850s in the broader context of women's associationalism in general, and here I do the same for the 1860s and early 1870s. The rapid growth of non-Catholic male-led associations in post-1867 Mexico, well-documented by Forment, leads us to expect to see the formation of numerous women's groups and societies that were dedicated to other interests or causes than the protection and preservation of the Catholic church. However, Forment found almost no autonomous women's groups and relatively few women's branches of men's groups.[92]

Forment's goal was to test whether voluntary associations were "democratic," with inclusionary practices (of admission and operation), so from his point of view, male-led groups that admitted women—of which there were few, but more than in the previous period—were entirely relevant. But for my purposes, the near-absence of autonomous women-led organizations in the story Forment tells is so unlike the story of men's associations that I felt that I needed to dig a little deeper to reassure myself that this picture was accurate. Since there is no study of Mexican women's associationalism during this period, I used newspapers to explore the extent to which autonomous or semi-autonomous groups of women formed nonreligious associations such as charitable groups or literary societies.[93] This is not, obviously, an entirely satisfactory stand-alone source, not least because most of the newspapers come from Mexico City, but I think I was able to gain an acceptable level of insight into nonreligious women's associations for the purpose of comparison to the Catholic groups.

I found that separate women's societies did increase in number somewhat more than Forment documents, but mainly in the form of auxiliaries to men's groups. And they were a particular kind of auxiliary. Unlike a large number of the women's branches of Catholic service organizations (the Sociedad Católica de Señoras and the women's conferences of the Society of St. Vincent de Paul, that is, the Ladies of Charity), which as we have seen might be the only group in some towns, the nonreligious women's groups were virtually never autonomous within their cities or towns.[94] They almost always existed alongside the men's group and were broadly governed by it, even when they were given separate domain over some particulars. In their relationship to the men's branches, then, they were more like the women's branch of the Archicofradía del Santísimo in Oaxaca—the one whose male leaders formed a women's branch to boost attendance and collect more alms, and who closely supervised them—than like the women's branch of the Escuela de Cristo de Señoras (chapter 3), which engaged in the same practices as the men's Escuela (on different days of the week) and operated parallel to, not subject to, the men.[95]

The largest nonreligious women's auxiliary, and one that fits the model of a women's association that was subject to the men's, continued to be the juntas or commissions of Señoras of the Compañía Lancasteriana, the society formed to help fund Lancaster schools in cooperation with national and local governments (see chapter 3 for its pre-Reform history). By 1870 the purview of the ladies' commissions had expanded slightly beyond handing out prizes and examining prospective teachers in sewing, and there is some indication that they were trying to carve out a larger role for their group. For example, they agreed in a January 1869 meeting to continue trying to improve the physical plant of various schools in Mexico City, to place sewing machines in all the girls' schools, and to explore teaching bookkeeping. A year later the "many" Señoras—led by the widow of the great liberal orator and editor Francisco Zarco—who staffed the ladies' commission were praised as having worked harder than the men on behalf of the youth of the city, including "going from house to house asking for donations of clothing so that poor girls in the Lancaster schools could present themselves decently in public."[96] It was still the case, however, that the men's commission examined potential candidates for teachers in girls' schools in the academic subjects, and for this reason it remained impossible for a Junta de Señoras to exist in any town without there also being a men's group to supervise them.

Further, the evidence for the women of the Lancaster societies becoming more active and engaging in more activities than in the 1830s and 1840s is all from Mexico City. It is unclear how many auxiliaries existed outside the national capital, and what their scope of action may have been. We do know that ladies' commissions were established in some places. Readers of *El Siglo Diez y Nueve* learned that new groups had formed in La Paz, Baja California, in 1871, and Mier, Tamaulipas, in 1873, and that their officers wished to establish communication with the "numerous" other women's groups of the interior (by which it seems fairly clear they meant Mexico City and its environs).[97] Baja California appears to have been a center for Lancaster schools; there were eighteen such schools there, six of which were probably girls' schools, so there was almost certainly a Junta de Señoras as well.[98] There were also new Lancaster schools—and therefore Lancaster societies—established in Guadalajara and in the states of Durango, San Luis Potosí, Sonora, and Michoacán.[99] However, despite these new foundations, the general trend was for Lancaster schools—which had always taught Christian doctrine as part of their curriculum—to languish after 1867, as they were slowly displaced by public, municipally funded schools that taught, or were supposed to teach, a nonreligious curriculum. For this reason it seems likely that the opportunity to join the Lancaster society, never anywhere near as widespread as the opportunity to join Catholic associations, remained limited.

In addition to the Lancaster societies, there was a small number of women's voluntary associations dedicated to mutual assistance. In Mexico City the association called "La Estrella del Porvenir," open to single women who were schoolteachers, was established in 1871, and a year later a mutual help society for Señoras was formed; by 1874 it had one hundred fifty members.[100] "Various señoritas," *El Correo del Comercio* reported in 1875, "were working to organize a mutual aid society called Luz y Constancia" (the newspaper added that these young ladies did more to help society than those who had signed the "famous" pro-Catholic protests—see chapter 6).[101] *El Eco de Ambos Mundos* reported in 1874 that "soon" there would be a ladies' auxiliary to the Sociedad de Socorros Mutuos "Esperanza" in which the "principal ladies" of Veracruz would be inscribed, and a similar society seems by that time to already exist in Yucatán.[102] Mutual help organizations (of which there were dozens open to men of different occupations in Mexico City) were of course extremely useful in light of the demise of the cofradías, which had previously provided similar sickness, death, and survivor benefits. And these were clearly voluntary associations, not just paper organizations that provided insurance but never met as a group. The Sociedad Mutua Particular de Señoras, for example, met once a week and had four elected officers.[103] But it does not seem that there were others even in Mexico City, and it is unlikely that there were too many outside of the capital.

The Lancaster groups and the mutual assistance societies were the two main kinds of non-Catholic voluntary association that had female leadership. Other groups to which women belonged were, as far as I have been able to determine, not voluntary and did not operate as a complex organization (with elections for officers, a treasury, etc.). Women, for example, were named to boards of hospitals or charitable organizations by government authorities, alongside male members. This happened fairly often during wartime, and after the wars women were sometimes appointed to the boards of state-run philanthropic organizations such as the Poor House. Women did constitute half of the members of the commission that supervised the Mexico City Poor House under the empire, and Maximilian's inclusion of women in official charitable institutions seems to have been imitated in at least some parts of provincial Mexico; I found references to female Juntas de Beneficencia in San Juan del Río and Colima in the mid-1860s.[104] The ladies' board of the Poor House continued after the republic was restored and indeed was given control over the day-to-day management of the institution until it closed four years later, in 1871.[105] Still, the number of women serving on these boards was quite limited. In sum, it appears that *El Monitor Republicano*, a liberal newspaper, accurately depicted the situation when it lamented that women had not "imitated" men who had formed associations. "There are a variety of associations of women among us, and yet," the editors wrote, ignoring Catholic associations, "they are few in number; we very much wish that the spirit of association would spread among the weaker sex, in the way it has among the stronger one."[106]

The relative dearth of nonreligious women's voluntary associations does not mean that women were entirely closed out of the nonreligious public sphere. Besides the board memberships just noted, as Forment points out they were allowed to join more clubs or groups than before the Reform (although that is not saying too much), and as of 1874 the first newspaper edited and run by women, *Las Hijas de Anahuac*, appeared, with an agenda of promoting the idea of intellectual equality between men and women.[107] One of the most impressive penetrations of the public sphere by women was their inclusion in and even, at least briefly, leadership of the Liceo Hidalgo, an important literary society originally founded in 1850 but revived, after many years of quiescence, in 1872.[108] Soon after it was restored, the society approved a proposal to allow women to serve as president.[109] Apparently the only female member at that time was Satur López de Alcalde, who had been recently nominated by "some of our most recognized writers, D. Guillermo Prieto, D. Ignacio

Ramírez, D. Vicente Riva Palacio," but in July 1873 two more accomplished writers, Laureana Wright de Kleinhans and Elena Castro, were also invited to join.[110] Less than a year later Castro, by then—rather amazingly—president of the Liceo, caused a scandal with a speech "rich in the great ideas of reform, progress, and liberty," in which she praised the Mexican hero Servando Teresa de Mier, and agreed with him that the "miracle" of the appearance of the Virgin of Guadalupe was not credible.[111] Despite this breakthrough, the number of women in the Liceo remained small, and male control over who was invited to join was barely disturbed by this one unusual female presidency, an office which Señorita Castro apparently resigned, presumably under pressure from the negative attention her brave speech had generated.[112]

Conclusion

Why did nonreligious associations for women fail to gain traction in this era of great enthusiasm for nonreligious men's associations in Mexico (and great enthusiasm for both secular and religious women's associations in the US and Europe)?[113] I think there are two compelling answers. First, the very fact that the women's Catholic associations were so vibrant, satisfying, numerous, and well-established preempted the formation of other clubs or societies for women. As we have seen in this and previous chapters, Catholic associations had a great deal to offer women: leadership, responsibility, community, prestige, and purpose—whether that purpose was saving their own souls or those of others; providing Catholic charity; aiding their parish priests in multiple ways; or, as we saw in chapter 4 and will see again in chapter 6, joining in the defense of Catholicism and the Catholic church. Demography contributed to the dominance of Catholic associations. For the same reason that it was hard for both the Ladies of Charity and the Sociedad Católica to coexist in a single location, it was hard for nonreligious groups to get off the ground when Catholic associations already existed: they needed the same kind of members, with time and energy on their hands, that the Catholic organizations already monopolized. Obviously people could and did belong to more than one organization, as we have seen in the case of the Catholic associations, but to the extent that membership in any association required commitments of time and money, there was a limit to the number of them that any one woman might be able to join.

There were women, however, like Elena Castro—who had disparaged the myth of Guadalupe in her speech at the Liceo Hidalgo—who surely can be thought of as unlikely to join even a Catholic service association (which, after all, expected members to save souls by persuading the people they served to be better Catholics), much less a devotional one. Why did these women not form their own voluntary associations in greater numbers? It was not because their needs were already being met by the Catholic associations. The second possible answer, then, lies with the fact that liberals had spent the middle months of 1856 lambasting the church for allowing (or forcing) Catholic women to emerge from their proper domain, the home (chapter 4). With this rhetorical move they painted their own wives and daughters and sisters and mothers into a corner: women who stayed at home to take care of their family were good, while women who entered the public sphere were at best deluded and at worst malign influences on their families.

Clearly the liberals meant to target Catholic women who left the home to participate in politics, not women who left the home in order to go to the meetings of a sewing circle or a musical society. In Europe and the US, in fact, the ideology of domesticity was entirely compatible with some forms of associational life, especially those—like charitable or philanthropic organizations—that could be seen, or portrayed by women who wished to found or join them, as extensions of the domestic sphere.[114] But in Mexico, the negative discourses spun by liberals about women who entered the public sphere, and the praise heaped on women who stayed home, were powerful. Even founding a benign and apolitical association might have seemed difficult under these circumstances. In any event, for whatever combination of reasons, women like Elena Castro did not participate in the spirit of association, other than to join the handful of male associations that would accept them.

In sum, the proliferation of both service and devotional Catholic women's groups in the 1860s and 1870s expanded the process that began in the 1840s—in which women's relationships to their parish priests and their local churches changed in rather dramatic fashion—from a regional phenomenon to a national one. Not only were there were more women's Catholic associations, but their goals enlarged, from filling the gaps left by failing male-led cofradías to defending the church against triumphant liberalism. It makes sense, then, as chapter 6 shows, that the next major political intervention made by Catholic women had not only a national scope but an intensity that the petition campaign of 1856, for all its passion, could not match.

CHAPTER SIX

"We'll See Who Wins: Them with Their Laws, or Us with Our Protests"

THE *LEY ORGÁNICA* AND THE
1874–1875 PETITION CAMPAIGN

> We intended to hold our tongues with regard to this barbarous law . . . but considering that even the female sex, with manly valor instead of its characteristic weakness, has parted its innocent lips to condemn those who call themselves the representatives of the suffering Mexican people, we must speak up.
>
> —PROTEST OF THE [MALE] RESIDENTS OF MATEHUALA, FEBRUARY 5, 1875[1]

THE PROLIFERATION OF PIOUS ASSOCIATIONS, especially women's organizations, between 1856 and 1875 (chapter 5) was accompanied by bolder and more demonstrative political acts by women. By "accompanied" I do not mean to suggest that lay associations were always the organizers of these events. In fact, far from a linear intensification over time of the connection between associationalism and political activity, what we see after the 1856 petition campaign—in which I argued that lay associations played an important role—is that all Catholic women, whether members of a lay organization or not, seem to have felt more empowered to act politically. In the intervening years between 1856 and the second major national petition campaign in 1874–75, however, most women's political actions were local, that is to say, initiated locally and not seeking to coordinate with other petitioners or protesters.

In 1861, for example, when the government of the Federal District ordered that no bells should be rung when the Host was carried from the church in viaticum and that the process should be carried out privately and without fanfare or distinction of any kind, Father Atenógenes Lombardini of the parish of Santa Veracruz violated the prohibition on bell ringing and was imprisoned. This led his "animated" female parishioners into the streets to accompany the Host out of the parish church, which in turn forced the priest's release from jail.[2] In a similar case, in February 1863, only months before the Liberals were forced to leave Mexico City in advance of the arrival of the French army, twenty-one women, one man, and the priest of the parish of Santa Veracruz were sent to prison for having carried lanterns (*luminarias*) while they accompanied the Host, another violation of the law.[3] A more sedate protest against this same law came in 1861 from over one hundred fifty women of the parish of San Miguel in Mexico City, who, explicitly invoking the right of petition, asked the president to allow them to accompany the Host when it was taken to the homes of the moribund during the night, as they said they had always been allowed to do.[4] (The petition was denied.) Catholic women also enjoyed a brief period when their political actions could be in praise of a conservative government. In early 1858, during the War of the Reform, for example, a commission of six Mexico City women, in representation of seven hundred others, called on President Zuloaga to congratulate him for having revoked the Reform-era Lerdo Law, which had ordered the sale of church property.[5]

In a different category are local protests of national issues that might have had broad resonance, but seem not to have been picked up by many women, probably because of external circumstances that militated against such a spread. To illustrate, a group of eighty-three women in Toluca protested the new Reform law passed in July 1859 that turned novices out of the convents and offered nuns the return of their dowries in the unlikely event that (as the outraged petition put it) they were willing to "divorce their celestial spouse."[6] This was an issue of concern nationally and it is entirely possible that the Toluca ladies either imitated another similar protest or expected to be imitated or both, but the timing of the petition in the middle of the War of the Reform worked against the survival of such petitions and may also have worked against their spread. In another local protest against a national law, a delegation of twenty women met with President Lerdo in May 1873 to discuss and protest his government's expulsion of foreign priests (mainly Jesuits).[7] The dialogue was presented in the conservative paper *La Voz de México* in such a way as to make it seem that the women got the better of the president, not just on moral grounds but also analytically and rhetorically. This time there were no wartime circumstances to prevent widespread petitioning on this score, but I found little protest against that law by anyone else.[8] In another case that may have come close to the level of a regional campaign, according to Pablo Mijangos y González women played a key role in the mobilization of communities in the central plateau in early 1857 against the despised (by Catholics) requirement that all public employees (and all municipal presidents on behalf of their communities) pledge allegiance to the new liberal constitution.[9] Unfortunately he does not provide more details.

There was one interesting case of pre-1874 women's petitioning in which a local protest did gain some traction and spread modestly. On December 27, 1864, Emperor Maximilian sent a letter to his minister of justice, Pedro Escudero, in which he signaled that he was ready to support at least some parts of the most controversial elements of the Reform. He expressed his desire to "reduce the controversies that surround the so-called laws of the Reform" and thus "satisfy the true needs of the country."[10] More specifically, he asked the minister to propose a plan to review all the sales of church property that had taken place after the Lerdo Law in 1856, and to ratify those that had been carried out without fraud and in conformity with the law. He also (somewhat ambiguously) suggested that religious tolerance should be respected: "You should act in accordance with the broadest liberal principles of religious tolerance without losing sight of the fact that the religion of the State is the Catholic, Apostolic, and Roman religion."[11]

When the contents of the letter to Escudero were published a week or so later, they created some odd new bedfellows. At least one liberal newspaper in Mexico City was supportive of Maximilian's posture (as *La Cuchara* put it, "We are for the laws of the Reform. . . . It matters not whether they are promulgated by Juan or by Pedro [or by the emperor]").[12] Meanwhile, conservatives, some of whom had actively recruited Maximilian and almost all of whom had applauded his arrival in Mexico eight months earlier, were naturally upset, but temporarily paralyzed by uncertainty about how to proceed.

The first public pronouncements against the *carta imperial* came from a group of women in Mexico City in 1865. A commission led by Doña Concepción Valdivielso de Malo, daughter of a member of the titled nobility, presented an "exposition" to the emperor, probably on January 6 or 7 (though possibly earlier), asking him not to decree religious tolerance.[13] It was signed by a "multitude" of señoras.[14] It read in part: "A rumor has reached us that . . . Your Majesty, surely against your pious instincts, may consider allowing the terrible decree of religious tolerance to stand. Justly alarmed, as Catholics, as loyal subjects of the Empire, and as wives and mothers, we fear for the holy Church, for Your Majesty, and for our sons and husbands."[15]

The petition was commented on with caution by the conservative *La Sociedad*, who wrote that they wished the ladies had used fewer "harsh" words that, "no matter how true, contradict the character of the sex to which the signers belong."[16] The editors would also have preferred that the women limit themselves to asking the emperor to let the pope negotiate matters such as these. The liberal newspapers, meanwhile, had a field day with the spectacle of Catholic women registering their objections to the actions of the emperor. "The ladies discussing questions of political convenience! The ladies writing expositions against a document that has been sanctioned and recognized by the government! It shocks us that the same persons who shouted 'vivas' to the Emperor at the top of their feminine lungs in June now attack him. Then he was a God; today he is a man, as fallible as Juárez, a heretic like the old president.... Either the Emperor merits our confidence, our dear female politicians, or not."[17]

The women did not back down. When, apparently, none of the conservative newspapers was willing to publish the names of the signers, they wrote a note ("which smelled of violets") to the editors of *La Orquesta*, asking them to persuade *El Pájaro Verde* to list the names.[18] Confronted with the criticism of *La Sociedad* that they should simply have asked the emperor to let the pope settle these questions of law, they responded that when they sent their exposition the December 27 carta imperial had not been published, and they were just acting on a rumor. But, they said unrepentantly, if the letter's contents had been known, they would nonetheless have asked him to suspend its recommendations, "and that is all we have to say about your disapproval of our actions."[19] They then addressed the criticisms of *L'Estafette* (and other newspapers) that women had no business entering politics. "Two great European nations are governed by women [England and Spain], and Empress Carlota not only plays an active role in the governing of Mexico and is aware of the vital questions of the day, but she has been named Regent in case of the death of her husband.... Thus there are occasions in which women can and must take part in public business."[20]

The ladies' petition did not inspire a major nationwide campaign, but it did have imitators. Similar petitions came from the women of Orizaba, Cholula, Lagos, and Tehuacán; from the "heads of family" of Puebla; and from the vecinos of Lagos, Guadalajara, and Tehuacán.[21] The señoras of Puebla sent one to the Empress Carlota.[22] It is even possible to view the petition from the archbishops of Mexico and Michoacán and the bishops of Oaxaca and Querétaro, also asking for the suspension of the directives of the December 27 letter, as having been inspired, at least in a very general way, by the Mexico City women's exposition, since it came several days after the ladies submitted theirs.[23] Under the headline "It's Raining Expositions!" the liberal *La Cuchara* printed a verse about the petitions which concluded, "What does the government have to say about this? It gathers up all the paper and says: 'to the garbage bin, for I do not waste my time on such trivial nonsense.'"[24]

The only other semi-coordinated political action taken by Catholic women before late 1874 was a letter-writing and fundraising campaign to support the pope in 1871 in his attempt to hold onto temporal power in Italy. Despite the fact that this was not a petition drive that had anything directly to do with Mexican politics, it is relevant here because of the role of the Sociedades Católicas de Señoras in orchestrating the campaign.[25] The Sociedad Católica of Oaxaca, for example, raised the substantial sum of 600 pesos and sent a letter to the pope signed by 226 women.[26] The Sociedad Católica of San

Luis Potosí sent even more (1,333 pesos) along with their letter.[27] Sociedades Católicas (both men's and women's) were also involved in organizing public demonstrations of faith in mid-1871 in the context of anticlerical publications, political turmoil around the question of Juárez's reelection, and the anniversary of the pope's "captivity" in the Vatican.[28] It should not surprise us, then, that, as we will see later in this chapter, some of the direct evidence of lay association involvement in the 1874–75 petition campaign came from the Sociedades Católicas de Señoras. Let us turn to that campaign.

The Ley Orgánica

When Benito Juárez died in office in July 1872, his successor, Sebastián Lerdo de Tejada, although not as personally popular as Juárez, benefited from Juárez's efforts to consolidate the liberal victory over Maximilian and the conservative army. These efforts included a not-too-aggressive stance against the church. But in September 1873 Lerdo felt strong enough to take on the church in what he considered to be the next step in cementing Mexican liberalism: elevating to constitutional status the Reform laws that had been decreed by Juárez, mainly in 1859 and 1860, during the War of the Reform.[29] These included religious tolerance, as well as a number of other laws, such as the requirement for secular education in public schools, that had been either not enforced at all or under-enforced since their decree.[30]

There were isolated protests against Lerdo's move in late 1873 and 1874, including the first stirrings of armed uprising in the center-west, especially in the state of Michoacán.[31] In December 1874, however, a regulatory law, the Ley Orgánica de Adiciones Constitucionales, was passed by the congress. This law was meant to clarify and explain exactly how the vaguer and/or forgotten and/or previously unenforced laws of Reform would now work, and to establish clearly, once and for all, the principle of the subjection of the church to the state.[32] It turned out that the devil (literally, for many of the faithful) was in these details, and in the promise implicit in them that some of the Reform-era laws that had been decreed but often ignored, such as the banning of religious processions, would now be effectively enforced. These "clarifications" were interpreted by the Catholic public as an *expansion* of the original laws of the Reform, and indeed some of them were.

The Ley Orgánica immediately caused an uproar. Among the most objectionable provisions of the law were:

- Article 3, which abolished all religious holidays from work. This law had been decreed in 1859 but had been mainly unenforced.
- Article 4, which prohibited religious instruction in the public schools. This law had been decreed at the time of the Reform but in very vague language, and enforcement after 1860 depended on the state. In the

state of Mexico, for example, the prohibition had gone into effect in 1867, but in some states it had not been enforced at all.

- Article 5, which prohibited public displays of religiosity (such as processions). All religious activities were to be confined to the inside of the churches. It also prohibited ministers from wearing distinctive clothing (such as the priest's collar). Another often-unenforced law before 1875.
- Article 6, which prohibited ringing of church bells for any purpose other than during religious acts. Previously sporadically and inconsistently enforced.
- Article 11, which prohibited ministers from preaching disobedience of any laws or fomenting any kind of civil infraction, on pain of arrest by the authorities. This article did represent an expansion of the Reform-era laws, which had not specifically addressed sedition or subversive speech from the pulpit.
- Article 12, which placed the churches under the vigilance of the police and allowed the police to arrest people inside the churches "when the situation demands." Again, those who claimed this was an "expansion" of the laws of the Reform had a point.
- Articles 19 and 20, which prohibited the existence of monastic orders and defined "monastic order" in a very capacious way so that even previously exempted nuns—specifically, the Sisters of Charity (Hermanas de la Caridad)—were now covered by this prohibition. Cloistered nuns had been required to leave the convents in 1863 in the areas under liberal control, and in areas under conservative control they were expelled after the restoration of liberal rule in 1867. But at the time of the Reform, the Sisters had been exempted because they were active, not contemplative, nuns, and because they had not taken solemn vows to commit to this estate for life. Now they were to be treated as any other monastic women.
- Article 21, which required all public employees to swear allegiance to the constitution, including the provisions of the Ley Orgánica. This was an impossible promise for committed Catholics to make, and it ensured that the congresses were comprised of mainly liberals. This article was the proximate cause of much of the armed unrest in Michoacán, triggered by Catholic refusal to swear allegiance.

For both men and women but perhaps particularly for women, the provision that the Sisters of Charity must disband and cease living in community was extraordinarily inflammatory. When most of the Sisters chose exile over disbandment and they departed on ships for California or France amid much sentimental gnashing of teeth, mobilization of the faithful was made that much easier. The Catholic campaign had its face, and it was the image of four hundred "angels of mercy" being dragged out of their homes, forced onto waiting ships, and sent across dangerous seas to new homes where they did not speak the language, leaving behind the miserable, the poor, the disabled, the orphaned, and a generation of children who would now grow up without the benefit of a Catholic education.

The "Burning Question," the "Question of the Moment": The Petitions [33]

The Ley Orgánica set off the second great Catholic petition campaign.[34] This time there were many more petitions than in 1856: 230 whose male or female authorship is known were submitted to the authorities and/or to editors of Catholic newspapers in Mexico, and 127 (55 percent) of them were from women.[35]

While petitioning was obviously not the same as armed rebellion, at the same time some of the petitions—and more the women's than the men's— struck a decidedly fiery and even militant tone. The one sent by the señoras of Guanajuato set the standard for angry petitioning. Their protest, as had happened with the petition of the Mexico City ladies in 1856, was cited repeatedly as an inspiration. Nineteen of the other women's petitions published in the Catholic press specifically stated that they were in full agreement with the "heroic" ladies of Guanajuato and were grateful to them for having "shown us the way."[36] Theirs was not the first by a group of women (petitions from the women of Guadalajara, Puebla, Monterrey, San Francisco del Rincón [Guanajuato], and Lagos preceded the December 31, 1874, Guanajuato petition), and it was by no means the most heavily subscribed petition, with only 45 signatures, as opposed to 1,071 from just one of the two Guadalajara petitions, or 2,493 from Monterrey or, later, 2,330 from the small town of La Piedad. But the language of the Guanajuato señoras caught the attention of everyone. It was shockingly intemperate, immodest, and aggressive.

Far from apologizing for their entry into politics or trying to disarm their readers by saying that they knew politics was not the proper realm for women, the señoras of Guanajuato seized the right to speak "granted by our magna carta, in the liberal spirit of hearing the complaints of the oppressed" (although a few sentences later, they called the constitution of 1857 that "miserable hodgepodge of nonsensical laws").[37] Striking a bitter note that was found in a number of both men's and women's petitions, they stated that they did not expect to be heard because the deputies had been "blinded by partisan spirit": "once a Mason has received his marching orders, he is not capable of turning back even if the universe is afire." Nonetheless, they had not only the right but the duty to vent their anger at the "iniquity" of the delegates who had voted for the Ley Orgánica: "We speak to protest your tyrannical laws. We speak so that you will know the true sentiments of the nation of which we form half, and so that the rest of the world, indignant at your barbarity, will not attribute to our sane, sensible, and long-suffering nation the madness and wickedness of its leaders."

Following this in-your-face introduction, the señoras launched into a diatribe against the "expulsion" of the "angels of Charity," which left thousands of children without education, and hundreds of sick without assistance.[38] With this one action, they accused the congress, "you have caused so many tears to be shed that they exceed the volume of liquor that you guzzle at your banquets."[39] In the law disbanding the Sisters of Charity, they wrote, "the absurd shakes hands with the unjust, and the ridiculous with the infamous."[40] Since, they wrote, the law defined a monastic order as "any association that has particular rules and is subject to one or more superiors," a family could be considered a monastic order, as could the secular clergy, as well as any town that was subject to its parish priest. Indeed, the entire population of the Republic, which was subject to the ecclesiastical hierarchy, could, by this law, "suffer the pain of persecution and exile!" "With what right do you pursue Catholicism, señores? With what right do you tax its temples, organize espionage in its sanctuaries, expel its ministers and demolish its most beautiful institutions?"[41]

But the most shocking language was the señoras' characterization of "men who call themselves 'Catholics'" as peace-loving Quakers:

> And now that fear has converted men who call themselves "Catholics" into Quakers, we women swear to disobey, with all the means at our disposal, the edicts of these modern Julians; we swear to obey to the death our priestly superiors . . . we swear to disown as brothers, husbands and even sons any who have participated in the iniquitous expulsion of the Sisters, and finally we swear to suffer, with pleasure and with courage, all the persecutions that our honest manifesto brings.[42]

For all their vitriol against the congress, the special wrath of the ladies of Guanajuato was saved for Catholic men who were reluctant to confront the Lerdo administration and risk a third war of religion within a single generation.

It is true that many of the other women's protests were tamer, using the kind of modest, gentle, and humble language—apologizing for entering politics and for raising their "weak voices"—that was the dominant tone of most of the 1856 petitions. The señoras of Amanalco, for example, wrote simply but almost poetically that "although we were born among rocks and thorns, we have a heart and a Religion because from the time we were little girls we used to look upon the rustic cross that crowns the peak of the mountains that surround our village, and there we could see the sacred standard of the Religion of our parents: we have never seen nor practiced any other Religion than that of the Crucified One!"[43] The señoras of Orizaba wrote that "knowing the place that Providence has assigned us in the world, we are not accustomed to speaking outside the confines of our houses; there is where we make our influence felt on the people we love, protecting them from danger and preventing them from becoming contaminated in their unavoidable dealings with unbelievers."[44]

But the militant tone of many of the 1874-75 petitions is striking. The women of Coroneo (Guanajuato) threatened that "civil war is inevitable if contempt for the vast majority of Mexicans continues."[45] The señoras of Puebla, who were among the many particularly outraged by what they considered the expulsion of the Sisters of Charity, wrote to Lerdo that by sending "your assassins of evil to throw these modest women out of their houses," "you have left our youth to drink the venom of immorality in the government schools ... but you have been deceived: we will convert ourselves into apostles of Christian education, and not one of our children will ever cross the threshold of these dungeons, these sewers of corruption, where libertinage and sensualism predominate, dressed up as the rights of man and universal fraternity."[46] On the topic of the Sisters, the señoras of Mexico City wrote that "Voltairian liberalism and freemasonry, without doubt more savage than the barbarians of our frontiers, have dragged these holy messengers of God's mercy from their native land. Over three and a half centuries, hundreds and hundreds of ships have transported our nation's mineral wealth to Europe; now in a few days Europe will receive on its shores another Mexican treasure, more precious than all the gold and silver of our mines."[47]

As in 1856, the subject matter of the women's petitions was different from the men's, despite overlap on the issue of the Sisters of Charity, which both sexes deplored. Many of the men's petitions took up the Reform laws' impacts on property, foreign investment, the government's program for material improvements, states' rights, taxation, public works, constitutional issues of freedom of assembly and freedom of speech, besides directly addressing the offending articles of the Ley Orgánica.[48] Although women in 1874-75 sometimes ventured into the relatively ungendered territory of the meanings of liberty, democracy, and modernity (usually pointing out liberal "hypocrisies" like their enshrinement of freedom of speech even as they encouraged "spies" to snoop on priests and allowed police to enter the temples), their protests tended to stick to arguments against specific articles of the Ley Orgánica, especially the "unfair" way the Sisters had been treated. In tone, on balance the men's petitions in 1874-75 seem somewhat milder than the women's petitions—less angry, more matter-of-fact. Some even thanked their representatives for trying to preserve space for Catholicism.[49] This could well be a reflection of the fact that at least the middle-class male signers had more to lose than women in the unsettled political arena, where they were being required by the Ley Orgánica to swear their loyalty to the constitution if they wished to hold a government job.

What do we make of the differences between the 1856 women's petitions and the ones in 1874-75? On the surface it seems logical to conclude that the more militant language and aggressive tone of the women's petitions in 1874–75 means that men (editors, priests, Catholic laymen) were more involved in the writing process than in 1856. This was certainly the view of the liberal press, as we'll see in more detail below. "If a woman had written the protest [from Guanajuato], she would have employed a more restrained and less emphatic tone," wrote *El Correo del Comercio*; instead, it is full of insolence, and "by its pedantic style, makes clear that it was written by some fashionable preacher."[50] It is hard to disagree with this conclusion.

But we should at least probe it. There are some reasons to think that there may have been more female authors and a greater women's contribution to the writing process in this second campaign than in the first one. It makes sense to think about priests having a strong role in writing the approximately one-third of the petitions that came from very small towns, including some mainly indigenous towns. In places like these it is hard to imagine women who were educated enough to pen any but the shortest and most modest texts. But for the bigger towns and cities, where schooling for middle- and upper-class girls was common and where often enough this schooling came in Catholic or parochial schools, there is a possibility that women had important input or even did some authoring, especially in light of the expanded petitioning by women between 1856 and 1874.

Even in the case of the aggressive, sarcastic, bombastic language of the señoras of Guanajuato and others, there seems to be an undercurrent of genuine female resentment, especially in two areas. First, they were devastated by the way the Sisters of Charity were treated. The clearly special relationship between laywomen and the Sisters of Charity comes through in many of the petitions. This was a relationship that had roots in the close relationship during the colonial period between nuns and laywomen, who often visited daily and sought to live near the convents. The convent was a valued part of Mexican laywomen's religious lives, and nuns were involved in the lives of many secular women and families. Some women may have felt keenly the closing-off of a Mexican religious community just at the time that in Catholic Europe there was an explosion of female vocations.[51] The close relationship was also built into the structure of the Vincentian charities in Mexico, with the resurgent Ladies of Charity serving as a complement to the Sisters. In any event, the anguish over the departure of some four hundred sisters comes through in the petitions as not just authentic but personal, in a way it would not be to most men.

Second, the way the women expressed their resentment of the way the liberal press had disparaged their capability to hold opinions and author the petitions seems convincingly specific. The Guanajuato petition included a line referring back to 1856. "You," they wrote, addressing the congress, "insulted our sex . . . saying that we did not know what we were signing when we protested against religious tolerance, as if we, like you, spoke or wrote with our brains deranged by drink and vice!"[52] (The obsession with the deputies' use of alcohol also feels female-authored to me.) The señoras of San Miguel de

Allende were prepared to prove they both signed and wrote the petition: "some will say that our signatures are fictitious; we are ready to legalize them. Others will say that priests compelled us. To this we say that the person who was in charge of expressing our sentiments is prepared to publish her name."[53]

Intending to belittle the process of women's petition-writing, one liberal writer—in a piece we will examine in more detail below—may have hit upon a fairly accurate image of what actually happened in many cases:

> I can picture [the author] sitting at his desk with pen in hand, ears burning, and the shadow of half a dozen wild-haired women watching with rapt attention as each line is penned. I can picture him imposing silence: "Silence, girls!" and then reading out loud:
> "And now that fear has converted into Quakers those men who call themselves 'Catholics,' we women swear to disobey . . ."
> I hear the "Hurrah" of the old women.[54]

If we filter out the negative images of "wild-haired" (read: unladylike) old women and grant them a little more agency than just yelling "Hurrah," the image of collaboration in the writing of the Guanajuato petition that this writer conjures up is actually not improbable. The women are present at the moment of composition, and they are signaling their engagement in and approval of every line the male author writes. Even if this scenario is not an exact match for the way all petitions got off the ground, it captures a plausible relationship between women and (possible) male authors that was characterized by cooperation and collaboration on a project of mutual interest.

Gender and Protest in Liberal Discourse, 1874–75

Let's look more closely, now, at the liberal reception of the petitions. As with the petitions themselves, there were certain themes from 1856 that were repeated in the liberal press's reactions to the 1874–75 campaign, but there were also changes in the ways the press covered the story, including significant shifts in the tone of the coverage and in the sheer amount of it. As it had done in 1856, the liberal press tended to refer to the petitions as the "representaciones de las señoras" or the "protestas de las señoras," or even referred to *all* the petitions as if they came from women, although almost half of them in 1874–75 came from men. *El Defensor de la Reforma* in 1875 called one Catholic publication "the newspaper of the protestas de señoras," despite the fact that that paper regularly published petitions from both sexes.[55] *El Monitor Republicano*, in an article titled "Las Protestas," suggested that in the next session of congress, "all the señoras" who had signed the petitions would be asked to attest to the validity of their signatures; this not only suggested that women didn't know what they were signing (whereas men did), but it also had the desirable effect of feminizing the protests.[56]

In 1856 the liberal press had depicted priests as hiding "behind" women, but in 1875 the invasion became more personal: priests now were to be found under women's petticoats or among their skirts or even under their bosoms. In 1875 *El Defensor de la Reforma* sarcastically noted that "we republicans don't have the retrogrades' great talent of writing and conspiring from under [women's] crinolines."[57] Petticoats were invoked by *El Monitor Republicano*, as well, in 1875, which primly noted in reference to an anonymous letter that "the *mochos* [a pejorative term for excessively devout and conservative people] think it is appropriate to attack and then hide under petticoats, but liberals ought to be better than that."[58] The same daily made a similar reference to "the insults launched by the clergy from their sacristies, hiding among the silk skirts of the Mexican ladies," while Guillermo Prieto in *El Correo del Comercio* held up the image of the "erudite authors" of the protests sheltering under women's bosoms.[59] In short, we see the feminizing language used by liberals against priests ramped up in 1874–75: they are trying to make priests even more in need of women's protection than twenty years earlier, a rhetorical move that had the effect of giving women power in the religious sphere, a result that was quite intentional.

The women among whose skirts priests were to be found were depicted as either clueless or wizened and old. "How much shall we bet that not even the know-it-alls (*bachilleronas*) who are orchestrating this female sedition have any idea what they are talking about" wrote *La Bandera de Ocampo* (Morelia).[60] These tropes were not unfamiliar in the 1856 press coverage of the petitions but began to dominate in the press's treatment of women in the 1865 petition campaign against Maximilian's decision to accept religious tolerance, and became even more prevalent and meaner in 1875. There were a few lingering comments such as those of one writer in *El Defensor de la Reforma* to the effect that "women, precisely because of the delicacy of their sex and the gentleness of their hearts, should abstain from politics."[61] But it was now more common to be scathingly negative about Catholic women. *El Monitor Republicano*, for example, featured on the front page a satirical piece ridiculing women's frivolity and their commitment to, and understanding of, politics. The author imagined conversations between two girls, Lola and Lupe, and their two mothers. The dialogue begins with the girls:

—Did you already sign the *protesta*, Lola?
—Of course, *chula*, you know that it is all the vogue to protest.
—How many times have you protested?
—Just once.
—Well, I have signed four times.
—Ay! Where can I go to protest more? I want to protest ten times . . .
—My goodness, niña, you ought to be ashamed to have only protested once! What are you thinking? . . .

Meanwhile the mothers are sharing strategies for racking up more signatures:

>—And you haven't even sent your maids to go protest?
>—What do you think, Juanita? The maids are so useless. Yesterday I allowed the bedroom maid and the seamstress to go to church for Ash Wednesday and to sign a protest; they got the ashes on their foreheads but then went on a canoe ride in Santa Anita . . .
>—What about getting Lucecita to sign?
>—But she is only three years old.
>—It doesn't matter; why not? . . .

And back to the daughters:

>—Do you worry that people will say we should not interfere in matters that don't concern us?
>—Don't worry about them, *chula*, I am content for now with my four protests, but I can't wait for Congress to open, because if they present a budget, then I will protest and go out and collect signatures; if they pass a railroad law, I'll protest again; whatever they do, I will protest. Those damn heretics! It's for this that we will protest and re-protest until kingdom comes. We'll see who wins: them with their laws, or us with our protests.
>—Very good, my child (says one of the mothers); above all we must defend religion, even if it means having to leave your boyfriends.
>—*Oye*, Lola, is it really necessary to leave our boyfriends?
>—When it is necessary we will do it; didn't you see that the señoras of Guanajuato have renounced their children, their fathers, and their husbands?
>—Well, then, this is serious![62]

If these four women seem to have been born shallow, the idea that politics changes women from good wives into bad continued to be articulated, as it had in 1856. But the rhetoric of 1856 had been somewhat cautious on this subject, since the women's petitions revolved around tolerance as a threat to the sanctity of marriage, and many liberals were reluctant to accuse the women signers themselves of threatening marriage. But the liberal rhetoric in 1875 didn't hold back. "WAR IN THE HOME!" cried *El Defensor de la Reforma*. "Warning, Compatriots! A hidden hand has begun to plant the seed of discord in the core of the family!"[63] *El Monitor Republicano* warned that "a sad situation is already notable in more than one family . . . in which the dissipated woman neglects her children, because caring for them steals time from the business of fanaticism."[64] References to women's beauty, gentleness, and naivete yielded in the 1870s to biting comments about their willing participation in the political process and the danger it held to the family and the honor of their husbands and fathers.⁶⁵ This was of course symbolized by the much-quoted señoras of Guanajuato and their frontal attack not just on the Ley Orgánica but on Catholic men.

By 1875, although there were still frequent insinuations that women had been duped into signing the petitions, more liberals than before seem to have accepted that women had knowingly and self-consciously entered politics. The distinction is subtle, but priests were seen more as conniving with willing women than deceiving totally gullible ones; put another way, the women who organized and wrote the 1875 petitions were seen as less naive than the women of 1856, and more as active accomplices of the clergy. "FUROR PROTESTATIVO" read one headline in Morelia's *El Defensor de la Reforma*. "A furor of protestation has gripped the ladies of the clerical party of Guadalajara, and it has spread—we do not know whether by imitation or contagion—to the parrots and loyal companions of our own rebels [*Comuneros*]."⁶⁶ Two weeks later *El Defensor* praised the women of Uruapan for resisting pressure from the "henchmen" of the clerical party and refusing to sign a protest of their own: "That's the way it's done, ladies of Guanajuato," they wrote, referring to the famous Guanajuato petitioners. "Read and don't forget the lesson of dignity and delicacy that the modest and admirable daughters of a small but decent town have given you."⁶⁷ (This praise looked a bit hollow two months later, when the ladies of Uruapan did in fact submit an anti–Ley Orgánica petition, in which they mentioned having been humiliated by *El Defensor*'s characterization of them as having refused to sign.)⁶⁸

One long story, featured on page one in *El Monitor Republicano* from 1875, combines all these negative images of women and priests in a way that Francisco Zarco—who ridiculed women in 1856 for believing that religious tolerance would require them to join a harem—would applaud, though he would never have used imagery that so strongly recognized women's self-consciousness. For Zarco, women were nothing but pawns of priests. For *El Monitor* in 1875, after the publication of the Guanajuato manifesto and others by women who proudly adhered to it, active and militant and self-conscious women are at the center of the fable. The author of the piece pretends to be writing to his niece, whose name he says he saw on the list of signers of an "insolent protest." Fortunately, her name was "obscure," otherwise he would have died of anger and shame when he saw her name on this "ridiculous piece of paper."⁶⁹ But, he continued, "I can guess why you have committed such an imprudent act, and why so many other modest señoras have also done so." He then imagines how the Guanajuato manifesto was created. Two or three *beatos* (sanctimonious men) "with a sweet and feminine smile on their closely shaved lips, who have lived all their lives among women," were joined by some resentful old women who hate men because they were "left at the ball." "I assure you," the letter continues, "that the protest you signed was created with the help of various persons of this type. You can see in it the obsequious but cruel character of women of a certain age." He continues:

> I can picture one of the *beatos* sitting at his desk with pen in hand, ears burning, and the shadow of half a dozen wild-haired women watching with rapt attention as each line is penned. I can picture him imposing silence: "Silence, girls!" and then reading out loud:
> "And now that fear has converted into Quakers those men who call themselves 'Catholics,' we women swear to disobey..."
> I hear the "Hurrah" of the old women....
> My child, an honest young women like you can lose... the patrimony of your honor... What do you have in common with those women who abuse your piety, drag you along under a banner formed by kitchen rags, to fight, cross in hand, for the interests of men you don't even know and ought not ever know in your life? Keep yourself isolated as always in your modest little house. There, alone, on your knees, raise your beautiful eyes to heaven and to your God of infinite consolation, whom neither we nor the priests can apprehend.[70]

This author's advice to his niece—"keep yourself isolated as always in your modest little house"—epitomized the liberal view (the only view available to them, given their excoriation of Catholic women's public activism) that women's place is at home. Some of the most effective statements along these lines, and the ones most damaging to the emergence of liberal women as political beings, were made by women themselves. During the 1874–75 protesta "crisis," *El Monitor Republicano* kept up a running battle with the conservative newspapers *La Voz de México* and *El Pájaro Verde*, in part by encouraging women to write in with a retraction of their signatures on the protests. These were dozens of these. Almost all of them in one way or another said that they would never have signed, or didn't mean to sign, because they considered commenting on politics to be, in the stock phrase, "foreign to my sex." Clementina L. de Calápiz was a little more effusive: "Dear Sir: In no. 29 of the popular newspaper that you direct... I noticed my name... and since there ought not exist in this city another person with this same given name and married name, its appearance could give the impression that I had intervened in a politico-religious matter, which is very much alien to a mother who is dedicated to inculcating in the hearts of her children ideas of rectitude, morality, and respect for the law, without making a vain ostentation of her beliefs, whatever these may be."[71] Clementina de Calápiz was a poster child for the perfect liberal woman.

For almost three months from January 1875 to the middle of March, there was scarcely a day that *El Monitor* and *El Siglo Diez y Nueve* did not feature some comment on the women's petitions and women's role in politics—including the two long imagined scenarios that I have quoted at length here—much back-and-forth with the conservative newspapers, retractions and counter-retractions of signatures, and numerous editorials. At the height of the liberal response in mid-February, there were days when there were five or six related items. Oddly, since the liberals *won* the battle to keep the Ley Orgánica, where they had lost the 1856 battle to include religious tolerance in the 1857 constitution, the commentary was characterized by a heightened degree of hysteria, compared to 1856. One explanation is the threat of religious rebellion, a reality in the west where the *religioneros*, as Brian Stauffer shows, challenged the Ley Orgánica in their own way. But another part of the explanation may lie in the militant language of the 1874–75 petitions themselves, which generally lacked the respectfulness of the 1856 petitions, the stated willingness to play by the rules of proper politics and proper gender relations. This is a point to which I will return in the chapter's conclusion.

Gender and Protest in Conservative Discourse, 1874–75

The conservative press coverage of the petition campaigns changed more fundamentally between the two episodes than was true for the liberal press. Conservatives made two major rhetorical moves and, in cooperation with women, one important strategic move. In 1856 the Catholic press, like the liberal press, had been taken aback by the number of women's petitions and by the attention they received. They shared with liberals the view that women didn't belong in politics, and the tone of their writing on women's entry into politics *on their side* was more defensive than celebratory, as we saw in chapter 4. In fact, they appeared to be more concerned with liberals' disrespect for women than with attacking the liberal view that women ought to stay out of the political arena. By the 1870s, however, conservatives, at least those writing in the press, were active and (mainly) enthusiastic supporters of women's roles in politics, and they embraced the image of women as warriors in the cause of Catholicism.

The conservative defense of women's political actions in 1856—that in signing the protests they were acting *religiously* not *politically*—was roundly rejected by *La Voz* in 1875. The paper was critical of four women who had recently retracted their support for the part of the petition that had to do with criticism of the Ley Orgánica, stating that their signatures only applied to the "religious part" (the farewell to the Sisters of Charity). "Without putting down the ladies who expressed themselves in this way . . . the distinction that they made between allowing their signatures to stand where religion is concerned and not where politics is concerned is an impossible distinction . . . at present [women] cannot live far removed from the public sphere, because public power, which attacks and insults Catholic belief, has obliged them to lift their voices when they see their faith threatened. . . . It could not be any other way."[72]

La Voz and *El Pájaro Verde* also attacked the hypocrisy of liberals—who they said claimed to support female emancipation—in attempting to keep women out of the political arena. Whereas the liberal José María Vigil in 1856 had applauded the *idea* of female equality with men, he had lamented the cause they had taken up (religious tolerance) and the tactics they were using (according to him, trying to seduce the congress). By 1874–75, however, it was the conservatives who were enthusiastically in support of (limited) female emancipation. They made fun of the liberals' continuing insistence that women should stay at home: *La Voz de México* quoted the liberal *El Eco* as saying that "the Mexican woman was born for family and home, not for getting involved with political and social questions." "What happened," *La Voz* asked sarcastically, "to emancipation? Now it's not convenient anymore."[73] *La Voz* had fun pointing out the knots into which one liberal paper had tied itself. The paper had commented that the government punished public employees when their female relatives signed the protests not because of the protests themselves, which were of no consequence, but rather because the men "could not control the skirts." "¡Ola!" *La Voz* exclaimed. "What do we have here? The government meddling in domestic affairs! . . . What about the emancipation of women? When a woman's husband, brother, etc. allows a woman to protest, it is not because he is dominated by skirts but out of respect for freedom of opinion and of conscience, a glorious victory of the century of light."[74] In a more intense vein, *La Voz* editorialized in 1875 that the liberal press, whose ideology celebrated emancipation and equality, "has no hesitation now in declaring that it is repugnant for the lovelier sex to take part in the turmoil of politics."

> What does it matter to women that they die of hunger, or see their sons degenerate, or see their religion persecuted? To the spinning wheel, to the sewing kit, to the boring routine of domestic work to which they exclusively are condemned, while men, from the back rooms of government to the mysterious machinations of the clubs, arbitrarily dictate their well-being, their lives and their consciences. Is this really consistent with your theories of liberalism and democracy?[75]

But it was the political results of female emancipation that the conservative press embraced with true enthusiasm. Women who defended the faith by petitioning were regularly praised by the press for possessing attractively manly characteristics. Catholic discourse had, of course, always featured women who were warrior saints, brave martyrs, or courageous nuns.[76] The difference now was that the petitioners were not saints, not martyrs, but rather tens of thousands of ordinary women whom the press made into embattled heroines: "They have leaped into the field of combat . . . with the valor that only Christianity has known how to inspire in women, they have thrown themselves in front of their tormentors . . . protesting energetically against infamy and sacrilege!"[77] "With manly force and noble indignation they raise their voice against the untold injuries to our religion! ... In spite of everything, they have no fear."[78] *La Voz* even argued that the ladies of Guanajuato were right: men *were* too accepting of the threat to religion; "we men ought to have provided examples of dignity and honesty, of valor and energy, but instead these examples came from this distinguished group of believers. When they say that we have been converted into Quakers, their beautiful lips utter the most just of reproaches."[79] *La Voz* also gleefully published a letter from thirty-five women from Mexico City who applauded the manly valor of the ladies from Guanajuato. "We who love Catholicism more than ... our own families and more than life itself, which we would sacrifice gladly, adhere with the vehemence of our souls as Mexican Catholics, to the memorable protesta of the *simpáticas* ladies of Guanajuato."[80]

Besides these changes in tone and theme, the conservative press and Catholic women also changed their more concrete strategies of persuasion between 1856 and 1875. In 1856 few of the petitions were actually published in the press, and most did not include the names of the signatories. As we saw, the señoras of Guanajuato in their 1874 petition noted their chagrin that in 1856 their authorship of the petitions and their awareness of what they had signed had been too easy for liberals to impugn. Thus in 1875 the strategy was to publish hundreds of petitions (by both men and women) in the Catholic press, including every signature. The appearance of tens of thousands of names in the newspapers had real visual impact.

And if this were not enough, the editor of *El Pájaro Verde* also orchestrated the collection and republication of these petitions *and* the signatures in a volume titled *El libro de las protestas*, which came out less than a year after the original protests. (Interested buyers, according to the advertisements on page 4 of *El Pájaro*, could choose whether or not to buy a roughly 330-page edition, a 600-page edition, or the full 1,125 page edition—which accounts for the fact that the handful of US libraries that hold *El libro de las protestas* have three different editions.) An additional element of the strategy to make sure the protests were taken seriously was that while *El libro de las protestas* was edited by a man, it was presented as having been conceived of and brought to fruition (in ways that the editor does not specify) by Catholic women. In other words, a volume containing protests from both sexes was said to have been orchestrated by women, giving the women's protests contained therein an additional importance and power. In 1876 one appreciative (male) supporter of this project wrote that "perhaps it was believed that those who signed were not representative of their sisters, that the majority of señoras were as removed from religion as from the other concerns of politics."[81] But, he continued, they were mistaken. "Well done, Señoras, well done!" "You have given the world solemn testimony of the true religion, and provided your Patria with a service of incalculable transcendence! ... *El libro de las protestas* is your initiative, formed by your names and informed by your example, and on it will rest the favorable judgment of history as we pass through these trying times." The massive protests against the Ley Orgánica and their publication in *El libro de las protestas* showed that "You, Señoras, have revealed yourselves to be more politically astute than the politicians" ("más políticas que los políticos").[82]

It is worth noting that while presenting *El libro de las protestas* as having been conceived by women was a strategic move, it may also be at least partly true. We know of one call for direct national action by women in which the women were clearly out ahead of the conservative press and the hierarchy. In mid-January a group of women from Celaya reached out to "all of our sisters" to participate in a demonstration in Mexico City. Their invitation was published by the Guadalajara paper *La Religión y la Sociedad*.[83] The plan was for each town and city in Mexico to name a commission of two women and one man from every town. The commissions would bring with them to Mexico City on March 25 (the first day of the new session of congress) the petitions asking for the derogation of the laws of the reform, with all signatures "legalized" so there could be no doubt whom the commissions were representing. After presenting the petitions to the congress they would proceed to the Basilica of Guadalupe, either to give thanks if their mission was successful, or to ask the virgin to give them strength to continue the fight if it failed. Women from all over the country began to make plans to come to Mexico City, including a group from faraway Chiapas.[84]

However, while the conservative press was unambiguously in favor of women's petition-writing, it was not so sure about direct political action. The Celaya call for what amounted to a women's march on the congress was a little too much. The editors of *La Religión y la Sociedad* dragged their feet for over a month before publishing the invitation. *El Pájaro Verde* shed crocodile tears over the "fact" that husbands and fathers would never permit this "necessary" but "unrealizable" and "utopian" protest to take place.[85] *La Voz de México* condescendingly argued that women had already done a great deal with their petitions, that they should keep them coming, but that they should let men, who had the right to vote, elect new officials who would amend the constitution to restore official Catholicism.[86] Petitioning was absolutely to be encouraged. Women in the streets, especially with political goals and a destination of the congress, were not.

Women's Lay Associations and the 1874–75 Petition Drive

As was true in 1856, it is logical to suppose that the proliferating women-led lay associations during the period leading up to the 1874–75 petition campaign were important parts of the national story of Catholic women in politics, but hard evidence is skimpy. There are three possible reasons why such evidence might be difficult to find. One is that the petitions were entirely priest-directed and that lay associations played no role. I don't find this explanation fatally flawed (and, as noted above, I actually find it likely in the case of the petitions that came from very small towns where the priest might be one of the only literate people in town), but for the majority of towns and cities that sent petitions I find it much less compelling than the idea that the production of women's petitions actually involved women. Those women weren't necessarily members of lay associations, but they are extremely likely to have been: by this time there were so many women's lay associations that activist Catholic women who were not members of such associations must have been very rare. Instead, it seems probable that lay associations were once again vehicles and facilitators for women's involvement in the writing and distribution of petitions, for the reasons developed in earlier chapters: that these associations gave women experience dealing with priests as partners in the promotion of parish well-being (chapters 3 and 5), and that they provided leadership, connections, and womanpower to collect hundreds of signatures (chapter 4).

The second reason that we have so little direct evidence of what seems such a logical connection may be that lay associations, as they seem to have done in 1856, actively tried to hide their connection to the petitions. Even more than in 1856—now that the laws of the reform had outlawed cofradías, and now that "pious associations," as lay groups were innocuously relabeled, were required by both church and state to stay out of politics—it was important for petitions to be seen as coming from individuals, not from groups that were church-supported or church-affiliated.[87] We get a hint of the Catholic press's desire to construct the petitions as coming from individuals and not from church-affiliated groups in an article in *La Voz*, which refuted a liberal claim that the famous Guanajuato petition was signed by women who were primarily Hijas de María: "They say that the majority of the signers are Hijas de María, as if the membership registers of this association did not give this accusation the most solemn lie."[88] The newspaper's use of the word "accusation" and its quick rebuttal of the idea that the Hijas de María had orchestrated the petition suggests that they knew signing as members of a lay association (especially a lay association like the Hijas, which was oriented to devotion and not service, and was seen as particularly fanatical and emotion-driven) was a negative.[89]

Finally, it made sense from a strategic point of view to make the petitions about individuals coming together to protest, not about lay associations sponsoring them. The more people who signed a petition, the better, especially after the decision was made to publish every name. If a petition was to carry as much weight as possible, it would be desirable, even if it was a lay organization that initiated the petition drive, to go outside its own membership and collect as many signatures as possible. In other words, lay associations could have been deeply involved in collecting signatures, but did not sign as a corporate group because their own efforts had ensured that the list of signatories included many more people than just the members.

In chapter 4 the most convincing piece of circumstantial evidence that lay associations had a role to play in organizing the 1856 petitions was the almost perfect overlap between the then-new women-led lay associations and the towns and cities that sent petitions. By no means did all towns with women-led lay associations send petitions, but every town whose women petitioned, save one, had a lay association with female officers; in other words, they had leadership and an administrative structure that could be put to use in writing the petitions or at the very least collecting signatures. By 1875, however, there were not only many more petitions but also many more cities and towns with women's lay associations (chapter 5), not all of which were captured by my research (which, as noted in chapter 2, is strongest for the center-west because of the integrity of the church archives in Michoacán and Jalisco). This means that the mapping exercise employed in chapter 4 cannot be used as confidently in this chapter to test the strength of the connection between associations and petitions in the second campaign.

Nonetheless, there are some signs that the presence of women-led lay associations continued to correlate with women's petitioning. If we focus on the center-west, where my research on the presence of lay associations is fairly complete, we can discern two distinct profiles among the towns and cities from which the sixty-six women's petitions that originated in this region came. One pattern conforms to the 1856 model: towns with large women-led lay associations. Petitions from this kind of town numbered forty-six, or 70 percent of the regional total. The other twenty included a few fairly sizeable mestizo towns that would seem to belong to the first category (for example, Sahuayo, Michoacán, and Mascota, Jalisco), but they did not have a women's lay association, or at least not one my research uncovered. But the majority were very small entities (sometimes not even pueblos), probably not large enough to support a women's lay association (e.g., the ranchería of Tecario de Salazar or Rancho del Capulín).[90] In these small places it seems likely that the priest was the prime mover behind the petitions.

But in the forty-six towns with women's associations, a strong role for them is plausible. The fact that the center-west towns disproportionately sent petitions—53 percent of the national total came from this region, despite having only 33 percent of the population—and continued disproportionately to have women-led lay associations suggests this connection, though it obviously does not prove it.[91] As I also pointed out in chapter 4 with regard to the 1856 petitions, lay associations, like the enthusiasm for petitioning, may have been an outgrowth of the demographics and religious history of the small, pious Hispanic towns in the region, and not any kind of cause of or precondition for petitioning. In other words, both phenomena may have had the same root cause. Thus, ideally, if we are to hypothesize that lay associations did have a role to play in petitioning, we would like to see some direct evidence of such a role. Let's see what we've got.

There is more direct evidence of lay association involvement in producing the petitions than there was in 1856, but not overwhelmingly so. Among the many women's petitions, only four (one from Jalapa, one from Cosalá, one from Tlaltlauquitepec, and one from Mexticatlán) frankly stated that they were sent in, respectively, by the Hijas de María, the Vela Perpetua, the Ladies of Charity, and the Sociedad Católica.[92] Brian Stauffer writes that in 1875 the Vela and the local Sociedad Católica authored the petition from Coalcomán against the Ley Orgánica, and his fine-grained local history of the town convinces me that he knows the names of the women in those associations and can match them with the signatures on the petition. But the petition itself does not acknowledge the corporate authorship, so without Stauffer's contextualizing research we would not know from the petition alone that lay associations were involved.[93] It stands to reason that the Coalcomán case was not the only one in which a lay association orchestrated a petition drive but did not so acknowledge in the petition itself.

There is also evidence that the home-visit method of signature collection in 1874–75—a method that lends itself to thinking of lay associations as organizing such visits—was used to mount the campaign. Some of the best evidence of this comes, ironically, from the testimonials published in the liberal press from women who wanted to retract or disavow their signatures. Many of these described a similar scene: a "commission of ladies" or a "commission in charge of collecting signatures" came to someone's house and asked them if they wanted to sign.[94] *La Voz*, a few years later in the context of a different petition campaign, refers to "the commissions of señoras in charge of collecting signatures" in a tone that suggests that it was common knowledge that signatures were gathered in this way.[95] Additional evidence of a sort comes from the satirical conversation among Lola and Lupe and their mothers that appeared in *El Monitor Republicano* (see above). One of the mothers says, "Listen, niña, why don't you come with us to look for signatures? All of us in the Vela Perpetua . . . go around collecting signatures; we go into the tenements, which besides being a good work, because many women sign, is a lot of fun."[96] Associating the Vela with these airheads could have been intended by the author to damage the reputation of the Vela, but this was not the central point of the piece, and I am more inclined to view this as a clue than as a dig at the Vela. It worked as satire, in other words, because it had a basis in observable or believable fact.

In sum, hard evidence to support the logic of women-led lay associations having a role to play in women's petitioning is once again not plentiful, but combining it with the indirect statistical evidence allows us to imagine that the scene described by Lola and Lupe was more or less accurate; that the ladies of the Vela Perpetua, who sat vigil two-by-two in adoration of the Blessed Sacrament, or the women of the Sociedad Católica, who worked together on so many parish projects, or other members of women-led or women-dominated associations channeled their zeal into petitioning and organizing commissions to go door-to-door collecting signatures.[97]

Conclusion

On March 19, 1875, the archbishops of Mexico, Michoacán, and Guadalajara issued a joint pastoral condemning the Ley Orgánica and calling for peaceful protest through petitioning.[98] The objective, as Cecilia Bautista García puts it, was to "motivate Catholics and citizens to produce numerous petitions against laws that were considered anti-Catholic, and to bring about their suppression."[99] This statement implies that the archbishops gave marching orders to the laity, who responded with the petition drive.[100] But the pastoral was not published until mid-March, by which time the petition drive had already peaked, and at least one hundred petitions had already been submitted. At this point the pastoral's approval of the value of petitioning was not so much prescriptive as reflecting an ongoing reality. Although it is hard to imagine that the petitions were undertaken months earlier without some nod of approval by the hierarchy—perhaps communicated in a quiet way to the Catholic press who then found a way to get the message to priests and laity—all we know for sure is that on paper, the petitions significantly preceded the pastoral. This appears, then, to have been a petition campaign whose narrative arc was substantially driven by the Catholic press and the laity and joined later by the hierarchy.[101]

Comparing this petition campaign to the one in 1856, one is struck by how the changes over time in both the petitions and the press coverage of them were in the direction of a harsher and even more gendered politics of religion. Clearly liberals still feared the power of the church, and they specifically feared the power of women allied with the church. Their diatribes against women entering politics, their sarcasm about women's understanding of what they were doing, the sheer number of articles they published that attacked the petitions and the women who signed them, and their constant efforts to question the authorship of the petitions as well as the validity of the signatures all show us that they continued to take the power of Catholic women seriously.

This tells us something interesting about the difficulties of consolidating liberal power during the Restored Republic (the period between the expulsion of the French in 1867 and the rise of Porfirio Díaz, who would rule for thirty-five years, in 1876), and it provides some insight into not only the emergence of Díaz but also the nature of his government. The Lerdo regime had doubled down on enforcing the laws of the Reform, incurring the wrath of the devout. Although the only armed rebellion against the Ley Orgánica—the "war of the religioneros" in Michoacán—failed to spread much beyond the state, Stauffer argues that it was a factor in Porfirio Díaz's decision to challenge Lerdo in 1876 and then to take a different tack in his dealings with the church.[102] If so, then the role of Catholic women, supported by the Catholic press and their own priests, can also be seen as a factor in the weakness of Lerdo, and thus the ambition, and success, of Díaz. The debates over the Ley Orgánica were vigorous and well known to a wide swath of the population, and, along with the religionero rebellion, made Lerdismo start to feel oppressively polarizing. Moderate liberals who might not approve of women writing petitions, especially angry ones, might nonetheless go over to Díaz's side because they thought he would bring some calm to this question. And he did. The solution to the problem of how to curb the overt expression of Catholic political power was the one that the Díaz regime embraced: reconciliation with the church.

Liberalism, of course, despite its core ideological confidence in progress, was by no means irreversible. In 1863 the US federal government began to try to dismantle the country's most glaringly illiberal institution: slavery. But in 1877 it abandoned its commitment to establishing the full individual rights of former slaves. Likewise, in 1856 Mexico began to try to disempower its own glaringly illiberal institution: the Catholic church. The 1874 Ley Orgánica was an attempt to advance that project by making the laws of the Reform a part of the constitution. But Catholic opposition was strong—as was conservative resistance to the full and meaningful pursuit of racial equality in the US—and in 1876, under Porfirio Díaz, the Mexican government began to water down the liberal commitment to a strict interpretation of the Reform laws and to seek accommodation with the church. Catholic men's and women's resistance to enforcement of liberal anticlerical legislation helped draw clear lines for the Díaz government regarding how far it could extend liberalism. The answer was: not as far as Lerdo had tried to go. For the rest of his thirty-five years in power, Díaz acted upon this insight and allowed the church to exist so comfortably that by 1910 it had regained much of its former economic power, rebuilt some of its old institutions and created new ones, and forged ahead on a highly successful political agenda based on lay organizing, recruitment, and cultural power, as we will see in more detail in chapter 8. It also tried to regain its control over women, though without relinquishing the alliance with them that had in many ways allowed the church to bend but not break, to resist liberalism over and over again until a group of liberals made peace with it.

There is one other point made in this chapter that I would like to underscore here: that the emergence of Catholic women as relatively powerful urban political actors unwilling to play by the rules of proper (masculine) politics and proper (hierarchical) gender relations had as its corollary a sharpened and heightened idealization of the liberal woman who stayed home and stayed out of politics. In the small literature on gender roles in nineteenth-century Mexico, a preference for women to stay home and raise children to be productive and moral citizens is usually assigned, implicitly or explicitly, to both liberals and conservatives.[103] Scholars have seen, in other words, a generalized cult of domesticity more than a Catholic or liberal one, in which the ideal woman was an *angel del hogar* ("angel of the home").[104]

Jean Franco has pointed out that for nineteenth-century liberals "the ideal of domestic life [became], if anything, more circumscribed than that described by Fray Luís de León in his classic essay on married life, *La Perfecta Casada*, written in the sixteenth century and the basis for the Catholic ideal of the family."[105] Franco went on to observe, without venturing much of an explanation, that while "women writers all over the continent" (she mentions Gertrudis Gómez de Avellaneda in Cuba, Clorinda Matto de Turner in Peru, and Harriet Beecher Stowe in the US) "struggled to find spaces for themselves within the debate on national formation . . . there are no parallels to these women in Mexico . . . Mexican women were slow to challenge the domestication of women and often fearful of taking a step into areas where their decency would be put into question."[106] She is right that liberal women in Mexico were comparatively silent. She misses an obvious explanation: that Catholic women had been so un-silent. The liberal critique of activist Catholic women in politics was shrill and powerful and, discursively, trapped liberal women in the roles that Catholic women had to a certain extent escaped through the petition drives: mothers and wives who stayed at home.

In the next chapter we will see what happened to gender roles, women's lay organizing, and women's activism in a period of softened conflict between church and state.

PART III

The Porfiriato

CHAPTER SEVEN

"Excellent Assistants of the Priest"

WOMEN AND LAY ASSOCIATIONS, 1876–1911

A REPORT ISSUED IN 1910 in Guadalajara by the directors of the Apostolate of Prayer (Apostolado de la Oración), one of the most important new lay associations to appear in the last quarter of the nineteenth century, offers valuable insights into the gendered appeal of this organization. The report promised that during the month of June—the Month of the Sacred Heart of Jesus—any household that carried out devotions dedicated to the Sacred Heart would enjoy "happiness and luck," and "a more loving husband, a more tender wife, more obedient children and more faithful and hard-working servants."[1] Painting a gentle picture of familial togetherness in devotion, it continued:

> The whole family can become involved in the holy rituals of the Sacred Heart. . . . The children can take turns preparing the altar, and you can even give them a little prize for doing so. In the houses of the wealthy the servants can take part in the family prayers, as in ancient times, and the poor can invite their neighbors to join them. . . . No house ought to be without an image of the Sacred Heart, even if it is just made of paper, since Jesus said: "I will bless the houses in which an image of my Heart is displayed and honored."[2]

In the schools, the report urged, an image of Jesus as an adolescent should be displayed, because this would appeal to the youth, and at the end of the month there should be a procession of the image through the halls and patios of the school. "Thus educated in devotion to the Sacred Heart, our youth will serve in the vanguard of future struggles for the good cause, the salvation of the family and of society."[3] In short, the members of the Apostolado constituted an "army of Apostles" in defense of Catholicism. It was an army that prayed but also took action.

That was the problem, however, as the report made clear. The defense of Catholicism needed action, but action was "a quality more widely held by men than women."[4] Men were "more influential, more solid, more persevering, and even more help for the priest," so much so that "recruiting one man is better than recruiting five women."[5] But as national reports indicated and cell-by-cell statistics confirmed, men were grossly underrepresented in the Apostolado.[6] "What can be done to encourage men to join?" the report asked plaintively. The solutions were not obvious. It could only offer the weak recommendation that men should be reminded that this was not a very onerous lay association, since the "only essential obligation of the members is to pledge to God every day that you will act during the day according to the intentions of the Sacred Heart of Jesus. All the other useful and valuable pious practices are voluntary."[7]

This chapter (like the odd-numbered chapters that preceded it) analyzes changes over time in the nature of lay associations, with particular attention to gender. In this case the temporal focus is a long one, from the end of the petition campaign of 1874–75 to end of the Díaz regime in 1911. This period has coherence because of the steady growth of lay associations that was permitted by the politics of conciliation with the church practiced by Porfirio Díaz (more on this policy in chapter 8), and encouraged by the Vatican's late nineteenth-century modernization of church administration and institutions.[8] These modernizations, embedded in a program of reform often referred to as "Romanization," were meant to more effectively battle secularism, "godless" ideologies like liberalism and socialism, and Protestantism. The chapter explores what those changes did and did not accomplish in Mexico. It shows that the church was in many ways successful in bringing about what is sometimes called the "re-Christianization" of Mexico. One of the most significant elements of Romanizing reform was the project to reseed parishes where piety and the lay associations that organized piety had withered or become decadent, with new Vatican-promoted associations that would excite the population and bring people back to church (as the homegrown Vela Perpetua had done beginning in the 1840s). However, despite efforts to encourage male participation in these lay associations—primarily by segregating male and female groups and reasserting gender hierarchy—and despite increasing insistence on the part of the Vatican and Catholic writers that women were "born for the domestic sphere," women absolutely dominated them, even some that are usually assumed to have had mostly male members.[9] This dominance put them in the vanguard of the church's political projects, as we will see in chapter 8.

"Romanization" and Lay Associations in Mexico

Romanization refers to the process by which the Vatican, beginning with the ecumenical council held in 1869–70 (Vatican I), attempted to standardize and generalize certain favored dogmas and devotions, such as the Immaculate Conception and the Sacred Heart, and later centralize ecclesiastical administration and orient it more toward Rome.[10] Clerical control over spectacular events like the coronation of the Virgin of Guadalupe in 1895 (for more on this event, see chapter 8) also increased compared to earlier grand occasions.[11] In the later stages of Romanization we see stepped-up recruitment of and improved seminary training for priests. Ideally priests would be indoctrinated with the Vatican's ethos of centralized control, exposed to the new devotions and lay associations that the Vatican particularly approved of, and taught the importance of using the tools of the modern age (schools, the press, bureaucratic organizational structures, and mass mobilizations) to achieve the church's goals. A more effectively mobilized laity, under the close supervision of the modern priest, was the goal, though better control over parish priests was also a desired outcome.

Centralization and restructuring happened everywhere in the Catholic world to some extent, with different timetables and outcomes. In Mexico, as elsewhere in Latin America where the original colonial ecclesiastical jurisdictions were huge and unwieldy, a key feature of Romanization was the creation of new bishoprics, new parishes, and new seminaries. The Vatican, in cooperation with the Mexican church, added eleven new bishoprics between 1876 and 1911 as well as ten new seminaries; created hundreds of new parishes and new priests; and brought dozens of young men to Rome for training, many of whom eventually ended up as bishops and archbishops. Other centralizing features included the introduction of new means of connecting parish priests to each other, to the hierarchy, and to Rome, such as the publication of *Boletines Eclesiásticos* that contained news of Catholic happenings all over the world; an increased pace of meetings of councils of bishops; and, in Mexico after the turn of the century, four Catholic congresses in which laymen and priests together debated the pressing issues of the day and formulated solutions.[12] All these efforts had the effect of strengthening ties among priests and Catholic men, without much attention to Catholic women, and were thus consistent with the (marginally effective) moves (which we will examine later in the chapter) to reintroduce gender hierarchies in lay associations.

More, better-trained, and better-supported priests were expected to promote the formation of lay associations that would in turn organize and mobilize the laity. Lay associations clearly increased in number in the 1890s and the first decade of the twentieth century, and most historians have assumed that this was directly tied to Romanization. They have further assumed that the new associations imported from Europe and imposed at the parish level did indeed subordinate the laity to a newly energized clergy.[13] A few scholars have questioned this priest-centric picture of religious change in the era of Romanization. Both Edward Wright-Ríos and Benjamin Smith, for Oaxaca, have emphasized that, as Wright-Ríos puts it, the "foundations upon which clergymen . . . proposed to build . . . were not as weak as they claimed. Oaxacan communities sustained rich religious institutional cultures that seasoned their response to ecclesiastical efforts to alter local organizational structures."[14] Similarly, Smith writes that the "top-down initiatives designed to modernize, Europeanize, and purify Mexican Catholicism . . . were always subject to reinterpretation and modification."[15] Instead of seeing Romanized devotions and associations as imposed willy-nilly on the pueblos, Smith emphasizes that a kind of organic re-Christianization at the local level, based on older institutions and practices, was the dominant process, and that local Catholics incorporated new institutions and practices introduced from above selectively, if at all.

Oaxaca—hypothetically along with other mainly indigenous regions or subregions of Mexico—appears to have been a case in which efforts by priests to bring in new organizations came up against the continued power of the old. Priests had to accept that their efforts would be "seasoned," as Wright-Ríos put it, by existing practices and institutions.[16] But Luis Enrique Murillo, writing on Michoacán, a state squarely in the middle of the highly Hispanized center-west, puts even more weight on the importance of local desires and actions in shaping Catholic practice during the Porfiriato than do Wright-Ríos and Smith for Oaxaca. Data showing the number of new parishes created, he writes, imply "an active Catholic Church extending its hegemonic control over a passive population. In rural Michoacán, however, it was local communities that were demanding a greater Catholic Church presence."[17]

I find these authors' emphases on the importance of local actors to be attractive at a theoretical level and to align with my own conclusions about the importance of local actors in the earlier part of the nineteenth century. However, as I show in this chapter, Romanization enjoyed considerable success in both the archdiocese of Mexico and the archdiocese of Michoacán, at least as measured by the ubiquity with which new Vatican-approved associations appeared in parish after parish, often creating lay organizations where there had been none before. For me the question is not whether Romanization was a major force—it clearly was—but whether and how the nature of its success (from the Vatican's point of view) changes when we take into consideration the outsized role of women in organizing and administering the new lay associations.

I will argue that gendering Romanization makes it appear to be more than just an inexorable imposition of Vatican control over lay piety, and more like a joint effort between priests and (mainly) women that was in some ways an extension of the dynamic formation of the new associations in the earlier part of the century, such as the Vela Perpetua when it came to devotional associations, or the conferences of St. Vincent de Paul when it came to Catholic service and charity. In other words, Romanization brought priests who wanted to reform and modernize their parishes even more closely into line with the women of the parish who had been embracing these outlets for female energies for decades.

Associations New and Old

Although Mexico's bishops and archbishops were keen to introduce into every parish the new Vatican-approved devotions and associations that were sweeping Catholic Europe, the difficulty of doing so in the more isolated and largely indigenous parishes of Mexico is clear from a parish survey of the archbishopric of Mexico conducted in 1897 (and lends further weight to Wright-Ríos's and Smith's argument that in indigenous Oaxaca it was not always easy to "Romanize" devotional life). The survey indicates that most of the parish head towns (*cabeceras*) in the late 1890s had at least two or three lay associations (the average was three, not including Mexico City parishes). But it was quite rare for the smaller towns and settlements subject to the cabecera to have any independent associations at all, most likely because they did not have a permanent priest who could supervise the organization.[18] A few priests indicated that some of the people in the pueblos were members of associations in the head towns, but descriptions of the roads connecting many of these populations to the centers make it unlikely that they were regular participants in much more than the annual functions.

The parish priest of Tasquillo narrated an extreme case. He began his response to the questionnaire by saying that his parish was very beautiful, but that religious indifference reigned in it.[19] In the cabecera, the single lay association was the Vela Perpetua, with only twenty female members. Outside of the cabecera, there was nothing. In the pueblo of San Juanico, some ten miles from Tasquillo, Mass was only said once a year (this was true of all the pueblos). There were no lay associations, and the municipal authorities were vigilant opponents of religion. To illustrate this point, the priest recounted an episode that occurred during Carnival. The townspeople, "as is their custom," brought their personal or household images (*santos*) to the Mass, accompanied by drums and whistles. But after the Mass, as people were leaving the church, the municipal president seized the santos and put them in jail. The images remained in prison for three or four days, until the priest could persuade the president to release them to their owners.

In terms of the project to use lay associations to "moralize" the more remote rural populations and bring them firmly into the Romanized world, then, the church had limited success, as the Oaxaca cases studied by Wright-Ríos and

Smith also suggest.[20] In the cities and larger towns, however, as always, lay associations were plentiful and in most places were clearly on the increase during the Porfiriato. In fact, overlap in some cities became a problem. Dolores de la Vega, president of the Asociación de la Purísima established in the church of La Concepción in Mexico City, had a rude surprise in 1899 when she was informed that during the brief time her organization had been suspended while it awaited the appointment of a new chaplain, a similar association had been founded in the same church, and she would need to find a new church for hers.[21] In San Juan de los Lagos in 1909 there was a long discussion about whether the Asociación de Hijas de María, whose members wore the Miraculous Medal, was sufficiently distinct from the Asociación de la Medalla Milagrosa that both could be allowed to exist in the same church.[22] And in Mexico City in 1885 the archbishop responded to a request by the women of the Guardia de Honor del Santísimo Sacramento, housed in the church of Santa Catalina de Sena, to move to the Sagrario by saying that the Vela Perpetua had existed in the Sagrario for many years and that the Guardia should find a church in which a vigil before the Host wasn't already established.[23]

Where lay associations were concerned, perhaps the most striking phenomenon during this period was the rather sudden appearance of three Vatican-favored associations dedicated to the Sacred Heart of Jesus.[24] Jesuits had promoted this devotion in New Spain since the 1730s, but at least in the colonial records I have examined, lay associations dedicated to advancing the devotion were not widespread. But in the Catholic world of the late nineteenth century there was an explosion of such associations. The Apostolado de la Oración and the Guardia de Honor del Sagrado Corazón de Jesús were both relatively recent inventions, and the older Asociación del Sagrado Corazón de Jesús was now newly endorsed by Rome.

Papal interest in promoting the Sacred Heart began in the middle of the nineteenth century, and it had political implications from the beginning, quickly becoming associated in France with anti-liberal political elements, a posture that lined up nicely with the feelings of the Mexican church and laity alike in the post-Reform era.[25] In the mid-1870s Pius IX urged his bishops to exhort the faithful to consecrate themselves to the Sacred Heart. In response, bishops and priests in Mexico energetically encouraged the devotion and the lay associations dedicated to it. As we will see below, the Sacred Heart had a particular appeal to women, historically and emotionally. But it was also appealing to a church that was looking for exciting new devotions with which to help expand, fortify, mobilize, and control the Catholic base.

We are fortunate to have mid or late Porfirian parish surveys in three archdioceses—Mexico, Michoacán, and Oaxaca—that covered a large majority

Table 7.1. Ten most popular associations in the archdiocese of Mexico (1896), Michoacán (1896), and Oaxaca (1908) according to the parish surveys conducted in those years

Archdiocese of Mexico	Archdiocese of Michoacán	Archdiocese of Oaxaca
Sagrado Corazón de Jesús (n = 38)	Vela Perpetua (n = 50)	Apostolado de la O. (n = 22)
Vela Perpetua (30)	Guardia Honor SCJ (31)	Sgdo Corazón de Jesús (12)
San José (28)	Apostolado de la O. (25)	Sgdo Corazón de María (11)
Apostolado de la O. (26)	Hijas de María (21)	Carmen (11)
Guadalupe (24)	Ladies of Charity (14)	Rosario (10)
Hijas de María (21)	Third Orders (10)	Propagación de la Fe (9)
Guardia Honor SCJ (11)	San José (9)	Santísimo Sacramento (6)
Santísimo Sacramento (11)	Carmen (9)	Guadalupe (6)
Ladies of Charity (10)	Escapulario Carmen (7)	San José (5)
La Purísima (7)	Rosario (7)	Asoc. del Catequismo (4)
		Vela Perpetua (4)

Total

206 (75 percent of total number of associations in survey, n = 275)	183 (78 percent of total, n = 235)	100 (77 percent of total, n = 130)

Sources: AHAMex parish surveys from 1896–97, AHAMich parish surveys from 1896, AHAO parish surveys from 1908. In all three cases the surveys are scattered in different boxes, so they do not include all parishes. It is particularly important to note that the parishes in the archdiocesan capitals were not included in these surveys, for reasons that remain unclear. They may have been surveyed differently or were under the direct purview of the archbishop, unlike the outlying parishes (although an 1885 survey of the archbishopric of Mexico did include Mexico City parishes). This omission most obviously skews the data for the Archdiocese of Mexico because of the importance of Mexico City. Further, the rural/provincial city bias means that associations such as the Conferencias de San Vicente de Paul are underrepresented here, since they tended to cluster particularly in urban settings. Outside of the capitals, however, the parishes that answered the survey represent a fairly large proportion of all parishes, especially for Mexico and Michoacán. For Mexico, I found surveys from 72 parishes and 25 vicarías fijas, or about 73 percent of the total number of parishes and 42 percent of the *vicarías fijas* in the archdiocese; for Michoacán, I found 55 parishes or 86 percent of the total (I also found 6 vicarías); for Oaxaca, I have 45 parishes, or 34 percent. Many thanks to Eddie Wright-Ríos for making his notes from the Oaxaca survey available to me. Parish totals from Vera, *Catecismo*.

of parishes and allow us to make some generalizations about the extent to which "Roman" associations like those dedicated to the Sacred Heart, as well as others promoted by the diocesan hierarchy, had penetrated the spiritual landscape (see Table 7.1). Of the three Sacred Heart associations, the Archicofradía del Sagrado Corazón de Jesús was the most structurally similar to other devotional associations: the faithful paid a small fee to join a local association, committed to giving alms to support the annual function and monthly masses, and elected the usual officers to govern the association and liaise with the priest. The devotion invited the faithful to identify with the sufferings of Jesus, and respond to the sacrificial offering of grace by Jesus by making amends.[26] The main purpose of the association was to make sure members had access to last rites before dying.[27]

The two newer Sacred Heart organizations changed how the image was venerated.[28] The Apostolado de la Oración, which first appeared in Mexico in the mid-1870s, was, as its name implies, more "apostolic" than the archicofradía: it actively sought to recruit new members, working to place images of the Sacred Heart in dormitories and classrooms and hospitals and other public places, urging members to wear the scapular, distributing issues of the Catholic press, handing out prayer topics for each month.[29] June was "Mission month," when special efforts to recruit new members were made. To this apostolic end, the association was highly organized, with a national headquarters, local centers, and "guardians" (*celadores*) who not only governed the members of their "choir" but also monitored their religious compliance and morality. The Apostolado was easy to join: you just had to add your name to the register and there was no fee—although there was a clear expectation that new members would purchase the scapular or medal of the organization. It was also easy to practice. It required daily prayer in the morning (suggested topics were printed in newspapers like *La Idea Católica* and distributed at meetings), and a daily rosary in honor of the Virgin Mary "since it is easier to approach Jesus through his Holy Mother."[30] The Apostolado was first founded in Mexico in Querétaro in 1874 and spread rapidly in the center-west.[31] In Guanajuato, it was said to be "flourishing" by 1877, and multiple associations also existed in Jalisco and Michoacán by then.[32] It did not really take off nationally until the 1890s, but then it thrived; it was by far the most common lay association in Oaxaca by 1908, and already by 1896 it was the third most common in both Mexico and Michoacán among the associations in the surveys.[33]

The 1890s were also the years when the third of the big Sacred Heart associations, the Guardia de Honor del Sagrado Corazón de Jesús, began to catch fire after having been brought to Mexico in the late 1880s.[34] It appears that the great success of the Apostolado built up enough enthusiasm for the Sacred Heart that a somewhat more demanding devotion could also thrive. The archbishop of Michoacán, in founding the Guardia de Honor in Morelia in 1889, took note of the rapid development of the cult of the Sacred Heart in the diocese in the past decade, which he attributed to the work of the Apostolado.[35] The Guardia de Honor divided the hours of the day among its members, and required them to pray in front of the Host for an hour.[36] Despite this significant demand on members' time, it was extremely popular, especially in Michoacán, where there were thirty-one Guardias de Honor dedicated to the Sacred Heart counted in the 1896 survey, making it was the second most popular lay association in the late nineteenth century for that archdiocese (see Table 7.1).

There were also other associations favored by the Vatican. One of the most popular was the Asociación del Culto Perpetuo del Señor San José. This was a favorite of Leo XIII and was also heavily promoted by Archbishop Pedro Loza in the 1870s in Guadalajara, which had an Asociación de San José in almost every parish by the early 1880s, and by 1888 was said to have half a million members.[37] There had been an older, colonial-era lay association dedicated to San José but the new association was meant to replace it. In fact, in 1901 the archbishop of Michoacán was annoyed that some of the "now extinguished" older associations still existed, while the new version was not yet present in every parish (as he had ordered in 1899).[38] Priests, he instructed, must immediately dissolve all but the "true" association, the only one authorized in the archdiocese. The new Asociación de San José was popular with the hierarchy during this period in part because it was a vehicle for collecting funds to support the grooming and training of young men for the priesthood.[39] As we have seen, improved training for priests was one of the goals of the Vatican during this period. This new function of the devotion to St. Joseph complemented the still-useful "message" of the older association that indigenous men should model their behavior on Joseph's piety and acceptance.

To reiterate, the Vatican especially fostered all four of these associations—the three dedicated to the Sacred Heart plus the Asociación de San José. They constituted approximately one-third of the associations in the Mexico and Michoacán surveys in 1896 and the Oaxaca survey in 1908. But the other four top associations overall in Table 7.1 were more vigorously promoted by bishops, parish priests, and members of the Jesuit and Misionero orders located in Mexico than by the papacy.[40] They were highly valued by these officials for their fundraising ability, energy, piety, and good example. The Vela Perpetua, for example, remained very attractive to hierarchy and laity alike.[41] During his visits in the 1870s and 1880s, Guadalajara's Pedro Loza included, in his instructions to every priest whose parish did not already have a Vela, some formulaic but at the same time impassioned language to the effect that it was very much in the spiritual interests of his flock to establish one as soon as possible.[42] His insistence appears to have paid off; by 1885 it seems there were few parishes in Guadalajara that did *not* have a Vela: a Vela de Señoras, at least, and fairly often a Vela de Señores, as well, was recorded in twenty-three of the twenty-seven parishes that were visited by Loza between 1880 and 1885. In the archbishopric of Michoacán, the Vela was present in fifty out of sixty-one parishes represented in the 1896 survey, some of them smaller, poorer parishes that might not have taken the initiative to establish a Vela without episcopal pressure. By 1912 there was a Vela in every one of the archdiocese's sixty-four parishes, including ten that had both a men's and a women's group.[43] Nor did the bishops stop at pressing the Vela on the poorer parishes. In Guadalajara there was a major push to establish Velas not just in parish churches but also in the smaller *vicarías* in the first decade of the twentieth century. Virtually all the numerous Velas that were founded between 1902 and 1913 in Guadalajara were established not in parish churches but in auxiliaries. The extent to which the bishopric tried to make founding a Vela as easy as possible is suggested by the mass production of an approval form in which the name of the town and the name of the priest in charge could simply be filled in. In the archbishopric of Mexico, the presence of the Vela Perpetua in smaller indigenous towns often came as part of a mission visit, helping to account for the strong presence of the organization throughout the archbishopric.[44] In Oaxaca, however, the Vela never caught on; there were only four Velas out of the 130 associations listed in the 1908 questionnaire.

The new/old Asociación de Hijas de María also continued to be pushed by bishops and missions. As we saw in chapter 5, the Hijas de María had originally been established among the girls taught by the Sisters of Charity in the early 1860s, and when the Sisters were disbanded by the Lerdo regime in 1875, expectations that the new association would survive were low. But new Catholic girls' schools such as the Colegio de Niñas de Nuestra Señora de Guadalupe in Morelia and new associations such as the Hijas de María Josefinas, a kind of disguised active monastic order founded by Cesárea Ruiz de Esparza y Dávalos in 1872, took over where the Sisters left off and made sure that young schoolgirls were still enlisting in the Hijas and setting an example of morality and virtue.[45] In 1898 there were over three hundred Hijas de María associations in Mexico, an increase of over two hundred fifty since 1875.[46] The Hijas were tied with the Guardia del Honor del Sagrado Corazón and the Asociación del Sr. San José as the fourth most common association in the three archbishoprics combined.

The next of the overall top associations was strongly favored by Mexican bishops, and especially the archbishop of Mexico, Pelagio Antonio Labastida y Dávalos, who led the campaign to crown the virgin in 1895. This was the Asociación de Nuestra Señora de Guadalupe. It is true, however, as Table 7.1 shows, that at the time of the surveys its popularity was mainly limited to the archbishopric of Mexico. One of the main problems afflicting the Mexican church, according to one priest who sought to animate the cult of Mary in the late 1870s, was "great indifference in devotion toward the Virgen de Guadalupe."[47] The association did not begin to thrive in Michoacán until after 1900, and in 1908 was still not very common in Oaxaca.[48] It was strong enough in the archdiocese of Mexico, however, to rank seventh overall among the associations represented in the three surveys.

Finally, the eighth overall were the conferences of señoras of St. Vincent de Paul. Underrepresented here because of the rural/small-town bias of the surveys (as noted in Table 7.1, the Mexico City parishes did not report, nor did those in Morelia or Oaxaca City), the conferences were tolerated and mildly encouraged by the Vatican but did not fall into the category of easy-to-join, easy-to-practice, accessible devotions that the Vatican especially favored.[49] But they were much lauded by bishops and priests, for whom their charitable efforts were essential to the reputation of the church locally. As the conservative paper *El Tiempo* wrote in 1884, priests invested great effort in expanding membership in this society (as well as the Hijas de María), "so that the good works performed by them, to the applause of the Catholic world and to the benefit of many souls, will increase every day."[50] The Catholic press regularly reported the numbers of sick who had been cured and clothes that had been distributed and souls that had been saved by the various conferences, according to their annual reports. A 1905 report to the archbishop from the Consejo Central Arquidiocesano de las Conferencias de Señoras in Michoacán notes that the growth of the conferences "has been powerful this year" thanks to a pastoral letter that called for their establishment in every parish, vicario, and capellanía, all reporting to the Consejo Central. A circular from Archbishop Jacinto López y Romo in Guadalajara in 1900 also called for a conference of men and one of women in every parish, by which time there were already nine conferences in the capital city alone and nineteen in the rest of the archdiocese, with over eleven thousand members ("What a phalanx!" commented *El País*.)[51] By 1911 the number of active conference members nationally had more than quintupled since 1875, to over twenty-one thousand.[52]

Table 7.2 shows that the top eight associations overall, all of which we know to have been highly promoted by either the Vatican or the hierarchies or both, comprised about two-thirds of the associations that appeared in the surveys from Mexico and Michoacán.[53] Despite the continued presence in Oaxaca of a range of more traditional cofradías—there the Vatican-favored associations only accounted for 38 percent of the associations in the surveys, especially striking given that the Oaxaca survey was conducted over a decade later than the other two—I think we still have to interpret these results as a fairly impressive Romanization success story. It was not unusual to find parishes in which some combination of these eight represented the only lay associations in existence. Although there is no parish survey for the last years of the Díaz regime in Mexico and Michoacán, my sense is that these eight would still be dominant, with the Apostolado perhaps at the top of the list by 1910 and associations dedicated to Guadalupe more important than before, but the others still very prominent.

The predominance of the lay organizations we associate with Romanization and/or episcopal centralization and standardization was not, of course, as these numbers indicate, complete, and indeed an alternate way to interpret the data is to emphasize the continued variety of lay associations. Anywhere from two-thirds of the associations (in Oaxaca) to about one-third (in Michoacán and Mexico) were associations that only appeared in a small number of parishes.

Table 7.2. Distribution of the eight most common associations in order of overall numbers

Archdiocese of Mexico	Archdiocese of Michoacán	Archdiocese of Oaxaca
Vela Perpetua (30)	Vela Perpetua (50)	Vela Perpetua (4)
Apostolado de la Oración (26)	Apostolado de la Oración (25)	Apostolado de la Oración (22)
Sagrado Corazón de Jesús (38)	Sagrado Corazón de Jesús (0)	Sagrado Corazón de Jesús (12)
Señor San José (28)	Señor San José (9)	Señor San José (5)
Hijas de María (21)	Hijas de María (21)	Hijas de María (0)
Guardia de Honor del SCJ (11)	Guardia de Honor del SCJ (31)	Guardia de Honor del SCJ (0)
N.S. de Guadalupe (24)	N.S. de Guadalupe (0)	N.S. de Guadalupe (6)
Conferencia de SVP (10)	Conferencia de SVP (14)	Conferencia de SVP (0)
Total		
188 (68 percent)	150 (64 percent)	49 (38 percent)

Sources: AHAMex parish surveys from 1896, AHAMich parish surveys from 1896, AHAO parish surveys from 1908.

These were sometimes colonial holdovers, seemingly a more common phenomenon in the archbishoprics of Mexico and Oaxaca than in Michoacán.[54] This makes sense considering the devastation of the cofradía system in Michoacán (see chapter 2).[55] But they were also relatively new associations formed to support local devotions, like the Virgen de la Salud in Pátzcuaro, the Virgen de la Paz in Indaparapeo, or El Señor de la Piedad in La Piedad (all in Michoacán). This means that in the larger parishes that could support multiple lay organizations, the strikingly common presence of some of the Romanizing associations like the Sacred Heart or the Apostolado, or increasingly national episcopally encouraged organizations like the Vela, were balanced by at least a degree of local variety.

It is also true that not all Romanizing associations thrived. The Sagrada Familia, for example, seems to have been a bust in all three archbishoprics during this period (though let us keep in mind that the Mexico City parishes did not report).[56] It started out with strong support from both the papacy and the hierarchy: the pope ordered it to be established in every parish in 1892, and the archbishop of Mexico reiterated the order in 1898.[57] Obediently, many priests tried to drum up enthusiasm for it. But as the priest of San Antonio Polotitlán said in 1898, he had established the association in 1893, and convinced 147 families to join, but there the project had stalled.[58] Meanwhile, the priest of Soyamiquilpan had only been able to sign up nine families, and the priest of Tepetlaoxtoc stated that despite doing everything he could to "reanimate" the association, only a few people remained.[59] In 1907 the archbishop of Mexico again insisted that the Sagrada Familia be founded in every parish. The new disposition, he said, was necessary because despite the 1892 papal brief and his own decree, the association had either not been introduced, had failed, or had neglected to send a report to the national director of the association (which probably implied failure).[60] In neither the 1896 Michoacán nor the 1908 Oaxaca questionnaire did the Sagrada Familia appear in a single parish.[61] Why? The reasons are not obvious, especially since the Sagrada Familia did achieve more success in the later twentieth century than at this time. One difference between it and other Roman or episcopal favorites was that it was directed at men, especially working-class men, as heads of their families. The data presented in the next section leads me to hypothesize that the most successful associations, by contrast, were ones that were not only open to women but also invited them to lead and organize.

Women and Men in Lay Associations
MOTIVATIONS FOR JOINING

Before turning to the evidence that women continued to dominate lay associations in the Porfiriato, it makes sense first to consider gendered motivations for joining. The women who made decisions to become members of lay associations in the late nineteenth century were over a generation removed from the women who, with their priests, reenvisioned the lay association as capable of being led by women in the 1840s. Can we discern any changes in the reasons why women, in particular, were attracted to joining the new associations in the Porfiriato?

The new women's devotional associations that began to appear in the 1840s—with their emphasis on inside-the-church practices, personal connection to Jesus, and simplified business practices—were both highly appealing to women and also more suited for female leadership and female dominance than the colonial cofradías. The late nineteenth-century devotional associations doubled down on those characteristics of emotional access and practicality. The Vela Perpetua had made friendship with Jesus and accompanying him so he would not be alone in the church an important element of the vigil. The Sacred Heart associations continued and built upon that emotional connection between Jesus and women. Historians have pointed to the Sacred Heart's non-elitist inclusivity and its accessible and emotion-inspiring imagery—the "fleshy" wounded heart that burned with the flames of Christ's love for all mankind—to explain its appeal to both men and women, but especially women, not only because they could identify with Jesus's sacrifice for his "children," but also because it was a devotion derived from visions of Christ experienced by a woman, sister Margaret Mary Alacoque, that women since the seventeenth century had pressured the Vatican to recognize and elevate.[62]

The late nineteenth-century devotional associations also greatly simplified becoming and remaining a member of a lay association and fully participating in its practices. As we saw in chapter 1, colonial cofradías put limitations on how much women's pious energy could be enlisted in advancing the organization, but the post-1840 associations, including the new ones in the Porfiriato, tapped those energies by providing ways for individual women, at any hour of the day that was convenient to them, to participate in the activities of the association as well as establish a one-on-one relationship with a particular saint, Jesus, or an advocation of Mary. The new associations were, if anything, even easier to join and participate in (as the report of the Apostolado summarized at the beginning of this chapter indicated), often just requiring adding your name to a list. And if they were sometimes more complicated to run than the Vela—they might be wealthier and they might be connected to a national or regional office and responsible for reporting to them—by this time there was no question that female treasurers and secretaries could easily handle the demands of office.

Meanwhile, the service organizations that also appeared first in the 1840s and really came into their own in the 1860s had a different kind of appeal—more bound up with service to the community and the ability to bask in community approbation, and more suited to middle- and upper-class women who could devote a lot of time and energy to the organizations. But they shared with the devotional associations an administrative structure that was manageable by female officers, an opportunity for female leaders to shine, and the knowledge that their activities were saving souls as well as improving material conditions for the Catholic poor. There were not as many new service organizations in the Porfiriato as there were devotional ones. This seems strange in light of the fact that the roots of Social Catholicism in Mexico were in this period. But Social Catholicism did not really begin to thrive in Mexico until after the turn of the century, and when it did, its focus was more on workers' circles than on "traditional" service organizations (more on this below). Nonetheless, both the Sociedad Católica and the conferences of St. Vincent de Paul continued to operate and (especially in the case of the Vincentian association) grow, if more slowly than the exploding number of devotional associations. It is worth mentioning here (though I will come back to it in the epilogue) that the earliest version of the best-known women-led lay association in post-revolutionary Mexico, the Damas Católicas, was a service organization very much in the mold of the post-1860s ones. An innovation of both devotional and service organizations during the Porfiriato was an emphasis on recruitment: getting friends, family, and neighbors to join. This was an area in which women were well-suited to excel, and it inclined female-dominated associations to reproduce gender balances in favor of women.

Finally, women in the late nineteenth century may also have been particularly drawn to the new associations because they put such an emphasis on shaping and reinforcing Catholic values, especially among the young. The dangers of losing Catholic youth to crime and suicide and debauchery were constantly impressed on the readers of Catholic newspapers, as we will see in more detail in chapter 8. The desire to instill Catholic morality in the young seems to have increased during this period when the secular state became more fully consolidated every year and secular schools, which were forbidden to teach Catholic doctrine, multiplied. Imparting "morality" had long been considered the primary job of mothers, whether liberal or Catholic, and so the lay associations' commitment to *moralización* may have had a particular appeal to women.

CRUNCHING THE NUMBERS

The data are so compelling that I do not need to dwell excessively on these numbers, but since the literature does not appreciate the extent to which women formed the leadership and usually the large majority of members in lay associations, it is important to establish this fact quite clearly and unequivocally. I use two methods to show the dominance of women in the leadership and membership of lay associations during the Porfiriato. First, I provide a global look at all associations in the archbishopric of Mexico, whose 1896–97 parish survey was the only one to include data for most parishes on gender makeup and officers in lay associations. Second, I offer snapshots of selected parishes and institutions outside of the archbishopric of Mexico.

The answers to the parish association questionnaire sent in by priests in the archbishopric of Mexico allows us to identify 127 associations that were either all-female or mixed-sex with female leadership, and only 25 associations that were either all-male or mixed-sex with male leadership. As Table 7.1 shows, there was a big drop-off in the number of associations in the archbishopric between the top six and the bottom four. So in the interest of limiting mind-numbing statistics, I will concentrate here on these top six, all dominated by women.[63]

Twenty-four of the 28 associations dedicated to San José—an association that some might assume to have been directed toward men, since St. Joseph had been seen since the colonial period as a model for men, and particularly indigenous men—reported at least some details on membership and leadership composition by gender, and of these, 15 were led by women and nine by men.[64] The membership in the female-led organizations was approximately double that of the male-led organizations.

In the other five top associations of the archbishopric, the dominance of women is even more striking. Of the 29 Sacred Heart cofradías that gave gender balance information, 27 were led by women.[65] Similarly, there were 17 women-led Apostolados and only three led by men.[66] Twenty-seven Vela Perpetuas were either all women, or had mixed-sex membership but female officers. There were only three parishes with both a Vela de Señoras and a Vela de Señores: Malinalco, where the women's group had 450 members and the men's 50; Villa del Carbon, where the women numbered 444 and the men 82; and Chicoloapan, with 36 men and 32 women. Like the others, women dominated the associations dedicated to Guadalupe: 17 of the 24 that submitted detailed reports were either all-female or mixed with female officers. (Contrary to some historians' assumption that Marian associations were women's associations, the Guadalupan associations and others did attract men, and there were seven with male leadership, including two all-male associations.)[67] The 21 Asociaciones de Hijas de María, finally, were by definition all-female.

As noted, this detailed data is all from the archbishopric of Mexico. To gauge whether the pattern of female dominance prevailed elsewhere, we turn to snapshots of individual towns or associations. Let's begin with an exemplary parish (from the point of view of the church) in which both men and women, energized by their priests, were active in lay associations: La Piedad, Michoacán.[68] La Piedad was a small city of 33,000 served by only five priests, and yet the population was, as membership figures show, highly mobilized in the service of the church. The episcopal visitor in 1904 listed 18 associations, many of them with huge memberships. The Vela Perpetua de Señores, for example, with 1,060 members, must have been one of the largest men's Velas in the republic. But in La Piedad the Vela de Señoras dwarfed it, with 4,119 members. The gender imbalance between men and women in the two Apostolados was less stark: there were 3,437 men in their gender-segregated organization, and 4,587 women in theirs, though the visitor commented that the women's group "works harder and reaches a larger population" than the men. He credited the Apostolado with achieving in four years what through other means would have been unattainable: that something like 4,000 men and "a much larger number of women" from the rancherías around the town received confession and Communion twice a year. In addition to the men's and women's Velas and Apostolados, there were also the following all-female organizations: the Corte de María (one each for señoras and señoritas), the Congregación de San Luis Gonzaga (one each for niñas and señoritas), the Madres Católicas, the Cofradía de Nuestra Señora del Carmen with 2,003 female members, the Hijas de María with 151 members, and the Conferencia de San Vicente de Paul for señoras. In addition there were three mixed-sex cofradías: the Archicofradía del Ynmaculado Corazón de María, the Cofradía de Nuestra Señora del Rosario, and the "very numerous" Cofradía del Sr. de la Piedad. The only other all-male association besides the men's Vela and the men's Apostolado was the Obreros Católicos, about which the visitor did not comment other than to note its presence, so we do not know how large or active it was. La Piedad, then, is a town in which the male population was far from reluctant to participate, indeed was quite enthusiastic about joining Catholic societies. But associations were still dominated by women.

In other places, the contrast was even more vivid. Combined, the five lay associations in Salamanca (Guanajuato) in 1896 included 1,200 women members and 220 men.[69] In Tehuacán (Puebla), where "piety, above all on the part of the fair sex, is very complete," the women's Apostolado numbered over 4,000 female members in 1887, while the men's group had 400.[70] In Huanímaro, Guanajuato, in 1899 the Asociación Josefina had 409 women and 22 men.[71] The Asociación del Sr. San José in Villa Morelos, Michoacán had over 900 female members and about 200 men in 1911.[72] Finally, in the archbishopric of Guadalajara in 1910, of 39 Apostolados that provided information on their officers, 26 had female officers (12 of them were all-female associations, 14 were mixed sex), and another 7 were mixed sex with both male and female officers. Only 4 were mixed sex with male officers, and there were just two all-male associations.[73]

Social Catholicism and Men's and Women's Workers' Circles

Before turning to the relationship between priests and women leaders of associations during the Porfiriato, we should account for a different kind of new lay organization: Catholic workers' associations. The earliest Catholic workers' groups were fairly simple mutual aid societies, a subsection of a larger group of non-church-affiliated *mutualistas* that began to develop in the absence of cofradías in the late 1860s, and flourished in the 1880s and into the 1890s.[74] It is difficult to know how many of these mainly artisan (or wives of male artisans) and mainly male groups should be identified as "Catholic" since many of them participated in church events, such as the annual procession to honor the Virgin of Guadalupe, without being otherwise affiliated with the church. But Catholic workers' societies in Mexico City are definitely undercounted in the most straightforward source of information about the mutualistas as a group, the directories regularly published in *La Convención Radical Obrera*. "El Alma de María," for example, a women's group that debuted in 1886 to great fanfare in a function attended by the archbishop, does not appear on the list.[75] It operated as a mutualista but was not a workers' organization and called itself instead a Sociedad Católica de Beneficencia. Its stated goal, besides mutual aid for members, was to provide the children of workers with a school that would teach religion and separate them from "pernicious and destructive" doctrines. The Workers' Congress and *La Convención Radical Obrera* were not fans of this Catholic society; the congress did not recognize it, and so it did not appear in the annual directory.[76] (As an aside, the directory did include at least one other mutual aid society that was explicitly not composed of workers but rather of "señoras y señoritas de hogar": "Esperanza de la Patria.")[77]

As industrialization and factory organizing increased in the late 1890s, mutual aid societies declined in favor of associations that were more aggressive about wages, work conditions, and strikes.[78] This provided an opening for the Catholic workers' societies that became a priority of the church after the turn of the century as part of the growing strength of the doctrine of Social Catholicism.[79] Most famously articulated in 1891 by Leo XIII in the encyclical *Rerum Novarum: Rights and Duties of Capital and Labor*, Social Catholicism called for owners and workers to come together under the church's moralizing gaze in order to improve working conditions through class harmony (not revolution or class struggle).[80] The movement was predicated on the idea that the local priest would facilitate the formation of Catholic working-class organizations with social as well as religious goals; these groups would then identify worker needs and contribute funds to meet these needs through dues. Catholic Workers' Circles sponsored and helped fund professional development in the form of night schools, libraries, and vocational schools; provided family assistance (e.g., childcare centers, recreational centers); and developed financial institutions that would serve workers, like credit unions and savings banks. They also supported workplace issues like higher wages and bans on child labor.

In these functions the Catholic Workers' Circles were superficially comparable to the other working-class organizations of the period, but they also bore fundamental similarities to other Catholic lay associations, in that they shared the core goals of maintaining and promoting the Catholic faith and Catholic morality. Failure to maintain moral standards as defined by the church (no drunkenness, for example) might result in loss of access to benefits.[81] A story in *El Tiempo* about the rapidly growing Sociedad de Obreros Católicos de Santa María de Guadalupe, in Aguascalientes, spelled out the difference between the goals of secular unions and Catholic unions: "Catholic mutualism opens a path that allows workers to avoid the unhealthy and disastrous ideas of socialism and remain under the holy auspices of Religion. In Aguascalientes we applaud this triumph of Religion over the worker who just wants to live an orderly and solid life of honest labor, without envying the good fortune of the rich or falling victim to the illusion of false self-enrichment by means of violence."[82]

Social Catholicism and its attitude toward labor in particular has been an attractive topic for some historians of the Mexican church during the Porfiriato because it puts the church in a somewhat progressive and modern light, even anticipating some of the labor reforms of the revolutionary era.[83] But from the perspective of Mexican social and labor history in the Porfiriato, and definitely from the perspective of women's history, Social Catholicism was not as important as it may be in intellectual history narratives. First, its influence in Mexico was quite late; most historians of the movement do not claim that it had much impact until the first decade of the twentieth century, certainly not before the foundation of the Catholic newspaper *El País*—an advocate of Social Catholicism—in 1899 and probably not before Leo XIII's last encyclical in 1902, which articulated the idea of Christian democracy and "inspired many young Catholics to redouble their commitment to 'social action,'" or the first of the four major Catholic congresses that were held in Mexico in the first decade of the twentieth century, the one at Puebla in 1903.[84] (Many of the ideas and projects articulated at these congresses did become a prominent part of the church's agenda after the Revolution, when "social action" took center stage in Catholic efforts to combat the social agenda of the Revolution.)

Second, while there is no question that Social Catholicism–inspired workers' organizations were new features of the associational landscape and represented a notable effort by the church to compete with socialists and anarchists for the loyalty of workers, in the end the number of Catholic Workers' Circles was not huge compared to other lay associations. Archbishop Atenógenes Silva of Michoacán promoted workers' circles perhaps as vigorously as any other ecclesiastical leader, and in 1905 there were said to be 36,000 members in 30 associations of Obreros Católicos in the archdiocese.[85] This seems quite impressive for a region without a major industrial presence. But if we recall that in one small town in Michoacán, La Piedad, there were over 8,000 members of a single association (the Apostolado de la Oración), we gain some perspective on the impact of the Obreros Católicos. And in other dioceses the number of workers' groups seems to have been far less than in Michoacán. The Catholic newspaper in Puebla, for example, lamented that there were "very few" Catholic workers' associations, and that those that did exist were "purely religious," rather than having the social goals that were called for by Leo XIII in 1891.[86] An early attempt to confederate Catholic workers, the Liga Católica (1891) lasted only three years and was dissolved "with great bitterness."[87] Another attempt (the Unión Católica Obrera) was not made until 1907, and according to Manuel Ceballos Ramírez, only nine Círculos in Mexico City joined the UCO in 1908; it also failed to incorporate important centers of Catholic workers' organization in Guadalajara and Zamora.[88] In 1911 the UCO had only about 5,000 members in approximately 40 workers' circles.[89]

Third, and most important for my purposes, the implication of much of the literature on Catholic Workers' Circles is that they were overwhelmingly male. This is clearly not the case, although firm numbers are hard to come by. We know that some of the *Obreros* could in fact be mostly female despite the (ambiguously) masculine name, as was the case in Colima in 1904, where the new Sociedad de Obreros included "female servants, female workers in textile and cigarette factories, washerwomen, seamstresses, ironers of clothes, and in general all women who do manual labor."[90] In other cases there are hints that even when the number of male Catholic workers was substantial, the number of female ones was at least as large if not larger. The 1906 pilgrimage to Morelia for the June celebration of the Sacred Heart, for example, included 1,500 Obreros and 1,010 *Obreras*.[91] Even more strikingly, in Guadalajara the 1910 festivities associated with the month of June celebrations featured 2,000 members of the Obreros and 5,000 members of the Obreras.[92]

Participation in processions is not, of course, a definitive reflection of the numbers of members, but it does quite clearly indicate an enthusiasm gap between Catholic men and women workers. There is other evidence that men's groups were inconsistent, at best, in their active support of the church. An early Catholic workers' group, the Círculo Patriótico Religioso de Artesanos, made up of 11 trade organizations and 2,000 workers, was first organized in 1887 to participate in the coronation of the Virgin of Guadalupe.[93] But when the coronation planned for 1888 fell through, they lost almost all their members. The organizers kept it afloat but lamented that discord had "sown its cursed seed in the very breast of the Circle," and by 1909 they had been forced to reorganize several times. In Huetamo (Michoacán), a small city of 26,000, in 1902 there was a men's Catholic Workers' Circle that had 228 members.[94] But according to the priest, only 10 men were active. (For comparison, the Apostolado in Huetamo had 120 members of whom 70 were said to be active; the Asociación del Catequismo had 240 members with 200 active; and the Vela Perpetua had 295 members with 100 active.) A Mexico City newspaper article from 1905 praised the presence of "around one thousand female workers" who formed "the largest contingent" in a procession of workers celebrating the tenth anniversary of the crowning of the Virgin of Guadalupe.[95] In short, the Catholic Workers' Circles were no doubt aimed at male workers, but the number of women's circles should not be underestimated and the active participation of the men's circles should not be overestimated.

Relations between Hierarchy, Priests, and Women

The frustration about the dominance of women as officers and members exhibited by the directors of the Guadalajara Apostolado in the report discussed at the beginning of this chapter was not invariably shared by priests, who did not necessarily find men to be either "more solid," "more persevering," or "more help for the priest" than women. Many parish priests continued to prefer women as officers in parish lay associations and were not troubled at all by the fact that women governed men in mixed-sex groups. After all, although female officeholding in all-female associations was the most common form of leadership in the archbishopric of Mexico in 1897, according to the survey results, there were at least forty groups that were mixed-sex with female leaders, compared to fifteen mixed-sex groups with male leadership.

As had been true since the 1840s, many parish priests probably preferred, in a perfect world, more traditional gender relations in lay associations, but they understood what it took to make a successful lay association and apparently felt that in many cases male leadership would not produce the desired results. The priest commissioned to supervise the election of new officers of a mixed-sex lay association in the temple of La Encarnación in Mexico City, for example, commented that the (female) members and the (all-female) officers of the association "are performing their duties well, and indeed to a large extent it is due to them that there is religion at all in the church."[96] *La Defensa Católica* recommended that priests pay attention first to the women of the Apostolado, making sure they are "burning with the love of the Sacred Heart," because they are "excellent assistants to the Priest" in the project of bringing men back to the church.[97] In Puebla the women of the Apostolado formed a "holy beehive" of action in support of the association and devotion to the Sacred Heart: "those with wealth give money; those that lack wealth are in charge of collecting alms; those with the ability to confect admirable arrangements of artificial flowers, tat fine lace, embroider, among a thousand other skills, dedicate themselves to adornment of the altars, while others take charge of beautifying the rest of the church."[98]

Men, by contrast, were not as present in support of the day-to-day activities of the church. Out of the twenty-eight scheduled days of procession through the streets of Guadalajara at the end of the Porfiriato, for example, seven were devoted to adult female groups and two to adult men's groups. On the day that the men's groups—the Liga Eucarística, the Junta Guadalupana del Comercio, the Caballeros de la Corte de Santa María de Guadalupe, the Sociedad Católica de Señores and the law school it supported, and the lawyers, doctors, engineers, pharmacists, merchants and agriculturalists of the city—were to march, it was said that they had to be "begged insistently to show up."[99] Many priests, then, continued to make the calculation that it was impossible to both eliminate female governance of men and expand the number of associations and members. If they wished to have strong, active lay associations with good membership totals, they would have to work with women. This had been true since the 1840s.

But in a number of cases, as the threats to the church from the state eased up under the Díaz policy of conciliation and clerical finances stabilized and then improved, there was a discernible tendency, especially on the part of the hierarchy, to push back against women's power and to try to restore traditional gender relations both within the organizations and between the female leaders and their priest/directors. Perhaps greater "normalcy" and stability in politics and finances awakened a preference for more "normal" gender relations. The comments by the directors of the Apostolado reflect these ecclesiastical anxieties. Several of the more prominent innovations of the period, without explicitly stating that this was a goal, re-masculinized the church's public image: the four Catholic congresses held in the first decade of the twentieth century, to which laymen but not laywomen were invited; the recruitment of young men to go to Rome to study at the Colegio Pío Latinoamericano (what Sergio Francisco Rosas Salas calls a key element in the "Romanization" of the Mexican clergy because of the disproportionate number of future bishops trained there); the promotion of workers' circles (even if many of them turned out to attract women as much as men); the militarization of the names of men's associations (e.g., the Knights of Columbus); and the creation of special devotions just for men (e.g., the Adoración Nocturna, which opened churches to men only in the evenings).[100] As Matthew Butler observes, it is an oversimplification to see this "masculinization" as counter-feminization, but at the same time there is a clear sense in which efforts to restore "proper" gender relations by bringing in more men inevitably had a negative impact on women's power in the relationship between women and priests.[101]

The goal of reestablishing gender hierarchy in the lay associations was pursued in two ways. The most obvious was to reiterate the principle of gender segregation, in order to avoid what the promotor of the archbishopric of Mexico in 1887 called the "very improper and very unsuitable" spectacle of women governing men.[102] In other words, gender relations were upside down, in his view, when there were female leaders of a mixed-sex association. As another official put it, "men and women members of a lay association may worship together in the Church, but outside of the Church itself separation is necessary."[103] Segregated men's and women's groups allowed women to continue to serve the church and assist the priest, but (theoretically) guaranteed that there would be men in positions of power as well. When one Vela Perpetua association led by women submitted a new set of rules for approval by the archbishop's office in Mexico City, the archbishop rejected it in part because it proposed to allow men to join, noting that it was "more appropriate to form a different and separate association for men."[104] The priest, we can guess, had allowed men to join because this was the best way to enlist men in the first place. This was also the case in 1911 when the priest of the church of San Jerónimo in Mexico City tried to establish an Asociación del Señor de la Penitencia. His proposed set of rules was rejected by the archbishop because they included only women in the *junta directiva* of the association and only female celadoras, but admitted men as members. The hierarchy objected: "If at all possible, men should form a separate association with their own *junta* and *celadores*."[105]

The archbishop's office was more blunt in an 1894 case. Father Francisco Oviedo had proposed the canonical formation of the Hermandad del Espiritu Santo in the church of La Enseñanza in Mexico City, but one adviser to the bishop objected to the fact that men and women would both be admitted and would both be present in the meetings. The point of a "brotherhood," he argued, is that the members should form bonds as if they were brothers, but when men and women are together in this way "who can fail to see that this can turn into scandal? What would Padre Oviedo say if in the convents they admitted both friars and nuns without regard to their sex?"[106] In another Mexico City case, the rules of the Asociación de Santa Teresa de Jesús were approved by the archbishop in 1891 as long as it was made clear that "as far as leadership, meetings, etc., the men would be totally separate from the women."[107]

In an early (1875) example of priests trying to nurture separate men's groups, women tried to enter the church of La Encarnación for the nighttime vigil of the Eucharist. The chaplain complained to the bishop that the government required the doors of the church to remain open, and this allowed the women to enter, which they did, saying that "the Church is for everyone." The archbishop's office answered that if they could not prevent the entry of women by putting guards (*celadores*) at the doors, "tell them [the women] that if they insist on entering this exercise will cease to be practiced, and they will have to take responsibility for this result."[108] Segregation, the reader will recall, had always been preferred by the hierarchy, beginning with the foundation of separate men's and women's Velas in Guadalajara in the 1840s (chapter 3). But during the Porfiriato it seems to have become a point of emphasis, rather than a simple preference that might or might not have been realistic under the circumstances. It should be noted that women did not usually object, at least to judge by the archival traces available, to being segregated from men, and it is possible, of course, that they sometimes preferred it.

The other way to restore traditional gender relations was for priests and higher officials alike to emphasize gender hierarchy (more than "just" segregation), making clear the dominant role of the priest in his relationships with women in associations. There are numerous examples of clerical officials putting this principle—to which women *did* regularly object—into practice. (There were also cases in which priests and the hierarchy displayed their desire to control male association leaders, but they are many fewer in number. Of course it is also true that there were far fewer male-led associations than female-led ones.) The statutes of the new Corte de María, for example, established in the church of La Profesa in Mexico City in 1878, make it clear that "the Association will be governed solely and exclusively by a priest. There will never be in said Association a [female] president nor [female] deputies . . . nor will the [female] members of the association intervene at any time in the administration or functioning of the Association; instead, everything, even the most insignificant detail, is under the charge of the Director at all times and in all circumstances."[109] The priest of San Pablo in 1896, claiming that the (female) members of an association under his direction were demanding that he return possessions they had never given him in the first place, asked the archbishop for permission to deal with the son of the presidenta of the association, since unlike his mother "he seems to me to be a little rational and somewhat prudent."[110] And in 1897 an association was dissolved by the archbishop because its president, Doña Refugio Ocampo de Leyva, was, according to the priest, "ignorant, and of stubborn and turbulent character."[111] The language in these cases is of course quite similar to that used in numerous cases in the 1840s and 1850s in which priests complained of uncooperative women leaders and tried to reassert their authority over them. But at that time the bishops either rebuked them or let the case drop on its own. Extinguishing a valued lay association because the priest couldn't get along with the presidenta was unheard of. Now such extinction was a real threat.

As in the midcentury cases, control over the treasuries of the associations was an issue. In Cuautla in 1884 the priest railed from the pulpit against the women of the Vela because they refused to pay for paving the atrium of the parish church (they wanted instead to buy a new piano), and another accused a priest sympathetic to the women of being the "blind instrument of Doña Justa Martínez."[112] And in 1895 the priest of Tepetlaoxtoc was locked in battle with the female officers of the Asociación del Sagrado Corazón de Jesús, the Guardia de Honor, and the Vela Perpetua, who refused to turn over their funds to him so that he could use them as he saw fit.[113] "What right does the Treasurer have to withhold funds?" he thundered. "She and the few other insignificant persons who side with her are the only ones who have systematically opposed my dispositions." One imaginative way to restore gender hierarchy and control over what priests considered to be uncooperative lay associations was employed by Father Manuel Tortolero in Tlalnepantla in 1895: after long disputes with the Asociación de Nuestra Señora de Guadalupe, a women's lay organization, he decided to create a *junta general* composed of male heads of household and "free persons" of the villa who would choose the leaders of the Guadalupan asociación and the one other women's lay association that was not yet canonically approved, thus bypassing the election process within the associations.[114]

Finally, a telling case from 1906 shows that even the most self-assured priests could not always assert their power over women when social class factored against them, even though they were willing to try. The chaplain of the church of San Diego in Mexico City attempted, and failed, to disempower the women of the Archicofradía del Perpetuo Socorro. Threatening the "public and authorized extinction" of the association if its president did not comply with his wishes, he wanted to establish new rules: members shouldn't speak out of turn at the meetings, shouldn't raise their voices, shouldn't bring in unauthorized (by him) topics of discussion, and shouldn't meet without the director present.[115] But the apparently well-to-do women who led the association (both Angela G. Buch y Yguarte and Saturnina Núñez Vda. de Carpio had cards or stamps with their names printed on them, indicating a certain level of disposable wealth) prevailed, accusing the chaplain of putting innumerable obstacles in the way of the progress of the association and of using words from the pulpit ("for which there are hundreds of witnesses") that, "besides hurting the members of the Archicofradía, are offensive to the spirit of charity that ought to characterize the seat of the Holy Spirit." They sought and received permission to move their organization to a different church.

That restoring gender segregation and hierarchy was part of the project of Romanization is an insight that is generally absent in the existing literature, because the emphasis is on presumably gender-neutral efforts to bring Catholics more effectively under the control of their priests and by extension the hierarchy and the Vatican. Understanding the process as gendered, however, makes it clear that while the project to introduce new European and Vatican-approved associations and use them to organize and mobilize the laity was quite successful in terms of the overall numbers of new associations and members, to the extent that the goal was to enlist both women and men, its success was far more ambiguous.

Non-Catholic Women's Associations

In Puebla the editor of the Catholic newspaper *El Amigo de la Verdad* claimed in 1888 that "there may not be a single decent and honorable Señora who does not belong to a pious association or *cofradía*," and indeed there is every indication, as we have seen, that female membership in Catholic societies was as high as it had ever been.[116] But in the Porfiriato we finally begin to see a solid increase in the number of women's clubs and associations that were not affiliated with the church. They offered a chance for female sociability outside of the church-affiliated groups that for decades had provided virtually the only such opportunities. The phenomenon was notable enough to be made fun of: in 1909 *El Diario* satirized the club scene with a faux report on the "Orden del Botón Azul," dedicated to abolishing the social kiss, which was said to be sweeping the land and attracting the most respectable ladies.[117]

I focus on the clubs that were founded before 1909, since the political clubs that began to crop up in that year—and included quite a few for and by women—have already received a fair amount of attention in the literature.[118] Non-Catholic women's groups, like the lay associations that are at the core of our story, were for most of the period politically neutral, at least on the surface. Some, perhaps many, members of non-church organizations may also have been members of Catholic associations. It is not hard to imagine some of the girls who got together to found a recreational club also belonging to, say, the Corte de María. Most probably married both civilly and in the church, attended Mass, and considered themselves Catholic (as did many, probably most, liberal men). Nonetheless, the fact that there were secular organizations to which women could belong gave them, for the first time, a broadly available alternative to Catholic lay associations. Establishing a secular mode of sociability in the earlier clubs, even if their purpose was not overtly political, paved the way for the more political clubs of the immediate pre-Revolution years.

Most of the new groups for women continued to be located in Mexico City, but "secular" clubbing and organizing was clearly much more of a national experience than in previous decades. The Club Recreativo Rosa, for example, was formed in Orizaba in 1904, for the purpose of organizing dances for its "aristocratic" members.[119] Luisa P. de Overton started a club in Zacatecas in 1908 "to put on dances periodically and organize diversions to soothe the spirit and foment the sense of sociability among the members."[120] The women of Guanajuato seem to have been the first to establish a temperance society, in 1877 (though it should be noted that women never dominated temperance societies in Mexico as they did in the US).[121] In Monterrey a women's bicycling club was founded in 1899.[122]

Non-church-affiliated charitable organizations began to compete with or work parallel to the well-established Catholic charitable associations like the Ladies of Charity. The women of Morelia formed the Sociedad del Socorro in 1899 to provide clothing for the poor, for example, and women from Saltillo formed a similar charity in 1896.[123] The Sociedad Feminista de Cultura Moral in Mexico City even used some language and concepts reminiscent of the Vincentian conferences: founded in 1908, it proposed—like the Ladies of Charity—to foment both the physical and moral health of its clients. Specifically, it planned to collect clothes from merchants to distribute among female prisoners, found a school within the prison for the children of the interned, promote the handiwork made by the prisoners and advise them on the design of their work "since many lack aesthetic inspiration," and hold "conferences" to discuss various moral themes.[124] This society worked with the authorities of the Federal District and the Secretaría de Gobernación. Cooperation with government agencies also characterized several of the other new charitable groups. In 1881, for example, the legislature of Veracruz authorized the Sociedad Femenil de Beneficencia, allowing it to establish a lottery whose proceeds would go to found an asylum, an orphanage, and a poorhouse.[125]

The number of women's mutual assistance organizations also slowly increased along with the number of women in the workforce. *La Convención Radical Obrera* in 1894 listed eight exclusively female mutualistas (seven of them in Mexico City), out of a total of fifty-four.[126] Some were founded by the workers themselves, but the social anxieties produced by expanding opportunities for women to enter the workforce—a phenomenon that has been well-documented throughout Latin America in the late nineteenth and early twentieth centuries—seem to have elicited male patronage and official encouragement of women's organizations that promised to organize, assist, and control women workers. Men involved in the professions that women had recently entered in large numbers had a particular interest in organizing relevant women's groups, and men who also managed male mutualistas established quite a few women's mutual aid groups.[127] Some of these women's workers' associations were among those who were politicized after the rise of the Partido Liberal Mexicano (PLM), an group with anarcho-syndicalist tendencies (despite their name), including the Hijas de Anáhuac, which was founded in 1907 by textile workers in Mexico City and met weekly in the home of sisters María del Carmen and Catalina Frías until the group was suppressed by Porfirio Díaz.[128]

One of the most striking characteristics shared by secular women's associations during this period was the importance attached to inaugural and annual social functions. In 1902 a group of "beautiful and elegant young ladies from the best families of Veracruz society" formed the Club Violeta, a beneficence society; one of their first actions was to put on a banquet for the poor, complete with music from the band of the 23rd Battalion and the recitation of various "sonorous and allusive" verses by the presidenta of the society.[129] An association of schoolteachers in San Luis Potosí, the Sociedad Protectora de Profesoras "Josefa Negrete," celebrated its anniversaries with concerts, speeches, decorations, a lunch, and an "animated ball."[130] The Sociedad de Empleadas de Comercio's first actions in 1906 were to plan an evening soiree featuring music and poetry.[131] Even the mutual aid societies were regularly launched with the most lavish events they could afford. The Sociedad Fraternal de Costureras Mexicanas, for example, celebrated its honorary president, Carmen Romero Rubio (Díaz's wife), with a "magnificent" event attended by not only the workers and their families but also the "most distinguished families of our society"; in a unique twist, two "luxurious" sewing machines, filled with bouquets of flowers, flanked the stage on which appeared the usual musical performances, speeches, and poetry.[132]

It is hard not to see this preference for and expectation of a showy social event as connected, at least subconsciously, to the as-splendid-as-possible annual functions formerly sponsored by cofradías. But not every group adopted this practice. The meetings of the Sociedad Mexicana Para el Cultivo de las Ciencias, for example, seem to have consisted of presentations by female authors of works on "physics, applied chemistry, meteorology, astronomy, natural history, telegraphy, and much more."[133] And my sense is that a more rigorous study of non-Catholic associations might find the practice of emphasizing the social event diminishing over time; it was seemingly ubiquitous among the mutualistas of the 1880s and 1890s, but seems at least slightly less common in the later foundations (except, of course, the recreational clubs that were founded for the purpose of organizing balls).

To what should we attribute this expansion of non-Catholic women's clubs and societies in the Porfiriato? Context is important. The relative peace of the Porfiriato and the growing prosperity and size of the middle classes are surely part of the story. Women of the middle and upper classes saw an increase in disposable time, energy, and money, which they could invest in social or cultural causes, using clubs as vehicles. The new charitable and social/recreational clubs probably benefited most from political stability and the expansion of the middle class. But men's non-Catholic associationalism had thrived in an earlier period without Porfirian "order and progress," while women's organizations had not, so this explanation can only take us so far.

Another contextual factor may be more explanatory. I have already touched on the rise of a female working class that included women who worked as both manual laborers (like seamstresses or tobacco factory workers) and as office or retail workers.[134] These new workers needed protections; as we have seen, they joined mutual aid societies to gain at least some insurance in case of injury or illness, and perhaps joining these associations led to an increased interest in joining more generally. The research on this point is scant. But a subgroup of working women, schoolteachers, *has* been studied enough for us to see them as active joiners and participants in associational life (as well as in other elements of civil society that are not the subject of this book, such as writing for and editing newspapers for women).[135] The increasing number of elementary schoolteachers who began to graduate from the official state normal schools in the late 1870s and 1880s became a notable feature of the associational landscape. Almost all single, these women sought forms of sociability outside the classroom, and joined or founded clubs that ranged from the purely recreational, to mutual aid, to the literary/intellectual, and, in the late Porfiriato, to the political.[136]

Like the Porfirian women's associations in general, most of the associations founded by and/or for teachers appear to have been ideologically neutral through the 1870s, 1880s, and 1890s, such as the teachers' mutual aid society founded in San Luis Potosí in 1897, whose aim was simply to help cover expenses for *maestras* if they fell ill, and to pay burial expenses if they died.[137] In 1907 *profesoras* and alumna of the Escuela Lerdo de Tejada founded the Sociedad "Felipe Villanueva" as an "artistic and recreational" society.[138] Its inaugural fiesta, with the usual elaborate musical and literary program, was presided over by minister of public education Justo Sierra and his subsecretary Ezequiel A. Chávez.[139] Professor Luis G. León founded the Sociedad Mexicana Para el Cultivo de las Ciencias in 1898, dedicated to the presentation of women's scientific, literary, and musical work.[140]

But in time, while many teachers sought ways to teach Catholic doctrine even if it required them to do so illegally, others imbibed the messages of the government-run normal schools and began to harbor antagonism toward the church.[141] In the 1880s there were a small number of women's Masonic associations—with similar anti-Catholic rhetoric to the male lodges—founded and populated by teachers.[142] At the time these female affiliates of the Masons gathered, the number of public schoolteachers was still limited. After the turn of the century, however, teachers were more numerous, and the socialist-anarchist critique of the Díaz regime being mounted by the PLM was beginning to take shape, offering an organizational structure to channel any anti-Catholic sentiments that public schoolteachers might harbor. When James Creelman's 1908 interview of Porfirio Díaz introduced the possibility that Díaz might not run again for the presidency, this prompted political stirrings across the spectrum, and a number of schoolteachers, along with a handful of professional women and some workers, stepped into the fray through the vehicle of anti-reelectionist clubs.

One association founded by teachers deserves special mention as a link between the older, non-confrontational style of association and a newer, more "feminist" and politicized stance that would appear after 1908. This was the Sociedad Protectora de la Mujer Mexicana, founded in 1904.[143] The Sociedad Protectora sent ambiguous messages in its early stages that could easily be interpreted as signs that this association was similar to those that had come before. The liberal newspaper *La Patria* understood the Sociedad's mission to be a kind of combination of a literary association and a beneficence association: the members, it reported, would organize musical auditions, poetry readings, and drama presentations that showcased their talents; these events would raise money for a Banco Fraternal that would be used to promote the material well-being of the "humble classes," including classes on hygiene and assistance for the sick and disabled.[144] *El Mundo* reported that the Sociedad's project was to "organize trips to the countryside, artistic and literary salons, concerts, and all manner of gatherings of an educational and recreational nature," including a trip by train and either horse or carriage to the "famous waters of Chimalixtac" in the district of San Angel in 1905.[145] Even the Catholic newspaper *El Tiempo* reported positively on the enthusiasm for this new organization, commenting, "It is easy to predict that this Society will prosper rapidly."[146]

But the Sociedad Protectora was not like most of the other non-Catholic women's associations. In its actions and through the magazine *La Mujer Mexicana*, also established in 1904 by many of the founders of the Sociedad, it backed civil matrimony and proposed to teach working women about its importance.[147] This was clearly a political (because it was anti-Catholic) position.[148] Logically, considering that the preponderance of members were teachers, the Sociedad was also a defender of public education, another position in conflict with the commitment of many Catholic activists to religious education. Moreover, the Sociedad's and *La Mujer Mexicana*'s posture in favor of feminism and the "progress" of the female sex was well understood to imply that "progressive" women would either give up their devotion to Catholicism or at the very least practice a less ultramontane version of it. As *El Colmillo Público* put it in 1904, the year the Sociedad Protectora was founded, "the day that women become educated and intellectually emancipated, they will be the first enemy of fanaticism."[149] The Catholic paper *La Voz de México* seemed to agree when it observed ominously that "feminism" was advancing in Mexico, calling this development "imprudent, given the physical impossibility for women to carry out responsibilities that should be exclusive to men."[150] Teachers, in short, were not the only women keen to associate in the Porfiriato, but they were an important and influential subgroup of joiners, and they were at the core of some of the anti-Díaz feminist groups that cropped up as the regime began to collapse, especially after 1908.

Conclusion

This chapter has shown that Romanization was a success in the sense that lay associations grew rapidly in number, most of them sponsored by either the Vatican or the bishops—a sign that the desired centralization of Catholic practice was proceeding as hoped (though the process was never uniform, as shown by significant differences between the associational life of parishioners in the archbishoprics of Mexico, Michoacán, and Oaxaca). What did not go according to plan was that a large majority of these clubs were led and populated by women. There is evidence that some members of the clergy were uncomfortable with women's continued dominance in lay associations, and sought—now that the financial and social position of the church was on firmer ground than it had been in almost a century—to return to a kind of colonial model of lay association, in which men were the clear lay leaders of the organizations, priests were the clear spiritual leaders and directors, and disputes over control of the association did not have a gendered dimension. At the same time, other priests continued to accept that growing lay associations meant tolerating (indeed, welcoming) women as leaders and members. A gendered division of labor where lay associations were concerned—in which women shouldered the main burdens of maintaining both devotional and charitable life in the church—that had begun in the 1840s out of clerical desperation had now settled in, in practice if not in rhetoric.

Meanwhile, it is important to recognize that while they remained far less numerous than Catholic groups, secular women's clubs and societies were also growing during this period when associationalism continued to be understood as a key feature of a modern nation. Liberal discourse around gender roles still celebrated mothers and women who stayed at home. But in the absence of angry Catholic women activists for liberals to rail against (as we will see in chapter 8, Catholic women's politics became less confrontational as the liberal government itself became less confrontational after 1876), their admonitions about the proper role of women became more abstract, less clearly something that secular-minded women had to pay attention to in order to distinguish themselves from the manly and virile Catholic women (chapter 6).[151] Perhaps even more important, Catholic anti-feminist rhetoric about women's roles as mothers and the desirability of women staying at home began to sound quite like the liberal discourses on gender, as we will see in more detail in chapter 8.[152] Reflecting the essentially non-partisan nature of ideas about domesticity in this period, literary scholar Nancy LaGreca calls the widespread embrace of women as "angels of the home" a "national ideology."[153] As this gender ideology was embraced by both liberals and conservatives, it freed both Catholic and liberal women to associate in ostensibly apolitical associations that were now seen as an extension of "proper" roles for women, such as charity or event organizing.

There were no clear equivalents during the Porfiriato of the petition campaigns described in chapters 4 and 6. For priests and bishops, whether they were anxious or tolerating or welcoming of women in positions of power in lay associations, it must have been a bit of a relief to see Catholic women out of the headlines. But this does not mean that they did not want women to be engaged in the church's broader political projects. They might wish more men would join lay associations, but they were well aware that subtracting women would greatly weaken the behind-the-scenes political goals of the church: regaining not only some of its economic power but, more importantly, its moral power. And moral power was women's turf. We now turn to that political project and the role of women's lay associations in it.

CHAPTER EIGHT

"The Men Are Somewhat Preoccupied. Fortunately, the Mexican Woman Carries the Standard of Our Beliefs"

WOMEN AND CATHOLIC POLITICS
IN THE PORFIRIATO

IN JANUARY 1888, the historian Joaquín García Icazbalceta, in his role as national president of the Society of St. Vincent de Paul, wrote to the archdiocese of Mexico.[1] Should the Vincentian conferences, he wanted to know, continue to provide assistance to families who chose to send their children to public schools instead of Catholic schools? The response to García Icazbalceta's question offers a window into how the church's politics had changed in Porfirian Mexico, and how they had not.

García Icazbalceta guessed that parents would remove their children from the municipal schools if they were threatened with the loss of support from the conferences. But this would not necessarily be a good thing, he warned, since it was far from certain that they would enroll them instead in Catholic schools, "to which they have demonstrated great aversion, finding a thousand reasons to avoid sending their children there, as experience has shown us."[2] If this happened, children would receive no education at all, either religious or civil: "It is deplorable if they do not receive the first of these," García Icazbalceta wrote, "but it is even worse if they have neither." For this reason and others, García Icazbalceta asked for more time during which to evaluate a family's particular situation and to determine whether withdrawing the support of the conferences would do more harm than good.[3]

The provisor's response was firm: the conferences must not support Catholic families who refused to send their children to Catholic schools, because "before the great good of a religious education the benefits of civil education disappear."[4] He did extend the deadline by which the conferences must stop supporting these families from two months to six months (giving them the rest of the year), but he absolutely rejected García Icazbalceta's notion that in some cases it might be better for children to remain in a government school than no school at all, and he insisted that in the future families be required to comply from the outset of their relationship with the conferences.

The case highlights the church's continued resistance to the secular state and its institutions, but it also reveals the way church politics had changed during the Porfiriato. Despite ongoing under-the-radar efforts to regain some of its economic power, the church's main political goals had shifted to the cultural realm.[5] Now its principal concern—shared with other national Catholic hierarchies and the Vatican itself as they responded to secularization campaigns mounted across the Catholic world—was to reenergize and organize the laity and to spread and deepen Catholic culture. García Icazbalceta's association could not be allowed to go easy on families that would not commit to imbuing their children with Catholic values in every way possible.

The project of instilling Catholic values was partly entrusted to a new generation of priests, as we saw in the previous chapter's discussion of Romanization. But its success was fundamentally dependent on the laity, and especially the organized laity. Lay associations supported the Catholic schools, the Catholic family, Catholic social work, the Catholic press, and Catholic workers. They were key to keeping Catholicism and the church visible and active in the community, in an era when liberal legislation had tried to relegate all evidence of Catholic practice to behind church doors. Before "Catholic Action" became a named movement in the 1930s, this was already an era during which the church called upon Catholics to organize and then to act "collectively," as the archbishops of Mexico, Michoacán, and Guadalajara put it in their 1875 pastoral.

Middle-class and elite women as leaders and members of lay associations were at the forefront of this new Catholic political project. Yet the work they did outside the home on behalf of the church's political agenda during the Porfiriato has been underacknowledged and all but unanalyzed.[6] This chapter shows that the women-dominated lay associations that we met in chapter 7 played vital roles in advancing the new Catholic politics, including expanding religious education, building a parochial school system, challenging the Reform laws' prohibitions on external displays of religion, bolstering the Catholic press, and in general rebuilding the church's prestige and moral power after the military defeats of the 1850s and 1860s. In short, women were crucial elements in the Mexican version of Catholic revival.

Church Politics in the Porfiriato

The political activities of Catholic women and men look different in the Porfiriato than in the era of the Reform, and not just because the goals of church politics had changed. Díaz's policy of "conciliation" toward the church allowed Catholic politics to be less openly combative than during the earlier periods. Díaz himself announced this policy in a circular issued in January 1877. Accordingly, conciliation was long seen by historians as primarily a government project, one that the regime undertook from a position of power—since the church no longer was a threat to the state—because it served government ends, especially to forestall any further religion-inspired rebellions (such as the one that had risen up in the center-west in 1873–74 against the Lerdo regime). Recently, other historians have seen in conciliation a more active role for the church, interpreting it as a "pact" (to use Cecilia Bautista García's word) between the state and the ecclesiastical hierarchy that was sought as much by the church as by the Díaz regime.[7] Social stability, which the church could offer as part of its end of the bargain, would create the conditions for both economic growth and Catholic revival.[8] A picture of coexistence with some assumption of mutual benefit (if not going quite as far as Bautista García's suggestion that there was an active and ongoing pact) remains the most common interpretation.[9] In this picture, Catholics took advantage of the forbearance of the state to strengthen church institutions.

Dramatic examples of conciliation include Díaz's decision to ask the archbishop to preside over his marriage to Carmen Romero Rubio in 1881 (admittedly when he was temporarily out of office), and the government's tolerance of the public celebrations around the crowning of the Virgin of Guadalupe in 1895. But there were many other signs.[10] The number of churches more than doubled, as the government signaled it would not oppose new construction projects, and the number of seminaries tripled. Over two dozen new religious orders, both male and female, were permitted to establish themselves in Mexico, beginning little more than a decade after the highly controversial and inflammatory "expulsion" of the Hermanas de la Caridad. Most of them were dedicated to opening Catholic schools or carrying out missions to indigenous populations.

At the same time, conciliation, while serving both church and state, was not embraced in all places by all Catholics or all liberals. In fact, it masked both considerable Catholic resistance to liberalism (at both the grassroots level and in the Catholic press), and liberal anger at the resurgence of the church.[11] Religious liberty, long resisted but now enshrined in the constitution, became a weapon in the Catholic resistance, by allowing Catholics to argue that they had the right to send their children to schools that taught doctrine; disseminate anti-liberal and pro-Catholic ideas in the press; wear badges and medals proclaiming their membership in Catholic associations; and carry out religious processions within certain limits. Meanwhile, more than a small faction of liberals resented what they saw as Catholics' perverse use of the 1857 constitution, with the intention of undermining its fundamental values and spreading retrograde ideas. Despite the constitution's blueprint for a church that was entirely removed from the political arena, there was no question in the minds of liberals that the church sought new ways to exert itself politically. "The clergy's determination to . . . recover its domination over the State is notorious," wrote *El Siglo Diez y Nueve* in 1896.[12]

Although my primary goal in this chapter is to examine the changes in the nature of women's activism on behalf of the church and the concrete ways that the lay associations dominated by women were involved in promoting the church's agenda, it is necessary first to establish the contours of the culture wars, since the argument that women's activism and their work in lay associations was political work hinges on appreciating the extent to which culture wars were an important way that politics played out during the dictatorship. Edward Wright-Ríos, writing about Porfirian interpretations of Madre Matiana—a supposedly historical nun from the colonial period who predicted the disasters that Mexico would undergo if it turned away from the church and who served during this period as a "Mexican beacon of universal Catholic resurgence"—calls this an era of "superheated Catholic rhetoric."[13] It was also an era of superheated anticlerical and anti-Catholic rhetoric, despite official conciliation.

Porfirian Culture Wars

RELIGIOUS EDUCATION

One of the most prominent features of the culture wars was the battle over religious education. Historians have recognized the importance of public schools to the liberal state as transmitters of new, secular values that emphasized loyalty to the nation above all other institutional loyalties.[14] They may not fully appreciate the extent to which the Catholic hierarchy and the Catholic press vigorously resisted, in the press and from the pulpit, the new "atheist" government schools.[15] The 1875 joint pastoral signed by the archbishops of Mexico, Michoacán, and Guadalajara had first warned of the dangers of religionless education and called for laypeople to develop a "Catholic option" to counter the expansion of public schools, making full use of the "freedom that the Constitution of the nation guarantees citizens to promote and foment the kind of education that they choose for their children."[16]

A much-used trope in Catholic discourse was the government schools' "poisoning" of Mexican children. Michoacán's *Junta de Instrucción Católica Primaria* in 1884 wrote that Satan "has perfectly well understood that the easiest means of dechristianizing the world is to poison the souls of our schoolchildren."[17] *La Voz de México* lamented in 1897 that unlike in Guadalajara and Puebla, where there were many Catholic schools, "in Mexico City thousands of children drink daily from the poisoned well of the secular school."[18] A priest commented that he was often asked if it was acceptable for Catholics to enroll their children in a "school without God." His stock answer to the question was "Is it acceptable for a father to give deadly poison to his children?"[19]

The specific effects of this "poisoning" were frightening. The Catholic press published spurious statistics from laicized France and anecdotal evidence from Mexico claiming a dramatic increase in suicide attributable to the absence of religious education.[20] Dueling, libertinism, gambling, drinking, criminality—in short, every possible manifestation of immorality—were also blamed squarely on the public schools.[21] And even if parents were not convinced that government schools could be held accountable for these terrible woes, wrote *El Amigo de la Verdad*, anyone could compare these schools, where they would see children "vomiting torrents of insolence and writing obscene words on the walls," to the Catholic schools where students "converse on innocent matters or play children's games."[22]

It was particularly terrible for girls to attend the public schools, since these schools would instill a "lack of pious sentiments and ... ignorance of their religious duties, the very things that make a home solid and happy"; the girls so-indoctrinated would become "very dangerous women to society."[23] The prospectus for a Catholic girls' secondary school in Puebla echoed that view: "to educate a boy is to educate a man; but to educate a women is to educate a family. To regenerate itself, the world only needs good mothers."[24] *La Voz*, under the 1901 headline "A Poisoned Flower," pointed with horror to a "feminist's" suggestion that the members of her club (not identified in the article) pledge not to participate in the sacraments of baptism and marriage. It blamed her heresy on the public schools: "Oh *escuela laica*, you are bearing the fruits of death!"[25]

Although there were many shades of liberalism, especially where views on the dictatorship were concerned, there was widespread agreement among diverse liberal groups that religious education was just as terrible as the Catholics thought secular education was: it corrupted the young and produced social dysfunction. *La Patria* called religious education a "monstrous octopus that has sucked dry the nation's ability to think" and has formed only "fanatics, when it doesn't create imbeciles."[26] *La Convención Radical Obrera* called religious schools "factories producing hypocritical altar boys ... whose perversities ... sink the nation in an abyss of misery."[27] It was not the public schools but the Catholic schools who sent the most people to the cantinas and gambling dens, and who exhibited the most scandalous behavior in balls and public diversions, claimed *El Siglo Diez y Nueve*.[28] The same newspaper wrote: "Everywhere we see Catholic schools being founded, not to teach, because the clergy and the Catholics are utterly ignorant, but rather to tear our youth out of the lay schools and create a generation that is reactionary, fanatical, and sanctimonious."[29] Like the Catholic press, the liberal press characterized the debates over education as war. *El Siglo Diez y Nueve* called the church "an enemy that you cannot wound with just a pinprick; you need an axe to the head."[30] "The clerics are alarmed," wrote *La Convención Radical Obrera*; "they utter their war cries and prepare themselves for combat.... We have pushed the clergy to its ultimate stronghold: the school. In order for us to triumph completely ... the clerical school must disappear and upon its ruins we can build the foundation for the secular school, which alone can ensure progress."[31]

Like Catholics, liberal writers saw the education of women as a key to the future. For many, women were undermining the progress made since the Reform: "The evil that we have in our homes, bewitching and seductive, serves as the terrible weapon of our adversary ... How can we combat this evil ... ? Only with obligatory secular education for women."[32] *La Patria* wrote in 1900 that religious education for women "is one of our greatest social evils, since mothers inculcate the Catholic religion in their children, making it very hard later to liberate their intelligence from the absurd notions of causality ... like the existence of 'miracles'; ... Religious education for women retards the intellectual development of their children and prepares the clergy for the economic domination of society."[33] The future minister of education, Justo Sierra, added that women who received a religious instead of a secular education were likely to despise the ideas of their emancipated husbands and fathers, leading to discord in the family and the nation.[34] A speech at a meeting of Masons in 1895 agreed that women's religious fanaticism was dangerous, and that the only way to mitigate the danger was her emancipation by way of the public school: "the future is not in our hands, but rather in the hands of women, who today have as the principal element of their education, a book of prayers; as their principal center of activity, the church; and as the only guide of their consciences, the confessional."[35]

PUBLIC DISPLAYS OF RELIGIOSITY

Another dimension of the culture wars revolved around the prohibition on public religious expression.[36] The Reform laws that were elevated to constitutional status in December 1874 stated that no religious act (such as a procession) could be carried out in public outside a church, and neither priests nor members of religious orders could wear clothing that identified them as clergy, nuns, or friars on the street.[37] The law also prohibited bell ringing except when strictly necessary as defined in police regulations. Violation carried a fine or imprisonment. Enforcement of these constitutional provisions was mixed, and the Díaz government itself was more tolerant than some local and state officials. But whether or not there was vigorous enforcement is not as important as either the perception of unjust persecution of Catholic practice or the perception of widespread evasion of the law; in other words, as seems to be a consistent feature of culture wars, both sides saw the issues as more black-and-white than they were in actuality.[38]

The liberal press was kept busy with reports from all over the country denouncing violations of this law and calling it a flouting of the constitution. They blamed both the clergy and complicit or weak-minded authorities for willfully breaking the law. "The government of the priests is enthroned in Tlaxcala, making a mockery of the Reform laws," wrote *La Patria* in 1882. "The district judge denies that religious acts are being carried out in public, but we cannot believe him because he is among the participants, bringing with him the employees of the court and even imposing fees to cover the cost of religious functions."[39] The political chief of Celaya, similarly, was accused of allowing a "scandalous manifestation of public religion" on the occasion of a visit from the bishop of León, and authorities in San Luis Potosí were accused of "converting to clericalism, and forgetting the liberal principles that gave them life and political importance."[40] In Aguascalientes, it was reported in *La Patria* in 1898, "the domination of the clergy in this city is accentuated more every day by the protection that our Governor provides for it . . . allowing clerics to roam the plazas and streets on Sundays soliciting alms, and permitting the viaticum to be out on the streets every afternoon."[41]

The Catholic press, meanwhile, regularly denounced the laws of the Reform prohibiting *culto externo* as "ridiculous, tyrannical, and foolish," and condemned the "stupid persecution" of priests and Catholics just trying to practice their religion, as they claimed the constitution allowed.[42] *El Tiempo* in 1887 recounted an illustrative story. A priest in Silao had been fined 100 pesos or fifteen days in prison because the driver of the carriage that carried the viaticum to a sick person had removed his hat. The priest refused to pay because he said he had infringed upon no law, and this led the chief of police to station officers at all the doors of the atrium and *casa cural* in order to apprehend him. When the priest refused to go quietly, according to *El Tiempo*, the police returned with twenty-six soldiers from the cavalry and a foot patrol, all armed with rifles and machetes. The priest was conducted to jail along with some distinguished members of local society.[43] In another case, a butcher in Puebla who had always hung an image of the Virgin of Guadalupe above his display case decided to decorate the picture with flowers and ribbons. According to the outraged author of the letter reporting this incident, "this seemed to the police a grave violation of the laws and they demanded the removal of the image, even though it was inside his establishment" and not, for this reason, a public display of religion.[44] Catholics cited the constitution's individual guarantees to complain that these laws limiting personal freedom were unconstitutional and "anti-liberal," as an 1896 article put it.[45] "*Liberal* liberty ties the hands of good men with a heavy chain and prevents them from doing good," wrote *La Rosa del Tepeyac* (Zacatecas); "we condemn with all our strength such oppressive freedom."[46]

A flash point throughout the Porfiriato was the practice of procession. *El Diario del Hogar* despaired that liberals had given up on enforcing the laws of the Reform regarding public processions. "The government ... thinking that the old elements of disorder have disappeared ... ignores the work of the reactionaries and the clergy ... Processions are being held all over the Republic and when they are punished at all it is with a small fine."[47] The liberals condemned either the absence or the inconsequence of fines that were levied against priests who led the processions or the faithful who participated in them, insufficient to deter them in the future and perhaps even serving as badges of honor.[48]

Reports on the lead-up to and aftermath of the crowning of the Virgin of Guadalupe in 1895 offer good insight into the Catholic effort to stay just within the limits of the law.[49] The crowning itself and the procession of the faithful carrying images or standards representing their associations would take place entirely inside the church, as permitted by law. But the thousands of dignitaries, associations, and ordinary pilgrims who would attend had to get to the church over city streets in an orderly fashion. That is, there had to be an organized procession of sorts, because otherwise chaos would result. On this point the municipal government agreed, and the advance publication of times of departure for various groups and the streets they would take was not a point of particular contention. The question, however, was how openly devout this procession to the church could be, without crossing the line.

According to the liberal *El Diario del Hogar*, unnamed clerics had a plan to deceive the government by adorning the houses along the avenue leading to the Basilica in legal fashion—that is, without images—and then adding the images at the last minute when it would be too late for the authorities to stop them without angering the thousands of pilgrims. Fortunately, it continued, when it found out about this plan and made it public, the good-liberal prefect of the district of Guadalupe made it clear that not even a slight infraction of the law would be tolerated.[50] But *El Diario* had a point; the Catholics were clearly trying to make this a procession as close to the old-fashioned processions as possible. *La Voz de México*, two days before the coronation, ran an article expressing outrage that the authorities would even consider fining a group of pilgrims from Puebla who planned to carry a standard along the route to the Basilica. They were not displaying it, the newspaper insisted, for the purpose of veneration, but merely transporting it to the interior of the church for the legal, inside-the-church procession. "The only thing the law prohibits is public worship [*culto público*]; but, we repeat, the mere exhibition of a sacred and religious object is not a call to worship. Is the government of the District going to punish the ladies who wear medallions around their neck or carry the rosary in their hands?" The indignant author continued: "And in any event, this was a standard of the Sociedad de Empleados of Puebla, entirely secular, without any sacred attribute. You might as well punish someone for carrying a watch."[51] From the descriptions of the crowded streets and the decorations of the houses and shops in the city—including the house of Eduardo González Gutiérrez, Vergara 12, which, besides multiple floral arrangements and silk drapes on the balconies, featured hundreds of electric bulbs, including forty-nine that spelled out the name "María"—it appears that the frustration of *El Diario del Hogar* was justified: the planners of the coronation seem to have carefully instructed the faithful in how to be as openly religious as possible while remaining within the law.[52]

It is possible that historians have underestimated the incidence and even the duration of the battles over processions and other demonstrations of religion. Moisés González Navarro, in the *Historia moderna de México*, wrote that most of the friction between authorities and the faithful came in the smaller pueblos, who "insisted on staging their processions outside the temples."[53] He quoted *El Tiempo* to the effect that "in the big cities, it seems that God is obliged to remain hidden in the temples ... but in the pueblos, his true children, far from hiding him, take him out amidst general rejoicing."[54] As a broad generalization this is probably true. Brian Stauffer has shown that resistance to "modern" reforms of their "baroque" practices could be intense (indeed, the Religionero rebellion in 1873–75 in Michoacán was strongly motivated by resentment of religious reform).[55] During the Porfiriato hundreds of violations of the law were reported in small towns. But other places with riots and protests and resistance to the law were not pueblos; they were small only by comparison with the national capital: San Luis Potosí, Guanajuato, Zacatecas, Lagos de Moreno, Pénjamo, Puruándiro, La Huacana, Tepejí del Río, Celaya, Pátzcuaro, Matehuala, Hermosillo, Lagos, and Torreón, to name a few, all saw clashes over this issue. It seems to be true, as Karl Schmitt claims, that there were more of these clashes earlier in the Porfiriato than later, but we continue to see them throughout the period.[56]

But José Alberto Moreno Chávez, who has carefully studied devotional practices in Mexico City, where closer adherence to the laws of the Reform than in the provinces or the countryside was posited by González Navarro and others, shows that "exhibitions of public devotion were made with absolute normality," and that liberal reclamations against such practices, though they were frequent, never rose to the level of "persecution," as the Catholic press claimed.[57] It is entirely possible that some kinds of public displays were better tolerated by the government than others; particularly baroque and defiant displays probably antagonized liberals more than carefully crafted and organized public celebrations of the Virgin of Guadalupe or the Sacred Heart. Class was surely a factor too. As Sergio Francisco Rosas Salas shows, in Puebla the elite-directed Círculo Católico pursued a strategy of slow change in the direction of more public displays of religiosity between 1887 and 1900.[58] These public displays, he argues, were no less political for being less aggressive, but they were more tolerated. As we will see, this trend toward nonviolent insistence on the right to express religiosity publicly opened more space for women, especially middle-class and elite women who were so supportive of the new Roman devotions (chapter 7), to participate.

FREEDOM OF THE PRESS

The culture wars were fought *in* the press but they were also fought *about* the press.[59] There were more non-Catholic newspapers than Catholic ones, but few cities, even small ones, failed to have both.[60] One purpose of both the liberal and Catholic press was, as I have emphasized above, to protest the actions and ideas of the other side in the culture wars (and indeed to construct the "other side" as monolithic, to paint all Catholics or all liberals as the same—which was true of neither liberalism nor Catholicism).[61] But press actions were also a site of culture warfare, as editors advanced their own ideas about what adherence to the principles of a "free press" should look like, and how their enemies' understandings of freedom of the press were wanting.

Catholic newspapers frequently ran articles critical of freedom of the press during the Porfiriato. Their attack was two-pronged. First, they argued that the liberal papers' freedom to publish "anything they wanted to" yielded too easily to abuse (*libertinaje*). The phrase "absolute freedom of the press" was always pejorative, and was always bound up with dangers to morality. An 1879 front-page article in *La Voz* captures the gist of this argument:

> Freedom of the press: to what has it been reduced in Mexico? It is sad to report. For every work of some usefulness, for every article that does not attack morality and customs, there are thousands of indecent pamphlets and novels that flaunt good taste . . . and drown out any semblance of virtue; for every newspaper that employs measured tones and elegant language, there are swarms of dailies that abound in nauseating sentences, in uncontrolled impudence, in impious insults, and disrespectful ridicule of the highest authorities. Private life, family honor, the sanctity of religion, everything that is cultured and civilized, is exposed daily to the venomous sarcasm of editors without knowledge and without conscience.[62]

Second, the Catholic press claimed that the restrictions on complete freedom of the press were applied unfairly. The "impious" press, it claimed, enjoyed "impunity" from harassment by the authorities, even when it "insulted, libeled, and offended Catholics," while the Catholic press was persecuted and its editors jailed.[63] This periodically repeated argument, supported by specific outrages, was at the heart of a movement in 1890 to form a new Catholic

Associated Press, splitting from the press association to which all newspapers had belonged. The idea was first floated by *La Voz*, and was quickly taken up by *El Tiempo*, who wrote that "we ourselves have recently had a difficult experience that confirms the truth of what *La Voz* says: just today we have been denounced and are in danger of being sent to [the prison of] Belén by the words and accusations of *La Patria*."[64] It does not appear that anything came of this secessionist movement, but from time to time the Catholic newspapers noted approvingly the formation of a Catholic press association in the United States.[65]

But for all its condemnations of too much freedom of the press or too differentially applied standards of decency, it is clear that the Catholic press understood that it needed to defend press freedom at least in some form, since the right to "sustain our beliefs by making use of freedom of the press" was an important element of their political projects after 1875.[66] Editors consistently upheld the principle of press freedom when it came to their own publications, and were quick to cry "hypocrisy" when, as happened from time to time, the liberal press expressed disgust for the Catholic press in terms that seemed to question their right to proclaim their faith. What "delicious irony," wrote *El Tiempo* in 1910, when the "anti-Catholics contend that not all opinions are equally respectable. Magnificent! . . . The free thinkers negating free thought, when it comes to the freedom of thought of the Catholics."[67]

Toward the end of the Porfiriato, the Catholic press ramped up its attack on its liberal counterparts, calling on the faithful to try to prevent anyone from buying or reading any book or newspaper that was not published by a Catholic press. Reading the "impious" or even the religiously indifferent press would do great harm to society, as *La Voz* put it in 1907, adding that "we consider it our duty, almost our most important duty, to combat this press that sows error and, while pretending to operate in good faith, is carrying our society down paths that lead nowhere."[68] Applauding a papal letter of 1910, *El Tiempo* put "uncontrolled freedom of the press" on a par with socialism as "terrible dangers" that must be resisted. By this time the Catholic population in Mexico, along with Catholics in Europe and Latin America, had responded, as we will see below, with a campaign of boycotts that aimed to silence published impieties.

The liberal press matched the virulence of the adjectives used by the Catholic press against it: "Every page [of the Catholic newspapers]," wrote *La Convención Radical Obrera* in 1892, "reveals the scandal-mongering, jesuitical casuistry, and bad intentions that abound in all those nests of vipers they call sacristies."[69] Mirroring the Catholic press's accusation of liberal press hypocrisy, *La Patria* in 1897 complained that the "reactionary newspapers" were profoundly hypocritical, enjoying the freedom to say anything they want, but then protesting when they were caught (probably a reference to the jailing of some editors). "They say that they do not enjoy freedom of the press. This is like the thief complaining because he is prevented from thievery, or the delinquent because he is punished for his delinquency."[70]

The liberal press was in at least as awkward a position as the Catholic press. If Catholic editors condemned freedom of the press despite relying on it, the liberal press condemned the Catholic press but was philosophically committed to press freedom, in a way that the Catholic press was not. *El Diario del Hogar* in 1896 admitted the dilemma: as much as it disdained the words and actions of the clerical press, it was unwilling "to deny it the right to publish political propaganda. In the intellectual fight all ideas ought to be allowed to contest, which is the only way that false and laughable ones can be defeated."[71] The best liberals could do was to try to shame the Catholic press for being excessively political.

This was a task that some liberal writers thought would be made easier after the apostolic visitor Monseñor Nicolas Averardi, in 1896, told the Catholic newspapers that they should tame their language and write only about religion, not about politics: "The Catholic press should not pursue any goal that is not Religion."[72] Speaking directly to three newspaper editors he had summoned for an audience, he continued: "With regard to the constituted public authorities, show them respect, obedience, and compliance; with regard to private persons, show deference, gentleness, and consideration; always there should be an absence of hatred, resentments, acrimony, and virulence in your language and style." *El Diario del Hogar* gloated that this put the Catholic press "between the sword and the wall: if they do as he instructs . . . goodbye plans for worldly aggrandizement! Goodbye ambitious dreams of power!"[73] But the Catholic press was defiant. As *El Monitor Republicano* wrote three weeks later, "We expected that when [Monseñor Averardi] went back to his own country, the Catholic press would once again adopt the anti-religious, inconvenient, and discourteous stance that it had always taken." But "we thought that given the seriousness of [his] words, his benign influence would at least last as long as the Apostolic Delegation remained in Mexico."[74] The Averardi effect, however, had only lasted eighteen days. By May 13, as *El Monitor* pointed out, *La Voz*, with Averardi still in Mexico for some time to come, had attacked *El Universal* in intemperate language and was back to its old ways, "given over in body and soul to politics, not religion."[75]

WOMEN AND WOMEN'S ACTIVISM IN CATHOLIC DISCOURSE

Scholars depict the church's view of women in this period as a full—indeed, fuller than ever—embrace of traditional gender hierarchies.[76] We saw in chapter 7 that the hierarchy was trying to reestablish gender hierarchy in lay associations, and discursively, too, the church redoubled its efforts to promote traditional gender roles. The famous 1891 papal encyclical *Rerum Novarum* was centrally about labor, but it also "reaffirmed the husband's authority within the home and promoted women's domesticity."[77] Motherhood as the highest calling for a woman and the need for women to stay at home, raising their children and supporting their husbands, was a constant refrain. As we saw above, this womanly ideal was at work in the context of calls for religious education for girls, deemed of supreme importance because future mothers needed to be taught Christian values and doctrine. And as historian Sofía Crespo Reyes observes, if anything these rigid definitions of appropriate roles for women were an even more important part of church discourse in the Porfiriato than earlier in the nineteenth century.[78] She notes that the church in Argentina, Chile, France, England, and Italy, as well as Mexico, redoubled efforts in the last third of the nineteenth century to promote women's "traditional" role as the "axis on which family life turned, the guardian and protector of domestic space, the housewife, wife, and mother, the 'angel of the home.'"[79] In an echo of liberal critiques about Catholic women during the petition campaigns, female agitators for women's rights and the dreaded feminists ("thank God" only to be found in the US and England) were held up as unwomanly.[80]

Catholic women themselves, for the most part, seem to have agreed with this view. The establishment of multiple Catholic secondary schools during the Porfiriato meant that the year-end examinations and celebrations usually included a speech by one of the graduates or profesoras, and there were also speeches given by the female directors of these schools at the time the school opened. Almost always, as we might expect, given the occasions, these speeches dwelled on the importance of education for women, which was bound up with training for the moral and material demands of motherhood. Saturnina Jasso's 1889 speech upon the opening of the Colegio de Santa Teresa de Jesús in Puebla extolled the great mothers in history.[81] An 1888 speech by María de Jesús Gutiérrez, a professor at the Colegio de Santa María de Guadalupe in Morelia, praised the church for "never forgetting the sublime mission of the woman, who, before she is an educated person, is a daughter, sister, wife, or mother."[82] In order to shine, she continued, all that is necessary is her "humility as a daughter, her modesty as a virgin, her tenderness as a wife, her abnegation as a mother, her delicacy and her religion as a woman." And the director of a girls' school in Pátzcuaro assured parents that she was teaching their daughters to "fulfill the most important functions in human society: taking care of the family, educating its children, guiding it along the path of reason and justice, watering and fertilizing this hard ground and preparing it to flourish."[83]

But the very fact that these were speeches by women, given in public spaces with men in the audience, and praised by the newspapers that reprinted them, suggests that public roles for women were quite not as taboo as the rhetoric of the speeches themselves might indicate. And in fact, María de Jesús Gutiérrez of Morelia, while ultimately coming down in favor of traditional roles for women, also made clear that times had changed: the "apprenticeship of women today is not limited to preparing her for the honorable chores of the domestic life; she spins in a much bigger orbit because she is being pulled by an era that wants to take away the spinning wheel and the needle and replace them with the telescope and the scalpel."[84] It was no longer unthinkable, she orated, that the "queen of the home" might involve herself in "political, social, and philosophical debates; belong to clubs; go to cafes and casinos; and aspire to the congress and the law."[85]

A more powerful sign of ambivalence in Catholic discourse about the proper roles for women had to do with the cautious but intensifying praise in the press for foreign women who were activists on behalf of the church. This was a late-Porfirian phenomenon for the most part, and one initiated by the comparatively moderate *El Tiempo*. The earliest example I found was a short article in 1903 condemning the Italian government for trying to put nonreligious textbooks in the schools, and applauding the one thousand mothers of Brescia who signed a protest against this "masonic imposition."[86] In 1905 an approving report on a movement of French Catholic women, Acción Social Cristiana de la Mujer, occupied the better part of three columns on page one of *El Tiempo*.[87] In 1907 another front-page article about the Uruguayan League of Catholic Women's campaign against legalizing divorce was the most effusive yet. It contrasted the persistence and effectiveness of Uruguayan Catholic women with the ineffectual behavior of Catholic men, and quoted the archbishop of Montevideo as calling for the "female Catholic element" to organize, in imitation of the "valiant" Patriotic League of French women."[88] *El Tiempo* included in the article information about how the league was organized, its relationship to congregations and pious associations, whom it invited to adhere to the League, and the various commissions that were created within the League. In other words, it offered a blueprint for Mexican women, without quite saying so.

In 1908 the conservative *La Voz de México* got into the act, with an article carrying the headline "An Active Life is What is Needed."[89] The article was concerned, as the previous article in *El Tiempo* had been, with Uruguayan women's activism, but it was long and passionate, with praise for activist women not only in Uruguay and France but also Belgium, Germany, and other places where men were not acting and women were. The Catholic press of Mexico was moving closer and closer to outright calls for Mexican women to organize and act.

CATHOLIC POLITICS, MEXICAN WOMEN, AND WOMEN-LED LAY ASSOCIATIONS

Women's political work on behalf of the church during the Porfiriato was not, for the most part, in the form of organized protests—certainly not on the scale of either of the petition drives discussed in chapters 4 and 6. Moreno Chávez mentions that women were present in several marches and demonstrations after the turn of the century, including one in favor of a priest who had been accused of seducing a parishioner, and as we'll see below, I, too, have found cases of local protesting and petitioning.[90] But I have discovered only one early petition campaign that was intended to be national: an effort directed at women by *La Voz de México* to convince incoming president Díaz (as the "odious" presidency of Manuel González was ending in 1884) to allow the return of the Sisters of Charity.[91] But it seems to have fizzled, perhaps because it did not originate with women or women's groups, but rather with the exhortations of *La Voz*. Although the Guadalajara newspaper *La Voz de la Patria* claimed that a "multitude" of women's petitions in response to *La Voz*'s call were coming in daily, only six were published either there or in *La Voz* itself, and they were from smallish towns like Celaya, Atlacomulco, and Tepoztlán.[92]

Instead, women advanced the church's political agenda in quieter ways, often through the vehicle of lay associations. The actions of both service and devotional associations—helping the poor; visiting and providing for the sick; holding raffles and kermesses to raise money for the church; visiting the prisons; performing rituals, devotions, and prayer inside the church; and adorning the interior of the churches for special occasions in as splendid and awe-inspiring fashion as possible—all had clear political impacts. They bound the casual Catholic more closely to the church, influenced susceptible young children, bolstered the visibility and moral prestige of the church, and kept the church in the public eye and attractive to the faithful. But while liberals did not find these actions innocuous, they did not (generally) condemn them, except for the occasional comment about them being a waste of time or money. They were not seen as clearly "political" and so escaped the kind of opprobrium that women's petitioning had come in for in the earlier period.

Even in the three highly controversial arenas of the culture wars discussed above, the political work done by women and women's lay associations did not provoke much gendered criticism by liberals.[93] In other words, liberals issued vehement warnings about the increase in the number of Catholic schools, but they did not specifically blame Catholic women for driving this trend. They bitterly complained about violations of the spirit of the Reform laws where public displays of religion were concerned, but did not call out women's groups for being behind these displays. The liberal anxiety about women in Catholic politics, then, was notably weakened during the Porfiriato, translated into an anxiety about Catholic schools or the Catholic press that was largely ungendered in its attribution of causation. As for the Catholic perspective, women who quietly supported Catholic schools, rather than writing angry petitions lambasting secular schools, required no defense, in contrast to the petitioners of the 1850s and 1870s. So the Catholic press, until late in the period, was also fairly muted on the topic of women's political activities.

This lack of attention in the press makes it harder for the historian to recover the actions that were taken by women, but it is clear that they were neither inactive nor silent. I concentrate here on the activity of Catholic women and women's lay associations in advancing the church's political agenda in the three areas of most controversy: public displays of religion, the press, and schools.

PUBLIC DISPLAYS OF RELIGION

The most energetic protests by women against the laws of the Reform came at the local level, and especially with regard to public displays of religion, as they organized petitions and commissions to approach local authorities, asking them either to allow a religious procession or display, or to request that civic events not be permitted to interfere with sacred holidays. The Catholic ladies of Puebla, for example, asked the municipal authorities not to illuminate or allow music to be played in the kiosk of the Paseo Viejo on Good Friday.[94] Women in Zacatecas requested the city council to make an exception to the laws of the Reform and allow the church bells to ring throughout the day on October 12, 1895, to coordinate with the coronation of Guadalupe in Mexico City.[95] Further research in municipal archives or possibly the archive of the Basilica of Guadalupe might show these kinds of small local actions by women to have been quite common; they only came to the attention of the press when they raised a fuss, which most of them did not, because they were rejected by municipal authorities. We have already seen that quite a few municipal authorities were sympathetic and allowed processions and bell-ringing to go forward, in which case they often produced liberal outrage—but in those cases the outrage was directed at the priest or the municipal authorities, not the original petitioners, whose identity was not mentioned in the press accounts.

The most common way that women resisted the spirit of the Reform was by elevating their long-standing responsibility of adorning the interior of churches—allowed by the Reform laws—into a political statement. The most famous of these actions was the 30,000 pesos in "rings, earrings, necklaces, watches, and any other jewels of value" that women donated to embellish the Virgin of Guadalupe's crown in her 1895 coronation, a mass donation that both Catholics and liberals understood to be laden with political meaning.[96] Liberals took the opportunity to imply that Father Antonio Plancarte, the organizer of the coronation, did something fishy with these jewels, or at the very least duped women into contributing them.[97] But on a smaller level, women, and especially women in lay associations, could make a political statement by doing what cofradías and pious associations had always done, which is take responsibility for ensuring that the adornments of the church in ordinary times and on special occasions was as spectacular and awe-inspiring as possible.

In 1882 the "humble and virtuous ladies" of Puebla took politicized religious display into the streets when they organized the elaborate decoration of many houses in the city center for the day of Santa Teresa de Jesús. According to *El Amigo de la Verdad*, Puebla's Catholics, angered by anticlerical acts taken by the city government, had refused to participate in civic ceremonies on September 16.[98] Not content with passively staying indoors for the *fiestas patrias*, however, the women of Puebla decided to orchestrate a competing act of civic adornment, much more elaborate than the one the city government had managed. At least according to *El Amigo*, they succeeded: "You could stand at any intersection and look in all four directions and see every house" featuring tapestries, banners, flags, pennants, flowers, arches made of greenery, such that "it appeared as if a magician with supernatural power had taken charge of embellishing the city in honor of the saint." That this was a political statement was emphasized by *El Amigo*: "Everyone wanted to demonstrate that although the Catholics of Puebla are oppressed, their faith does not decay, their hope endures. . . . saying in mute but eloquent language: Here there is Catholicism, here there is faith."[99]

Although we cannot be sure that the Catholic ladies of Puebla who formally protested civic celebrations during Holy Week and arranged the decoration of the downtown to compete with the fiestas patrias were members of lay associations, it seems highly likely, since the Puebla lay associations were extremely active and well-organized. We know that in 1888 a similar display was indeed organized by "various cofradías of Señoras" of Puebla, who coordinated the tossing of flowers and confetti from balconies as the bishop's carriage passed through the city in such profusion that "it seemed as if they were raining on him."[100] Like the adornment of downtown houses, and like the petition campaigns of 1856 and 1874–75, this was the kind of group action, involving door-to-door organizing, at which lay associations—and particularly women's lay associations—excelled.

Another way that lay associations after the turn of the century expressed their willingness to challenge the prohibition on external displays of religion had to do with the medallions and insignias that the associations required their members to wear. The sale of these items raised money for the organization, but they were also a way to manifest faith publicly in a way that was impossible to forbid for a regime that was, at least superficially, committed to individual freedoms. Almost every lay association added this requirement, beginning early in the Porfiriato, including the Apostolado de la Oración, which had as one of its few requirements that members wear the scapular and medal of the association.[101]

Toward the end of the period, Catholic women teachers in the public schools began to wear medallions featuring the images of saints and other "religious propaganda" in their classrooms. This was too much for liberals, who condemned this practice as a violation of the laws of the Reform; the Secretaría de Instrucción Pública forbade it in 1907, and the state of Mexico did the same in 1909.[102] This produced a predictable outcry from the conservative press on the grounds of freedom of conscience. "This is yet another example of the odious intolerance of those who constantly brag about how religiously tolerant they are," thundered *El Tiempo*.[103] "If wearing these medallions is a public demonstration of religion, which is against the law, then no señora or señorita should be allowed to wear them; public school teachers should not be singled out." It seems clear that the young teachers who displayed these images in the classroom knew what they were doing, and were choosing to risk the disapproval of their employers in order to defend Catholicism.

A variation on the theme of challenging the prohibition on public displays of religion was the ostentatious modesty in dress and behavior modeled self-consciously by members of women's lay associations.[104] The church had tried to dictate the way women dressed for well over a century, but mainly from the pulpit. Now lay associations became the mechanism through which the members embodied morality. The Hijas de María in particular were believed by many priests to be an essential lay association to establish in their parishes because they provided "a strong shield against corrupt customs" in part through the modesty of their dress, as one priest put it, "so important when girls were young."[105] Public perceptions of morality had much to do with dress and behavior, and lay associations were keen to be sure that their members looked the part. In 1887 the Sociedad Católica of Puebla published and distributed leaflets that called on both women and men to abstain from participating in two "recent bad customs": a promenade, and a serenade on Good Friday.[106] The promenade caused scandal because it reflected a desire to be seen and admired: "vanity and ostentation are characteristics that Catholics should reject," the leaflet admonished. Instead, the public should emulate the behavior of the members of the Sociedad, including the "most distinguished ladies of Mexican society, who dressed during Holy Week in the simplest clothes, with absolutely no jewels, and avoided entertainments and distractions." The rules of the Asociación de la Corte de María in Mexico City called for members not to be "slaves of style" and only to adopt new fashions that did not undermine the "decency and dignity of a Señora or young Christian lady."[107] Similarly, the objective of the Asociación de Nuestra Señora de Lourdes was to "distance the youth from vanity and dangerous diversions, and accustom them to respect and modesty in church."[108] The Corte de Guadalupe in Morelia also listed among its principle goals to model resistance to immorality by "reading sacred books, engaging in pious conversations, and practicing good customs such as trying to procure an end to drunkenness."[109] In 1909 the Sociedad Antipornográfica was founded in Mexico City, with the purpose of "moralizing public spectacles and . . . protecting the spectators from indecent situations."[110] Finally, one of the main purposes of the Obreros Católicos was to combat vice, among the male workers, of course, but also among their families. Many of these associations had a salon in which they sponsored "theatrical spectacles, lectures, projections of the magic lantern, etc. . . . all of which serve as honest recreation for the male workers, the female workers, and their families who are fleeing from the impious spectacles that the public movie houses and theaters offer."[111]

THE PRESS

One of the most dramatic entries of Catholic women and women in lay associations into the political arena came late in the period, in connection with the battle between the "good" (Catholic) press and the "bad" (liberal) press. In 1909 the women of the small city of Zamora, Michoacán, were outraged by a caricature of General Bernardo Reyes in the image of the Immaculate Conception, which had been printed in the liberal *El Heraldo*.[112] The women found this image sacrilegious and insulting and wrote a manifesto condemning it, calling for signatories to disallow in their homes any newspaper that directly or indirectly attacked religion, boycott any businesses that advertised in such newspapers, persuade friends and family to stop reading and subscribing to the impious press, support the "good press," pray for the conversion of the "bad" newspapermen, and unite with other women "in this glorious enterprise."[113] Soon after, Catholics—sometimes just women, sometimes both men and women but almost always many more women than men—signed petitions of support or formed new leagues to combat the liberal press in Mexico City, Guadalajara, Cholula, Córdoba, Orizaba, Toluca, and Morelia, among others.[114] In March 1910 *El Tiempo* ran an admiring article about the crucial role played by Catholic women in Buenos Aires, Montevideo, and Santiago in developing the Catholic press, and specifically praised the women of Zamora for getting such a movement underway in Mexico.[115]

Lay associations had in fact been involved earlier in combating the "mala prensa," following the lead of Catholic Europe.[116] In 1898 the Círculo Católico of Puebla created a League of Women that would be in charge of distributing "good" reading material and "making war on the bad."[117] But after the 1909 Zamora manifesto the cause was quickly adopted by several other lay associations, most notably the Apostolado de la Oración.[118] The 1910 report on the activities of the Apostolado in the archdiocese of Guadalajara registered the collection of fifty thousand printed (by the Apostolado) "promises" not to read any book or periodical that was in any way contrary or hostile to the Catholic faith.[119] The faithful signed them and deposited them in front of the congregation; those collected in the Santuario de Señor San José in Guadalajara, for example, were placed in a special "elegant silver-plated urn."[120] Those who made these promises constituted the Liga del Sagrado Corazón de Jesús, a subgroup within the Apostolado that was meant to be especially vigilant against the impious press.[121] The report also credited members for generating almost nine thousand subscriptions to *La Restauración Católica*. As for the "bad books," the report detailed elaborate plans to collect, display, count, and then burn such publications. A separate new lay association, the Asociación del Espiritu Santo, was also founded in Guadalajara, specifically to foment the Catholic press.[122] All over the country, women were urged by *El País* to take the lead in this campaign, since the editors argued, they were ideally suited to distribute good newspapers through their societies and social connections and thus assure the triumph of the Catholic press.[123] They should band together, *El País* urged, like the "Damas de la Buena Prensa" in Germany and the Liga Protectora de la Prensa Católica, a women's group in Bilbao, Spain, not only to distribute Catholic newspapers but also to promote subscriptions, advertising, and protection for the Catholic press.[124]

Catholic women, in sum, as members of lay associations or leagues of women, challenged two of the most contentious aspects of liberalism: laws against public displays of religiosity and battles over the meaning of the free press. We turn now to the role of women in lay associations in promoting Catholic education, perhaps the most contentious issue of all from the point of view of the national (and international) culture wars.

LAY ASSOCIATIONS AND RELIGIOUS EDUCATION

In 1890 *La Voz de México* ran an article with the headline "Catholic Associations: Protectors of Religious Instruction."[125] But clearly the article—which called for establishing lay associations dedicated to promoting religious education in the nation—was more aspirational than a reflection of reality.[126] Lay associations, the article argued, had a big role to play in improving Catholic schooling. But even the Sociedad Católica, which had been founded with a mandate to expand religious education, had not extended its reach very far outside of the cities and larger towns.

I think we can assume that at the turn of the century there were no more than three hundred schools in the whole country either run by lay associations or for which lay associations supplied the bulk of the operating budget.[127] According to the 1896 parish survey of the archbishopric of Michoacán, for example, where lay associations were abundant, not a single one was mentioned as supporting any of the thirteen parochial schools included in the survey.[128] (The reader should recall that the survey is not comprehensive; I only found surveys for 86 percent of the parishes in the archbishopric.) There were quite a few private Catholic schools, but parents or hacienda owners funded them. In the archbishopric of Mexico outside of Mexico City, according to the 1897 parish survey, there were thirty-three parochial schools and over seventy private Catholic schools (here I found surveys from 73 percent of the total parishes in the archbishopric). The men's and women's Societies of St. Vincent de Paul each supported one private school in Atzcapotzalco, and the Sociedad Católica helped support two parochial schools in Pachuca. That was the extent of lay association involvement in funding Catholic schools outside Mexico City.

In the capital, where there were many Catholic schools, the situation was a little different. By the mid-1890s there were at least twenty-five parochial schools, eight schools supported by the archbishop, seventy schools for nonpaying students, and over one hundred fifty private Catholic schools.[129] But the role of lay associations in supporting this variety of Catholic schooling was still not major. The Congregación de la Buena Muerte, the Sociedad Católica, the Sociedad Guadalupana, the Asociación de Señoras "El Alma de María," and the Sagrado Corazón de Jesús ran or contributed to fewer than twenty of them.[130]

Although I don't have survey data from the archbishoprics of either Puebla or Guadalajara, my impression is that lay associations in those archdioceses were more involved in education than was the case in Mexico and Michoacán.[131] In Puebla, through the 1890s the Sociedad Católica (both men's and women's) ran ten schools in the capital city alone, seven for boys and three for girls.[132] They had estimated in 1887 that in order to reach all the children of Puebla, they would need twenty; there were probably not many other cities in Mexico where *all* Catholic schools at this time were able to reach half the population, much less Catholic schools supported by a single lay association.[133] There were also a fair number of schools outside the city.[134] And in the archbishopric of Guadalajara, in the mid to late 1870s and 1880s pastoral visits to seventy parishes show that the Sociedad Católica was maintaining at least one school in ten of them, and often more than one—in San Gabriel they ran twenty-four schools—while in Atotonilco an Asociación de María supported a large girls' school, and in Arandas and Zapotlanejo the Ladies of Charity supported multiple schools.[135] Unfortunately I have not found systematic reporting for later in the Porfiriato, but we know that the Sociedad Católica continued to be strong in that archbishopric and that archbishops there continued to emphasize the need for Catholic schools. I would be surprised to learn that there were fewer than 60 schools supported at least in part by lay associations at the turn of the century, given that there were 104 parochial schools alone (that is, not including Catholic private schools) by 1900.[136]

Why, despite the furious national rhetoric around religious education, did lay associations not play a larger role in helping to bolster the Catholic school system in the first two and a half decades of the Porfiriato? Part of the explanation is that beginning in the late 1880s, European religious orders began to arrive in Mexico, most of them as educators. Most schools run by these orders were found in the cities, but some served smaller towns, and wherever they were they obviated the need for parish schools or private schools financed by parents or the community.[137]

There were three other reasons, however. First, establishing a school was an ambitious proposition. They were very difficult to staff, especially in rural areas. Priests in the 1885 parish survey conducted by the archbishopric of Mexico constantly complained about how hard it was to find teachers willing to teach in a rural school, while parents (and the priests as well) complained about the quality of the teachers who were willing to do so.[138] The schools were also expensive. Most needed at the very least 25 pesos a month to pay the salary of one teacher as well as necessary supplies and rent on a room or building.[139] A modest school, then, would cost 300 pesos a year, a fairly substantial amount even if there were several sources of funds available that could be combined to meet expenses. The priest of Teocuitatlán (Guadalajara) in 1885 noted that the Sociedad Católica had sponsored two schools in his parish, one for boys and one for girls, for nine years, from 1873 to 1882.[140] But in 1882 the schools ceased to exist for lack of funds, because the Sociedad could not keep up its monthly stipend, and the priest could not make up the difference because of the money he had to expend in the "work of the church."

This last comment points to the second reason that lay associations were not more involved in supporting parochial schools: no matter the panic in the Catholic newspapers over religious education, priests perceived more urgent needs than establishing schools, and the priority of the parish associations was to help the priest. After the consolidation of the Díaz regime and the onset of the first extended period of relative peace and prosperity for many decades, repair and restoration of the physical plant and material needs of the church were understandably seen as more pressing than establishing schools. As the priest of Tanhuato (Michoacán) put it, when he arrived in his parish there were no schools, not even a municipal school, and although he "understood that this was one of the most urgent necessities," he "could not attend to it immediately because there were other needs that were even more essential, including stocking the Sacristy with the necessary instruments of the Mass."[141] As it happened, this clerical priority of providing for the church and making it possible to conduct the Mass with decency aligned with the preferences of many women, and as had been true from the early days of the Vela Perpetua in the 1840s, lay associations in the 1880s and 1890s regularly assisted with new purchases such as the liturgical vestments for the parish that the ladies of the Vela Perpetua in Tecolotlán (Jalisco) paid for in 1881, or the cost of painting the inside of the church and gilding the main altar (which was "completely destroyed") that the Vela in Valle de Santiago (Guanajuato) helped fund in 1894.[142]

Third, priests de-prioritized establishing expensive schools because they were frequently quite satisfied with the existing state of religious education in their parishes. In some parishes this was because of the religiosity of the public school teachers and their willingness to teach doctrine in the schools, sometimes in defiance of the law. I have calculated elsewhere that in the archbishopric of Mexico in 1885 almost two-thirds of the public schools taught doctrine, despite the fact that in the state of Mexico it was forbidden to do so and teachers often had to teach Catholicism surreptitiously.[143] Similarly, in Guadalajara—where the friendly state government instructed the municipal schools not to hold class on Thursday afternoons or Saturdays so that students could receive religious instruction—in parish after parish priests professed themselves to be entirely satisfied with the religious instruction that students were receiving in the public schools.[144]

In other parishes, parochial schools were not seen as essential because private Catholic schools were abundant. As the priest of Celaya put it, he could not, with his parish income, afford to support a parochial school, but "there are plenty of Catholic schools for both boys and girls, sustained by private funds and supervised by me."[145] In Pátzcuaro there was no parochial school but there were twelve private Catholic schools to serve the small city's population.[146] The vecinos of Mezquitan (Jalisco) petitioned the archbishop for funds with which to establish a Catholic boys' school in 1906, but they were willing to live without a girls' school since there were two private schools for girls.[147] The number of private schools was greatly increased in the late 1890s and especially in the first decade of the twentieth century by the arrival from Europe of new teaching orders: the Salesians, the Ursulines, the Marists, and many others, including two "home-grown" women's teaching orders, the Guadalupanas and the Josefinas.[148]

But lay associations did figure prominently in religious education, despite not running or supporting very many Catholic schools (at least until late in the period, as we will see shortly). How? By providing the essential services of offering religious instruction, teaching the catechism (in the church and in afterschool or Saturday or Sunday classes), and preparing children for First Communion, tasks that priests found burdensome and repetitive. It would be difficult to underestimate the number of families into which members of lay associations intervened in order to bring their children to church and instruct them in how to be a good Catholic. Almost all lay associations dedicated part of the time of qualified members to these crucial endeavors, which not only reproduced Catholicism in families generation after generation, but also brought new or strayed members back into the church. These efforts were at the core of the church's political agenda in the late nineteenth and early twentieth centuries.

Besides the Sociedades Católicas de Señoras and the Hijas de María, which had always dedicated themselves to teaching the catechism and preparing children for their First Communions, there were new associations created for the specific purposes of helping the priest in these areas of religious education.[149] An 1898 pastoral letter from archbishop of Mexico Próspero Alarcón urged the creation of the Congregación del Catechismo, and within two years the new association ran twenty-three catechism "schools" for boys and nineteen for girls in Mexico City, and another eighteen outside of the city.[150] The all-female Cofradía de la Doctrina Cristiana later joined the Congregación in dedicating itself to the teaching of doctrine, and it spread rapidly.[151] Active members actually did the teaching, while "protectors" donated money, stamps, books, sweets, and other little gifts to reward the children for their accomplishments. Members earned particularly attractive indulgences by going out into the countryside to teach doctrine.[152] The importance of the association for providing religious instruction can be gauged by the fact that there were sixty-two active members in the small parish of Tacámbaro (Michoacán) alone.[153]

After the Latin American Plenary Council in Rome in 1899—attended by four archbishops and nine bishops from Mexico—ordered parish priests to found parochial schools anywhere they did not already exist, we do begin to see lay associations move more noticeably into direct support of parochial schools.[154] In response to this order the archbishop of Michoacán circulated a questionnaire asking parish priests, among other things, what means they proposed to amass enough resources to support a school.[155] Common answers were raffles, creating local Juntas de Instrucción, pressuring landowners to contribute, and, most significant for our purposes, tapping the funds of lay associations. Priests especially named the Vela Perpetua, which had very rarely been involved in helping fund schools in its sixty-year history.

Soon after, we begin to see evidence that the Vela was changing its spending practices to include regular support for parish schools. To cite just one example, in Morelia the Vela contributed twenty pesos a month to support a girls' parochial school that enrolled five hundred girls "of all social classes" when it was founded in 1902.[156] Other lay associations that had previously supported the parish by donations of time and money for improvements also shifted to supporting the parochial school project. The parish priest of Tanhuato, for example, in 1905 lined up support from the Vela Perpetua (two pesos a month), the Asociación del Sagrado Corazón de Jesús (two pesos), and the Obreros Católicos (five pesos), which, along with five pesos from his parish funds and five pesos from the parents of the students, added up to nineteen of the twenty-five pesos needed to pay the salary of the teacher.[157] He hoped that the archbishop would cover the rest (if not, he wrote, the project will be unsustainable). The Apostolado de la Oración, which, like the Vela, had previously infrequently dedicated money to support schools, became a significant source of funds in the twentieth century. In Zacapu (Michoacán) just over 230 pesos out of the approximately 330 pesos collected by the Apostolado from alms and the sale of medals and other objects signifying membership in the organization went to the parish schools.[158] The Ladies of Charity also moved more decisively into schooling while maintaining their traditional roles as home, hospital, and prison visitors. In Ameca (Jalisco), the conference of Señoras ran five parochial schools and thirty Sunday schools, covering all the neighborhoods in the small city.[159] And the new Catholic workers' associations were a natural fit for a relationship between lay associations and schools. Free schools for the children of workers were extremely attractive, and probably a majority, perhaps even a large majority, of these associations prioritized the establishment of schools. In Matamoros, the Sociedad de Obreras

Católicas founded a free school for girls in 1902.[160] Obreras also supported a girls' school in Senguio, Michoacán.[161] Both Obreras and Obreros in La Piedad sponsored schools; two hundred twenty girls attended the one, and three hundred boys attended the other.[162]

This flurry of activity on the part of lay associations helped make for an increase in the number of Catholic schools in the last decade of the Porfiriato. How much of an increase is hard to say because statistics on this topic are quite problematic, and totals for the whole country are not reliable.[163] But I think it is safe to draw some conclusions from the official reports sent in by individual states, where it is easier to spot strange numbers and we do not have to worry about states that failed to report skewing the totals. The official statistics collected in the *Anuario estadístico de la República Mexiana* on church-run schools, which were mostly parish elementary schools, show that some states added only a few such schools or even lost some between 1902 and 1907 (among them Tepic, Hidalgo, Puebla, and Veracruz).[164] But others showed fairly significant increases. Between 1894 and 1905, for example, Jalisco, which already had made a serious commitment to parish schools beginning in the 1870s, increased the number of these schools from 74 to 165.[165] If we assume that, on average, 80 percent of the private schools accounted for in the *Anuario* were Catholic (a conservative estimate, I think), and additionally assume that 50 percent of the small number of schools said to be run by "associations" also taught doctrine, and we add those to the reported number of church-run schools, then Catholic schools constituted between 40 percent and 50 percent of the total number of primary schools in Guanajuato, Aguascalientes, San Luis Potosí, Querétaro, Jalisco, and Michoacán by 1907.

Conclusion

On the surface, Catholic women appear to have been surprisingly politically quiescent in the Porfiriato, compared to their previous activism, and in light of both the importance of the culture wars from the perspective of the Catholic press, and the example of Catholic women in other countries organizing, petitioning, and making waves. The success of the Romanization project (chapter 7) may explain this apparent passivity. Romanization was intended to reestablish the power differential between priest and parishioner, but a semi-unintended consequence was that it made the relationship between priest and *useful* parishioners, who could help him accomplish the long list of things that the Vatican hoped he would accomplish, closer and less combative. I found far less evidence of women challenging or arguing with their priests than I did in the previous periods, which could reflect the reality that middle-class and elite women who led the associations had aligned their own interests with those of their priests. Improved training for parish priests toward the middle and end of the period may also have given them better tools for achieving this kind of alignment than priests possessed in the earlier part of the century.

To reiterate a point I have made throughout this chapter, however, to interpret women's lack of dramatic politicking as an absence of politics would be a mistake. Women were not doing less of the church's political work—they were doing more of it. Church politics had changed after military defeats in Mexico and challenges to the power of the church globally. These cultural politics were the kind that women were well-suited to advance, especially through the lay associations they led and dominated numerically, which were more numerous, more prosperous, and more active than they had ever been. Another way to think about women and Catholic politics in the Porfiriato is to see instilling Catholic morality, as against what Catholics viewed as amoral or morally neutral liberalism—the ideology of the "scientists"—as the overarching goal of the church. And there was no group of Catholics more prepared to make morality matter than women.

EPILOGUE

Catholic Women and Politics, 1910–1940

CATHOLIC WOMEN'S ACTIVISM in the 1910s, 1920s, and 1930s has attracted the interest of a growing number of historians since the 1990s. Almost without exception, these scholars have assumed that the highly visible petition drives, letter-writing campaigns, marches, demonstrations, defiant processions, coordinated symbolic protests, and even military actions (during the Cristero rebellion in the late 1920s) were Catholic women's first entries into politics.[1] As they see it, the extreme anticlericalism and anti-Catholicism of the revolutionary state drove women to act politically as they had never done before.[2]

They also seem to suggest that Catholic women's political actions effectively ended in the 1940s (though this period is scarcely studied at an archival level, especially with attention to gender). Women had seemingly been won over by conciliatory gestures from the post-1940 state, one that was prepared to find common ground with the church around anticommunism, and preferred to court women with the carrots of subsidized consumption, welfarism, modest protections for women's rights within marriage, and eventually suffrage, rather than continue to antagonize them by, for example, mandating sex education. The broad narrative, then, is one of the twentieth-century "rise and fall" of female Catholic activism, closely paralleling the dominant "rise and fall" narrative of the Revolution to which Catholic women objected.

This book, however, writes a different story. It decenters the Revolution by showing that Catholic women had been politically aware and active since the late 1840s. The actions of women in the 1910s, 1920s, and 1930s, then, were not pioneering or anomalous forays into politics. For Catholic women in Mexico, the era of the Reform—more than the era of the Revolution—was the major turning point. This was when the state committed to a secular state, secular education, a secular regime of property ownership, and to promoting secular culture, positions anathema to many Catholics. From the

Reform forward, governments might bear down on secularism or ease off, but they never considered a return to a world in which Catholicism would regain official status as a state religion or public schools would be allowed to teach doctrine. Catholic politics thus became a politics of attenuation, sometimes desperate, sometimes confident, sometimes fiercely waged, and sometimes quietly. Catholic women were a key to the success of all Catholic politics, and at no time between 1850 and 1940 were they sidelined or irrelevant. Like Catholic politics itself, the nature of their engagement did vary in intensity and visibility, but it was never absent.

Since most readers' only image of Mexican Catholic women as political actors comes from their military actions during the Cristero war (1926–29) and perhaps the protests against sex education during the Cárdenas regime (1934–40), a survey of women's lay associations and Catholic activism after 1910 makes sense, so that we can more effectively think about what a deeper genealogy of Catholic women's associationalism and activism in the postrevolutionary period means for the history of Mexico, the history of women, and the history of Catholicism in Mexico. Accordingly, this chapter figures as both an epilogue and a conclusion, with my thoughts on that genealogy woven into the story of what happened after 1910 and summarized at the end.

Catholic Women, Lay Associations, and Politics in the 1910s

One of the twentieth-century women's lay associations that has drawn substantial attention from scholars is the Asociación de Damas Católicas Mejicanas [sic] (ADCM), founded in Mexico City in 1912. At first, the Damas appeared to be another church-run charitable and philanthropic association, like the Ladies of Charity or the Sociedad Católica, distinguished mainly by the fact that it had been founded by the archbishop and not by groups outside the direct purview of the hierarchy.[3] The basic outlines of the Damas' social work—combining attention to schools and the teaching of doctrine, the press, and moral improvement of their communities and the working classes—were not only quite like those of the Ladies and the Sociedad Católica, but also resembled the great variety of devotional associations like the Apostolado de la Oración, the Vela Perpetua, and the Hijas de María. Like the earlier service organizations, they were active in supporting schools, clinics, hospitals, schools, daycare centers, soup kitchens, clothing drives, and prison libraries.[4] Like many Porfirian associations, both service and devotional, they distributed pro-church newspapers. And like most of the Porfirian associations—again, both service and devotional—they were very concerned about maintaining moral standards and promoting Catholic values. Some of the events they organized, like baseball games, were meant to provide "a moral alternative to spending time in cantinas."[5]

Were the Damas fundamentally different from the Porfirian or Reform-era associations in terms of their engagement with politics? Several historians have argued that the Damas were designed with the direct advancement of Catholic politics in mind. According to Jorge Adame Goddard, the Damas' main political purpose was to support the work of the new Catholic political party, the Partido Católico Nacional (PCN).[6] This aspect of the Damas' work, however, was short lived since the PCN was disbanded less than two years after the Damas were founded. Randall Hanson, in a 1994 dissertation, highlights a different political connection in emphasizing the role of Alfredo Méndez Medina, a Jesuit priest who called for the establishment of a national association of Catholic women in part to combat the recent foundation of the YMCA in Mexico.[7] But while the Protestant threat was always present in the minds of churchmen and Catholic women, it was more of a cultural or moral threat than a political one. Francisco Barbosa Guzmán points to yet a third political goal of the Damas: to support the fledgling association of (male) Catholic students, the Asociación Católica de la Juventud Mexicana (ACJM).[8] However, although the ACJM would later play a key political role in the Catholic resistance to revolutionary anticlericalism, at the time of its founding this highly politicized future was not yet clear.

More convincingly, the Damas can be seen as advancing indirect political goals. As historian Sofía Crespo Reyes argues, its ecclesiastical founders hoped that by enhancing ties of sociability among Catholic women, their social and philanthropic activities would be molded into a kind of political practice.[9] This is surely a likely motivation for the foundation. But the suggestion that the Damas were the first to bring Catholic women together in association and thereby make it easier for them to be politicized, politicize each other, and politicize their clients is incorrect. In fact, compared to the sociability provided by the nineteenth-century associations, which allowed women to associate and lead in ways they never had before, the value added by the Damas was probably marginal, since my guess is that the mainly elite and middle-class members were almost all already members of another lay association. In short, the Damas' political actions and potential (at least until the very end of the decade), like their social agenda, did not go much beyond those of women's associations during the Porfiriato.

The Damas were initially very successful, perhaps because 1912 turned out to be a good year to organize. The Revolution had not yet created chaos in Mexico City, but it had begun to exacerbate poverty and what the ladies saw as "immorality," giving rise to the perception that something must be done by those who had the means to do so. By October 1912 the third convocation of the Damas was attended by over nine hundred women (all "belonging to the best society"). They were organized by their ecclesiastical directors into sections (schools, libraries, press, etc.), with three ladies at the head of every section. Their responsibility would be to go block by block "so that in the end there is not a single woman in the city that does not belong to the Association."[10]

During the regime of Francisco Madero (1911–February 1913), the strategy seemed to be working: the Damas of Mexico City grew to over 10,000 members; a new foundation in Guadalajara quickly enrolled 10,200 members; and there were early foundations in Toluca and Zamora.[11] But the Huerta dictatorship of 1913–14, to which the Catholic hierarchy and the PCN had acquiesced to at least a certain degree, brought discredit to the church and the Catholic party, civil war to Mexico City, and disaster to the Damas organization in the capital.[12] With the fall of Huerta in mid-1914, the victorious Constitutionalists under Venustiano Carranza tolerated and even encouraged sometimes-violent anticlericalism, justifying it by referencing the church's and the PCN's support of Huerta. These persecutory actions affected the Damas institutionally and individually and led to the cancellation of meetings in Mexico City and the flight of the presidenta out of Mexico.[13] Finances were desperate. Only eight women regularly attended meetings in Mexico City, and eventually the chapters in towns on the outskirts of the capital that were most affected by the war disappeared.[14] Although later in the decade new chapters were formed in Colima (1917), Guanajuato and Puebla (1918), and San Luis Potosí, La Paz, Durango, Oaxaca, Morelia, Querétaro, and Celaya (1919), as late as 1920 the Mexico City Damas' activities were still reduced, both in terms of the number of chapters and the number of committees that remained active.[15]

In Guadalajara, however, the Damas, founded in 1913, remained vibrant, and it is perhaps for this reason that here is where we begin to get a glimpse of how Catholic women's political participation would ratchet up in the revolutionary and post-revolutionary contexts. In 1918 a series of petitions, mass protests, economic boycotts, and political theater brought numerous women's associations into the political foreground, including (prominently) the Damas, but also the Vela Perpetua, the Ladies of Charity, the Hijas de María, the Asociación de Santa Zita, and several female catechistic associations.[16] Their ire was directed against a decree issued by the governor of the state of Jalisco which, among other objectionable things allowed by the 1917 Constitution, limited the number of priests in the state and permitted only one church per 5,000 faithful, converting the rest to state use, like schools.[17] The Damas, many of whose chapters in and around the city submitted petitions protesting both the decree and the subsequent expulsion of the archbishop of Guadalajara, expressed their reasoning in a broadside that read: "There are times when a woman, naturally resigned to suffering, cannot but make herself heard. . . . She will remain silent confronted with offense made toward her person; but confronted with assaults on her Faith, her life's force and vigor, woman must always respond with the sublime cry of protest."[18] This is language that could easily have been found in the petitions of 1856 or 1874–75.

Besides the petitions, the protests also included a boycott of transportation and of two newspapers, as well as a powerful symbolic performance: Catholics placed black bows over their doors and in their windows as a sign of mourning. These actions of protest went on for a year and were successful in getting the state government of Jalisco to repeal the decree in early 1919.[19] In fact, the success of this movement surely contributed to the policy of President Álvaro Obregón (1920–24) not to encourage state and local officials to strictly enforce the anticlerical provisions of the constitution.

Catholic Women and Politics in the 1920s

In the aftermath of the military phase of the Revolution, the church and Mexican Catholics, including many women—though including many men as well, some of whom had tolerated anticlericalism but were frightened by the anti-Catholicism of the Revolution—worked hard to shore up loyalty to the church.[20] Revolutionary governments sought not only to deal a powerful blow to the church but also to deliver on the social agenda that had emerged over the course of the Revolution. The church countered with a renewed social agenda of its own. The emphasis on social action was partly a global Catholic initiative, but for the Mexican church there was also the powerful impetus that Catholic social action could be used to counter revolutionary social action.[21] In an ideal world, there would be a corresponding Catholic institution for every state institution: the Catholic answer to the public school was the Catholic school; to the labor union, the Catholic workers' union; to the revolutionary press, the Catholic press; to state charity, Catholic charity; to public libraries, Catholic libraries; to the nationalism of the Revolution, a Catholic nationalism built around the Virgin of Guadalupe. None of these initiatives was new, of course, but in the 1920s, the heyday of Social Catholicism in Mexico, they seem to have been understood as constituent parts of a world that was fully parallel to the one being offered by the Revolution.[22] As Roberto Blancarte puts it, "Catholic social doctrine, like its revolutionary counterpart, tried to offer an answer to the social problems caused by the modern relations of production, but one based on Christian morality."[23]

But a full commitment to Social Catholicism was not the only feature of Catholic politics in the 1920s. Continued—indeed increased—anticlericalism seemed to require not only a social action response but also a political response, as had been mounted in Jalisco in 1918–19.[24] The social and political projects overlapped, since most of the social action associations encouraged by the church also participated in the many political actions with which Catholics provoked the state and responded to provocations.

In 1920 the church formalized the social action effort by creating a national umbrella organization of lay associations devoted to Social Catholicism called the Secretariado Social Mexicano (SSM). The SSM aimed to centralize, modernize, and coordinate efforts among its component associations, which included three associations structured by age and gender: the Damas (now renamed the Unión de Damas Católicas Mejicanas, UDCM) for adult women, the Caballeros de Colón (Knights of Columbus) for adult men, and the ACJM for young men.[25] (The Juventud Católica Femenina Mexicana [JCFM], for young women, was founded in 1926.) Thus the SSM was structured in a way that on the surface embraced a substantial degree of gender parity.[26] The role of the two women's groups in the SSM was clearly understood to be important, and indeed Hanson identifies the Damas as having the "most rigorous social program" of the four age/gender groups.[27] They also had by far the largest membership, with almost twenty-three thousand members in 1925, compared to seven thousand in the ACJM and five thousand in the Caballeros.[28]

How did the Damas' sociocultural functions and goals change in the 1920s? Overall, they seem to have become more specialized in providing social services for working women, and not just poor families generally, than before 1920.[29] Among the more notable efforts on behalf of working women was the Damas' activity in organizing unions for female workers, including clerical workers, telephone workers, tobacco workers, seamstress, and teachers.[30] Other female-oriented services included night schools for women workers, normal schools to train Catholic teachers, day care for the children of women workers—all of which had Porfirian antecedents—and rehabilitation houses (casas de regeneración) for former prostitutes. Finally, as lay associations had in the Porfiriato and the decade of revolution, the Damas continued to fulminate against bad morals when it came to dances, fashion, movie houses, and theaters, a stepped-up campaign from the early years of the organization that fit nicely here because it was mainly directed at women.[31] The concern with working-class morals, always present, may have become a more central part of the Damas' program in the aftermath of the Revolution and in the context of global cultural models and changes that seemed very frightening: 1920s cinema, fashion, and the imported phenomenon of the flapper-like *chica moderna*.[32]

Some historians have seen these activities and priorities as evidence that the Damas had been influenced by maternalism, a loose set of ideas around maternal and child welfare that were circulating internationally in the early twentieth century.[33] This was probably the case; the Damas were well-educated, worldly women, and in the 1920s they actively sought international contacts. But what was "new" about maternalism in the international arena was primarily that it idealized an alliance between women and the state, an element of the Damas' "maternalism" that was lacking, for obvious reasons. There is no question that the Damas were interested in child welfare and mothers, probably no more so than the Ladies of Charity or the Sociedad Católica, but interested nonetheless. However, the implication that this elevation of the role of the mother in child welfare in the Damas' rhetoric and mission first gave Catholic women a political platform in the 1920s does not accord with the evidence presented in this book. In the nineteenth century, as we have seen, Catholic women's self-proclaimed basis for political action had also sought to highlight their traditional roles as mothers and guardians of youth, if perhaps more their moral state than their physical well-being. The idea that women must take the lead in socializing their families and their communities into Catholicism was, implicitly if usually not explicitly, at the core of every lay association (both devotional and service) founded or led by women, and their roles as mothers were repeatedly held up as a justification for their venture into political petitioning in 1849, 1856, and 1874–75.

What about the Damas' more concrete political roles? And how did theirs differ from the roles of other lay associations or from Catholic women's activism in general? To answer these questions, we need to briefly summarize the escalating climate of tension between Catholics and the revolutionary state in the 1920s. There were multiple serious clashes during the Obregón years (1920–24).[34] Anticlerical acts in the early 1920s that registered on the national consciousness included the bombing of the archbishop's home and the Basilica of Guadalupe in 1921, and the expulsion of the apostolic delegate for having taken part in the consecration of a monument to Christ in the state of Guanajuato in 1923. Catholics provoked the state with mass movements that defied the law against public displays of religion, like the monument to Christ itself and the 1921 coronation of the Virgin of Zapopan in the cathedral of Guadalajara, accompanied by a procession of some twenty thousand people.

The punch/counterpunch quality of many incidents is well illustrated by a series of episodes in Morelia in 1920 and 1921. In 1920 several lay associations planned a huge procession to celebrate the 25th anniversary of the coronation of the Virgin of Guadalupe, even though the event violated both the constitution and specific prohibitions issued by the police chief of Morelia. When members of various lay associations persisted in distributing fliers advertising the procession, the radical governor of Michoacán, Francisco J. Múgica, ordered the leaders of these associations to be arrested.[35] A few months later, a group of labor activists occupied the cathedral on Labor Day and flew the red-and-black flag of the labor movement from the clock tower. To protest this desecration, as they saw it, thousands of Morelia's Catholics, led by several priests and lay associations, tried to march from the church of San Diego, on the outskirts of the city, into the city center. Confronted by police, the march turned violent and the leader of the Socialist party in Michoacán, Isaac Arriaga, was killed.[36] Further reprisals against Catholics followed.

Catholic women regularly joined these and other marches, pilgrimages, processions, petition campaigns, and other actions that were intended to protest restrictions on religious liberty. For Jalisco, María Guadalupe García Alcazar writes that women "constituted the largest contingent in the demonstrations and marches" in that state.[37] For Chihuahua, Franco Savarino Roggero calls the presence of women in petitioning and lobbying "significant and leading," and points to the invasion of the state congress of Chihuahua in 1923 by six hundred "belligerent" women protesting the implementation of the 1917 constitution and the subsequent three-thousand-person demonstration ("almost all women") in further protest a few days later.[38] In a 1924 speech in San Luis de la Paz, Guanajuato, the revolutionary party candidate, Plutarco Elías Calles, lambasted Catholicism, and women in attendance shouted him down with cries of "Viva Cristo Rey!"[39]

Although it seems likely that lay associations played a role in these protests (as the Morelia case makes clear), it is just as hard to pinpoint those roles as it was for the nineteenth-century petitions. But as with the petitions, there are strong hints that their impact was significant. One of the lay associations that took a lead in publicizing the Morelia procession was a women's group, the Asociación de Madres de Familia, and we know that the Damas Católicas continued to send and publish letters of protest (as they had in Jalisco in 1918), designed to spur other groups to register their own protests.[40] When Calles ordered the closing of the church of the Sagrada Familia in Mexico City on May 26, 1926, on the pretext that foreign priests were officiating there, the Damas, along with the affiliated association of Santa Zita (made up of domestic workers), blocked the entrance to the church and refused to leave. When they were attacked with water hoses, they responded by advancing on the soldiers with rocks. Some five thousand women marched to the national palace in protest, where they, too, were attacked. The Damas' newspaper, *La Dama Católica*, evaluated the scene in a way reminiscent of the Guanajuato women's shaming of men in 1874: "Men of the Republic," it wrote, "there are your models. Go hide your shame in the dark caverns of our forests."[41] In short, it is clear that Catholic women's participation in political protests before the Cristero war broke out in late 1926 was widespread and visible, and we know that women's lay associations, including the Damas, were front and center in at least some of them, though as we will see shortly, the Damas held a special position in the Catholic resistance in the later part of the decade.

The lead-up to the war began in earnest when Calles took over the presidency in December 1924. Calles was not prepared—as Obregón had been, at least to a certain extent—to treat the church in a conciliatory fashion. As Sarah Osten puts it, "Calles argued that the most urgent ... political obstacle that Mexico faced was the enduring threat of a conservative (Catholic) reaction against the Mexican Revolution."[42] It was Calles who first used the full power that the constitution of 1917 granted the state to regulate the church. The Calles Law, as it was labeled, of June 1926 called for severe penalties for any infraction of the five articles of the constitution that governed church-state relations.[43]

When the Calles Law was enacted, the Catholic resistance was ready. In February 1925, just a few months after he took office, Calles had supported the installation of a schismatic Mexican church that disavowed the Vatican, hired non-celibate clergy, used tortillas instead of wafers in the Communion, and consecrated the Host with mezcal instead of wine.[44] Many Catholics and the entire hierarchy agreed that this was something that could not be met by the massive but relatively uncoordinated protests that had formed the core of the Catholic response so far. Two weeks later the hierarchy and key lay organizations—including the Damas, the ACJM, the Knights of Columbus, the Catholic labor confederation, and the national parents' association, in other words, the main components of the SSM—formed what David Espinosa calls a "Catholic umbrella resistance organization," the Liga Nacional Defensora de la Libertad Religiosa (LNDLR).[45]

Once the Calles Law was promulgated, the Liga called upon the Damas to help advance the organization in a variety of ways, including publicizing the LNDLR in their magazine and urging readers to join.[46] Damas used their networks to organize the dissemination of LNDLR propaganda: "Dressed in black as a sign of mourning for the evils suffered by the church and as a symbol of the austerity that they proposed," Juan Pablo Vivaldo Martínez writes, "they walked the streets distributing the LNDLR's call to action."[47] As women were the main organizers of consumption in their families, they were key parts of the LNDLR-organized boycott of all nonessential businesses in 1926. They helped the Liga coordinate huge pilgrimages to the Basilica of Guadalupe during the fiesta of Christ the King; in 1928 something like two hundred thousand pilgrims in Mexico City participated.[48] The JCFM, too, offered its services to the Liga, recruiting members and raising funds. Its first donation to the Liga, a modest 200 pesos, came from members' work as hairdressers and hat repairers.[49]

The UDCM formally disassociated itself from the Liga once the organized military rebellion began in January 1927 under Liga direction.[50] But many individual members of the Damas continued to support the war, as did other women. Damas and others provided hiding places for priests and nuns; printed and spread propaganda; sent letters and telegrams of protest to the president; participated in boycotts; organized masses in private homes to give priests an income and maintain the faith; fed prisoners taken during the war; baptized babies; conducted clandestine masses; and paid for priests' and nuns' journeys into exile.[51] There were numerous incidents in which Damas were arrested and jailed for distributing propaganda, wearing mourning for the church, or hiding priests.[52]

The Damas were politically active, then, though their role has been overshadowed by the more famous Brígadas Femeninas de Santa Juana de Arco. These were young women, most from the middle and lower classes, who enlisted as members of a full military organization (each brigade had seven hundred fifty members under a colonel, lieutenant colonel, and five majors, each of whom was served by captains, lieutenants, and sergeants).[53] They came to number some twenty thousand. Unlike the Damas, the Brigadas continued to recognize the Liga's leadership, though the tensions between the female-led Brigadas and the male-led Liga were intense.[54] Some of their most dangerous work involved smuggling ammunition and supplies (María Luisa Aspe Armella calls their role "decisive"); they also carried documents, cared for the wounded, and made explosives. Many were killed or arrested in the process.[55] When the Cristero rebellion ended in June 1929, many Catholic women—from the Damas to the *brigadistas*—were profoundly disappointed in the outcome.

Acción Católica Mexicana and Catholic Women in the 1930s

Since the 1860s, as we have seen, liberal and revolutionary governments had consistently prohibited lay associations from directly engaging in political activity. But when the Cristero rebellion ended, the negotiated peace settlement put extra pressure on the Mexican church to comply with this injunction.[56] The Catholic cause had not prevailed, and the war had been costly in human and reputational terms. The hierarchy agreed to completely renounce political activity, in exchange for which they extracted a pledge from the government not to enforce anticlerical provisions in the constitution "in a hostile manner."

Not wanting to risk reprisals for venturing out of the spheres in which the accords allowed the church to operate, in late 1929 the SSM drew up statutes for a new organization that was called simply Acción Católica Mexicana (ACM), or Catholic Action, as opposed to the Catholic *social* action that had guided the church and lay associations in the 1920s.[57] The ACM consisted of four core groups structured along lines of age and gender.[58] For adult women there was the Unión Femenina Católica Mexicana (UFCM), whose original incarnation was of course the Damas Católicas.[59] For young women, there was the JCFM. For adult men the Unión Católica Mexicana (UCM) replaced the Knights of Columbus (which had been a part of the militant LNDLR during the Cristero war); and for young men the ACJM was purged of its Cristero connections and transformed into a defanged youth organization with no resemblance to the old version.[60] All were meant in their activities and rhetoric to emphasize the spiritual and moral over the social, and to the exclusion of the political.

After almost twenty years of promoting an activist Social Catholicism, the church's narrowed insistence on moralization and spiritual instruction instead of (as opposed to in conjunction with) political and even to a certain extent social action was difficult for many laypeople to accept. Roberto Blancarte and María Luisa Aspe Armella see this as a contradiction: members had integralist inclinations, in the sense that they saw moral, social, political, and spiritual projects as connected; but both the church and the state prohibited this kind of integration.[61] Another contradiction was that while the hierarchy had to work through laypeople to accomplish their goals, they also wanted to control the laity so no rogue actions violated the accords.[62] (This was a predicament not unlike the one faced by the hierarchy after the victory of the liberals in 1867, when, as we saw in chapter 5, they feared being seen as organizing lay associations but also worried about excessive lay autonomy.) The ACM thus came into existence with the potential for lay resistance to both its mission and the way it was intended to function. Perhaps for this reason the women's groups within the ACM enjoyed the special trust of ecclesiastical officials. They could, the hierarchy thought, be trusted to be "submissive daughters of the Church," just the ticket for an ACM that prioritized control over the laity.[63]

In the new, supposedly more apolitical ACM, the two women's organizations were put in charge of a set of familiar tasks: restoring faith and devotion to the church, as well as confronting cultural secularism with moralization in the home, the parish, and the elementary schools.[64] I would not characterize any of these three sites of Catholic moralization as "apolitical," but it was especially difficult to avoid politics in the schools. As chapter 8 showed, the role of religion in education had long been highly controversial.[65] Now schools became even more of a political battleground. Tensions between the revolutionary government and Catholics moved from a post-Cristero simmer to a full boil in 1934, when the Secretaría de Educación Pública (SEP) intensified its attack on religious education, following through on the belief shared by many liberals and revolutionaries that Catholicism was not compatible with nationalism.[66] In late 1933 the revolutionary party included in its Six-Year Plan the proposal that "primary and secondary education should be based on the principles of the socialist doctrine that the Mexican Revolution supports."[67] Resistance to "socialist education" grew dramatically, especially when it was recommended a month later that the curriculum for grades one through six should include sex education (see Figure 9.1).[68]

The ecclesiastical hierarchy came close to violating the letter and spirit of the peace accords with a joint pastoral urging Catholics to resist. They did. The furious lay response was spearheaded by parents and especially by women. Women's groups organized marches against socialist education and sex education and went door-to-door urging fellow Catholics to boycott public schools.[69] In Guadalajara in 1934 over thirty thousand Catholic women demonstrated against socialist education, despite being met with tear gas and water hoses.[70] Women's lay associations opened clandestine schools where Catholic instruction would be offered, in homes and churches and other spaces, and the UFCM alone was administering approximately twenty-five hundred schools throughout Mexico by 1936.[71] I have not found any information on gender balances in the Unión Nacional de Padres de Familia (UNPF),

FIGURE 9.1. Women marching against sex education. Photograph courtesy of the Instituto Nacional de Antropología e Historia de México and Mediateca INAH. From the Casasola collection.

which was among the groups leading the opposition to sex education, but it appears that the "mothers'" branch of the organization was especially active, and one UNPF plan revolved around mothers individually sending letters of protest to the Mexican president, with copies sent to the leading dailies.[72] And in a different register, women were perhaps surprisingly often perpetrators of the horrific violence committed against public school teachers.[73] One admittedly biased observer wrote in 1936 that "the men play nothing more than secondary roles in this battle full of ignominy and wickedness. It is the women who work the invisible strings of all the propaganda against the educational work. It is women who unite an infinite number of children in the annexes of El Sagrario to teach them the catechism. . . . It is women who have gone from house to house to persuade [students] . . . to quit attending classes."[74]

By 1936 the regime was beginning to realize that, as Adrian Bantjes put it, "Catholic resistance, combined with rising opposition from conservative groups within the revolutionary family . . . threatened the very future of the Revolution."[75] The state backed off gradually.[76] As it did, the hierarchy responded by providing important support for Cárdenas's nationalization of the foreign-owned oil companies in 1938, issuing cautious praise for some government social programs, and relaxing its prohibition on Catholics working in or attending public schools.

Not all lay Catholics accepted the conciliatory posture of the church and the ACM after 1936, any more than they had after the Cristero rebellion.[77] Catholic violence against public schoolteachers or agents of the revolutionary state did not end; a "second Cristero war" (*la segunda*) continued into the late 1930s and beyond.[78] But by 1940 pilgrimages and processions began to occur without government interference, and Cárdenas's successor, Manuel Ávila Camacho, famously stated that he was "a believer." The desire on the part of the revolutionary state to combat the influence of the church did not go away. But the strategy for cultivating hearts and minds changed from harsh methods of elevating the nation over the church—closing churches, persecuting priests, exiling bishops, burning saints, and prohibiting religious practices—to more positive methods like stressing nationalism and patriotism through music, dance, festivals, art, and education.[79]

The ACM and Catholic Women in the 1940s and 1950s

Servando Ortoll implies in his 1986 dissertation that the ACM was "unpopular" with "active" Catholics because it was increasingly "relegated to the role of an organization for women."[80] This is a statement whose dismissive tone Ortoll would be unlikely to defend today, but substantively he had a point. In 1938 the two women's organizations within the ACM constituted about 80 percent of the membership, which was under two hundred thousand people. Twenty years later the ACM reached a zenith of half a million members, 80 percent of whom were still women.[81]

Hypothetically, this overwhelmingly feminine cast to the ACM might explain why, in an effort to bring in more men (an old historical challenge, as chapter 7 shows), new groups were formed or incorporated into the ACM: its directors may have hoped they would attract more men.[82] These included the Legion of Decency, which was brought into the ACM in 1938; the UNPF, which had been in tenuous existence since the 1910s but began to come into its own in the 1930s as a leader of the movement against socialist education; and the Movimiento Familiar Cristiano (MFC), founded in 1958. All had male participation (though we don't know what the gender ratios of the membership were).[83] Like the women's groups in the ACM, they were centered on the need for Christian education and Catholic moralization.[84]

Anne Rubenstein calls the moralization campaigns organized by these and other Catholic groups in the 1940s, 1950s, 1960s, and 1970s expressions of "moral panic," showing that there were times when calls for censorship of comic books, "pornographic" books and magazines, cinema, and even statues like the one of Diana on Avenida Reforma (whose nakedness the wife of one president wanted covered) were especially heated.[85] But it is important also to see the underlying desire for moralization—the key, Catholics believed, to family preservation—as an acute concern at least since the challenge to

Catholic values from secular values began in the mid-nineteenth century. From this perspective the women and men of the ACM and the Legion of Decency and the other associations dedicated to defending Catholic morals were connected to the nineteenth-century lay associations and the petitioners of 1849, 1856, 1874–75, as well as to the activists of the 1920s and 1930s, all of whom were also profoundly worried about the threats to the family—represented by "godless" ideologies or non-Catholic religions—that the secular state allowed to exist and even encouraged. When apostolic delegate Leopoldo Ruiz y Flores in 1934 called socialism a system in which "the child belongs to the State and not to the family," he channeled the fears of mothers since the mid-nineteenth century.[86]

The moralization campaigns of the ACM groups and its offshoots helped smooth the path for an alignment of church and state around anticommunism. In the aftermath of World War II and the Allied victory, the Mexican government joined other Western states in opposition to Soviet influence globally and within Mexico itself. This positioning had geopolitical motivations, not religious ones, but it made communism a shared target of Catholics and PRIistas (supporters of the official party the PRI, or Partido Revolucionario Institucional). The period 1940–60 was, then, one of "relative reconciliation" between church and state in which lay associations and Catholic women, as active in both moralizing and anticommunist actions, played a large role.[87] No wonder the Mexican government finally saw it as safe, even as an advantage, to offer the franchise to women, who were granted the vote in 1953.

Catholic Women, Lay Associations, and Catholic Politics after 1960

In the 1960s the ACM began to decline as a national organization. By 1965 the membership had fallen from half a million in the 1950s to four hundred thousand, and by 1985 it did not even reach one hundred thousand, almost 90 percent of whom were women.[88] The global backlash that began in the 1960s against rigid moralities was surely implicated in this loss of membership. Moreover, Vatican II (1962–65) and the related rise of liberation theology caused a "crisis" in the ACM because of the voice they gave to liberalizing, even radical, tendencies within the church (at odds with the "traditional" values of the ACM), and because they encouraged Catholics to demand more say in their parishes and in the church (at odds with the ACM's top-down structure).[89]

Since the ACM was comprised so heavily of women, does the decline in membership mean that more and more Catholic women, reconciled to a post-1940 state that could be seen as defending families and upholding Catholic moral values by fighting communism and other threats, were gaining a more secular outlook?[90] Were more of them willing to reject at least some of the strict positions taken by Rome and the Vatican with regard to gender, marriage, sexuality, and reproductive rights?

Without better research on this period, it is difficult to know. Obviously, as we saw in the discussions of liberal women in chapters 3, 5, and 7, not all Mexican women felt as powerful a connection to the church and Catholic values as the women self-selected to join and lead Catholic lay associations; in other words, there had always been degrees of adherence to church teachings even among self-identified Catholics.[91] It is certainly possible, even likely, that loyalty to the church after 1960 was weakening among women. The birth control pill, the ability to divorce and remarry, and even abortion rights were clearly attractive to some Catholic women, and in the 1970s the language of second-wave feminism arguably gave them the courage to break, at least partially, with the church well before a Mexican branch of Católicas por el Derecho a Decidir (Catholic Women for the Right to Choose) was founded in 1994, institutionalizing this progressive element within the population of Mexican Catholic women.[92]

But I think we should be cautious in drawing conclusions about the degree and nature of secularization from scant data about joining patterns in one organization that suffered a sharp decline. First, the drop in the numbers of people who belonged to ACM groups may not even tell the whole story for these groups. Some seem to have remained relevant at least into the 1980s. Guillermo de la Peña and Renée de la Torre, for example, characterize the role of the ACM in the neighborhood of Santa Teresita in Guadalajara in the 1940s as still strong and active into the 1980s, though less involved in organizing workers and peasants over time and more centered on improving the parish, providing suitable recreation for parishioners, supporting parish schools, and of course encouraging religious observance.[93]

Second, one given since the colonial period in Mexican associational life has been that new associations rise in popularity and old ones often fade. We have already observed this kind of dynamism in the associational landscape; it happened throughout the nineteenth century, as we have seen, and in the period under consideration here we see new national-level associations formed in the 1930s, 1940s, and 1950s, like the Legion of Decency and the MFC. Since then other new associations seem to have captured the mood of the religious right better than the ACM, with its historic commitment to advancing Catholic politics indirectly. Two stand out as more willing to engage national politics, especially concerning gender politics, than the ACM, and may therefore have been more attractive to activist conservative Catholic women and the religious right more generally. One is the Mexican pro-life movement, Pro-Vida, which began in 1978 when ten thousand women from across the country marched to the Basilica of Guadalupe to protest proposals to legalize abortion.[94] The march has become an annual event; in October 2021 there were marches in seventy cities, with over a million participants protesting the Mexican

FIGURE 9.2. The March for Women and Life, Mexico City, Oct. 3, 2021. Photograph courtesy of David Ramos, ACI Prensa.

Supreme Court's recent decision to decriminalize abortion.[95] The other is the Frente Nacional por la Familia, formed in 2016 to protest legalized same-sex marriages in Mexico; it sponsored a million-person march in the year it was founded, and has made powerful connections with both the Partido Acción Nacional (PAN), which was founded in 1939 as a Catholic party, and the PRI, as well as, ironically, with evangelical Protestant groups.[96]

Third, and most relevant for this book, there are the parish associations. Even during the decade of the Revolution in the 1910s, the Damas Católicas was far from the only association Catholic women wanted to join. In fact, the formation of new women's associations that were *not* the Damas continued at a steady pace.[97] In the 1920s and 1930s, we see the same thing: non-ACM groups were alive and well.[98] The continued importance, from the perspective of parish priests, of these groups is indicated by the order in which the new priest of Zapotiltic in 1929 went about establishing new lay associations: first he committed to rejuvenating the Vela Perpetua and reorganizing the Hijas de María, among others, before turning in late 1930 to founding ACM organizations. By the end of the decade, Zapotiltic had twelve well-functioning lay associations in addition to the four ACM groups.[99]

We know very little about these parish associations in the period 1910–40, though we catch glimpses of them working alongside the ACM groups to resist the revolutionary project in the 1930s. Kristina Boylan's informants, for example, consistently remember the Hijas de María acting politically in the archbishopric of Guadalajara in the 1930s and into the 1940s, and Ben

Fallaw points to the Hijas, the Asociación de Catequistas, the Damas de Caridad, and the Asociación de la Medalla Milagrosa as among the "beatas" who "forged informal networks based on their parish organizations . . . to resist the revolutionary project" in 1930s Guerrero.[100] After the 1940s they disappear even more thoroughly from the historiography, but this does not mean that they were not still active in the parish, not still nurturing and strengthening community piety; it just means that scholarly attention focused on the ACM groups and their predecessors (the Damas, the UDCM) has largely concealed them from view.[101]

Conclusion

I emphasize the importance of these parish groups not only because they have been lost in the historiographical shadow of the Damas and the women's ACM groups, but also because they are the main actors in this book. From the colonial period to at least 1940 and probably beyond, parish associations continued to bring women, who formed the majority in most of them and led many of them, into close, working relationships with priests and each other. This institutional base and experience of leadership meant they were positioned to act politically at the local or regional level when the need arose. Parish associations generally practiced a quiet politics that could be transformed—either by the members themselves or the parish priest, or the two in tandem, as I suggested often happened in the 1850s and 1870s—into a more aggressive politics. When they did enter national politics, it was temporary. Sometimes their efforts contributed to fleeting successes, as in 1856. Sometimes they made for a more enduring victory, as in the 1874–75 petitions, which helped bring about the overthrow of Lerdo by the more conciliatory Díaz, and in the 1930s, when they successfully pushed the Cárdenas regime to soften official anticlericalism and effectively end socialist education. But afterward they returned, figuratively, to the parishes. Beneath the surface of the "rise and fall" narrative of Catholic women's activism, then, the parish continued to be the place from which women, though lay associations, either acted directly on national issues or acted locally to nurture Catholic practices, to moralize and socialize Catholic youth, and therefore to advance the Catholic political project.[102]

If the parish has been for many years the locus and strength of Catholic politics, this gives important context to the negotiations of the ecclesiastical hierarchy with the state, that is, to church-state relations. Some scholars have persuasively attributed the persistence and expansion of Catholic political power in Mexico since the 1960s to the hierarchy's skill at political maneuvering.[103] The archbishops are seen as having achieved surprising victories, in light of the ostensible commitment of the state to laicism. Their efforts culminated in the 1992 constitutional reform that restored many of the privileges that had been lost to the church since the era of the Reform.[104] Eight years later the PAN was victorious in the 2000 presidential election; president-elect Vicente Fox

FIGURE 9.3. Cover of *Los supermachos* featuring Doña Eme, Sept. 8, 1966. © Eduardo del Rio, with permission of his estate. The bubbles read: Doña Eme: "The League of Decency prohibited it!" Juan Calzonzin: "Ah, then it must be a good movie."

celebrated with a banner of the Virgin of Guadalupe and a crucifix on prominent display.[105] Frustrated progressive commentators have railed against the seemingly phoenix-like power of the church to throw its political weight around, from the great political cartoonist and humorist Eduardo del Río (Rius)—who consistently critiqued the church in the 1960s, using, among others, his character Doña Eme (appropriately for this book, a member of the Vela Perpetua; see Figure 9.3)—to two leading scholars of the church in Mexico, Bernardo Barranco V. and Roberto Blancarte, who recently published a book called *AMLO y la religión. El estado laico bajo amenaza* (AMLO [the Mexican president, 2018–24] and religion: The secular state under threat). The title speaks for itself.[106]

But without disputing ecclesiastical shrewdness, in this book I have focused not on the actions of the bishops but on how religious practices were maintained and reinforced in the community, notably by women in parish lay associations. The constant, not phoenix-like, presence of a loyal laity with a track record of voicing discontent when threatened has given the hierarchy the power to negotiate with the state. The book does not aim to prove that the laity was out ahead of the hierarchy (though there were a couple of incidents where I suggest they may have been), or more important than the hierarchy, or that the hierarchy was dependent on laypeople. But it does remind us that the church has strength because of the people who trust it and actively support it. This seems obvious, but is not always clearly taken into account in analyses of church-state relations.

Besides offering a perspective that emphasizes the parish rather than the bishops and church-state relations, this book has shown the importance of using a framework of gender in order to understand change over time in the ways religion and religious practice are organized and promoted. Scaled-back religious celebrations, multiplying complaints about impiety, the growth of anticlerical rhetoric, and the gradual installation of national (nonreligious) institutions and celebrations have all been taken as part of a story of declension, evidence of a decline in the practice of religion in nineteenth-century Mexico. But focusing on Catholic women tells a completely different story, one in which the very sources of deterioration (the wars for independence, the transition to nationhood) give rise to new ways of performing religion and rejuvenating community religious practice. We have seen that the church accepted and later sought a new relationship with women in the context of grave economic and political threats. It did not mean to be emancipatory, I think it is fair to say, but the effect of its choice to give the women who sought it institutional power within the parish was to raise up generations of women whose loyalty to the church, cemented in these new relationships, was a key element of the church's political successes.

Instead of trying to account for this changing experience as a product of papal initiatives to mobilize and inspire women throughout the Catholic world in the late nineteenth century, the book establishes the deep and autochthonous roots of women's religious participation in Mexico, back to the colonial period. Taking proper account of the transnational in national histories has been an important historical project in recent decades, but there is still much to be learned from a closer focus that does not dilute the particularity of experience. The book shows that there *was* a feminization of religion in Mexico, demographically speaking, as there was elsewhere in the Western world, just as there was an emergence in the early twentieth century of Catholic women's political activism and willingness to challenge male authority that some have called "Catholic feminism." But these processes had their own rhythm and historical contexts in Mexico—most obvious, though it was far from the only factor distinguishing the Mexican experience, was that both feminization of formerly male-dominated institutions and of Catholic political action happened significantly earlier in Mexico than elsewhere—and are not productively shoehorned into broad global patterns or categories that cause the Mexican women's religious experience to lose its unique historical characteristics.[107]

Though I consider it valuable to have presented a new set of female actors besides the liberal women who emerged in the context of the Revolution and the post-Revolution and who have dominated writing about Mexican women and politics, I have also strived to see liberal women as part of the story told here. Catholic women's associational successes seem to have had the figurative effect of taking out of the room the oxygen needed by nonreligious voluntary associations to truly thrive, as men's groups did. And reactions by the Catholic and liberal press to Catholic women's political actions also had a negative impact on liberal women. The Catholic press was forced to find ways to approve of women who acted politically outside the home in defense of the church. They were uncomfortable with Catholic "feminism," and rejected it later, but they supported women's petitioning in both the 1850s and the 1870s. But the liberal press, by gleefully calling attention to the horrors of Catholic women entering into politics, made it harder for liberal women to act politically. It took the imminent fall of Porfirio Díaz to mobilize large numbers of liberal women, many of them trained as schoolteachers in government schools, and to give them a powerful voice in Mexican politics.

For Mexican history more generally, this book fits into ongoing work by historians who question and decenter the role of the Revolution in Mexican history. By highlighting the importance of religion in the development of cultural and political divides, the book locates the major sea change in modern Mexican history around the time of the Reform, not—as has so often been the case in the historiography—at the 1910 Revolution. The deep genealogy of 1920s and 1930s activism provided in this epilogue underscores that the activism of Catholic women is best interpreted not as having been given life by the Revolution, but as a long-standing pattern of response to the strong strains of anticlericalism and the early glimmers of anti-Catholicism that began to take shape before the Reform. The fact that Mexican women became politically involved in the wars over Catholicism, the culture wars, around the time of the Reform puts them at the center of this periodization.

Finally, beyond Mexican history, the book suggests that examining how churches serve laypeople and how laypeople serve churches at the community level may be the best way to understand how religion-based national political movements emerge from their local contexts at particular moments, sometimes seemingly out of the blue from the perspective of elite observers who have not been paying attention to what is going on in church or in the homes of the faithful. When religion is "privatized," Jon Butler writes, it is assumed to be "irrelevant to public deliberations."[108] But private religion—and, I would add, community religious practice, kept vibrant by lay associations—is alive and influential and can move into the public arena when it perceives itself to be threatened. We will not understand the failures of progressive projects, in Mexico or anywhere else, until we take seriously the religious opposition to them, not just when it is organized for battle but also when it is quietly nurtured in the community, where the women are in charge.

APPENDIX

Foundations of the Vela Perpetua 1840–1860

Place	Date(s) of foundation
Silao (Guanajuato)	1841
Acámbaro (Guanajuato)	by 1841
Zinapécuaro (Michoacán)	by 1841 and 1847
Maravatío (Michoacán)	by 1841 and 1859
Guanajuato (Guanajuato)	1842
Pátzcuaro (Michoacán)	1842 and 1847
Santa Clara (Michoacán)	1842
Querétaro (state of Mexico)	by 1843
Tacámbaro (Michoacán)	1843
Morelia (Michoacán)	1843, 1845, 1847
Guadalajara (in church of the University)	1843
Celaya (Guanajuato)	1843
León (Guanajuato)	1843
Dolores Hidalgo (Guanajuato)	1843
Lagos (Jalisco)	1843
Tepic (Nayarit)	1843
San Luis Potosí (San Luis Potosí)	1843
La Barca (Michoacán)	1844
San Juan de los Lagos (Jalisco)	1844
Villa de San Felipe (Guanajuato)	1844
Zapotlán el Grande (Jalisco)	1844
Tepatitlán (Jalisco)	1844
Zapopan (Jalisco)	1844
Mexticacan (Jalisco)	1844

Place	Date(s) of foundation
Jocotepec (Jalisco)	1844
Uruapan (Michoacán)	1845
Encarnación (Jalisco)	1845
Cocula (Jalisco)	1845
Arandas (Jalisco)	1845
Zacapu (Michoacán)	1846
Ario (Michoacán)	1846
La Piedad (Michoacán)	1846
Teocaltiche (Jalisco)	1846
Purépero (Michoacán)	by 1846
Chilchota (Michoacán)	1846
San Juan de la Vega (Guanajuato)	1846
Salamanca (Guanajuato)	1847
Yuririapúndaro (Guanajuato)	1847
Jiquilpan (Michoacán)	1847
Tinguindín (Michoacán)	1847
Cotija (Michoacán)	1847
Mexico City	1848
Tamazula (Jalisco)	1848
Techaluta (Jalisco)	1848
Zacatecas (Zacatecas)	by 1848
San Diego del Biscocho (San Diego de la Union) (Guanajuato)	1849
Apaseo (Guanajuato)	1849
San Sebastián del Oeste	1849 and 1855
Nochistlán (Zacatecas)	1849
Zacoalco (Jalisco)	1850
Ahuacatlán (Nayarit)	1850
Zináparo (Michoacán)	1853
Tuxpan (Michoacán)	1853
Amoles (mineral de Mellado) (Guanajuato)	1853
Mineral de Rayas (Guanajuato)	1853
Zapotiltic (Jalisco)	1853
San José de Gracia (Michoacán)	1854
Tonila (Jalisco)	1854
Sayula (Jalisco)	by 1854
Autlán (Jalisco)	by 1854
La Huacana (Michoacán)	1854
Tarímbaro (Michoacán)	1854
Chucándiro (Michoacán)	1854
Numerán (Michoacán)	1854

Place	Date(s) of foundation
Tlaxcala (Puebla)	1854
Huamantla (Puebla)	1854
Tangancícuaro (Michoacán)	1855
Huango (Michoacán)	1855
Tlalpuhajua (Michoacán)	1855
Oaxaca (Oaxaca)	1855
Tecolotlán (Jalisco)	by 1855
Tanhuato (Michoacán)	1856
Tlasasalca (Michoacán)	1856
Jaral (Guanajuato)	by 1856
Tuxpan (Nayarit)	1856
Jalostotitlan	by 1856
Tototlán (Jalisco)	by 1857
Durango (Durango)	1858
San Pedro de los Pozos (Guanajuato)	1858
Pénjamo (Guanajuato)	1858
Chamacuaro (Guanajuato)	by 1858
Tanhuato (Michoacán)	by 1859
Coeneo (Michoacán)	by 1860
Puruándiro (Michoacán)	by 1860
Huaniqueo (Michoacán)	by 1860
Toluca	around 1860
Chalchihuites (Zacatecas)	by 1863; probably before 1860

Sources: Multiple documents located in AHAMich, AHAG, AHAMex, AHAD, AHAO, AGN. The author will gladly supply specific locations upon request.

NOTES

I have retained the original spellings, capitalizations, and phrasings of the titles of the archival documents, rather than change them to dictionary-perfect orthography and phrasing. I think this choice conveys something about the authors and their contexts that would be lost in a cleanup. But perhaps contradictorily, I have included accents, although in many cases there were none in the originals. I did this because this book was substantially researched before cell phone cameras allowed us to take huge numbers of photographs, so I cannot go back to each document to double check that I use accents only where the original had them. The absence of accents is jarring, at least to me, in a way that variations in spelling are not, so not being confident of the accuracy (where accents are concerned) of my hand-typed notes, I decided to err on the side of inclusion rather than exclusion.

Introduction

1. The War of the Reform (1858–61); the War of the French Intervention (1862–67); the Revolution of 1910 (1910–20); and the Cristero war (1926–29).

2. Robles de Mendoza, *La evolución*, 84.

3. For a relatively recent broad survey of writing on gender and religion in history, see De Groot and Morgan, "Beyond the 'Religious Turn'?"

4. For a strong recent survey of the field with particular attention to Catholic intellectuals and the need to see Catholic history on its own terms and not just as a reaction to liberalism, see Alarcón Menchaca, Martínez Villegas, and Mora Muro, *Intelectuales católicos*.

5. Braude, "Women's History."

6. Wright-Ríos, *Searching*, 4, and throughout Part I.

7. Differences included their bases of financial support (land or herds belonging to the community for the indigenous cofradía, vs. the rental of donated properties or the loan of donated funds for the urban cofradía); their leadership (for the indigenous cofradía, often some overlap with the leadership of the village—though Chance and Taylor, "Cofradías," make clear that they were not part of the same structure); their number (there was usually just one church in an indigenous village and often only one cofradía); the nature of their spirituality (indigenous cofradía members tended to seek assistance or intercession from the object of devotion, vs. members' focus on salvation in the urban ones); and their devotional practices (annual fiestas were important for both but especially important for the indigenous cofradías). On indigenous cofradías, see Taylor, *Magistrates*, especially chapter 12; Taylor, "Indian Pueblos"; Chance and Taylor, "Cofradías"; Gruzinski, "Indian Confraternities"; Serrera Contreras, *Guadalajara*; Pérez-Rocha, "Mayordomías"; Bechtloff, *Las cofradías*; Martínez Aguilar, "Las cofradías"; Farriss, *Maya Society*.

8. On urban cofradías, see von Germeten, *Black Blood Brothers*; Bazarte Martínez, *Las cofradías*; Brading, *Church and State*, chapter 8; Larkin, "Confraternities and Community"; Larkin, *The Very Nature of God*; Martínez de Codes, "Cofradías y capellanías"; Pescador, *De bautizados*; García Ayluardo, "Ceremonia y cofradía"; García Ayluardo, *De tesoreros y tesoros*; Carbajal López, "Devoción."

9. ACM, Caja 90, exp. 6, Cofradía del Smo Rosario de la Purísima Virgen María, Madre de Dios, patentes de varios cofrades y algunos recibos de los años de 1779–1786. There were four wheel firecrackers, five dozen fireworks cannons, six dozen large sky rockets, eight dozen small sky rockets, eight dozen serpent firecrackers, and fifteen exploding fireworks.

10. AHAD, consulted on microfilm at New Mexico State University, Las Cruces, Roll 522, Frame 745. Contracto de los Sugetos que la subscriben que hande componer la Música que sirve de acompaniamiento al Smo Sac cuando va de beatico, Jul. 1, 1816.

11. AGN, Cofradías, Vol. 18, exp. 7, Informe que presentó el Arzobispo de México, sobre las cofradías y hermandades de las iglesias y capillas de Nueva España, 1794. Payments tended to range between fifteen to twenty-five pesos, and wages of day workers were about two reales, one-quarter of a peso, a day.

12. Another drain on the income of some cofradías was their charitable obligations, from funding a school for the poor, to providing dowries for poor girls or orphans, to feeding prisoners on Sundays, to supplying clothes for the poor. Two of the wealthiest cofradías in Mexico City supported schools for the poor. The largest and wealthiest cofradía in Mexico City, the Archicofradía del Santísimo Sacramento, famously provided dowries for poor girls, but others in the provinces emulated it on a smaller scale, as did all the Third Orders of Franciscans, who also fed prisoners. See Muriel, *La sociedad*; Loreto López, *Los conventos*, 72; Victoria Moreno, *El Convento*, 114, 172–78; and Belanger, "Between the Cloister," 157–77, 164.

13. It is difficult to be precise about the breakdown among the types of cofradía. We can assume that after 1794 a larger proportion than before were cofradías de retribución (meaning that they paid death and survivor benefits) because the archbishop, who extinguished four hundred fifty cofradías that year, favored this type of cofradía, especially in poor parishes. AGN, Cofradías, Vol. 18, exp. 7, Informe que presentó el Arzobispo de México, sobre las cofradías y hermandades de las iglesias y capillas de Nueva España, 1794. O'Hara, *Flock*, 134, however, identified many informal cofradías in Mexico City that were presumably not even on the archbishop's list at all; Rugeley, *Of Wonders*, documents the survival of what were called *gremios* (guilds) in the Yucatan; and Brading, *Church and State*, 139–141, also emphasizes the diversity of "cofradías."

14. Brading, *Church and State*, 133.

15. Calling a town "Hispanic" or "mestizo" does not mean that there were no indigenous people living in it. It just distinguishes such towns from indigenous landholding villages. The indigenous people living in a "Hispanic" town were migrants to the town from their villages.

16. It is surprisingly difficult to establish how many cofradías existed in Mexico City in the late colony, even though all estimates build off of the 1794 report that Archbishop Núñez de Haro submitted to the king, supplemented by the reports that priests submitted to the archbishop to be used in the preparation of that 1794 report. (AGN, Cofradías, Vol. 18, exp. 7, Informe que presento el Arzobispo de México, sobre las cofradías y hermandades de las iglesias y capillas de Nueva España, 1794; and AGN, BN, Vol. 1170/1, Expediente formado sobre el informe de los curas de esta capital, para dar el que pidió el Exmo Senor Virrey, Quaderno 3, 1794.) The reason is that it is very hard to be consistent about whether to count as a single cofradía those that had been been consolidated from two or more into one, either much earlier or as a result of actions taken by Núñez de Haro in the early

1790s, or whether to count them as separate cofradías. The archbishop's own report shows 95 cofradías in Mexico City before he consolidated them into 52, but some authors clearly double, triple, or even quadruple-count at least some of those 52—and not unreasonably, since they had at one time been two or more cofradías. At one end of the spectrum is García Ayluardo, "Confraternity, Cult, and Crown," 283–90, who uses both reports to compile a list of 157 cofradías in Mexico City in the eighteenth century. Bazarte Martínez, *Las cofradías*, appendix, gives 110 cofradías in Mexico City from 1526–1795, with only six marked as ones that no longer existed in 1794. Pescador, *De bautizados*, 327, says there were 73 at the end of the eighteenth century. Complicating matters further, O'Hara, *Flock*, 134, found the Núñez de Haro survey to have undercounted cofradías and cofradía-like collectivities (hermandades, devociones).

17. AHAMich, Diocesano, Gobierno, Visitas, Informes, Caja 508, exp 97, Visita Guanajuato; AHAMich, Diocesano, Gobierno, Visitas, Informes, Caja 510, exp. 106, Autos de visita en fines de 92 y principio de 93; AHAMich, Diocesano, Gobierno, Visitas, Informes, Caja 509, exp. 103, General visita San Miguel el Grande, 1791; AGN, Cofradías, Vol. 18, exp. 4, fs. 143–45; AHAMich, Diocesano, Gobierno, Visitas, Informes, Caja 507, exp. 91, Visita Puruándiro. This is a much lower per capita level of cofradías than in Spain, where there were 143 cofradías for 60,000 people in Toldeo in the sixteenth century, 100 for 30,000 in Valladolid; at least 600 in Madrid; and in Zamora, 150 for a population of only 8,600. Sánchez de Madariaga, "Cultura religiosa," 27–28. I am not aware of a detailed analysis of this difference between the Old World and the New, but it surely has to do with three factors: the absence of a medieval confraternity tradition in the Americas, as well as a weak guild system (guilds historically having been associated with a particular cofradía); the practice in America of authorizing or encouraging only a single cofradía in indigenous villages; and the settlement of the New World for the most part during the post-Tridentine era, an era in which bishops (of which there were many fewer in the Americas than in Europe) were meant to exert greater control over popular religion.

18. In Mexico City there were multiple exceptions to this rule of diversity—there were cofradías exclusive to men born in a certain region in Spain, for example—but in the smaller cities and mestizo towns, diversity was the rule.

19. Critics of the feminization of religion as a theory include Braude, "Women's History"; Butler, "Eucharistic Angels"; Shiels, "Feminization"; Schuyler, "Inventing"; Bilhartz, "Sex"; Reynolds, "Feminization Controversy"; Langlois, *Le catholicisme*; Pasture, "Beyond the Feminization Thesis"; Blaschke, "Unrecognized"; Imhoff, "Myth"; De Groot and Morgan, "Beyond the 'Religious Turn'?"

20. Although the impoverishment of the female convents after independence and the expulsion of nuns from their convents in the 1860s meant that Mexico was not a part of the European trend toward more religious vocations among women in the nineteenth century.

21. Putnam, *Bowling Alone*; Putnam, *Making Democracy Work*; Rendall, *Origins*; Reid, "Measuring"; Clarke, *Piety and Nationalism*. Studies of US women's associations and their connections to politics have been particularly helpful. Scott, *Natural Allies*; Ryan, *Cradle*; Cott, *Grounding*; Boylan, *Origins*; Zaeske, *Signatures*. There is little comparable work on associations for Latin America but Carlos Forment's sociological and quantitative analysis of associations in Mexico and Peru in the nineteenth century is invaluable. Forment, *Democracy*. See also Londoño-Vega, *Religion*; Hoogen, "Romanization."

22. Aceves Ávila, "*Que es bueno*," emphasizes the importance of the priest and bishop as directors of lay associations.

23. The first to articulate the connection between associations and democracy was of course Tocqueville, *Democracy*. Hoffmann and others have pointed out that there is a correlative, not causative, relationship between the mania for associations in the nineteenth

century and the rise of democracy in the same century, and that in fact "a vibrant associational life could entail antidemocratic effects," as seems to have happened in Germany. Hoffmann, "Democracy," 299.

24. For Latin America, see Maza Valenzuela, "Catholicismo"; Sanders, "A Mob"; Leavitt-Alcántara, *Alone*; Londoño-Vega, *Religion*; Serrano, *¿Qué hacer*; Sullivan-González, *Piety*; Cowan, *Securing Sex*; Weld, "Holy War"; Weld, "Spanish Civil War"; Weld, "Other Door"; Finchelstein, *Ideological Origins*, especially chapters 2 and 3; Deutsch, "Gender"; Deutsch, "Spartan"; Helgen, *Religious Conflict*; Power, *Right-Wing Women*; Borges, "Catholic Vanguards." For Catholic Europe, see Anderson, *Practicing*; Smith, *Ladies*; Enders, "'And We Ate'"; De Grazia, *How Fascism*. For the US, see McGirr, *Suburban*; Griffith, *God's Daughters*; Nickerson, *Mothers*; Cox, *Dixie's Daughters*; Janney, *Burying*.

25. Okin, *Women*, 314.

26. Power, *Right-Wing Women*; Weinstein, "Inventing the 'Mulher Paulista'"; Rosemblatt, *Gendered Compromises*; Deutsch, "Gender and Sociopolitical Change"; Carey Jr., *I Ask for Justice*; Guy, *Women Build the Welfare State*; Hutchison, *Labors Appropriate to Their Sex*; Olcott, *Revolutionary Women*; Tinsman, *Partners in Conflict*; Tinsman, *Buying into the Regime*; Amador, "Women Ask Relief"; Cano, *Se llamaba*; Galeana de Valadés, ed., *La revolución de las mujeres*; Mitchell, "Revolutionary Feminism"; James, *Doña María's Story*; Levenson-Estrada, "Loneliness"; French and Cluff, "Women"; Baldez, *Why Women Protest*; Kaplan, *Taking Back the Streets*. See also the contributions by Power and Deutsch to Blee and Deutsch, *Women of the Right*, for interesting comments about how their thinking about right-wing women has changed since their pioneering studies over twenty years ago.

27. Liberals and republicans in France and elsewhere in the Catholic world constructed this narrative, many drawing on Jules Michelet's well-known diatribe against priests in the confessional and their hold over women, published in 1845. As Ruth Harris observes with regard to France, "It was a classic republican cliché of the era to link women's rejection of the Revolution and republican principles to their apparent submission to priests . . . So important was this vision of women outside the control of husbands and masculine, republican rationality that it remained—and in some sense still remains—a central, if unspoken, feature of anticlerical ideology." Harris, *Lourdes*, 213–14.

28. Outside of chapters in several good anthologies or broad histories, the most comprehensive analysis was Arrom, *Women*, which remains a key text.

29. Connaughton, *Ideología*; Adame Goddard, *El pensamiento*; Ceballos Ramírez, *El catolicismo*; Blancarte, *El pensamiento*; Blancarte, *Historia*.

30. For many years, for the twentieth century, there were only Jean Meyer's 1970 treatment of the Cristero conflict, *La Cristiada*, in which he paid significant attention to Catholic women's contributions; Barbara Miller's excellent 1980 dissertation, "The Role of Women in the Mexican Cristero Rebellion," and a couple of articles that came out of it (Miller, "Women and Revolution"; Miller, "The Roles of Women"); and Laura O'Dogherty's article, "Restaurarlo," on the Damas Católicas. From the mid-1990s to around 2000, however, four important dissertations were completed that prominently featured women and religion: Hanson, "Day of Ideals"; Schell, "Teaching the Children"; Boylan, "Mexican Catholic Women's Activism"; and Fernández-Aceves, "Political Mobilization." A number of influential articles came out of these dissertations, though only Schell published her findings as a book: Schell, *Church*. For the nineteenth century, Moreno Chávez, *Devociones*; Stauffer, *Victory*; and Smith, *Roots*, take gender seriously in their studies of church/religion and politics, though it is not the primary unit of analysis. Outside of Mexico the post-independence chapters of Leavitt-Alcántara, *Alone*, nicely integrate gender, religion, and politics, as do Londoño-Vega, *Religion*, and Sanders, "A Mob," for Colombia, and Serrano, *¿Qué hacer*, for

Chile. For a fuller accounting of works on gender, church, and politics in twentieth-century Mexico, see the epilogue.

31. There has also been a burst of relatively recent work on gender, religion, and politics in nineteenth- and early twentieth-century Spain, which faced similar culture battles as Mexico. See Romeo Mateo, "¿Sujeto católico"; Mínguez-Blasco, "Between Virgins"; Mínguez Blasco, *Evas*; Duch Plana, "Mundo"; and Blasco Herranz, "Género y religión."

32. For the nineteenth century this debate is implicit, in the sense that there is no scholarship that examines it as such, but Fallaw, *Religion*, observes a similar tension in the literature for the 1930s, and his book is in part an exploration of "how Catholics could both fight a Kulturkampf and at the same time collude and cooperate in the creation of a postrevolutionary state" (9). On "culture war" as an organizing concept in nineteenth-century history, see Clark and Kaiser, *Culture Wars*; and Ivereigh, *Politics*.

33. Bautista García, *Las disyuntivas*; Moreno Chávez, "Nuevas perspectivas"; Loaeza, *La restauración*; Barranco V., "Posiciones"; Blancarte, *Historia*; Mijangos y González, "Tres momentos."

34. Butler, *Popular Piety*; Moreno Chávez, *Devociones*; Stauffer, *Victory*; Fallaw, *Religion*; Wright-Ríos, *Revolutions*; Curley, *Citizens*; Boylan, "Mexican Catholic Activist Women"; Díaz Patiño, *Católicos*. For several cases in which attending to religious conflict at the local level reveals authorities who could be persuaded or who volunteered to ignore anticlerical legislation (that is, for cases where "church-state" conflict did not materialize), see Curley and Mota, "Catolicismo cívico."

35. Moreno Chávez, *Devociones*, 254.

36. These five archbishoprics cover a large number of Mexican states: Mexico, Morelos, Guerrero, Hidalgo, Tlaxcala, San Luis Potosí, Guanajuato, Michoacán, Colima, Nayarit, Jalisco, Zacatecas, Aguascalientes, Oaxaca, Durango, and part of Puebla and Chihuahua.

Chapter 1

The quotation in the chapter title comes from the following source: AHAMex, CL 23, no. 3, Visita Pastoral de Francisco Antonio Lorenzana 1766–67, Tulancingo.

1. AGN, Indiferente, Caja 248, exp. 9, Libro de cobranza de los hermanos de la Cofradía de Nuestra Señora del Tránsito que comiensa hoy 20 de mayo de 1724 con los jornalillos desde 13 de marzo hasta dicho día.

2. The best treatment of poor, single, urban women and their devotional habits—including cofradía membership—in colonial Latin America is Leavitt-Alcántara, *Alone*.

3. AGN, BN, Leg. 190, exp. 4 (1727–28), Libro de la Hermandad de Nuestra Señora de la Guía.

4. AGN, Indiferente, Caja 4896, exp. 1, Libro de haciento de los Hermanos Cofrades de NS de la Purificación, fundada con authoridad apostólica en la Capilla de SS José de Españoles cita en el Combento de NSPS Francisco de esta Corte, y empiesa a correr desde fin de el mes de marzo de 1762.

5. The advantage of this source is its detail about the individuals from whom fees were being collected—their names, sometimes their relationships within their households, sometimes their occupations, how regularly or irregularly they paid their dues, even whether the collector tracked them down on the street, at home, at work, and so on. This source, then, reflects the particular territories covered by collectors over (usually) a limited span of years, making it a useful snapshot of a neighborhood. But it has limitations as well. It is not a list of every member of the cofradía. Some collectors might have been assigned neighborhoods of higher or lower status or more or fewer women, as was the case with one of the collectors for the Cofradía de San Ygnacio Loyola in Mexico City around 1770,

whose main responsibility was collecting dues from the mostly female workers at the royal cigarette factory (Pescador, "Devoción y crisis demográfica," 781). And duplication of names can be very hard to detect: sometimes just first names were used, and sometimes names were spelled differently from one week to the next.

6. This source is mainly useful for the lists of payouts that some cofradías had to make when members died. Many cofradías functioned as a kind of mutual aid society, and the death benefits paid to the members' survivors were recorded in the annual expenses, almost always by name of the deceased. The lists of deceased members each year do not usually provide a very large sample unless the account books cover multiple years, but I did use this source to confirm the ratios of men to women from other sources for the same cofradía, and occasionally on its own.

7. These lists lack the detail of either kind of account book, but they are a better source than either for developing a gender-and-status profile of the entire membership, not just the members assigned to a single collector, and not just the small number of deceased each year. Because this is a list of the whole cofradía membership, the problems of unintended double-counting or neighborhood peculiarities skewing the data are avoided.

8. There are thousands of these certificates in the archives, sometimes one or two of them scattered among other documents, sometimes large bundles of them. When a member joined a cofradía that provided death benefits, he or she received a printed document—typically with an image of the object of the cofradía's adoration at the top, and a description of the indulgences the joiner would earn—with their names and the date they joined filled in by the secretary of the cofradía (see Figure 1.1). Patentes cannot be used to generate absolute numbers of members, obviously, because the size of each bundle is a function of the archival habits and length of career of the treasurer, and cannot be assumed to count all deaths or all joiners. But they can be used cautiously to gauge status (most secretaries were careful to note whether someone was a don or doña), and they can be used with even more confidence to generate statistics about gender balance. There may be some undercounting of elite members, who might not turn in their certificates because they were wealthy enough to pay for their burial expenses on their own. But the spiritual rewards of cofradía membership obviously crossed social classes, and "collecting" on those spiritual rewards required turning in the patente, so I would not expect this undercounting to be significant.

9. It should be noted that because I used fee collectors' books and especially patentes, the sample is skewed toward cofradías that paid death benefits. I do not have the sense that gender balances in other cofradías were markedly different, since, as will be shown below, the vast majority of cofradías fell into a relatively tight range. I cannot claim to have great insight into gender balances in the more informal small brotherhoods that O'Hara found to be numerous in eighteenth-century Mexico City. O'Hara, *Flock*, especially chapter 4.

10. Pescador, *De bautizados*, Cuadro I (pp. 64–67), lists 119 Mexico City cofradías, 1526–1795. Forty-four of them had either been incorporated into other cofradías or had disappeared by 1794. Of course some new ones were established over the course of the eighteenth century. My estimate that twenty-seven constituted one-quarter to one-third of the total at any given time is based on these numbers. The two with majority men were the unified cofradías of the Preciosa Sangre de Cristo, Dolores, and Ánimas in the church of the Santísima Trinidad, at 72 percent men and 28 percent women (virtually the only women who belonged were the wives of the merchants who dominated the membership rolls) and the Third Order of Penitents of San Francisco, at 54 percent men and 46 percent women. See Table 1.1 notes for my decision to include the Third Orders.

11. The best documentation comes from the bishopric of Michoacán (eighteen of the thirty-seven data sets come from the extraordinarily rich cathedral archives in that diocese), so there is a possibility that a different pattern might prevail in some of the other

bishoprics if more data were available. Still, this seems unlikely, since the average female majority in the Michoacán cofradías, at 59.4 percent, was almost exactly the average for the other fifteen scattered across five other dioceses.

12. If we divide the ordered data sets into quartiles and measure the distance between the data points at the top and bottom of the middle range (the two quartiles on either side of the median), the interquartile range for Mexico City was a quite tightly clustered 8, while the IQ for the provinces was 22.

13. Pescador, *De bautizados*.

14. Larkin, *The Very Nature of God*.

15. The literature on Mexico acknowledging strong female presence in cofradías is limited to my own work (Chowning, "Catholic Church"; Chowning, "La feminización"), in which I briefly summarized what I here analyze more fully; von Germeten, *Black Blood Brothers*, chapter 3, who shows that women formed majorities in Afro-Mexican (and some indigenous) cofradías; and Carbajal López, "Mujeres," who studies the constitutions of cofradías that were reviewed by the crown between 1770 and 1820. Of these constitutions, 51 allowed women to join, out of 133. These include both rural and urban cofradías. There is no indication of how many women were actually members. Carbajal López seems to believe that there were probably more than these 51 that allowed women but that the constitutions did not explicitly state it. For Europe, much of the literature still leaves the impression that most European confraternities were all-male. See Black, *Italian Confraternities*, 32; Dinan, "Confraternities"; Davis, *Society and Culture*, 75; Vovelle, *Piété baroque*; Flynn, "Rituals of Solidarity." Hufton, *Prospect*, 398, observes that one of the "triumphs" of the sixteenth-century Council of Trent was to get women out of confraternities. But on the growth and/or presence of female confraternities, see Casagrande, "Confraternities," who identified nine female confraternities in Perugia in the late sixteenth century; Poska and Lehfeldt, "Redefining Expectations," 24, who mention the possibility of female leadership in mixed-sex confraternities in early modern Spain, as well as noting the presence of all-female confraternities (but commenting that little is known about them); Desan, *Reclaiming*, 210, who names two provincial all-female confraternities in eighteenth-century France; Clark, "By All the Conduct," who notes female presence in and leadership of confraternities in eighteenth-century French New Orleans; Norberg, "Women," who documents several all-female charitable confraternities in seventeenth-century France and speculates that there were hundreds of them; and Hufton, *Prospect*, who notes that "confraternities dedicated to specific charitable ends directed by women grew very considerably in Italy in the late sixteenth and seventeenth centuries" (398).

16. O'Hara, "Supple"; Delgado, *Laywomen*; Greenleaf, "Inquisition Brotherhood"; Lavrin, "La congregación de San Pedro."

17. Delgado, *Laywomen*.

18. AHAMich, XIX, Caja 818, exp. 2, Constituciones que ha de observar la Archicofradía del Divinísimo Señor Sacramentado de la ciudad de Salvatierra, 27 Dec. 1802.

19. AHAG, Gobierno, Cofradías, 1771–1780, Caja 10, exp. 1771–1778, Archicofradía del Santísimo Sacramento del Parroquial de Fresnillo, Año de 1777, Mayordomo and diputados to arzobispo.

20. AGN, Cofradías, Vol. 18, exp. 7 (257–311), "Informe que presentó el Arzobispo de México, sobre las cofradías y hermandades de las iglesias y capillas de Nueva España . . . 1794." San Sebastián. For this practice in Spain, see Callahan, *Church*, 58.

21. AGN, Cofradías, Vol. 18, exp. 7 (257–311), Informe que presentó el Arzobispo de México, sobre las cofradías y hermandades de las iglesias y capillas de Nueva España, 1794.

22. This cofradía had been combined with that of Nuestra Señora de la Asunción, and therefore had more cofrades to care for and more feast days to finance than before the amalgamation, in part accounting for its financial shortfalls.

23. AGN, BN, vol. 1170/1, Expediente formado sobre el informe de los curas de esta capital, para dar el que pidió el Exmo Senor Virrey, Quaderno 3. 1794. Santa María la Redonda." They also said that they relied on the "zeal of our priest, who has foregone many of his parochial fees and has maintained out of his own funds the Cart that transports Jesus Christ." Similar contributions from wealthy officers were noted for the parish of Santa Catalina Virgen y Martir in the same document.

24. Bazarte Martínez, *Las cofradías*.

25. Carbajal López, "Mujeres."

26. One cofradía in Seville in 1804 explicitly affirmed that women could only "participate" in the activities of the cofradía, and that they were impeded "for good cause" from exercising the same voting and other rights as men ("voz y voto"). But as Carbajal López points out, in most cases spelling out the roles for women was not a priority for the constitution-writers, probably because it was simply assumed that the sexes would not mix in the meetings where votes were held. Carbajal López, "Mujeres." Exclusion of women from office-holding in mixed-sex confraternities was apparently all but universal in Europe, too, though Black's discussion of women in cofradías in sixteenth-century Italy and Casagrande's study of lay female religiosity in Umbria, also in the sixteenth century, show how much regional and institutional variation could exist in terms of how female members of cofradías were treated. Black, *Italian Confraternities*, 34–38; Casagrande, "Confraternities." Casagrande concludes that while women were more or less full participants in devotional activities, they were marginalized from administrative activities. The only exception I have seen is one confraternity in Spain in 1523 that allowed "full participation of both men and women in its administration and activities," constantly repeating the expression "order[ing] and command[ing] a brother or sister to . . ." Gavala González, "Original Statutes," 3, 5. This is a clear but pre-Tridentine exception to the rule. Terpstra observes that the exclusion of women from officeholding in Bologna derived from the fact that the confraternities were "governed on the model of artisanal guilds," and could not "include in their councils a sex that played no administrative part in the guilds." Terpstra, "Women." In Mexico the guild system was linked to cofradías in Mexico City, but the system itself—even in the viceregal capital—was weaker than in Europe and by no means were all cofradías connected to guilds. In fact, by the eighteenth century relatively few were.

27. Von Germeten, *Black Blood Brothers*, 69. The Cofradía de Ánimas in Sultepec (state of Mexico) allowed women to serve as "rector," the most important office, but if a woman was elected she was to be represented by the (male) governing board. See also Carbajal López, "Mujeres."

28. AHAMex, CL 23, no. 3, Visita Pastoral de Francisco Antonio Lorenzana 1766–67, Tulancingo.

29. Von Germeten, *Black Blood Brothers*; 48. According to Strocchia, "Sisters in Spirit," 735–36, formal associations of pious women were rare in Italy before 1600, when they were "spawned by the Catholic and Counter-Reformations." See also Casagrande, "Confraternities"; Norberg, "Women"; and Clark, "'By All the Conduct.'" The New Orleans confraternity studied by Clark, like the one referred to here, was formed in a convent but was open to other women.

30. This document indicates that there was a group of women who occasionally went on a retreat sponsored by the men's group. AGN, Cultos Religiosos, vol. 1, exp. 1, 1797–1802, Expediente formado a virtud del Real Cédula sobre que se informe del número de Escuelas de Cristo que hay en esta Ciudad y demas puntos.

31. Carbajal López, "Mujeres."

32. AHAD, Roll 203, Frames 403–7, Solicitud a procesión nocturna en Parral. Madres de la Hermandad de Nuestra Señora de la Soledad, cita en la Yglecia de S. Juan de Dios de Parral, al Sr. Cura Vicario y Juez Eclesiástico, 1800.

33. Independent female cofradías seem to have been more common in Europe, as early as the sixteenth century. Flynn, "Rituals of Solidarity"; Norberg, "Women"; Terpstra, "Women."

34. AGN, Bienes Nacionales, Leg. 871, exp. 3, Varios patentes, Tercer Orden de Santo Domingo (includes a loose document, undated but around 1780, that names the officials in this Third Order).

35. Victoria Moreno, *El Convento*, 102–7.

36. Victoria Moreno, *El Convento*, 107–8. See also Belanger, "Between the Cloister," 159, for the exclusion of women from the Mesa in the Third Order of Franciscans of Querétaro.

37. Victoria Moreno, *El Convento*, 101.

38. Victoria Moreno, *El Convento*, 107.

39. Larkin, *The Very Nature of God*, 94–95, distinguishes between types of processions without mentioning gender, but writes that "in [the] smaller processions, all members of the neighborhood community could participate" (95); Staples, "Sociabilidad," 105. See also Davis, "City Women," for the comment that in early modern France "parish processions led by priests on Corpus Christi and at other times included men, women, and children" (75).

40. AHAO, Parroquial, Disciplinar, Cofradías, 1870–1899, Caja 453, Copia de las constituciones hechas en la innovación de la espresada archicofradía [del Santísimo Sacramento] en 31 de Marzo del año del Señor 1748. Rapley, *The Dévotes*, reports that in seventeenth-century France, also, "women seldom took part in the organized activities of the religious confraternities" (4). Black, *Italian Confraternities*, for seventeenth-century Italy, also notes that in "various confraternities" women "were only partial or inferior members" (35).

41. AHAO, Parroquial, Disciplinar, Cofradías, 1870–1899, Caja 453, Copia de las constituciones hechas en la innovación de la espresada archicofradía [del Santísimo Sacramento] en 31 de Marzo del año del Señor 1748.

42. AHAD, Roll 183, Frames 543–53, Expediente sobre congregación de alumbrado y vela.

43. Carbajal López, "Mujeres."

44. Carbajal López, "Mujeres."

45. There is in fact little direct evidence that colonial women filled these roles; the cofradía constitutions did not assign them to them. But there are hints that these were their accustomed duties. For one case in which women in a cofradía were explicitly assigned to sweep the church, see AGN, Clero Regular y Secular, vol. 72, exp. 20, fs. 383–500, Sobre cofradías de la capital (de la Intendencia de SLP), y demas Parroquias de su distrito. 31 Dec. 1798. Vicente Bernabeu to Intendent.

46. The case is from 1831 but this does not seem likely to have been a post-independence innovation, so it is probably safe to assume that this kind of assignment happened in the colonial period as well. AHAM, XIX, Caja 108, exp. 23, Apuntes sobre varios temas: Convento de la Nueva Enseñanza, testamentos, leyes, etc. 1833 [says 1836].

47. Carlos María Bustamante, quoted in Staples, "Sociabilidad," 105.

48. Even if the definition of "beauty" changed over time, from baroque splendor to the more classical and spare aesthetics of the eighteenth and nineteenth centuries. Larkin, *The Very Nature of God*.

49. On this point, besides Larkin for Mexico City, see also Eire, *From Madrid to Purgatory*.

50. Larkin, *The Very Nature of God*, 109–115; 183–84; 212–13.

51. Larkin, *The Very Nature of God*, 95.

52. Carbajal López, "Mujeres."

53. AHAMich, XVIII, Caja 484 (1733–34), exp. 27, Constituciones de la Hermandad de la Sangre de Christo para su observancia y buen Govierno, 1729; AHAG, Gobierno,

Cofradías, 1760–1771, Caja 9, exp. 1770–1799, Expediente de varios insertos que en Copia y manera de Testimonio, se han sacado; consernentes a la Cofradía del Santo Entierro de Christo, 1777; AHAG, Gobierno, Cofradías, Caja 14, 1801–1808, exp. Tizapan, 1802, Expediente formado a instancia de D. Antonio Abad Panoja sobre la erección de una Cofradía del Smo Sacramento que pretenden fundar en la Parroquia del Pueblo de Tizapan el Alto, 1802.

54. In Spain, too, inclusion remained a key value of cofradías. Eire, *From Madrid to Purgatory*; Flynn, "Rituals of Solidarity." The appearance of inclusivity may have been particularly prized in cofradías in the New World, with its vast social divides underscored by racial difference. Terpstra, "Women," argues that gender inclusivity in Bologna was "a calculated move by patricians concerned less with religious expression than social control" (194); inclusive public rituals would achieve this political purpose.

55. Tutino, *Making a New World*; Arrom, *La Güera Rodríguez*; Guevara Sanginés, *Guanajuato diverso*; Delgado, *Laywomen*; Taylor, *Drinking*; Tutino, *Mexico City, 1808*.

56. For their conception and implementation in the Spanish context, see Callahan, "Confraternities"; Romero Samper, *Las cofradías*; López Muñoz, "Las cofradías"; Martín García, "Ilustración." On both the Spanish context and the Mexican implementation, see Brooks, "Parish and Cofradía." On the European context, see Dewald, ed., *Europe, 1450–1789*.

57. Teófanes Egido, quoted in López Muñoz, "Las cofradías," 5; Brooks, "Parish and Cofradía," 100.

58. O'Hara, *Flock*, draws our attention to the "flock of sheep" model in the title of his 2010 book. The definitive work on the changing role of the priest in eighteenth-century Mexico is Taylor, *Magistrates*.

59. AGN, Cofradías, Vol. 18, exp. 7 (257–311), Informe que presentó el Arzobispo de México, sobre las cofradías y hermandades de las iglesias y capillas de Nueva España, 1794. It seems that the other bishops of New Spain were less draconian in their adherence to the principle of streamlining and refocusing cofradía activities, but the anti-cofradía movement was by no means limited to the archbishopric.

60. Larkin, *The Very Nature of God*, 8. On Catholic reformism in Mexico, see also Brading, *Church and State*; Brooks, "Parish and Cofradía"; Voekel, *Alone Before God*; Larkin, "Confraternities"; Belanger, "Secularization"; Herrejón Peredo, *Del sermón*; Tapia Santamaría, *Campo religioso*, 104–117, 125–26; Zahino Peñafort, *Iglesia y sociedad*; Jaramillo Magaña, *Hacia una iglesia*. There is a much larger literature on Catholic reformism in Spain, but notable books with an emphasis on cofradías include Romero Samper, *Las cofradías*; Arias de Saavedra y López Munoz, *La represión*.

61. In the archbishopric of Mexico, almost 440,000 pesos belonging to cofradías was turned over to the Consolidación, about 9 percent of the total collected in the archbishopric. For New Spain as a whole, the percentage of Consolidación funds provided by cofradías was about 10.5 percent. Von Wobeser, *Dominación colonial*, 154, 228.

62. Some of the cases involve cofradías associated with churches of the regular orders, which the crown was trying to suppress or restrict.

63. I have written briefly about this cofradía in a different context. Chowning, "Catholic Church." See also Carbajal López, "Devoción," who evaluates the Real Congregación as an example of late colonial royal emphasis on the Santísimo Sacramento and reform of the cofradías.

64. *Constituciones de la real congregación del alumbrado y vela al SS. sacramento del altare: establ. en la capilla del real palacio desde etc. 1789* (Madrid: Imprenta real, 1790), xiii–xiv, http://bibliotecavirtualmadrid.org/bvmadrid_publicacion/i18n/catalogo_imagenes/grupo.cmd?path=1035309; AGN, Bienes Nacionales, Leg. 851,

exp. 17, El Exmo y Illmo S. Arzobispo sobre alumbrado perenne del Smo. 1793. https://bibliotecavirtualmadrid.comunidad.madrid/bvmadrid_publicacion/es/catalogo_imagenes/grupo.do?registrardownload=0&path=1034607&presentacion=pagina&posicion=14.

65. *Constituciones de la real congregación del alumbrado y vela al SS. sacramento del altare: establ. en la capilla del real palacio*, x.

66. According to one document (concerning a different cofradía) that included in its supporting documentation an excerpt from the constitution of the Real Congregación in Mexico City, another innovation was to alternate vigil days between men and women. I have seen no corroboration of this, however, and there is no mention of it in these documents from the late 1790s, so it may have been a later amendment of the practices of the Mexico City congregation. AGN, BN, Leg. 851, exp. 17, Año de 1794, Testimonio de los Documentos que se expresan pertenecientes a la Real Congregación del Alumbrado y Vela del Smo Sacramento fundada en la Parroquia de Sn Sebastian de México, 1792; AGN, Cofradías, vol. 14, exp. 4, 1805, "Sobre establecer en esta capital una congregación de Oblatas"; AGN, Cofradías, vol. 14, exp. 4, 1805, *Indulgencias Perpetuas Concedidas a las Congregantes de la Insigne real congregación del Alumbrado y Vela Continua al Smo Sacramento, fundada canónicamente en la Parroquia de S Sebastián de esta corte, a imitación de la erigida en la Real Capilla de Madrid de que son Hermanos Mayores perpetuos los Reyes Nuestros Señores*. 1793.

67. AGN, BN, Leg. 851, exp. 17, Testimonio de los Documentos que se expresan pertenecientes a la Real Congregación del Alumbrado y Vela del Smo Sacramento fundada en la Parroquia de San Sebastián de México, 1792.

68. AGN, BN, Leg. 851, exp. 17, Testimonio de los Documentos que se expresan pertenecientes a la Real Congregación del Alumbrado y Vela del Smo Sacramento fundada en la Parroquia de San Sebastián de México, Archbishop Alonso Núñez de Haro to Marqués de Branciforte, Sept. 19, 1794. All quotes in the next several paragraphs are from this letter, unless otherwise indicated.

69. AGN, BN, Leg. 851, exp. 17, Testimonio de los Documentos que se expresan pertenecientes a la Real Congregación del Alumbrado y Vela del Smo Sacramento fundada en la Parroquia de San Sebastián de México. Informe del Conde del Valle de Orizaba.

70. I count fifty-two officers in the March 1794 list of officers in the Spanish congregation. AGN, BN, Leg. 851, exp. 17, Nominación y aumento de oficiales de la Junta Primitiva.

71. *Constituciones de la real congregación del alumbrado y vela al SS. sacramento del altare: establ. en la capilla del Real Palacio*, xiii.

72. AGN, BN, Leg. 851, exp. 17, Nominación y aumento de oficiales de la Junta Primitiva.

73. Technically the king was the hermano mayor of all the many congregations that were to be established, each of which was then headed by a local vice hermano mayor. Another Mexican innovation was to ask the queen to serve as vice hermana mayor, a position that was not required in an all-male officer corps.

74. AGN, BN, Leg. 851, exp. 17, El Exmo y Illmo S. Arzobispo sobre alumbrado perenne del Smo. 1793. Promotor Fiscal [Cisneros] to Arzobispo Núñez de Haro, Apr. 30, 1806. There were two intertwined issues: whether a Minister of the Audiencia should preside, and whether the vice hermano mayor of the Madrid congregation should be considered also to be the vice hermano mayor of all the other congregations in the kingdom, with the local presidents taking the title of teniente vice hermano. If the archbishop, in order to justify naming female officers, claimed that the Mexico City congregation was using the same constitution as the Madrid congregation, with minor and insubstantial alterations, then (the Madrid congregation claimed) was not the Mexico City congregation a "branch" of the Madrid one, meaning that the Madrid officers must govern the Mexico City officers?

And if this was so, then was there a requirement for a Minister of the Audiencia to be present, as was required of other cofradías that were more clearly local and autonomous? The archbishop was in an unappealing position, but he ended up preferring that the Mexico City congregation be considered a branch of the Madrid one, in order to obviate the presence of a royal minister. It is unclear how much he conferred with the male officers of the Mexico City congregation in all this; certainly they were being consulted, but there is no direct correspondence that sheds light on their roles or positions.

75. Clause Three of the Madrid constitution allowed the hermano mayor and the other four officers to call for "private meetings" (*juntas particulares*) whenever necessary. The archbishop here leaves unaddressed the question of why the hermana mayor and the other female officers held a different status vis-à-vis the ability to call such meetings. *Constituciones de la real congregación del alumbrado y vela al SS. sacramento del altare: establ. en la capilla del real palacio*, x.

76. Sixty would be the daily required number if the church was open from 6:00 a.m. to 9:00 p.m.

77. We do not know how many other Reales Congregaciones were founded in Mexico. Certainly there were not as many as the king envisioned. There are many documents relating to a successful foundation in Durango. There was one in Orizaba as well and probably one in Querétaro. AHAD, Frame 63, Cuenta corriente de cargo y data de la Hermandad de los Veladores del Smo Sac que dió principio el dia 3 de mayo de 1804; The Church of Latter Day Saints, "Family Search Records," Veracruz, Mexico, Catholic Church Records, 1590–1978, Orizaba, San Miguel, Cofradías 1818–1869, Frames 20–63. There were also foundations in Buenos Aires and Lima: Bernardo Mendel, *Instruccion á los hermanos de la Real Congregación del Alumbrado y Vela continua al santísimo sacramento reservado en los santos sagrarios, sobre el espiritu y práctica de su santo instituto, é indulgencias perpetuas que le están concedidas* (Lima, 1808); *Constituciones de la real congregación del alumbrado y vela continua al Santísimo Sacramento reservado en los santos sagrarios: fundada en Madrid el año de 1789 por los reyes nuestros señores, y establecida ahora en la Santa Iglesia Catedral de la Capital de Buenos-Ayres, con algunas adiciones respectivas, y análogas al espíritu de tan piadoso instituto* (Buenos Aires: Real Imprenta de Niños Expositos, 1799).

78. I conclude this because there was some overlap in the officer corps of the two associations (at least three women were prominently involved in both groups: the Marquesa de Guardiola, the Marquesa de Ribascacho, and Doña María Josefa Fagoaga y Villarrutia), and because the Asociación de Señoras en la Ciudad de México made explicit reference to copying elements of the mode of operation of the Real Congregación.

79. Rapley, *The Dévotes*; Diefendorf, *From Penitence to Charity*; Vidal Galache, "Porque Usía es condesa."

80. AGN, Cofradías, vol. 14, exp. 4, 1805, Sobre establecer en esta capital una congregación de Oblatas. Viceroy Iturrigaray to Archbishop Lizana, Dec. 28, 1804.

81. AGN, Cofradías, vol. 14, exp. 4, 1805, Sobre establecer en esta capital una congregación de Oblatas. Archbishop Lizana to Viceroy Iturrigaray.

82. AGN, Cofradías, vol. 14, exp. 4, 1805, Sobre establecer en esta capital una congregación de Oblatas. Constituciones de la Asociación de Señoras en la Ciudad de México con el fin de exercitar la Caridad con las Enfermas pobres en los Hospitales; enseñar la Doctrina en las Escuelas de Niñas y otros designios piadosos, baxo la protección de María Ssma con el título de divina Pastora.

83. AGN, Cofradías, vol. 14, exp. 4, 1805, Sobre establecer en esta capital una congregación de Oblatas. Constituciones de la Asociación de Señoras en la Ciudad de México.

84. AGN, Cofradías, vol. 14, exp. 4, 1805, Sobre establecer en esta capital una congregación de Oblatas. Constituciones de la Asociación de Señoras en la Ciudad de México.

85. AGN, Cofradías, vol. 14, exp. 4, 1805, Sobre establecer en esta capital una congregación de Oblatas. Constituciones de la Asociación de Señoras en la Ciudad de México, and Señoras [de la Congregación de Oblatas] al Fiscal Civil. Another model for requiring no set fee was the Real Congregación, with which several of the ladies were also associated; indeed, part of the constitution of the Real Congregación was copied into their document as evidence of a precedent for a cofradía with no required contribution.

86. Diefendorf, *From Penitence to Charity*, 226–236; Arrom, "Mexican Laywomen," 52–53.

87. Diefendorf, *From Penitence to Charity*, 226–236; Dinan, "Confraternities," 197, 202, 208, 210; Rapley, *The Dévotes*, 82.

88. Hernández Martín, "Las Hijas de la Caridad," 41.

89. For women's gifts to cofradías and other church projects, see Leavitt-Alcántara, *Alone*.

Chapter 2

The quotation in the chapter title comes from the following source: AHAMich, XIX, Caja 690, 1846–1859, exp. 43, Mayordomos of Morelia to Provisor, Oct. 20, 1846.

1. AHAMich, XIX, Caja 689, exp. 41, José Alejandro Quesada to Lic. D. José María Arizaga, Srio del Gobierno Diocesano, Feb. 12, 1845.

2. Van Young, *Other Rebellion*, 82. Scholars who have taken a regional approach to understanding the economic impact of the wars for independence include Cañedo Gamboa, "Merchants"; Chowning, *Wealth and Power*; Sanchez Santiró, "Ingresos"; Tutino, *Mexican Heartland*, 153; Van Young, *Other Rebellion*, 75–86; Hamnett, "Royalist Counterinsurgency"; Hamnett, "Anastacio Bustamante"; Hamnett, "Economic and Social Dimension"; and Hamnett, *Roots of Insurgency*.

3. My data comes from the archiepiscopal records of the archbishoprics of Mexico, Michoacán, Guadalajara, Durango, and Oaxaca. These data cover the present-day states of: for the center, Mexico, Morelos, and parts of Tlaxcala, Hidalgo, Puebla, and Guerrero; for the north, Durango, Chihuahua, Sonora, and Sinaloa; for the south, Oaxaca; and for the center-west, Jalisco, Colima, Zacatecas, Aguascalientes, Guanajuato, and Michoacán.

4. AHAG, Gobierno, Cofradías, Caja 15, exp. 1814, Dr. Huerta to Promotor Fiscal, Jun. 1, 1814. The Guadalajara records are especially rich in loans from one cofradía to another. See AHAG, Gobierno, Cofradías, Caja 15, 1809–1815.

5. AGN, Justicia Eclesiástica vol. 19, Estado que manifiesta las Cofradías, Hermandades, del obispado de Puebla, 1822.

6. AGN Justicia Eclesiástica vol. 19, 1822.

7. AGN Justicia Eclesiástica vol. 19, Estado que manifiesta las Cofradías . . . Provincia de Guanajuato, 1822.

8. AHAMich, XIX, Caja 818, exp. 9. Noticia que el Cura de Piedragorda remite a la Sria del gobierno Diocesano de las cofradías legalmente erectas en la Parroquia de su cargo, según orden de 1832, y sus rendimientos.

9. AHAG, Gobierno, Cofradías, 1820–1824, Caja 17, exp. 1824, Libro de la cofradía de NS del Rosario, Colima, 1824–1850; AHAMich, XIX, Caja 819, exp. 6, Cuentas 1826, Cofradía del Rosario, Valladolid; AHAMich, XIX, Caja 833, exp. 25, San Luis Potosí.

10. Hutchinson, "Asiatic Cholera," 15–21.

11. Hutchinson, "Asiatic Cholera," 22.

12. See especially AHAMich, XIX, Caja 61, exp. 75 and exp. 82. On the horrifying aspect and emotional impact of the epidemic, see Stevens, *Mexico in the Time of Cholera*, chapter 9.

13. On how epidemics strained cofradía stability even before the extra burden of the independence wars, see Schroeder, "Jesuits." For one cofradía that was financially destroyed by an epidemic that cost them 15,000 pesos in sixty days, see Pescador, "Devoción," 782, 789.

14. AHAMich, XIX, Caja 821, exp. 35, Estado que manifiesta el Yngreso y Egreso de la Cofradía del Divinísimo Señor Sacramentado, Nov. 30, 1842.

15. AHAMich, XIX, Caja 839, exp. 13, Cofradía del Rosario pide licensia . . . Morelia, 1833.

16. AHAMich, XIX, Caja 833, exp. 23, Estracto de las cantidades que en el año de 1832 se colectaron en la Cofradía de Nuestra Señora de la Merced, Morelia; AHAMich, XIX, Caja 834, exp. 53, Alejo Ortega, Miguel Valdespino, and José María Contreras to Provisor, 1840; AHAMich, XIX, Caja 689, exp. 44, José María Contreras y Miguel Valdespino piden permiso, Morelia, 1847.

17. AHAMex, 51 CL, exp. 1, Libro de actas de los cabildos generales y particulares de la mesa de la Cofradía del Santísimo Sacramento de la parroquia de San Pedro Tepotzotlán, 1824–1838.

18. AHAMich, XIX, Caja 689, exp. 30, Francisco Javier Orozco to Promotor Fiscal, Dec. 29, 1831.

19. I have shown elsewhere (Chowning, "Management") that many branches of the church in Michoacán were selling off property, not just cofradías. A reason is rarely given, but in a few cases there is a strong suggestion that the national political discussion around church property (after all, the 1804 Consolidación had already shown the royal government willing to force the sale of some church property) was motivating a desire to get rid of property. On the other hand, some mayordomos of convents were trying to convert financial capital into rental property, on the idea that it was easier to collect local rent than interest from often-distant borrowers (see Chowning, *Rebellious Nuns*).

20. AHAMich, XIX, Caja 839 alone has almost one hundred such requests.

21. Bazant, *Alienation*, 25.

22. AHAMex, Caja 23, L1, Libro de cuentas de la Cofradía de Jesús Nazareno, Amecameca, 1743–1833; see entries for 1806, 1826, 1827, 1831, and 1832.

23. This was part of the objective of an 1829 circular from the office of the bishop of Michoacán, which called for uniformity in the administrative structure and practices of all cofradías in the bishopric, including careful supervision of extraordinary costs. AHAMich, XIX, Caja 818, exp. 6, Constituciones Generales para todas las Cofradías del Obispado de Michoacán, 1829.

24. AHAG, Gobierno, Visitas Pastorales, Guadalajara, Caja 10, exp. 1853, Libro 3º Visita por el Ilmo. Sr. Aranda.

25. AHAMich, XIX, Caja 824, exp. 83, José María Arriaga to Sres Rectores y Vocales de la V[enerable] M[esa] del Santísimo, Jun. 21, 1855.

26. AHAMex, Caja 147, Libro 2, Cuentas del Santísimo Sacramento de Amecameca, Sept. 12, 1841.

27. It is impossible to study systematically the effect of financial and political problems on membership levels in the cofradías. There are very few cases in which I was able to compare lists within a single cofradía before and after 1810, and the sources, as explained in chapter 1, are not reliable for ascertaining membership totals.

28. AHAMich, XIX, Caja 235, exp. 94, Pénjamo.

29. AGN, Bienes Nacionales, Leg. 418, exp. 7, Solicitud que el Cura Proprio y Juez Ecco de la Parroquia de Teloloapam hase a nombre de la Hermandad del Smo Sac y Maria Sma del Rosario, 1851.

30. AHAMich, XIX, Caja 83, exp. 41, Lista de los únicos cofrades de SS José que existen hoy 23 de enero de 1838.

31. Stevens, *Mexico in the Time of Cholera*, chapter 1. It is of course impossible to know whether people were really more impious after 1810 than they had been in the colonial period. The colonial records show plenty of complaints from priests about impiety and "licentiousness," often suggesting—as their post-independence counterparts did—that things were much worse than they had been in some earlier, more idyllic era.

32. Pescador, *De bautizados*, esp. 341–51, attributes the loss of membership in all the cofradías in the parish of Santa Catarina (Mexico City) to this perception.

33. AHAMich, XIX, Caja 834, exp. 51, Lista de los actuales cofrades en la Archicofradía de N.S. de la Merced, 1840; AHAMich, XIX, Caja 834, exp. 53, Lista de los cofrades de esta Archicofradía del Santísimo Rosario; AHAMich, XIX, Caja 834, exp. 53, Lista nominal en donde constan los hermanos de esta cofradía de N.S. del Transito.

34. AHAG, Gobierno, Cofradías, Caja 15, 1809–1815, exp. 1815, Cuentas de la Cofradía del Smo, Aguascalientes, 1815–1850.

35. AGN, Templos y Conventos, Leg. 315, exp. 7, Libro tercero en que se escriven los hermanos de la Concordia del Sr S. Joseph fundada en la capilla del venerable orden 3ro de penitencia de NPS Agustín de México. This cofradía had declined in overall size from around 500 members in the 1750s to around 220 members in the years 1812–13.

36. AHAD, Roll 519, Frames 587–618, Libro en el que constaran todos los Yndividuos que se alistaren en esta cofradía del Transito de NS, fundada con autoridad Real en el convento Hospital Rl de San Cosme y San Damián de la Ciudad de Durango, y lo que cada uno diere por su asiento; AHAD, Roll 520, Frames 100–23; Roll 521, Frames 426–898.

37. AHAMich, XIX, Caja 247, exp. 389, Ydea del Curato de Turicato, su posesión, extensión y población, 1867.

38. AHAMich, XIX, Caja 652, exp. 42, José Vicente Navarro to Provisor, Zacapu, Jun. 18, 1823.

39. In addition to Stevens, *Mexico in the Time of Cholera*, on the topic of the grave and increasing dangers of impiety, see Pani, "Una ventana," on what happens to Mexican youth without religious education.

40. For the success with which French women socialized their sons into Catholicism, producing a vibrant Catholic male bourgeoisie by the later part of the century, see Seeley, "O Sainte Mère."

41. Voekel, "Liberal Schism"; Mijangos y González, "Secularización." This phenomenon of widespread agreement among different political leanings and among both men and women on the properness of the separation of spheres has been observed in most of the Western world. See, for example, Davidoff and Hall, *Family Fortunes*.

42. Pani, "Una ventana," 76. Mínguez-Blasco, "Between Virgins," 98–99, also makes this point.

43. Seminal works on the masculinization of the public sphere include Landes, *Women*; Cott, *Bonds of Womanhood*; Hunt, *Family Romance*; Kerber, Women of the Republic.

44. Since both the masculinization of the public sphere and the ideologies that called for curbing the public power of the churches gained strength almost everywhere in the Western world around the late eighteenth and early nineteenth centuries, many scholars have seen the nineteenth century as one in which religion was most "feminized." The alliance between two displaced or disestablished groups—women and Protestant ministers—was at the core of the feminization "thesis" advanced in 1977 by Ann Douglas (and which had been advanced less aggressively a few years earlier by Barbara Welter). Douglas, *Feminization*, and Welter, "Feminization." Although the thesis was first applied to the Protestant world (see also Ryan, *Cradle*; Stout and Brekus, "Declension"; Davidoff and Hall, *Family Fortunes*), feminist scholars of Catholicism quickly began to explore its implications for Catholic Europe. The process was most clearly visible in France during the Revolution,

when women literally brought church services into the home after dechristianization took hold (Desan, *Reclaiming*; Hufton, "Reconstruction"; Outram, *Body*), but something similar seemed to have happened in a less dramatic way elsewhere and at other times in France (Grew, "Liberty"; Seeley, "O Sainte Mère"; Smith, *Ladies*; Ford, *Divided Houses*.) For the Spanish case, see Mínguez-Blasco, "Between Virgins," who emphasizes the importance of discursive feminization. For a recent assessment of the assignment of both women and religion to the private sphere, see Scott, *Sex*, especially chapter 1.

45. Pani, "'Ciudadana'"; Arrom, *Women*.

46. Seeley, "O Sainte Mère," 866.

47. Forment, *Democracy*.

48. The renter of a house belonging to one Mexico City cofradía claimed that "simulated sales" were taking place, in which a property was sold at below-market prices to members of the cofradías, causing the "disappearance from one night to the next morning of the numerous properties that form the wealth of those establishments, as they pass into the hands of the members themselves." AGN Justicia Eclesiástica, Vol. 125, fs. 384–85, Letter from Fernanda de la Barrera, 1842.

49. AHAD, Roll 522, Frames 51–52, Diputados de la Archicofradía del Smo Sacramanto del Altar al Yllmo Sor. Obispo Marqués de Castañiza, Sept. 25, 1818. The solution these deputies came to was to tap a "private fund" controlled by the cofradía, in order to avoid having to change the "public and accustomed" practices of the cofradía.

50. AHAO, Diocesano, Gobierno, Parroquias, 1818–19, Humilde demostración que como mayordomo que fui de la Cofradía, Jan. 10, 1820. In this long and self-serving letter, the mayordomo recounted the efforts and personal expense involved in rebuilding the cofradía, which he said was essential to organize and fund the rebuilding of the Templo de las Nieves that was in total abandonment, "its pious doors closed" and the building fetid from the corpses buried there. "I had to create a new governing board . . . then print a sufficient number of Patentes to enlist 154 new members, which, with the 16 who were the only ones left, made for a total of 170." He also rehabilitated some of the houses owned by the cofradía so that they produced more rental income than before. Finally, he claimed to have purchased or solicited the purchase of almost 1,000 pesos' worth of new utensils and equipment and to have resumed sponsoring masses and festivities.

51. AHAD, Roll 271, Frames 469–79, Mayordomos de Chihuahua, 1832.

52. AHAO, Parroquial, Disciplinar, Cofradías, 1820–1833, Libros de cofradía del año de 1832 al año de 1841.

53. AHAD, Roll 518, Frame 542 passim. Descargo que Mariano Larrasolo da a las observaciones que los señores comisionados . . . han hecho en las cuentas de la Fábrica Espiritual y Archicofradía del Smo, Villa de Allende, March 2, 1844.

54. AHAD, Roll 518, Frame 666, Estado que manifiesta las Fincas que reconosen capitales a rédito a favor de la Cofradía del Rosario de esta Parroquia [de Hidalgo], 1840.

55. AHAD, Roll 301, Frames 220–28, Los Mayordomos del Smo Sacramento en el Mineral de S. Pedro de los Chalchihuites ante VSY . . . Jun. 23, 1844; and Frame 229, Lista de los Sres y Señoras que se han presentado, voluntariamente para ser hermanos de la Cofradía del Smo Sacramento que se trata de establecer en ese Mineral . . . 1844; AHAD, Roll 518, Frames 553–54, Distribución de lo que gastan las Cofradías en un año, Durango, no date but appears to be 1843; AHAD, Roll 518, Frames 555–64, Cofradía de Nuestra Señora del Carmen fundada en . . . Sombrerete . . . depósito irregular, 1842.

56. It was explicitly stated that no women were allowed to be one of the eight, no matter how respectable they were. AHAO, Diocesano, Gobierno, Parroquias, 1830–33, Proyecto apuntes para la formación del reglamento que en los tiempos venideros deve regir en el Govierno de la Archicofradía de NS de Xuquila, 1831.

57. AHAO, Parroquial, Disciplinar, Cofradías, 1820–1833, Libros de cofradía del año de 1832 al año de 1841.

58. AGN, Justicia Eclesiástica, vol. 19, fs. 452–468, Consejo del Estado, La sección de Justicia del consejo de Estado que suscribe se ha impuesto detenidamente de las constituciones formadas por el Sr. cura de S. Agustín Tlalpan BD Manuel Sánchez Soriano para el establecimiento de una cofradía en su parroquia.

59. AGN, Bienes Nacionales, Leg. 671, exp. 16. Expediente sobre aprobación de las constituciones hechas por la hermandad del Smo Sac erigida en el Pueblo de S. Fco Temascatlepec del Valle, 1843.

60. AGN, Bienes Nacionales, Leg. 418, exp. 7, Solicitud que el Cura Proprio y Juez Ecco de la Parroquia de Teloloapam hase a nombre de la Hermandad del Smo Sacramento y María Sma del Rosario, 1851.

61. AGN, Bienes Nacionales, vol. 145/83, Diligencias promovidas por el C. Ygnacio Santos García, como Diputado de la Cofradía del Santísimo Sacramento de este Pueblo [de Jilotepec], 1844; and Informe del Cura, Jun. 17, 1844.

62. AHAM, Caja 23, L1, Libro de cuentas de la Cofradía de Jesús Nazareno, Amecameca, 1743–1833; AGN, Bienes Nacionales, Leg. 418, exp. 13, El señor cura vicario Foraneo [de Amecameca] sobre que se le permita vender unos terrenos pert. a la cofradía de Jesús Nazareno, 1853.

63. There are no rigorous, statistics-based comparisons of economic destruction from the insurgency across regions, but this is the clear sense of the scholars who have tried to generalize, including Tutino, *Mexican Heartland*, 153; Van Young, *Other Rebellion*, 75–86; Hamnett, "Royalist Counterinsurgency"; Hamnett, "Anastacio Bustamante"; Hamnett, "Economic and Social Dimension"; and Hamnett, *Roots of Insurgency*.

64. This could cause resentment among those who did *not* qualify for interest forgiveness. Vicente Herrera, of the town of Los Reyes in Michoacán, complained in 1827 that he had paid interest on his 1,700-peso loan from a cofradía throughout the "challenging days of the revolution," since unlike many "unfortunate farmers," he had been in possession of his property throughout the insurgency. But in 1822, upon learning that some borrowers had been allowed to cancel interest owed for the decade of insurgency, he refused to pay. AHAMich, XIX, Caja 689, exp. 25, Perivan, Cofradía del Santísimo, 1827.

65. AHAMich, XIX, Caja 834, exp. 41, Lista de los únicos cofrades de SS José que existen hoy 23 de enero de 1838.

66. AHAMich, XIX, Caja 834, exp. 48, Cofradía de San José, 1839.

67. AHAMich, XIX, Caja 835, exp. 109, Lista de los cofrades de S. San José Morelia que están corrientes y pagan su cornadillo, Jan. 1855.

68. AHAMich, XIX, Caja 834, exp. 41, Lista de los únicos cofrades de SS José que existen hoy 23 de enero de 1838.

69. AGN Justicia Eclesiástica, Vol. 183, 260, Estado general de las cofradías y congregaciones piadosas establecidas en las respectivas dioceses con espresión de sus bienes y sus deudas, 1856; Rugeley, *Of Wonders*, 74.

70. AHAG, Gobierno, Visitas Pastorales, Guadalajara, Caja 10, exp. 1853, Libro 3º Visita por el Illmo Sr. Aranda.

71. AHAMich, Diocesano, Gobierno, Parroquias, Informes, multiple boxes.

72. AHAMich, XIX, Caja 833, exp. 13. Informe que el B. D. Ygnacio Alvis cura y juez ecco de la Villa de San Felipe remite de las cofradías.

73. AHAMich, XIX, Caja 232 (1822–24), exp. 46. Chilchota. 1822. Les remito un plan instructivo de las cinco cofradías que hay fundadas en este Curato.

74. AHAMich, XIX, Caja 406, exp. 22, Vicente Casas Navarrete, cura Guadalcazar, to Sr. Vicario Capitular, 28 Jun. 1824.

75. The 1829 expulsion of Spaniards, among whom were numerous merchants who had often contributed to religious functions because they brought customers in from the surrounding towns and haciendas, may also have affected the well-being of the cofradías and the mood of the mayordomos, though the numbers of Spaniards outside of Mexico City by this date was relatively small. On balance, the epidemic seems a more likely explanation.

76. AHAG, Gobierno, Parroquias, 1842–1849, Caja 3, exp. 1844, Cura Juan María de Dios Piñera to Arzobispado, 6 Sept. 1844.

77. AHAMich, XIX, Caja 690 (1846–1859), exp. 47, Silao. Sobre nombramiento de mayordomo y colector gral de las cofradías y obras pias de aquella provincia. José Dolores Farías to Provisor, Oct. 23, 1850. In the colonial period convent mayordomos seem usually to have received a 4 percent commission.

78. AHAMich, XIX, Caja 690 (1846–1859), exp. 49, Sobre que se declaran Obras Pías las cofradías de San Miguel Allende excepto las de la Purísima y San Pedro, 1852.

79. AHAMich, XIX, Caja 655 (1829–1835), exp. 121, Francisco Ávila to Provisor, July 7, 1832, and Mayordomo Archicofradía de la Sma. Trinidad to Provisor, 10 Jul. 1832.

80. AHAMich, XIX, Caja 834, exp. 53, Alejo Ortega, Miguel Valdespino, and José María Contreras to Provisor, 1840.

81. AHAMich, XIX, Caja 835, 1845–1856, exp. 88, Sobre restablecimiento de la Cofradía de San Roque de esta ciudad, Morelia 1848.

82. AHAMich, XIX, Caja 689, exp. 41, José Alejandro Quesada to Lic. D. Jose Maria Arizaga, Srio del Gobierno Diocesano, Feb. 12, 1845.

83. AHAMich, XIX, Caja 690 (1846–1859), exp. 49, Sobre que se declaran Obras Pías las cofradías de San Miguel Allende excepto las de la Purísima y San Pedro, 1852.

84. For Mexico and Guadalajara, see Taylor, *Magistrates*, 24. Brading, *Church and State*, 108, shows that the number of priests living in some towns in the diocese of Michoacán nearly doubled between 1770 and 1809. Partly this increase was due to the new opportunities for men from poor or middling backgrounds to become priests in the late colony. The new diocesan seminary in Valladolid (later Morelia), for example, which was founded in 1770, reserved thirty spots for scholarship students. García Alcaraz, *La cuna*, 58, 194.

85. Aguirre Salvador, *El mérito*, 290.

86. Manuel Abad y Queipo, from an 1811 edict, quoted in Brading, *Church and State*, 108. Priests also had other reasons for disgruntlement. Taylor, *Magistrates*, 24, characterizes the disaffection felt by late colonial parish priests as political at its core: they found themselves increasingly "on the defensive" because of the Bourbon state's new limitations on their temporal power. One of the by-products of the state's undermining of priestly authority was an increase in complaints about clerical misconduct and lawsuits filed against priests by both parishioners and district governors. Priests, for obvious reasons, found these criticisms frustrating, in light of their perception that the state had opened the door to them. A slightly different take on this "political" interpretation is Connaughton, "El cura párroco," who emphasizes priests' loss of their role as "interlocutors" between the pueblo and the broader society.

87. At the top were the small number of well-educated, well-connected, generally well-born, and well-placed ministers who occupied the diocesan hierarchy or the richest parishes. In the middle were priests who served in poor to middling parishes; vicars, ordained assistants to whom priests paid a modest but respectable salary; and chaplains, who served specific institutions such as convents, schools, or haciendas and might or might not have a comfortable stipend, depending on the institution. Also in the middle were some unemployed ministers who held benefices or trusts (*capellanías*) that provided them with a (usually) small annual income. At the bottom were those who had neither independent sources of income nor a parish position (even as a vicar).

88. Taylor, *Magistrates*, 78; Aguirre Salvador, *El mérito*, 289-90.

89. AHAMich, XVIII, Caja 509, exp. 103, General visita 1791, Lista de el Número de Yndividuos de el Clero Secular, San Luis Potosí.

90. Capellanías could be granted by the bishop (and these were usually quite small, 1,000 or 2,000 pesos, providing an income of 50 to 100 pesos a year) or privately, usually by family members wishing to provide a son or nephew a regular income. These, too, could often be on the small side—the most common private capellanía was 4,000 pesos, which provided an income of 200 pesos a year—but a few priests held more than one capellanía, making it possible for them to live very comfortably even without a parish or a position in the diocesan government. The modest income from capellanías meant that many priests who held them also engaged in outside endeavors (commerce, agriculture) and sought occasional parish employment during feast days and annual functions like Corpus Christi.

91. The parish priest of Dolores paid his vicar 365 pesos a year plus the income from manuales (alms for performing sacraments); in San Luis de la Paz the vicar was paid 300 pesos plus manuales; in Santa María del Río one vicar was paid 300 and another 400, plus manuales; in Pátzcuaro in 1794, vicars were paid 500 pesos. AHAMich, XVIII, Caja 509, exp. 103, General visita 1791, Lista de el Número de Yndividuos de el Clero Secular; AHAMich, XVIII, Caja 511, exp. 109, Pátzcuaro. A day laborer probably earned about 75 pesos a year. The glut of priests and the need for many of them to constantly seek out ways of supplementing their income may have been part of the reason why Dr. Juan Antonio de Tapia, representing the bishop of Michoacán in the 1792 visita, found the large population of secular clergy living in San Miguel el Grande to be shockingly negligent in their dedication to the crucial task of confession, for which priests could charge no fee. AHAMich, XVIII, Caja 510, exp. 106, Autos de visita en fines de 92 y principio de 93, Report of Dr. D. Juan Antonio de Tapia, San Miguel el Grande, Feb. 7, 1792.

92. Brading, *Church and State*, summarizes the fees for various services for which cofradías might pay: "whereas a sung mass cost 8 ps. and a solemn high mass with vigil 16 ps., the rate for an ordinary 'low' mass was 1 ps. For a novena of masses organised for the celebration of a feast one paid 27 ps., or 18 ps., according to whether they were sung or not. Anniversary masses for the dead cost 6 ps., and any sung mass which was accompanied by a procession and vespers, as was regularly provided by confraternities, 8 ps" (143-44). Out of these fees, priests had to support their assistants (vicars, deacons, sub-deacons, sacristans).

93. AHAMich, XVIII, Caja 509, exp. 103, General visita 1791, San Luis Potosí, San Miguel el Grande, Celaya.

94. AGN, BN, vol. 1170/1, Expediente formado sobre el informe de los curas de esta capital, para dar el que pidió el Exmo Senor Virrey... Quaderno 3, Report from priest of Santa Cruz Acatlán, 1794.

95. Taylor, *Magistrates*, includes an appendix with the names of all the priests known to have joined the insurgency.

96. AHAMich, XIX, Caja 233, exp. 68, Zinapécuaro, Juan Bautista Figueroa to bishop, Dec. 11, 1835.

97. Taylor, *Magistrates*.

98. On the archbishopric of Mexico, see Pérez Iturbe, "Lázaro de la Garza," 139; and O'Hara, *Flock*, chapter 6. On the archdiocese of Guadalajara, see Staples, *La iglesia*, 133, 134. Some municipal authorities took the opposite stance and defended their priests against criticism. The town of Santa Ana Tianguistengo, for example, defended its priest, Joaquín Aldaz, against accusations that he was ineffective, pointing out that many of his apparent failures came because he was very obese, nearly blind, and prone to falling whenever his strong eyeglasses fogged up. Pérez Iturbe, "Lázaro de la Garza," 141, 142. Pérez

Iturbe found that the number of cases against priests brought by municipal authorities in the 1850s was more than double the number of "positive collaborations" between town councils and priests.

99. AHAMich, XIX, Caja 833, exp. 24, José Ygnacio Losano to Promotor, Jun. 19, 1832.

100. AHAMich, XIX, Caja 690, exp. 43, Ramón Magaña to Provisor, Aug. 7, 1846; Mayordomos of eight cofradías to Provisor, Oct. 20, 1846; Magaña to Provisor, Feb. 17, 1847; Provisor disposition, Jun. 30, 1847.

101. Staples, *La iglesia*, 133–34; Rugeley, *Of Wonders*, 76. The priest of Guadalcázar in 1852 accused the cofradías of his parish of failing for over a decade to pay what they owed to the Fábrica Espiritual (the building fund), the sacristy, the priest himself, and the alms that were supposed to be applied to the vicars. AHAMich, XIX, Caja 690, exp. 47, Cura Guadalcázar to Provisor, Feb. 23, 1852.

102. Quoted in Mijangos y González, *Lawyer*. Ocampo was excoriated by the "anonymous priest of Michoacán," who accused him of trying to "usurp the church's sovereignty, to secularize religious society and to impose civil power over and above the divine jurisdiction of the bishops" (140–41).

103. AHAMich, XIX, Caja 231, exp. 33, Félix de la Fuente cura interino Apaseo to Vicario Capitular, May 16, 1851. Parish priests and interims like De la Fuente suffered from reduced income, but priests who depended on their capellanías were also in trouble. In the cathedral city of Valladolid in 1827, there were forty-nine priests in residence. Fifteen of them depended on their capellanías, but only five enjoyed up-to-date payments on those capellanías from individuals who had borrowed funds from the Juzgado de Testamentos y Capellanías. One other borrower was partially up to date. The rest depended for their income on properties that were either in bankrupcy or were so far behind they might as well have been. AHAMich, XIX, Caja 236, exp. 106, Estado en que se manifiesta el número de eccos de esta capital de Morelia, 1827.

104. AHAMich, XIX, Caja 27, exp. 244, Sobre asignación del tercio de Rosas a las Parroquias del Obispado; AHAMich, Diocesano, Gobierno, Colegios, Santa Rosa, Caja 19, exp. 145, Noticia del colegio de Sta Rosa María en la Ciudad de Morelia. In 1855 the bishopric restored the one-third proportion. AHAMich, Diocesano, Gobierno, Colegios, Santa Rosa, Caja 27, exp. 244, Sobre asignación del tercio de Rosas a las Parroquias del Obispado. In the colonial period, interim priests were required to turn over one-third of their emoluments, but in Michoacán this was reduced to one-quarter in 1823 because of the financial problems interim priests were experiencing.

105. De la Fuente also notes that priests were earning fewer fees because of the decline in relatively elaborate annual functions and funerals, which he attributed to "the enlightenment of our century." AHAMich, XIX, Caja 231, exp. 33, Félix de la Fuente cura interino Apaseo to Vicario Capitular, May 16, 1851.

106. The crown had exercised this right since the conquest, but with independence the Vatican wanted to renegotiate the terms of state patronage, and the new Mexican state resisted. It was not until 1831 that an agreement between Mexico and the Vatican allowed new bishops to be appointed.

107. Ricker, "Lower Secular," 46–50.

108. AGN Justicia Eclesiástica vol. 19, f. 307, Mejico, May 1825 or 1826 (ink has run). In 1820 the bishopric of Michoacán already had seventy-eight vacancies. AHAMich, XIX, Caja 231, exp. 30, Nos el Dr. D. Manuel de la Bárcena, Arcedeano dignidad de esta Obispado . . . por el Yllmo Sr D. Manuel Abad Queypo . . . 1820.

109. Ricker, "Lower Secular," 47; Aceves Ávila, *"Que es bueno,"* 402.

110. *Memoria del Ministerio de Justicia y Negocios Eclesiásticos*, 1850, Estado 13. Even after 1831, some bishops may have continued intentionally to appoint interim priests rather

than permanent curates because of the flexibility it gave them. Sullivan-González, *Piety*, 23–24, for Guatemala points out that interim appointments allowed the church to continue to control the appointment process, while permanent appointments had to be approved by the state. The curia may also have continued to appoint interim priests for financial reasons: because of the provision that, as we just saw, interim priests were obligated to turn over one-third of their income—after the purchase of essentials like wine, wax, and oil—to the curia. Thus the curia, whose own income had been reduced in 1834 by new legislation that made payment of the tithe voluntary, benefited from interim appointments.

111. AHAMich, XIX, Caja 559, exp. 1; exp. 2; exp. 3; Caja 560, exp. 4; exp. 8; Caja 584, exp. 114–21; Caja 585, exp. 122–25; Caja 603, exp. 212–18; Caja 604, exp. 220–23; Caja 605, exp. 224–29; Caja 606, exp. 230, 232–36; Caja 607, exp. 237.

112. For the 1790s (based on twenty-three parishes): AHAMich, XVIII, Caja 509, exp. 103, General visita 1791; AHAMich, XVIII, Caja 510, exp. 106, Autos de visita en fines de 92 y principio de 93; AHAMich, XVIII, Caja 511, exp. 108 and 109, 1794–95. For the 1820s and 1830s (based on thirty parishes): AHAMich, XIX, Cajas 229, 230, 231, 232, 233, 234, 235. Note that even the colonial ratio is significantly higher than the contemporary ratio of priests to parishioners in some parts of Catholic Europe, which in eighteenth-century France was around 1:700, and in late eighteenth-century Milan was 1:127. In Ireland, on the other hand, the ratio in the eighteenth century was higher, by one estimate 1:970. Atkin and Tallett, *Priests*, 75; Po-Chia Hsia, *World of Catholic Renewal*, 125; Fenning, *Undoing*, 285.

Chapter 3

The quotation in the chapter title comes from the following source: AHAMich, XIX, Caja 238, exp. 134, Sobre erección de la Congregación del alumbrado y vela continua del SSMo Sacramento en la Parroquia de San Miguel de Allende.

1. For the modest revival of silver mining and its effect on hacienda agriculture, see Urrutia de Stebelski and Nava Oteo, "La minería (1821–1880)," 128; Bazant, *Cinco haciendas*; Brading, *Haciendas and Ranchos*, 136, 202; del Raso, *Notas estadísticas*; Salvucci and Salvucci, "Crecimiento económico"; Muñoz, "La minería." On the midcentury economic recovery in Michoacán, see Chowning, "Contours"; Chowning, "Reassessing"; Chowning, *Wealth and Power*. For the recovery of the economy outside of Michoacán, see Sánchez Santiró, "Ingresos fiscales"; Mayo, *Commerce*; Pérez Herrero, "'*Crecimiento*'"; Grosso, "Producción"; Thomson, "Continuidad"; Wiemers, "Agriculture"; Cañedo Gamboa, "Merchants"; Moncada González, *La libertad comercial*.

2. On separation as both subordination and autonomy, see Dunn, "Saints and Sisters"; Freedman, "Separatism as Strategy"; Kerber, "Separate Spheres."

3. The Third Order organizations provided an earlier alternative model, with their parallel men's and women's structures, but they were not cofradías. Some Afro-Mexican cofradías and some indigenous cofradías, as we saw in chapter 1, had female officers or branches, but they seem to have been relatively few in number by the nineteenth century.

4. For the Querétaro and Mexico City mentions in the Vela foundation documents, see AHAMich, XIX, Caja 238, exp. 134, Sobre erección de la Congregación del alumbrado y vela continua del SSMo Sacramento en la Parroquia de San Miguel Allende. For the Orizaba Congregación, see Church of Latter Day Saints, Veracruz, Mexico, registros parroquiales y diocesanos, 1590–1978, FamilySearch (https://familysearch.org/ark:/61903/3:1:33SQ-GP4N-9C8Z?cc=1883382&wc=3PQ4-DP8%3A176854501%2C176850802%2C178963501, May 21, 2014, Orizaba, San Miguel, Cofradías 1818–1869, image 21–117 of 603.

5. Carbajal López, "Devoción," 381, notes the late colonial foundation of the Real Congregación in Durango, Puebla, Atlixco, Aguascalientes, and Orizaba. For Durango see also

AHAD, Roll 183, Frames 543–53, various documents concerning the foundation of the Real Congregación in the cathedral of Durango, 1793.

6. On the practices of the Santa Escuela, see O'Hara, "Supple." The Escuelas de Cristo proved to be quite popular in the eighteenth century, and by 1810 there were at least thirty-two in Mexico, most of them founded after 1740. Twelve were in Mexico City, and fourteen of the twenty provincial Escuelas were located in eighteen different cities/towns in the center-west. O'Hara, "Supple," Table 1; Hernández, *La soledad*, 50.

7. Bazarte Martínez and Cruz Rangel, "Santas Escuelas de Cristo," 184. As noted in chapter 1, there was the theoretical possibility of a women's Escuela, but a royal interrogatory in 1797 determined that there was no such organization in Mexico City. Von Germeten, *Black Blood Brothers*, 53, reports a women's Escuela de Cristo in Analco, Puebla, but the relationship of that "Escuela" to the men's version is unclear, since the leadership positions held by the women of Analco, among them "porters" and "nurses," are not ones that accorded with the didactic and penitential nature of the men's Escuela. See also Labarga García, "La Santa Escuela," 524.

8. Celaya, Salamanca, and Valle de Santiago are all within sixty kilometers of each other. Morelia, at ninety kilometers from Valle de Santiago, is a little farther away but very clearly in the same subregion. AHAMich, XIX, Caja 5, exp. 1 (De Cristo), Silvestre Verdusco to Luis Macouzet, Salamanca, ca. Oct. 15 1876; AHAMich, XIX, Caja 840, exp. 57, Solicitud de Da. Maria Inés Farfan Aguilar sobre que se establezca en esta ciudad la Santa Escuela para Señoras, a imitación de la que ai fundada en la iglesia de la Sta Cruz de esta capital, Morelia, Sept. 1, 1854.

9. It is also possible, as happened in the Michoacán archives, that some material on the Escuelas is misfiled under "schools," instead of "cofradías" or "pious associations."

10. AHAMich, XIX, Caja 5, exp. 1 (De Cristo), Trinidad Ramírez to Luis Macouzet, Oct. 6, 1876; Silvestre Verdusco to Luis Macouzet, Oct. 1876.

11. The implication is that both the men's group and the women's group were involved in these renovations, although the document describing them (based on documents in the archive of the Escuela) was written decades later, so the roles of the men's versus the women's groups are impossible to reconstruct.

12. Chapter 22 of the standard constitution allowed local groups to introduce amendments if the changes were approved by a two-thirds majority of the governing council (*junta de ancianos*) in two separate votes. *Constituciones de la Congregación y Santa Escuela de Cristo* (1836), 191. The material here comes from a section entitled "Adiciones que ha puesto a sus constituciones, la Santa Escuela de Cristo Señor Nuestro fundada en el Convento del Espíritu Santo de México."

13. *Constituciones de la Congregación y Santa Escuela de Cristo* (1836), 191. In 1798 the Santa Escuela in Zacatecas agreed to something similar, that is, that during the men's spiritual retreats the exercises that were held at night would not involve either darkness or discipline, but rather a period of mental prayer. AHAG, Gobierno, Visitas Pastorales, 1798–99, Caja 7, Memorial presentado por D. Pedro Joaquin de Aguilera, Director de la Santa Escuela . . . Santa Visita de Zacatecas, 1798.

14. *Constituciones de la Congregación y Santa Escuela de Cristo* (1836), 191–92.

15. *Constituciones de la Congregación y Santa Escuela de Cristo* (1836), 196–200, 199.

16. *Constituciones de la Congregación y Santa Escuela de Cristo* (1836), 198.

17. An 1834 constitution from Mexico City does not include the additions; I have not located any constitutions printed after 1836. Thanks to Dr. Hortencia Calvo at Tulane Library for looking up this information in the 1834 constitution, held in Tulane's rare book library. An 1865 constitution for the Santa Escuela in Madrid, the only constitution I have been able to find that postdates 1836, continued to include discipline and the banquillo. *Constituciones de la Congregación y Escuela de Cristo* (1865).

18. AGN, Cultos Religiosos, vol. 1, exp. 1, 1797–1802, Expediente formado a virtud del Real Cédula sobre que se informe del número de Escuelas de Cristo que hay en esta Ciudad y demas puntos.

19. AHAG, Gobierno, Visitas Pastorales, 1798.

20. De la Flor, "Pantalla," 723.

21. AHAMich, XIX, Caja 244, exp. 304, Sobre restablecimiento del Sagrado Depósito y Vela Perpetua en la Casa de Ejercicios de la Parroquia de Silao. Morelia, 1849. The date is imprecise because two different dates, 1837 and 1841, were given in the document.

22. I include in the six center-western cofradías the four Escuelas de Señoras that we know of, the Cofradía del Sr. San José in Aguascalientes, and the Arca de la Alianza in San Miguel de Allende. The latter was elaborately planned but seems not to have been approved, at least the first time it was submitted. The others are: the Archicofradía de la Santa Veracruz in Mexico City, the Archicofradía del Santísimo Sacramento of Mérida, and the Cofradía del Santísimo Sacramento in Hunucmá (Yucatan). AHAG, Gobierno, Parroquias, Aguascalientes, Caja 6, exp. 1842–1855, Sobre erección de la cofradía de SSJosé en la parroquia de Aguascalientes, 1855; AHAMich, XIX, Caja 829, exp. 11, 1853, "Sobre fundación de una hermandad"; *Constituciones de la muy Ilustre Archicofradía de ciudadanos de la Santa Veracruz*, in *Colección de papeles varios*, MS Bancroft Library; Rugeley, *Of Wonders*, 78, 80.

23. On the Sisters, why they were so valued by many Mexicans, and the politics behind their expulsion, see O'Brien, "'If They Are Useful.'"

24. Reyes Pavón, "Las Hermanas," ii; AHAMich, XIX, Caja 829, Fundaciones, exp. 8, "Sobre Hermanas de la Caridad" (several exchanges of correspondence in this packet from 1842–45); *Diario del Gobierno de la República Mexicana*, Feb. 22, 1845, "Remitidos" [por José Guadalupe Romero].

25. *El Siglo Diez y Nueve*, Jan. 6, 1844, 2, "Interior"; *Diario del Gobierno de la República Mexicana*, Apr. 24, 1844, 4, "Establecimiento de las Hermanas de la Caridad en la República Mexicana"; *Diario del Gobierno de la República Mexicana*, Nov. 20, 1844, 3, "Remitido: Las Hermanas de la Caridad"; *Diario del Gobierno de la República Mexicana*, Nov. 12, 1844, 3, "Interior. Departamento de Veracruz"; Carta del P. Armengol al P. General México, in *Historia de las Hijas de la Caridad*.

26. AHAMich, XIX, Caja 70, exp. 286, Buenaventura Armengol to bishop, Oct. 27, 1850 and Nov. 30, 1850; *El Siglo Diez y Nueve*, Feb. 15, 1850, 4, "Hermanas de la Caridad."

27. *El Siglo Diez y Nueve*, Nov. 19, 1854, 4, "Las Hermanas de la Caridad."

28. *Historia de las Hijas de la Caridad*. The ten cities where the Hermanas had houses by 1860 were Mexico City, Puebla, Monterey, Saltillo, Toluca, Silao, Guanajuato, Guadalajara, Lagos, and Zacatecas; five of these were in the center-west. By 1873 they were established in a total of twenty-three cities. Of these twenty-three, thirteen were in the center-west (five in Guanajuato, two in Michoacán, three in Jalisco, plus Zacatecas, San Luis Potosí, and Colima), three were in Puebla, three were in the state of Mexico (including the DF), three were in the north, and one was in Veracruz.

29. On the Sisters' authority over men, see O'Brien, "'If They Are Useful,'" 427. As we saw in chapter 1, an effort to found an organization similar to the Ladies of Charity in 1806 seems never to have come into being, probably because of the political turmoil that began in 1808 and turned into warfare in 1810.

30. The Mexican conferences were branches of the international Dames de la Charité headquartered in Paris, revived in 1840 after quiescence during the French Revolution. Originally founded in the seventeenth century, the Dames' rebirth followed the creation of the male Society of St. Vincent of Paul in 1833, which was itself modeled after the seventeenth-century laywomen's organization. Arrom, *Volunteering*, 77. On the history of the Misioneros in Mexico, see De Dios, "Fundación de la Congregación de la Misión."

31. Thirty-two men's conferences were founded between 1845 and 1854. Of these, twelve were in Mexico City and thirteen were in the center-western states of Guanajuato, Michoacán, and Jalisco. Another ninety-four were founded between 1855 and 1874; by 1874 the state of Guanajuato had an impressive twenty-four men's conferences. Arrom, *Volunteering*, 28–29; 44 (Table 2.2).

32. AHAMich, XIX, Caja 245, exp. 354, Ciudad de León de los Aldamas a los 12 días del mes de Mayo . . . reunidas las Sras de la Caridad en asamblea general . . . , May 13, 1856.

33. Arrom, Volunteering, 78; AHAMich, XIX, Caja 245, exp. 354, Ciudad de León de los Aldamas a los 12 días del mes de Mayo . . . reunidas las Sras de la Caridad en asamblea general . . . , May 13, 1856; AHAMich, XIX, Caja 840, exp. 66, Establecida en esta ciudad [de Guanajuato] desde el dia 26 de julio la asociación de las Señoras de la caridad . . . 1861.

34. Not including two chapters founded as part of missions to the pueblos of Huichapán and Nopola in the state of Hidalgo. De Dios, *Historia*, 542.

35. *El Siglo Diez y Nueve*, Feb. 14, 1845, 3, "Bases propuestas por el Sr. Director de las Hijas de la Caridad de esta república, D. Benaventura Armengol, y aprobadas por el presbítero Lic. D. José Guadalupe Romero, para plantear una fundación de dichas Hermanas en la villa de Silao."

36. AHAMich, XIX, Caja 238, exp. 134, Sobre erección de la Congregación del Alumbrado y Vela Continua del Santísimo Sacramento en la Parroquia de San Miguel Allende, Morelia, 1840.

37. The only other case I have found in which women (and no men) were the instigators of a new association was the Oblatas de María proposed in 1806, discussed in chapter 1.

38. The San Miguel reglamento is reproduced more legibly in AHAMich, XIX, Caja 829, exp. 7, Apr. 23, 1842. "El Exmo Sor. Gobernador del Departamento [de Guanajuato] ha dirigido a esta Prefectura con fecha 19 del que rige el oficio que copio."

39. AHAMich, XIX, Caja 237, exp. 134, Promotor Fiscal (Lic. Pelagio Antonio de Lavastida) to Bishop Portugal, May 8, 1840.

40. Each of the cabezas de día would line up two women to sit vigil for half an hour, from 6:00 a.m. to 6:00 p.m., with male veladores coming in after 6:00 p.m.

41. AHAMich, XIX, Caja 237, exp. 134, Provisor y Vicario General (Lic. Mariano Rivas) to Bishop Portugal, May 23, 1840; AHAMich, XIX, Caja 237, exp. 134, Departmental Junta to Bishop Portugal, Jun. 27, 1840. Technically all new cofradías were to be approved by the civil authorities—this was also true in the colonial period. But in practice it was a very pro forma exercise.

42. AHAMich, XIX, Caja 237, exp. 134, Departmental Junta to Bishop Portugal, Jun. 27, 1840.

43. "Nos el Dr. D. Pedro Espinosa, 8–9."

44. AHAMich, XIX, Caja 238, exp. 134, Sobre erección de la Congregación del Alumbrado y Vela Continua del Santísimo Sacramento en la Parroquia de San Miguel Allende, Morelia, 1840; AHAMich, XIX, Caja 829, exp. 7, El Exmo Sor. Gobernador del Departamento [de Guanajuato] . . . Apr. 23, 1842; AHAMich, XIX, Caja 829, exp. 7, Jun. 17, 1842, Presbítero Rafael Ortiz, Cura y Juez Eclesiástico de Pascuaro; AHAMich, XIX, Caja 829, exp. 11, 1853, Jungapeo.

45. AHAG, Gobierno, Parroquias, Lagos, 1842–49, Caja 3, exp. 1843, Dec. 5, 1843.

46. AHAMich, XIX, Caja 237, exp. 134, Lic. José Manuel Fernández to Bishop Portugal, Apr. 16, 1840.

47. AHAG, Gobierno, Parroquias, Tepic, Caja 3 (1841–54), exp. 1843, Rafael Homobono Taver to Bishop Aranda, Dec. 16, 1843; AHAG, Gobierno, Parroquias, Tepic, Caja 3 (1841–54), exp. 1845, Andrés Gonzalez to Bishop Aranda.

48. AHAMich, XIX, Caja 829, exp. 7, Presb. Domingo María Montero de Espinosa to Sr. Provisor y Vicario Gral, Apr. 29, 1842.

49. AHAG, Gobierno, Parroquias, La Barca 1819–1854, Caja 2, exp. 1843–46; AHAG, Gobierno, Parroquias, Lagos, Caja 3, exp. 1843; AHAMich, XIX, Caja 829, exp. 14, Solicitud del Párroco de Tlasasalca sobre establecimeinto de la VP al Smo Sac en su parroquia, 1856.

50. AHAMich, XIX, Caja 835, exp. 89, Presb. Vicente Reyes, cura Zinapécuaro to Provisor, 1847; AHAMich, XIX, Caja 835, exp. 89, Sobre fundación de la Vela Perpetua en la Parroquia de Tinguindín, 1854; AHAMich, XIX, Caja 835, exp. 89, Varias señoras prales [de Yuririapúndaro] . . . 1847; AHAMich, XIX, Caja 829, exp. 11, Deseando varios vecinos del pueblo de Jungapeo . . . 1853; AHAMich, XIX, Caja 829, exp. 11, D. José Noguera Cura Juez Eclesiástico del partido de Tlasasalca to Provisor.

51. AHAMex, Base Siglo XIX, Caja 77, exp. 12, Sobre que se establezca la Vela Perpetua en el Sagrario. 1848.

52. AHAD, Roll 183, Frames 543–45, Chaplain of Durango to Sr. D. José Merlo Aug. 12, 1793; AHAMex, Labastida, Caja 163, exp. 47, El Capellán de La Encarnación sobre que la Asociación del Santísimo . . . se agregue a la de Santa Clara, 1884.

53. In one case the constitution appears to have been misinterpreted: in 1847 in Cotija, Michoacán, twenty-one señoras and ten señores were listed as cabezas de día, and they elected a man, José María Oseguera, as treasurer. AHAMich, XIX, Caja 835, exp. 89, Cotija, 1847. Alumbrado y Vela perpetua del Santísimo Sacramento.

54. AHAMich, XIX, Caja 817, exp. 1, Lic. Manuel Tiburcio Orozco, Canonigo, Provisor y Vicario Gral interino, por el Sr. D. Juan C. Portugal, aprobación de la fundación del alumbrado y vela perpetua en honor del SS en varias parroquias de este obispado . . . Jul. 29, 1843.

55. AHAMich, XIX, Caja 829, exp. 11, Queja de algunos vecinos de San Diego del Biscocho contra el Parroco D. Esiquio Degollado, 1853.

56. Though less of a challenge to the gender hierarchies so embedded in Catholic doctrine and practice than the early Michoacán Velas, the creation of a separate men's and women's Vela was almost as much of a break with colonial tradition. As we saw in chapter 1, cofradías that were single-sex by constitution were relatively uncommon in Mexico in the late colonial period. The principle of gender inclusiveness was reiterated in Michoacán just ten years before the first Vela was founded: an 1829 circular insisted that all cofradías should be open to "ambos sexos," as well as all castes ("calidades"). AHAMich, XIX, Caja 818, exp. 6, Constituciones Generales para todas las Cofradías del Obispado de Michoacán . . . 1829.

57. AHAG, Gobierno, Parroquias, Lagos, 1842–49, Caja 3, exp. 1844.

58. AHAG, Gobierno, Cofradías, Vela Perpetua, 1843–1907, Libro en que se lleva la cuenta de las limosnas colectadas para el culto Divino en la Cofradía de la Vela Continua del Santísimo Sacramento de la Yglecia de la Universidad de Guadalajara, y de su imberción, desde 1 de julio de 1843.

59. AHAG, Gobierno, Cofradías, Vela Perpetua, 1843–1907. Caja 1, exp. 1850, Inventario general de entrega que hago de las cosas pertenecientes a la vela del Santíssimo Sacramento en representación de la Sra mi Madre Da. María Ygnacia Ortiz de Alba, ya difunta, Hermana mayor que fue de dha vela; AHAG, Gobierno, Cofradías, Vela Perpetua, 1843–1907. Caja 1, exp. 1850, Vela Perpetua en la Universidad, julio de 1843.

60. AHAG, Gobierno, Cofradías, Vela Perpetua, 1843–1907, Caja 1, exp. 1850, Vela Perpetua en la Universidad, julio de 1843. Libro en que se lleva la cuenta de las limosnas . . .

61. AHAG, Visitas Pastorales, Guadalajara, Caja 9, San Juan de los Lagos.

62. AHAG, Visitas Pastorales, Guadalajara, Caja 9, exp. 1846, Arandas.

63. AHAG, Visitas Pastorales, Caja 10, Visita [a Aguascalientes] por el Ilmo arzobispado Pedro Loza, 1871.

64. AHAG, Visitas Pastorales, Caja 10, Libro 3º, Visita por el Ilmo Sor. Aranda [a Zapotlán el Grande].

65. AHAMex, Base Siglo XIX, Caja 77, exp. 12, Sobre que se establezca la Vela Perpetua en el Sagrario, 1848. See also AHAMex, Labastida, Caja 189, exp. 26, Presbítero D. Samuel Arguelles sobre la vela perpetua que trata de establecer en S. Bernardo, 1887. In this document the promotor notes that the Vela in the Sagrario "parece ser la mas antigua," because no reglamento exists for any earlier one.

66. The only other Vela foundation in the archbishopric before the 1870s was in Jilotepec in 1855, as far as I have been able to determine. AHAMex, Base Siglo XIX, Caja 91, exp. 59, El Cura de Zempoala D. Tiburcio Lorenzo Zepea sobre que se apruebe el establecimiento de una hermandad que ha erigido en su parroquia. [Actually the parish is that of Jilotepec], 1855.

67. It is reasonable to ask why they did not just ask the bishops of Michoacán or Guadalajara for guidance, but I have noticed during this period a hermeticism within bishoprics, that is, that they did not regularly share information or know what was going on in other bishoprics nearly as much as they would later, in the last third or so of the nineteenth century. Brian Stauffer in a personal communication felicitously called this "diocesan patriachiquismo." Brian Stauffer, personal communication with author, Aug. 9, 2020.

68. AHAMex, Alarcón, Caja 7, exp. 49, Chapa de Mota, El Parroco Fr. Francisco de S. Lira, sobre que se apruebe el Reglamento de la Vela Perpetua, 1892 and AHAMex, Alarcón, Caja 6, exp. 16, El RP Cura Fr. Francsico de S. Lira sobre erección de la Vela Perpetua, 1892. The archbishop disapproved of missionary Fray Francisco de S. Lira's proposed reglamento for a Vela Perpetua in Chapa de Mota because it was written in an "obscure" fashion and he recommended that Fray Francisco just adapt a reglamento that had already been approved; Fray Francisco replied that he had looked at a reglamento from Jilotepec, but it did not satisfy him ("pues si bien es cierto que pudiera copiar el que existe ya en algunas parroquias en donde está establecida la misma devoción, he visto el de la de Jilotepec y no me satisface"). To this the archbishop replied curtly: "We declare the Vela Perpetua to be canonically erected [in Chapa de Mota] and to be subject to the reglamento of the Sagrario Metropolitano." The lack of consistency in the Velas' constitutions had also come to annoy the bishop of Michoacán: in 1861 he issued a uniform constitution that all the Velas were to follow. AHAMich, XIX, Caja 836, exp. 128, Constitutión de la Hermandad de la Vela Perpetua o Adoración del Santísimo Sacramento que se han de Observar en la Arquidiócesis de Michoacán, 1861.

69. AHAO, Parroquial, Disciplinar, Cofradías, 1840–1863, Caja 452, Carta de Esclavitud y patente de admisión a la sociedad del alumbrado y velación perpetua del santísmo Sacramento de la Eucaristía, fraternal y devotamente establecida en la parroquia del Sagrario de Oaxaca el dia 1 de enero de 1855. The next foundation I located was in Tlalpan in 1877, but this foundation made reference to a previous foundation in Tlaxeo. AHAO, Diocesano, Gobierno, Parroquias, 1876–77, Caja 608.

70. Rugeley, *Of Wonders*.

71. AGN Justicia Eclesiástica vol. 19, fs. 408–12.

72. I do not know the reason for this, though the reader should remember that the Real Congregación (chapter 1) also worked like this, and it was treated by the ladies of the Vela in San Miguel as a precedent for their own organization, so it is not shocking that there might be a variant like this elsewhere in Mexico.

73. Chowning, "Talking Back."

74. Lavrin, *Brides of Christ*, 283, 292. See also van Deusen, "Circuits."

75. Cofradías had always stood up to meddlesome priests and had always used defiant language. In the parish of Tizapan el Alto (Jalisco), when the Cofradía del Santísimo

Sacramento was originally founded in 1766, its officers insisted on calling it an "hermandad" (brotherhood) instead of a "cofradía," specifically in order to put it at a remove from the control of the priest. "In case any future Bishops or Vicars and Priests who administer this pueblo want to interfere in [the management of the cofradía]," the original constitution read, "from now and forever we refuse to consent, and if [priests] persist in trying to control or exert authority over it, [the cofradía] should be demolished and ended." AHAG, Gobierno, Cofradías, Caja 14, 1801–1808, exp. Tizapan, Expediente formado a instancia de D. Antonio Abad Panoja sobre la erección de una Cofradía del Smo Sacramento que pretenden fundar en la Parroquia del Pueblo de Tizapan el Alto, 1802.

76. AHAMich, XIX, Caja 840, exp. 57, Vela Perpetua. La Huacana. 1854.

77. AHAG, Gobierno, Parroquias, Arandas, 1845–63, Caja 2, exp. 1849–52, Trinidad Romo to bishop, Sept. 23, 1850.

78. AHAMich, XIX, Caja 825, exp. 98, Tesorería de la Vela Perpetua, Cuenta de cargo y data . . . Ario, 1854–1862.

79. AHAMich, XIX, Caja 823, exp. 68, Cuenta que manifiesta la distribución de los fondos que la Sra. Tesorera de la Vela Perpetua ha ministrado a la Hermana Mayor para los gastos de la misma Hermandad, Jul. 1, 1847–Jun. 30, 1848.

80. AHAG, Gobierno, Cofradías, Vela Perpetua, 1843–1907, Caja 1, exp. 1850, Inventario general de entrega que hago de las cosas pertenecientes a la vela del Santíssimo Sacramento en representación de la Sra. mi Madre Da. María Ygnacia Ortiz de Alba, ya difunta, Hermana mayor que fue de dha vela; AHAG, Gobierno, Cofradías, Vela Perpetua, 1843–1907, Caja 1, exp. 1850, Vela Perpetua en la Universidad, Jul. 1843.

81. AHAG, Gobierno, Cofradías, Caja 22, exp. Lagos, 1845, El Presb. Clemente de Sanromán Cura interino de esta Ciudad to VSY, Jan. 25, 1845.

82. In Silao, too, the Vela celebrated itself too much for the taste of the priest, who was upset that the Vela had spent a lot of money to buy a "large Musical instrument" that could be heard in the street and was meant to call the public to attend the celebration of the foundation of the Vela itself. AHAMich, XIX, Caja 835, exp. 82, José Dolores Farías to Provisor Munguía, Silao, Jul. 1846.

83. This letter represents his next move in the dispute with the Vela: in it he (unrealistically) asked the bishop to make him the "President in perpetuity" of the Vela and to limit the number of veladoras, presumably so as to restrict the amount of money that went into the coffers of the Vela.

84. AHAMich, XIX, Caja 836, exp. 124, Rafael Herrera to Sras. Cabezas de Día, Aug. 22, 1863.

85. AHAMich, XIX, Caja 690, exp. 47, José de Jesús Robledo to Sr. Provisor del Obispado. Jaral, Oct. 10, 1850. Here we can detect not only gendered resentment but also echoes of the Bourbon-era complaints by priests that their parishioners do not sufficiently respect them and indeed treat them like subordinates.

86. AHAMich, XIX, Caja 690, exp. 47, Victoriano Treviño to Sra. Hermana Mayor de la Vela Perpetua, Sept. 3, 1850; AHAMich, XIX, Caja 690, exp. 47, Da. María de la Luz Sierra to Victoriano Treviño, Sept. 5, 1850.

87. Forment, *Democracy*, 107.

88. Staples, "Sociabilidad," 111. According to the entry for Compañía Lancasteriana in Pérez Hernández, *Diccionario geográfico*, 727–28, the idea of founding a girls' school and a Compañía de Señoras to support it first surfaced in 1831, but events intruded and it was not until 1837 that another attempt was made to organize the association, and it too failed. Thus is was not until 1841 that the "many times proposed" Compañía de Señoras was finally approved and officers were named, and 1842 before it began to function.

89. Arrom, *Containing*, 180.

90. Arrom, *Containing*; Staples, "Sociabilidad," 110–11.

91. Arrom, *Women*, 45.

92. Arrom, *Women*, 46, also writes that she found no record of female societies active in Mexico by the late 1850s.

93. *El Monitor Republicano*, Mar. 20, 1847, 3, "Secretaría de gobierno del Estado de S. Luis Potosí."

94. Staples, "Sociabilidad," 111–13.

95. *Semanario de las Señoritas Mexicanas*; *Panorama de las señoritas*; *El presente amistoso*; *La semana de las señoritas mejicanas*; and *La camelia*. Vega, "Difundir la instrucción."

96. As a point of comparison, in the US, where joining was rampant (in the cities at least) during this period, religion and church were important in the expansion of clubs and societies founded and run by women. Many of the non-church organizations that women founded and joined had a vaguely religious underpinning, so that poor relief, for example, was couched in terms of Christian morality and duty. But there was also a wide variety of women's literary, benevolent, and reform organizations (sometimes in alliance with men, sometimes not), and most of them were not concerned with advancing a specific denomination or religion. Boylan, *Origins*, 219–26, identified seventy-eight women's associations founded in New York and Boston during the period from 1797 to 1840, only twenty of which had a connection with a single denomination. Of these, eight were African American Methodist, Baptist, or Presbyterian organizations, two were Jewish, and five were Catholic; the other five were divided among other Protestant churches. In addition to these there was a handful of societies with a connection to Protestantism but not a particular sect: bible societies, tract societies, missionary societies, Sunday school societies. But the majority of the associations were more secular than religious. Their actions were not meant to advance a particular church; at most they meant to advance Christian moral principles.

97. We see this happening in the agricultural sector in some parts of Mexico in the 1830s, 1840s, and 1850s, as owners of haciendas that had been severely damaged in the wars of insurgency or in their aftermath had to innovate to try to stay afloat: building new infrastructure, experimenting with new crops, buying new equipment, trying out new labor arrangements. Chowning, "Reassessing"; Tutino, "Hacienda Social Relations"; Tutino, *Mexican Heartland*.

98. Aranda (bishop of Guadalajara, 1836–1853), as we saw above, was highly complimentary of the Velas de Señoras in his parish visits, while Gómez de Portugal (bishop of Michoacán, 1831–50) was one of the founders of the Sisters of Charity in Silao, Guanajuato, and approved the foundation of the very first Vela. There is no evidence that I know of that might allow anything more than speculation as to why bishops/archbishops in other dioceses might not have been as supportive of new female associations as these bishops. It is possible that entrusting indigenous women with lay authority was not seriously entertained by ecclesiastical authorities, so that in the archbishopric of Mexico and the bishopric of Oaxaca, for example, with a relatively large number of indigenous towns, the notion of female-led lay associations was not on the top of the mind of authorities. Even in the center-west, where female authority in the cofradías was pioneered, women's Velas in the more traditionally indigenous parishes were not encouraged from the top authorities or seemingly by parish priests either until the late nineteenth century. However, this does not explain what appears to be a lack of female-led associations in bishoprics like Puebla or Durango, despite a Hispanic-mestizo racial/ethnic profile roughly like that of the center-western bishoprics. These cases suggest to me the superiority of the hypothesis advanced in this chapter, that cofradía financial and leadership crisis was a necessary trigger to the formation of female-led associations.

Chapter 4

The quotation in the chapter title comes from the following source: *El Monitor Republicano*, Jul. 24, 1856, 1, "Uso y Abusos de las Creencias Religiosas."

1. *El Omnibus*, Jul. 17, 1856, 2, "Otra Esposición."
2. This does not appear to have been the Vela Perpetua that had been established in the Sagrario in 1848 and was the only Vela Perpetua in Mexico City until the 1870s. Rather it was probably the Vela Continua that had been established in the church of San Sebastián in 1793 (chapter 1) and which still functioned. As such, these ladies would have been members of the women's auxiliary.
3. For the US, see Boylan, *Origins*; Scott, *Natural Allies*; Ryan, *Cradle*; Gilmore, *Gender*; Cott, *Grounding*; Zaeske, *Signatures*; Lasser and Robertson, *Antebellum Women*; Fletcher, *Gender*; Portnoy, *Their Right*; Vaon, *We Mean to Be Counted*; Jeffrey, *Great Silent Army*; Salerno, *Sister Societies*.
4. Curley, *Citizens*, 154.
5. The database *Historical Abstracts*, consulted July 10, 2021, lists over thirty articles with petitions as a key unit of analysis published since 2014.
6. Carpenter, *Democracy*, 476.
7. Zaeske, *Signatures*, 3.
8. Masters, "Thousand"; Heerma van Voss, *Petitions*, 3.
9. The main change was to allow property owners to stretch out repayment of their church loans over a period of several years, instead of requiring them to pay them off all at once. Von Wobeser, *Dominación*, 88–98. Eleven of the *representaciones* are collected in Sugawara, ed., *La deuda pública*.
10. On the transformation of petitioning in the context of early democracy in the US, see Carpenter, *Democracy*.
11. Some observers made a distinction between the right to petition and the right to initiate legislation (*derecho de iniciativa*), saying that the later included an obligation on the part of the legislative power to take into consideration the proposals presented to it, while the former could only urge that a law be enacted. But my sense is that this distinction was seen as splitting hairs, and the widespread assumption that petitions would be discussed and acted upon continued to prevail. *El Siglo Diez y Nueve*, Oct. 11, 1844, 3–4, "Segunda Contestación al *Censor* de Veracruz."
12. Chowning, *Wealth and Power*, 139–40. Their plan was foiled because they found that in fact a slim majority of the state population was indeed represented by the petitions.
13. Fowler, *Pronunciamiento*. Zaeske, *Signatures*, 3, notes that in the US, too, by the Jacksonian era, "men were frequently using organized mass petitioning to agitate public opinion."
14. Heerma van Voss, *Petitions*, 4; *Aguila Mexicana*, Jan. 16, 1826, 2, "Cámara de Senadores . . . discusión en lo general de un dictamen de la comisión de puntos constitucionales sobre arreglo del derecho de petición."
15. *El Sol*, Feb. 25, 1831, 1–2, "Gobierno General."
16. *El Fénix de la Libertad*, Apr. 14, 1833, 2–3, "Discurso que pronunció el Sr. Ramírez en la sesión"; AHCEMich, Caja 6, exp. 4, "Pronunciamiento de Pátzcuaro a favor del cambio de sistema de gobierno." It appears that the states of Zacatecas and Querétaro had made the most progress toward establishing rules for petitions. *Correo de la Federación Mexicana*, Feb. 8, 1828, 2. An effort in the senate to make rules for petitioning seems to have died in committee. *Correo de la Federación Mexicana*, Feb. 11, 1828, 1–2.
17. *El Gladiador*, Mar. 29, 1831, 1–2, "Interior. San Luis Potosí"; *El Fénix de la Libertad*, Apr. 13, 1833, 1–2, "Proposición que el Sr. Ramírez"; *El Universal*, Apr. 16, 1850, 1, "Contraste. Derecho de petición violado."

18. The updates came in the "Acta de Reformas" in 1847. The relevant article was article 2: "It is the right of all citizens to vote in elections, exercise their right to petition, assemble to discuss public matters, and belong to the National Guard." http://www.ordenjuridico.gob.mx/Constitucion/1847.pdf.

19. Arrom, *Women*, 42.

20. *Diario de la Revolución*, Nov. 18, 1833, 3–4, "Voz del Bello Secso, o sea Representación de las señoras de Guadalajara pidiendo derogación de la ley núm. 519."

21. Fowler, *Pronunciamiento*, "Pronunciamiento de las mujeres de Zacatlán." I also found a petition from the early 1840s from about one hundred twenty women of the town of Tanhuato (Michoacán) defending their priest against accusations leveled against him by Indians; in this case there was an identical petition signed by the men of the town as well. There are likely more petitions of this nature in the ecclesiastical archives, that is, separate but identical men's and women's petitions dealing with entirely local and not-squarely-political issues. AHAMich, XIX, Caja 243, exp. 261, Petición de los vecinos de Tanhuato.

22. The orator was José María Mata, whose speech was printed in *El Monitor Republicano*, Aug. 4, 1856, 2.

23. Using various library catalogs in the US and Mexico (for printed petitions) and the two newspapers (*El Siglo Diez y Nueve* and especially *La Voz de la Religión*) that regularly published notice of petitions received by the congress, I have identified over forty petitions that either the congress acknowledged receiving or we know to have been published. Most of them came from the larger cities and towns of the republic. Another forty small towns—mainly in the states of Puebla, Veracruz, Guerrero, and Jalisco—were named in the text of a petition from Puebla as having also sent petitions (*La Voz de la Religión*, Feb. 28, 1849, 5, "Respetuosa escitativa que los Vecinos de Puebla dirigen a las supremas autoridades de la república, contra la tolerancia de cultos"). Although we cannot verify that these towns did in fact send petitions, if we assume that the Puebla petition was correct and they did, it is likely that there were small towns in other states of which the Puebla petitioners were not aware—perhaps, as a very rough estimate, as many as one hundred (if there were forty in the four states that the Puebla petitioners knew of).

24. Martínez Baez, *Representaciones*, 12.

25. On religious tolerance in Mexico, see Mijangos y González, *Lawyer*; Martínez Albesa, *La constitución*; Santillán Salgado, "La secularización"; Mendoza García, "Libertad de concienca"; Cortés Guerrero, "'Viva la religión.'"

26. *El Siglo Diez y Nueve*, Jul. 30, 1856, 1–2, "Crónica Parlamentaria"; Olveda, "Proyectos"; Pérez Acevedo, "Legislación." This is ironic in light of the fact that Texas colonization set in motion the events that resulted in the dismemberment of Mexico in the first place.

27. *El Monitor Republicano*, Nov. 29, 1849, 4, "Editorial. Matrimonios." Earlier colonization laws in Coahuila-Texas did encourage intermarriage, so this possibility was not a figment of the imagination (Brian Stauffer, personal communication with author, Aug. 27, 2020).

28. *La Voz de la Religión*, Jan. 31, 1849, 136–39, and Feb. 3, 1849, 150–56, "Representación que el Bello Secso de Orizava hace al soberano congreso, pidiendo no se admita en la república la libertad de cultos"; *La Voz de la Religión*, Feb. 7, 1849, 165–67, "Representación del Bello Secso de Oajaca al Supremo Gobierno de la Unión sobre que no se permita en la república la tolerancia de cultos"; *La Voz de la Religión*, Apr. 4, 1849, 421–28, "Representación que el Bello Secso de Querétaro dirige al Exmo Sr. Presidente de la Republica, pidiendo no se apruebe la ley que permite la tolerancia de cultos en la nación mexicana."

29. *El Universal: periódico independiente/periódico político y literario*, Jan. 6, 1849, 4, "Tolerancia." *La Voz de la Religión*, which published the petition, said there were 2,224 signatures.

30. *El Monitor Republicano*, Feb. 9, 1849, 4, "El bello sexo de Oajaca."

31. *El Observador Católico*, Mar. 3, 1849, 517–18, "El Monitor Republicano—El Bello Sexo—La Tolerancia."

32. *La Voz de la Religión*, Nov. 15, 1848, 7, "Representación que los habitantes de Puebla elevan al soberano congreso de la unión, contrariando los conatos que para establecer la tolerancia religiosa en nuestro País, aparecen hoy desgraciadamente."

33. *El Siglo Diez y Nueve*, Dec. 18, 1848, 4, "Representación."

34. *El Monitor Republicano*, Aug. 6, 1856, 1, "El art. 15 del proyecto de Constitución—Importancia política de la muger."

35. The "big three" laws of the Reform in 1855 and 1856 were the Ley Juárez, which provided that members of the clergy and the military could no longer enjoy special courts but must be tried in civil courts; the Ley Lerdo, which forced corporate entities including the church and indigenous villages to sell their property; and the Ley Iglesias, which regulated ecclesiastical fees for Catholic sacraments.

36. On the point that many liberals were anticlerical and/or anti-baroque religion but by no means against a kind of pure and simple Christianity, see Mijangos, "Tres momentos"; Connaughton, "La religiosidad"; Voekel, "Liberal Religion."

37. For the debate in the press, see Ruiz Castañeda, *La prensa*.

38. Gilbert, "'Long Live,'" 164. A "chronicle" of the efforts of the congress was also published daily in *El Siglo Diez y Nueve*, a liberal newspaper edited by Zarco.

39. See *El Monitor Republicano*, Aug. 6, 1856, 3, "La Cuestión Religiosa"; *El Siglo Diez y Nueve*, Jul. 31, 1856, 2; *El Monitor Republicano*, Aug. 2, 1856, 2 (speech by Guillermo Prieto).

40. Quoted in Martínez Baez, *Representaciones*, 15. *El Omnibus* noted that as of September 1, well after the victory of the campaign against tolerance, "petitions from all over the country continue to rain down on congress." *El Omnibus*, Sept. 1, 1856, 3, "La Libertad de Cultos." As noted above in the context of the 1848–49 petition campaign, José María Mata adopted a different discursive strategy, contrasting the "thousands" of anti-tolerance petitions in 1848–49 to the "just a few" ("apenas unas cuantas representaciones") that had been received in 1856. *El Monitor Republicano*, Aug. 4, 1856, 3.

41. I used the crónicas in *El Monitor Republicano* and *El Omnibus*, the latter the leading conservative daily, and the former one of the two leading liberal dailies. I also consulted the other liberal daily, *El Siglo Diez y Nueve*, but the digitalization is poor for that newspaper during this period, and *El Monitor* was more reliable.

42. Romeo Mateo, "¿Sujeto católico," 87. See also Wright-Ríos, *Searching*, chapter 2, for a discussion of the conservative publishers that published the petitions in pamphlet form.

43. The ten that I know of that went straight to a publisher were: *Representación de los indígenas de Zalatitan*; *Representación que el vecindario de Tototlán*; *Representación del ayuntamiento y vecindario de la Villa de Calvillo*; *Representación que los vecinos de Etzatlán*; *Representación que los vecinos de Guadalajara*; *Representación que los vecinos del Pueblo de Pihuamo*; *Representación del vecindario de Hostotipaquillo*; *Representación . . . Pueblo de Tlalnepantla Cuautenca*. The ninth is the representation from the women of Guadalajara, which was republished in Martínez Baez, *Representaciones*. The tenth is from Zamora, in Michoacán, "Representación que los habitantes de Zamora."

44. The two that were not part of the congressional record were, like the men's petitions that didn't arrive in time, from Jalisco: *Representación que las señoras de Guadalajara*; *Representación que las Señoras de Etzatlán*. The petition from Puebla came from a corporation, not the "señoras" of the city (as was true of all the others). The corporation was the Sisters of Charity.

45. *El Republicano*, Jul. 7, 1856, 3, "Las Mexicanas Vueltas Bloomeristas." On bloomers in the US, see Lerner, *Grimké Sisters*, 240; Smith and Greig, *Women in Pants*, 13.

46. *Diario Oficial del Supremo Gobierno de la República Mejicana*, Jul. 9, 1856, 3, "Noticias. Congreso Constituyente."
47. *El Monitor Republicano*, Jul. 21, 1856, 3, "La Representación de las Señoras," reprinted from *El Interés General*; *El Monitor Republicano*, Jul. 10, 1856, 3, "Firmas."
48. *El Monitor Republicano*, Aug. 5, 1856, 2, Zarco speech; *El Monitor Republicano*, Aug. 6, 1856, 1, "El art. 15 del proyecto de Constitución—Importancia política de la muger."
49. *El Omnibus*, Jul. 11, 1856, 2, "Otra Representación." The women's petition was read and reprinted in *El Omnibus* on Jul. 8, and the men's on Jul. 12.
50. *El Monitor Republicano*, Jul. 23, 1856, 3, "Gacetilla de la Capital. Morelia. Correspondencia Particular."
51. Sinkin, *Mexican Reform*, 128.
52. Wright-Ríos, *Searching*, cites the liberal Manuel Payno as saying that broad female mobilization against liberal reform was a major factor in "forestalling religious tolerance laws" (82).
53. *El Monitor Republicano*, Jul. 16, 1856, 4, "La Representación."
54. *El Monitor Republicano*, Jul. 21, 1856, 3, "La Representación de las Señoras," reprinted from *El Interés General* (Puebla).
55. *El Monitor Republicano*, Jul. 15, 1856, 4, "Representaciones."
56. *El Monitor Republicano*, Jul. 21, 1856, 3, "La Representación de las Señoras," reprinted from *El Interés General* (Puebla).
57. *El Siglo Diez y Nueve*, Jul. 6, 1856, 4, "Firmas," reprinted from *El Heraldo*.
58. *El Monitor Republicano*, Aug. 4, 1856, 3, "El Señor Mata."
59. *El Monitor Republicano*, Aug. 5, 1856, 2, "El Señor Zarco."
60. *El Monitor Republicano*, Jul. 10, 1856, 3, "No les está bien."
61. *El Monitor Republicano*, Jul. 21, 1856, 3, "La Representación de las Señoras," reprinted from *El Interés General*.
62. *El Monitor Republicano*, Jul. 21, 1856, 3, "La Representación de las Señoras," reprinted from *El Interés General*.
63. *El Monitor Republicano*, Jul. 24, 1856, 1, "Uso y Abusos de las Creencias Religiosas."
64. *El Siglo Diez y Nueve*, Aug. 5, 1856, 2, "El Señor Zarco."
65. *El Monitor Republicano*, Jul. 21, 1856, 3, reprinted from *El Interés General*.
66. Zarco, *Historia*, 661.
67. *El Monitor Republicano*, Aug. 2, 1856, 4, "Gacetilla de la Capital: Correspondencia Particular."
68. *El Monitor Republicano*, Aug. 6, 1856, 1, "El art. 15 del proyecto de Constitución.—Importancia política de la muger," reprinted from *El País*.
69. *El País*, reprinted in *El Monitor Republicano*, Aug. 6, 1856, 1, "El art. 15 del proyecto de Constitucion—Importancia política de la muger."
70. *El Monitor Republicano*, Aug. 6, 1856, 1, "El art. 15 del proyecto de Constitución—Importancia de la muger."
71. *El Omnibus*, Jul. 10, 1856.
72. *El Omnibus*, Jul. 10, 1856, 3, "Esposición de las Señoras Mexicanas," reprinted from an unnamed "colleague."
73. *El Omnibus*, Jul. 12, 1856, 3, "Confesion de parte."
74. *El Omnibus*, Jul. 14, 1856, 3, "Intento Frustrado."
75. For Chile, Maza Valenzuela, "Catolicismo," writes that "women [in an 1856 case] felt that it was proper and largely accepted for them to intervene in public affairs over matters of religious and Church concerns" (8).
76. *El Omnibus*, Jul. 14, 1856, 3, "Al Heraldo, Siglo, Acolito, y Comparsa."
77. *El Omnibus*, Jul. 9, 1856, 1, "Breves observaciones sobre la tolerancia religiosa."

78. *El Omnibus*, Jul. 9, 1856, 3, "Crónica Parlamentaria."
79. *El Omnibus*, Aug. 6, 1856, 3, "Crónica. La Esperanza."
80. *El Omnibus*, Jul. 10, 1856, 2, "El congreso constituyente."
81. Leavitt-Alcántara, *Alone*; Sanders, "A Mob"; and Maza Valenzuela, "Catolicismo," offer interesting comparisons to Guatemala, Colombia, and Chile, respectively, on the topic of mid-nineteenth-century conservative acceptance of women entering politics.
82. Romeo Mateo, "¿Sujeto católico," 93.
83. "Representación . . . Orizaba," Jan. 31, 1849, 136. Curley, "Sociólogos," 207, makes the point that Catholic thinkers had always promoted the idea that pagan societies had perverted the proper relationship between husbands and wives, considering the wife as a slave and tolerating divorce, adultery, and sensuality; and that Jesus Christ had rescued women from this condition.
84. "Representación . . . Orizaba," Jan. 31, 1849, 138, 139.
85. "Representación . . . Orizaba," Feb. 3, 1849, 150–51.
86. "Representación . . . Orizaba," Feb. 3, 1849, 151, 153.
87. "Representación . . . Orizaba," Jan. 31, 1849, 138, 136.
88. The petition mangled the story slightly. The woman of Tekoa was not actually a widow who had lost two sons, but rather was posing as such at the behest of David's general, who saw that David was grief-stricken at the prospect of the loss of Absalom, and thought that bringing the woman to him and having her solicit his wise council, urging her to protect her living son, would show him that he, too, ought to protect Absalom and not allow him to be killed.
89. "Representación . . . Orizaba," Feb. 3, 1849, 155–56.
90. The seminal work on Catholic thinkers' defense of the idea of the nation is Connaughton, *Ideología*.
91. Sosenski, "Asomándose"; Gilbert, "'Long Live'"; Voekel, "Liberal Religion"; Pani, "Una ventana"; Martínez Baez, *Representaciones*; Wright-Ríos, *Searching*, 80–82; Sinkin, *Mexican Reform*, 128; Arrom, *Women*. McGowan, *Prensa*, chapter 9, analyzes the petitions as a whole.
92. Sosenski, "Asomándose," 55, 59–60, 62.
93. Wright-Ríos, *Searching*, 80, 82.
94. *La Voz de la Religión*, Jan. 10, 1849, 38, "Representación que el Pueblo y Clero de Orizava Elevan al Soberano Congreso Nacional, pidiendole no autorice la introducción de falsas religiones en la República Mexicana." Philip Melancthon was a German Lutheran reformer and collaborator with Martin Luther.
95. Gilbert, "Long Live," 85, 171.
96. *La Voz de la Religión*, Feb. 7, 1849, 165, "Representación . . . Oajaca"; *La Voz de la Religión*, Apr. 4, 1849, 421, "Representación . . . Querétaro."
97. *La Voz de la Religión*, Feb. 7, 1849, 165, "Representación . . . Oajaca."
98. *La Voz de la Religión*, Apr. 4, 1849, 422, "Representación . . . Querétaro."
99. Again, I recognize that women might have had access to such allusions. Until there is better research on this question, however, I stand by my sense that the sheer number of literary and historical references is beyond what most women would likely use.
100. *La Cruz*, Jul. 3, 1856, 491; *La Cruz*, Nov. 5, 1857, 181.
101. *El Monitor Republicano*, Aug. 5, 1856, 1–2, Speech of Sr. Zarco. In an earlier speech (*El Monitor Republicano*, Jul. 31, 1856) Zarco was less circumspect: "some of the petitions were invited by the clergy and sooner or later we will know their authors, for example, that of Morelia is immediately recognizable as having been formulated by Sr. D. Clemente Munguía."
102. "Representación . . . señoras mexicanas," 21–22.

103. "Representación que las mexicanas de los barrios de San Pablo, San Miguel y la Palma hemos elevado al soberano congreso constituyente, pidiendo sea desaprobado el articulo 15"; "Representación que las señoras de Toluca elevan al soberano congreso constituyente"; "Representación que las señoras de Silao elevan al soberano congreso constituyente"; "Representación que las señoras de San Luis Potosí elevan al soberano congreso constituyente," in Martínez Baez, *Representaciones*.

104. Sosenski, "Asomándose," 59–60, also calls for this move.

105. *El Observador Católico*, tomo II, num. 22, Mar. 3, 1849, 520.

106. Heerma van Voss, *Petitions*, 3.

107. For Mexico City, *El Omnibus*, Jul. 10, 1856, 3, "Esposición de las Señoras Mexicanas"; for Guadalajara, *Representación que las Señoras de Guadalajara*; for Lagos, *El Omnibus*, Jul. 23, 1856, 2–3, "Esposiciones"; for Toluca, *El Omnibus*, Jul. 25, 1856, 2, "Tolerancia de Cultos"; for Silao, *El Omnibus*, Aug. 1, 1856, 1, "Siguen las representaciones"; for Guanajuato, *El Omnibus*, Aug. 8, 1856, 2, "Siguen las esposiciones"; for Etzatlán, *Representación que las Señoras de Etzatlán*.

108. *El Monitor Republicano*, Jul. 4, 1856, 4, "Firmas"; *El Monitor Republicano*, Jul. 5, 1856, 4, "Firmas"; *El Omnibus*, Jul. 9, 1856, 1, "Breves Observaciones sobre la tolerancia Religiosa."

109. *El Monitor Republicano*, Jul. 23, 1856, 3, "Gacetilla de la Capital. Morelia. Correspondencia Particular."

110. Ponciano Arriaga quoted in Sosenski, "Asomándose," 58.

111. *El Omnibus*, Aug. 4, 1856, 2, "Hermanas de la Caridad."

112. *La Voz de la Religión*, Apr. 4, 1849, 421–28, "Representación . . . Querétaro."

113. México, Veracruz, registros parroquiales y diocesanos, 1590–1978, FamilySearch (https://familysearch.org/ark:/61903/3:1:33SQ-GP4N-9C8Z?cc=1883382&wc=3PQ4-DP8%3A176854501%2C176850802%2C178963501, May 21, 2014, Orizaba, San Miguel, Cofradías 1818–1869, image 21–117 of 603.

114. Arrom, *Women*.

115. *El Omnibus*, Jul. 9, 1856, 1, "Breves observaciones sobre la tolerancia religiosa."

116. Griffith, *Moral Combat*.

117. Mijangos y González, "Secularización," 207.

118. *El Observador Católico*, Mar. 3, 1849, 517–18, "El Monitor Republicano—El Bello Sexo—La Tolerancia."

Chapter 5

The quotation in the chapter title comes from the following source: AHAMex, Labastida, Caja 92, exp. 70, Sociedad Católica de Méjico, Sobre su nuevo organización, 1873.

1. Forment, *Democracy*, 240; Palti, *La invención*, 306–11.
2. Palti, *La invención*, 308.
3. *Almanaque Estadístico . . . 1874*, 359.
4. Leal, *Del mutualismo*.
5. Bautista García, *Las disyuntivas*; García Ugarte, *Poder político*; Voekel, "Liberal Religion"; Ruiz Guerra, "Los dilemas"; Bastian, "La lucha"; Mijangos, *Lawyer*; Mijangos, "Tres momentos"; Connaughton, "La religiosidad"; Adame Goddard, *El pensamiento*; Vázquez, "Centralistas."
6. Lomnitz, *Return*, 91.
7. AHAMich, XIX, Caja 659, exp. 334, Establecimiento de la Vela Perpetua en Acuitzio . . . Abril 1863.
8. *Memoria de la Sociedad Católica*, 4–5, 21.

9. Komonchak, "Modernity," and many others.
10. Larkin, "Devotional Revolution," 645.
11. *Memoria de la Sociedad Católica*, 5.
12. García Ugarte, *Poder político*.
13. Adame Goddard, *El pensamiento*, 100.
14. This is a point made, with different emphases, by García Ugarte, *Poder político*; Bautista García, *Las disyuntivas*; and Mijangos y González, *Lawyer*.
15. Ramos, "Ascenso Liberal," 119; Stauffer, *Victory*.
16. The law read: "It is prohibited to found or erect archicofradías, cofradías, congregaciones or hermandades religiosas, whatever the form they take or the name that is applied to them." AHAMex, Labastida, Caja 87, exp. 3, El Padre Capellán, sobre licencia para el establecimiento de la Asociación de Veladores de la Santa Casa de Loreto, 1874.
17. AHAMex, Labastida, Caja 92, exp. 70, Sociedad Católica de Méjico, Sobre su nueva organización, 1873.
18. AHAMex, Labastida, Caja 92, exp. 70, Sociedad Católica de Méjico, Sobre su nueva organización, 1873.
19. Those that had the best chance of surviving were ones that served the parishes; the older cofradías associated with the regular orders had few champions, after the convents and monasteries were forcibly disbanded in 1863.
20. Like most traditional cofradías, this elite, exclusive, all-male archicofradía had supported its activities from rents on its properties and interest earned by accumulated reserves; now it adapted by reducing its expenses "to the ultimate limit" and adding members, whose annual fixed contribution was the main source of income for the organization. It expanded from twelve to twenty-five members and eventually to thirty-three. Needless to say each member had to commit to a very large yearly donation. Vallebueno Garcinava, *La archicofradía*, 28; AHAD Roll 325, Frame 263, Año de 1872, Copia autorizada de las nuevas constituciones de la Muy Ylustre Archicofradía del Santísimo Sacramento de esta Ciudad, aprobadas en superior auto de 23 de julio del corriente año; AHAD Roll 528, Frame 273, Libro de Actas de la Archicofradía del Smo Sac Durango, 1872, Feb. 1897.
21. AHAO, Parroquial, Disciplinar, Cofradías, 1870–1899, Caja 453, Libro de Actas de la Ylustre Archicofradía del Santísimo Sacramento establecida con autoridad apostólica en el Sagrario de esta Santa Yglesia Catedral, Actas, Mar. 24, 1870, and Feb. 27, 1873.
22. AHAO, Parroquial, Disciplinar, Cofradías, 1870–1899, Caja 453, Libro de Actas de la Ylustre Archicofradía del Santísimo Sacramento, Actas, Mar. 24, 1870.
23. AHAO, Parroquial, Disciplinar, Cofradías, 1870–1899, Caja 453, Libro de Actas de la Ylustre Archicofradía del Santísimo Sacramento, Actas, May 24, 1875, and Mar. 16, 1880.
24. AHAO, Parroquial, Disciplinar, Cofradías, 1870–1899, Caja 453, Libro de Actas de la Ylustre Archicofradía del Santísimo Sacramento, Actas, Feb. 28, 1882. A variation on the theme of adding formal roles for women to bolster the cofradías was the alternation of men and women in the position of president of the cofradía, as in the pious association dedicated to Nuestra Señora del Claustro in Santo Domingo Ocotlán, Oaxaca. This does not appear to have been very common, however. AHAO, Diocesano, Gobierno, Parroquias, 1870–1871, Caja 605, 1870, Reglamento de las Asociación piadosa y de caridad en Santo Domingo Ocotlán Cabecera de parroquia.
25. *El Siglo Diez y Nueve*, Jan. 18, 1856, 3, "El Sr. Presbítero D. Ponciano Jauregui." As we saw in chapter 4 and will see again in chapter 6, liberal accusations that priests used subterfuge to gain signatures was a constant during this period.
26. Zavala, "El tiempo precioso."
27. *La Voz de México*, Jun. 7, 1871, 1, "Noticias Religiosas" (earliest mention of Vela in the Iglesia de Monserrate); *La Voz de México*, Jun. 19, 1870, 1, "Iglesia Parroquial de

S. Sebastián" (early mention of the rejuvenated Congregación de la Vela Perpetua in the original church of the Real Congregación, San Sebastián).

28. These were in Pachuca, Cuautla, Toluca, Almoloya, Zinacantepec, San Juan del Río, Tezontepec, Sultepec, Mazatepec, Polotitlán, Tepetitlán, Cuautitlán, Calpulapán, and Tlalquiltenango. Three of these were canonically founded in the late 1870s, but since this often followed the de facto erection of the association by several years, I am including them here. This was definitely the case for both Pachuca and Cuautla. AHAMex, Labastida, Caja 130, exp. 50, Pachuca, El S. Cura sobre licencia para establecer la Velación de la Vela Perpetua, Sept. 1880; AHAMex, Labastida, Caja 164, exp. 67, Con relación a la Hermandad de la "Vela Perpetua," Rosario Rivas to Arzobispo, Cuautla de Morelos, Sept. 19, 1884; AHAMex, Labastida, Caja 72, exp. 72, El Vicario fijo sobre establecer la vela perpetua, Almoloya, 1872; AHAMex, Labastida, Caja 102, exp. 15, El Sr. Cura pide licencia para establecer la velación nocturna, Zinacantepec, 1876; AHAMex, Labastida, Caja 106, exp. 20, El Sor Cura sobre Velación del Smo, Tezontepec, 1876 and Fr. Luis G. Garduno Cura Coadjutor de la Parroquia de Tezontepec; AHAMex, Labastida, Caja 105, exp. 56, El Vicario Fijo sobre establecer la Vela Perpetua y el ejercicio de la Hora Santa, Sultepec, 1877; AHAMex, Labastida, Caja 109, exp. 59, El encargado sobre erección de la Vela Perpetua, exposición y obra de la Yglesia, Tepetitlán, Nov. 1877; AHAMex, Labastida, Caja 70, exp. 37, Doña Eustaquia Guerrero, sobre lo que expresa, May 1872, Cuautitlán; *Estadística de la Sociedad Católica de Señoras*, 13; *Memoria de la Sociedad Católica*, 145.

29. "Devoción que practican . . . Guaymas"; "Hermosillo y los archivos," 3; *El libro de las protestas*, "Protesta que hacen los vecinos católicos de Cosalá," Jun. 11, 1875, 479; AHAD, Roll 274, Frames 194–95, Reglamento de la Vela Continua del Divinísimo Señor Sacramentado [Sagrario cathedral of Durango]; AHAD, Roll 556, Frames 620–22, "Constitutiones del la Hermandad de la Vela Perpetua al Smo Sacramento en la Yglesia Parroquial de Sn. Dimas," 1877; AHAD, Roll 290, Frame 333. Constituciones para la congregación de la Vela del Santíssimo Sacramento [S. Pedro de los Chalchihuites]; *Estadística de la Sociedad Católica de Señoras*, 14.

30. These were in Izúcar de Matamoros, Atlixco and San Agustín Tlaxco in Puebla, and Tlalpan and Tlaxeo in Oaxaca. While Puebla would eventually have quite a few Velas, they were never very popular in Oaxaca at least up to the end of the Porfiriato (see chapter 7). The sources I used to track the spread of the Vela outside of the areas covered in my own archival research were two. First and most important, the ADABI (Apoyo y Desarrollo de Archivos y Bibliotecas de México) project's published inventories of most parish archives in the states of Mexico, Tlaxcala, Puebla, Veracruz, Oaxaca, and Morelos, which are easily searchable for dated mentions of the Vela Perpetua. Newspapers provide a second and less systematic source of information about lay associations. My archival research complements the ADABI records for the states of Mexico, Morelos, the parts of Tlaxcala that belonged to the archbishopric of Mexico, and Oaxaca, so there are probably not too many new Vela foundations that are unaccounted for in those states. For Puebla and Veracruz, covered by the ADABI project, I am less confident that I have captured all the Velas, since it appears that the parish archives inventoried in that project are richest, at least where cofradía and pious association records are concerned, for the late nineteenth and twentieth centuries, and may not be entirely reliable for the 1860s and 1870s. The parish inventory project has not reached the northern states yet, so we have only my own research in the diocesan archive of Durango and a few random documents to help us track the spread of the Vela there.

31. AHAMEX, Labastida, Caja 163, exp. 47, El Capellán de La Encarnación sobre que la Asociación del Santísimo . . . se agregue a la de Santa Clara, 1884, which includes the reglamento of "La Guardia del Santísimo," dated 1873.

32. AHAD, Roll 519, Frames 229–89, Libro de registros para la Asociación del Sr. S. José, fundada canónicamente en esta Yglesia de los Santos Cosme y Damián.

33. For an interesting comparison to the Mexican Hijas, who were connected to the Vincentians, see Leavitt-Alcántara, *Alone*, for a discussion of the Jesuit-affiliated Hijas in Guatemala. Most of the Marian societies founded during this period were *not* dedicated to the Virgin of Guadalupe. One exception is the Asociación de Nuestra Señora de Guadalupe in Puebla, founded by the Sociedad Católica de Señoras between 1870 and 1874; it was composed of thirty-one señoritas from the "best families." *Estadística de la Sociedad Católica de Señoras*, 31. The biggest wave of Marian associations in general did not occur until the 1880s and after.

34. During the war with the United States, some members of the liberal press began to turn on the Sisters, whom they accused of running the hospitals poorly, catering to the rich, and refusing to enter the battlefields to care for soldiers.

35. The schools were in Mexico City, Silao, Guanajuato, Monterey, Toluca, Zacatecas, Saltillo, and Lagos. *Fundación de las Hijas de la Caridad*, n.p.

36. They founded two more schools in Mexico City, as well as two in Puebla; two in Guadalajara; and one in Morelia, Zapotlán (Jalisco), Jiquilpan, San Miguel Allende, San Luis Potosí, Cuernavaca, Irapuato, León, Amozoc, Izúcar de Matamoros, San Andres Chalchicomula, and Veracruz. *Fundación de las Hijas de la Caridad*, n.p.

37. AHAMex, Labastida, Caja 138, exp. 62, Boletín de las Hijas de María, Apuntes históricos sobre la Asociación de Hijas de María en México," May 1927, 136–37, 142–44; De Dios, *Historia*, 568; *La Sociedad*, Jan. 22, 1865, 1, "Bautismo solemne."

38. Taves, *Household*, 37.

39. Chávez, *La bandera*, 112.

40. *Catholic Encyclopedia*, entry for "Children of Mary."

41. AHAMex, Labastida, Caja 138, exp. 62, Boletín de las Hijas de María, Apuntes históricos sobre la Asociación de Hijas de María en México," May 1927; Chávez, *La bandera*, 115.

42. De Dios, *Historia*, 566, 568. The six earliest foundations were in Mexico City, Toluca, Guanajuato, Silao, Monterey, and Lagos de Moreno.

43. The Vincentian priest José María Vilaseca was instrumental in this unification. A few years later Vilaseca divided the organization into the Hijas de María Inmaculada, and the Hijas de María y del Señor San José, or the Josefinas; the latter were girls who wished to become Sisters and who, after the end of the order in Mexico in 1875, took on the burden of educating young girls.

44. Boylan, "Mexican Catholic Women's Activism," 305.

45. Chávez, *La bandera*, 114.

46. Arrom, *Volunteering*, 78, 82.

47. Arrom, *Volunteering*, 78; AHAMex, Labastida, Caja 110, exp. 35, Asociación de las Señoras de la Caridad dirigida por los PP Paulinos, Mexico, 1902. The figure of 4,022 members and "some 300" chapters in 1875 comes from the 1902 report, which does not list the chapters in existence in 1875 by name. The same report gave a figure of only 127 conferences and 2,877 members in 1872. An 1878 report that does name each chapter shows 122 reporting with 3,003 active members. Another 23 existing associations were named but because they did not send in their statistics, their members were not counted. If we accept that the 23 associations that did not send in their statistics should nonetheless be counted, there would have been 145 chapters and perhaps 3,500 to 3,600 members in 1878. This makes the 1875 figures given in the official history appear to be somewhat suspect, especially where the number of chapters is concerned. If all else was equal it would seem unlikely that the number of chapters could leap from 127 in 1872 to some 300 in 1875 and

then fall back to 145 in 1878. However, as chapter 6 will show, in late 1874 and 1875 there was a major challenge to the church and a major mobilization of women, so a big jump in the number of chapters in response (and then some loss of energy afterward) may not be as anomalous as it appears.

48. Arrom, *Volunteering*, 43, 44. The reader will recall that the men's groups had a head start since they began to be established in the mid-1840s.

49. Arrom, *Volunteering*, 111.

50. Arrom, *Volunteering*, 94.

51. Arrom, *Volunteering*, 95. Several chapter foundations in Guadalajara were also attributed to their female presidents.

52. De Dios, *Historia*, 555.

53. Arrom, *Volunteering*, 100.

54. Arrom, *Volunteering*, 102.

55. *Memoria de la Sociedad Católica*, 5.

56. *Memoria de la Sociedad Católica*, 6; Stauffer, *Victory*, 92.

57. *Memoria de la Sociedad Católica*, 72.

58. Velasco Robledo, "Institución," 167.

59. Bautista García, *Las disyuntivas*, 236–37.

60. *Memoria de la Sociedad Católica*, 23.

61. *Memoria de la Sociedad Católica*, 82–83.

62. *Memoria de la Sociedad Católica*, 4–5.

63. AHAMich, XIX, Caja 248, exp. 409, Title page missing, Proposal for Sociedad Católica, Mexico, Aug. 2, 1872, Officers to José Ignacio Arciga, archbishop of Michoacán.

64. *El Pájaro Verde*, Nov. 23, 1874, 1, "Religiosos. Sociedad Católica."

65. *El Monitor Republicano*, Oct. 24, 1873, 3, "Sociedad Católica." In their pragmatism about living with the liberal state, they resemble García Ugarte's characterization of the archbishop of Mexico during this time, Pelagio Antonio de Labastida. García Ugarte, *Poder político*.

66. Goddard, *El pensamiento*, 19–27; Velasco Robledo, "Institución."

67. *Memoria de la Sociedad Católica*, 20. A separate commision called "free schools" was established in 1872, to separate the support of schools of higher education from those aimed at poor boys, and in 1873 a commission on Catholic workers was added; its main purpose was to form night schools for workers.

68. Arrom, *Volunteering*, chapter 4, shows that the activities of men's and women's Conferences of St. Vincent de Paul were also gendered, that is, they each tended to provide different kinds of support for the organization.

69. *Estadística de la Sociedad Católica de Señoras* counts 9,738 *socias*, but many chapters did not provide the number of members; see also *El Ferrocarril*, May 6, 1872, 2, "Noticias Diversas," for an estimate of the number of members of the female societies as 8,000 to 10,000 in just 87 chapters. The 1877 men's *Memoria* said that the "recent revolutions" had interrupted correspondence so that they had no data to report from the "many other" chapters that existed. *Memoria de la Sociedad Católica*, 146.

70. *Memoria de la Sociedad Católica*, 155, 160–61.

71. Stauffer, *Victory*, 93. The exact language the priest used to describe the men's chapter's floundering was "*salió borrego*," meaning to fail to honor one's obligations. Thanks to Brian Stauffer for this nugget.

72. Adame Goddard, *El pensamiento*, 26–27. Velasco Robledo, "Institución," 168, 155, surveyed *La Voz de México* with an eye to trying to see if Adame Goddard's conclusion that the Sociedad was defunct by 1878 is correct. She found a total of 115 mentions of the Sociedad, making her think that it was not dead, but she does not specify either a time frame or

whether she is writing about just the men's Sociedad, just the women's, or (perhaps) both. We know that the men's Sociedad in Guadalajara continued to operate the law school there well into the Porfiriato, and the men's as well as women's Sociedades in Puebla were strong into the 1890s. On balance, though, the men's societies do seem to have been much less active than the women's after 1876.

73. For Oaxaca City, see Wright-Ríos, *Revolutions*, 105; for Puebla, see *El Amigo de la Verdad*, Feb. 9, 1899, "La Sociedad Católica de Señoras."

74. An 1875 pastoral specifically encouraged the formation of Vincentian conferences. Arrom, *Volunteering*, 131.

75. AHAM, CL 14, exp. 7, Libro de visita, 1871, Parroquia de S. Agustín de las Cuevas Tlalpan, Nov. 21, 1871.

76. There were 146 conferences of the Ladies of Charity in 92 cities or towns. Unfortunately the 1902 report that gave the number of women's conferences of St. Vincent de Paul in 1872 as 127 and in 1875 as 300 did not list the individual conferences; the 1878 list, compiled during a period of temporary institutional crisis, only lists 100 conferences but is the closest in time to the period under consideration that does specify the towns where the conferences existed. *Estadística de la Sociedad Católica de Señoras*; *Memoria que el Consejo Superior de Señoras de la Caridad*.

77. AHAG, Visitas Pastorales, Caja 11, exp. Libro 4º visita 1874, Arandas. The founder of the Guadalajara Ladies of Charity was also a member of the Sociedad Católica. Thanks to Silvia Arrom for this information.

78. *Estadística de la Sociedad Católica de Señoras*, Atotonilco, Guadalajara, Oaxaca, Cotija, and Zamora.

79. Stauffer, *Victory*, 84; *Estadística de la Sociedad Católica de Señoras*, for San Sebastián [Concordia], Calpulalpan, and Cuquio; Villanueva y Francesconi, ed., *El libro de las protestas*, "Protesta que hacen los vecinos católicos de Cosalá," 479.

80. *El Monitor Republicano*, Jan. 16, 1872, 1, "Boletín del Monitor."

81. Pani, "'Ciudadana,'" 14; and Voekel, "Liberal Religion," 89.

82. *Estadística de la Sociedad Católica de Señoras*, 18, 39, 50, 58, 17.

83. Arrom, *Volunteering*, 90. They also bought items for churches and paid for priests' salaries.

84. *El Siglo Diez y Nueve*, Jul. 13, 1873, 3, "Tiene Gracia."

85. Moreno Méndez, "Chavinda," 12.

86. Stauffer, *Victory*, 129. In both cases, Stauffer characterizes the essential conflict as that between the "baroque" religious practices of indigenous and mulatto parishioners, and modernizing priests allied with women's groups and other mainly middle-class, parish-oriented, "modern" Catholics.

87. Stauffer, *Victory*, 161–62.

88. AHAMex, Labastida, Caja 70, exp. 37, Doña Eustaquia Guerrero, sobre lo que expresa, Cuautitlán, May 1872.

89. Stauffer, *Victory*, 204.

90. AHAMex, Labastida, Caja 84, exp. 53, El Sr. Cura de Tacuba respecto a la Asociación de SVP, Apr. 7, 1874.

91. AHAMich, XIX, Caja 5, exp. 1, Silvestre Verdusco to Luis Macouzet, Oct. 1876.

92. The associations that Forment names that allowed women members include the Gran Círculo de Obreros, the Junta Menor Municipal of Mexico City, the Sociedades Filarmónicas, some of the Patriotic Societies, and the Hermandad Cosmopólita. The only autonomous group he includes was the Sociedad Ruth, an organization of elite women that trained indigenous and orphaned girls to enter domestic service, hardly an exemplar of liberal associationalism. The only group with a women's auxiliary he names was the Masons,

who established "a" chapter for women, presumably in Mexico City. Forment, *Democracy*, 251, 253–54, 257, 259, 264; *La Voz de Mexico*, Apr. 17, 1875, 3, "Sociedad Ruth."

93. Perales Ojeda, *Las asociaciones*.

94. I only found one other autonomous association besides the Sociedad Ruth: this was El Ramillete de Flores, a literary association founded in late 1873 that was apparently quite short-lived. *El Siglo Diez y Nueve*, Dec. 20, 1873, 3, "Gacetilla. El Ramillete de Flores"; *El Monitor Republicano*, Dec. 21, 1873, 1, "Charla de los Domingos."

95. Of course the Escuela de Señoras, like the Vela Perpetua de Señoras (when there were separate men's and women's Velas) and numerous other pious associations, were subject to the direction of the priest; but they were not subject to the direction of the male branch of the society.

96. *El Siglo Diez y Nueve*, Jan. 1, 1869, 3, "Noticias Nacionales. Junta de Señoras"; *El Siglo Diez y Nueve*, Jan 30, 1870, 1, "Editorial. Revista de la Semana. Premios de la Junta Lancasteriana."

97. *El Federalista*, Nov. 16, 1871, 3, "Bravo, Señoras"; *El Monitor Republicano*, May 2, 1873, 4, "La Compañía Lancasteriana."

98. González y González, et al, *Historia moderna de México . . . la vida social*, 680.

99. González y González, et al, *Historia moderna de México . . . la vida social*, 680.

100. *El Federalista*, Feb. 13, 1871, 3, "Gacetilla"; *Almanaque Estadístico . . . 1874*, 364–65.

101. *El Correo del Comercio*, Feb. 5, 1875, 2, "Bien pensado."

102. *El Eco de Ambos Mundos*, Feb 18, 1874, 3, "Sociedad de Socorros Mutuos"; *La Razón del Pueblo: Periódico Oficial del Estado de Yucatán*, Mar. 18, 1874, 4, "La Sociedad de Socorros Mutuos Esperanza y Caridad."

103. *Almanaque Estadístico . . . 1874*, 364–65.

104. Arrom, *Containing*, 244, 247; *La Sociedad*, Jul. 9, 1864, 3, "Acta y Alocución"; *La Sociedad*, Oct. 26, 1865, 1, "Prensa de los Departamentos."

105. Arrom, *Containing*, 260–62; *La Iberia*, Nov. 26, 1867, 3, "Beneficencia."

106. *El Monitor Republicano*, Sept. 15, 1878, 1, "Charla de los Domingos."

107. Infante Vargas, "Igualdad."

108. Perales Ojeda, "El Liceo Hidalgo." The Sociedad Concordia, another literary society that was more or less a contemporary of the Liceo, also admitted women, as did the Society of Nezahualcoyotl at least as honorary members, since we know that Laureana Wright de Kleinhans was admitted in 1869, at the request of its founders, Manuel Acuña and Gerardo M. Silva. *El Siglo Diez y Nueve*, Feb. 6, 1874, 3, "Nombramientos."

109. *La Voz de México*, Oct. 24, 1872, 3, "El Liceo Hidalgo."

110. *El Imparcial*, Oct. 17, 1872, 3, "La Sra. Satur López de Alcalde." Wright de Kleinhans had also joined the scientific society *El Porvenir* in 1872, where she published several of her poems.

111. *El Monitor Republicano*, Feb. 15, 1874, 1, "Charla de los Domingos." On the much-talked-about speech, see also *La Voz de México*, Mar. 1, 1874, 1–2, "La Presidenta del Liceo Hidalgo y el Dr. Mier"; *El Siglo Diez y Nueve*, Feb. 11, 1874, 3, "Velada Literaria."

112. *El Radical*, Jan. 25, 1874, 1, "Editorial."

113. On the US and Europe, see Scott, *Natural Allies*; Fuchs and Thompson, *Women*, 137–55.

114. Fuchs and Thompson, *Women*, 138.

Chapter 6

The quotation in the chapter title comes from a satirical piece ridiculing women's protests in *El Monitor Republicano*, Feb. 21, 1875, 1, "Charla de los Domingos."

1. *El libro de las protestas*, "Protesta de los Vecinos de Matehuala," 1025.
2. Voekel, "Liberal Religion," 87; *Legislación Mexicana*, Núm. 5140, Enero 5 de 1861, "Orden del gobierno del Distrito. Como debe ser conducido el Sagrado Viático, y prevenciones sobre el uso de las campanas." The episode is recounted in Malo, *Diario*, 593.
3. *El Pájaro Verde*, Sept. 25, 1863, 3, "Apuntes Históricos . . . Febrero de 1863."
4. Voekel, "Liberal Religion," 87; *El Pájaro Verde*, Feb. 8, 1861, 2–3, "Crónica de la Capital. El Sagrado Viático"; *El Siglo Diez y Nueve*, Feb. 13, 1861, 2, "El Exmo Sr. presidente interino."
5. Malo, *Diario*, 509–10.
6. *Diario Oficial del Supremo Gobierno*, Sept. 1, 1859, 3, "Parte Oficial."
7. *La Voz de México*, 31 May 1873, 1, "Editorial. La Diputación de Señoras."
8. *La Voz* did report on a protest against the expulsion signed by some two hundred men from Mexico City, causing the liberal *El Monitor Republicano* to mock the small number of signatories out of the two hundred fifty thousand people in the city. *El Monitor Republicano*, 8, 1873, 3, "Una observación." The male residents of San Juan de los Llanos in their petition against the Ley Orgánica (see below) mentioned that there were "many" petitions against the ex-claustration of nuns in February 1863 and the expulsion of the Jesuits in early 1873, but I have not seen any published examples. *El libro de las protestas*, "Exposición de los Vecinos de San Juan de los Llanos," 374.
9. Mijangos y González, "La respuesta," 264.
10. Quoted in Olimón Nolasco, "La iglesia católica."
11. Olimón Nolasco, "La iglesia católica."
12. *La Cuchara*, Jan. 25, 1865, 1–2, "Variaciones."
13. *La Sociedad*, Jan. 8, 1865, 2, "El *Espíritu Público* ha dado ayer." The exposition also asked Maximilian to provide financial support for clergy and nuns. It did not address the Lerdo Law.
14. *La Sociedad*, Jan. 7, 1865, 3, "El "Espíritu Público."
15. *El Pájaro Verde*, Jan. 9, 1865, 1, "Noticias Religiosas. Esposición elevada a S. M. I. por las señoras de esta capital."
16. *La Sociedad*, Jan. 11, 1865, 2, "Actualidades"; *La Sociedad*, Jan. 13, 1865, 2, "Actualidades. Una de las señoras."
17. *La Cuchara*, Jan. 20, 1865, 1–2, "Una fraterna a las señoras (Con el debido respeto.)"
18. *La Orquesta*, Jan. 18, 1865, 3, "Otra Vez la Exposición de las Señoras."
19. *La Sociedad*, Jan. 13, 1865, 2, "Actualidades. Una de las señoras."
20. *La Sociedad*, Jan. 13, 1865, 2, "Actualidades. Una de las señoras."
21. *La Cuchara*, Jan. 27, 1865, 4, "Las Orizabeñas"; *La Sociedad*, Feb. 2, 1865, 2–3, "Cholula del Imperio"; *La Sociedad*, Jan. 15, 1865, 2, "Puebla"; *La Sociedad*, Feb. 2, 1865, 3, "Representaciones"; *La Razón de México*, Feb. 5, 1865, 1, "Representaciones sobre la Carta Imperial." In Cholula expositions also came from thirty-six indigenous pueblos, from the twelve towns in the municipality of Cholula, and from the vecinos of the city. All were reportedly submitted together.
22. *La Sociedad*, Feb. 2, 1865, 3, "Más Esposiciones."
23. *El Pájaro Verde*, Jan. 11, 1865, 3, "Esposiciones"; *La Sociedad*, Jan. 13, 1865, 2–3, "El Episcopado."
24. *La Cuchara*, Feb. 6, 1865, 2, "¡Llueven Esposiciones!"
25. The Sociedades Católicas also participated in local political actions, though none (until the petition campaign) that were coordinated with other groups of women in other places. For example, in 1872 the señoras of the Sociedad Católica of Rioverde sent a telegram to the president asking for a pardon for the prisoners that government forces had taken. *Iberia*, Apr. 11, 1872, 3, "Petición."

26. *La Idea Católica*, Sept. 10, 1871, 2, "Carta de la Sociedad Católica de Oaxaca al Santo Padre."

27. *La Idea Católica*, Sept. 3, 1871, 2, "Carta de la Sociedad Católica de Señoras de San Luis al Santo Padre."

28. *La Idea Católica*, Jul. 16, 1871, 1, "Demostración Católica," and 4, "Aviso"; *La Idea Católica*, Sept. 10, 1871, 1, "A las Señoras Presidentas de las Sociedades Católicas de Señoras."

29. On Lerdo's decision to make this move, see Pi-Suñer, "Sebastián Lerdo de Tejada."

30. The famous "Lerdo Law," which required the church to sell its property, had been incorporated into the 1857 constitution at the time of its promulgation, as had the abolition of the church's special privileges in the judicial arena (*fueros*), the suppression of the Jesuit order, and supresion of the tithe and parish fees. But other laws that came later, in 1859–63, were obviously not part of the constitution of 1857. The laws of the Reform that were elevated to constitutional status in 1873 included the laws providing for civil matrimony, civil registry of births and deaths, secularization of cemeteries, suppression of religious work holidays, suppression of religious activities outside the church, ex-claustration of nuns and friars, suppression of cofradías, and secular education.

31. On the Cristero war in Michoacán, see Stauffer, *Victory*.

32. The text of the law can be found at: http://www.memoriapoliticademexico.org/Textos/5RepDictadura/1874LRD.html.

33. *El Monitor Republicano*, Feb. 21, 1875, 1, "Charla de los Domingos."

34. There is almost no attention paid by historians to this petition campaign, though Stauffer, *Victory*, and Iñiguez Mendoza, "'¡Viva la religión'" touch on it briefly.

35. *El Pájaro Verde* collected all the petitions it received in a volume called *El libro de las protestas*. I consulted the 1,175-page version (available on microfilm from Emory's theological seminary); two shorter versions, more commonly found in libraries, also circulated. I also used the Guadalajara newspaper *La Religión y la Sociedad* and what is available of the Morelia newspaper *El Pensamiento Católico*. Both included some protests sent exclusively to them; although many petitions were sent to multiple newspapers, not all were, and *El libro de las protestas* just covered the ones received by the Mexico City press, likely a majority but clearly not the entirety. *La Religión y la Sociedad* ceased publication in April 1875, so any protests it received after that were not covered (though the protests were beginning to become sparser by the middle of March). Camacho Pérez, "La iglesia," 234, mentions four protests to the state congress of Nuevo León that appeared in the Catholic newspaper *La Luz* but not in *El libro de las protestas*. As this example shows, exploring more of the provincial press would surely uncover more petitions than I have been able to account for; thus the total may be more like 350 or perhaps even more.

36. The señoras of Amatlán, *El libro de las protestas*, "Manifestación de las Señoras de Amatlán," 678, used the phrase. The señoras of Toluca, *El libro de las protestas*, "Protesta que hacen las Señoras de Toluca," wrote that they shared "the same ideas and sentiments as our compatriots the señoras of Guanajuato," and that they "adhere in all parts to their protest" (303). The others were Malacatepec, Comitán, Aguascalientes, Acatlán, Tlaxcala, Zacapoaxtla, Irapuato, Córdoba, Tehuacán, Zamora, La Piedad, Aculco, Jilotepec, Tenancingo, Chilapa, Villa de la Encarnación, Cuapiaxtla.

37. *El libro de las protestas*, "Protesta que las Señoras de Guanajuato hacen al congreso de la Unión contra la ley orgánica de las adiciones constitucionales," 249, 250.

38. Liberals repeatedly noted that the Sisters had not been expelled, just forced to disband; if they left the country it was because they chose to do so.

39. *El libro de las protestas*, "Protesta . . . Señoras de Guanajuato," 250.

40. *El libro de las protestas*, "Protesta . . . Señoras de Guanajuato," 250.

NOTES TO CHAPTER 6 [299]

41. *El libro de las protestas*, "Protesta . . . Señoras de Guanajuato," 250.

42. *El libro de las protestas*, "Protesta . . . Señoras de Guanajuato," 251. "Modern Julián" is a reference to Emperor Julián, notorious for his anti-Christian sentiments and actions.

43. *El libro de las protestas*, "Protesta que hacen las señoras católicas de Amanalco," 341. "Rustic cross" may be a reference to Chalma, nearby.

44. *El libro de las protestas*, "Protesta de las Señoras de Orizaba," 837.

45. *El libro de las protestas*, "Manifestación de las Señoras de Coroneo," 1076.

46. *El libro de las protestas*, "Nueva Protesta de Las Señoras de Puebla," 226.

47. *El libro de las protestas*, "Protesta que hacen las Señoras Católicas de la Capital," 308.

48. For example, see *El libro de las protestas*, "Representación que hacen los vecinos de Guadalajara," 258; "Representaciones que los Vecinos de Morelia Dirigen al Congreso del Estado y al de la Union," 143–47; "Protesta de los vecinos de La Barca," 452–53; "Protesta de los Señores de Pueblo Nuevo de Irapuato," 703–6; "Protesta de los Vecinos de Zamora," 751–53.

49. *El libro de las protestas*, "Representación que hacen los Vecinos de Jalostotitlán," 501; *El libro de las protestas*, "Exposición de los Vecinos de San Juan de los Llanos," 374.

50. *El Correo del Comercio*, Jan. 29, 1875, 2, "Protesta."

51. McNamara, *Sisters*, especially chapters 17, 18, 19; Ford, *Divided Houses*; Lannon, *Privilege*; Anderson, "Limits of Secularization," 653; Caffiero, "From the Late Baroque"; Scaraffia, "'Christianity Has Liberated Her'"; Mangion, *Contested Identities*; Magray, *Transforming Power*, 8–11; Coburn, *Spirited Lives*; Londoño-Vega, *Religion*, chapter 2.

52. *El libro de las protestas*, "Protesta que las Señoras de Guanajuato hacen," 251.

53. *El libro de las protestas*, "Protesta de las Señoras de San Miguel Allende," 819. The adjective "prepared" (*dispuesta*) is feminine, which is why I translate "su nombre" as "her name."

54. *El Monitor Republicano*, Feb. 13, 1875, 1, "Las Protestas."

55. *El Defensor de la Reforma*, Feb. 11, 1875, 4.

56. *El Monitor Republicano*, Feb. 21, 1875, 3, "Las Protestas."

57. *El Defensor de la Reforma*, Feb. 18, 1875, 1.

58. *El Monitor Republicano*, Feb. 20, 1875, 3, "Una Carta."

59. *El Monitor Republicano*, Feb. 3, 1875, 1, "Las Protestas"; *El Correo del Comercio*, Feb. 6, 1875, 1, "Las Protestas de las señoras de Mexico, Guadalajara, y Guanajuato."

60. *La Bandera de Ocampo*, Jan. 10, 1875, 4, "La reforma está perdida," quoted in Mendoza García, "Libertad," 99.

61. *El Defensor de la Reforma*, Jan. 27, 1875.

62. *El Monitor Republicano*, Feb. 21, 1875, 1, "Charla de los Domingos."

63. *El Defensor de la Reforma*, Mar. 18, 1875, 4, "LA GUERRA EN EL HOGAR."

64. *El Monitor Republicano*, Feb. 10, 1875, 1, "Editorial. Necesidad de la Instrucción."

65. Particularly vehement on the topic of the damage to men's honor being done by their wives and daughters signing the petitions is Guillermo Prieto in *El Correo del Comercio*, Feb. 6, 1875, 1, "Las Protestas de las señoras de Mexico, Guadalajara, y Guanajuato."

66. *El Defensor de la Reforma*, Jan. 13, 1875, 4, "Furor Protestativo."

67. *El Defensor de la Reforma*, Feb. 11, 1875, 3.

68. *El libro de las protestas*, "Ocurso de las Vecinas de Uruapan," 650–51.

69. *El Monitor Republicano*, Feb. 13, 1875, 1, "Las Protestas."

70. *El Monitor Republicano*, Feb. 13, 1875, 1, "Las Protestas."

71. *El Monitor Republicano*, Feb. 5, 1875, 3, "Una aclaracion."

72. *La Voz de México*, Feb. 9, 1875, 1, "Editorial. Las firmas 'in partibus.'"

73. *La Voz de México*, Feb. 3, 1875, "Siempre no habrá nada."

74. *La Voz de México*, Feb. 28, 1875, 3, "Por la tangente."
75. *La Voz de México*, Feb. 21, 1875, 1, "Editorial. Al Buen Callar Le Llaman Sancho."
76. Witschorik, *Preaching*.
77. *El Pájaro Verde*, Feb. 6, 1875, 2, "En un impreso suelto."
78. *La Idea Católica*, Jan. 31, 1875, 3, "El Por Que de la Protesta."
79. *La Voz de México*, Jan. 16, 1875, 3, "La protesta de las Señoras de Guanajuato."
80. *La Voz de México*, Feb. 4, 1875, 3, "Gacetilla. Remitido."
81. *La Idea Católica*, Sept. 17, 1876, 4, "Algunas Reflexiones sobre la Ley Orgánica de las Adiciones y Reformas a la Constitución."
82. *La Idea Católica*, Sept. 17, 1876, 4, "Algunas Reflexiones."
83. *La Religión y la Sociedad*, Feb. 20, 1875, 380, "Invitación que, á todas las señoras católicas de la gran República Mexicana, hacen las hijas de la ciudad de la Purísima Concepción de Celaya."
84. *El libro de las protestas*, 719–20, "Protesta de las Señoras de Acatlán"; *La Voz de México*, Mar. 31, 1875, 3, "Remitido."
85. *El Pájaro Verde*, Mar. 6, 1875, 2, "Prensa de los Estados. Una Cruzada Santa." Reprinted from *El Amigo de la Verdad*, Puebla.
86. *La Voz de México*, Mar. 23, 1875, 1, "Editorial. Al Amigo de la Verdad."
87. Camacho Pérez, "La iglesia," 232–34, while observing that Catholic societies were proscribed from openly protesting the government, notes that members of such associations were very active in the petition movement in Nuevo León. Edwards, "Messages Sent," notes that "Catholic leaders were reluctant to encourage Catholic political participation lest it be taken as accepting liberals' secularization program" (3).
88. *La Voz de México*, Feb. 10, 1875, 2, "Remitido."
89. A classic example of disdain for the Hijas is the Juan Rulfo short story "Anacleto Morones," in *El llano en llamas*.
90. The data from the center and center-east regions roughly confirm what I have outlined for the center-west. Twenty petition-sending towns in the states of Mexico, Querétaro, Tlaxcala, Hidalgo, Morelos, Puebla, and Veracruz are known to have had women-led lay associations. The twenty-five that do not appear to have had such associations were overwhelmingly small and mostly indigenous.
91. Mendoza García, "Libertad," breaks down the state of Michoacán into more conservative Catholic and more liberal subregions, and shows that the petitions came from the more conservative regions. Her identification of "liberal" and "conservative" regions comes from a few secondary sources. Population figures from "Resumen comparativa," Dirección General de Estadística . . . 1900.
92. *La Voz de México*, Feb. 14, 1875, 2, "La Asociación de Hijas de María en Jalapa al C. Presidente de la República Mexicana"; *El libro de las protestas*, "Protesta que hacen los vecinos católicos de Cosalá," 479; *La Voz de Mexico*, May 6, 1875, 1, "Representaciones contra la Ley orgánica"; *La Religión y la Sociedad*, May 22, 1875, 506, "Ciudadanos diputados del Congreso de la Unión."
93. Stauffer, *Victory*, 174; *La Idea Católica*, Apr. 25, 1875, 3, "Representaciones contra la Ley Orgánica de la Reforma"; *La Voz de México*, Apr. 9, 1875, 2, "Voto de Gracias."
94. *La Voz de México*, Feb. 20, 1875, 2, "Jilotepec" (in this unusual case the account was published in the conservative newspaper because it was a complaint by women in this town that the commission in charge of collecting signatures had not stopped at their house); *La Voz de México*, Feb. 2, 1875, 3, "Rectificación"; *La Voz de México*, Feb. 23, 1875, 2, "Al Sr. Rábago." I did find one case in which two women claimed that they had been approached by "un Don Fulano" who asked them to sign a petition to the archbishop to celebrate masses in a certain temple, when he really wanted them to sign one of the protests. However, two days

later the newspaper that printed this retraction/explanation said that someone had forged one of the women's signatures on the notice about retractions. Further, the same woman was also named in another article saying that "various women had approached them to collect signatures." It is not out of the question that individual collectors, even men, might have operated alongside the women's commissions that are more frequently referenced, but it does not seem we should have great confidence in this one particular case. *El Correo del Comercio*, Feb. 16, 1875, 3, "Siguen las firmas"; *El Correo del Comercio*, Feb. 18, 1875, 3, "Quien suplantó la firma?"; *El Monitor Republicano*, Feb. 14, 1875, 3, "Contraprotestas de señoras."

95. *La Voz de México*, Jan. 23, 1885, 1–2, "Excitativa al Bello Sexo Mexicano." In the 1871 protests against the treatment of the pope, the women's Sociedad Católica of Veracruz's petition used this language to conclude the protest: "the signatures of the *socias*, of a multitude of *señoras* outside the Sociedad, of the chaplain of the Sociedad, of the parish priest, and of many men in the population." *La Idea Católica*, Oct. 8, 1871, 2, "Protesta."

96. *El Monitor Republicano*, Feb. 21, 1875, 1, "Charla de los Domingos."

97. Borges, "Catholic Vanguard," 41, observes that it was "probably" the Brazilian Apostolados who mobilized women for the Catholic petition drive of 1898 against a divorce law.

98. The pastoral is reprinted in *El libro de las protestas*, 33–60.

99. Bautista García, *Las disyuntivas*, 241.

100. This view of the archbishops as in the lead is adopted by many scholars of Mexican Catholicism. See Ruiz Massieu, *La relación del estado*, 4–5; García Ugarte, *Poder político*, vol. 2, 1508–9. Without connecting it to the petitions, Adame Goddard, *El pensamiento*, and Stauffer, *Victory*, 72–73, also place great weight on the pastoral as a kind of foundational document of post-Reform Catholicism.

101. The bishop of León did publish a manifesto on Dec. 24, 1874, that is to say, after some of the lay protests but before most of them. That manifesto, however, did not call for petitioning or mention any protests except those that the hierarchy had published in 1847, 1849, and 1856. His longer criticism and the short December 24 manifesto are in *El libro de las protestas*, 61–136. The short manifesto is on 81–83.

102. Stauffer, *Victory*, chapter 6. Adame Goddard also gave credit to the armed rebellion, as well as the protestas, in making Díaz realize that he needed to be able to count on the church in order to govern. Adame Goddard, *El pensamiento*, 101.

103. Pani, "'Ciudadana'"; Pacheco, "Periódicos Católicos"; Pani, "Una ventana"; Franco, *Plotting Women*; Torres Septién, "Un ideal femenina"; Ramos Escandón, "Señoritas Porfirianas"; Tuñón Pablos, *Mujeres en México*; Bazant, "Feisty."

104. Clarke, "Parish," 194–95.

105. Franco, *Plotting Women*, 85.

106. Franco, *Plotting Women*, 92–93.

Chapter 7

The quotation in the chapter title comes from the following source: *La Defensa Católica*, Mar. 22, 1888, 2, "La Vuelta de los Hombres a la Frecuencia de Sacramentos."

1. AHAG, Gobierno, Cofradías, Caja 3 de Vela Perpetua and Apostolado de la Oración, 1955–1960, exp. El Apostolado de la Oración en la Arquidiocesis de Guadalajara, de julio de 1909 a junio de 1910. Folleto publicación por la dirección Diocesana del Apostolado de la Oración, 9.

2. AHAG, Gobierno, Cofradías, Caja 3 de Vela Perpetua and Apostolado de la Oración, 1955–1960, 9.

3. AHAG, Gobierno, Cofradías, Caja 3 de Vela Perpetua and Apostolado de la Oración, 1955–1960, 10.

4. AHAG, Gobierno, Cofradías, Caja 3 de Vela Perpetua and Apostolado de la Oración, 1955–1960, 21–22.

5. AHAG, Gobierno, Cofradías, Caja 3 de Vela Perpetua and Apostolado de la Oración, 1955–1960, 21–22.

6. Wright-Ríos, *Revolutions*, 111. Wright-Ríos uses the *Boletín Oficial y Revista Eclesiástica de Antequera* for national statistics counting five hundred branches and two hundred fifty thousand affiliates in 1901, with women in a 9:1 ratio to men.

7. AHAG, Gobierno, Cofradías, Caja 3 de Vela Perpetua and Apostolado de la Oración, 1955–1960, exp. El Apostolado de la Oración en la Arquidiocesis de Guadalajara, de julio de 1909 a junio de 1910, 22.

8. A highlight of the period of condemnation was the publication of the Syllabus of Errors (1864), a condemnation of eighty heresies afoot in the modern world.

9. Quoted in Weiner, "Trinidad Sánchez Santos," 341.

10. On the Vatican push to introduce new devotions in Mexico, see Díaz Patiño, *Católicos*.

11. Matovina, *Theologies*, 131–32.

12. Edwards, *Roman Virtues*; O'Dogherty, "El acenso."

13. Menéndez Rodríguez, *Iglesia y poder*; Díaz Patiño, "El catolicismo social."

14. Wright-Ríos, *Revolutions*, 101.

15. Smith, *Roots*, 181, 200–01.

16. Wright-Ríos, *Revolutions*, 101. For Yucatán, see Rugeley, *Of Wonders*.

17. Murillo, "Politics," 134.

18. This pattern also holds in Oaxaca, but we cannot be sure that it held in Michoacán, because the interrogatory did not ask priests to specify whether the associations were in the cabeceras or the pueblos. In the colonial period it is safe to presume that many of these communities would have had a cofradía, but the assault on indigenous associations in the Reform's anti-cofradía provisions and its focus on privatization of communally owned property greatly damaged them.

19. AHAMex, Alarcón, Caja 36, exp. 32, 1897, Noticias estadísticas de las parroquias de Tenango del Valle, Tlalmanalco, Tepejí del Río, Almoloya, Texcaliacac, Pachuca, Tasquillo, Tecozautla, Zacualpan, Tulyehualco, Tlalpan Tenancingo y Texcoco.

20. The other great moralizing institution, Catholic schools, was also rare in the pueblos, though most of them had a municipal school. Chowning, "Culture Wars."

21. AHAMex, Alarcón, Caja 87, exp. 20, Sra. de la Vega con respecto a la Asociación de la Purísima, 1899.

22. AHAG, Gobierno, Cofradías, 1895–1919, Caja 29, San Juan de los Lagos, Aug. 12, 1909.

23. AHAMex, Labastida, Caja 165, exp. 21, Da. Luisa Mancera de Herrera pide licencia para que la Asociación del Smo Sac establecida en Sta Catalina, se traslade a la Parrqouia del Sagrario, Nov. 28, 1884; AHAMex, Labastida, Caja 165, exp. 21, Da. Loreto Araiz de Villagrán, primera celadora, y a nombre de sus 24 veladoras et al," Jan. 5, 1885; AHAMex, Caja 165, exp. 21, Determination of archbishop, Jan. 9, 1885.

24. For a lengthy and valuable treatment of the devotion to the Sacred Heart in Guadalajara, see Aceves Ávila, *"Que es bueno."*

25. Jonas, *France*; Moreno Chávez, *Devociones*, 38–50, and chapter 3.

26. Morgan, *Sacred Heart*, 13.

27. Moreno Chávez, *Devociones*, 117.

28. For more background and analysis of the two new organizations, see Moreno Chávez, *Devociones*, 57–58, and chapter 3.

29. AHAG, Gobierno, Cofradías, Caja 3 de Vela Perpetua and Apostolado de la Oración, 1955–1960, x and 58.

30. *La Idea Católica*, Oct. 4, 1874, 4, "Apostolado de la Oración"; AHAG, Gobierno, Cofradías, Caja 3 de Vela Perpetua and Apostolado de la Oración, 1955-1960, exp. El Apostolado de la Oración en la Arquidiocesis de Guadalajara, de julio de 1909 a junio de 1910; *La Voz de México*, Apr. 17, 1889, 2, "El Apostolado de la Oración." There were three "levels" of participation, and the "lowest" level simply committed to praying every day that their actions would be consistent with the intentions of the Sacred Heart. The second level, in addition to the daily prayer, recited an Our Father and ten Hail Marys. The third level added a weekly or monthly communion of reparation (*comunión reparadora*). Examples of the suggested prayer topics included the liberty of the captive pope, Catholic schools, Catholic associations, an increase in the charity of the faithful, and the "bad Catholics" who sought "impossible alliances between Catholicism and liberalism." These are from *La Idea Católica*, Jan. 10, 1875, 4, "Apostolado de la Oración. Intenciones para el mes de Enero de 1875."

31. AHAMex, Labastida, Caja 86, exp. 86, Sobre que se nombre Director Central de la asociación titulada "Apostolado de la Oración," 1874.

32. *La Voz de México*, Oct. 11, 1877, 1, Correspondencia de los Estados. Guanajuato; AHAG, Visitas Pastorales, Caja 11, 1874-1878 . . . [1942], exp. Libro 4º visita Diocesana 1874, entries for Lagos and Magdalena; AHAG, Gobierno, Cofradías, Caja 30, 1920-1939, exp. Apostolado de la Oración 1920.

33. In the archbishopric of Mexico, a 1909 questionnaire asking when the Apostolados were founded in various parishes shows none established before 1889 outside of Mexico City, though it appears to have been well subscribed in the capital by then. AHAMex, Alarcón, Caja 61, exp. 19, Regarding the Apostolado de la Oración and the Guardia de Honor del Sgdo Corazón de Jesús; Bautista García, *Las disyuntivas*, 267.

34. *La Voz de México*, Dec. 25, 1886, 1-2, "Dos Palabras sobre la Segunda serie del Mensajero del Corazón de Jesús," says that the Guardia de Honor was founded "a year and a half ago" in the republic. AHAMich, XIX, Caja 187, exp. 167, Decreto, Jun. 1889. In this document the archbishop of Michoacán says the cofradía had just been authorized in Mexico City, in the temple of Santa Brígida, which would serve as the center for the whole Republic.

35. AHAMich, XIX, Caja 187, exp. 167, Decreto, Jun. 1889.

36. *La Voz de México*, Apr. 17, 1889, 2, "El Apostolado de la Oración."

37. AHAG, Gobierno, Cofradías, 1895-1919, Caja 29, 1877 document inserted into the magazine *El Josefino*, regarding circular from archbishop to priests on indulgences for the Asociación del Señor San José; AHAMex, Labastida, Caja 81, exp. 7, El cura de S. José con respecto a una Asociación Josefina; AHAG, Visitas pastorales, Caja 10, Visitas of Pedro Loza; *El Propagador de la devoción*; *Historia moderna de México, El Porfiriato, Vida Social*, Vol. 4, 493.

38. Archdiocese of Michoacán, *Boletín Eclesiástico*, 1905, 10.

39. AHAMex, Alarcón, Caja 20, exp. 20, Catálogo de las Fundaciones Josefinas y del personal que las desempeña.

40. See Wright-Ríos, *Revolutions*, chapter 1, for a rich and nuanced portrait of Archbishop Gillow and the extent to which he independently promoted some devotions, while at the same time hewing to the ideals of Romanization.

41. Cejudo, "Católicas," 43, counts only thirty-five to forty lay associations in Sonora in 1913, but the top two by a wide margin were the Vela Perpetua and the Apostolado.

42. AHAG, Visitas Pastorales, Caja 10, Visita of Pedro Loza to Parroquia de Jesús María, 1870.

43. AHAMich, XX, Caja 10, 1900-14, exp. 4, Libro de las asociaciones de la Vela Perpetua en el Arzobispado, 1905-1912.

44. AHAMex, Alarcón, Caja 6, exp. 16, Chapa de Mota, El RP Cura Fr. Francsico de P. Lira sobre erección de la Vela Perpetua, 1892.

45. ACM, Caja 181, Fojas 808-812, Memoria que hace el Director del Colegio de Niñas de Nuestra Señora de Guadalupe en el presente año de los trabajos escolares del mismo Colegio, y que fue leida en la solemne distribución de premios, y día cuatro de Diciembre de 1878; *El Faro*, Nov. 15, 1887, 4, "Los Protestantes de México"; Chávez, *La bandera*, 92–93; Pérez, "Cesárea Ruiz."

46. AHAMex, Alarcón, Caja 24, exp. 40, Con relación a unos estatutos para erigir una asociación de la iglesia parroquial de San Miguel, 1898; De Dios, *Historia*, 566, 568.

47. AHAMex, Labastida, Caja 118, exp. 72, El Presbítero D. Sotero García sobre Reglamento de la Asociación Mariana, 1877.

48. AHAMex, Alarcón, Caja 39, exp. 19, 1901–1921, documents on the foundation of asociaciones guadalupanas; Murillo, "Politics," 175–76.

49. The surveys show fourteen conferences in the archdiocese of Michoacán, for example, but an annual report from 1905–6 shows thirty. *El Tiempo*, Oct. 13, 1906, "Las conferencias de S. Vicente de Paul en Michoacán."

50. *El Tiempo*, Aug. 26, 1884, 1–2, "Del Vaticano."

51. Aceves Ávila, "*Que es bueno*," 432; *El País*, Oct. 9, 1901, 1, "Los milagros de la caridad."

52. Arrom, *Volunteering*, 85–86.

53. Stauffer, *Victory*, 156–57, comments that compared to the diocese of Zamora, the establishment of the new Romanized devotional associations lagged behind in the archdiocese of Michoacán, which means that Zamora was even more blanketed with the new associations than Michoacán.

54. Besides the Asociación del Sr. S. José, colonial holdovers included the associations dedicated to Nuestra Señora del Rosario, now more about stimulating the praying of the rosary than in the colonial era. On papal encouragement of the Rosary, see AHAMich, XIX, Caja 187, exp. 167, Se ha comunicado desde Roma al Illmo Señor Arzobispo Dr. D. José Igo Arciga con fecha 26 de Julio anterior [1883]. Another older cofradía that still survived, especially in the archbishopric of Mexico, was Nuestra Señora del Carmen, pushed by the Carmelite friars after their return to Mexico, but unlike the Rosary association, the hierarchy was not always happy with this association and occasionally disbanded it when given the opportunity. See AHAMex, Alarcón, Caja 66, exp. 68, Con relación a la Cofradía de NS del Carmen establecida en Guadalupe, Feb. 8, 1897.

55. In Michoacán the colonial cofradías that were present during an 1831 survey had almost completely disappeared by 1896. In eighteen towns in which we know specifically which cofradías existed in both 1831 and 1896, forty-eight of the ones present in 1831 had disappeared by 1896, and only four survived. Not a single Cofradía de las Benditas Ánimas still functioned; nor did any of the Nuestro Amos or most of the Santísimos, not even as non-canonically-approved associations. (Of course, as pointed out in chapter 5, if some of the Blessed Sacrament cofradías had disappeared they were usually replaced by some other pious association that adored the Sacrament, like the Vela or la Adoración Nocturna.) Some of the 1831 organizations were noted by the responding priests to have been extremely weak financially, and it is most likely that they failed soon after and were slowly replaced by the first wave of new associations in the 1840s, 1850s, and 1860s. These were then joined later in the century, typically—in Michoacán—by the Apostolado and/or the Guardia de Honor. Both the 1831 survey and the 1896 survey are found in AHAMich, Diocesano, Gobierno, Parroquias, Informes, multiple boxes.

56. For Oaxaca, see Wright-Ríos, *Revolutions*, 110; for Mexico and Michoacán, see the 1896 interrogatories.

57. AHAMex, Alarcón, Caja 74, exp. 23, Carta pastoral del Illmo Sr. D. Próspero María Alarcón; AHAMex, Alarcón, Caja 74, exp. 16, Carta Pastoral de Alarcón, sobre el establecimiento de la Congregación del Catecismo y de la Asociación Universal de la Sagrada Familia,1898.

58. AHAMex, Alarcón, Caja 80, exp. 62, Con respecto a la Asociación de la Sagrada Familia, 1898.

59. AHAMex, Alarcón, Caja 80, exp. 62, Con respecto a la Asociación de la Sagrada Familia, 1898; AHAMex, Alarcón, Caja 79, exp. 97, Respecto a la Asociación de la Sgda Familia, Tepetlaoxtoc, 1898.

60. AHAMex, Alarcón, Caja 129, exp. 29, Con respecto a dos circulares, 1907.

61. Some of the other unsuccessful new associations were the Asociación de Caballeros y Damas de Nuestra Señora de Loreto, the Asociación de la Divina Providencia, the Asociación de "La Semana Devota" (to extend devotion to Nuestra Señora del Carmen), the Asociación de la Santísima Virgen del Pronto Socorro, the Asociación Reparadora, and the charmingly named Compañía de Seguros para el Cielo. AHAMex, Alarcón, Caja 57, exp. 44, Con relación a la Asociación de Caballeros y Damas, Loreto, 1896; AHAMex, Alarcón, Caja 114, exp. 62, El Capellán [de la iglesia de Jesús María] con relación a la Asociación de la Divina Providencia, 1903; AHAMex, Alarcón, Caja 112, exp. 7, Fray Liberato, con respecto a la Asociación "La Semana Devota" [en la iglesia del Carmen], 1902; AHAMex, Alarcón, Caja 122, exp. 37, El cura de Tacuba con respecto a la erección canónica de una cofradía de la capilla de Popotla,1905; AHAMex, Labastida, Caja 112, exp. 34, El RP Cura de San Miguel con relación a la Asociación Reparadora, 1878; AHAMich, XX, Caja 109. 1901–1915, exp. 1, Seguros, 1901.

62. Marin, "Fleshy Heart"; Morgan, *Sacred Heart*.

63. All four of the associations below the top six (the Guardia de Honor del Sagrado Corazón de Jesús, the Santísimo Sacramento, the Conferencias de San Vicente de Paul, and the associations dedicated to La Purísima Concepción) were also strongly female in leadership and composition.

64. Four were all-female, nine were mixed-sex with female officers, seven had mixed membership with male officers, and two had parallel men's and women's groups, each with their own officers.

65. Twenty-two were all-female, three others were mixed-sex with female officers, and two more parishes had parallel male and female organizations, such as happened in Pachuca where there was an all-female Sagrado Corazón de Jesús with 356 members, and an all-male association with 80 members. There was only one mixed-sex association with male officers.

66. Eight were all-female, nine were mixed-sex with female officers, and three were mixed-sex with male officers.

67. For example, Bautista García, *Las disyuntivas*, 262, 263, implies that Marian asociaciones were all-female.

68. AHAMich, XIX, Caja 286, exp. 41, Visita, La Piedad, 1904.

69. AHAMich, XIX, Caja 249, exp. 470, Lista ... Salamanca, 1896.

70. *El Tiempo*, Aug. 9, 1887, 2, "Tehuacán. El Apostolado de la Oración."

71. AHAMich, XIX, Caja 250, exp. 482, Libro no. 1 donde constan los nombres de las celadoras y demás personas que forman los coros de la Asociación Josefina, establecida en Huanímaro hoy 1º de mayo de 1899.

72. AHAMich, XX, Caja 109, exp. 1, San José. The estimate is based on the fact that the association had twenty-eight female celadoras and six male celadoras.

73. AHAG, Gobierno, Cofradías, Caja 3 de Vela Perpetua and Apostolado de la Oración, 1955–1960, 39–105.

74. Leal and Woldenberg, *Del estado liberal*; Rivas Jiménez, "Las asociaciones"; Ávila Espinosa, "Una renovada misión."

75. AHAMex, Labastida, Caja 182, exp. 52, Toca al expediente relativo a la Asociación de "El Alma de María," 1886.

76. *La Convención Radical Obrera*, May 1, 1887, 4, "Para Solaz de nuestros lectores." Among other Catholic-identifying mutual aid societies not included in *La Convención Radical*'s directory were the Asociación de Hijas del Sagrado Corazón de Jesús (AHAMex, Labastida, Caja 18, exp. 47, Asociación de Hijas de S. Corazón de Jesús. Informe relativo a dicha Asociación, 1887); and the men's groups Unión y Amistad del Señor de Chalma (AHAMex, Labastida, Caja 21, exp. 10, Reglamento General de la Sociedad Unión y Amistad del Señor de Chalma. Fundada el 1 de Abril de 1888) and Sociedad de S. Felipe de Jesús (AHAMex, Labastida, Caja 238, exp. 1, Sobre instalación de la Mesa Directiva de esa Sociedad de S. Felipe de Jesús, 1887).

77. *El Diario del Hogar*, Mar. 15, 1891, 2, "Inauguración de una Sociedad."

78. Hart, *Anarchism*; Lear, *Workers*; Porter, *Working Women*, 74.

79. On workers' circles as part of Social Catholicism, see Adame Goddard, *El pensamiento*; Ceballos Ramírez, *El catolicismo social*; Bautista García, *Las disyuntivas*; Romero de Solís, *El agujón*; Ávila Espinosa, "Una renovada misión."

80. Social Catholicism as understood in Mexico included workers' circles prominently, but not exclusively. It was also concerned with Catholic education and "moral" activities for the working class.

81. AHAMich, XX, Caja 109, exp. 3, Modificación, adiciones y supresiones del reglamento de la Sociedad de O. C. estab. en esta Parroquia [Santa Cruz, GTO], 1903.

82. *El Tiempo*, Feb. 24, 1910, 8, "Aguascalientes."

83. Adame Goddard, *El pensamiento*, 250–58, for example, lines up the provisions of Article 123 of the 1917 constitution and various Social Catholic texts, mainly from the congresses held in the last decade of the Porfiriato, to show how closely they were aligned and to suggest a Social Catholic origin for the labor provisions of the constitution. For some historians, Social Catholicism represented—as the subtitle of Manuel Ceballos Ramírez's classic on the subject indicates—a "third way" that was neither capitalism nor socialism, but rather a means of confronting the injustices of liberal capitalism while preserving a place for religion in society. Ceballos Ramírez, *El catolicismo social*. Most see it as much closer to liberal capitalism, in its calls for employers to treat their workers more fairly but not for major changes in the relationship between labor and capital or in property regimes. Bautista García, *Las disyuntivas*.

84. Wright-Ríos, *Revolutions*, 102; García Ugarte, "Etapa." Adame Goddard, *El pensamiento*, makes a case for *Rerum Novarum* having an impact on Catholic intellectuals within a few years of its publication. But he agrees with others that the social effects did not come until at least the foundation of *El País*. Savarino Roggero, "Catholics of the North," 16, points out that there was "initial resistance" to the encyclical on the part of the Mexican hierarchy.

85. *El Tiempo*, Mar. 4, 1905, 3, "Rectificación"; *El Tiempo*, Oct. 11, 1904, "La Fiestas Jubilares de Morelia."

86. *La Voz de México*, Apr. 16, 1907, 1, "Unión de los Obreros Católicos" [reprinted from *El Amigo de la Verdad*].

87. Ceballos Ramírez, "Rerum Novarum," 160.

88. Ceballos Ramírez, "Rerum Novarum," 161; Ceballos Ramírez, "La encíclica," 30.

89. Ceballos Ramírez, "Rerum Novarum," 161.

90. *El Tiempo*, Nov. 18, 1904, 3, "Obreros Católicos."

91. Archdiocese of Michoacán, *Boletín Eclesiástico*, 1906.

92. AHAG, Gobierno, Cofradías, Caja 3 de Vela Perpetua and Apostolado de la Oración, 1955–1960, 41.

93. AHAMex, Mora y del Río, Caja 125, exp. 34, Informe sobre el Círculo Patriótico Religioso de Artesanos, 1909.

94. AHAMich, XX, Caja 61, exp. 6, Movimiento religioso, Huetamo, 1902.

95. *El Tiempo*, Oct. 3, 1905, 2, "El octavo día del novenario en la Basílica de Guadalupe. La función de los Obreros y Artesanos."

96. AHAMex, Alarcón, Caja 77, exp. 77, El Pbro Ycaza con relación a las asociaciones del templo de la Encarnación, Jul. 1898.

97. *La Defensa Católica*, Mar. 22, 1888, 2, "La Vuelta de los Hombres a la Frecuencia de Sacramentos."

98. *El Amigo de la Verdad*, Jul. 2, 1892, 1, "Una Función en el Templo de la Compañía."

99. AHAG, Vela Perpetua/Apostolado de la Oración, Caja 3, "Informe del Apostolado de la Oración, 1910," 40–41.

100. Rosas Salas, "De le República," 242. On masculinization of Catholic practice, for Mexico, see Butler, "Eucharistic Angels" and "La coronación"; for the Catholic world, see Blaschke, "Unrecognized," 40–41.

101. Butler, "Eucharistic Angels."

102. AHAMex, Labastida, Caja 189, exp. 24, Promotor to D. Manuel Monsuri sobre aprobación del reglamento de la Asociación de la Sma Virgen de los Dolores, Sept. 3, 1887.

103. AHAMex, Labastida, Caja 185, exp. 7, Sobre aprobación del Reglamento de la Sociedad Guardia de Honor de la Inmaculada Concepción de María, 1886.

104. AHAMex, Labastida, Caja 99, exp. 27, Dr. Ambrosio Lara to Fr. Nicolás Arias, cura de la parroquia de S. Sebastián, May 12, 1876.

105. AHAMex, Mora y del Río, Caja 3, ex. 33, Pbro Dr. D. Benjamin Sánchez, con respecto a un reglamento, 1911.

106. AHAMex, Alarcón, Caja 20, exp. 84, El Pbro D. Francisco Oviedo con relación a la "Hermandad del Espíritu Santo," 1894.

107. AHAMex, Labastida, Caja 8, exp. 89, El Sr. Pbro Dr. D. Antonio J. Paredes, sobre que se apruebe el reglamento de la "Asociación de Santa Tereza de Jesús, del Profesorado Mexicano," 1891.

108. AHAMex, Labastida, Caja 89, exp. 76, El Padre Capellán respecto a la velación nocturna del Smo Sacramento, Jan. 14, 1875.

109. AHAMex, Labastida, Caja 130, exp. 11, El R. P. Fr. Rafael López sobre la aprobación de la Sociedad de la Corte de María. Estatutos de la Corte de María, establecida en la Yglesia de la Profesa de México," 1878.

110. AHAMex, Alarcón, Caja 56, exp. 66, El Cura de San Pablo con relación a las socias de NS de la Merced, Feb. 1896.

111. AHAMex, Alarcón, Caja 64, exp. 47, Canónigo Arguelles con relación a la Archicofradía de NS del Carmen, Jul. 21, 1897.

112. AHAMex, Labastida, Caja 164, exp. 67, Sept. 19, 1884, Con relación a la Hermandad de la "Vela Perpetua"; AHAMex, Labastida, Caja 163, exp. 48, Dn. Salvador Paredes Lozada, sobre lo que expresa.

113. AHAMex, Alarcón, Caja 166, exp. 56, La Vicepresidenta de la Sociedad del Sagrado Corazón de Jesús con relación al Parroco, Tepetlaoxtoc, 1895.

114. AHAMex, Alarcón, Caja 47, exp. 13, Circular a todos los jefes de familia y personas libres de esta población, 1895.

115. AHAMex, Alarcón, Caja 127, exp. 34, Con relación a la Archicofradía del Perpetuo Socorro, 1906.

116. *El Amigo de la Verdad*, Jun. 9, 1888, 4, "Joco-série."

117. *La Iberia*, Jun. 22, 1909, 1, "Croniquillas. El Botón Azul"; *El Diario*, Jul. 14, 1909, 5, "El Botón Gana Terreno Día a Día."

118. Fernández-Aceves, "La lucha," 133; Rocha Islas, "Visión"; Rocha Islas, *Los rostros*, 332, 335–38; Macías, *Against*; Soto, *Emergence*. There was a sharp increase in the number of political clubs after Porfirio Díaz's interview with the American journalist James Creelman in 1908, in which he indicated that he would tolerate political opposition as early as the 1910 presidential election. But there was some previous political activity. The Club Liberal Ponciano Arriaga, associated with the anarcho-syndicalist Partido Liberal Mexicano (PLM), was founded in 1900, and its manifesto was signed by some women, including Juana Belén Gutiérrez de Mendoza, who founded the Guanajuato daily *Vésper* in 1901, in support of miners and against the clergy and the Díaz regime, and later, in 1907, founded the women's organization Hijas de Cuauhtémoc, a group of three hundred women demanding better work conditions for women. On Juana Belén, see Lau Jaiven, "La participación," 30–32.

119. *La Opinión*, Jul. 28, 1904, 1, "Noticias de Orizaba."

120. *El Diario*, Sept. 12, 1908, 3, "Llegada del Gobernador."

121. *La Gacetilla*, Oct. 31, 1877, "En Guanajuato." There appear to have been just three female temperance societies in Mexico City by 1904, all Protestant, and around seven hundred members of these and others nationally. *El Abogado Cristiano Ilustrado*, Feb. 25, 1904, "De Actualidad. La Campaña Anti-alcohólica de la Señora Fields."

122. *El Continente Americano*, May 2, 1899, 2, "Quisicosas."

123. *El Comercio de Morelia*, Dec. 16, 1899, 1, "La Sociedad del Socorro"; *La Convención Radical Obrera*, Mar. 1, 1896, 2, "Discurso pronunciado por la Srita. Rebeca Plata, al Inaugurarse el 27 del pasado Enero la 'Asociación de Mujeres Coahuilenses' en el Saltillo."

124. *El Imparcial*, Jul. 21, 1908, 1, "Otra Institución Feminista en México."

125. *El Centinela Español*, Jul. 28, 1881, 3, "Gacetilla."

126. Soto, *Emergence*, 16.

127. In the late 1880s there were at least two scandals regarding men's intrusions into the management of women's groups, with hints in one case that the male treasurer was embezzling funds, and in the other that the male director was treating accomplished women like children. *La Convención Radical Obrera*, May 1, 1887, 4, "Las Sociedades de Señoras y sus Directores"; *La Convención Radical Obrera*, May 1, 1887, 4, "Para Solaz de nuestros lectores"; *El Nacional*, Aug. 24, 1888, 2, "Escandaloso é Interesante."

128. Soto, *Emergence*, 15.

129. *El Popular*, Feb. 10, 1902, 1, "Banquete Dado a los Pobres por el Filantrópico 'Club Violeta.'"

130. *El Contemporáneo* (SLP), Aug. 11, 1903, 2, "Aniversario."

131. *El Correo Español*, Nov. 23, 1906, 2, "La Sociedad de Empleadas de Comercio."

132. *El Siglo Diez y Nueve*, Jun. 2, 1888, 1, "Charla Semanaria." Besides the seamstresses' group, Carmen Romero Rubio was asociada con "La Buena Madre," "Fe, Esperanza y Caridad," and "Josefa O. de Domínguez," along with General Hermenegildo Carrillo and his wife, Manuela Arango de Carrillo.

133. *El Imparcial*, Feb. 25, 1898, 1, "Sociedad Mexicana para el Cultivo de las Ciencias"; *El Diario*, Oct. 2, 1908, 4, "La Sociedad Mexicana Para el Cultivo de las Ciencias."

134. Porter, *Working Women*; Porter, *From Angel*.

135. Accompanying the establishment of women's secular associations was a wave of magazines and newspapers published by and/or for women including (besides the short-lived Las Hijas del Anáhuac of 1873; see chapter 5) *La Mujer* (1880), *El Album de la Mujer* (1883–90), *El Correo de las Señoras* (1883–93), *Violetas de Anáhuac*

(1887–89), *La Siempreviva* (1870, in Mérida); and *La Mujer Mexicana* (1904–8) (more on the latter below). Infante Vargas, "Igualdad"; González Jiménez, "Normal"; Pasternac, "El periodismo."

136. González Jiménez, "The Normal School," 34–35; Schell, *Church*, 66.

137. *El Contemporáneo*, Mar. 27, 1897, 1, "La 'Sociedad de Socorros Mutuos de Profesoras.'"

138. *El Correo Español*, Dec. 24, 1907, 2, "Nueva Sociedad Recreativa."

139. *El Correo Español*, Dec. 26, 2, "La Sociedad 'Felipe Villanueva.'"

140. *El Nacional*, Aug. 7, 1898, 3–4, "La Aristocracia Intelectual Femenina en México."

141. Chowning, "Culture Wars"; more on this point in chapter 8.

142. *Boletín Masónico*, Aug. 1, 1893, "La Mujer en la Masonería," 531–32; Velasco López, "La mujer y la masonería."

143. Also in 1904 an organization described by González Navarro, *El porfiriato*, 415, was founded by a journalist, Laura N. Torres, in order to diffuse ideas about women's emancipation: the Admiradoras de Juárez. I have not been able to find out anything else about this group.

144. *La Patria*, Mar. 23, 1904, 2, "Sociedad Feminista"; *La Patria*, Mar. 24, 1904, 2, "La Sociedad Protectora de la Mujer."

145. *El Mundo*, Jun. 8, 1905, 2, "La Protección a la Mujer."

146. *El Tiempo*, Apr. 29, 1904, 3, "Sociedad Protectora de la Mujer Mexicana."

147. On *La Mujer Mexicana*, see Rocha Islas, *Los rostros*, 335–38.

148. *La Patria*, Mar. 24, 1904, 2, "La Sociedad Protectora de la Mujer"; *El Abogado Cristiano*, Mar. 23, 1905, 4–5, "El Feminismo y los Toros."

149. *El Colmillo Público*, Jul. 10, 1904, 3, "Feminismo Católico."

150. *La Voz de México*, Dec. 12, 1900, 1, "Boletín."

151. Piccato, *Tyranny*; Ramos Escandón, "Género"; LaGreca, *Rewriting*, chapter 1; Carner, "Estereotipos"; Macías, *Against*; Parcero, *Condiciones*; Ramos Escandón, "Señoritas"; Tuñón Pablos, *Women*.

152. LaGreca, *Rewriting*, 41–44; Trejo, "Educar"; Weiner, "Trinidad Sánchez Santos"; Pani, "Una ventana."

153. LaGreca, *Rewriting*, 34.

Chapter 8

The quotation in the chapter title comes from the following source: *El Tiempo Ilustrado*, Feb. 6, 1910, 82, "Notas de la Semana."

1. AHAM, Labastida, Caja 192, exp. 43, Joaquín García Icazbalceta to Mitra, Jan. 9, 1888; Ygnacio Martínez Barrosa to Joaquín García Icazbalceta, Mar. 24, 1888; AHAM, Labastida, Caja 192, exp. 43, Joaquín García Icazbalceta to Mitra, May 2, 1888.

2. AHAM, Labastida, Caja 192, exp. 43, Joaquín García Icazbalceta to Mitra, Jan. 9, 1888. He does not elaborate on the reasons for this aversion, whether anticlerical attitudes, an ideological preference for secular education, the cost or inconvenience of Catholic schools, or some other reason.

3. García Icazbalceta also pointed out that although there were quite a few Catholic elementary schools, there were almost no free-of-charge institutions at the upper levels, making advancement difficult for poor children who might be capable of pursuing a literary or scientific career. He further argued that many of the teachers in the public schools were good Catholics and would do no moral harm.

4. If Protestant families needed the support of the conferences, it should be offered, since providing charity to Protestants would instill a love of Catholicism and that was the

best way to convert the whole family. AHAMex, Labastida, Caja 192, exp. 43, Ygnacio Martínez Barrosa to Joaquín García Icazbalceta, Mar. 24, 1888.

5. It was fairly widely asserted by contemporaries that the church had already regained "the majority" of its wealth, putting it in the hands of trusted individuals. *El Siglo Diez y Nueve*, Jul. 13, 1888, 1, "La Lucha Periodística." That is what Juárez, *Reclaiming*, observed for Guadalajara and I (Chowning, *Wealth and Power*, chapter 7) observed for Michoacán.

6. Though for a clear acknowledgment, see Aceves Ávila, "*Que es bueno*," 413–14.

7. Bautista García, *Las disyuntivas*. See also Ceballos Ramírez, *El catolicismo*, 48, and chapter 3, who periodizes the Catholic attitude toward conciliation and sees at least a ten-year period during which Catholics sought to make something like a pact with the government. From 1867 to 1892 he characterizes the dominant Catholic faction as traditionalist and oppositionist, but from 1892 to 1900 Catholic liberals sought an understanding with the regime and favored conciliation. From 1899 to 1909 Catholic social critics of the regime still operated under the umbrella of conciliation, but began to see the social costs of capitalist progress under Díaz.

8. Bautista García, *Las disyuntivas*, 232.

9. Butler, *Popular Piety*, 39; Guerra, *México*, 220–24; Bastian, "La lucha"; Díaz Patiño, "El catolicismo social."

10. Schmitt, "Catholic Adjustment," 189.

11. Many decades ago Schmitt, "Díaz Conciliation Policy," 520–25, captured the fact that "conciliation" was not ubiquitous, but recent historians have been more inclined to see collaboration than resistance. See Butler, *Popular Piety*, 44–47; Guerra, *México*, 225; Murillo, "Politics," 1–3. Ceballos Ramírez, *El catolicismo*, shows that late in the regime there was also resistance to conciliation on the part of some Catholics because they did not see it as capable of solving the "social problem" (18). See Stauffer, *Victory*, chapter 6, on the difficulty of Díaz's balancing act between appeasing the church and maintaining the support of liberals.

12. *El Siglo Diez y Nueve*, Jul. 8, 1896, 1, "La Política Conservadora."

13. Wright-Ríos, *Searching*, 129, 145.

14. Bazant, *Historia de la educación*; Staples, *Recuento*; Vaughan, *State*; Vázquez de Knauth, *Nacionalismo*; Dumas, "El discurso"; Loaeza, "La iglesia."

15. Schmitt called religious instruction an area of "minor friction" with the state, but his sources emphasized the local accommodations that were often made with public schoolteachers and the public displays of cooperation rather than the much more combative national-level rhetoric. My own research confirms his intuition that at the local level the debate was generally not as intense as at the national level, but the national level debates shaped both public policy and church policy. Schmitt, "Díaz Conciliation," 515–520; Chowning, "Culture Wars."

16. Quoted in Bautista García, "La educación privada," 84.

17. *La Voz de México*, Jan. 8, 1885, 2, "Junta de instrucción católica primaria del Arzobispado de Michoacán."

18. *La Voz de México*, Feb. 27, 1897, 2, "Futuros Candidatos a la Horca."

19. *El Siglo Diez y Nueve*, Jun. 16, 1896, 1, "Más Ataques a la Escuela Laica."

20. *El Colaborador Católico*, Sept. 1, 1885, 2, "El Suicidio"; *La Voz de México*, Feb. 27, 1897, 2, "Futuros Candidatos a la Horca"; *El Siglo Diez y Nueve*, May 10, 1895, 1, "Otra Calumnia Más."

21. *La Libertad*, Jun. 22, 1880, 2, "Remitido" (quoting *La Ilustración Católica*); *El Amigo de la Verdad*, Mar. 15, 1900, 1, "La inmoralidad amenaza devorar a la Sociedad."

22. *El Amigo de la Verdad*, Feb. 28, 1900, 1, "Lo que Valen los Maestros Laicos."

23. *El Tiempo*, Jul. 8, 1887, 1, "Remitidos . . . de Guadalajara a México."

24. ACM, Caja 181, fojas 820–824, Colegio de Santa Teresa de Jesús para Señoritas, Fundado en Puebla de los Angeles . . . Dirigido por Profesoras de los Establecimientos de Sta Teresa de Jesús en España, 1889. The line from the prospectus was repeated in a speech given by the Directora. *El Amigo de la Verdad*, Feb. 9, 1889, 2, "Discurso que, al inaugurarse en Puebla el Colegio de Santa Teresa de Jesús, pronunció la Directora del mismo Doña Saturnina Jassa."

25. *La Voz de México*, Feb. 21, 1901, "Una Flor Envenenada."
26. *La Patria*, Feb. 10, 1881, 1, "Editorial. La Instrucción Religiosa."
27. *La Convención Radical Obrera*, Jun. 23, 1889, 1, "El Congreso de Instrucción Pública."
28. *El Siglo Diez y Nueve*, May 22, 1895, 1, "La Enseñanza Laica."
29. *El Siglo Diez y Nueve*, May 1, 1896, 1, "Siguen las tandas por la Compañía Averardi."
30. *El Siglo Diez y Nueve*, Apr. 27, 1896, 1, "Aspiraciones Reaccionarias."
31. *La Convención Radical Obrera*, Jun. 23, 1889, 1, "El Congreso de Instrucción Pública."
32. *El Demócrata*, Oct. 19, 1895, 1, "Mal de Zapa."
33. *La Patria*, Jul. 14, 1900, 1, "Altar Suntuoso."
34. *El Contemporáneo*, Nov. 6, 1902, 1, "El Sr. Lic. Justo Sierra y la Enseñanza de la Mujer."
35. *El Siglo Diez y Nueve*, Dec. 26, 1895, 1–2, "Festividad Masónica."
36. Díaz Patiño, *Católicos*.
37. Schmitt, "Díaz Conciliation," 523, says that graveside rites were exempted until late in the regime.
38. Rosas Salas, "De la República," 241–42, observes that the Díaz government permitted public Catholic practices.
39. *La Patria*, Mar. 15, 1882, 2, "Tlaxcala."
40. *El Diario del Hogar*, Aug. 9, 1887, 2, Gacetilla. "Al Observador"; *El Diario del Hogar*, Jul. 12, 1896, 3, "San Luis Potosí."
41. *La Patria*, Apr. 12, 1898, 2, "Estado de Aguascalientes."
42. *El Tiempo*, Oct. 15, 1885, 2, "En el Estado de México"; *El Tiempo*, Apr. 26, 1887, 1, "Jalisco"; *El Tiempo*, Dec. 11, 1895, 1, "Los defensores de las leyes de Reforma."
43. *El Tiempo*, Nov. 16, 1887, 3, "¡A última hora! ¡Siguen las arbitrariedades y prisiones en el Estado de Guanajuato!"
44. *El Tiempo*, Oct. 20, 1895, 1, "Ecos de la Coronación."
45. *El Tiempo*, Oct. 17, 1896, 2, "Las Leyes de Reforma. Un artículo de D. Francisco Bulnes."
46. *El Tiempo*, Dec. 28, 1887, 3, "También en Zacatecas."
47. *El Diario del Hogar*, Aug. 27, 1895, 1, "Manifiesto del 'Grupo Reformista y Constitucional.'"
48. See the praise heaped on those who happily paid the fine by the Catholic newspaper in Zacatecas. *El Tiempo*, Dec. 28, 1887, 3, "También en Zacatecas."
49. On the logistics and special features of the celebration, see Brading, *Mexican Phoenix*, chapter 12; Trasloheros, "Señora."
50. *El Diario del Hogar*, Sept. 24, 1895, 1, "Las infracciones a la ley proyectadas con motivo de la Coronación Guadalupana."
51. *La Voz de México*, Oct. 10, 1895, 2, "La multa impuesta a los Peregrinos de Puebla."
52. Moreno Chávez, *Devociones*, 201–10, gives an excellent account of the political impact and implications of the coronation.
53. *Historia moderna de México. El Porfiriato. Vida social*, 494.
54. *El Tiempo*, Jun. 14, 1884, 1, "La Fiesta de Corpus-Christi en el campo."

55. Stauffer, *Victory*.
56. Schmitt, "Díaz Conciliation," 514.
57. Moreno Chávez, *Devociones*, 109. In fact, Moreno Chávez sees the occasional outburst of criticism against public displays as a positive for the hierarchy, because they allowed bishops and archbishops to crack down on popular religiosity in favor of the Vatican-approved devotions and practices.
58. Rosas Salas, "El Círculo," 40.
59. For an extended treatment of debates over freedom of the press from the perspective of printers and editors, see Zeltsman, *Ink*.
60. In Michoacán during the Porfiriato, Pineda Soto, "La prensa religiosa," 77–78, identified no fewer than forty-one Catholic newspapers.
61. For a close examination of one Catholic newspaper that shows its differences from others, see Rosas Salas, "Trinidad Sánchez Santos."
62. *La Voz de México*, May 24, 1879, 1, "Escándalo."
63. *El Tiempo*, Mar. 25, 1887, 1, "El Partido Liberal"; *La Voz de México*, May 13, 1896, 1, "El Edicto Diocesano y 'El Universal.'"
64. *El Tiempo*, Jul. 1, 1890, 2, "De Acuerdo"; *La Voz de México*, Jun. 28, 1890, 1, "La Prensa Católica."
65. *La Voz de México*, May 20, 1891, 2, "Segundo Congreso de la Asociación de la Prensa Católica de Estado Unidos"; *El Tiempo*, Jan. 4, 1899, 1, "Proyecto de Prensa Católica Asociada."
66. *La Voz de México*, Jul. 6, 1881, 2, "Correspondencia de los Estados. Durango."
67. *El Tiempo*, Dec. 6, 1910, 5, "Los librepensadores pintados por ellos mismos."
68. *La Voz de México*, Dec. 18, 1907, 1, "Gutta Cavat Lapidem. La Mala Prensa."
69. *La Convención Radical Obrera*, Jun. 5, 1892, 2, "Misión de la Prensa Clerical."
70. *La Patria*, Jun. 15, 1897, 1–2, "La prensa reaccionaria. Su actitud hostil."
71. *El Diario del Hogar*, May 2, 1896, 1, "Entre la Espada y la Pared."
72. As reported by *La Voz de México*, Apr. 25, 1896, 1, "La Prensa Católica de Mexico. Importantísimas declaraciones del Ilustrísimo Señor Visitador Apostólico." Some liberal newspapers saw in Averardi's declaraciones a conspiracy to lull the liberal press into complacency, while the church quietly went about the business of focusing on actions "designed to little by little negate the Reform and give victory to the clergy." See *El Monitor Republicano*, May 16, 1896, 1, 'Boletín del 'Monitor.'"
73. *El Diario del Hogar*, May 2, 1896, 1, "Entre la Espada y la Pared."
74. *El Monitor Republicano*, May 15, 1896, 1, "Boletín del 'Monitor.'"
75. *El Monitor Republicano*, May 15, 1896, 1, "Boletín del 'Monitor'"; *La Voz de México*, May 13, 1896, 1, "El Editor diocesano y 'El Universal.'"
76. Weiner, "Trinidad Sánchez Santos"; Pani, "Una ventana"; Pineda Soto, "La prensa religiosa"; Trejo, "Educar"; Curley, "Sociólogos peregrinos."
77. Schell, "Honorable Avocation," 79.
78. Crespo Reyes, "Entre la filantropía," 9.
79. Crespo Reyes, "Entre la filantropía," 9.
80. *La Voz de México*, Jun. 23, 1880, 1, "Extranjero. Meetings de mujeres."
81. *El Amigo de la Verdad*, Feb. 9, 1889, 2, "Discurso que, al inaugurarse en Puebla el Colegio de Santa Teresa de Jesús, pronunció la Sra. Directora del mismo Doña Saturnina Jassa, en la noche del 3 de Febrero de 1889."
82. AHAMich, XIX, Caja 6, exp. 51, "Alocución pronunciada por la Srita. Profesora Jesús Gutiérrez."
83. AHAMich, XIX, Caja 11, exp. 5, "Memoria que la que suscribe presenta, en el presente año escolar a la justa espectación de los padres de familia de esta ilustrada Ciudad de Pátzcuaro."

84. AHAMich, XIX, Caja 6, exp. 51, "Alocución pronunciada por la Srita. Profesora Jesús Gutiérrez."

85. AHAMich, XIX, Caja 6, exp. 51, "Alocución pronunciada por la Srita. Profesora Jesús Gutiérrez."

86. *El Tiempo*, May 28, 1903, 1, "La Cruzada de las Madres de Brescia."

87. *El Tiempo*, Sept. 23, 1905, 1, "Un Congreso de damas Catolicas francesas. Acción Social Cristiana de la Mujer."

88. *El Tiempo*, Dec. 17, 1907, 1, "Las damas uruguayas antes la persecución de la fe. La Liga de Damas Católicas—Una Gran Obra." On the Uruguayan Catholic activists, see Ehrick, *Shield of the Weak*.

89. *La Voz de México*, Jan. 12, 1908, 1, "Vida Activa es lo Necesario."

90. Moreno Chávez, *Devociones*, 169.

91. *La Voz de México*, Jan. 23, 1885, 1–2, "Excitativa al Bello Sexo Mexicano"; *La Voz de México*, Nov. 16, 1884, 1–2, "Insistimos"; *El Tiempo*, Feb. 13, 1885, 2, "El Pacto Federal."

92. *La Voz de la Patria*, Feb. 15, 1885, 317, "Las Hermanas de la Caridad"; *La Voz de México*, Feb. 10, 1885, 1–2, "Petición"; *La Voz de México*, Mar. 8, 1885, 2, "Las Hermanas de la Caridad"; *El Tiempo*, Feb. 13, 1885, 1, "Cartas de los Estados." Other petitions came from the women of Tacubaya, Sierrahermosa (Zacatecas), and San Pedro (Jalisco). *La Voz de México*, Feb. 12, 1885, 2, "Las Hermanas de la Caridad"; *La Voz de México*, Feb. 11, 1885, 2, "Las Hermanas de la Caridad"; *La Voz de la Patria*, Mar. 22, 1885, "Petición de las Señoras de la Villa de San Pedro al Soberano Congreso de la Unión, en favor de las Hermanas de la Caridad."

93. Though as Moreno Chávez, *Devociones*, 160–67, shows, there was no slowdown in the liberal criticism of women as dupes of priests, as destroying the home through embrace of the practice of confession, which they claimed "was converted into a lockbox [*buzón*] of denunciations" (162).

94. *El Amigo de la Verdad*, Apr. 6, 1887, 4, "A Última Hora."

95. *El Siglo Diez y Nueve*, Nov. 25, 1895, 1, "Fin de la Cuestión Clerical de Zacatecas."

96. *El Siglo Diez y Nueve*, Nov. 18, 1895, 1, "Se despejó la incognita"; *El Amigo de la Verdad*, Oct. 12, 1895, 3, "La Corona de la Virgen de Guadalupe"; Congregación Hijas de María Inmaculada, *Proceso*. The letters in ACHJMI (Archivo de la Congregacion Hijas de María Inmaculada), Serie Correspondencia Emitida, vols. 2, 3, and 4, "A sus amigos," which I consulted at the Colegio de Michoacán in Zamora, contain multiple mentions of necklaces, pearls, bracelets, and so on, that were given to Plancarte as donations to the colegiatura de Guadalupe, from 1888 forward.

97. *El Monitor Republicano*, Oct. 23, 1895, 2, "Los Diamantes de la Corona." On the preparations for the coronation and the controversies around Plancarte's actions, see Poole, *Guadalupan*, chapter 3.

98. *El Amigo de la Verdad*, Oct. 21, 1882, 1, "¡Victoria!"

99. *El Amigo de la Verdad*, Oct. 21, 1882, 1, "¡Victoria!"

100. *El Amigo de la Verdad*, Sept. 1, 1888, 2, "Solemne Ovación." The dangers of such actions were hinted at in the article, which followed applause for the actions of the lay associations with praise for parishioners who abstained from doing things that would give fuel to the liberals, such as unhooking the mules that pulled the carriage and transporting it on their shoulders.

101. AHAMex, Labastida, Caja 115, exp. 62, Da. Soledad Marenco de Berazueta sobre licencia para colocar la imagen de nuestra Sra de Lourdes en uno de los altares de la Yglesia de S. Cosme y para formar una Asociación de Señoras, 1878; AHAMex, Labastida, Caja 210, exp. 8, Vicario fijo D. Braulio Jiménez, sobre licencia para establecer la Asociación de la Vela Perpetua, 1889, Atlapulco; AHAMex, Alarcón, Caja 35, exp. 56, Refugio Ocampo

de Leyva solicita erección de una sociedad religiosa, 1894, Villa de Guadalupe Hidalgo; AHAG, Gobierno, Cofradías, 1895–1919, Caja 29, Cura Parroquia de Santa María de Guadalupe y Director de la Asociación de las Señoras del Centro establecida en este Santuario [de Yatlahuacan], Feb. 9, 1910; AHAG, Gobierno, Cofradías, Caja 3 de Vela Perpetua and Apostolado de la Oración, 1955–1960, exp. Apostolado de la Oración en la Arquidiocesis de Guadalajara, de julio de 1909 a junio de 1910, 35.

102. *El Diario*, Nov. 12, 1907, 1, El Profesorado Oficial no Puede Hacer Una Propaganda Religiosa; *El Tiempo*, Jul. 22, 1909, 2, "La intolerancia jacobina de los liberales."

103. *El Tiempo*, Jul. 22, 1909, 2, "La intolerancia jacobina de los liberales."

104. For a discussion of continued concern in the 1920s on the part of Catholic moralists with fashion and entertainment, see Schell, "Social Catholicism."

105. AHAMex, Alarcón, Caja 35, exp. 10, Pbro Fco Reyes sobre la instalación de la Sociedad de "Hijas de María," Jonacatepec, 1894.

106. *El Amigo de la Verdad*, Apr. 6, 1887, 3, "El Paseo del Viernes Santo."

107. AHAMex, Labastida, Caja 216, exp. 52, Reglamento de la Corte de María, 1886.

108. AHAMex, Alarcón, Caja 6, exp. 52, El Párroco Dr. D. Daniel Escobar [Sta Veracruz] sobre que se apruebe el reglamento de la Asociación de NS de Lourdes, 1892.

109. AHAMich, XX, Caja 109, exp. 2 (Santa María de Guadalupe), Reglamento General de la Corte de la Exelsa Reina y Amorosa Madre de los Mexicanos, la Santísima Virgen de Guadalupe . . . 1904.

110. Moreno Chávez, *Devociones*, 168–69.

111. AHAMex, Mora y del Río, Caja 3, exp. 25, Con respecto al círculo Católico de Obreros, 1910, Guadalupe Hidalgo.

112. *El Tiempo*, Aug. 20, 1909, 1, Los Católicos de Córdova protestan contra 'El Heraldo.'"

113. *El Tiempo*, Aug. 17, 1909, 1, "Solemne protesta."

114. *El Tiempo*, Aug. 17, 1909, 1, "Solemne protesta"; *El Faro*, Aug. 20, 1909, 5, "El Colmo del Fanatismo"; *El Tiempo*, Sep. 4, 1909, 1, "'Liga contra las malas lecturas,' iniciada por las damas católicas de Cholula"; *El Tiempo*, Aug. 20, 1909, 1, Los Católicos de Córdova protestan contra 'El Heraldo'"; *El Tiempo*, Aug. 26, 1909, 1, "Otra Protesta"; *El Tiempo*, Sep. 10, 1909, 1, "La Sociedad de Toluca protesta contra 'El Heraldo'"; *El Tiempo*, Aug. 26, 1909, 1, "Más adhesiones á la protesta contra 'El Heraldo.'"

115. *El Tiempo*, Mar. 11, 1910, 2, "Las damas católicas y la prensa."

116. For example, a congress of Catholic associations in Germany resolved at an 1867 congress that all their members would abstain from reading, buying, or subscribing to "bad newspapers." *El Tiempo*, Sep. 10, 1884, 1, "Prensa Extranjera."

117. Rosas Salas, "El Círculo," 57.

118. See also AHAG, Gobierno, Cofradías, 1895–1919, Caja 29, Feb. 9, 1910, "Cura Parroquial de Santa María de Guadalupe y Director de la Asociación de las Señoras del Centro"; and *La Voz de México*, Jun. 14, 1905, 2, "Contra la mala prensa," which calls for the Hijas de María of México to follow the example of the Hijas of Pamplona, Spain, who pledged not to receive or read certain newspapers.

119. AHAG, Gobierno, Cofradías, Caja 3 de Vela Perpetua/Apostolado de la Oración, "Apostolado de la Oración, 1910," 112–14.

120. AHAG, Gobierno, Cofradías, Caja 3 de Vela Perpetua/Apostolado de la Oración, "Apostolado de la Oración, 1910," 55.

121. AHAG, Gobierno, Cofradías, Caja 3 de Vela Perpetua and Apostolado de la Oración, 1955–1960, exp. El Apostolado de la Oración en la Arquidiocesis de Guadalajara, de julio de 1909 a junio de 1910, 12.

122. AHAG, Gobierno, Cofradías, 1895–1919, Caja 29, exp. Asociaciónes Piadosas/Correspondencia al Sr. Obispo, 1895–1912, "Reglamento de la Asociación del Espiritu Santo para fomentar la buena prensa en la Arquidiocesis de Guadalajara."

123. *El País*, May 4, 1908, 4, "Para las damas: La Mujer y la Prensa."

124. *El País*, May 4, 1908, 4, "Para las damas: La Mujer y la Prensa"; *El País*, Jun. 25, 1903, 2, "Por el Orbe Católico: Las Señoras Católicas de Bilbao."

125. *La Voz de México*, Jun. 28, 1890, 1, "Asociaciones Católicas: protectoras de la instrucción religiosa."

126. The article articulated very twenty-first-century concerns about how to improve the prestige of elementary school teaching and achieve lower student-teacher ratios.

127. Bautista García cites a figure of 209 in 1875, which accords well with the annual reports of the men's and women's Sociedades Católicas in the late 1870s. Bautista García, *Las disyuntivas*, 282. By the turn of the century, some of the Sociedad Católica schools had disappeared, but there a few other new lay associations took up some slack. Still, it is unlikely that there were more than 100 of these.

128. This number did not include schools in Morelia, whose parishes did not report.

129. Vaughan, "What Catholics Have Done," 122–24.

130. AHAMex, Alarcón, Caja 8, exp. 64, La Sra. Da. Concepcion C. de Mansouri, sobre que se le asigne una pensión para la Escuela que sostiene, 1892; Vaughan, "What Catholics Have Done," 122–24; Bautista García, *Las disyuntivas*, 282.

131. The number of parishes represented in the survey information I have for Oaxaca and the type of data included does not seem sufficient to generalize on this topic.

132. *El Amigo de la Verdad*, Mar. 16, 1898, 3, "Noticia de las Escuelas de la Sociedad Católica establecidas en esta Ciudad."

133. *El Amigo de la Verdad*, Jan. 1, 1887, 2, "Conferencia 26—Deberes de los católicos en la lucha actual." Two other schools in Puebla were funded by the conferences of St. Vincent de Paul. *El Amigo de la Verdad*, Jan. 16, 1897, 4, "Enseñanza católica gratuita y beneficiante."

134. There were several, for example, in Zacatlán and at least one each in Tlaxco, Tehuacán, Tezuiltlán, and Tlascala. *El Amigo de la Verdad*, Aug. 10, 1899, 2, "Velada literaria y musical"; *Estadística de la Sociedad Católica*. The Apostolado de la Oración did not usually get involved in supporting schools, but one exception was a girls' school in Tehuacán. *El Tiempo*, Aug. 9, 1887, 2, "Tehuacán. El Apostolado de la Oración."

135. AHAG, Visitas Pastorales; O'Dogherty, "La política," 146. Schmitt, "Catholic Adjustment," 195, uses but does not specifically cite an "educational survey" in 1880 showing that almost half the schools of Guadalajara city were Catholic schools, at least some supported by the Sociedad Católica. And in 1910 the Sociedad Católica de Señoras was still supporting schools in Guadalajara proper and Zapotlán, while the Sociedad Católica de Señores continued to fund the Escuela de Jurisprudencia, founded in the 1870s. AHAG, 1910, Vela Perpetua/Apostolado, Caja 3, Annual report of the Apostolado de la Oración, 40, 105.

136. O'Dogherty, "La política," 147.

137. Torres Septién, *La educación*.

138. See several cases in Chowning, "Culture Wars."

139. A budget for nine schools run by the Sociedad Católica in Puebla in 1892 shows that the average teacher's salary was a generous forty-five pesos a month, with another fifteen pesos a month needed for rent and supplies. *El Amigo de la Verdad*, Jan. 23, 1892, 2, "Remitidos." More typical was the twenty-five pesos a month that the parish priest of Tanhuato, Michoacán, had allocated for his new parochial school, or the parish school in a poor district of Mexico City where teachers were paid sixteen pesos a month and other costs increased the budget to twenty-three pesos. AHAMich, XX, Caja 48, exps. 7 and 8, "Escuelas Católicas del Arzobispado," 1905; AHAM, Labastida, Caja 174, exp. 53, La Santísima Trinidad, Mexico City. Salaries went up over time, and by 1905 one priest in rural Michoacán noted that he would have to pay a teacher twenty-five pesos a month

(not including supplies). AHAMich, XX, Caja 48, exps. 7 and 8, "Escuelas Católicas del Arzobispado," 1905.

140. AHAG, Visitas Pastorales 1879–1885, Teocuitatlán, 1885.

141. AHAMich, XX, Caja 48, exps. 7 and 8, "Escuelas Católicas del Arzobispado," 1905.

142. AHAG, Visitas Pastorales 1879–1885, Tecolotlán, 1881; AHAMich, XIX, Caja 840, exp. 77, Valle de Santiago, 1894.

143. Chowning, "Culture Wars."

144. AHAG, Visitas Pastorales 1879–1885.

145. AHAMich, XIX, Caja 239, exp. 143, Celaya, 1896.

146. AHAMich, XX, Caja 48, exps. 7 and 8, "Escuelas Católicas del Arzobispado," 1905.

147. Curley, "Slouching," 70.

148. Torres Septién, *La educación*, 59–60.

149. See AHAMich, XX, Caja 61, exp. 5, Ynforme del movimiento parroquial desde el cinco de Febrero al seis de junio del corriente año [1902], Ario y Tacámbaro.

150. AHAMex, Alarcón, Caja 102, exp. 59, Libro en donde se encuentran los títulos de los Colegios aprobados por el Centro General de la Congregación del Catecismo. 1899; AHAMex, Alarcón, Caja 89, exp. 41, El párroco con respecto a la Congregación del Catecismo, Tepejí del Río, 1898.

151. AHAMich, XX, Caja 111, exp. 1 (Reglamentos), Reglamento de la Cofradía de la Doctrina Cristiana estab. en la Iglesia del Beaterio, Nov. 25, 1906.

152. AHAG, Gobierno, Cofradías, 1895–1919, Caja 29, exp. Asociaciones Piadosas/Correspondencia del Sr. Obispo 1912–1918, Sumario de las Indulgencias y privilegios, concedidos a la Archicofradía de la Doctrina Cristiana . . . 6 de junio de 1912.

153. AHAMich, XX, Caja 61, exp. 32, Lista de las Señoritas Catequistas socias activas de la Ynstitución de la Doctrina Cristiana en la Parroquia de Tacámbaro.

154. Schmitt, "Catholic Adjustment," 193.

155. AHAMich, XX, Caja 61, exp. 7, Various responses to questionnaire (ca. 1900).

156. AHAMich, XX, Caja 4, exp. 9 (Sagrado Corazón), 1911, Fr. Gabriel M. Soto to Sagrada Mitra. The other funds came from the archbishop (eighty pesos), the parish (thirty), and the parish building fund (twenty). By 1911 enrollments had declined to only three hundred, as the better-off girls dropped out, probably enrolling instead in one of the schools run by religious orders.

157. AHAMich, XX, Caja 48, exps. 7 and 8, "Escuelas Católicas del Arzobispado," 1905.

158. AHAMich, XX, Caja 109, exp. 2 (Apostolado de la Oración), Cuentas, Parroquia of Zacapu, 1905–15.

159. Arrom, *Volunteering*, 149.

160. *La Voz de México*, Apr. 29, 1902, 2, "Sociedad de Obreras Católicas."

161. AHAMich, XX, Caja 48, exps. 7 and 8, "Escuelas Católicas del Arzobispado," 1905.

162. AHAMich, XX, Caja 61, exp. 19, "Informe escrito que el Pbro Nicolas Corona, Cura encargado de la Parroquia de La Piedad . . . 1914."

163. Most historians of education in the Porfiriato have relied on the *Anuario estadístico de la República Mexicana*, published from 1894 to 1907. But while the *Anuario* seems to be fairly reliable about the number of federal, state, and municipal schools, it is incomplete and inconsistent for schools run by the clergy, private schools, and schools run by associations. For example, in 1904 (*Anuario . . . 1904*, 246–47) it lists just four private and church-run schools in Guanajuato, whereas in 1902 (*Anuario . . . 1902*, 192–93) there had been 226 such schools, and in 1905 there were 217 (*Anuario . . . 1905*, 216–17). Schmitt, "Catholic Adjustment," 196, asserts confidently that there were 28 parochial schools in Tabasco, but in 1907 (*Anuario . . . 1907*, 254) the state only reported six church-run schools. There are quite a few instances in which the church-run and private schools are lumped

together (sometimes also including schools run by associations), which makes sense in light of the archival data presented above that suggests that private Catholic schools were quite a bit more numerous than parochial schools. So if you were drawing conclusions from the *Anuarios* about the number of Catholic schools just using the data in the category of "establecimientos sostenidos por el clero," you would be significantly underestimating the presence of Catholic schools.

164. Monsignor Francis Kelley, in his testimony before the US Senate on Mexican affairs in 1920, claimed that official statistics about the number of Catholic schools in Mexico could not be trusted, because "Catholics have been obliged to be very reticent regarding the number of schools they had in Mexico." Where officially there were only 24 Catholic schools in Puebla, he claimed, the real number was 300; in Michoacán officially there were 69, but there were actually 270. US Senate, Kelley testimony, 2679, 2680; *Anuario . . . 1902*; *Anuario . . . 1907*.

165. *Anuario . . . 1894*, 466–67; *Anuario . . . 1905*. Over the same period, Aguascalientes went from 4 schools to 34, and between 1894 and 1907 the number of church schools in Zacatecas increased from 11 to 35. Aguascalientes, according to the 1907 *Anuario*, fell back to 13 but this seems a very large decline in just two years. Michoacán did not report in 1894, but in 1902 it gave the number of church-run schools as 69, which increased to 101 in 1905 before declining to 81 in 1907. *Anuario . . . 1902*; *Anuario . . . 1905*; *Anuario . . . 1907*.

Epilogue

1. A small number of historians (Crespo Reyes, "Entre la filantropía"; Barbosa Guzmán, "El catolicismo social") do draw ties between pre- and post-1910 Catholic women's social action, but not their political actions.

2. Another factor contributing to Mexican Catholic women's politicization, alluded to by a few scholars, mostly quite briefly, is global church policy encouraging a Catholic women's movement based on the image of the "angel of the home." See Crespo Reyes, "Entre la filantropía," 9; Andes, *Mysterious Sofía*, 204–18. On anticlericalism in the revolutionary and post-revolutionary years, see Bantjes, "Mexican Revolutionary"; Bantjes, "Idolatry"; Fallaw, "Varieties"; Curley, "Anticlericalism"; Butler, "*Sotanas*"; Smith, "Anticlericalism"; Blancarte, "Personal"; Bantjes, *As If Jesus*; Becker, *Setting*; Vaughan, *Cultural Politics*; Fallaw, *Religion*.

3. The founders of the Damas were the archbishop of Mexico, José Mora y del Río, and Carlos María Heredia, a Jesuit adviser, appointed by Mora y del Río to found the institution. The reader will recall that the Ladies of Charity were run by the Vincentians and the Sociedad Católica was lay-administered.

4. On the work of the Damas in the early years, see Schell, "Honorable Avocation"; Hanson, "Day of Ideals"; Crespo Reyes, "Entre la filantropía"; O'Dogherty, "Restaurarlo"; Dávila Garibi, *Memoria*.

5. Schell, "Honorable Avocation," 84.

6. Adame Goddard, *El pensamiento*, 236–38. See also the Toluca foundation in 1913 in AHAMex, Mora y del Río, Caja 65, exp. 77, "Con respecto a la Asociación de las Damas Católicas de Toluca. 1913. Bases para establecer." The PCN was one of the parties that was formed in the aftermath of Díaz's surprise 1908 announcement that he would welcome a political opposition. Adame Goddard writes that the Damas's "main task" was to collect funds for Catholic works through a campaign of small donations (the *óbolo católico nacional*), of which half would go to the hierarchy and half to the PCN. The PCN had six hundred centers throughout the country and was therefore thought to be in a good position to spend this money wisely on fomenting the Catholic press, Catholic congresses, Catholic

Workers' Circles, and "in general, all of the projects associated with Social Action." Adame Goddard, *El pensamiento*, 238. The close connection between the PCN and the Damas was epitomized in the fact that the mother and wife of two of the leaders of the PCN served as the presidenta and vicepresidenta of the Damas in Mexico City. Crespo Reyes, "Entre la filantropía," 83.

7. Hanson, "Day of Ideals," 175–77, 188. Méndez Medina, who had published articles on "Feminine Social Action and the Awakening of a People" in mid-1911, believed that women were superior to men in their organizational and administrative skills (citing their patience, tenacity, tact, delicacy, and ability to ingratiate); and he thought they would be better than men at propagandizing "good ideas" and creating "good institutions" like "good" magazines and newspapers, popular libraries, study circles, centers for religious and social instruction, female trade unions, employment agencies, domestic service schools, and consumer leagues.

8. Barbosa Guzmán, "El catolicismo social."

9. Crespo Reyes, "Entre la filantropía," chapter 2.

10. *El País*, Oct. 5, 1912, 4, "La tercera sesión de Damas Católicas Mejicanas." Crespo Reyes, "Entre la filantropía," chapter 2, has excellent detail on the way the organization was structured to reach and recruit more and more women. The division into sections was another similarity between the Damas and the Sociedad Católica, which had also had (similar) sections.

11. *El País*, Mar. 7, 1913, 5, "Una Peregrinación a la Basílica de Guadalupe"; O'Dogherty, "Restaurarlo," 134; AHAMex, Mora y del Río, Caja 65, exp. 77, "Con respecto a la Asociación de las Damas Católicas de Toluca. 1913. Bases para establecer."

12. On the PCN's and church's relationship to the Huerta dictatorship, see García Ugarte, "La Iglesia"; O'Dogherty Madrazo, *De urnas*; González Morfín, "Entre la espada." Meyer, *La cristiada*, 65–68, argues that neither the church nor the PCN were as firmly linked to Huerta as Venustiano Carranza—an old-school liberal in his thinking on the church—and many of the other Constitutionalists such as Adalberto Tejada and Antonio Villarreal, made them out to be.

13. Meyer, *La cristiada*, vol. 2, 68, 95; Hanson, "Day of Ideals," 190–92.

14. On the efforts of President Elena Lascurain de Silva to keep the Mexico City chapter afloat, and the difficulties it endured, see Crespo Reyes, "Entre la filantropía," 90–96.

15. Hanson, "Day of Ideals," 190–91; O'Dogherty, "Restaurarlo," 134; Crespo Reyes, "Entre la filantropía," 105. Crespo Reyes, "Entre la filantropía," 102, adds that between 1917 and 1920 the director of the Damas, Leopoldo Icaza, also traveled to León and Texcoco with the goal of founding new branches of the association, but she does not say that they were founded. How did the Revolution financially affect other lay associations besides the Damas? The scholarship on this question is, to my knowledge, almost totally nonexistent. But we can assume, I think, that all lay associations, both the devotional and the social action ones, had setbacks because of the wars. The report presented to the archbishop in 1920 about the state of the Apostolado de la Oración in the diocese of Guadalajara was full of comments about the negative effects of the Revolution on their operations. In Juchitlán, for example, there were vacancies in the officer corps, meetings were not held, and neither copies of the newsletter "El Mensajero" nor the list of suggested monthly prayers arrived regularly, "all due to the inquietude, alarm and great damage suffered by this hard-working pueblo because of the Revolution." AHAG, Gobierno, Cofradías, Caja 30, 1920–1939, exp. Apostolado de la Oración 1920, Datos presentados al Ilmo. y Rmo. Sr. Arzobispo de Guadalajara . . . tomados de los informes que dieron los Señores Directores de los Centros Locales del Apostolado de la Oración, que tuvieron a bien contestar la Circular que la Dirección Diocesana . . . dirigió a todos los Centros, June 30, 1920.

16. Dávila Garibi, *Colección*, 16, 21, 2, 24, 30, 34, 36, 38, 117. Santa Zita was comprised primarily of female servants, and it was affiliated with the Damas. Boylan, "Mexican Catholic Women's Activism," 216. Initially the written protests were dominated by women; Robert Curley estimated that signatures ran 8:1 in favor of women. Curley points out, however, that official intimidation of men was greater than it was of women, which may account for the bias. Later petitions included more men's signatures than women's. Curley, *Citizens and Believers*, 156, 160.

17. The best analysis of this movement is Curley, *Citizens and Believers*, 149–62.

18. Quoted in Curley, *Citizens and Believers*, 155.

19. There are many references to the need to keep up the symbols of mourning in the various protests collected in Dávila Garibi, *Colección*.

20. See Weis, *For Christ*, for a vivid picture of some members of this generation of Catholic zealots.

21. Schell, "Honorable Avocation," has good comparative information on global Catholic social action.

22. De la Torre, "Los laicos," 419; for Social Catholicism in Chihuahua, see Savarino Roggero, *El conflicto*.

23. Blancarte, "Intransigence," 71.

24. Anticlericalism could take the form of local, state, national, and semi- or non-official anticlericalism (for example, the actions of the state-supported labor confederation, the CROM, or those of the Socialist party). Some examples are given below.

25. The Knights had been established in Mexico in 1905 by American Knights. The Caballeros later became the Unión de Católicos Mexicanos (UCM), in 1929. Other service/charitable organizations, like the Ladies of Charity, that were not supervised directly by the ecclesiastical hierarchy, as well as the multitude of devotional associations, were not a part of the SSM.

26. The SSM also included a new confederation of Catholic workers' unions (the Confederación Nacional Católica del Trabajo), a parents' association (the Asociación Nacional de Padres de Familia), and a confederation of other Catholic lay associations, which seems to have been relatively inactive.

27. Hanson, "Day of Ideals," 407.

28. Hanson, "Day of Ideals," 394.

29. There were also administrative changes. The Damas' name change from the Asociación de Damas Católicas to the Unión de Damas Católicas signified both the consolidation of the Mexico City base as the head of a nationwide organization (the Damas were now a "union" of "associations") and their increased interest in liaising with international Catholic women's movements, which required a national headquarters. On the significance of the name change, see Crespo Reyes, "Entre la filantropía," chapter 3. Another administrative change was abandoning the block-by-block organization in favor of concentrating and organizing the work of the Damas in the parish, where the parish priest could increase his influence over the Damas. Crespo Reyes, "Entre la filantropía," 104.

30. Schell, "Honorable Avocation," 90; Fernández-Aceves, "Political Mobilization," 188–19.

31. Schell, "Honorable Avocation," 84–92; Schell, "Social Catholicism"; Hanson, "Day of Ideals," 407–08; Crespo Reyes and Fuentes, "Bodies and Souls"; Vivaldo Martínez, "La Unión," 103–5, 116–18; O'Dogherty, "Restaurarlo"; Fernández-Aceves, "Political Mobilization"; Crespo Reyes, "Entre la filantropía."

32. On the *chica moderna*, see Hershfield, *Imagining*.

33. See especially Crespo Reyes, "Entre la filantropía." On maternalism, broadly considered, in Mexico and Latin America, see Sanders, "Protecting Mothers"; Lavrin, *Women*;

Pieper-Mooney, *Politics of Motherhood*; Guy, "Politics of Pan-American Cooperation"; Blum, *Domestic Economies*; Mead, "Beneficent Maternalism."

34. Most historians have viewed Obregón as wary of antagonizing Catholics and even somewhat conciliatory; they see most of the anticlerical and anti-Catholic actions as taken by non-state actors. Valenzuela, "Antecedentes"; Meyer, *La cristiada*, vol. 2, 110–61; Hanson, "Day of Ideals," chapter 9; Miller, "Role of Women," 24–29; Fernández-Aceves, "Political Mobilization," 139–56; García Ugarte, "Etapa"; Tapia R-Esparza, "Los festejos." For an argument that there was less conciliation under Obregón than is generally thought, see Savarino Roggero, "La delegación."

35. AGHPEM, MX/16053/Asuntos Religiosos, Caja 2, exp. 33, "Denuncia," Oct. 12, 1920.

36. Romero de Solís, *El aguijón*, 277–78; Nava Hernández, *Isaac Arriaga*. A monument in honor of Arriaga can be seen today at the spot where he was shot.

37. García Alcazar, "El Centro Jalisco," n.p.

38. Savarino Roggero, "Catholics of the North," 22; Savarino Roggero, *El conflicto*, 122.

39. Valenzuela, "Antecedentes," 210–12.

40. Vivaldo Martínez, "La Unión," 113–14.

41. This episode is recounted in Miller, "Role of Women," 41.

42. Osten, *Mexican Revolution's Wake*, 242.

43. Articles 3, 5, 24, 27 and 130.

44. Ortoll, "Catholic Organizations," 3; Butler, "*Sotanas*"; Andes, *Vatican*.

45. Espinosa, *Jesuit*, 41.

46. Crespo Reyes, "Entre la filantropía," 208.

47. Vivaldo Martínez, "La Unión," 146–47.

48. Butler, "Trouble," 156–58.

49. Álvarez Pimentel, "Guerra Fría," paragraph 7.

50. On the Cristero rebellion, see the classic Meyer, *La cristiada*; Vaca, *Los silencios*; Butler, *Popular Piety*; Young, *Mexican Exodus*; González, *Pueblo*; Purnell, *Popular Movements*; Bailey, *Viva Cristo*; Boyer, *Becoming*; Padilla Rangel, *El catolicismo social*; Puente Lutteroth, *Movimiento cristero*.

51. For a relatively recent historiographical analysis of women's roles in the Cristiada, with annotated bibliography, see Vivaldo Martínez, "Las mujeres." For evidence of these activities, see Meyer, *La Cristiada*; Miller, "Role of Women"; Hanson, "Day of Ideals"; Butler, "'Su Hija Inés'"; Butler, *Popular Piety*; Schell, "Gender"; Vivaldo Martínez, "La Unión de Damas"; Vaca, *Los silencios*; Boylan, "Mexican Catholic Women's Activism"; Savarino Roggero, "Catholics of the North."

52. Crespo Reyes, "Entre la filantropía," 222–26.

53. Miller, "Role of Women," 68.

54. Miller, "Role of Women," 71–86.

55. Aspe Armella, *La formación*, 23; Miller, "Role of Women," chapter 5.

56. In exchange the government agreed not to not enforce the anticlerical provisions in the constitution "in a manner hostile to the church."

57. Acción Católica was a global Catholic movement, so the Mexican church was in step with the rest of the Catholic world in setting up the ACM; nonetheless, the timing of the decision to move from an emphasis on Social Catholicism to Catholic action seems to have obeyed Mexican triggers more than transnational ones.

58. In fact, besides the four age/gender groups, the SSM had also included among its main components the Catholic labor confederation and the parents' association; now the ACM's core groups were all age/gender defined.

59. On the new structure of the UFCM, see Crespo Reyes, "Entre la filantropía," 234–35.

60. Other Catholic associations could petition to join the ACM as "confederated" groups, though they had to jump through many hoops to do so, and they received no access to the prestige or leadership roles enjoyed by the core groups. One historian referred to them as the "patitos feos" or "ugly ducklings." The national groups that did choose to affiliate were the Knights of Columbus (Caballeros de Colón), the Unión Nacional de Estudiantes Católicos (UNEC), the Brigadas Femeninas de Santa Juana de Arco; the Legión Mejicana de la Decencia; the Bibliotecas Populares del Sagrado Corazón; the Sociedad EVC ("El Verdadero Catolicismo"); the Scouts de Méjico; the Ladies of Charity; the Guías de México; the Hijas de María Inmaculada de la Medalla Milagrosa; and the Congregaciones Marianas. Torres Septién, "Archivo Histórico," 9. For the ugly duckling comment, see Trasloheros, review of Aspe Armella.

61. Aspe Armella, *La formación*, especially 19–20; Blancarte, *Historia*, 8. Fallaw, *Religion*, gives this contradiction a more intentional spin by arguing that it was the church's strategy to decentralize resistance. Andes, *Vatican*, offers a look at the international organization and its Mexican (and Chilean) branches. See also Barranco V., "Posiciones."

62. Aspe Armella, *La formación*, 20, 273.

63. Archbishop Pascual Díaz, quoted in Aspe Armella, *La formación*, 273. Though historians agree that the aim of the church was to centralize and control the laity, some see laypeople in religious networks as capable of resisting the weakened hierarchy and retaining considerable autonomy, notably Ben Fallaw and Kristina Boylan. Fallaw, *Religion*; Boylan, "Mexican Catholic Women's Activism."

64. Crespo Reyes, "Entre la filantropía," 247–48; De la Torre, "Los laicos," 422; O'Dogherty, "Restaurarlo," 153; Boylan, "Feminine 'Apostolate in Society.'"

65. On education as a battlefield earlier, see also Chowning, "Culture Wars"; Guerra Manzo, *Del fuego*; Vaughan, *State*.

66. In the 1920s, as in the Porfiriato, despite the strong liberal critique of religious schools, the SEP grudgingly tolerated Catholic schools because of the public service they provided. In fact, as Patience Schell has documented, under José Vasconcelos the SEP cooperated with Catholic schools. Schell, *Church*, 94.

67. 1933 Plan Sexenal, quoted in Brown, "Mexican Church-State," 202.

68. Brown, "Mexican Church-State," 202, 203.

69. On the 1930s actions see Cejudo, "Católicas"; Loyo, "Popular," Fallaw, *Religion*; Boylan, "Mexican Catholic Women's Activism"; Hanson, "Day of Ideals"; Piña, "Different."

70. Macías, *Against*, 139.

71. Boylan, "Feminine 'Apostolate in Society,'" 174; Fallaw, *Religion*.

72. Zavala Ramírez, "¿De quién," 176–77. The UPF was founded in 1917 but became particularly active in the 1930s. To my knowledge the archive of the organization has not been exploited; membership demographics might be found there. We do know that all the presidents of the organization were men until 2009. Ornelas Méndez, *Inventario*, 16–17. See also García Alcazar, "El Centro Jalisco."

73. Kloppe-Santamaría, *In the Vortex*, chapter 2; see also Vaughan, *Cultural Politics*; García Alcazar, "El Centro Jalisco"; Raby, *Educación*.

74. Becker, *Setting*, 139.

75. Bantjes, "Idolatry," 118. See also Espinosa, *Jesuit*.

76. Specifically, the state did not retract any articles of the 1917 constitution, but it signaled it would tolerate private schools that taught Catholic doctrine and would allow public displays of religion.

77. The Knights of Columbus took years to renounce armed movements in defense of the church, and an important student organization, the Unión Nacional de Estudiantes Católicos (UNEC), bragged about their rejection of the peace agreements, calling them

"disagreements." On the divide between conciliatory clergy and "combative" clergy, see Romo Aguilar, "Las asociaciones." The most significant dissident Catholic organization was the pacifist (but still intransigent) Unión Nacional Sinarquista (UNS), which was founded in 1937. The origin of the UNS came earlier in the decade. A secret organization founded by Jesuits in 1932, *Los Legiones*, was deemed by some to be more interested in appeasement than in tapping into the passions of ordinary Catholics; it was transformed into the militant *La Base* within a few years, and finally became the UNS. The UNS was a peculiar organization, partly mystical (it envisioned creating a new Christian social order), partly nationalist (and against the *indigenista* version of nationalism in favor of *hispanismo*), partly anti-agrarian reform. By 1938 it had over three hundred fifty thousand members, more than the number of members in the four ACM core groups. On the UNEC, see Aspe Armella, *La formación*. On the UNS and its origins, see Álvarez Pimentel, "Guerra fría"; Ortoll, "Catholic Organizations"; Romo Aguilar, "Las asociaciones"; Campos López, "Movimientos"; Ludlow, "Formación"; Meyer, *El sinarquismo*; González Flores, "Los motivos." The role of women in the UNS has been explicitly studied by a few scholars; see Márquez Sandoval, "Si el hombre"; Rodríguez Bravo, "El sufragio"; Pérez Rosales, "Las mujeres." Another approach to solving the problem of the church's prohibition on political activity came in 1939, with the foundation of a conservative political party, the Partido Acción Nacional (PAN), which represented a "secularized right" but clearly espoused alternatives to revolutionary values and revolutionary nationalism that were recognizably Catholic. There is a vast literature on the PAN, but see especially Loaeza, *El partido*.

78. On continued Catholic violence and *la segunda*, see Kloppe-Santamaría, *In the Vortex*, chapter 2; also see Fallaw, *Religion*.

79. Bantjes, "Idolatry," 119–20.

80. Ortoll, "Catholic Organizations," 135.

81. Loaeza, "La Guerra Fría," location 5380; Pérez Rosales, "Censura," 107–8.

82. Though it is true that the foundation of new lay associations to invigorate the associational landscape was a long-standing strategy and need not have had anything to do with attracting more men.

83. The small amount of research on groups affiliated with the church and the ACM in the postwar era has not taken a gender perspective, to my knowledge, so I have not been able to find out anything about the gender composition of the membership or the changing roles of Catholic women in these organizations, though since the MFC is comprised mainly of couples, we can presume this organization to have had a fairly equal gender balance. All I have been able to glean about the Legion of Decency and the UNPF is that they always seem to have had male officers (in a throwback to the colonial cofradías). The leadership of the MFC, like the membership, was/is comprised of wives and husbands who partnered as officers in the organization. On postwar religious movements and associations, see De la Torre, "Los laicos"; Muro, "Iglesia."

84. On the ACM moralization campaigns, see Sanders, "Women"; Pérez Rosales, "Censura"; Torres Septién, *La educación*; Andes, *Mysterious Sofía*.

85. Rubenstein, *Bad Language*. See also Zolov, *Refried Elvis*.

86. Quoted in Guerra Manzo, *Fuego sagrado*, 294.

87. Blancarte, "Intransigence," 70.

88. From an official publication of the Mexican episcopate, quoted in Barranco V., "Posiciones."

89. On the lay desire for more voice, see Blancarte, "Intransigence," 83. There is a large literature on liberation theology in Latin America, but for a concise treatment see Hughes, "The Catholic Church."

90. This is the view of Loaeza, "La secularización," and De la Torre, "La Iglesia Católica." See also Barranco V., "Posiciones"; Aspe Armella, *La formación*.

91. See Weis, *For Christ*, for example, on "sugar Catholics," women and men who called themselves Catholics but were attracted in the 1920s to the kind of cultural imports (like Hollywood movies) that the Damas and some zealous Catholic men railed against.

92. See, for example, De la Torre, "La Iglesia Católica," who analyzes a 2003 poll suggesting that "subjective secularization" was taking place among Mexican Catholics, including many women, who favored reproductive freedoms and the right to abortion, among other gendered causes.

93. De la Peña and De la Torre, "Religión," 582. Meetings of ACM groups were often devoted to organizing work brigades to make up for the lack of city-supplied services like potable water, garbage collection, and street paving.

94. Pro-Vida is a civil association, technically, but it has the explicit support of the bishops.

95. See Muro, "Iglesia," on the many Catholic or pro-Catholic associations formed between 1970 and 1990, and on the Pro-Vida march, see Muro, "Iglesia," 93. On the 2021 march, see "Convocatoria Nacional a la marca 'Por la mujer y por la vida,'" https://www.cem.org.mx/Slider/831-Convocatoria-Nacional-a-la-marcha--Por-la-mujer-y-por-la-vida.html.

96. Mijangos y González, "La derecha religiosa"; López, "Anuncia sociedad." Also worth noting is the group of lay associations (I have not been able to identify them by name) that in December 2017 organized a "Gran Acto de Reparación, Desagravio y Consagración de la nación mexicana" in the national stadium in Mexico City in the wake of earthquakes that organizers attributed in part to God's wrath against the "evils of our times," abortion, and the "perverse ideology of gender."

97. A list of Guadalupan associations in the archbishopric of Mexico in the period 1901–21 shows that there were at least as many foundations during the decade of Revolution as in the last decade of the Porfiriato. The archbishop of Guadalajara in 1912 and 1913 alone authorized the foundation of ten new Hijas de María associations and fifteen new Vela Perpetuas, along with many other devotional groups, and in 1917 approved a Eucharistic association called "Jardineras del Santísimo," which was said to have made "marvelous progress in just two months" and already had 180 female members and 23 celadoras. AHAMex, Mora y del Río, Caja 39, exp. 19, Request for information about the presence of Asociaciones de Guadalupe, 1901–1921; AHAG, Gobierno, Cofradías, 1895–1919, Caja 29, exp. Asoc. Piadosas/Correspondencia al Sr. Obispo, 1895–1912.

98. In 1935, in the parish of the Sanctuary of Guadalupe in Guadalajara City, besides the four core ACM associations, there were eighteen others, including several that were specifically noted to be "thriving," including the Apostolado, the Corte de Honor de Caballeros, the Corte de Honor de Damas, and the Cruzada de Penitencia. All four ACM groups existed in Ocotlán in the 1930s, but there were also the Apostolado, the Vela, the Hijas de María, and fourteen other pious associations. This pattern held throughout the parishes of the city. In the vicaría of San Vicente all four Acción Católica groups were listed (consisting of some three hundred women in the two women's associations, and forty-four in the two men's associations), but there were also six other associations, most with more members than the social action associations. AHAG, Acta de la Visita Pastoral a la Parroquia del Santuario de Guadalupe de esta ciudad, Dec. 21, 1935; *El Informador*, Sept. 24, 1939, 3, "Principió la Feria de Ocotlán"; AHAG, Acta de la Visita Pastoral a la vicaría de San Vicente, 1935.

99. Boylan, "Mexican Catholic Women's Activism," 303–5. Also see Boylan, "Mexican Catholic Women's Activism," chapter 4, for evidence of the continued strength of these

non–Acción Católica associations in the archbishop of Guadalajara into the 1960s and beyond. Lay associations seem to have remained just as overwhelmingly female as ever. For example, the Apostolado in the archbishopric of Guadalajara in 1920 had five times as many women members as men, and the UNPF in Guerrero in 1932, although it had a male chief, was also dominated by women. AHAG, Gobierno, Cofradías, Caja 30, 1920–1939, exp. Apostolado de la Oración 1920, Datos presentados al Ilmo. y Rmo. Sr. Arzobispo de Guadalajara . . . tomados de los informes que dieron los Señores Directores de los Centros Locales del Apostolado de la Oración, que tuvieron a bien contestar la Circular que la Dirección Diocesana . . . dirigió a todos los Centros, June 30, 1920.

100. Boylan, "Mexican Catholic Women's Activism"; Fallaw, *Religion*, 111, 116.

101. Fernández-Aceves, "Political Mobilization," 363, for example, in a list labeled "women's organizations in Guadalajara during the 1930s," only includes as religious organizations the JCFM and the UFCM.

102. This is probably still substantially the case, though the rise of social media may have begun to bypass lay associations and the parish as essential spaces of political organizing and joining.

103. Some of these strategies for which the hierarchy are given credit are supporting the government's anticommunist and some other postures in the postwar period, beginning to criticize the PRI in the 1960s when others were also doing so, and pushing for constitutional reform in the 1980s that resulted in the 1992 constitutional reform. See Blancarte, "Intransigence"; Butler, "Catholicism"; Loaeza, *La restauración*; Martínez Assad, "La iglesia"; De la Torre, "La Iglesia Católica."

104. The constitutional reform included the right to provide religious instruction in private schools, the right to practice religion in public, and especially recognition of the juridical personality of religious associations and the freedom to organize. Blancarte, "El contexto," 256–57; González Schmal, "La libertad." Though see Butler, "Catholicism," 15–16, who points out that not everything was undone, noting particularly that the exclusively lay character of public education was upheld.

105. De la Torre, "La Iglesia Católica," para. 9.

106. Barranco V. and Blancarte, *AMLO*. The authors are concerned about the blurring of lines between not just the Catholic church and the state but also between evangelicals and the state.

107. On Catholic feminism in Spain and Latin America, see Blasco Herranz, "Género y religión"; Crespo Reyes, "Entre la filantropía"; Espino Armendáriz, "Feminismo"; Kaplan, "Female Consciousness"; Álvarez Pimentel, "Guerra Fría"; Verba, *Catholic Feminism*; Mínguez-Blasco, "Between Virgins." See also a summary of discussions about religious feminism more broadly in De Groot and Morgan, "Beyond the 'Religious Turn'?"

108. Butler, "Jack-in-the-Box Faith," 1361.

BIBLIOGRAPHY

Aceves Ávila, Roberto. *"Que es bueno y útil invocarles": continuidad y cambio en las prácticas y devociones religiosas en Guadalajara, 1771-1900*. Zapopan, Jalisco, Mexico: El Colegio de Jalisco, 2018.
Adame Goddard, Jorge. *El pensamiento político y social de los Católicos mexicanos. 1867-1914*. Mexico City: Universidad Nacional Autónoma de México, 1981.
Aguirre Salvador, Rodrigo. *El mérito y la estrategia: clérigos, juristas y médicos en Nueva España*. Mexico City: Centro de Estudios sobre la Universidad, Universidad Nacional Autónoma de México, Plaza y Valdés, 2003.
Alarcón Menchaca, Laura, Austreberto Martínez Villegas, and Jesús Iván Mora Muro, eds. *Intelectuales católicos: conservadores y tradicionalistas en México y Latinoamérica, 1910-2015*. Guadalajara: El Colegio de Jalisco, 2019.
Álvarez Pimentel, Ricardo José. "Guerra Fría, Guerra Cristera, Guerreras Católicas: el conservadurismo y femenismo católico de la Juventud Católica Femenina Mexicana (JCFM), 1926-1939," Nuevo Mundo/Mundos Nuevos (2017). Online publication. https://journals.openedition.org/nuevomundo/71299.
Amador, Emma. "'Women Ask Relief for Puerto Ricans': Territorial Citizenship, the Social Security Act, and Puerto Rican Communities, 1933-1939." *Labor: Studies in Working Class History of the Americas* 13, no. 3 (Dec. 2016): 105-29.
Anderson, Margaret Lavinia. "The Limits of Secularization: On the Problem of the Catholic Revival in Nineteenth-Century Germany." *Historical Journal* 38, no. 3 (1995): 647-70.
Anderson, Margaret Lavinia. *Practicing Democracy: Elections and Political Culture in Imperial Germany*. Princeton, NJ: Princeton University Press, 2000.
Andes, Stephen J. C. *The Mysterious Sofía: One Woman's Mission to Save Catholicism in Twentieth-Century Mexico*. Lincoln: University of Nebraska Press, 2019.
Andes, Stephen J. C. *The Vatican and Catholic Activism in Mexico and Chile: The Politics of Transnational Catholicism, 1920-1940*. Oxford: Oxford University Press, 2014.
Archdiocese of Michoacán de Ocampo. *Boletín Eclesiástico del Arzobispado de Michoacán*. Morelia, Michoacán, Mexico: Agustín Martínez Mier, 1905; 1906.
Arias de Saavedra, I., and M. L. López Muñoz. *La represión de la religiosidad popular. Crítica y acción contra las cofradías en la España del siglo XVIII*. Granada: Universidad de Granada, 2002.
Arrom, Silvia Marina. *Containing the Poor: The Mexico City Poor House, 1774-1871*. Durham, NC; London: Duke University Press, 2000.
Arrom, Silvia Marina. *La Güera Rodríguez: The Woman and the Legend*. Oakland: University of California Press, 2021.
Arrom, Silvia Marina. "Mexican Laywomen Spearhead a Catholic Revival: The Ladies of Charity, 1863-1910." In *Religious Culture in Modern Mexico*, edited by Martin Austin Nesvig, 50-77. Lanham, MD: Rowman and Littlefield Publishers, 2007.
Arrom, Silvia Marina. *Volunteering for a Cause: Gender, Faith, and Charity in Mexico from the Reform to the Revolution*. Albuquerque: University of New Mexico Press, 2016.
Arrom, Silvia Marina. *The Women of Mexico City, 1790-1857*. Stanford, CA: Stanford University Press, 1985.

Aspe Armella, María Luisa. *La formación social y político de los católicos mexicanos*. Mexico City: Universidad Iberoamericana/Instituto Mexicano de Doctrina Social Cristiana, 2008.

Atkin, Nicholas, and Frank Tallett. *Priests, Prelates and People: A History of European Catholicism since 1750*. Oxford; New York: Oxford University Press, 2003.

Ávila Espinosa, Felipe Arturo. "Una renovada misión: las organizaciones católicas de trabajadores entre 1906 y 1911." Estudios de historia moderna contemporánea, no. 27 (Jan./Jun. 2004): 61–94. http://www.scielo.org.mx/scielo.php?script=sci_arttext&pid=S0185-26202004000100061&lng=en&tlng=en#fn4.

Bailey, David C. *Viva Cristo Rey! The Cristero Rebellion and the Church-State Conflict in Mexico*. Austin: University of Texas Press, 1974.

Baldez, Lisa. *Why Women Protest: Women's Movements in Chile*. New York: Cambridge University Press, 2002.

Bantjes, Adrian A. *As If Jesus Walked on Earth: Cardenismo, Sonora, and the Mexican Revolution*. Wilmington, DE: Scholarly Resources, 1998.

Bantjes, Adrian A. "Idolatry and Iconoclasm in Revolutionary Mexico: The De-Christianization Campaigns, 1929–1940." *Mexican Studies/Estudios mexicanos* 13, no. 1 (Winter 1997): 87–120.

Bantjes, Adrian A. "Mexican Revolutionary Anticlericalism: Concepts and Typologies." *The Americas* 65, no. 4 (Apr. 2009): 467–80.

Barbosa Guzmán, Francisco. "El catolicismo social en la diócesis de Guadalajara, 1891–1926." PhD diss., Universidad Autónoma de México, Iztapalapa, 2004. http://148.206.53.231/tesiuami/UAMI11054.pdf.

Barranco V., Bernardo, and Roberto Blancarte. *AMLO y la religión. El estado laico bajo amenaza*. Mexico City: Grijalba, 2019.

Barranco V., Bernardo. "Posiciones políticas en la historia de la Acción Católica Mexicana." In *El pensamiento social de los católicos mexicanos*, edited by Robert J. Blancarte, 39–70. Mexico City: Fondo de Cultura Económica, 1996.

Bastian, Jean-Pierre. "La lucha por la modernidad religiosa y la secularización de la cultura en México durante el siglo XIX." In *Memoria del I Coloquio Historia de la Iglesia en el siglo XIX*, edited by Manuel Ramos Medina, 423–35. Mexico City: Condumex, 1998.

Bautista García, Cecilia Adriana. *Clérigos virtuosos e instruidos: un proyecto de romanización clerical en un arzobispado mexicano: Michoacán, 1867–1887*. Morelia, Michoacán, Mexico: Universidad Michoacana de San Nicoláas de Hidalgo, Coordinación de la Investigación Científica, 2017.

Bautista García, Cecilia Adriana. *Las disyuntivas del Estado y de la Iglesia en la consolidación del orden liberal, México, 1856–1910*. Mexico City: Colegio de México, Fideicomiso Historia de las Americas, Universidad Michoacana de San Nicolás Hidalgo, 2012.

Bautista García, Cecilia Adriana. "La educación privada en Jacona: una propuesta alterna al proyecto liberal decimonónico." *Estudios Michoacanos*, no. 9 (2001): 75–104.

Bazant, Jan. *Alienation of Church Wealth in Mexico: Social and Economic Aspects of the Liberal Revolution, 1856–1875*. Cambridge, Eng.: Cambridge University Press, 1971.

Bazant, Jan. *Cinco haciendas mexicanos. Tres siglos de vida rural en San Luis Potosí (1600–1910)*. Mexico City: Colegio de México, 1975.

Bazant, Mílada. "A Feisty Woman in Nineteenth-Century Mexico: Laura Méndez de Cuenca (1853–1928)." *Journal of Women's History* 27, no. 1 (Spring 2015): 13–37.

Bazant, Mílada. *Historia de la educación durante el Porfiriato*. Mexico City: Colegio de México, 1993.

Bazarte Martínez, Alicia. *Las cofradías de españoles en la ciudad de México (1526–1860)*. Mexico City: Universidad Autónoma Metropolitana, 1989.

Bazarte Martínez, Alicia, and José Antonio Cruz Rangel. "Santas Escuelas de Cristo en la segunda mitad del siglo XVIII en la Ciudad de México." *Fuentes Humanísticas* vol. 38 (2009): 179–99. http://zaloamati.azc.uam.mx/bitstream/handle/11191/2312/Santas _escuelas%2038_13.pdf?sequence=1.

Bechtloff, Dagmar. *Las cofradías en Michoacán durante la época de la colonia: la religión y su relación política y económica en una sociedad intercultural*. Zinacantepec, Mexico: Colegio de Michoacán, Colegio Mexiquense, 1996.

Becker, Marjorie. *Setting the Virgin on Fire: Lázaro Cardenas, Michoacán Peasants, and the Redemption of the Mexican Revolution*. Berkeley; Los Angeles: University of California Press, 1995.

Belanger, Brian C. "Between the Cloister and the World: The Franciscan Third Order of Colonial Querétaro." *The Americas* 46, no. 2 (Oct. 1992): 157–77.

Belanger, Brian Conal. "Secularization and the Laity in Colonial Mexico: Querétaro, 1598–1821." PhD diss., Tulane University, 1990.

Bilhartz, Terry D. "Sex and the Second Great Awakening: The Feminization of American Religion Reconsidered." In *Belief and Behavior: Essays in the New Religious History*, edited by Philip R. Vendermeer and Robert P. Swierenga, 15–37. New Brunswick, NJ: Rutgers University Press, 1991.

Black, Christopher. *Italian Confraternities in the Sixteenth Century*. Cambridge, Eng.; New York: Cambridge University Press, 1989.

Blancarte, Roberto. "El contexto socio-histórico en el proceso de las reformas constitucionales en materia religiosa." In *Relaciones estado-iglesia: encuentro y desencuentros*, edited by Patricia Galeana de Valadés, 249–58. Mexico City: Secretaría de Gobernación, 2001.

Blancarte, Roberto. *Historia de la iglesia católica en México*. Mexico City: Colegio Mexiquense y Fondo de Cultura Económica, 1992.

Blancarte, Roberto. "Intransigence, Anticommunism, and Reconciliation: Church/State Relations in Transition." In *Dictablanda: Politics, Work, and Culture in Mexico, 1938–1968*, edited by Paul Gillingham and Benjamin T. Smith, 70–88. Durham, NC: Duke University Press, 2014.

Blancarte, Roberto, ed. *El pensamiento social de los católicos mexicanos*. Mexico City: Fondo de Cultura Económica, 1996.

Blancarte, Roberto. "Personal Enemies of God: Anticlericals and Anticlericalism in Revolutionary Mexico, 1915–1940." *The Americas* 65, no. 4 (Apr. 2009): 589–99.

Blaschke, Olaf. "The Unrecognized Piety of Men: Strategies and Success of the Remasculinisation Campaign around 1900." In *Christian Masculinity: Men and Religion in Northern Europe in the Nineteenth and Twentieth Centuries*, edited by Yvonne Maria Werner, 21–46. Leuven: University of Leuven Press, 2011.

Blasco Herranz, Inmaculada. "Género y religión: de la feminización de la religión a la movilización católica femenina. Una revisión crítica." *Historia Social* 53 (2005): 119–36.

Blee, Kathleen M., and Sandra McGee Deutsch, eds. *Women of the Right: Comparisons and Interplay Across Borders*. University Park: Pennsylvania State University Press, 2012.

Blum, Ann. *Domestic Economies: Family, Work, and Welfare in Mexico City, 1884–1943*. Lincoln: University of Nebraska Press, 2009.

Borges, Dain. "Catholic Vanguards in Brazil." In *Local Church, Global Church: Catholic Activism in Latin America from Rerum Novarum to Vatican II*, edited by Stephen J. C. Andes and Julia G. Young, 21–49. Washington, DC: Catholic University of America Press, 2016.

Boyer, Christopher. *Becoming Campesinos: Politics, Identity, and Agrarian Struggle in Post-revolutionary Michoacán, 1920–1935*. Stanford, CA: Stanford University Press, 2003.

Boylan, Anne M. *The Origins of Women's Activism: New York and Boston, 1797–1840*. Chapel Hill; London: University of North Carolina Press, 2002.

Boylan, Kristina A. "The Feminine 'Apostolate in Society' versus the Mexican State: The Unión Femenina Católica Mexicana, 1929–1940." In *Right-Wing Women: From Conservatives to Extremists Around the Globe*, edited by Paola Bacchetta and Margaret Power, 169–82. New York: Routledge, 2002.

Boylan, Kristina A. "Gendering the Faith and Altering the Nation: The Unión Femenina Católica Mexicana and Women's Revolutionary and Religious Experiences." In *Sex in Revolution: Gender, Politics, and Power in Modern Mexico*, edited by Gabriela Cano, Jocelyn Olcott, and Mary Kay Vaughan, 199–222. Durham, NC: Duke University Press, 2006.

Boylan, Kristina A. "Mexican Catholic Women's Activism, 1929–1940." PhD diss., University of Oxford, 2000.

Brading, D. A. *Church and State in Bourbon Mexico: The Diocese of Michoacán 1749–1810*. Cambridge, Eng.: Cambridge University Press, 1994.

Brading, D. A. *Haciendas and Ranchos in the Mexican Bajío: León, 1700–1860*. Cambridge, Eng.: Cambridge University Press, 1978.

Brading, D. A. *Mexican Phoenix: Our Lady of Guadalupe: Image and Tradition Across Five Centuries*. Cambridge, Eng.: Cambridge University Press, 2001.

Braude, Ann. "Women's History *Is* American Religious History." In *Retelling U.S. Religious History*, edited by Thomas A. Tweed, 87–107. Berkeley: University of California, 1997.

Brooks, Francis Joseph. "Parish and Cofradía in Eighteenth-Century Mexico." PhD diss., Princeton University, 1976.

Brown, Lyle C. "Mexican Church-State Relations, 1933–1940." *Journal of Church and State* 6, no. 2 (Spring 1964): 202–22.

Butler, Jon. "Jack-in-the-Box Faith: The Religion Problem in Modern American History." *Journal of American History* 90, no. 4 (Mar. 2004): 1357–78.

Butler, Matthew. "Catholicism in Mexico, 1910 to the present." In *Oxford Research Encyclopedia of Religion*, edited by William H. Beezley, published online Nov. 22, 2016. https://oxfordre-com.libproxy.berkeley.edu/latinamericanhistory/view/10.1093/acrefore/9780199366439.001.0001/acrefore-9780199366439-e-23?rskey=UE29I8&result=2.

Butler, Matthew. "Eucharistic Angels: Mexico's Nocturnal Adoration and the Masculinization of Postrevolutionary Catholicism, 1910–1930." In *Local Church, Global Church: Catholic Activism in Latin America from Rerum Novarum to Vatican II*, edited by Stephen J. C. Andes and Julia G. Young, 53–90. Washington, DC: Catholic University Press, 2016.

Butler, Matthew. *Popular Piety and Political Identity in Mexico's Cristero Rebellion: Michoacán, 1927–29*. Oxford, Eng.; New York: Oxford University Press, 2004.

Butler, Matthew. "*Sotanas Rojinegras*: Catholic Anticlericalism and Mexico's Revolutionary Schism." *The Americas* 65, no. 4 (Apr. 2009): 535–58.

Butler, Matthew. "'Su Hija Inés': Católicas laicas, el Obispo Luis María Martínez, y el conflicto religioso michoacano, 1927–1929." *Historia Mexicana* 67, no. 4 (Apr.–Jun. 2018): 1249–93.

Butler, Matthew. "Trouble Afoot? Pilgrimage in Cristero Mexico City." In *Faith and Impiety in Revolutionary Mexico*, edited by Matthew Butler, 149–66. New York: Palgrave Macmillan, 2007.

Caffiero, Marina. "From the Late Baroque Mystical Explosion to the Social Apostolate, 1650–1850." In *Women and Faith: Catholic Religious Life in Italy from Late Antiquity to the Present*, edited by Lucetta Scaraffia and Gabriella Zarri, 176–204. Cambridge, MA: Harvard University Press, 1999.

Callahan, William J. *Church, Politics, and Society in Spain, 1750–1874*. Cambridge, MA: Harvard University Press, 1984.

Callahan, William. "Confraternities and Brotherhoods in Spain, 1500–1800." *Confraternitas* 12, no. 1 (Spring 2001): 17–25.

Camacho Pérez, Fidel. "La iglesia católica en Nuevo León: Sociedades católicas y oposición ante liberalismo y anticlericalismo (1872–1874)." *Humanitas Digital* num. 42 (Mar. 2015), 221–40. https://humanitas.uanl.mx/index.php/ah/article/view/11.

Campos López, Xochitl Patricia. "Movimientos de la derecha religiosa mexicana." *El Cotidiano*, no. 185 (May-Jun. 2014): 33–45. https://www.redalyc.org/articulo.oa?id=32530725004.

Cañedo Gamboa, Sergio Alejandro. "Merchants and Family Business in San Luis Potosí: The Signs of an Economic Upsurge, 1820–1846." PhD diss., University of California at San Diego, 2011.

Cano, Gabriela. *Se llamaba Elena Arizmendi*. Mexico City: Tusquets, 2010.

Carbajal López, David. "Devoción, utilidad y distinción. La reforma de las cofradías novohispanas y el culto del Santísimo Sacramento, 1750–1820." *Hispania Sacra*, 68, no. 137 (Jan.-Jun. 2016): 377–89.

Carbajal López, David. "Mujeres y reforma de cofradías en Nueva España y Sevilla, ca. 1750–1830." *Estudios de Historia Novohispana* 5 (Jul.-Dec. 2016): 64–79, http://www.sciencedirect.com/science/article/pii/S1870906016300048#fn0450.

Carey Jr., David. *I Ask for Justice: Maya Women, Dictators, and Crime in Guatemala, 1898–1944*. Austin: University of Texas Press, 2014.

Carner, Françoise. "Estereotipos femeninos en el siglo XIX." In *Presencia y transparencia: La mujer en la historia de México*, edited by Carmen Ramos Escandón, 95–110. Mexico City: Colegio de México, 1987.

Carpenter, Daniel. *Democracy by Petition: Popular Politics in Tranformation, 1790–1870*. Cambridge, MA: Harvard University Press, 2021.

Casagrande, Giovanna. "Confraternities and Lay Female Religiosity in Late Medieval and Renaissance Umbria." In *The Politics of Ritual Kinship: Confraternities and Social Order in Early Modern Italy*, edited by Nicholas Terpstra, 48–66. Cambridge, Eng.: Cambridge University Press, 2000.

The Catholic Encyclopedia, http://www.newadvent.org/cathen/03659d.htm.

Ceballos Ramírez, Manuel. *El catolicismo social: un tercero en discordia, Rerum Novarum, la cuestión social" y la movilización de los católicos mexicanos (1891–1911)*. Mexico City: Colegio de México, 1991.

Ceballos Ramírez, Manuel. "La encíclica Rerum Novarum y los trabajadores católicos en la Ciudad de México (1891–1913)." *Historia Mexicana* 33, no. 1 (Jul.-Sept. 1983): 151–70.

Ceballos Ramírez, Manuel. "Rerum Novarum en México: cuarenta años entre la conciliación y la intransigencia (1891–1931)." *Revista mexicana de sociología* 49, no. 3 (Jul.-Sept. 1987): 151–70.

Cejudo, Elizabeth. "Católicas y Ciudadanas: Mujeres laicas organizadas contra la campaña desfanatizadora de Sonora (1932–1939)." PhD diss., Universidad Nacional Autónoma de México, 2019.

Chance, John K., and William B. Taylor, "Cofradías and cargos: an historical perspective on the Mesoamerican civil-religious hierarchy." *American Ethnologist* 12, no. 1 (Feb. 1985): 1–26.

Chávez, Gabino. *La bandera de la pureza al fin del siglo. Ojeada sobre la Asociación de las Hijas de María Inmaculada, su origen e institución, su naturaleza y desarrollo, su incremento e influencia social*. Mexico, Imp. J. de Elizalde, 1900. https://babel.hathitrust.org/cgi/pt?id=txu.059172017759640;view=1up;seq=85.

Chowning, Margaret. "The Catholic Church and the Ladies of the Vela Perpetua: Gender and Devotional Change in Nineteenth-Century Mexico." *Past & Present* 221 (Nov. 2013): 197–237.

Chowning, Margaret. "The Contours of the Post-1810 Depression in Mexico: A Reappraisal from a Regional Perspective." *Latin American Research Review* 27, no. 2 (Spring 1992): 119–50.

Chowning, Margaret. "Culture Wars in the Trenches? Public Schools and Catholic Education (1867–1897)." *Hispanic American Historical Review* 97, no. 4 (Nov. 2017), 613–49.

Chowning, Margaret. "La feminización de la piedad en Mexico: género y piedad en las cofradías de españoles. Tendencias coloniales y pos-coloniales en los arzobispados de Mexico, Michoacán, y Guadalajara." In *Religión, identidad, y política en México en la época de la independencia*, edited by Brian Connaughton, 475–514. Mexico City: Universidad Autónoma Metropolitana, 2010.

Chowning, Margaret. "The Management of Church Property in Michoacán, Mexico, 1810–1856: Economic Motivations and Political Implications." *Journal of Latin American Studies* 22, no. 3 (Oct. 1990): 459–96.

Chowning, Margaret. "Reassessing the Prospects for Profit and Productivity in Nineteenth-Century Mexico." In *How Latin America Fell Behind: Essays on the Economic Histories of Brazil and Mexico, 1800–1914*, edited by Stephen H. Haber, 179–215. Stanford, CA: Stanford University Press, 1997.

Chowning, Margaret. *Rebellious Nuns: The Troubled History of a Mexican Convent, 1752–1863*. New York: Oxford University Press, 2006.

Chowning, Margaret. "Talking Back: Nuns, *Beatas*, and *Colegialas* Invoke Rights and Constitutional Principles in Late Colonial and Early Nineteenth-Century Mexico." *Colonial Latin American Review* 29, no. 1 (Feb. 2020): 115–38.

Chowning, Margaret. *Wealth and Power in Provincial Mexico: Michoacán from the Late Colony to the Revolution*. Stanford, CA: Stanford University Press, 1999.

Clark, Christopher, and Wolfram Kaiser, eds. *Culture Wars: Secular-Catholic Conflict in Nineteenth-Century Europe*. Cambridge, Eng.: Cambridge University Press, 2003.

Clark, Emily. "'By All the Conduct of Their Lives': A Laywomen's Confraternity in New Orleans, 1730–1744." *William and Mary Quarterly* 54, no. 4 (Oct. 1997): 769–94.

Clarke, Brian. "The Parish and the Hearth: Women's Confraternities and the Devotional Revolution among the Irish Catholics of Toronto, 1850–85." In *Creed and Culture: The Place of English-Speaking Catholics in Canadian Society, 1750–1930*, edited by Terrence Murphy and Gerald Stortz, 185–203. Montreal; Kingston; London; Buffalo: McGill-Queens University Press, 1993.

Clarke, Brian. *Piety and Nationalism: Lay Voluntary Associations and the Creation of an Irish-Catholic Community in Toronto, 1850–90*. Montreal: McGill-Queen's University Press, 1993.

Coburn, Carol. *Spirited Lives: How Nuns Shaped Catholic Culture and American Life, 1836–1920*. Chapel Hill: University of North Carolina Press, 1999.

Congregación Hijas de María Inmaculada de Guadalupe. Proceso de canonización del Siervo de Dios J. Antonio Plancarte y Labastida. Unpublished document, typewritten in Mexico City in 1992. Consulted at the Colegio de Michoacán.

Connaughton, Brian. "El cura párroco al arribo del siglo XIX: el interlocutor interpelado." In *El historiador frente a la historia: religión y vida cotidiana*, edited by Alicia Mayer and José Rubén Romero Galván, 189–214. Mexico City: Universidad Nacional Autónoma de México, 2008.

Connaughton, Brian. *Ideología y sociedad en Guadalajara (1788–1853)*. Mexico City: Consejo Nacional para la Cultura y las Artes, 1992.

Connaughton, Brian. "La religiosidad de los liberales: Francisco Zarco y el acicate de la economía política." In *Presencia internacional de Juárez*, edited by Patricia Galeana de Valadés and Miguel León Portilla, 69–84. Mexico City: Centro de Estudios de Historia de México Carso-Condumex; Asociación de Estudios sobre la Reform, la Intervención Francesa y el Segundo Imperio, 2008.

Constituciones de la Congregación y Santa Escuela de Cristo, fundada bajo del Patrocinio de la Santísima Vírgen María Nuestra Señora, y del glorioso S. Felipe Neri. Mexico City, Imprenta de Luis Abadiano y Veldés, 1836.

Constituciones de la real congregación del alumbrado y vela continua al Santísimo Sacramento reservado en los santos sagrarios: fundada en Madrid el año de 1789 por los reyes nuestros señores, y establecida ahora en la Santa Iglesia Catedral de la Capital de Buenos-Ayres, con algunas adiciones respectivas, y análogas al espíritu de tan piadoso instituto. Buenos Aires: Real Imprenta de Niños Expositos, 1799.

Constituciones de la real congregación del alumbrado y vela al SS. sacramento del altare: establ. en la capilla del real palacio desde etc. 1789. Madrid: Imprenta real, 1790. http://bibliotecavirtualmadrid.org/bvmadrid_publicacion/i18n/catalogo_imagenes/grupo.cmd?path=1035309.

Cortés Guerrero, José David. "'Viva la religión y mueran sus enemigos': Oposición a la tolerancia religiosa en México a mediados del siglo XIX." *Anuario Colombiano de Historia Social y de la Cultura* 33 (2006): 209–46.

Cott, Nancy. *The Bonds of Womanhood: "Women's Sphere" in New England, 1780-1835.* New Haven, CT: Yale University Press, 1977.

Cott, Nancy. *The Grounding of Modern Feminism.* New Haven, CT: Yale University Press, 1987.

Cowan, Benjamin A. *Securing Sex: Morality and Repression in the Making of Cold War Brazil.* Chapel Hill: University of North Carolina Press, 2016.

Cox, Karen L. *Dixie's Daughters: The United Daughters of the Confederacy and the Preservation of Confederate Culture.* Gainesville: University Press of Florida, 2003.

Crespo Reyes, Sofía. "Entre la filantropía y la Práctica Política. La Unión de Damas Católicas Mexicanas en la Ciudad de México (1860-1930)." PhD diss., Instituto Mora, 2016.

Crespo Reyes, Sofía, and Pamela J. Fuentes. "Bodies and Souls: A Fight Between the Revolutionary State and Catholic Women Over the Sexuality of Prostitutes in the 1920s." *Mexican Studies/Estudios mexicanos* 36, no. 1/2 (Summer 2020): 243–69.

Curley, Robert. "Anticlericalism and Public Space in Revolutionary Jalisco." *The Americas* 65, no. 4 (Apr. 2009): 511–33.

Curley, Robert. *Citizens and Believers: Religion and Politics in Revolutionary Jalisco, 1900-1930.* Albuquerque: University of New Mexico Press, 2018.

Curley, Robert. "Slouching towards Bethlehem: Catholics and the Political Sphere in Revolutionary Mexico." PhD diss., University of Chicago, 2001.

Curley, Robert. "Sociólogos peregrinos: Teoría social católica en el fin-de-régimen porfiriano." In *Catolicismo social en México.* Vol. 1: *Teoría, fuentes e historiografía*, edited by Manuel Ceballos Ramírez and Alejandro Garza Rangel. Monterrey, Mexico: Academia de Investigación Humanística, 2000.

Curley, Robert, and Jorge Omar Mota. "Catholicismo cívico, reforma liberal y política moderna en el Jalisco rural, 1867-1890." *Historia Mexicana* 71, no. 2 (Oct.-Dec. 2021): 851–97.

Davidoff, Leonore, and Catherine Hall. *Family Fortunes: Men and Women of the English Middle Class, 1780-1850.* Chicago: University of Chicago Press, 1987.

Dávila Garibi, J. Ignacio. *Colección de documentos relativos a la cuestión religiosa en Jalisco*, vol. 2. Guadalajara: Imprenta J. M. Yguiniz, 1920.

Dávila Garibi, J. Ignacio. *Memoria histórica de las labores de la Asociación de Damas Católicas.* Guadalajara: Tipografía, Litografía y Encuadernación J. M. Iguíniz, 1920.

Davis, Natalie Zemon. "City Women and Religious Change in Sixteenth-Century France." In *Society and Culture in Early Modern France*, edited by Natalie Zemon Davis, 65–96. Stanford, CA: Stanford University Press, 1975.

De Grazia, Victoria. *How Fascism Ruled Women: Italy, 1922–1945*. Berkeley: University of California Press, 1992.

De Groot, Joanna, and Sue Morgan. "Beyond the 'Religious Turn'? Past, Present and Future Perspectives in Gender History." *Gender & History* 25, no. 3 (Nov. 2013): 395–422.

De la Flor, Fernando R. "Pantalla total: La casa de ejercicios espirituales como *locus* del imaginario Jesuítico." In *Emblemática trascendente: hermenéutica de la imagen, iconología del texto*, edited by Rafael Zafra Molina and José Javier Azanza López, 719–30. Pamplona: Universidad de Navarra, 2011.

De la Peña, Guillermo, and Renée de la Torre. "Religión y política en los barrios populares de Guadalajara." *Estudios sociológicos* 8, no. 24 (1990): 571–602.

De la Torre, Renée. "La Iglesia Católica en el México contemporáneo: Resultados de una prueba de contraste entre jerarquía y creyentes." *L'Ordinaire des Amériques* [online] 210 (2008). http://journals.openedition.org/orda/2616.

De la Torre, Renée. "Los laicos en la historia de las relaciones iglesia-estado en México durante el siglo XX." *Anuario del Instituto de Estudios Históricos y Sociales* 24 (2009): 417–44.

Del Raso, José Antonio. *Notas estadísticas del departamento de Querétaro*. Mexico City: J. Mariano Lara, 1848.

Delgado, Jessica L. *Laywomen and the Making of Colonial Catholicism in New Spain, 1630–1790*. Cambridge, Eng.: Cambridge University Press, 2018.

Desan, Suzanne. *Reclaiming the Sacred: Lay Religion and Popular Politics in Revolutionary France*. Ithaca, NY; London: Cornell University Press, 1990.

Deutsch, Sandra McGee. "Gender and Sociopolitical Change in Twentieth-Century Latin America." *Hispanic American Historical Review* 71, no. 2 (May 1991): 259–306.

Deutsch, Sandra McGee. "Spartan Mothers: Fascist Women in Brazil in the 1930s." In *Right-Wing Women: From Conservatives to Extremists Around the World*, edited by Paola Bachetta and Margaret Power, 155–68. New York: Routledge, 2002.

Devoción que practican las hermanas de la Vela Perpetua de la ciudad de Guaymas. Guaymas, Sonora, Mexico: Imprenta de R. J. Taboada, 1874.

Dewald, Jonathan, ed. *Europe, 1450–1789: Encyclopedia of the Early Modern Era*. Scribner's, 2004, entry on "confraternities."

Díaz Patiño, Gabriela. "El catolicismo social en la arquidiócesis de Morelia, Michoacán (1897–1913)." *Tzintzun. Revista de Estudios Históricos* 38 (2003): 97–160.

Díaz Patiño, Gabriela. *Católicos, liberales y protestantes: el debate por las imágenes religiosas en la formación de una cultura nacional (1848–1908)*. Mexico City: Colegio de México, 2016.

Diefendorf, Barbara B. *From Penitence to Charity: Pious Women and the Catholic Reformation in Paris*. Oxford; New York: Oxford University Press, 2004.

Dinan, Susan Eileen. "Confraternities as a Venue for Female Activism During the Catholic Reformation." In *Confraternities and Catholic Reform in Italy, France, and Spain*, edited by John Patrick Donnelly and Michael W. Maher, 191–214. Sixteenth Century Essays & Studies, Vol. 44. Kirksville, MO: Thomas Jefferson University Press, 1999.

De Dios, Vicente. "Fundación de la Congregación de la Misión en México." 1993. http://vincentians.com/es/fundacion-de-la-congregacion-de-la-mision-en-mexico/.

De Dios, Vicente. *Historia de la familia vincentina en México, 1844–1994*. 2 vols. Salamanca: Editorial CEME, 1993.

Dirección General de Estadística. *Censo General de la República Mexicana 1900*. https://www.inegi.org.mx/programas/ccpv/1900/.

Douglas, Ann. *The Feminization of American Culture*. New York: Knopf, 1977.
Duch Plana, Montserrat. "Mundo, Demonio y Carne. Proceso de secularización, feminización de la religión y sociabilismo católico en la diócesis de Tarragona." *Feminismo/s* 28 (Dec. 2016): 269–92.
Dumas, Claude. "El discurso de oposición en la prensa clerical conservadora de México en la época de Porfirio Díaz (1876–1910)." *Historia Mexicana* 39, no. 1 (Jul./Sept. 1989): 243–56.
Dunn, Mary Maples. "Saints and Sisters: Congregational and Quaker Women in the Early Colonial Period." *American Quarterly* 30, no. 5 (1978): 582–601.
Edwards, Lisa M. "Messages Sent, Messages Received? The Papacy and the Latin American Church at the Turn of the Twentieth Century." In *Local Church, Global Church: Catholic Activism in Latin America from Rerum Novarum to Vatican II*, edited by Stephen J. C. Andes and Julia G. Young, 3–20. Washington, DC: Catholic University Press, 2016.
Edwards, Lisa M. *Roman Virtues: The Education of Latin American Clergy in Rome, 1858–1962*. New York: Peter Lang, 2011.
Ehrick, Christine. *The Shield of the Weak: Feminism and the State in Uruguay, 1903–1933*. Albuquerque: University of New Mexico Press, 2005.
Eire, Carlos. *From Madrid to Purgatory: The Art and Craft of Dying in Sixteenth-Century Spain*. Cambridge; New York: Cambridge University Press, 1995.
El Propagador de la devoción al señor S. José y la Sagrada Familia. Boletín destinado principalmente a propagar el culto del santísimo patriarca conteniendo además el Sacerdocio católico. Mexico City: Tip. Religiosa de M. Tornier y Cía., 1875.
Enders, Victoria L. "'And We Ate Up the World': Memories of the *Sección Femenina*." In *Right-Wing Women: From Conservatives to Extremists Around the World*, edited by Paola Bacchetta and Margaret Power, 85–99. New York: Routledge, 2002.
Espino Armendáriz, Saúl. "Feminismo católico en México: la historia del CIDHAL y sus redes transnacionales (c. 1960–1990)." PhD diss., Colegio de México, 2019.
Espinosa, David. *Jesuit Student Groups, the Universidad Iberoamericana, and Political Resistance in Mexico, 1913–1979*. Albuquerque: University of New Mexico Press, 2014.
Estadística de la Sociedad Católica de Señoras hasta el día 2 de febrero de 1874. Mexico City: Imprenta de José Mariano Fernández de Lara, 1874. https://play.google.com/books/reader?id=7gI5AQAAMAAJ&printsec=frontcover&output=reader&hl=en&pg=GBS.PA1.
Falcón, Romana. "El arte de la petición: Rituales de obediencia y negociación, México, segnda mitad del siglo XIX." *Hispanic American Historical Review* 86, no. 3 (Aug. 2006): 467–500.
Fallaw, Ben. *Religion and State Formation in Postrevolutionary Mexico*. Durham, NC: Duke University Press, 2013.
Fallaw, Ben. "Varieties of Mexican Revolutionary Anticlericalism: Radicalism, Iconoclasm, and Otherwise, 1914–1935." *The Americas* 65, no. 4 (Apr. 2009): 481–509.
Farriss, Nancy M. *Maya Society under Colonial Rule: The Collective Enterprise of Survival*. Princeton, NJ: Princeton University Press, 1992.
Fenning, Hugh. *The Undoing of the Friars of Ireland: A Study of the Novitiate Question in the Eighteenth Century*. Louvain: Publications universitaíres de Louvain, 1972.
Fernández-Aceves, María Teresa. "The Political Mobilization of Women in Revolutionary Guadalajara, 1910–1940." PhD diss., University of Illinois at Chicago, 2000.
Fernández-Aceves, María Teresa. "La lucha por el sufragio femenino en Jalisco, 1910–1958." *Revista de Estudios de Género. La Ventana* 2, no. 19 (Jun. 2004): 131–51.
Finchelstein, Federico. *The Ideological Origins of the Dirty War: Fascism, Populism, and Dictatorship in Twentieth Century Argentina*. Oxford, Eng.; New York: Oxford University Press, 2014.

Fletcher, Holly Berkley. *Gender and the American Temperance Movement of the Nineteenth Century*. New York: Routledge, 2008.
Flynn, Maureen. "Rituals of Solidarity in Castilian Confraternities." *Renaissance and Reformation/Renaissance et Réforme* 13, no. 1 (1989): 53–68.
Ford, Caroline. *Divided Houses: Religion and Gender in Modern France*. Ithaca, NY; London: Cornell University Press, 2005.
Forment, Carlos. *Democracy in Latin America, 1760–1900: Civic Selfhood and Public Life in Mexico and Peru*. Chicago: University of Chicago Press, 2003.
Fowler, Will. *The Pronunciamiento in Independent Mexico, 1821–1876*. Online database. https://arts.st-andrews.ac.uk/pronunciamientos/index.php.
Fowler, William R., and Humberto Morales Moreno, eds. *El conservadurismo mexicano en el siglo XIX*. Puebla: Universidad Autónoma de Puebla, 1999.
Franco, Jean. *Plotting Women: Gender and Representation in Mexico*. New York: Columbia University Press, 1989.
Freedman, Estelle. "Separatism as Strategy: Female Institution Building and American Feminism, 1870–1930." *Feminist Studies* 5, no. 3 (Fall 1979): 512–29.
French, John D., with Mary Lynn Pedersen Cluff. "Women and Working-Class Mobilization in Postwar São Paulo, 1945–1945." In *The Gendered Worlds of Latin American Women Workers: From Household and Factory to the Union Hall and Ballot Box*, edited by John D. French and Daniel James, 176–207. Durham, NC: Duke University Press, 1997.
Fuchs, Rachel G., and Victoria E. Thompson. *Women in Nineteenth-Century Europe*. New York; Hampshire, Eng.: Palgrave Macmillan, 2005.
Galeana de Valadés, Patricia. *Historia de las mujeres en México*. Mexico City: Instituto Nacional de Estudios Históricos de las Revoluciones de México, 2015.
Galeana de Valadés, Patricia. *Las relaciones estado-iglesia durante el segundo imperio*. Mexico City: Siglo XXI, 2015 [1991].
Galeana de Valadés, Patricia. *La revolución de las mujeres en México*. Mexico City: Instituto Nacional de Estudios Históricos de las Revoluciones de México, 2016.
García Alcaraz, Agustín, *La cuna de la independencia*. Morelia, Michoacán: Fimax, 1971.
García Alcazar, María Guadalupe. "El Centro Jalisco de la Unión Nacional de Padres de Familia (UNPF), 1917–1965." *Revista Mexicana de Investigación Educativa* 1, no. 2 (1996): n.p. https://www.redalyc.org/pdf/140/14000211.pdf.
García Ayluardo, Clara. "Ceremonia y cofradía: la Ciudad de México durante el siglo XVIII." In *Identidad y prácticas de los grupos de poder en México, siglos XVII-XIX*, edited by Rosa María Meyer Cosío. Mexico City: Instituto Nacional de Antropología e Historia, 1999.
García Ayluardo, Clara. "Confraternity, Cult, and Crown in Colonial Mexico City: 1700–1810." PhD diss., Cambridge University, 1989.
García Ayluardo, Clara. *De tesoreros y tesoros: la administración financiera e intervención de las cofradías novoespañas*. Mexico City: CIDE, 2002.
García Ugarte, Marta Eugenia. "Etapa de intransigencias: disputa por el espacio social." In *Estado, iglesia y sociedad en México, siglo XIX*, edited by Alvaro Matute, Evelia Trejo, and Brian Connaughton, 399–425. Mexico City: Facultad de Filosofía y Letras, Universidad Nacional Autónoma de México, Group Editorial M.A. Porrúa, 1995.
García Ugarte, Marta Eugenia. "La Iglesia y la formación del Partido Católico Nacional en México: distinción conceptual y práctica entre católico y conservador, 1902–1914." *Lusitania Sacra* 30 (Jul./Dec. 2014): 15–52.
García Ugarte, Marta Eugenia. *Poder político y religioso: México, siglo XIX*, 2 vols. Mexico City: Miguel Ángel Porrúa/Universidad Nacional Autónoma de México, 2010.

Gavala González, Juan. "The Original Statutes of the Ancient and Royal Brotherhood of Our Lady Saint Anne in Dos Hermanas, Spain: Introduction." *Confraternitas* 24, no. 1 (Spring 2013): 3–6.

Gilbert, David Allen. "'Long Live the True Religion!'": Contesting the Meaning of Catholicism in the Mexican Reforma (1855–1860)." PhD diss., University of Iowa, 2003.

Gilmore, Glenda. *Gender and Jim Crow: Women and the Politics of White Supremacy in North Carolina, 1896–1920.* Chapel Hill: University of North Carolina Press, 1996.

González Flores, José Gustavo. "Los motivos del sinarquista. La organización y la ideología de la Unión Nacional Sinarquista." *Culturales* 3, no. 1 (Jan./Jun. 2015): 49–76. Online version: http://www.scielo.org.mx/scielo.php?script=sci_arttext&pid=S1870-11912015000100002.

González y González, Luis. *Pueblo en vilo: microhistoria de San José de Gracia.* Mexico City: El Colegio de México, 1968.

González y González, Luis, Emma Cosío Villegas, and Guadalupe Monroy. *Historia moderna de México: la república restaurada: la vida social.* Mexico City: Hermes, 1956.

González Jiménez, Rosa María. "The Normal School for Women and Liberal Feminism in Mexico City, Late Nineteenth and Early Twentieth Century." *Resources for Feminist Research* 34, no. 1–2 (Spring/Summer 2012): 33–55. *Gale Literature Resource Center*, https://link-gale-com.libproxy.berkeley.edu/apps/doc/A349721093/LitRC?u=ucberkeley&sid=LitRC&xid=3a3f9147.

González Morfín, Juan. "Entre la espada y la pared: el Partido Católico Nacional en la época de Huerta." *Anuario de historia de la Iglesia* 21, no. 21 (2012): 387–99.

González Schmal, Raúl. "La libertad religiosa como principio regulador de las relaciones Estado-Iglesia." In *Relaciones estado-iglesia: encuentro y desencuentros*, edited by Patricia Galeana de Valadés. Mexico City: Secretaría de Gobernación, 269–81.

Guerra Manzo, Enrique. *Del fuego sagrado a la Acción Cívica: los católicos frente al Estado en Michoacán (1920–1940).* Zamora; Mexico City: El Colegio de Michoacán, 2015.

Guevara Sanginés, María. *Guanajuato diverso: sabores y sinsabores de su ser mestizo (siglos XVI a XVII).* Guanajuato, México: Ediciones La Rana, 2001.

Greenleaf, Richard E. "The Inquisition Brotherhood: Cofradía de San Pedro Mártir of Colonial Mexico." *The Americas* 40, no. 2 (1982): 171–207.

Griffith, R. Marie. *God's Daughters: Evangelical Women and the Power of Submission.* Berkeley: University of California Press, 1997.

Griffith, R. Marie. *Moral Combat: How Sex Divided American Christians and Fractured American Politics.* New York: Basic Books, 2017.

Grosso, Juan Carlos. "Producción e intercambio en el centro de México. San Juan de los Llanos, 1780–1840." *Siglo XIX, Siglo XIX/Monterrey* 3, no. 8 (Jan./Apr. 1994): 7–44.

Gruzinski, Serge. "Indian Confraternities, Brotherhoods and *Mayordomías* in Central New Spain." In *The Indian Community of Colonial Mexico*, edited by Arij Ouweneel and Simon Miller, 203–21. Amsterdam: CEDLA, 1990.

Guardino, Peter. *The Time of Liberty: Popular Political Culture in Oaxaca, 1750–1850.* Durham, NC: Duke University Press, 2005.

Guerra, Francois-Xavier. *México: del antiguo regimen a la revolución.* Mexico City: Fondo de Cultura Económica, 1991 [1985].

Guy, Donna J. "The Politics of Pan-American Cooperation: Maternalist Feminism and the Child Rights Movement, 1913–1960." *Gender & History* 10, no. 3 (Nov. 1998): 449–69.

Guy, Donna J. *Women Build the Welfare State: Performing Charity and Creating Rights in Argentina, 1880–1955.* Durham, NC: Duke University Press, 2009.

Hamnett, Brian R. "Anastacio Bustamante y la guerra de independencia, 1810–1821." *Historia Mexicana* 28, no. 4 (Apr./Jun. 1979): 515–45.

Hamnett, Brian R. "The Economic and Social Dimension of the Revolution of Independence in Mexico, 1800–1824." *Ibero-amerikanisches Archiv* 6, no. 1 (1980): 1–27.

Hamnett, Brian R. *Roots of Insurgency: Mexican Regions, 1750–1824.* Cambridge, Eng.; New York: Cambridge University Press, 1986.

Hamnett, Brian R. "Royalist Counterinsurgency and the Continuity of Rebellion: Guanajuato and Michoacán, 1813–20." *Hispanic American Historical Review* 62, no. 1 (Feb. 1982): 19–48.

Hanson, Randall S. "The Day of Ideals: Catholic Social Action in the Age of the Mexican Revolution, 1867–1929." PhD diss., Indiana University, 1994.

Harris, Ruth. *Lourdes: Body and Spirit in the Secular Age.* London: The Penguin Press, 1999.

Hart, John M. *Anarchism and the Mexican Working Class, 1860–1931.* Austin: University of Texas Press, 1987.

Helgen, Erika. *Religious Conflict in Brazil: Protestants, Catholics, and the Rise of Religious Pluralism in the Twentieth Century.* New Haven, CT: Yale University Press, 2020.

"Hermosillo y los archivos." Online publication. http://www.adabi.org.mx/publicaciones/artEsp/archivistica/eclesiastica/perfiles/hermosilloArchivos.pdf.

Hernández, Jorge F. *La soledad del silencio: microhistoria del Santuario de Atotonilco.* Mexico City: Fondo de Cultura Económica, 1991.

Hernández Martín, Francisca. "Las Hijas de la Caridad en la profesionalización de la enfermería." *Cultura de los Cuidados* 10, no. 20 (Sept. 2006): 39–49.

Heerma van Voss, Lex, ed. *Petitions in Social History.* Cambridge, Eng.; New York: Cambridge University Press, 2002.

Herrejón Peredo, Carlos. *Del sermón al discurso cívico: México, 1760–1834.* Zamora, Michoacán, Mexico: Colegio de Michoacán, 2003.

Hershfield, Joanne. *Imagining la Chica Moderna: Women, Nation, and Visual Culture in Mexico, 1917–1936.* Durham, NC: Duke University Press, 2008.

Hijas de la Caridad: Fundación en México, online publication 2016. http://vincentians.com/es/hijas-la-caridad-fundacion-mexico-ii/ and http://vincentians.com/es/hijas-la-caridad-fundacion-mexico-4/.

Hoffmann, Stefan-Ludwig. "Democracy and Associations in the Long Nineteenth Century: Toward a Transnational Perspective." *Journal of Modern History* 75, no. 2 (Jun. 2003): 269–99.

Hoogen, Lisette van den. "The Romanization of the Brazilian Church: Women's Participation in a Religious Association in Prados, Minas Gerais." *Sociological Analysis* 50, no. 2 (1990): 171–88.

Hufton, Olwen. *The Prospect Before Her: A History of Women in Western Europe.* Vol. 1, *1500–1800.* New York: Vintage Books, 1998.

Hufton, Olwen. "The Reconstruction of a Church, 1796–1891." In *Beyond the Terror: Essays in French Regional and Social History, 1794–1815,* edited by Gwynne Lewis and Colin Lucas, 19–35. Cambridge, Eng.: Cambridge University Press, 1983.

Hughes, Jennifer S. "The Catholic Church and Social Revolutionaries." In *Religion and Society in Latin America: Interpretive Essays from Conquest to Present,* edited by Lee M. Penyak and Walter J. Petry, 243–67. Maryknoll, NY: Orbis Books, 2009.

Hunt, Lynn. *The Family Romance of the French Revolution.* Berkeley: University of California Press, 1992.

Hutchinson, C. A. "The Asiatic Cholera Epidemic of 1833 in Mexico." *Bulletin of the History of Medicine* 32, no. 1 (Jan. 1958): 1–23.

Hutchison, Elizabeth Quay. *Labors Appropriate to Their Sex: Gender, Labor, and Politics in Urban Chile, 1900–1930.* Durham, NC: Duke University Press, 2001.

Imhoff, Sarah. "The Myth of American Jewish Feminization." *Jewish Social Studies: History, Culture, Society* n.s. 21, no. 3 (Spring/Summer 2016): 126–52.
Infante Vargas, Lucrecia. "Igualdad intelectual y género en *Violetas del Anáhuac. Periódico Literario Redactado por Señoras* (Ciudad de México, 1887–1889)." In *Cuatro estudios de género en el México urbano del siglo XIX*, edited by Gabriela Cano and Georgette José Valenzuela, 129–56. Mexico City: Universidad Autónoma de México, 2001.
Informe del Consejo Central Arquidiocesano de las Conferencias de Señoras de S. Vicente de Paul, correspondiente al año económico de 1904 a 1905. Morelia, n.p., 1905.
Iñiguez Mendoza, Ulises. "'¡Viva la religión y mueran los *protestantes*!': Religioneros, catolicismo, y liberalismo, 1873–1876." PhD diss., Colegio de Michoacán, 2015.
Instruccion á los hermanos de la Real Congregación del Alumbrado y Vela continua al santísimo sacramento reservado en los santos sagrarios, sobre el espíritu y práctica de su santo instituto, é indulgencias perpetuas que le están concedidas. Lima, n.p., 1808. https://archive.org/details/instruccionloshe00cong_0.
Ivereigh, Austen. *The Politics of Religion in an Age of Revival: Studies in Nineteenth-Century Europe and Latin America*. London: Institute of Latin American Studies, 2000.
James, Daniel. *Doña María's Story: Life History, Memory, and Political Identity*. Durham, NC: Duke University Press, 2000.
Janney, Caroline E. *Burying the Dead But Not the Past: Ladies' Memorial Associations and the Lost Cause*. Chapel Hill: University of North Carolina Press, 2012.
Jaramillo Magaña, Juvenal. *Hacia una iglesia beligerante: La gestión episcopal de Fray Antonio de San Miguel en Michoacán (1784–1804): Los proyectos ilustrados y las defensas canónicas*. Zamora, Michoacán, Mexico: Colegio de Michoacán, 1996.
Jeffrey, Julie Roy. *The Great Silent Army of Abolitionism: Ordinary Women in the Antislavery Movement*. Chapel Hill: University of North Carolina Press, 1999.
Jonas, Raymond. *France and the Cult of the Sacred Heart: An Epic Tale for Modern Times*. Berkeley: University of California Press, 2000.
Juárez, José Roberto. *Reclaiming Church Wealth: The Recovery of Church Property after Expropriation in the Archdiocese of Guadalajara, 1860–1911*. Albuquerque: University of New Mexico Press, 2004.
Kaplan, Temma. "Female Consciousness and Collective Action: The Case of Barcelona, 1910–1918." *Signs: Journal of Women in Culture and Society* 7, no. 3 (Spring 1982): 545–66.
Kaplan, Temma. *Taking Back the Streets: Women, Youth, and Direct Democracy*. Berkeley: University of California Press, 2004.
Kerber, Linda K. "Separate Spheres, Female Worlds, Woman's Place: The Rhetoric of Women's History." *Journal of American History* 75, no. 1 (Jun. 1988): 9–39.
Kerber, Linda. *Women of the Republic: Intellect and Ideology in Revolutionary America*. Chapel Hill: University of North Carolina Press, 1980.
Kloppe-Santamaría, Gema. *In the Vortex of Violence: Lynching, Extralegal Justice, and the State in Post-Revolutionary Mexico*. Oakland: University of California Press, 2020.
Komonchak, J. A. "Modernity and the Construction of Roman Catholicism." *Cristianismo nella storia* 18 (1997): 353–85.
Labarga García, Fermín. "La Santa Escuela de Cristo. Una peculiar institución del Barroco hispano." *Anuario de Historia de la Iglesia* 21 (2012): 519–28.
LaGreca, Nancy. *Rewriting Womanhood: Feminism, Subjectivity, and the Angel of the House in the Latin American Novel, 1887–1903*. University Park: Pennsylvania State University Press, 2009.
Landes, Joan. *Women and the Public Sphere in the Age of the French Revolution*. Ithaca, NY: Cornell University Press, 1988.

Langlois, Claude. *Le catholicisme au féminin: les congrégations françaises à supérieure générale au XIXe siècle*. Paris: Cerf, 1985.
Lannon, Frances. *Privilege, Persecution and Prophecy: The Catholic Church in Spain, 1875-1975*. Oxford, Eng.; New York: Clarendon Press, 1987.
Larkin, Brian. "Confraternities and Community: The Decline of the Communal Quest for Salvation in Eighteenth-Century Mexico City." In *Local Religion in Colonial Mexico*, edited by Martin Austin Nesvig, 189-213. Albuquerque: University of New Mexico Press, 2006.
Larkin, Brian. *The Very Nature of God: Baroque Piety in Bourbon Mexico City*. Albuquerque: University of New Mexico Press, 2010.
Larkin, Emmet. "The Devotional Revolution in Ireland, 1850-75." *American Historical Review* 77, no. 3 (Jun. 1972): 625-52.
Lasser, Carol, and Stacey Robertson. *Antebellum Women: Private, Public, Partisan*. Lanham, MD: Rowman & Littlefield, 2010.
Lau Jaiven, Ana. "La participación de las mujeres en la revolución mexicana: Juana Belén Gutiérrez de Mendoza (1875-1942)." *Diálogos Revista Electrónica de Historia* 5, no. 1-2 (Apr.-Aug. 2005): 1-32. Online publication. https://www.redalyc.org/pdf/439/43926968005.pdf.
Lavrin, Asunción. *Brides of Christ: Conventual Life in Colonial Mexico*. Stanford, CA: Stanford University Press, 2008.
Lavrin, Asunción. "La congregación de San Pedro—Una cofradía urbana del México colonial, 1604-1730." *Historia Mexicana* 29, no. 4 (Apr./Jun. 1980): 562-601.
Lavrin, Asunción. *Women, Feminism, and Social Change in Argentina, Chile, and Uruguay, 1890-1940*. Lincoln: University of Nebraska Press, 1995.
Leal, Juan Felipe. *Del mutualismo al sindicalismo en México: 1843-1910*. Mexico City: Ediciones El Caballito, 1991.
Leal, Juan Felipe, and José Woldenberg. *Del estado liberal a los inicios de la dictadura porfirista*. Mexico City: Siglo XXI, Instituto de Investigaciones Sociales de la Universidad Nacional Autónoma de México, 1980.
Lear, John. *Workers, Neighbors, and Citizens: The Revolution in Mexico City*. Lincoln: University of Nebraska Press, 2001.
Leavitt-Alcántara, Brianna. *Alone at the Altar: Single Women and Devotion in Guatemala, 1670-1870*. Stanford, CA: Stanford University Press, 2018.
Lerner, Gerda. *The Grimké Sisters from South Carolina: Pioneers for Women's Rights and Abolition*. New York: Oxford University Press, 1967.
Levenson-Estrada, Deborah. "The Loneliness of Working-Class Feminism: Women in the 'Male World' of Labor Unions, Guatemala City, 1970s." In *The Gendered Worlds of Latin American Women Workers: From Household and Factory to the Union Hall and Ballot Box*, edited by John D. French and Daniel James, 208-31. Durham, NC: Duke University Press, 1997.
Loaeza, Soledad. "La Guerra Fría en México: La Santa Alianza entre la Iglesia y las Mujeres." In *La restauración de la Iglesia católica en la transición mexicana*, edited by Soledad Loaeza. Mexico City: El Colegio de México, 2013. Kindle.
Loaeza, Soledad. "La iglesia y la educación en México. Una historia en episodios." In *Historia de la educación y ensenanza de la historia*, edited by Pilar Gonzalbo Aizpuru, 173-94. Mexico City: Colegio de México, 1998.
Loaeza, Soledad. *El Partido Acción Nacional: la larga marcha, 1939-1994: oposición leal y partido de protesta*. Mexico City: Fondo de Cultura Económica, 2000.
Loaeza, Soledad. *La restauración de la iglesia católica en la transición mexicana*. Mexico City: Colegio de México, 2013.

Loaeza, Soledad. "La secularización de la identidad femenina. ¿La derrota de la iglesia?" In *La restauración de la Iglesia católica en la transición mexicana*, edited by Soledad Loaeza. Mexico City: El Colegio de México, 2013. Kindle.

Lomnitz, Claudio. *The Return of Comrade Ricardo Flores Magón*. New York: Zone Books, 2014.

Londoño-Vega, Patricia. *Religion, Society, and Culture in Colombia: Medellín and Antioquia, 1850–1930*. Oxford, Eng.: Oxford University Press, 2002.

López, Miroslava. "Anuncia sociedad civil e Iglesia en México megamarcha a favor de la mujer y de la vida." *Vida Nueva Digital* (Sept. 20, 2021). https://www.vidanuevadigital.com/2021/09/20/anuncia-sociedad-civil-e-iglesia-en-mexico-megamarcha-a-favor-de-la-mujer-y-de-la-vida/.

López Muñoz, Miguel Luis. "Las cofradías de penitencia de Granada en la edad moderna." *Gazeta de Antropología* 11, no. 12 (1995): 1–10. https://www.yumpu.com/es/document/read/14633281/las-cofradias-de-penitencia-de-granada-en-la-edad-moderna.

Loreto López, Rosalva. *Los conventos femeninos y el mundo urbano de la Puebla de los Angeles del siglo XVIII*. Mexico City: Colegio de México, 2000.

Loyo, Engracia. "Popular reactions to the educational reforms of Cardenismo." In *Rituals of Rules, Rituals of Resistance: Public Celebrations and Popular Culture in Mexico*, edited by William H. Bezley, Cheryl English Martin, and William E. French, 247–60. Wilmington, DE: Scholarly Resources, 1994.

Ludlow, Leonor. "Formación de una disidencia: El nacimiento de la Unión Nacional Sinarquista y del Partido Acción Nacional." *Estudios Políticos. 50 años del Partido Acción Nacional* 8, no. 3 (1989), 4–15.

Macías, Anna. *Against All Odds: The Feminist Movement in Mexico to 1940*. Westport, CT: Greenwood Press, 1982.

Magray, Mary Peckham. *The Transforming Power of the Nuns: Women, Religion, and Cultural Change in Ireland, 1750–1900*. New York: Oxford University Press, 1998.

Malo, José Ramón. *Diario de sucesos notables*. Mexico City: Editorial Patria, 1948.

Mangion, Carmen M. *Contested Identities: Catholic Women Religious in Nineteenth-Century England and Wales*. Manchester, Eng.: Manchester University Press, 2008.

Marin, Simonetta. "The Fleshy Heart of Jesus." *California Italian Studies* 5, no. 1 (2014): 131–74. https://escholarship.org/uc/item/5c14t6c2#author.

Márquez Sandoval, María Concepción. "Si el hombre da la cabeza, la mujer da el corazón: la participación femenina en la Unión Nacional Sinarquista." Paper presented at the II Coloquio Internacional Red de Enlaces Académicos de Género, 2010. https://cupdf.com/document/ma-concepcion-marquez-sandoval.html.

Martínez Aguilar, José Manuel. "Las cofradías novohispanas de Tzintzuntzan. Bienes, prácticas y espacios de devoción." *Relaciones: Estudios de Historia y Sociedad* 38, no. 151 (2017): 11–57.

Martínez Albesa, Emilio. *La constitución de 1857: Catolicismo y liberalismo en México*. Mexico City: Porrua, 2007.

Martínez Assad, Carlos. "La iglesia católica entre el pasado y el presente." In *Relaciones estado-iglesia: encuentro y desencuentros*, edited by Patricia Galeana de Valadés, 259–67. Mexico City: Secretaría de Gobernación, 2001.

Martínez Baez, Antonio. *Representaciones sobre la tolerancia religiosa*. Mexico City: Costa-Amic, 1959.

Martínez de Codes, Rosa María. "Cofradías y capellanías en el pensamiento ilustrado de la administración borbónica (1760–1808)." In *Cofradías, Capellanías y Obras Pías en la América Colonial*, edited by María del Pilar Martínez López Cano, Gisela Von Wobeser, and Juan Guillermo Muñoz Correa, 17–33. Mexico City, Universidad Autónoma de México, 1998.

Martín García, Alfredo. "Ilustración y religiosidad popular: el Expediente de Cofradías en la Provincia de León (1770–1772)." *Estudios Humanísticos. Historia* 5 (2006): 137–58.

Masters, Adrian. "A Thousand Invisible Architects: Vassals, the Petition and Response System, and the Creation of Spanish Imperial Caste Legislation." *Hispanic American Historical Review* 98, no. 3 (Aug. 2018): 377–406.

Matovina, Timothy. *Theologies of Guadalupe: From the Era of Conquest to Pope Francis.* New York: Oxford University Press, 2019.

Mayo, John. *Commerce and Contraband on Mexico's West Coast in the Era of Barron, Forbes & Co., 1821–1859.* New York: Peter Lang, 2006.

Maza Valenzuela, Erica. "Catolicismo, anticlericalismo y la extensión del sufragio a la mujer en Chile." Working Paper #214. Notre Dame, IN: The Helen Kellogg Institute for International Studies, 1995.

McGirr, Lisa. *Suburban Warriors: The Origins of the New American Right.* Princeton, NJ: Princeton University Press, 2001.

McGowan, Gerald L. *Prensa y poder, 1854–1857: La revolución de Ayutla, el Congreso Constituyente.* Mexico City: Colegio de México, 1978.

McNamara, Jo Ann Kay. *Sisters in Arms: Catholic Nuns through Two Millennia.* Cambridge, MA: Harvard University Press, 1996.

Mead, Karen. "Beneficent Maternalism: Argentine Motherhood in Comparative Perspective, 1880–1920." *Journal of Women's History* 12, no. 3 (Autumn 2000): 120–45.

Memoria del Ministerio de Justicia y Negocios Eclesiásticos. Mexico City: Tipografía de Vicente García Torres, 1850.

Memoria de la Sociedad Católica de la Nación Mexicana, que comprende el periodo trascurrido desde el 25 de diciembre de 1868, época de su fundación, hasta el primero de mayo de 1877. Mexico City: Imprenta de Francisco R. Blanco, 1877. https://babel.hathitrust.org/cgi/pt?id=txu.059172017759753;view=1up;seq=20.

Memoria que el Consejo Superior de Señoras de la Caridad de Mejico leyó en la asamblea general verificada en la Iglesia de la Encarnación de esta capital el día 23 de julio de 1878. Mexico City: Tipografía religiosa de Miguel Torner y Compañía, 1879.

Menéndez Rodríguez, Hernán. *Iglesia y poder: Proyectos sociales, alianzas políticas y económicas en Yucatán, 1857–1917.* Mexico City: Editorial Nuestra América, 1995.

Mendoza García, Leticia. "Libertad de concienca y tolerancia de cultos en Michoacán (1851–1876)." BA thesis, Universidad Michoacana de San Nicolás de Hidalgo, 2009.

Mexico. *Anuario estadístico de la República Mexicana*, various years. Mexico City: Dirección General de Estadística, 1903; Mexico City: Dirección General de Estadística, 1904; Mexico City: Dirección General de Estadística, 1905; Mexico City: Dirección General de Estadística, 1907; Mexico City: Dirección General de Estadística, 1908; Mexico City: Dirección General de Estadística, 1912.

Meyer, Jean A. *La cristiada: la guerra de los cristeros.* 2 vols. Mexico City: Siglo XXI, 1973.

Meyer, Jean A. *El sinarquismo, el cardenismo y la iglesia: 1937–1947.* Mexico City: Tusquets Editores, 2003.

Mijangos y González, Pablo. "La derecha religiosa en las elecciones mexicanas de 2018." *Letras Libres*, May 2, 2018. https://www.letraslibres.com/mexico/revista/la-derecha-religiosa-en-las-elecciones-mexicanas-2018.

Mijangos y González, Pablo. *The Lawyer of the Church: Bishop Clemente de Jesús Munguía and the Clerical Response to the Mexican Liberal Reforma.* Lincoln: University of Nebraska Press, 2015.

Mijangos y González, Pablo. "La respuesta popular al juramento constitucional en 1857: un esbozo de geografía político-religiosa del México de la Reforma." In *Entre Dios y la*

república: La separación Iglesia-Estado en México, siglo XIX, edited by Pablo Mijangos y González, 237–74. Valencia, Spain: Tirant lo Blanch, 2018.
Mijangos y González, Pablo. "¿Secularización o Reforma? Los orígenes religiosos del matrimonio civil en México." In *Entre Dios y la república: La separación Iglesia-Estado en México, siglo XIX*, edited by Pablo Mijangos y González, 197–221. Valencia, Spain: Tirant lo Blanch, 2018.
Mijangos y González, Pablo. "Tres momentos en la historiografía sobre el conflicto religioso de la Reforma." In *Entre Dios y la república: La separación Iglesia-Estado en México, siglo XIX*, edited by Pablo Mijangos y González, 17–34. Valencia, Spain: Tirant lo Blanch, 2018.
Miller, Barbara Ann. "The Role of Women in the Mexican Cristero Rebellion: A New Chapter." PhD diss., University of Notre Dame, 1980.
Miller, Barbara Ann. "The Roles of Women in the Mexican Cristero Rebellion: Las Señoras y las Religiosas." *The Americas* 40, no. 3 (Jan. 1984): 303–23.
Miller, Barbara Ann. "Women and Revolution: The Brigadas Femeninas and the Mexican Cristero Rebellion, 1926–1929." *Journal of Third World Studies* 15 (Mar. 1981): 57–66.
Mínguez-Blasco, Raúl. "Between Virgins and Priests: The Feminisation of Catholicism and Priestly Masculinity in Nineteenth-Century Spain." *Gender & History* 33, no. 1 (Nov. 2019): 94–110.
Mínguez Blasco, Raúl. *Evas, Marías y Magdalenas. Género y modernidad católica en la España liberal (1833–1874)*. Madrid: Asociación de Historia Contemporánea-Centro de Estudios Políticos y Constitucionales, 2016.
Mitchell, Stephanie. "Revolutionary Feminism, Revolutionary Politics: Suffrage under Cardenismo." *The Americas* 72, no. 3 (Jul. 2015): 439–68.
Moncada González, Gisela. *La libertad comercial: El sistema de abasto de alimentos en la ciudad de México, 1810–1835*. Mexico City: Instituto Mora, 2014.
Moreno Chávez, José Alberto. *Devociones políticas: cultura católica y politización en la Arquidiócesis de México, 1880–1920*. Mexico City: Colegio de México, 2013.
Moreno Chávez, José Alberto. "Nuevas perspectivas para los estudios de laicidad." *Cuicuilco* 61 (Dec. 2014): 49–56.
Moreno Méndez, Jorge. "Chavinda en el Archivo Diocesano." Unpublished manuscript, Zamora, Michoacán, 2001.
Morgan, David. *The Sacred Heart of Jesus: The Visual Evolution of a Devotion*. Amsterdam: Amsterdam University Press, 2008.
Muñoz, Joaquín. "La minería en México. Bosquejo histórico." *Quinto Centenario* 11 (1986): 145–56. https://revistas.ucm.es/index.php/QUCE/article/view/QUCE8686220145A.
Muriel, Josefina. *La sociedad novohispana y sus colegios de niñas*. Mexico City: Universidad Nacional Autónoma de México, 1995.
Murillo, Luis Enrique. "The Politics of the Miraculous: Local Religious Practice in Porfirian Michoacán, 1876–1910." PhD diss., University of California at San Diego, 2002.
Muro, Víctor Gabriel. "Iglesia y sociedad en México, 1970–1990." *Relaciones. Estudios de Historia y Sociedad* 47 (1991): 83–97.
Nava Hernández, Eduardo. *Isaac Arriaga: el humanismo militante*. Morelia: Archivo Histórico de la Universidad de Michoacán, 1999.
Nickerson, Michelle M. *Mothers of Conservatism: Women and the Postwar Right*. Princeton, NJ: Princeton University Press, 2012.
Norberg, Kathryn. "Women, the Family, and the Counter-Reformation: Women's Confraternities in the Seventeenth Century." *Proceedings of the Western Society for French History* 6 (Oct. 1978): 55–63.

O'Brien, Elizabeth. "'If They Are Useful, Why Expel Them?' Las Hermanas de la Caridad and Religious Medical Authority in Mexico City Hospitals, 1861–1874." *Mexican Studies/Estudios mexicanos* 33, no. 3 (2017): 417–442.

O'Dogherty, Laura. "El acenso de una jerarquía eclesial intransigente, 1890–1914." In *Memoria del I Coloquio Historia de la Iglesia en el Siglo XIX*, edited by Manuel Ramos Medina, 179–98. Mexico City: Condumex, 1998.

O'Dogherty, Laura. "La política de conciliación en la Arquidiócesis de Guadalajara." In *Relaciones estado-iglesia: encuentro y desencuentros*, edited by Patricia Galeana de Valadés, 139–51. Mexico City: Secretaría de Gobernación, 2001.

O'Dogherty, Laura. "Restaurarlo todo en Cristo: Unión de Damas Católicas, 1920–26." *Estudios de historia moderna y contemporanea de México* 14 (1991): 129–58.

O'Dogherty Madrazo, Laura. *De urnas y sotanas: el Partido Católico Nacional en Jalisco*. Mexico City: Conaculta, 2001.

O'Hara, Matthew. *A Flock Divided: Race, Religion, and Politics in Mexico, 1749–1857*. Durham, NC: Duke University Press, 2010.

O'Hara, Matthew. "The Supple Whip: Innovation and Tradition in Mexican Catholicism." *American Historical Review* 117, no. 5 (Dec. 2012): 1373–1401.

Okin, Susan Moller. *Women in Western Political Thought*. Princeton, NJ: Princeton University Press, 2013 [1979].

Olimón Nolasco, Manuel. "La iglesia católica y el segundo imperio mexicano. Antecedentes y principios de un entendimiento imposible." Unpublished paper (2014). http://www.olimon.org/manuel/ponencias/segundo_imperio.pdf.

Olveda, Jaime. "Proyectos de colonización en la primera mitad del siglo XIX." *Relaciones* 42 (Spring 1990): 23–47.

Ornelas Méndez, Candy E. *Inventario del Archivo Histórico de la Unión Nacional de Padres de Familia, Ciudad de México*. Apoyo al Desarrollo de Archivos y Bibliotecas de Mexico, 2017. https://www.adabi.org.mx/publicaciones/351.pdf.

Ortoll, Servando. "Catholic Organizations in Mexico's National Politics and International Diplomacy (1926–1942)." PhD diss., Columbia University, 1986.

Osten, Sarah. *The Mexican Revolution's Wake: The Making of a Political System, 1920–1929*. Cambridge, Eng.: Cambridge University Press, 2018.

Outram, Dorinda. *The Body and the French Revolution: Sex, Class and Political Culture*. New Haven, CT: Yale University Press, 1989.

Pacheco, Adriana. "Periódicos católicos mexicanos del siglo XIX. Conformación de la madre de familia durante la República Restaurada para trabajar por 'el otro Mexico.'" *Tinkuy: Boletín de Investigación y Debate* 21 (2014): 79–94. http://littlm.umontreal.ca/fileadmin/Documents/FAS/litterature_langue_moderne/Documents/2-Recherche/Tinkuy_21_2014.pdf.

Padilla Rangel, Yolanda. *El catolicismo social y el movimiento cristero en Aguascalientes*. Aguascalientes: Instituto Cultural, 1992.

Palti, Elías J. *La invención de una legitimidad: Razón y retórica en el pensamiento mexicano del siglo XIX*. Mexico City: Fondo de Cultura Económica, 2005.

Pani, Erika. "'Ciudadana y muy ciudadana'? Women and the State in Independent Mexico, 1810–30." *Gender & History* 18, no. 1 (Apr. 2006): 5–19.

Pani, Erika. "Una ventana sobre la sociedad decimonómica: los periódicos católicos, 1845–1857." *Secuencia: Revista de Historia y Ciencias Sociales* 36 (Sept./Dec. 1996): 67–88.

Parcero, María de la Luz. *Condiciones de la mujer en México durante el siglo XIX*. Mexico City: Instituto Nacional de Antropología e Historia, 1992.

Pasternac, Nora. "El periodismo femenino en el siglo XIX: Violetas del Anáhuac." In *Las voces olvidadas. Antología crítica de narradoras mexicanas nacidas en el siglo XIX*,

edited by Ana Rosa Domenella y Nora Pasternac, 399–418. Mexico City: El Colegio de México, 1991.
Pasture, Patrick. "Beyond the Feminization Thesis: Gendering the History of Christianity in the Nineteenth and Twentieth Centuries." In *Gender and Christianity in Modern Europe: Beyond the Feminization Thesis*, edited by Patrick Pasture and Jan Art. Leuven: Leuven University Press, 2012.
Perales Ojeda, Alicia. *Las asociaciones literarias mexicanas*. Mexico City: Universidad Nacional Autónoma de México, 2000.
Perales Ojeda, Alicia. "El Liceo Hidalgo." *Enciclopedia de la literatura en México*. Online publication, 2000. http://www.elem.mx/estgrp/datos/123.
Pérez, Angela. "Cesárea Ruiz de Esparza y Dávalos, fundadora de las Hermanas Josefinas." Online publication, 2013. http://vincentians.com/es/cesarea-ruiz-de-esparza-y-davalos-fundadora-de-las-hermanas-josefinas/.
Pérez, Juan E. *Almanaque Estadístico de las Oficinas y Guías de Forasteros y del comercio de la República para 1875*. Mexico City: Imp. del Gobierno, 1874.
Pérez Acevedo, Martín. "Legislación sobre extranjeros en México del siglo XIX." *Tzintzun: Revista de Estudios Históricos* 26 (1997): 9–28.
Pérez Hernández, José María. *Diccionario geográfico, estadístico, histórico, biográfico, de industria y comercio de la República Mexicana*. Vol. 3. Mexico City: Imprenta del Cinco de Mayo, 1875.
Pérez Herrero, Pedro. "'Crecimiento' colonial vs 'crisis' nacional en México, 1765–1854. Notas a un modelo explicativo." In *Cinco siglos de historia de México. Memorias de la VIII Reunión de historiadores mexicanos y norteamericanos*, 2 vols., edited by Virginia Guedea and Jaime E. Rodríguez O., 2:81–105. Mexico City; Irvine, CA: Instituto Mora/University of California Irvine, 1992.
Pérez Iturbe, Marco Antonio. "Lázaro de la Garza y Ballesteros y el clero secular del arzobispado de México 1851–1857. De la república católica a la liberal." MA thesis, Universidad Nacional Autónoma de México, 2006.
Pérez-Rocha, Emma. "Mayordomías y cofradías del pueblo de Tacuba en el siglo XVIII." *Estudios de Historia Novohispana* no. 6 (1978): 119–31.
Pérez Rosales, Laura. "Censura y Control: La Campaña Nacional de Moralización en los años cincuenta." *Historia y grafía* 37 (2011): 79–113.
Pérez Rosales, Laura. "Las mujeres sinarquistas: Nuevas Adelitas en la vida política mexicana (1945–1948)." In *Religión, política y sociedad. El sinarquismo y la iglesia en México (nueve ensayos)*, edited by Rubén Aguilar and Guillermo Zermeño, 169–94. Mexico City: Universidad Iberoamericana, 1992.
Pescador, Juan Javier. *De bautizados a fieles difuntos. Familia y mentalidades en una parroquia urbana: Santa Catarina de México, 1568–1820*. Mexico City: Colegio de México, 1992.
Pescador, Juan Javier. "Devoción y crisis demográfica: La Cofradía de San Ygnacio de Loyola, 1761–1821." *Historia Mexicana* 39, no. 3 (Jan./Mar. 1990): 767–801.
Piccato, Pablo. *The Tyranny of Opinion: Honor in the Construction of the Mexican Public Sphere*. Durham, NC: Duke University Press, 2010.
Pieper Mooney, Jadwiga E. *The Politics of Motherhood: Maternity and Women's Rights in Twentieth-Century Chile*. Pittsburgh: University of Pittsburgh Press, 2009.
Pi-Suñer, Antonia. "Sebastián Lerdo de Tejada y su política hacia la iglesia católica." In *Relaciones estado-iglesia: encuentro y desencuentros*, edited by Patricia Galeana de Valadés, 127–37. Mexico City: Secretaría de Gobernación, 2001.
Piña, Ulices. "The Different Roads to Rebellion: Socialist Education and the Second Cristero Rebellion in Jalisco, 1934–1939." *Letras históricas* 16 (Spring–Summer 2017): 165–92.

Pineda Soto, Adriana. "La prensa religiosa y el estado liberal en el siglo XIX: La perspectiva michoacana." In *Rompecabezas del papel: La prensa y el periodismo desde las regiones de México, siglos XIX y XX*, edited by Celia del Palacio Montiel, 74–96. Guadalajara: Porrúa, 2006.

Po-Chia Hsia, Ronald. *The World of Catholic Renewal 1540–1770*. Cambridge, Eng.; New York: Cambridge University Press, 2005.

Poole, Stafford. *The Guadalupan Controversies in Mexico*. Stanford, CA: Stanford University Press, 2006.

Porter, Susie S. *From Angel to Office Worker: Middle-Class Identity and Female Consciousness in Mexico, 1890–1950*. Lincoln: University of Nebraska Press, 2018.

Porter, Susie S. *Working Women in Mexico City: Public Discourses and Material Conditions, 1879–1931*. Tucson: University of Arizona Press, 2003.

Portnoy, Alisse. *Their Right to Speak: Women's Activism in the Indian and Slave Debates*. Cambridge, MA: Harvard University Press, 2005.

Poska, Allyson M., and Elizabeth A. Lehfeldt. "Redefining Expectations: Women and the Church in Early Modern Spain." In *Women and Religion in Old and New Worlds*, edited by Susan E. Dinan and Debra Meyers, 21–42. New York and London: Routledge, 2001.

Power, Margaret. *Right-Wing Women in Chile: Feminine Power and the Struggle Against Allende, 1964–1973*. University Park: Pennsylvania State University Press, 2002.

Puente Lutteroth, María Alicia. *Movimiento cristero: una pluralidad desconocida*. Mexico City: Progreso, 2002.

Purnell, Jennie. *Popular Movements and State Formation in Revolutionary Mexico: The Agraristas and Cristeros of Michoacán*. Durham, NC: Duke University Press, 1999.

Putnam, Robert D. *Bowling Alone: The Collapse and Revival of American Community*. New York: Simon & Schuster, 2000.

Putnam, Robert D. *Making Democracy Work: Civic Traditions in Modern Italy*. Princeton, NJ: Princeton University Press, 1992.

Ramos, Luis. "Ascenso Liberal. Intervención francesa. Consolidación del Estado Mexicano (1840–1876)." In *Hacia una historia mínima de la Iglesia en México*, edited by María Alicia Puente Lutteroth, 111–20. Mexico City: Editorial Jus; CEHILA, 1993.

Raby, David. *Educación y revolución social en México, 1921–1940*. Mexico City: Secretaría de Educación Pública, 1974.

Rapley, Elizabeth. *The Dévotes: Women and Church in Seventeenth-Century France*. Montreal: McGill-Queen's University Press, 1993.

Ramos Escandón, Carmen. "Género y modernidad mujeril: Las relaciones de género en el fin del siglo mexicano." *Anuario del Instituto de Estudios Histórico-Sociales* 16 (2001): 261–84.

Ramos Escandón, Carmen. "Señoritas Porfirianas: mujer e ideología en el México progresista." In *Presencia y transparencia: la mujer en la historia de México*, edited by Carmen Ramos Escandón, 143–62. Mexico City: Colegio de México, 1987.

Reid, Dylan. "Measuring the Impact of Brotherhood: Robert Putnam's Making Democracy Work and Confraternal Studies." *Confraternitas* 14:1 (Spring 2003): 3–12.

Rendall, Jane. *The Origins of Modern Feminism: Women in Britain, France and the United States, 1780–1860*. New York: Macmillan, 1985.

Representación de los indígenas de Zalatitan, San Gaspar y Rosario, contra la tolerancia de cultos. Guadalajara: Tip. de Rodríguez, 1856.

Representación del ayuntamiento y vecindario de la Villa de Calvillo al soberano congreso general contra la tolerancia de cultos en la república. Guadalajara: Tip. de Rodríguez, 1856.

Representación del vecindario de Hostotipaquillo contra la tolerancia. Guadalajara: Tip. de Rodríguez, 1856.

Representación que al soberano Congreso Constituyente hacen los vecinos del Pueblo de Tlalnepantla Cuautenca. Mexico City: Imp. de L. Inclán, 1856.

Representación que el vecindario de Tototlán dirige al Soberano Congreso Constituyente de la República contra la tolerancia de cultos. Guadalajara: Tip. de Rodríguez, 1856.

Representación que las Señoras de Etzatlán dirigen al Soberano Congreso Constituyente contra la tolerancia de cultos. Guadalajara: Tip. de Rodríguez, 1856.

Representación que las señoras de Guadalajara dirigen al soberano Congreso Constituyente sobre que en la carta fundamental que se discute, no quede consignada la tolerancia de cultos en la república. Guadalajara: Tip. de Rodríguez, 1856.

Representación que los habitantes de Zamora dirigen al Soberano Congreso Constituyente, pidiéndole que no se permita en la República la libertad de cultos. Mexico City: M. Murguía, 1856.

Representación que los vecinos de Etzatlán dirigen al s. congreso constituyente contra la tolerancia de cultos. Guadalajara: Tip. de Rodríguez, 1856.

Representación que los vecinos de Guadalajara dirigen al Soberano Congreso Constituyente: sobre que en la carta fundamental que se discute, no quede consignada la tolerancia de cultos en la República. Guadalajara: Tip. de Rodríguez, 1856.

Representación que los vecinos del Pueblo de Pihuamo en el estado de Jalisco, dirigen al Soberano Congreso Constitutyente, a fin de que no se sancione el artículo 15 del Proyecto de Constitución que se discute en la Carta Fundamental sobre tolerancia de cultos. Guadalajara: Tip. de Rodríguez, 1856.

Reyes Pavón, Leonor Eugenia. "Las Hermanas de la Caridad: Su labor asistencial y educativa en Yucatán, 1865–1875." MA thesis, Universidad Autónoma de Yucatán, 2013. https://www.academia.edu/16516685/Las_hermanas_de_la_caridad_Su_labor_asistencial_y_educativa_en_Yucat%C3%A1n_1865-1875.

Reynolds, David S. "The Feminization Controversy: Sexual Stereotypes and the Paradoxes of Piety in Nineteenth-Century America." *New England Quarterly* 53 (Mar. 1980): 96–106.

Ricker, Dennis Paul. "The Lower Secular Clergy of Central Mexico: 1821–1857." PhD diss., University of Texas at Austin, 1982.

Rivas Jiménez, Claudia P. "Las asociaciones mutualistas de trabajadores y la iglesia católica en Guadalajara, siglo XIX." In *Para la historia de las asociaciones en México (siglos XVIII-XX)*, edited by Isnardo Santos, 99–108. Mexico City: Palabra de Clio, 2014.

Robles de Mendoza, Margarita. *La evolución de la mujer en México*. Mexico City: Imp. Galas, 1931.

Rocha Islas, Martha Eva. *Los rostros de la rebeldía: Veteranas de la revolución mexicana, 1910–1939*. Mexico City: Secretaría de Cultura; Instituto Nacional de Estudios Históricos de las Revoluciones de México; INAH, 2016.

Rocha Islas, Martha Eva. "Visión panorámica de las mujeres durante la revolución mexicana." In *Historia de las mujeres en Mexico*, edited by Patricia Galeana de Valadés, 201–24. Mexico City: Secretaría de Educación Pública, Instituto Nacional de Estudios Históricos de las Revoluciones de México, 2015. https://inehrm.gob.mx/work/models/inehrm/Resource/1484/1/images/HistMujeresMexico.pdf.

Rodríguez Bravo, Roxana. "El sufragio femenino desde la perspectiva sinarquista-católica (1945-1958)." *Letras Históricas* 8 (Spring/Summer 2013): 159–84.

Romeo Mateo, María Cruz. "¿Sujeto católico femenino? Política y religión en España, 1854–1868." *Ayer: Revista de Historia Contemporánea* 106, no. 2 (2017): 79–104.

Romero Samper, Milagrosa. *Las cofradías en el Madrid del siglo XVIII*. Madrid: Universidad Complutense, 1998.

Romero de Solís, José Miguel. *El aguijón del espíritu: Historia contemporánea de la Iglesia en México (1895-1990)*. Mexico City: Instituto Mexicano de Doctrina Social Cristiana, 1994.

Romo Aguilar, Filiberto. "Las asociaciones políticas católicas en México entre 1924 y 1939." In *Para la historia de las asociaciones en México (siglos XVIII-XX)*, edited by Isnardo Santos, 239–46. Mexico City: Palabra de Clío, 2014.

Rosas Salas, Sergio Francisco. "El Círculo Católico de Puebla, 1887–1900." *Estudios de historia moderna y contemporánea de México* 43 (Jun. 2012): 35–67.

Rosas Salas, Sergio Francisco. "De la República católica al Estado laico: Iglesia, Estado y secularización en México, 1824–1914." *Lusitania Sacra*, no. 25 (Jan.–Jun. 2012): 227–44.

Rosas Salas, Sergio Francisco. "Trinidad Sánchez Santos: *El País*, el periodismo católico como constructor de la opinión pública en México, 1910–1912." In *Intelectuales católicos: Conservadores y tradicionalistas en México y Latinoamérica, 1910–2015*, edited by Laura Alarcón Menchaca, Austreberto Martínez Villegas, and Jesús Iván Mora Muro, 23–38. Guadalajara: El Colegio de Jalisco, 2019.

Rosemblatt, Karin. *Gendered Compromises: Political Cultures and the State in Chile, 1920–1950*. Chapel Hill: University of North Carolina Press, 2000.

Rubenstein, Anne. *Bad Language, Naked Ladies, and Other Threats to the Nation: A Political History of Comic Books in Mexico*. Durham, NC: Duke University Press, 1998.

Rugeley, Terry. *Of Wonders and Wise Men: Religion and Popular Cultures in Southeast Mexico, 1800–1876*. Austin: University of Texas Press, 2001.

Rulfo, Juan. *El llano en llamas*. Havana: Casa de las Américas, 1968.

Ruiz Castañeda, Carmen. *La prensa periódica en torno a la Constitución de 1857*. Mexico City: Universidad Nacional Autónoma de México, 1959.

Ruiz Guerra, Rubén. "Los dilemas de la conciencia: Juan Bautista Morales y su defensa liberal de la Iglesia." In *Memoria del I Coloquio Historia de la Iglesia en el Siglo XIX*, edited by Manuel Ramos Medina, 411–22. Mexico City: Condumex, 1998.

Ruiz Massieu, José Francisco. *La relación del estado con las iglesias*. Mexico City: Porrúa, 1992.

Ryan, Mary P. *Cradle of the Middle Class: The Family in Oneida County, New York, 1790–1865*. Cambridge, Eng.; New York: Cambridge University Press, 1981.

Salerno, Beth. *Sister Societies: Women's Antislavery Organizations in Antebellum America*. DeKalb: Northern Illinois University Press, 2005.

Salvucci, Richard, and Linda K. Salvucci, "Crecimiento económico y cambio de productividad en México, 1750–1895." *HISLA* 10 (1987): 67–89.

Sánchez de Madariaga, Elena. "Cultura religiosa y sociedad: las cofradías de laicos." *Historia social* 35 (1999): 23–42.

Sánchez Santiró, Ernest. "Ingresos fiscales y economía en México, 1790–1910." Unpublished paper, IX Congreso Internacional de la Asociación Española de Historia Económica (2008). https://www.aehe.es/wp-content/uploads/2008/09/Crecimiento-economico.pdf.

Sanders, James E. "'A Mob of Women' Confront Post-Colonial Republican Politics: How Partisan Ideology Affected Gendered Political Space in Nineteenth-Century Colombia." *Journal of Women's History* 20, no. 1 (Spring 2008): 63–89.

Sanders, Nichole. "Protecting Mothers in Order to Protect Children: Maternalism and the 1935 Pan-American Child Congress." In *Maternalism Reconsidered: Motherhood, Welfare and Social Policy in the Twentieth Century*, edited by Marian van der Klein, Rebecca Jo Plant, Nichole Sanders, and Lori R. Weintrob, 148–67. New York; Oxford, Eng.: Berghahn Books, 2012.

Sanders, Nichole. "Women, Sex, and the 1950s Acción Católica's Campaña Nacional de Moralización del Ambiente." *Mexican Studies/Estudios mexicanos* 36, no. 1/2 (2020): 270–97.

Santillán Salgado, Gustavo. "La secularización de las creencias. Discusiones sobre la tolerancia religiosa en México, 1821–1827." In *Estado, iglesia y sociedad en México, Siglo*

XIX, edited by Alvaro Matute, Evelia Trejo, and Brian Connaughton, 175–98. Mexico City: Universidad Nacional Autónoma de México; Porrúa, 1995.
Savarino Roggero, Franco. "Catholics of the North: The Catholic Mobilization in Chihuahua During the Religious Conflict." *International Journal of Latin American Religions* 4 (2020): 14–24.
Savarino Roggero, Franco. *El conflicto religioso en Chihuahua, 1918–1937*. Ciudad Juárez: El Colegio de Chihuahua, Universidad Autónoma de Ciudad Juárez, 2017.
Savarino Roggero, Franco. "La delegación apostólica y los orígenes del conflicto religioso en México (1921–1924)." In *Entre la pugna y la conciliación: iglesia católica y estado en México y Brasil*, edited by Laura Alarcón Menchaca, 21–42. Zapopan: El Colegio de Jalisco, 2017.
Scaraffia, Lucetta. "'Christianity Has Liberated Her and Placed Her alongside Man in the Family': From 1850 to 1988 (Mulieris Dignitatem)." In *Women and Faith: Catholic Religious Life in Italy from Late Antiquity to the Present*, edited by Lucetta Scaraffia and Gabriella Zarri, 249–80. Cambridge, MA; London, Harvard University Press, 1999.
Schell, Patience A. *Church and State Education in Revolutionary Mexico City*. Tucson: University of Arizona Press, 2003.
Schell, Patience A. "Gender, Resistance and Mexico's Church-State Conflict." In *New Approaches to Resistance in Brazil and Mexico*, edited by John Gledhill and Patience A. Schell, 184–203. London; Durham, NC: Duke University Press, 2012.
Schell, Patience A. "An Honorable Avocation for Ladies: The Work of the Mexico City Unión de Damas Católicas Mexicanas, 1912–1926." *Journal of Women's History* 10, no. 4 (Winter 1999): 78–103.
Schell, Patience A. "Social Catholicism, Modern Consumption and the Culture Wars in Postrevolutionary Mexico City." *History Compass* 5, no. 5 (2007): 1585–1603. https://onlinelibrary-wiley-com.libproxy.berkeley.edu/doi/epdf/10.1111/j.1478-0542.2007.00465.x.
Schell, Patience A. "Teaching the Children of the Revolution: Church and State Education in Mexico City, 1917–1926." PhD diss., University of Oxford, 1998.
Schmitt, Karl M. "Catholic Adjustment to the Secular State: The Case of Mexico, 1867–1911." *Catholic Historical Review* 48, no. 2 (Jul. 1962): 182–204.
Schmitt, Karl M. "The Díaz Conciliation Policy on State and Local Levels 1876–1911." *Hispanic American Historical Review* 40, no. 4 (Nov. 1960): 513–32.
Schroeder, Susan. "Jesuits, Nahuas, and the Good Death Society in Mexico City, 1718–1767." *Hispanic American Historical Review* 80, no. 1 (Feb. 2000): 43–76.
Schuyler, David. "Inventing a Feminine Past." *New England Quarterly* 51 (Sept. 1978): 291–308.
Scott, Anne Firor. *Natural Allies: Women's Associations in American History*. Urbana: University of Illinois Press, 1991.
Scott, Joan Wallach. *Sex and Secularism*. Princeton, NJ: Princeton University Press, 2017.
Seeley, Paul. "O Sainte Mère: Liberalism and the Socialization of Catholic Men in Nineteenth-Century France." *Journal of Modern History* 70, no. 4 (Dec. 1998): 862–91.
Serrano, Sol. *¿Qué hacer con Dios en la república? Política y secularización en Chile (1845–1885)*. Mexico City: Fondo de Cultura Económica, 2008.
Serrera Contreras, Ramón. *Guadalajara ganadera: Estudio regional novohispano, 1765–1805*. Sevilla: Escuela de Estudios Hispano-Americanos, 1977.
Shiels, Richard D. "The Feminization of American Congregationalism, 1730–1835." *American Quarterly* 33 (Spring 1981): 46–62.
Sinkin, Richard. *The Mexican Reform, 1855–1876: A Study in Liberal Nation-Building*. Austin: University of Texas Press, 1979.

Smith, Benjamin. "Anticlericalism, Politics, and Freemasonry in Mexico, 1920–1940." *The Americas* 65, no. 4 (2009): 559–88.

Smith, Benjamin T. *The Roots of Conservatism in Mexico: Catholicism, Society, and Politics in the Mixteca Baja, 1750–1962*. Albuquerque: University of New Mexico Press, 2012.

Smith, Bonnie. *Ladies of the Leisure Class: The Bourgeoises of Northern France in the Nineteenth Century*. Princeton, NJ: Princeton University Press, 1982.

Smith, Catherine, and Cynthia Greig. *Women in Pants: Manly Maidens, Cowgirls, and Other Renegades*. New York: Harry N. Abrams, 2003.

Sosenski, Susana. "Asomándose a la política: representaciones femeninas contra la tolerancia de cultos en México, 1856." *Tzintzun. Revista de estudios históricos* 40 (2004): 51–76.

Soto, Shirlene. *Emergence of the Modern Mexican Woman: Her Participation in Revolution and Struggle for Equality, 1910–1940*. Denver: Arden Press, 1990.

Staples, Anne. *La iglesia en la primera república federal mexicana, 1824–1835*. Mexico City: Secretaría de Educación Pública, 1976.

Staples, Anne. *Recuento de una batalla inconclusa: La educación mexicana de Iturbide a Juárez*. Mexico City: Colegio de México, 2005.

Staples, Anne. "Sociabilidad femenina a principios del siglo XIX mexicano." In *Persistencia y cambio: acercamientos a la historia de las mujeres en México*, edited by Lucía Melgar, 99–120. Mexico City: Colegio de México, 2008.

Stauffer, Brian A. *Victory on Earth or in Heaven: Mexico's Religionero Rebellion*. Albuquerque: University of New Mexico Press, 2019.

Stauffer, Brian A. "'Where the Cult is in the Hands of the People': Enlightened Catholicism and Colonization on the Texas Frontier." *Southwestern Historical Quarterly* 124, no. 3 (Jan. 2021): 241–69.

Stout, Harry S., and Catherine A. Brekus. "Declension, Gender, and the 'New Religious History.'" In *Belief and Behavior: Essays in New Religious History*, edited by Philip R. VanderMeer and Robert P. Swierenga, 15–37. New Brunswick, NJ: Rutgers University Press, 1991.

Stevens, Donald Fithian. *Mexico in the Time of Cholera*. Albuquerque: University of New Mexico Press, 2019.

Strocchia, Sharon T. "Sisters in Spirit: The Nuns of Sant'Ambrogio and Their Consorority in Early Sixteenth-Century Florence." *Sixteenth Century Journal* 33, no. 3 (Autumn 2002): 735–67.

Sugawara, Masae, ed. *La deuda pública de España y la economía novohispana, 1804–1809*. Mexico City: Instituto Nacional de Antropología e Historia; Secretaría de Educación Pública; Departamento de Investigaciones Históricas; Seminario de Historia Económica, 1976.

Sullivan-González, Douglas. *Piety, Power and Politics: Religion and Nation Formation in Guatemala, 1821–1871*. Pittsburgh: University of Pittsburgh Press, 1998.

Tapia R-Esparza, Francisco Javier. "Los festejos del primer centenario de la consumación de la independencia, nuevo impulso para el catolicismo social." *Tzintzun. Revista de Estudios Históricos* 52 (Jul.–Dec. 2010): 13–48.

Tapia Santamaría, Jesús. *Campo religioso y evolución política en el Bajío zamorano*. Zamora, Michoacán, Mexico: Colegio de Michoacán, 1986.

Taves, Ann. *The Household of Faith: Roman Catholic Devotions in Mid-Nineteenth-Century America*. Notre Dame, IN: University of Notre Dame Press, 1986.

Taylor, William B. *Drinking, Homicide and Rebellion in Colonial Mexican Villages*. Stanford, CA: Stanford University Press, 1979.

Taylor, William B. "Indian Pueblos of Central Jalisco on the Eve of Independence." In *Iberian Colonies, New World Societies: Essays in Memory of Charles Gibson*, edited by Richard L. Garner and William B. Taylor, 161–83. State College, PA: private printing, 1985.
Taylor, William B. *Magistrates of the Sacred: Priests and Parishioners in Eighteenth-Century Mexico*. Stanford, CA: Stanford University Press, 1996.
Taylor, William B. *Shrines and Miraculous Images: Religious Life in Mexico Before the Reforma*. Albuquerque: University of New Mexico Press, 2010.
Terpstra, Nicholas. "Women in the Brotherhood: Gender, Class, and Politics in Renaissance Bolognese Confraternities." *Renaissance and Reformation/Renaissance et Réforme* 14, no. 3 (Summer 1990): 193–212.
Thomson, Guy P. C. "Continuidad y cambio en la industria manufacturera mexicana, 1800–1870." In *La industria textil en México*, edited by Aurora Gómez-Galvarriato, 53–113. Mexico City: Instituto Mora; Colegio de Michoacán; Colegio de México; Instituto de Investigaciones Históricas-Universidad Nacional Autónoma de México, 1999.
Tinsman, Heidi. *Partners in Conflict: The Politics of Sexuality, Gender, and Labor in the Chilean Agrarian Reform, 1950–1973*. Durham, NC: Duke University Press, 2002.
Tinsman, Heidi. *Buying into the Regime: Grapes and Consumption in Cold War Chile and the United States*. Durham, NC: Duke University Press, 2014.
Tocqueville, Alexis de. *Democracy in America*, 2 vols. Indianapolis: Liberty Fund, 2012.
Torres Septién, Valentina. "Archivo Histórico de la Acción Católica Mexicana: un acervo para la historia de la educación." Online publication. http://www.comie.org.mx/congreso/memoriaelectronica/v09/ponencias/at09/PRE1177505581.pdf.
Torres Septién, Valentina. *La educación privada en México, 1903–1976*. Mexico City: Colegio de México; Universidad Iberoamericana, 1997.
Torres Septién, Valentina. "Un ideal femenina: los manuales de urbanidad, 1850–1900." In *Cuatro estudios de género en el México urbano del siglo XIX*, edited by Gabriela Cano and Georgette José Valenzuela, 97–127. Mexico City: Programa Universitario de Estudios de Género; Porrúa, 2001.
Trasloheros, Jorge E. "Review of María Aspe Armella, *La formación social y política de los católicos mexicanos. La Acción Católica Mexicana y la Unión Nacional de Estudiantes Católicos, 1929–1958*." In *Estudios de historia moderna y contemporánea de México* 37 (Jan.–Jun. 2009): 170–74. http://www.scielo.org.mx/scielo.php?script=sci_arttext&pid=S0185-26202009000100009.
Traslosheros, Jorge E. "Señora de la historia, Madre mestiza, Reina de México. La coronación de la Virgen de Guadalupe y su actualización como mito fundacional de la patria, 1895." *Signos históricos*, núm. 7 (Jan.–Jun. 2002): 105–147.
Trejo, Evelia. "Educar para la justicia o educar para la libertad: una disjuntiva al fin del siglo." In *Catolicismo social en México. Teoría, fuentes e historiografía*, edited by Manuel Ceballos Ramírez and Alejandro Garza Rangel, 141–94. Monterrey: Academia de Investigación Humanística, 2000.
Tuñón Pablos, Julia. *Mujeres en México: una historia olvidada*. Mexico City: Planeta, 1987. Translated as *Women in Mexico: A Past Unveiled*. Austin: University of Texas Press, 1999.
Tutino, John. "Hacienda Social Relations in Mexico: The Chalco Region in the Era of Independence." *Hispanic American Historical Review* 55, no. 3 (Aug. 1975): 496–528.
Tutino, John. *Making a New World: Founding Capitalism in the Bajío and Spanish North America*. Durham, NC: Duke University Press, 2011.
Tutino, John. *Mexico City, 1808: Power, Sovereignty, and Silver in an Age of War and Revolution*. Albuquerque: University of New Mexico Press, 2018.
Tutino, John. *The Mexican Heartland: How Communities Shaped Capitalism, a Nation, and World History, 1500–2000*. Princeton, NJ: Princeton University Press, 2018.

Urrutia de Stebelski, María Cristina and Guadalupe Nava Oteo. "La minería (1821–1880)." In *México en el siglo XIX (1821–1919): historia económica y de la estructura social*, edited by Ciro Cardoso, 119–45. Mexico City: Editorial Nueva Imagen, 1980.
US Senate, Investigation of Mexican Affairs, 66th Congress, 2nd session, 1919–1920, Vol. 2, Testimony of Francis G. Kelley.
Vaca, Agustín. *Los silencios de la historia: las cristeras*. Zapopan: Colegio de Jalisco, 1998.
Valenzuela, Georgette José. "Antecedentes políticos de la rebelión cristera." In *Relaciones estado-iglesia: encuentro y desencuentros*, edited by Patricia Galeana de Valadés, 205–23. Mexico City: Secretaría de Gobernación, 2001.
Vallebueno Garcinava, Miguel. *La archicofradía del Santísimo Sacramento*. Durango, Mexico: Conaculta, 2009.
Van Deusen, Nancy E. "Circuits of Knowledge among Women in Early Seventeenth-Century Lima." In *Gender, Race, and Religion in the Colonization of the Americas*, edited by Nora E. Jaffary, 137–51. Aldershot, Eng.: Ashgate, 2007.
Van Young, Eric. *The Other Rebellion: Popular Violence, Ideology, and the Mexican Struggle for Independence, 1810–1821*. Stanford, CA: Stanford University Press, 2001.
Vaon, Elizabeth R. *We Mean to Be Counted: White Women and Politics in Antebellum Virginia*. Chapel Hill: University of North Carolina Press, 1998.
Vaughan, Kenelm. "What Catholics Have Done for Education in Mexico." *The Catholic World* 59 (1894): 120–29.
Vaughan, Mary Kay. *Cultural Politics in Revolution: Teachers, Peasants, and Schools in Mexico, 1930–1940*. Tucson: University of Arizona Press, 1997.
Vaughan, Mary Kay. *The State, Education, and Social Class in Mexico, 1880–1928*. DeKalb: Northern Illinois University Press, 1982.
Vázquez, Josefina Zoraida. "Centralistas, conservadores y monarquistas 1830–1853." In *El conservadurismo mexicano en el siglo XIX (1810–1910)*, edited by Humberto Morales and William Fowler, 115–33. Puebla: Benemérita Universidad Autónoma de Puebla; Saint Andrews University; Gobierno del Estado de Puebla, 1999.
Vázquez de Knauth, Josefina Zoraida. *Nacionalismo y educación en México*. Mexico City: Colegio de México, 1970.
Vega, Rodrigo. "Difundir la instrucción de una manera agradable": Historia natural y geografía en revistas femeninas de méxico, 1840–1855." *Revista mexicana de investigación educativa* 16, no. 48 (Jan./Mar. 2011). Online publication. http://www.scielo.org.mx/scielo.php?script=sci_arttext&pid=S1405-66662011000100006.
Velasco López, Octavio. "La mujer y la masonería en el Jalisco del siglo XIX. Catalina Álvarez Rivera." In *Mujeres jalisciences del siglo XIX: cultura, religión, y vida privada*, edited by Lourdes Celina Vázquez Parada and Darío Armando Flores Soria, 110–31. Guadalajara: Universidad de Guadalajara, 2008.
Velasco Robledo, Dinorah. "'Institución bendita por Dios': *La Sociedad Católica de México* 1868–1878." In *Política y religión en la Ciudad de México, Siglos XIX y XX*, edited by Franco Savarino, Berenise Bravo Rubio, and Andrea Mutolo, 151–70. Mexico City: Asociación Mexicana de Promoción y Cultura Social, A.C., 2014.
Vera, Fortino Hipólito. *Catecismo geográfico-histórico-estadístico de la Iglesia Mexicana*. Amecameca, Mexico: Imprenta del Colegio Católico, 1881.
Verba, Erika Kim. *Catholic Feminism and the Social Question in Chile, 1910–1917: The Liga de Damas Chilenas*. Lewiston, NY: Edwin Mellen 2003.
Victoria Moreno, Dionisio. *El Convento de la Purísima Concepción de los Carmelitas Descalzos en Toluca. Historia documental e iconográfica*. 2 vols. Mexico City: Biblioteca Enciclopédica del Estado de México, 1979.

Vidal Galache, Florentina, and Benicia Vidal Galache. "Porque Usía es condesa." *Espacio, Tiempo y Forma* 5, no. 11 (1998): 57–72.
Villanueva y Francesconi, Mariano M., ed. *El libro de las protestas. Recopilación de las manifestaciones y protestas de los mexicanos católicos, contra la ley anticonstitucional orgánica de la Reforma, que ataca la libertad del culto y las inmunidades de la Iglesia de Jesucristo.* Mexico City: Imprenta del Cinco de Mayo, 1875.
Vivaldo Martínez, Juan Pablo. "Las mujeres en el movimiento cristero. Una aproximación crítica a la bibliografía." BA thesis, Universidad Autónoma Metropolitana-Iztapalapa, 2008.
Vivaldo Martínez, Juan Pablo. "La Unión de Damas Católicas Mexicanas (1912–1929). Una historia política." MA thesis, Universidad Autónoma Metropolitana-Iztapalapa, 2011.
Voekel, Pamela. *Alone Before God: The Religious Origins of Modern Mexico.* Durham, NC: Duke University Press, 2002.
Voekel, Pamela. "Liberal Religion: The Schism of 1861." In *Religious Culture in Modern Mexico,* edited by Martin Nesvig, 78–105. Lanham, MD: Rowman and Littlefield, 2007.
Von Germeten, Nicole. *Black Blood Brothers: Confraternities and Social Mobility for Afro-Mexicans.* Gainesville: University Press of Florida, 2006.
Von Wobeser, Gisela. *Dominación colonial: la consolidación de vales reales en Nueva España, 1804–1812.* Mexico City: Universidad Nacional Autónoma de México, Instituto de Investigaciones Históricas, 2003.
Vovelle, Michel. *Piété baroque et déchristianisation en Provence au XVIIIe siècle. Les attitudes devant la mort d'après les clauses des testaments.* Paris: Plon, 1973.
Weiner, Richard. "Trinidad Sánchez Santos: Voice of the Catholic Opposition in Porfirian Mexico." *Mexican Studies/Estudios mexicanos* 17, no. 2 (Summer 2001): 321–49.
Weinstein, Barbara. "Inventing the 'Mulher Paulista': Politics, Rebellion, and the Gendering of Brazilian Regional Identities." *Journal of Women's History* 18, no. 1 (Spring 2006): 22–49.
Weis, Robert. *For Christ and Country: Militant Catholic Youth in Post-Revolutionary Mexico.* Cambridge, Eng.: Cambridge University Press, 2019.
Weld, Kirsten. "Holy War: Latin America's Far Right." *Dissent* 67, no. 2 (Spring 2020): 57–65.
Weld, Kirsten. "The Other Door: Spain and the Guatemalan Counter-Revolution, 1944–54." *Journal of Latin American Studies* 51, no. 2 (May 2019): 307–31.
Weld, Kirsten. "The Spanish Civil War and the Construction of a Reactionary Historical Consciousness in Augusto Pinochet's Chile." *Hispanic American Historical Review* 98, no. 1 (Feb. 2018): 77–115.
Welter, Barbara. "The Feminization of American Religion: 1800–1860." In *Clio's Consciousness Raised,* edited by Mary Hartman and Lois Banner, 137–57. New York: Octagon, 1974.
Wiemers, Eugene L. "Agriculture and Credit in Nineteenth-Century Mexico: Orizaba and Córdoba, 1822–71." *Hispanic American Historical Review* 65, no. 3 (Aug. 1985): 519–46.
Witschorik, Charles A. *Preaching Power: Gender, Politics, and Official Catholic Church Discourses in Mexico City, 1720–1875.* Eugene, OR: Pickwick Publications, 2013.
Wright-Ríos, Edward. *Revolutions in Mexican Catholicism: Reform and Revelation in Oaxaca, 1887–1934.* Durham, NC: Duke University Press, 2010.
Wright-Ríos, Edward. *Searching for Madre Matiana: Prophecy and Popular Culture in Modern Mexico.* Albuquerque: University of New Mexico Press, 2014.
Young, Julia G. *Mexican Exodus: Emigrants, Exiles and Refugees of the Cristero War.* Oxford: Oxford University Press, 2015.
Zaeske, Susan. *Signatures of Citizenship: Petitioning, Antislavery and Women's Political Identity.* Chapel Hill: University of North Carolina Press, 2003.

Zahino Peñafort, Luisa. *Iglesia y sociedad en México, 1765–1800: Tradición, reforma y reacciones*. Mexico City: Universidad Nacional Autónoma de México, 1996.

Zarco, Francisco. *Historia del Congreso Estraordinario Constituyente, 1856–1857. Estracto de todas sus sesiones y documentos parlamentarios de la época*. Mexico: Imprenta de Ignacio Cumplido, 1857.

Zavala, Miguel María. *El tiempo precioso, ó sea, Modo de emplear mas provechosamente la media hora que están delante de Nuestro Sr. Jesucristo Sacramentado, las personas que pertenecen á la Vela perpetua*. Querétaro, Mexico: Imp. de Luciano Frías y Soto, 1868.

Zavala Ramírez, María del Carmen. "¿De quién son los niños? Estado, familia y educación sexual en México en la década de 1930." *Signos Históricos* 21, no. 41 (Jan./Jun. 2019): 154–91.

Zeltsman, Corinna. *Ink Under the Fingernails: Printing Politics in Nineteenth-Century Mexico*. Oakland: University of California Press, 2021.

Zolov, Eric. *Refried Elvis: The Rise of the Mexican Counterculture*. Berkeley: University of California Press, 1999.

INDEX

Boldface numbers refer to figures and tables.

abortion, 246–47
Acción Católica Mexicana (ACM), 241–48, 321–23n. *See also* Catholic Action
Adame Goddard, Jorge, 126–27, 136, 234
adornment of churches: and gendered labor, 32, 135, 138, 139, 221; as role of lay associations, 5, 48, 50, 76, 78, 91, 195
Aguascalientes, 47, 60, 88, 192, 212, 230; lay associations in, 52, **83**
Alacoque, Sister Margaret Mary, 187
Alarcón, Próspero, 228
Amigo de la Verdad, El, 199, 211
Anarchism, 193
anarcho-syndicalism, 200
anticlericalism, 94, 319n24; and anti-Catholicism, 202, 209; and liberalism, 14, 67, 94–95, 170; and public display of religion, 151; and Reform period, 123–25, 170–71; of revolutionary state, 232, 235–36, 238, 241, 248, 250–51; and women in lay associations, 4, 14
anticommunism, 232, 246
Anuario estadístico de la República Mexicana, 230
Apostolado de la Oración: and defense of Catholicism, 175–76, 222, 224, 229, 233; growth of, 180–82, 185–86, 188, 193–95; and women, 175–76, 189–91, 194, 195, 303n30, 303n33, 315n134, 323n98
Apostolate of Prayer. *See* Apostolado de la Oración
Aranda, Diego de, 50, 88, 95, 284n98
archbishops: and anticlericalism, 238; and Catholic education, 209, 225–29; and female leadership, 3, 28–29, 88; and lay associations, 36, 127, 136, 139, 179–81, 191, 193, 233; and Ley Orgánica, 169; as responsible for community faith, 207; and Romanization, 183–86; and sale of church property, 50; and

Vela Perpetua, 89, 196; and women's political activity, 114, 150, 169, 219
Archicofradía del Santísimo Sacramento: of Durango, 57–58, 128; of Lagos, 63; of Mexico City, 6; 258; of Oaxaca, 32; 128; 130, 142; of Pátzcuaro, 50
Argentina, 218
armed rebellion, 101, 116, 123, 153, 162, 208. *See also* religionero rebellion
Arriaga, Isaac, 238
Arriaga, Ponciano, 118
Arrom, Silvia, 94
Asociación Católica de la Juventud Mexicana (ACJM), 234, 237, 240
Asociación de Catequistas, 248
Asociación de Madres de Familia, 239
Aspe Armella, María Luisa, 241
Averardi, Nicolás, 217, 312
Ávila Camacho, Manuel, 244

Bandera de Ocampo, La, 158
Bantjes, Adrian, 243
baptism, 211
Barbosa Guzmán, Francisco, 234
Barranco V., Bernardo, 249
Basílica de Guadalupe, 165, 221, 240, 246; bombing of, 238
Bautista García, Cecilia, 134, 169
Bazant, Jan, 50
birth control, 246
bishops, 1, 50, 244, 249; and appointment of parish priests, 64, 68, 140; and cofradías, 51, 62–63, 66, 76, 80, 126–127; and new lay associations, 140–41, 179, 180, 184–85, 196–98, 204–5; and petitions, 99–100, 150; and Romanization, 177, 195; and the Vela Perpetua, 81–82, 84–85, 88–89, 91, 95–96; and women, 3, 35
Blancarte, Roberto, 236, 241, 249
bloomers, 106. *See also* feminism
Boletines Eclesiásticas, 15

[353]

Bourbon regime, 66, 274n86
boycotts, 216, 224, 235–36, 240, 242
Boylan, Kristina, 247, 231
Braude, Ann, 2–3
Brigadas Femininas de Santa Juana de Arco, 240–41
Buenos Aires, 224
burial societies. *See* cofradías
Butler, Jon, 251
Butler, Matthew, 196

Caballeros de Colón. *See* Knights of Colombus
Calles Law, the, 239–40
Calles, Plutarco Elías, 239
capellanías, 65, 185, 274n87, 275n90, 276n103
Carbajal López, David, 28–29, 32, 37, 263n15, 264n26
Cárdenas, Lázaro, 233, 243, 248
Carpenter, Daniel, 99
Carranza, Venustiano, 235
carta imperial, 149
Castro, Elena, 145
Catholic Action, 207. *See also* Acción Católica Mexicana
Catholic Associated Press, 215–16
Catholic intellectuals, 3–4, 11
Catholic press, 15, 135, 177, 182, 185, 207, 224–25; and freedom of the press, 215–17; and petitions, 12, 105–6, 149–50, 153, 158, 162–66, 169–70, 221; and religious tolerance, 104–5; and secular education, 209–15, 222–23; and the Sisters of Charity, 78–79; and women in politics, 14, 99, 109–10, 121–23, 170, 219, 230
Catholic schools, 156, 184, 189, 233; for boys, 228; for girls, 209–11, 218; and lay associations, 48, 207, 225–30, 233; liberal critique of, 210–11, 220–21; as parochial schools, 10, 138, 207, 225, 226–29, 243; as private schools, 225–26, 228, 230; religious education in, 135, 141, 175, 177, 191–92, 206–7, 208, 236–37; as secondary schools, 218
Catholic workers. *See* labor
Ceballos Ramírez, Manuel, 193, 310n7, 310n10
censorship, 244

center west (region of Mexico), 95, 151; and cholera epidemic, 47–48, 73; lay associations in, 14, 60–64, 69, 78, 121, 125, 129–30, 178, 182, 208; and political activity, 167, 300n90; Vela Perpetua in, 89, 133
Charles IV, 37–38
Chávez, Ezequiel A., 202
Chile, 218, 288–89n
cholera epidemic of 1833, 47–51, 62–63
Cholula: political activity in, 155, 224
Christian democracy, 192–93
Celaya, 228; lay associations in, 65, 75, 235; political activity in, 165, 212, 214, 220; Vela Perpetua in, **83**
Círculo Católico, 214
Cofradías: of Blacks or pardos, 29–30, 47; as burial societies with death benefits, 5–6, 21, 25–26, 32, 34, 44, 46, 48–49, 65–67, 137, 143; and business dealings, 19, 25–27, 28, 31, 37, 43, 46–51, 56–61, 63, 65, 86, 88, 90–91, 95, 128, 133; and control of funds by women, 35, 63, 86, 90–92, 139–40, 198; in convents, 6, 30, 36, 76–77, 264n29; and corruption, 60, 66; and economic crisis, 13, 28, 44–52, 57–64, 95, 122, 124–25, 250, 57–64; elections in, 27, 36, 42, 48, 57; and financial burden on officers, 27–28, 46–47, 50, 63; and financial crisis, 45, 50, 56–57, 63–64; and financial support for church and priests, 48, 64–67, 86, 90, 91, 138, 183; gender balances in, 20, 24–25, 45, 57; 73–75; gender roles in, 3, 4, 7, 9, 19–44, 50, 56, 60, 73; and governing boards, 26–28, 40, 57, 59, 61, 63–64; indigenous cofradías, 5, 7, 29, 263n, 183, 189; male leadership of, 20, 25–27, 33, 38, 44, 46, 51, 57–64, 66, 69, 73–75; role of mayordomo in, 47, 57–58, 49, 50, 59, 60–62, 66; and priests, 64–68
civil matrimony, 123, 199, 203
Colegio Pío Latinoamericano, 195
Colmillo Público, El, 203
Compañía Lancasteriana, 93–94, 142–43. *See also* Lancaster school system; Lancaster societies
Conferencias de Señoras [de San Vicente de Paul]. *See* Ladies of Charity
conservative press. *See* Catholic press

colonization projects, 102–4, 111, 286n26
conciliation, Díaz regime and church, 14, 170, 176, 195, 208–09, 232
Congress of Mechlin (Belgium), 126
Consolidación of 1804, 37, 100, 266n, 270n
constitutional reform of 1992, 248, 324n103
Convención Radical Obrera, La, 211, 216
convents: and female leadership, 35, 86; and laywomen, 156; nuns in, 14; as single-sex setting, 75, 196; suppression of, 131, 134, 137, 152, 259n20, 291n19; and compensation, 274n77, 274n87. *See also* cofradías; nuns
Correo del Comercio, El, 143, 156, 158
Council of Trent, 263n
Creelmen interview, 202
Crespo Reyes, Sofía, 218, 234
Cristero rebellion, 232, 233, 241–42, 244
Cruz, La, 113
Cuchara, La, 149
culture wars, 8, 261n32; and Catholic women, 1, 11, 220, 230, 251; and education, 209–17, 225. *See also* press; public display of religion; schools
Cuba, 171

Dama Católica, La, 239
Damas Católicas: founding of, 188; twentieth-century associations of, 233–35, 237–41, 247–48, 318–19n6, 319n15, 323n91
de Branciforte, Viceroy Marqués, 38
de Cienfuegos, Juan, 38, 40
de la Peña, Guillermo, 246
de la Torre, Renée, 246
de León, Fray Luis, 171
Defensa Católica, La, 195
Defensor de la Reforma, El, 157–58, 160
del Río, Eduardo (Rius), 249
Delgado, Jessica, 26–27
Diario, El, 199
Diario del Hogar, El, 213, 214, 217
Diario Oficial, 106
Díaz, Porfirio: and Catholic marriage, 201, 208; and liberalism, 14, 170; political resistance to, 202, 203, 251; regime of, 1, 123–24, 136, 227. *See also* conciliation, Díaz regime and church
disestablishment, 102
divorce, 111, 219, 246

domestic workers, 239
domestic sphere: as apolitical, 10; as ideal for women, 121–22, 158, 161–63, 170–71, 176, 211, 217–18; labor of women and, 31–35, 42, 107, 146, 163; as realm of religion, 55–56
Durango, 12, 86, 143; lay associations in, 5, 32, 52, **53**, 57–59, 128, 235; Vela Perpetua in, 83, 130

economic conditions. *See* economic crisis
economic crisis, 45, 46–51, 56–57, 60; and damage to regional economies, 60–65, 69; and insurgency, 45–46; recovery from, 73, 284; and wars for independence, 120
ecclesiastical hierarchy: and conciliation, 195, 208; and gender hierarchy, 217–18; relationship between government and, 243, 248, 250; role of, 11–12, 154, 125–27, 169; and Romanization, 177–78, 183, 185, 186; and Vela Perpetua, 81–82, 86, 87; and women, 3, 199, 235, 240, 241, 242, 250. *See also* bishops; archbishops; Vatican
Eco, El, 163
Eco de Ambos Mundos, El, 143
education of women, 109, 113, 203, 156. *See also* schools
elite women: and alliance with church, 41; and participation in cofradías, 20, 21, **23–24**, 25, 34, 52, 56; and participation in lay associations, 133, 207, 215, 234; and political activity, 68, 109, 207, 215; and relationship with parish priests, 85–86, 198, 230–31; and secular women's associations, 200–1
elites: and cofradía membership, 27, 68–69; in mestizo towns and cities, 6–7
Empress Carlota, 150
England, 56, 150, 218
Escuelas de Cristo, 95–96; women's branch of, 30, 75–78, 80, 95–96, 140–42, 278n7–9, 296n95
Esperanza, La, 110
Espinosa, David, 240
Europe: charitable and voluntary associations in, 43, 56, 78–79, 131, 134, 145, 152, 199; as creditor, 123; feminization of piety in, 55; and lay associations, 25, 41, 43, 73, 78–79, 95, 126, 176–80,

Europe (*continued*)
224, 225; political activism in, 98, 216; and religious education, 210; role of women in, 37–39, 98, 141, 156, 218, 219; and Sacred Heart devotion, 180
ex-claustration, 123, 149, 152
expulsion of foreign priests, 149
expulsion of Spaniards, 101–2, 274n75. *See also* Spain

Fallaw, Ben, 248, 321n61, 321n63
family, protection of: and religious tolerance, 103, 111–12, 115–17; and threats to, 9–10, 102, 121, 159–60, 215, 245; women responsible for, 8, 54–56, 121
family piety: and Catholic values, 207, 244–45; gender roles in, 3–4, 188–89, 210, 218
female leadership. *See* cofradías, lay associations, Vela Perpetua
feminization of piety, 7–9, 12–13, 45, 250, 259n19, 271–72n44
feminism: as antithetical to Catholicism, 203–4, 210; and Catholic women's activism, 3, 250–51; as historical focus, 112; second wave of, 246; in the United States, 106, 218
Forment, Carlos, 93, 124, 141, 144
Fowler, Will, 101
Fox, Vicente, 248–49
Franco, Jean, 171
French Intervention, 123, 127, 149, 169
Frente Nacional por la Familia, 247
Frías, Catalina, 201

García Alcazar, María Guadalupe, 238
García Icazbalceta, Joaquín, 206–7, 309n
gender roles, 4, 35, 52, 54–55, 77, 161, 170, 188–89, 205, 217–19, 231, 238, 246. *See also* cofradías; family piety; lay associations; processions; vigils
gender segregation, 8, 15, 29, 35, 54–56, 196–99
gender studies, 7–8
Germany, 9, 111, 219, 225
Gilbert, David, 104–05
Gómez de Avellaneda, Gertrudis, 171
Gómez de Portugal, Juan Cayetano, 95, 284n98
González, Manuel, 220
Griffith, R. Marie, 121

Guadalajara, 12, 47–48, 50, 64, 68; Acción Católica Mexicana (ACM) in, 246–47; Damas Católicas in, 235, 238; lay associations in, **53**, 60, 62, 69, 75, 77, 80, **120**, 129, 175, 191, 194–95; political activity in, 102–3, 105, 106, 116, **120**, 150, 153, 160, 165, 220, 224–27; schools in, 209; Social Catholicism in, 193, 207; Vela Perpetua in, 74, 82, **83**, **84**, 87–89, 91, 95, **120**, 183–85, 197
Guanajuato, 6, 7, 200; Damas Católicas in, 235, 238–39; lay associations in, 27, 33, 35, 46, 47, 48, 51, 60, 63, 69, **120**, 182, 191; political activity in, 105–6, 116, **120**, 153, 155–60, 164, 166, 214; and schools, 230; Vela Perpetua in, 82, **83**, **84**, 85, 87, 89, 92, **120**, 227

Hanson, Randall, 234, 237
Henry VIII, 111
Heraldo, El, 107, 109–10, 224
Hermanas de la Caridad. *See* Sisters of Charity
Hidalgo y Costilla, Father Miguel, 60, 65
Hijas de Anáhuac, 200–1
Hijas de María, 131, 180, **181**, 223; and Catholic values, 233, 228, 247–48; growth of, 184–86, 190, 323n97–98; and political activity, 166, 168, 235. *See also* Sisters of Charity; Vincentian organizations
Historia moderna de México, 214
hospitals, 94, 182; service organizations and, 42–43, 137, 139, 229, 233; and Sisters of Charity, 78, 79, 131; women as board members of, 144
Huerta dictatorship, 235

Idea Católica, La, 182
images of saints: and gendered labor, 26, 32–34, 57; and public display of religion, 5, 26–27, 37, 179, 212–13, 223; and Sacred Heart devotion, 175, 182
Immaculate Conception, devotion to, 126, 130, 177–78, 224
impiety, 51, 54, 250; and evils of the modern world, 126, 210, 211, 215, 223–24, 231, 237; and men, 52, 66–67; and secular schools, 155
independence, 41, 51, 56, 100; and cofradías, 3, 69, 25, 41, 44; female participation

in cofradías after, 36, 37, 51–57, 75; male leadership crisis after, 57–64; and parish priests, 65; and religion, 1, 3

indigenous populations: men, 2, 183, 189; missions to, 208; and parishes, 139, 179; and petitions, 99; regions of, center and south, 60, 178; and villages, 61, 104

individualism, 10, 25, 33. *See also* liberal ideology

industrialization, 190–91

Interés General, El, 108

interim priests, 64, 67–68, 276n104, 276–77n110

Italy, 218

Jalisco: lay associations in, 35, 60, 62, 63, 69, **120**, 167, 182, 229, 230; political activity in, 102, 105, 106, **120**, 167, 228, 235, 236, 238–39; Vela Perpetua in, **83**, 84, 85, 88–89, 91, 227

Jesuits, 77, 234

joint pastoral of 1875, 169, 207, 209

Juárez, Benito, 150, 151

Junta de Instrucción Católica Primaria, 209

Kelley, Francis, 317

Knights of Columbus, 196, 237, 240, 241, 319n25, 321n60

la segunda, 244. *See also* Cristero rebellion

Labastida, Pelagio Antonio de, 294n

labor: Catholic unions and workers' associations and, 190, 192–94, 207, 229, 236–37, 240; *La Convención Radical Obrera*, 190, 200; domestic workers, 239; labor unions, 190–92, 236–38; Obreros Católicos, 223–24, 229; Unión Católica Obrera, 193; and workers, 6, 188, 223–24, 233; workers' circles, 190, 195–96; Workers' Congress, 190; working women, 7, 193–94, 202, 237, 223–24. *See also* Social Catholicism

Ladies of Charity, 11, 43–44, 73, 138; female leadership of, 132–33; growth of, 78–80, 119–20, 132, 136, 142, 145, 156, 295n76; and new lay associations, 94–96, 119, 168, 200, 233, 235, 237; and politics, 321n60; and schools, 226, 229

Lagos, 214; lay associations in, 63, **120**; political activity in, 106, 110, 116, **120**, 150, 153; Vela Perpetua in, 84, 85, 87–88, 91, **120**

Lancaster school system, 93–94. *See also* Compañía Lancasteriana; Lancaster societies

Lancaster societies, 93, 142–44, 283n88. *See also* Compañía Lancasteriana; Lancaster school system

Larkin, Brian, 25, 33, 36–37

Las Hijas de Anahuac, 144

Latin America, 2, 10, 177, 200, 229

Lay associations, 3–5, 9–15, 95–96, 124–27, 176–91; and elections, 80, 91–92; and female leadership, 73–74, 81–82, 84, 86–89, 92, 96, 110, 127, 133, 139–46, 166–69, 178–79; 187–91, 194–99; gender balances in, 73, 75–77, 93, 188–91, 194; 204, 207, 209, 231, 244; and male leadership, 79–80, 194, 198, 204; relationship to priests, 90–92, 138–41, 194–99; and Romanization, 177–87. *See also individual lay associations*

Legion of Decency (Legión Mejicana de la Decencia), 244–45, 246, 322n83

Leo XIII, Pope, 126, 183, 186, 192, 193

León, 127; lay associations in, 47, 80, **120**; political activity in, 105, **120**, 212; Vela Perpetua in, 83, **83**, 129

Lerdo de Tejada, Sebastián, 125, 169–70, 184, 248

Lerdo Law, 149, 151, 298n30; Catholic resistance to, 148–49, 151, 154, 208; petitions against, 118, 155

L'Estafette, 150

Ley Orgánica, 151–53; debates over, 170; and ecclesiastical hierarchy, 169; and Laws of the Reform, 170; and petitions, 153–55, 160–65, 168

liberal press: on Catholic service organizations, 78, 135, 137, 144, 203, 220–21; coverage of petitions, 12, 98–99, 101, 103–10, 113, 118, 129–30, 150, 168–70; and critique of women in politics, 14, 121–22, 156–59, 162–64, 251; and free press, 224–25; and secular education, 211–17

Libro de las protestas, El, 164

Liceo Hidalgo, 144

Liga Católica, 193

Liga Nacional Defensora de la Libertad Religiosa, 240–41

literary societies, 142
Lizana, Francisco Xavier, 41–42
Lomnitz, Claudio, 125
López de Santa Anna, Antonio, 104
López Obrador, Antonio Manuel, 249
López y Romo, Jacinto, 185
Loza, Pedro, 183
Luz de Monterey, La, 135

Madero, Francisco, 235
Marian lay associations, 131
marriage; and Catholicism, 108, 110–12, 246; ceremony of, 67, 210; conservatives and, 121; divorce and, 110–12, 148, 219, 246; of Porfirio Díaz, 208; and same sex couples, 247; as threatened by religious tolerance, 110–15, 159; as threatened by women's political action, 159; women's rights in, 232
Masons, 6, 14, 202; Catholic critique of, 126, 153, 155, 219; and critique of women, 1, 3, 211
Masters, Adrian, 100
mass, 54, 82, 86, 179; gender roles and, 35, 52, 77; sponsored by cofradías, 5, 6, 26, 28, 47, 65, 91, 181, 227, 240; sponsored by cofradías for funerals, 26, 33, 48, 65
Mateo, Romeo, 111
Matto de Turner, Clorinda, 171
Maximilian I of México, Emperor, 123, 124, 149, 151, 158
Méndez Medina, Alfredo, 234
Mexican Revolution: and national narratives, 2, 251; and post-revolutionary women's political activity, 1, 3, 10, 98, 232–48, 251; and revolutionary state, 10, 122, 192–93
Mexico City, 6, 20 47, 61, 65, 142, 239; Catholic schools in, 210, 225, 226, 228; Damas Católicas in, 233–35, 240, 247; Lancaster Societies in, 143–44; lay associations in, 21–26, 28, 30–31, 33–40, 48, 52, **120**, 132, 180, 258–59n16, 259n18, 262n9–10, 264n26; non-Catholic associations in, 199–200; political activity in, 105–6, 107, 110, 115, 116, 118, **120**, 146, 149–50, 164–65; and public display of religion, 214, 221, 223–24; Santa Escuela de Cristo in, 75–77, 278n6–7, 279n22; Social Catholicism in, 133, 136, 191, 193–94; Vela Perpetua in, 75, **83, 84**, 85, 89, 91, 93–94, **120**, 130, 196; Vincentian organizations in, 43, 78–79, 133, 155, 293n47
Michoacán, 12, 143, 167, 178, 214, 238; lay associations in, 35, 48, 50, **53**, 59–64, 67–69, **120**, 180–87, 190–94; political activity in, 100, **120**, 150–52, 169, 207, 224–25; and schools, 209, 227–30; Vela Perpetua in, 74, 75, 82, **83, 84**, 85, 87–91, 95, **120**, 129, 139
Mijangos y González, Pablo, 121, 149
military action, 232, 233, 240
Miraculous Medal, 126, 131, 180
modernism, 2, 4, 104, 155, 236; and associations, 204, 177–79, 207; of Catholicism and church, 127, 133, 176–79, 192, 214; and gender roles, 218–19
Monitor Republicano, El, 103, 106–8, 109, 118, 135, 137, 144, 157–61, 168
Mora y del Río, José, 317
morality: and Catholic values, 2, 4, 12, 15, 182; and lay associations, 4, 54, 86, 192, 200, 223, 233–38, 241–45; as role of priest, 4, 36, 141, 178, 207, 248; and schools, 184, 189. *See also* family piety; gender roles
Morelia, 79, 184, 218, 223; lay associations in, 47, 48, 51, 52, 61, 63, 66, 75, **120**, 182, 184, 200; political activity in, 81, 105–06, 114, 118, **120**, 139, 158, 160, 193, 224, 238–39; Vela Perpetua in, 82, **83, 84**, 87, **120**, 229
Morelos, Father José María, 65
Moreno Chávez, José Alberto, 214, 219–20, 312n57, 313n93
Movimiento Familiar Cristiano (MFC), 244, 322n83
Múgica, Francisco J., 238
Mujer Mexicana, La, 203
Mundo, El, 203
Munguía, Clemente de Jesús, 289n101
music, 244
mutual aid, 125, 143, 200–1, 191

non-Catholic women's associations, 93–95, 122, 124–25, 141–45; 199–204, 284n96, 308n135
Nuñez de Haro, Alonso, 36, 38–40, 41–42, 258–59n16

nuns: and Catholicism, 163, 209; and cofradías, 6, 30, 90, 96, 240; expulsion of from convents, 14, 123, 148, 152; and gender segregation, 79, 196; and laywomen, 96, 156; religious practices of, 27, 86, 211. *See also* convents; ex-claustration; Sisters of Charity

Oaxaca, 12, 47–48; lay associations in, 32, **53**, 57–59, **120**, 134, 136, 142, 178–87, 204; political activity in, 103, 113–14, 119 120t, 150, 235; Vela Perpetua in, **83**, **84**, 89, **120**, 128, 129–30
Obregón, Álvaro, 236, 238
Observador Católico, El, 103, 116, 122
Ocampo, Melchor, 67
Omnibus, El, 106, 109, 110, 118, 185, 192
Orizaba: lay associations in, 30, 199–200; political activity in, 103, 111–15, **120**, 224; Vela Perpetua in, 75, 119, **120**, 150, 154–55
orphanages, 131, 200
Orquesta, La, 150
Ortoll, Severando, 244
Osten, Sarah, 239

País, El, 185, 192, 225
Pájaro Verde, El, 150, 161, 163, 164, 165
Palti, Elías, 124
Pani, Erika, 54
papacy, 126
Paris Commune, 126
parochial fees, 67
Partido Acción Nacional (PAN), 247, 248–49
Partido Católico Nacional (PCN), 234, 235, 317–18n6
Partido Liberal Mexicano (PLM), 200, 202
Partido Revolucionario Institucional (PRI), 245
patentes (certificates of cofradía membership), 21, **22**, 52, 262n8, 262n9
Patria, La, 203, 211, 212
Pátzcuaro, 218, 228: lay associations in, 47, 49, 50, **120**, 186; political activity in, 105–06, **120**, 214; Vela Perpetua in, 82, 84, **84**, 85, 91, 92, 113
Perfecta Casada, La, 171
Peru, 171
Pesado, José Joaquín, 113, 114
Pescador, Juan Javier, 25

petitions, 9, 79, 101, 129, 139–40, 228, 285n11; against Ley Orgánica, 14, 124, 147–71; against religious tolerance, 14, 104–7, 110–21, 146; conservative press and, 12, 109–10; and female authorship of, 112–16, 153, 169, 157; and lay associations, 4, 51–52, 88, 90, 96, 98, 122, 176–78, 183, 248; liberal press and, 12, 107–09; and men, 4, 28, 54, 68, 105, 107, 110–11, 155; and public display of religion, 220–22; and women, 4, 7, 10, 56, 97–122, 168, 191, 205, 218–19, 230, 235, 238–39, 248, 251; and the Vela Perpetua, 82, 85–86, 89
piety, 36, 37, 64, 54, 55
pilgrimage: and Catholic workers, 193; as display of piety, 37, 244; as protest, 238, 240
Pius IX, Pope, 126, 150–51, 180
politics: Catholic women's activism in, 35, 97–99, 205–31, 232–51; as demonstrations and marches, 98, 165, 219–21, 232, 238–43, 246–47; and gender in Catholicism, 1–14, 146, 204–5; informal practices of, 9–10, 99; and men, 68, 108, 153; at national level, 14–15, 97–122, 141–71, 199, 248; and non-Catholic groups, 200–201, 203. *See also* petitions
polygamy, 108, 112
priests: and coercion of lay women, 10, 98, 110, 117, 157–58, 160, 221; and collaboration with lay women, 90, 116, 119, 141, 146, 166, 240, 248; and community piety, 4, 36–37, 127, 207; and female leadership, 3, 9, 110, 194–99, 204–05, 230–31; financial support of by lay associations, 45–46, 54, 59, 65, 77, 145; and new lay associations, 73–96, 133–34, 138–41; and petitions, 156–58, 160; and public display of religion, 211–13, 223; ratio to parishioners, 68, 277n112; and Romanization, 177–83, 185–87, 190–91; and schools, 211, 226–29
Prieto, D. Guillermo, 144, 299
processions: and collective devotion, 34; and conciliation, 208–9, 211, 213–14, 221; and election of Vicente Fox, 248–49; and female-led associations,

processions (*continued*)
84, 96; gendered roles in, 26–27, 29, 30, 32–33, 35, 57, 128, 191, 193–94, 195; prohibition of, 1, 36–37, 151–52, 244; as protest, 232, 239; in schools, 175; sponsored by lay associations, 5–6, 40, 49, 54, 58, 181, 201

Protestants, 111, 247; and criticism of Catholics, 36; and female dominance in churches, 8; as threat, 109, 126, 176, 234

public display of religion, 25, 54, 211–15, 221–24, 238; badges and medallions as, 208–9, 221–24; bell ringing as, 147–48, 211, 221. *See also* processions

Puebla, 61, 210, 223, 230; and public display of religion, 212, 218, 221–24; lay associations in, 46, **53**, 80, 118, **120**, 136, 191, 193, 199, 226, 235; political activity in, 102, 103, 106, 107, 118, **120**, 150, 153, 155, 195, 213–14, 224; Vela Perpetua in, **83**, **84**, 89, 129, 130

Quakers, 154, 164
Querétaro, 230; lay associations in, **120**, 182, 235; political activity in, 103, 113–14, 119, **120**, 150; Vela Perpetua in, 75, **83**, **120**

Ramírez, D. Ignacio, 144–45
Real Congregación; female leadership and, 37–41, 44; as model for new cofradías, 73–75, 78, 81, 89, 95, 119
Reform, liberal, 8–9, 69; and constitution, 151, 169–70, 208, 211, 212, 248; laws of the, 104–5, 125, 165–66, 207, 211–14, 220–22, 287n35, 298n30, 302n18; and lay associations, 123–46, 149, 151; and petitions, 148, 149, 151–57; and public display of religion, 37; War of the, 123, 127, 148. *See also* Ley Orgánica
religionero rebellion, 162, 170, 214, 301n102
Religión y la Sociedad, La, 165
religious right, 246
religious tolerance, 1, 123, 163; petition campaigns against, 14, 97, 98, 102–13, 149–62
reproductive rights, 246–47
Republicano, El, 106

Rerum Novarum: Rights and Duties of Capital and Labor, 192, 217–18
Restored Republic, 127, 169
Reyes, General Bernardo, 224
Risorgimento, 126
Riva Palacio, Vicente, 145
Romanization, 126, 176–79, 185, 204; and women's lay associations, 198–99, 230
Romero Rubio, Carmen, 201, 208
Rosa del Tepeyac, La, 212–13
rosary, 126, 213–14
Rosas Salas, Sergio Francisco, 195, 214
Rubenstein, Anne, 244
Rugeley, Terry, 89

Sacred Heart. *See* Sagrado Corazón de Jesús
Sagrada Familia (Mexico City), 239
Sagrado Corazón de Jesús, 226, 229; growth of, 180–82, 184, **186**; female leadership of, 189–90, 198, 305n63.
San Luis Potosí, 65, 94, 143, 190, 202, 212, 230; lay associations in, 47, 60, 62, 66, **120**; political activity in, 105, 115, **120**, 214, 235; Vela Perpetua in, 83, **83**, 84, **84**, **120**, 190
San Miguel de Allende: lay associations in, 6, 45, 63, 64, 65, 120; political activity in, 106, 115, 120; Vela Perpetua in, 81, **83**, 83–84, **84**, 86, 89
San Miguel el Grande. *See* San Miguel de Allende
Santa Escuela de Cristo. *See* Escuelas de Cristo
Savarino Roggero, Franco, 238–39
Schmitt, Karl, 214
schools, Catholic, 136, 137, 208, 225–27, 230; for girls, 42–43, 156, 184; and Hijas de María, 131; and parish priests, 36, 226–27; in rural areas, 226–27; teachers in, 201–2; and Sisters of Charity, 79; vocational training and, 192, 237; women as founders of, 35. *See also* schools, public
schools, Lancaster, 93, 142–43
schools, public or government: Catholic education in, 11, 135, 151–52, 184, 206–7, 222–23, 233, 243, 310n15; and Catholic families, 206–7, 209–11, 236; normal schools (government-run), 202, 251;

secular education in, 123, 155, 189, 206–7, 209, 219; teachers in, 222, 243–44, 251. *See also* schools, Catholic
Secretaría de Educación Pública (SEP), 242, 321n66
Secretariado Social Mexicano (SSM), 236–37, 320n58
sex education, 233, 242–43
sexuality, 246
Sierra, Justo, 202, 211
Siglo Diez y Nueve, El, 78, 143, 209; and petitions, 103–5, 129–30, 161; and Catholic schools, 210–11
Sisters of Charity (also Hermanas de la Caridad): arrival and expansion in Mexico, 43, 78–80, 293n47; charity and education work of, 79, 131, 137, 184; as European service association, 43, 73; and Hijas de María, 131, 184; and petitions, 118, 120, 139; relationship to Ladies of Charity, 79, 119; suppression and expulsion of, 152, 154–56, 162, 208, 220. *See also* Vincentian organizations
Silva, Atenógenes, 193
Six-Year Plan, 242
Smith, Benjamin, 178
Social Catholicism, 188, 236–37, 240–41; and workers' circles, 188, 191–94, 195, 306n83
social services, 237
socialism, 176, 193, 216, 242
Socialist party, 238
Sociedad, La, 117, 149
Sociedad Católica, 294n67; founding and growth of, 126–27, 134, 188; men's branches of, 195, 294–95n72; and other lay associations, 136–37, 145, 233; and politics, 134–35, 150–51, 168, 223; and religious education, 225–28, 237, 315n127, 315n139; women's branches of, 133–42, 294–95n72, 315n127
Sosenski, Susana, 112
Spain, 29, 32, 43, 78–79, 105, 225
spiritual conferences, 76, 77
spiritual exercises, 138
spiritual retreats, 77–78, 135, 138
splendor: as central to religious practice, 33, 48–49, 54; as target of reform,

25, 37, 214. *See also* public display of religion
St. Louise de Marillac, 78
St. Vincent de Paul, 43, 78, 140. *See also* Vincentian organizations
Staples, Anne, 93, 94
Stauffer, Brian, 282n67, 286n27; on lay associations, 134, 136, 139–40, 294n71; on Reform, 162, 168–69, 214, 304n53
Stevens, Donald, 51
Stowe, Harriet Beecher, 171
suffrage, 32, 121, 122, 232

Taylor, William B., 66, 266n, 274n
Teresa de Mier, Servando, 145
The Life of St. Vincent de Paul, 78
Third Orders, 24, **181**, 258n12, 262n10; governance of, 28, 30–31, 95, 277n3
Tiempo, El, 185, 189, 203, 214, 219, 223–24

Unión de Damas Católicas Mejicanas (UDCM), 237, 240–41
Unión Femenina Católica Mexicana (UFCM), 241, 242–43
Unión Nacional de Padres de Familia (UNPF, also Asociación Nacional de Padres de Familia), 242–44, 322n83
Unión Nacional Sinarquista (UNS), 322n
United States: and associationalism, 98, 145; Catholic press in, 216; feminism in, 106, 218; and gender roles, 9, 141, 171; and liberalism, 98, 170; petitioning in, 99; Protestants in, 111
Universal, El, 101, 103
US-Mexico War (1846–1848), 67, 94, 102–4, 111, 121

Van Young, Eric, 45
Vatican: and Catholic values, 176, 207, 245–46; and gender roles, 176; and favored devotions, associations, 126, 183, 185–87, 199, 204; influence in Mexico, 67–68, 126, 129, 141, 240; and parish priests, 15, 126, 141; and Romanization, 176, 178–80, 230
Vatican I, 176
Vatican II, 246
Vela Perpetua, 64, 74–75, 80–91, 137, 179–90, 249; female leadership of, 81–89, 93–95; founding of, 95, 126,

Vela Perpetua (*continued*) 128–130, 133; growth of, 81–85, 292n30, 323n97–98; and new lay associations, 227, 229 233, 235, 247; and petitions, 118–120, 168–169; relationship of priests to, 138–141, 198, 227, 229; and schools, 229

Viceroy Iturrigaray, 41–42

Vigil, José María, 109, 163

Vigils: and gender roles, 32, 197; continuous, 37–40, 81, 86–88, 91, 96, 128, 130, 168, 180 (*see also* Vela Perpetua); as individual practice, 86, 96, 130, 187

Vincentian organizations, 156, 206, 220; growth of, 43, 73, 79, 131–33, 136–37, 184, 188; and women, 80, 156, 225. *See also* Conferencias de Señoras de San Vicente de Paul; Ladies of Charity; Sisters of Charity

Virgin of Guadalupe: appearance of, 145; associations dedicated to, 181, 184–85, 190, 192; coronation of, 177, 194, 208, 213, 221, 238; honoring of, 191, 212, 214, 221, 249; as national symbol, 236, 249. *See also* Basílica of Guadalupe

von Germeten, Nicole, 29

Voz de la Patria, La, 220

Voz de la Religión, La, 103

Voz de México, La, 148, 161–65, 168, 203, 210, 215–16, 220, 225

Weis, Robert, 323n91

welfare, 232

women's rights, 121

workers. *See* labor

Wright de Kleinhans, Laureana, 145

Wright-Ríos, Edward, 3, 112, 178, 179–80, 209

YMCA, 234

Zacatecas, 200; lay associations in, 27, 46, 47, 58, 60, 77, **120**, 138; political activity in, **120**, 213, 214, 221; Vela Perpetua in, **83**, **84**, **120**, 129

Zaeske, Susan, 99–100

Zamora, 127, 129, 224; lay associations in, **83**, 136, 193, 235

Zarco, Francisco, 104–5, 107–8, 113, 160

Zuloaga Trillo, Félix María, 149

GPSR Authorized Representative: Easy Access System Europe - Mustamäe tee 50, 10621 Tallinn, Estonia, gpsr.requests@easproject.com

www.ingramcontent.com/pod-product-compliance
Lightning Source LLC
Chambersburg PA
CBHW031752220426
43662CB00007B/371